Shaw's

Local Government Directory

2004/05

Edited by Matthew Barber

FAX: 01322 550553
DX: 400700 CRAYFORD

ISBN 0 7219 1508 6
ISSN 1462-821X

A CIP catalogue record
for this book
is available from
The British Library

Printed in Great Britain by Antony Rowe Ltd., Chippenham, Wiltshire.

CONTENTS

SHAW'S LOCAL GOVERNMENT DIRECTORY ON CD

The main content of this Directory is now also available on CD. This comprises all the local authority "function" listings with Chief Officer's names, addresses, telephone and fax numbers, in tabbed delimited plain text format, suitable for importing into any standard database application.

The disk is searchable by authority name, authority type and departmental function, and can be used to generate mailing labels and personalised letters. Each entry is fully editable.

For further details, please visit: www.lgdirectory.co.uk or contact Matthew Barber at Shaw & Sons on 01322 621100.

EDITOR'S NOTE

The purpose of Shaw's Local Government Directory is to provide information for the authorities, solicitors and the many others whose work brings them into contact with the local authorities. For each authority, the addresses, telephone and fax numbers of the principal offices are listed, as well as details of other main offices.

Also listed are the names and job titles of those having prime responsibility for a selection of functions: Education; Electoral Registration; Environmental Health; Finance; Housing; Legal Services; Leisure; Local Land Charges; Planning; Purchasing & Supplies; Social Services; Technical Services; and Trading Standards, as well as the Chief Executive. It should be noted, of course, that not all authorities provide all of these services.

The Gazetteer lists alphabetically the names of parish, town and community councils, and the names of many other towns and villages throughout the United Kingdom, identifying the authority into which each immediately falls, in whole or in part.

The 2004/05 edition has been fully updated with the assistance of the authorities themselves and I would like to thank all the people who have assisted me in this process. The information in this edition was collated between February and April 2004.

We have made every effort to ensure that the information in the Directory is accurate, but there are inevitably frequent changes.

May 2004

Shaw & Sons, the publishers of this Directory, produce a range of books for local government and the legal profession. We are always interested in considering suggestions for new titles and would like to hear from any prospective authors with ideas for books; please write to the Publications Director at the address on the first page of this book.

Shaws also offer a wide variety of other products and services for local government. Full details can be found on our website:

www.shaws.co.uk

ENGLISH UNITARY AUTHORITIES

BATH & NORTH EAST SOMERSET COUNCIL

www.bathnes.gov.uk

Principal Office; Chief Executive's Office; Resources
The Guildhall, High Street, Bath BA1 5AW
Telephone: (01225) 477000

Corporate Support Services; Education; Operations
Riverside, Temple Street, Keynsham, Bristol BS31 1LA
Telephone: (01225) 477000

Environmental & Consumer Services
9-10 Bath Street, Bath BA1 1SN
Telephone: (01225) 477000

Property & Legal Services
Northgate House, Upper Borough Walls, Bath BA1 1RG
Telephone: (01225) 477000

Leisure Services
Pavilion, North Parade Road, Bath BA1 4RU
Telephone: (01225) 477000

Economic & Environmental Development
Trimbridge House, Trim Street, Bath BA1 2DP
Telephone: (01225) 477000

Social & Housing Services
7 North Parade Buildings, Bath BA1 1NY
Telephone: (01225) 477000

Function	Chief Officer	Title	Location
Chief Executive	Mr J Everitt	Chief Executive	Guildhall
Education	Mr M Young	Education Director	Riverside
Electoral Registration	Carol Nicholds	Electoral Services Officer	Guildhall
Environmental Health	Mr H Nowell	Head of Environmental & Consumer Services	Bath Street
Finance	Jean Hinks	Resources Director	Guildhall
Housing	Jane Ashman	Strategic Director, Social & Housing Services	7 North Parade
Legal Services	Mr T McBain	Head of Property & Legal Services	N'thgate House
Leisure	Mr M Smith	Head of Leisure & Amenity Services	Pavilion
Local Land Charges	Mr H Nowell	Head of Environmental & Consumer Services	Bath Street
Planning	Mr D Davies	Head of Planning Services	T'mbridge Hse
Purchasing & Supplies	Mr E Hale	Purchasing Manager	Guildhall
Social Services	Jane Ashman	Strategic Director, Social & Housing Services	7 North Parade
Technical Services	Mr C Thomas	Strategic Director (Economic & Environmental Development)	T'mbridge Hse
Trading Standards	Mr H Nowell	Head of Environmental & Consumer Services	Bath Street

ENGLISH UNITARY AUTHORITIES

On 1 April 1996, Bath & North East Somerset Council took over from Bath City Council, Wansdyke District Council and, in part, from Avon County Council.

Parish Councils in the authority's area: Bathampton; Batheaston; Bathford; Cameley; Camerton; Charlcombe; Chelwood; Chew Magna; Chew Stoke; Claverton; Clutton; Combe Hay; Compton Dando; Compton Martin; Corston; Dunkerton; East Harptree; Englishcombe; Farmborough; Farrington Gurney; Freshford; High Littleton; Hinton Blewett; Hinton Charterhouse; Marksbury; Monkton Combe; Nempnett Thrubwell; Newton St Loe; Norton Malreward; Paulton; Peasedown St John; Priston; Publow; Saltford; Shoscombe; Southstoke; Stanton Drew; Stowey Sutton; Swainswick; Timsbury; Ubley; Wellow; West Harptree; Whitchurch.

Parish Meetings in the authority's area: Kelston; Northstoke; St Catherine.

Town Councils in the authority's area: Keynsham; Norton Radstock.

BLACKBURN WITH DARWEN BOROUGH COUNCIL

council.blackburnworld.com

Principal Office
Town Hall, Blackburn, Lancashire BB1 7DY
Telephone: (01254) 585585; FAX: (01254) 680870

Function	Chief Officer	Title	Location
Chief Executive	Philip Watson	Chief Executive	Town Hall
Education	Peter Morgan	Director of Education & Lifelong Learning	Town Hall
Electoral Registration	Linda Comstive	Director of Legal & Democratic Services	Town Hall
Environmental Health	Adam Scott	Director of Regeneration, Housing & Neighbourhoods	Town Hall
Finance	Alan Cotton	Director of Finance	Town Hall
Legal Services	Linda Comstive	Director of Legal & Democratic Services	Town Hall
Leisure	Steve Rigby	Director of Culture, Leisure & Sport	Town Hall
Local Land Charges	Linda Comstive	Director of Legal & Democratic Services	Town Hall
Planning	Adam Scott	Director of Regeneration, Housing & Neighbourhoods	Town Hall
Social Services	Stephen Sloss	Director of Social Services	Town Hall
Trading Standards	George Campling	Director of Rights Advice & Entitlements	Town Hall

Blackburn with Darwen Borough Council became a unitary authority on 1 April 1998.

Parish Councils in the authority's area: Eccleshill; Livesey; North Turton; Yate & Pickup Bank; Pleasington; Tockholes.

BLACKPOOL BOROUGH COUNCIL

www.blackpool.gov.uk

Principal Office
PO Box 77, Town Hall, Blackpool, Lancashire FY1 1AD
Telephone: (01253) 477477; FAX: (01253) 477101

Education; Housing; Leisure; Social Services
Progress House, Clifton Road, Blackpool FY4 4US

Environmental Services
125 Albert Road, Blackpool FY1 4PW
Telephone: (01253) 478300

Finance
PO Box 4, Town Hall, Blackpool FY1 1NA
Telephone: (01253) 478505

Legal and Democratic Services
PO Box 1066, Town Hall, Blackpool FY1 1GB
Telephone: (01263) 477477

Planning and Transportation
PO Box 17, Blackpool FY1 1GT
Telephone: (01253) 476200

Operational Services
Layton Depot, Blackpool FY3 7HW
Telephone: (01253) 476310

Technical Services
PO Box 117, Westgate House, Squires Gate Lane, Blackpool FY4 2TS
Telephone: (01253) 476150

Function	Chief Officer	Title	Location
Chief Executive	Mr S Weaver	Chief Executive	Town Hall
Education	Mr D Lund	Director of Education, Leisure & Cultural Services	Progress Hse
Electoral Registration	Miss K Drury	Senior Electoral Registration Assistant	Town Hall
Environmental Health	Mr K Garritty	Head of Environmental Services	Albert Road
Finance	Mr M Hanson	Director of Finance	Town Hall
Housing	Mr S Pullan	Director of Social Services & Housing	Progress Hse
Legal Services	Mr M Lewis	Head of Legal & Democratic Services	Town Hall
Leisure	Dr D Sanders	Strategic Director of Community	Progress Hse
Local Land Charges	Mr M Lewis	Head of Legal & Democratic Services	Town Hall
Planning	Mr R Haslam	Head of Planning & Transportation	Town Hall
Purchasing & Supplies	Mr G Sharrock	Head of Operational Services	Layton Depot
Social Services	Mr S Pullan	Director of Social Services & Housing	Progress Hse
Technical Services	Mr J Shaw	Head of Technical Services	Westgate Hse
Trading Standards	Mr K Garritty	Head of Environmental Services	Albert Road

Blackpool Borough Council became a unitary authority on 1 April 1998.

Parish Councils & Parish Meetings in the authority's area: none.

Town Councils in the authority's area: none.

BOURNEMOUTH BOROUGH COUNCIL

www.bournemouth.gov.uk

Principal Office
Town Hall, Bournemouth, Dorset BH2 6DY
Telephone: (01202) 451451; FAX: (01202) 451000; DX 7615 Bournemouth

Bournemouth International Centre
Exeter Road, Bournemouth BH2 5BH
Telephone: (01202) 456400; FAX: (01202) 456500

Education Department
Dorset House, 20/22 Christchurch Road, Bournemouth BH1 3NL
Telephone: (01202) 451451; FAX: (01202) 456105

Social Services Department
New Century House, 24 Christchurch Road, Bournemouth BH1 3ND
Telephone: (01202) 458700; FAX: (01202) 458730

Tourism Services
Tourist Information Centre, Westover Road, Bournemouth BH1 2BU
Telephone: (01202) 451718; FAX: (01202) 451743

Function	Chief Officer	Title	Location
Chief Executive	Mr Paul Godier	Chief Executive	Town Hall
Education	Mr Pratap Deshpande	Director of Education	Dorset House

Function	Chief Officer	Title	Location
Electoral Registration	Mr Tim Martin	Head of Law & Administration	Town Hall
Environmental Health	Mr Mike Edwards	Head of Environmental Health & Consumer Services	Town Hall
Finance	Mr Eric Fisher	Director of Central Services	Town Hall
Housing	Mr Nigel Higgins	Director of Environment & Community Services	Town Hall
Legal Services	Mr Tim Martin	Head of Law & Administration	Town Hall
Leisure	Mr Stephen Godsall	Director of Leisure & Tourism	Town Hall
Local Land Charges	Mr Tim Martin	Head of Law & Administration	Town Hall
Planning	Mr Mike Holmes	Head of Planning & Development Services	Town Hall
Purchasing & Supplies	Ms Wendy Meaden	Purchasing & Office Services Manager	Town Hall
Social Services	Mrs Pam Donnellan	Director of Social Services	New Century
Technical Services	Mr Roger Ball	Head of Technical Services	Town Hall
Trading Standards	Mr Mike Edwards	Head of Environmental Health & Consumer Services	Town Hall

Bournemouth Borough Council became a unitary authority on 1 April 1997.

Parish Councils & Parish Meetings in the authority's area: none.

Town Councils in the authority's area: none.

BRACKNELL FOREST BOROUGH COUNCIL

www.bracknell-forest.gov.uk

Principal Office
Easthampstead House, Town Square, Bracknell, Berkshire RG12 1AQ
Telephone: (01344) 424642; FAX: (01344) 352810; DX 33611 Bracknell

Education Department
Seymour House, 38 Broadway, Town Square, Bracknell RG12 1AU
Telephone: (01344) 424642; FAX: (01344) 351222

Environment Department; Leisure Department
Time Square, Market Street, Bracknell RG12 1JD
Telephone: (01344) 424642; FAX: (01344) 352187

Social Services & Housing Department
Time Square, Market Street, Bracknell RG12 1JD
Telephone: (01344) 424642; FAX: (01344) 351190

Function	Chief Officer	Title	Location
Chief Executive	Mr Timothy Wheadon	Chief Executive	E'stead Hse
Education	Mr Tony Eccleston	Director of Education	Seymour House
Electoral Registration	Mr Peter Driver	Head of Democratic Services	E'stead Hse
Finance	Mr Chris Herbert	Borough Finance Officer	E'stead Hse
Housing	Daphne Obang	Director of Social Services & Housing	Time Square
Legal Services	Mr Alex Jack	Borough Solicitor	Seymour Hse
Leisure	Mr Vincent Paliczka	Director of Leisure & Environment Services	Time Square
Local Land Charges	Ms Linda Bell	Land Charges Officer	Seymour Hse
Planning	Mr Vincent Paliczka	Director of Leisure & Environment Services	Time Square
Purchasing & Supplies	Mr Rob Atkins	Head of Procurement	E'stead Hse
Social Services	Daphne Obang	Director of Social Services & Housing	Time Square
Technical Services	Mr Vincent Paliczka	Director of Leisure & Environment Services	Time Square
Trading Standards	Mr Robert Sexton	Trading Standards Manager	Time Square

ENGLISH UNITARY AUTHORITIES

Bracknell Forest Borough Council became a unitary authority on 1 April 1998.

Parish Councils in the authority's area: Binfield; Crowthorne; Warfield; Winkfield.

Town Councils in the authority's area: Bracknell, Sandhurst.

BRIGHTON & HOVE CITY COUNCIL

www.brighton-hove.gov.uk

Principal Office
King's House, Grand Avenue, Hove BN3 2LS
Telephone: (01273) 290000

Environment and Housing
Bartholomew House, Bartholomew Square, Brighton BN1 1JP
Telephone: (01273) 290000

Function	Chief Officer	Title	Location
Chief Executive	David Panter	Chief Executive	King's House
Education	David Hawker	Director of Children, Families and Schools	King's House
Electoral Registration	Alan McCarthy	Director of Corporate Services	King's House
Environmental Health	Jenny Rowlands	Director of Environment	King's House
Finance	Chris Taylor	Chief Finance Officer	King's House
Housing	Ian Long	Director of Housing & City Support	King's House
Legal Services	Alan McCarthy	Director of Corporate Services	King's House
Leisure	Jenny Rowlands	Director of Environment	King's House
Planning	Jenny Rowlands	Director of Environment	King's House
Purchasing & Supplies	Alan McCarthy	Director of Corporate Services	King's House
Social Services	Ian Long	Director of Housing & City Support	King's House
Technical Services	Jenny Rowlands	Director of Environment	King's House

Brighton & Hove Council became a unitary authority on 1 April 1997. It took over from Brighton Borough Council and Hove Borough Council.

Parish Councils & Parish Meetings in the authority's area: Rottingdean.

Town Councils in the authority's area: none.

BRISTOL CITY COUNCIL

www.bristol-city.gov.uk

Principal Office
The Council House, College Green, Bristol BS1 5TR
Telephone: (0117) 922 2000; FAX: (0117) 922 2024; DX 7827 Bristol

Department of the Environment, Transport & Leisure
Colston House, Colston Street, Bristol BS1 5AQ
Telephone: (0117) 922 2000

Department of Neighbourhood Services & Housing
St Anne's House, St Anne's Road, St Anne's, Bristol BS4 4AB
Telephone: (0117) 922 2000

Department of Social Services & Health
Amelia Court, PO Box 30, Pipe Lane, Bristol BS99 7NB
Telephone: (0117) 922 2000

Function	Chief Officer	Title	Location
Chief Executive	Nick Gurney	Chief Executive	The Council Hse
Education	[Vacant]	Director of Education and Lifelong Learning	The Council Hse

Electoral Registration	Stephen McNamara	Head of Legal Services	The Council Hse
Environmental Health	Stephen Wray	Director of Environment, Transport & Leisure	Colston Hse
Finance	Carew Reynell	Director of Central Support Services/ Head of Paid Services	The Council Hse
Housing	Ian Crawley	Director of Housing & Neighbourhood Services	St Annes House
Legal Services	Stephen McNamara	Head of Legal Services	The Council Hse
Leisure	Stephen Wray	Director of Environment, Transport & Leisure	Colston Hse
Planning	Stephen Wray	Director of Environment, Transport & Leisure	Colston Hse
Social Services	Bill McKitterick	Director of Health & Social Services	Amelia Court
Trading Standards	Howard Thomas	Head of Operational Support	St Annes House

Bristol City Council became a unitary authority on 1 April 1996. It took over the services formerly provided in Bristol by Avon County Council and the old district authority.

Parish Councils & Parish Meetings in the authority's area: none.

Town Councils in the authority's area: none.

DARLINGTON BOROUGH COUNCIL

www.darlington.gov.uk

Principal Office
Town Hall, Darlington, Co Durham DL1 5QT
Telephone: (01325) 380651; FAX: (01325) 382032; DX 69280 Darlington 6

Environment Regulatory Services
11 Houndgate, Darlington DL1 5RF
Telephone: (01325) 388582

Leisure Services
Vicarage Road, Darlington DL1 1JW
Telephone: (01325) 347510/486987

Function	Chief Officer	Title	Location
Chief Executive	Mr Barry Keel	Chief Executive	Town Hall
Education	Mr Geoff Pennington	Director of Education	Town Hall
Electoral Registration	Mr Peter Kearsley	Borough Solicitor	Town Hall
Environmental Health	Mr Keith Atkinson	Assistant Director, Public Protection	Houndgate
Finance	Mr Paul Wildsmith	Director of Corporate Services	Town Hall
Housing	Mr Cliff Brown	Director of Community Services	Vicarage Road
Legal Services	Mr Peter Kearsley	Borough Solicitor	Town Hall
Leisure	Mr Steve Thompson	Leisure & Catering Manager	Vicarage Road
Local Land Charges	Mr Peter Kearsley	Borough Solicitor	Town Hall
Planning	Mr Richard Alty	Assistant Director, Development & Regeneration	Town Hall
Purchasing & Supplies	Mr D Scarr	Purchasing Manager	Vicarage Road
Social Services	Mrs Margaret Asquith	Director of Social Services	Town Hall
Technical Services	Mr J Buxton	Director Development & Environment	Town Hall
Trading Standards	Mr Nigel Green	Trading Standards Manager	Houndgate

Darlington Borough Council became a unitary authority on 1 April 1997.

Parish Councils in the authority's area: Bishopton; Heighington; High Coniscliffe; Hurworth; Low Coniscliffe & Merrybent; Low Dinsdale; Middleton St George; Neasham; Piercebridge; Sadberge; Whessoe.

Parish Meetings in the authority's area: Archdeacon Newton; Barmpton; Brafferton; Coatham Mundeville; Denton; East & West Newbiggin; Great Burdon; Great Stainton; Houghton-le-Side; Killerby; Little Stainton; Morton Palms; Sockburn; Summerhouse; Walworth.

DERBY CITY COUNCIL

www.derby.gov.uk

Principal Office
The Council House, Corporation Street, Derby DE1 2FS
Telephone: (01332) 293111; FAX: (01332) 255500

Education Department
Middleton House, 27 St Mary's Gate, Derby DE1 3NN
Telephone: (01332) 293111; FAX: (01332) 716920

Environmental Health and Trading Standards
Celtic House, Friary Street, Derby DE1 1QX
Telephone: (01332) 293111; FAX: (01332) 716264

Derby Homes
Floor 2, Southpoint, Cardinal Square, 10 Nottingham Road, Derby DE1 3QT
Telephone: (01332) 711003; FAX: (01332) 711001

Development & Cultural Services Department
Roman House, Friar Gate, Derby DE1 1XB
Telephone: (01332) 293111; FAX: (01332) 255989

Social Services Department
Middleton House, 27 St Mary's Gate, Derby DE1 3NS
Telephone: (01332) 293111; FAX: (01332) 716767

Function	Chief Officer	Title	Location
Chief Executive	Mr R H Cowlishaw	Chief Executive	Council House
Education	Mr Andrew Flack	Director of Education	Middleton Hse
Electoral Registration	Mr M Foote	Director of Corporate Services	Council House
Environmental Health	Mr Andrew Hopkin	Assistant Director of Environmental Health & Trading Standards	Celtic House
Finance	Mr Paul Dransfield	Director of Finance	Council House
Housing	Mr Phil Davies	Chief Executive of Derby Homes	Southpoint
Legal Services	Mr Stuart Leslie	Chief Legal Officer	Council House
Leisure	Mr Ray Rippingale;	Assistant Director of Cultural Services;	Roman House
	Ms Lesley Whitney	Assistant Director of Lifelong Learning & Community	Middleton Hse
Local Land Charges	Mr Stephen Dunning	Assistant Director of Democratic Services	Council House
Planning	Mr J Guest	Director of Development & Cultural Services	Roman House
Purchasing & Supplies	Mr C Earnshaw	Procurement Officer	Council House
Social Services	Mrs M McGlade	Director of Social Services	Middleton Hse
Technical Services	Mr J Guest	Director of Development & Cultural Services	Roman House
Trading Standards	Mr Andrew Hopkin	Assistant Director of Environmental Health & Trading Standards	Celtic House

Derby City Council became a unitary authority on 1 April 1997.

Parish Councils & Parish Meetings in the authority's area: none.

Town Councils in the authority's area: none.

ENGLISH UNITARY AUTHORITIES

EAST RIDING OF YORKSHIRE COUNCIL

www.eastriding.gov.uk

Principal Office

County Hall, Beverley, East Riding of Yorkshire HU17 9BA
Telephone: (01482) 887700; FAX: (01482) 884150

Function	Chief Officer	Title	Location
Chief Executive	Mr D Stephenson	Chief Executive	County Hall
Education	Mr J Mager	Director of Lifelong Learning	County Hall
Electoral Registration	Mr B Gillatt	Electoral Services Manager	County Hall
Environmental Health	Mr A Hunter	Director of Social Services, Housing & Public Protection	County Hall
Finance	Mr J Butler	Director of Finance & Information Technology	County Hall
Housing	Mr J Blackmore	Director of Social Services, Housing & Public Protection	County Hall
Legal Services	Mr N Pearson	Director of Law, Administration, Planning & Property	County Hall
Leisure	Mr J Mager	Director of Lifelong Learning	County Hall
Local Land Charges	Mr N Pearson	Director of Law, Administration, Planning & Property	County Hall
Planning	Mr N Pearson	Director of Law, Administration, Planning & Property	County Hall
Purchasing & Supplies	Mr H Roberts	Director of Operational Services	County Hall
Social Services	Mr J Blackmore	Director of Social Services, Housing & Public Protection	County Hall
Technical Services	Mr H Roberts	Director of Operational Services	County Hall
Trading Standards	Mr J Blackmore	Director of Social Services, Housing & Public Protection	County Hall

On 1 April 1996, East Riding of Yorkshire Council took over from Beverley Borough Council, East Yorkshire District Council and Holderness District Council; and, in part, from Humberside County Council and Boothferry Borough Council.

Parish Councils in the authority's area: Airmyn; Aldbrough; Allerthorpe; Asselby; Atwick; Bainton; Barmby Moor; Barmby on the Marsh; Barmston & Fraisthorpe; Beeford; Bielby; Bempton; Beswick; Bewholme; Bilton; Bishop Burton; Bishop Wilton; Blacktoft; Boynton; Brandesburton; Brantingham; Broomfleet; Bubwith; Bugthorpe/Kirby Und; Burstwick; Burton Agnes; Burton Constable; Burton Fleming; Burton Pidsea; Carnaby; Catton; Catwick; Cherry Burton; Coniston; Cottam; Dalton Holme; Easington; East Cottingwith; East Garton; Eastrington; Ellerby; Ellerker; Ellerton & Aughton; Elloughton cum Brough; Elstronwick; Etton; Everingham; Fangfoss; Fimber; Flamborough; Foggathorpe; Foston; Fridaythorpe; Full Sutton & Skirpenbeck; Garton; Gilberdyke; Goodmanham; Goole Fields; Gowdall; Grindale; Halsham; Harpham; Hatfield; Hayton & Burnby; Hollym; Holme on Spalding Moor; Holmpton; Hook; Hotham; Huggate; Humbleton; Hutton Cranswick; Kelk; Keyingham; Kilham; Kilpin; Kirkburn; Langtoft; Laxton; Leconfield; Leven; Lissett & Ulrome; Lockington; Londesborough; Lund; Mappleton; Melbourne; Middleton; Millington; Molescroft; Nafferton; Newbald; Newport; Newton on Derwent; North Cave; North Dalton; North Ferriby; North Frodingham; North & South Cliffe; Nunburnholme; Ottringham; Patrington; Paull; Pollington; Preston; Rawcliffe; Reedness; Rimswell; Rise; Riston; Roos; Rowley; Rudston; Sancton; Seaton; Seaton Ross; Shiptonthorpe; Sigglesthorne; Skeffling; Skerne & Wansford; Skidby; Skipsea; Skirlaugh; Sledmere; South Cave; Spaldington; Sproatley; Stamford Bridge; Sunk Island; Sutton on Derwent; Swanland; Swine; Swinefleet; Thorngumbald; Thornton; Thwing & Octon; Tibthorpe; Tickton & Routh; Twin Rivers; Walkington; Warter; Watton; Wawne; Welton; Welwick; Wetwang; Wilberfoss; Withernwick; Wold Newton; Woodmansey; Wressle; Yapham cum Meltonby.

Town Councils in the authority's area: Anlaby with Anlaby Common; Beverley; Bridlington; Cottingham; Driffield; Goole; Hedon; Hessle; Hornsea; Howden; Kirkella; Market Weighton; Pocklington; Snaith & Cowick; Willerby; Withernsea.

ENGLISH UNITARY AUTHORITIES

HALTON BOROUGH COUNCIL

www.halton.gov.uk

Principal Office
Municipal Building, Kingsway, Widnes, Cheshire WA8 7QF
Telephone: (0151) 424 2061; FAX: (0151) 471 7301; DX 24302 Widnes

Education Directorate; Environmental Services Directorate; Social Care, Housing & Health Directorate
Grosvenor House, Halton Lea, Runcorn WA7 2WD
Telephone: (0151) 424 2061

Social Care, Housing & Health Directorate
Town Hall, Heath Road, Runcorn, Cheshire WA7 5TD
Telephone: (0151) 424 2061; FAX: (0151) 471 7303

Function	Chief Officer	Title	Location
Chief Executive	Mike Cuff	Chief Executive	Municipal Bldg
Education	Graham Talbot	Executive Director (Education & Social Inclusion Directorate)	Municipal Bldg
Electoral Registration	Christine Kenny	Head of Committee & Member Services	Municipal Bldg
Environmental Health	Dick Tregea	Executive Director (Environment & Development Services Directorate	Municipal Bldg
Finance	Alan Hill	Executive Director (Resources & Corporate Services Directorate)	Municipal Bldg
Housing	Paul Mullins	Operational Director, Housing Management Division (Social Care, Housing & Health Directorate)	Town Hall
Leisure	Howard Cockcroft	Operational Director (Culture & Leisure Services)	Town Hall
Legal Services	John Tradewell	Council Solicitor	Municipal Bldg
Local Land Charges	John Tradewell	Council Solicitor	Municipal Bldg
Planning	Chris Brough	Operational Director (Planning)	Grosvenor Hse
Purchasing & Supplies	Greg Yeomans	Support Services Manager	Municipal Bldg
Social Services	Diana Terris	Executive Director (Social Care, Housing & Health Directorate)	Municipal Bldg
Technical Services	Alan West	Operational Director (Highways & Transportation)	Grosvenor Hse

Halton Borough Council became a unitary authority on 1 April 1998.

Parish Councils in the authority's area: Daresbury; Hale; Moore; Preston Brook.

HARTLEPOOL BOROUGH COUNCIL

www.hartlepool.gov.uk

Principal Office
Civic Centre, Victoria Road, Hartlepool TS24 8AY
Telephone: (01429) 266522; FAX: (01429) 523005; DX 60669 Hartlepool 1

Department of Environment & Development
Bryan Hanson House, Hanson Square, Hartlepool TS24 7BT
Telephone: (01429) 523004; FAX: (01429) 523599

Function	Chief Officer	Title	Location
Chief Executive	Paul Walker	Chief Executive	Civic Centre
Education	Jeremy Fitt	Director of Education	Civic Centre
Electoral Registration	Christine Armstrong	Corporate Services Officer	Civic Centre
Environmental Health	Raplh Harrison	Head of Public Protection & Housing	Civic Centre
Finance	Mike Ward	Chief Financial Officer	Civic Centre
Housing	Bernard Williams	Director of Neighbourhood Services	Civic Centre

Function	Chief Officer	Title	Location
Legal Services	Tony Brown	Chief Solicitor	Civic Centre
Leisure	Janet Barker	Director of Community Services	Civic Centre
Local Land Charges	Christine Armstrong	Corporate Services Officer	Civic Centre
Planning	Peter Scott	Director of Regeneration & Planning	B Hanson Hse
Purchasing & Supplies	[Vacant]	Purchasing Manager	Civic Centre
Social Services	Sallyanne Jonhson	Director of Social Services	Civic Centre
Technical Services	Ian Parker	Head of Technical Services	Civic Centre
Trading Standards	Ralph Harrison	Head of Public Protection & Housing	Civic Centre

Hartlepool Borough Council became a unitary authority on 1 April 1996. It took over, in part, from Cleveland County Council.

Parish Councils in the authority's area: Brierton; Claxton; Dalton Piercy; Elwick; Greatham; Hart; Newton Bewley.

THE HEREFORDSHIRE COUNCIL

www.herefordshire.gov.uk

Principal Office
Brockington, 35 Hafod Road, Hereford HR1 1SH
Telephone: (01432) 260000

Education Department
Education & Conference Centre, 4 Blackfriars Street, Hereford
Telephone: (01432) 260801

Function	Chief Officer	Title	Location
Chief Executive	Mr N Pringle	Chief Executive	Brockington
Education	Dr E Oram	Director of Education	Blackfriars Street
Environmental Health	Mr G Dunhill	Director of Environment	Brockington
Finance	Mr I Hyson	County Treasurer	Brockington
Legal Services	Ms M Rosenthal	Legal Practice Manager	Brockington
Leisure	Mr G Cole	Head of Culture, Leisure & Education for Life	Brockington
Local Land Charges	Ms T Farmer	Land Charges Manager	Brockington
Planning	Mr J Barrett	Head of Planning Services	Brockington
Social Services	Ms S Fiernes	Director of Social Services & Strategic Housing	Brockington
Technical Services	Mr S Oates	Head of Engineering Services	Brockington
Trading Standards	Mr A Tector	Head of Environmental Health & Trading Standards	Brockington

The Herefordshire Council came into existence on 1 April 1998. It took over from Hereford City Council, Leominster District Council (in part), Malvern Hills District Council (in part) and South Herefordshire District Council; and, in part, from the former Hereford & Worcester County Council.

Parish Councils in the authority's area: Abbeydore & Bacton Group; Acton Beauchamp Group; Allensmore; Almeley; Ashperton; Aston Ingham; Avenbury; Aymestrey; Bartestree & Lugwardine Group; Birley with Upper Hill; Bishop's Frome; Bishopstone & District Group; Bodenham; Border Group; Bosbury & Coddington; Brampton Abbots & Foy Group; Bredenbury & District Group; Breinton; Bridstow; Brilley; Brimfield & Little Hereford Group; Brockhampton; Brockhampton Group; Burghill; Callow & Haywood Group; Clehonger; Clifford; Colwall; Cradley; Credenhill; Cusop; Dilwyn; Dinedor; Dormington & Mordiford Group; Dorstone; Eardisland; Eardisley Group; Eastnor & Donnington; Eaton Bishop; Ewyas Harold Group; Fownhope; Foxley; Garway; Goodrich & Welsh Bicknor Group; Hampton Bishop; Hatfield & District Group; Hentland & Ballingham Group; Holme Lacy; Holmer & Shelwick; Hope Mansell; Hope under Dinmore Group; How Caple, Sollershope & Yatton Group; Humber, Stoke Prior & Ford Group; Huntington; Kentchurch; Kilpeck Group; Kimbolton; Kings Caple; Kingsland; Kingstone & Thruxton Group; Kington Rural & Lower Harpton Group; Kinnersley & District Group; Lea; Leintwardine Group; Linton; Little Birch; Little Dewchurch; Llangarron; Llanwarne & District Group; Longtown Group; Lower Bullingham; Luston Group; Lyonshall; Madley; Marden; Marstow; Mathon; Middleton-on-the-Hill & Leysters Group; Monkland & Stretford; Moreton on Lugg; Much Birch; Much Cowarne Group; Much Dewchurch; Much Marcle; North Bromyard Group; Ocle Pychard; Orcop; Orleton; Pembridge; Pencombe Group; Peterchurch; Peterstow; Pipe & Lyde; Pixley & District; Putley; Pyons Group; Richard's Castle; Ross Rural; Sellack; Shobdon; St. Weonards; Stapleton Group; Staunton-on-Wye & District Group; Stoke Lacy; Stretton Grandison Group; Stretton Sugwas; Sutton; Tarrington; Thornbury Group; Titley & District Group; Upton Bishop; Vowchurch & District Group; Walford; Wellington; Wellington Heath; Welsh Newton & Llanrothal Group; Weobley; Weston Beggard; Weston-under-Penyard; Whitbourne; Whitchurch & Ganarew Group; Wigmore Group; Withington Group; Woolhope; Wyeside Group; Yarkhill; Yarpole Group.

Parish Meetings in the authority's area: Aconbury; Dinmore; Hampton Charles; Stoke Edith.

Town Councils in the authority's area: Bromyard & Winslow; Kington; Ledbury; Leominster; Ross on Wye.

City of Hereford Charter Trustees.

ISLE OF WIGHT COUNCIL

www.iwight.com

Principal Office
County Hall, High Street, Newport, Isle of Wight PO30 1UD
Telephone: (01983) 821000; FAX: (01983) 823333; DX 56361 Newport (IoW)

Planning Services
Seaclose, Fairlee Road, Newport, Isle of Wight PO30 2QS
Telephone: (01983) 823552; FAX: (01983) 823563

Engineering Services
Jubilee Stores, The Quay, Newport, Isle of Wight PO30 2EH
Telephone: (01983) 823777; FAX: (01983) 520563

Consumer Services
St Nicholas House, 58 St Johns' Road, Newport, Isle of Wight PO30 1LT
Telephone: (01983) 823396; FAX: (01983) 823387

Social Services
17 Fairlee Road, Newport, Isle of Wight PO30 2EA
Telephone: (01983) 520600; FAX: (01983) 524330

Housing Services
7 High Street, Newport, Isle of Wight PO30 1SS
Telephone: (01983) 823040; FAX: (01983) 823050

Function	Chief Officer	Title	Location
Chief Executive	Mike Fisher	Chief Executive Officer for Corporate Services	County Hall
Education	David Pettitt	Strategic Director for Education & Community Development	County Hall
Electoral Registration	John Lawson	Head of Legal & Democratic Services	County Hall
Environmental Health	Derek Rowell	Strategic Director for Environment Services	County Hall
Finance	Paul Wilkinson	Head of Finance & Business Services	County Hall
Housing	Glen Garrod	Strategic Director for Social Services & Housing	17 Fairlee Rd
Legal Services	John Lawson	Head of Legal & Democratic Services	County Hall
Leisure	John Metcalfe	Head of Community Development & Tourism	County Hall
Local Land Charges	John Lawson	Head of Legal & Democratic Services	County Hall
Planning	Andrew Ashcroft	Head of Planning Services	Seaclose
Social Services	Glen Garrod	Strategic Director for Social Services & Housing	17 Fairlee Rd
Trading Standards	Rob Owen	Head of Consumer Protection	St Nicholas Hse

ENGLISH UNITARY AUTHORITIES

Isle of Wight Council became a unitary authority on 1 April 1995. It took over from Medina and South Wight Borough Councils.

Parish Councils in the authority's area: Arreton; Bembridge; Brighstone; Calbourne; Chale; Freshwater; Gatcombe; Godshilll; Gurnard; Lake; Nettlestone; Newchurch; Niton; Rookley; St Helens; Seaview; Shalfleet; Shorwell; Totland; Whitwell; Wootton Bridge; Wroxall.

Town Councils in the authority's area: Brading; Cowes; East Cowes; Sandown; Shanklin; Ventnor; Yarmouth.

KINGSTON UPON HULL CITY COUNCIL

www.hullcc.gov.uk

Principal Office
Guildhall, Alfred Gelder Street, Kingston upon Hull HU1 2AA
Telephone: (01482) 609100; DX 11934 Hull 1

Function	Chief Officer	Title	Location
Chief Executive	Mr Jan Didrichsen	Acting Chief Executive	Guildhall
Education	Ms Helen McMullen	Corporate Director	Guildhall
Electoral Registration	Mrs Sandra Holder	Electoral Registration Officer	Guildhall
Environmental Health	Mr David Duxbury	Head of Public Protection	Guildhall
Finance	Mr Martin Fox	Head of Corporate Finance	Guildhall
Housing	Mrs Janet Whipps	Head of Housing Strategy	Guildhall
Legal Services	Ms Margaret Taylor	Town Clerk	Guildhall
Local Land Charges	Ms Margaret Taylor	Town Clerk	Guildhall
Planning	Mr Andy Snowden	Corporate Director	Guildhall
Purchasing & Supplies	Mr Barry Henniker	Head of Procurement	Guildhall
Social Services	Mr Ken Foote	Corporate Director	Guildhall
Technical Services	Mr Andy Snowden	Corporate Director	Guildhall
Trading Standards	Mr David Duxbury	Head of Public Protection	Guildhall

Kingston upon Hull City Council became a unitary authority on 1 April 1996.

Parish Councils & Parish Meetings in the authority's area: none.

Town Councils in the authority's area: none.

LEICESTER CITY COUNCIL

www.leicester.gov.uk

Principal Office
New Walk Centre, Welford Place, Leicester LE1 6ZG
Telephone: (0116) 254 9922; FAX: (0116) 254 5531

Education & Lifelong Learning Department
Marlborough House, 38 Welford Road, Leicester LE2 7AA
Telephone: (0116) 252 7807; FAX: (0116) 223 2685

Function	Chief Officer	Title	Location
Chief Executive	Mr R Green	Chief Executive	New Walk Centre
Education	Mr S Andrews	Director of Education & Lifelong Learning	Marlborough Hse
Electoral Registration	Mr T Stephenson	Town Clerk and Director of Resources, Access & Diversity	New Walk Centre
Environmental Health	Ms T Brill	Director of Environment, Regeneration & Development	New Walk Centre
Finance	Mr M Noble	Chief Finance Officer	New Walk Centre
Housing	Mr M Forrester	Director of Housing	New Walk Centre
Legal Services	Mr T Stephenson	Town Clerk and Director of Resources, Access & Diversity	New Walk Centre

Leisure	Ms T Brill	Director of Cultural Services & Nieghbourhood Renewal	New Walk Centre
Local Land Charges	Mr T Stephenson	Town Clerk and Director of Resources, Access & Diversity	New Walk Centre
Planning	Ms T Brill	Director of Environment, Regeneration & Development	New Walk Centre
Technical Services	Ms T Brill	Director of Environment, Regeneration & Development	New Walk Centre
Trading Standards	Ms T Brill	Director of Environment, Regeneration & Development	New Walk Centre
Social Services	Mr A Cozens	Director of Social Care & Health	New Walk Centre

Leicester City Council became a unitary authority on 1 April 1997.

Parish Councils & Parish Meetings in the authority's area: none.

Town Councils in the authority's area: none.

LUTON BOROUGH COUNCIL

www.luton.gov.uk

Principal Office
Town Hall, Luton, Bedfordshire LU1 2BQ
Telephone: (01582) 546000; FAX: (01582) 546223; DX 5926 Luton

Lifelong Learning and Social Services Department
Unity House, 111 Stuart Street Luton LU1 5NP
Telephone: (01582) 546000

Finance Department
Stuart House, 37 Upper George Street, Luton LU1 2RD
Telephone: (01582) 546000; FAX: (01582) 546422

Purchasing & Supplies
Central Depot, Kingsway, Luton LU4 8AU
Telephone: (01582) 546867

Function	Chief Officer	Title	Location
Chief Executive	Mr D Singh	Chief Executive	Town Hall
Education	Mr T Dessent	Director of Lifelong Learning	Unity House
Electoral Registration	Mr J Harper	Head of Legal Democracy	Town Hall
Environmental Health	Mrs C Welfare	Head of Environment & Consumer Services	Town Hall
Finance	Mr D Kempson	Head of Corporate Finance	Stuart House
Housing	Ms J Cleary	Interim Director of Social Services & Housing	Unity House
Legal Services	Mr R Stevens	Head of Legal Services	Town Hall
Leisure	Mr D Sutton	Head of Leisure, Libraries & Culture	Unity House
Local Land Charges	Mr R Stevens	Head of Legal Services	Town Hall
Planning	Mr I Slater	Head of Planning	Town Hall
Purchasing & Supplies	Mr C Addey	Supplies Manager	Central Depot
Social Services	Ms J Cleary	Interim Director of Social Services & Housing	Unity House
Trading Standards	Mrs C Welfare	Head of Environment & Consumer Services	Town Hall

Luton Borough Council became a unitary authority on 1 April 1997. It took over from the former Luton Borough Council and, in part, from Bedfordshire County Council.

Parish Councils & Parish Meetings in the authority's area: none.

Town Councils in the authority's area: none.

MEDWAY COUNCIL

www.medway.gov.uk

Principal Office
Civic Centre, Strood, Rochester, Medway ME2 4AU
Telephone: (01634) 306000; FAX: (01634) 332756; DX 56006 Strood

Health & Community Services
Municipal Buildings, Gillingham ME7 5LA
Telephone: (01634) 306000

Development & Environment
The Compass Centre, Chatham Maritime, Chatham ME4 4YH
Telephone: (01634) 306000

Function	Chief Officer	Title	Location
Chief Executive	Ms Judith Armitt	Chief Executive	Civic Centre
Education	Ms Rose Collinson	Director of Education & Leisure	Civic Centre
Environment	Dr Richard Simmons	Director of Development & Environment	Compass Cntre
Finance	Mr Neil Davies	Director of Finance & Corporate Services	Civic Centre
Legal Services	Mr Mark Bowen	Assistant Director (Legal & Contract Services)	Civic Centre
Leisure	Ms Rose Collinson	Director of Education & Leisure	Civic Centre
Planning	Dr Richard Simmons	Director of Development & Environment	Compass Cntre
Social Services	Ann Windiate	Director of Health & Community Services	Municipal Bldgs

Medway Council, a unitary authority from 1 April 1998, took over from the former Gillingham Borough Council and Rochester upon Medway City Council, and, in part, from Kent County Council.

Parish Councils in the authority's area: Allhallows; Cliffe & Cliffe Woods; Cooling; Cuxton; Frindsbury Extra; Halling; High Halstow; Hoo St Werburgh; St James, Isle of Grain; St Mary Hoo; Stoke.

MIDDLESBROUGH COUNCIL

www.middlesbrough.gov.uk

Principal Office
Municipal Buildings, Middlesbrough TS1 2QQ
Telephone: (01642) 245432; FAX: (01642) 263827

Function	Chief Officer	Title	Location
Chief Executive	Brian Dinsdale	Chief Executive	Municipal Bldgs
Education	Terry Redmayne	Executive Director	Municipal Bldgs
Electoral Registration	Bryan Siswell	Electoral Registration Officer	Municipal Bldgs
Environmental Health	John Richardson	Executive Director	Municipal Bldgs
Finance	Paul Slocombe	Director	Municipal Bldgs
Housing	Bill Pearch	Director	Municipal Bldgs
Legal Services	Richard Long	Director	Municipal Bldgs
Planning	Kevin Parkes	Head of Planning	Municipal Bldgs

Middlesbrough Council became a unitary authority on 1 April 1996. It took over, in part, from Cleveland County Council.

Parish Councils in the authority's area: Nunthorpe; Stainton; Thornton.

ENGLISH UNITARY AUTHORITIES

MILTON KEYNES COUNCIL

www.miltonkeynes.gov.uk

Principal Office
Civic Offices, 1 Saxon Gate East, Milton Keynes, Buckinghamshire MK9 3EJ
Telephone: (01908) 691691; FAX: (01908) 252456; DX 31406 Milton Keynes 1

Learning and Development; Neighbourhood Services
Saxon Court, 502 Avebury Boulevard, Milton Keynes MK9 3HS
Telephone: (01908) 691691; FAX: (01908) 253556

Finance Department
Lloyds Court, 21 North Tenth Street, Milton Keynes MK9 3EE
Telephone: (01908) 691691; FAX: (01908) 252952

Technical Services
Bleak Hall Depot, Chesney Wold, Bleak Hall, Milton Keynes MK6 1LY
Telephone: (01908) 691691; FAX: (01908) 252861

Function	Chief Officer	Title	Location
Chief Executive	John Best	Chief Executive	Civic Offices
Education	James McElligott	Head of Education	Saxon Court
Electoral Registration	John Moffoot	Head of Democratic Services	Civic Offices
Environmental Health	Brian Sandom	Acting Strategic Director – Environment	Civic Offices
Finance	Peter Timmins	Chief Officer, Finance & Corporate Services	Lloyds Court
Housing	Kate Page	Strategic Director – Neighbourhood Services	Saxon Court
Legal Services	Mark Jones	Head of Legal & Property Services	Civic Offices
Leisure	Vanessa Gwynn	Strategic Director – Learning & Development	Saxon Court
Local Land Charges	David Hackforth	Head of Planning & Transport	Civic Offices
Planning	David Hackforth	Head of Planning & Transport	Civic Offices
Purchasing & Supplies	Mike Hood	Assistant Treasurer – Audit & Customer Support	Lloyds Court
Social Services	Kate Page	Strategic Director, Neighbourhood Services	Saxon Court
Technical Services	Graham Uppington	Deputy Head of Technical Services	Bleak Hall Dep
Trading Standards	Geoff Beck	Head of Environmental Services	Civic Offices

Milton Keynes Council became a unitary authority on 1 April 1997.

Parish Councils in the authority's area: Astwood & Hardmead; Bow Brickhill; Bradwell; Bradwell Abbey; Broughton & Milton Keynes; Campbell Park; Castlethorpe; Central Milton Keynes; Clifton Reynes & Newton Blossomville; Emberton; Great Linford; Hanslope; Haversham cum Little Linford; Kents Hill & Monkston; Lavendon; Little Brickhill; Loughton; Moulsoe; New Bradwell; North Crawley; Ravenstone; Shenley Brook End; Shenley Church End; Sherington; Simpson; Stantonbury; Stoke Goldington; Walton; Wavendon; West Bletchley; Weston Underwood; Woughton.

Parish Meetings in the authority's area: Calverton; Chicheley; Cold Brayfield; Filgrave & Tyringham; Gayhurst; Lathbury; Warrington.

Town Councils in the authority's area: Bletchley & Fenny Stratford; Newport Pagnell; Olney; Stony Stratford; Woburn Sands; Wolverton & Greenley.

NORTH EAST LINCOLNSHIRE COUNCIL

www.nelincs.gov.uk

Principal Office
Municipal Offices, Town Hall Square, Great Grimsby,
North East Lincolnshire DN31 1HU
Telephone: (01472) 313131; DX 13536 Grimsby 1

ENGLISH UNITARY AUTHORITIES

Education Department
7 Eleanor Street, Grimsby DN32 9DU
Telephone: (01472) 323051

Environmental Planning Department
The Knoll, Knoll Street, Cleethorpes DN35 8LN
Telephone: (01472) 313131

Community Care Services Department
Fryston House, Bargate, Grimsby DN34 5BB
Telephone: (01472) 313131

Function	Chief Officer	Title	Location
Chief Executive	Darryl Stephenson	Interim Chief Executive	Municipal Offices
Education	Geoff Hill	Executive Director of Learning & Child Care	Municipal Offices
Environmental Health	Ray Oxby	Executive Director of Environmental Services	Municipal Offices
Planning	Liz Jones	Executive Director of Policy, Performance & Development	Municipal Offices
Social Services	Julie Ogley	Executive Director of Community Care	Municipal Offices
Technical Services	Ray Oxby	Executive Director of Environmental Services	Municipal Offices

On 1 April 1996, North East Lincolnshire took over from Great Grimsby & Cleethorpes Borough Councils, and, in part, from Humberside County Council.

Parish Councils in the authority's area: Ashby cum Fenby; Barnoldby-le-Beck; Bradley; Brigsley; Habrough; Healing; Humberston; Irby upon Humber; Laceby; New Waltham; Stallingborough; Waltham.

Town Councils in the authority's area: Immingham.

NORTH LINCOLNSHIRE COUNCIL

www.northlincs.gov.uk
Principal Office
Pittwood House, Ashby Road, Scunthorpe, North Lincolnshire DN16 1AB
Telephone: (01724) 296296

Community Services Directorate
Cottage Beck Road, Scunthorpe, North Lincolnshire DN16 1TS
Telephone: (01724) 297801; FAX: (01724) 270078

Education & Personal Development Directorate
Hewson House, PO Box 35, Station Road, Brigg, North Lincolnshire DN20 8XJ
Telephone: (01724) 297011; FAX: (01724) 297243

Environment & Public Protection Directorate
Church Square House, PO Box 42, High Street, Scunthorpe, North Lincolnshire DN42 6XQ
Telephone: (01724) 297601; FAX: (01724) 297899

Social & Housing Services Directorate
The Angel, Market Place, Brigg, North Lincolnshire DN20 8LD
Telephone: (01724) 296401; FAX: (01724) 843992

Function	Chief Officer	Title	Location
Chief Executive	Mr Simon Driver;	Deputy Chief Executive (Governance);	
	Mr Mike Hunter	Deputy Chief Executive (Performance)	Pittwood House
Education	Mr David Lea	Head of Education, Learning & Attainment Services	Hewson House

Electoral Registration	Mr Mike Wood	Head of Legal & Democratic Services	Pittwood House
Environmental Health	Mr Keith Ford	Head of Neighbourhood & Environmental Services	Church Sq Hse
Finance	Mr Mike Wedgewood	Head of Finance	Pittwood House
Housing	Mr Richard Birchett	Head of Public Sector Housing	The Angel
Legal Services	Mr Mike Wood	Head of Legal & Democratic Services	Pittwood House
Leisure	Mr Ian Reekie	Head of Leisure Services	Hewson House
Local Land Charges	Mr Mike Wood	Head of Legal & Democratic Services	Pittwood House
Planning	Mr Tony Lyman	Head of Planning & Regeneration Services	Church Sq Hse
Social Services	Mr Nigel Richardson	Head of Social & Housing Services	The Angel

On 1 April 1996, North Lincolnshire Council took over from Glanford and Scunthorpe Borough Councils and, in part, from Humberside County Council.

Parish Councils in the authority's area: Alkborough; Amcotts; Appleby; Ashby Parkland; Barnetby le Wold; Barrow upon Humber; Belton; Bonby; Burringham; Burton upon Stather; Cadney/Howsham; Croxton/Kirmington; East Butterwick; East Halton; Eastoft; Elsham; Epworth; Flixborough; Garthorpe & Fockerby; Goxhill; Gunness; Haxey; Hibaldstow; Holme; Horkstow; Keadby with Althorpe; Luddington & Haldenby; Manton; Melton Ross; Messingham; New Holland; North Killingholme; Owston Ferry; Redbourne; Roxby-cum-Risby; Saxby-All-Saints; Scawby; South Ferriby; South Killingholme; Thornton Curtis; Ulceby; West Butterwick; West Halton; Whitton; Winteringham; Wooton; Worlaby; Wrawby; Wroot.

Town Councils in the authority's area: Barton upon Humber; Bottesford; Brigg; Broughton; Crowle; Kirton in Lindsey; Winterton.

NORTH SOMERSET DISTRICT COUNCIL

www.n-somerset.gov.uk

Principal Office

Town Hall, Walliscote Grove Road, Weston-super-Mare, North Somerset BS23 1UJ
Telephone: (01934) 888888; FAX: (01934) 888822; DX 8411 Weston-super-Mare

Function	Chief Officer	Title	Location
Chief Executive	Graham Turner	Chief Executive Officer	Town Hall
Education	Colin Diamond	Director of Education	Town Hall
Electoral Registration	Malcolm Nicholson	Solicitor to the Council	Town Hall
Environmental Health	David Lawrence	Assistant Director of Development & Environment	Town Hall
Finance	Jonathan Thompson	Director of Finance & Resources	Town Hall
Housing	Jane Smith	Director of Housing & Social Services	Town Hall
Leisure	David Lawrence	Assistant Director of Environment & Operations	Town Hall
Legal Services	Malcolm Nicholson	Solicitor to the Council	Town Hall
Planning	Karuna Tharmananthar	Assistant Director of Development & Policy	Town Hall
Local Land Charges	Karuna Tharmananthar	Assistant Director of Development & Policy	Town Hall
Social Services	Jane Smith	Director of Housing & Social Services	Town Hall
Technical Services	Karuna Tharmananthar	Assistant Director of Development & Policy	Town Hall
Trading Standards	Karuna Tharmananthar	Assistant Director of Development & Policy	Town Hall

On 1 April 1996, North Somerset District Council took over from Woodspring District Council and, in part, from Avon County Council.

Parish Councils in the authority's area: Abbots Leigh; Backwell; Banwell; Barrow Gurney; Blagdon; Bleadon; Brockley; Burrington; Butcombe; Churchill; Clapton-in-Gordano; Cleeve; Congresbury; Dundry; Easton-in-Gordano; Flax Bourton; Hutton; Kenn; Kewstoke; Kingston Seymour; Locking; Long Ashton; Loxton; Portbury; Puxton; Tickenham; Walton-in-Gordano; Weston-in-Gordano; Wick St Lawrence; Winford; Winscombe & Sandford; Wraxall & Failand; Wrington; Yatton.

Town Councils in the authority's area: Clevedon, Nailsea, Portishead & North Weston; Weston-super-Mare.

NOTTINGHAM CITY COUNCIL

www.nottinghamcity.gov.uk

Principal Office
The Guildhall, Burton Street, Nottingham NG1 4BT
Telephone: (0115) 915 5555; FAX: (0115) 915 4636; DX 719182 Nottingham 34

Development Department
Exchange Buildings North, Smithy Row, Nottingham NG1 2BS
Telephone: (0115) 915 5555; FAX: (0115) 915 5349

Education Department
Sandfield Centre, Sandfield Road, Lenton, Nottingham NG7 1QH
Telephone: (0115) 915 0600; FAX: (0115) 915 0603

Environmental Services Department
Lawrence House, Talbot Street, Nottingham NG1 5NT
Telephone: (0115) 915 5555; FAX: (0115) 915 6151

**Housing Department; Social Services Department;
Leisure & Community Services Department**
14/15 Houndsgate, Nottingham NG1 7BA
Telephone: (0115) 915 5555

Function	Chief Officer	Title	Location
Chief Executive	Mr G Mitchell	Chief Executive	Guildhall
Education	Ms H Tomlinson	Director of Education	Sandfield Ctre
Electoral Registration	Mr K Miller	Electoral Officer	Guildhall
Environmental Health	Mr B Horne	Director of City Development	Exchange Bldgs
Finance	Mr A Belton	Director of Corporate Services	Guildhall
Housing	Ms L Pennington	Director of Housing	Houndsgate
Legal Services	Mr G O'Connell	Head of Legal Services	Guildhall
Leisure	Mr M Williams	Director of Leisure & Community Services	Houndsgate
Local Land Charges	Mr G O'Connell	Head of Legal Services	Guildhall
Planning	Mr B Horne	Director of City Development	Exchange Bldgs
Purchasing & Supplies	Mr K Gordon	Head of Procurement	Guildhall
Social Services	[Vacant]	Director of Social Services	Houndsgate
Trading Standards	Ms C Ryan	Service Manager	Exchange Bldgs

Nottingham City Council became a unitary authority on 1 April 1998.

Parish Councils & Parish Meetings in the authority's area: none.

Town Councils in the authority's area: none.

PETERBOROUGH CITY COUNCIL

www.peterborough.gov.uk

Principal Office
Town Hall, Bridge Street, Peterborough, Cambridgeshire PE1 1PJ
Telephone: (01733) 747474; FAX: (01733) 452537; DX 12310 Peterborough 1

Community Services Department
Bayard Place, Broadway, Peterborough PE1 1HZ
Telephone: (01733) 747474; FAX: (01733) 742600

Contract Services Department
Central Depot, Maskew Avenue, Peterborough PE1 2AY
Telephone: (01733) 425300; FAX: (01733) 891226

Education & Children Department
Bayard Place, Broadway, Peterborough PE1 1HZ
Telephone: (01733) 747474; FAX: (01733) 748111

Environmental Services Department
Bridge House, Bridge Street, Peterborough PE1 1HB
Telephone: (01733) 747474; FAX: (01733) 890348

Adult Social Care Department
Town Hall, Bridge Street, Peterborough PE1 1FD
Telephone: (01733) 747474; FAX: (01733) 758555

Function	Chief Officer	Title	Location
Chief Executive	Ms G Beasley	Chief Executive	Town Hall
Education	Mr J Evans	Director of Education & Children	Bayard Place
Electoral Registration	Ms G Beasley	Chief Executive	Town Hall
Environmental Health	Mr T Gibson	Director of Environmental Services	Bridge House
Finance	Mr G Dobson	Director of Corporate Services	Town Hall
Housing	Mrs S Grant	Director of Community Services	Bayard Place
Legal Services	Mr M Hughes	Solicitor to the Council	Town Hall
Leisure	Mrs S Grant	Director of Community Services	Bayard Place
Local Land Charges	Mr M Hughes	Solicitor to the Council	Town Hall
Planning	Mr T Gibson	Director of Environmental Services	Bridge House
Purchasing & Supplies	Mr G Dobson	Director of Corporate Services	Town Hall
Social Services	Mr I Anderson	Director of Adult Social Care	Bayard Place
Technical Services	Mr G Dobson	Director of Corporate Services	Bayard Place
Trading Standards	Mr T Gibson	Director of Environmental Services	Bayard Place

Peterborough City Council became a unitary authority on 1 April 1998.

Parish Councils in the authority's area: Ailsworth; Bainton; Barnack; Borough Fen; Bretton; Castor; Deeping Gate; Etton; Eye; Glinton; Helpston; Marholm; Maxey; Newborough; Northborough; Orton Longueville; Orton Waterville; Peakirk; Southorpe; Sutton; Thorney; Thornhaugh; Ufford; Wansford; Wittering; Wothorpe.

Parish Meetings in the authority's area: St Martins Without; Upton.

PLYMOUTH CITY COUNCIL

www.plymouth.gov.uk

Principal Office
Civic Centre, Royal Parade, Plymouth, Devon PL1 2EW
Telephone: (01752) 668000; FAX: (01752) 304819

Lifelong Learning; Social & Housing Services
Windsor House, Tavistock Road, Derriford, Plymouth
Telephone: (01752) 668000

Function	Chief Officer	Title	Location
Chief Executive	Mr Mike Robinson	Acting Chief Executive	Civic Centre
Education	Ms Bronwen Lacey	Director for Lifelong Learning	Windsor House
Environmental Health	Mr Les Netherton	Head of Environmental Services	Civic Centre
Finance	Mr Alan Clifford	City Treasurer	Civic Centre
Housing	Mr Clive Turner	Director for Housing Services	Windsor House
Legal Services	Mr Dave Shepperd	Head of Legal Services	Civic Centre

ENGLISH UNITARY AUTHORITIES

REDCAR & CLEVELAND BOROUGH COUNCIL

www.redcar-cleveland.gov.uk

Principal Office
Town Hall, Fabian Road, South Bank, Yorkshire TS6 9AR
Telephone: (01642) 444000; FAX: (01642) 444588; DX 60041 Normanby

Education Department, Neighbourhood Services Department
Council Offices, Kirkleatham Street, Redcar, Yorkshire TS10 1XZ
Telephone: (01642) 444000

Social Services Department
Seafield House, Kirkleatham Street, Redcar, Yorkshire TS10 1SP
Telephone: (01642) 771500; FAX: (01642) 771560

Development Department
Belmont House, Rectory Lane, Guisborough, Yorkshire TS14 7FD
Telephone: (01642) 444000; FAX: (01287) 612335

Function	Chief Officer	Title	Location
Chief Executive	Mr C Moore	Chief Executive	Town Hall
Education	Mrs J Lewis	Director of Education	Council Offices
Electoral Registration	Mr R Short	Electoral Officer	Town Hall
Environmental Health	Dr J Rees	Director of Development	Belmont House
Finance	Mr R Richardson	Director of Finance, Performance & Procurement	Town Hall
Housing	Dr J Rees	Director of Development	Belmont House
Legal Services	Mr R J Frankland	Assistant Chief Executive (Legal & Democratic Services)	Town Hall
Leisure	Mrs C Barnes	Assistant Director (Advice & Culture)	Council Offices
Local Land Charges	Mr R J Frankland	Assistant Chief Executive (Legal & Democratic Services)	Town Hall
Planning	Dr J Rees	Director of Development	Belmont House
Purchasing & Supplies	Mr R Richardson	Director of Finance, Performance & Procurement	Town Hall
Social Services	Mr M Bates	Director of Health & Social Care	Seafield House
Technical Services	Dr J Rees	Director of Development	Belmont House
Trading Standards	Mr J Bell	Chief Trading Standards Officer	Council Offices

On 1 April 1996, Redcar & Cleveland Borough Council took over from Langbaurgh-on-Tees Borough Council and, in part, from Cleveland County Council.

Parish Councils in the authority's area: Lockwood; Saltburn, Marske & New Marske; Skelton & Brotton.

Town Councils in the authority's area: Guisborough, Loftus.

RUTLAND COUNTY COUNCIL

www.rutnet.co.uk/rcc

Principal Office
Catmose, Oakham, Rutland, LE15 6HP
Telephone: (01572) 722577; FAX: (01572) 758307; DX 28340 Oakham

Function	Chief Officer	Title	Location
Chief Executive	Mr Keith Franklin	Chief Executive	Catmose
Education	Ms Carol Chambers	Director of Education, Youth & Culture	Catmose
Electoral Registration	Mr Graham Carey	Central Services Manager	Catmose
Environmental Health	Mr Phil Trow	Director of Environmental Services	Catmose
Finance	Mr Neil Taylor	Director of Resources	Catmose
Housing	Mr John Bloxsom	Head of Housing	Catmose
Legal Services	Mr Geoff Pook	Head of Legal Services	Catmose
Leisure	Ms Carol Chambers	Director of Education, Youth & Culture	Catmose

ENGLISH UNITARY AUTHORITIES

Local Land Charges	Mr Geoff Pook	Head of Legal Services	Catmose
Planning	Mr Dorsan Baker	Head of Planning & Development	Catmose
Purchasing & Supplies	Mr Graham Carey	Central Services Manager	Catmose
Social Services	Mr Colin Foster	Director of Social Services & Housing	Catmose
Technical Services	Mr Phil Trow	Director of Environmental Services	Catmose
Trading Standards	Mrs Sue Lammin	Head of Environmental Protection	Catmose

Rutland County Council became a unitary authority on 1 April 1997. It took over from the former Rutland District Council and, in part, from Leicestershire County Council.

Parish Councils in the authority's area: Ashwell; Barrowden; Belton; Braunston; Caldecott; Cottesmore; Edith Weston; Empingham; Essendine; Exton; Great Casterton; Greetham; Ketton; Langham; Little Casterton; Lyddington; Manton; Market Overton; Morcott; North Luffenham; Ridlington; Ryhall; Seaton; South Luffenham; Stretton; Whissendine; Wing.

Parish Meetings in the authority's area: Ayston; Barleythorpe; Barrow; Beaumont Chase; Bisbrooke; Brooke; Burley; Clipsham; Egleton; Glaston; Gunthorpe; Hambleton; Horn; Leighfield; Lyndon; Martinsthorpe; Normanton; Pickworth; Pilton; Preston; Stoke Dry; Teigh; Thistleton; Thorpe by Water; Tickencote; Tinwell; Tixover; Wardley; Whitwell.

Town Councils in the authority's area: Oakham; Uppingham.

ISLES OF SCILLY COUNCIL

www.scilly.gov.uk

Principal Office
Town Hall, St Mary's, Isle of Scilly TR21 0LW
Telephone: (01720) 422537; FAX: (01720) 422202

Function	Chief Officer	Title	Location
Chief Executive	Mr P S Hygate	Clerk & Chief Executive	Town Hall
Education	Mr P S Hygate	Clerk & Chief Executive	Town Hall
Electoral Registration	Mr P S Hygate	Clerk & Chief Executive	Town Hall
Finance	Mr B Archer	Treasurer	Town Hall
Housing	Mr B Archer	Treasurer	Town Hall
Local Land Charges	Mr D Nicholas-McKee	Planning Officer	Town Hall
Planning	Mr D Nicholas-McKee	Planning Officer	Town Hall
Social Services	Mr A Lejk	Director of Social Services	Town Hall
Technical Services	Mr N Gardner	Chief Technical Officer	Town Hall

SLOUGH BOROUGH COUNCIL

www.slough.gov.uk

Principal Office
Town Hall, Bath Road, Slough, Berkshire SL1 3UQ
Telephone: (01753) 552288; FAX: (01753) 692499; DX 42270 Slough

Housing & Neighbourhood Services
Wellington House, PO Box 570, Slough SL1 1FA
Telephone: (01753) 552288

Function	Chief Officer	Title	Location
Chief Executive	Cheryl Coppell	Chief Executive	Town Hall
Education	Chris Spencer	Director of Learning & Cultural Services	Town Hall
Electoral Registration	Steven Quayle	Director of Legal, Democratic & Development Services	Town Hall
Environmental Health	Rosemary Westbrook	Director of Housing & Neighbourhood Services	Town Hall
Finance	Mike Suarez	Director of Finance	Town Hall

Housing	Rosemary Westbrook	Director of Housing & Neighbourhood Services	Town Hall
Legal Services	Steven Quayle	Director of Legal, Democratic & Development Services	Town Hall
Leisure	Janet Perez	Director of 'Heart of Slough' Project	Town Hall
Local Land Charges	Steven Quayle	Director of Legal, Democratic & Development Services	Town Hall
Planning	Steven Quayle	Director of Legal, Democratic & Development Services	Town Hall
Social Services	Dawn Warwick	Director of Social Services	Town Hall

Slough Borough Council became a unitary authority on 1 April 1998.

Parish Councils in the authority's area: Britwell; Colnbrook with Poyle; Wexham Court.

SOUTH GLOUCESTERSHIRE COUNCIL

www.southglos.gov.uk

Principal Office

The Council Offices, Castle Street, Thornbury, South Gloucestershire BS35 1HF
Telephone: (01454) 868686; FAX: (01454) 863067; DX 48357 Thornbury

Function	Chief Officer	Title	Location
Chief Executive	Amanda Phillips	Chief Executive	Council Offices
Education	Therese Gillespie	Director of Education	Council Offices
Electoral Registration	Roger Hopkins	Cabinet Secretary	Council Offices
Environmental Health	Ken Latimer	Assistant Director – Environmental Services	Council Offices
Finance	Paul Appleton	Acting Director of Corporate Resources	Council Offices
Housing	Andy Graham	Director of Housing	Council Offices
Legal Services	Kate Berry	Head of Legal & Democratic Services	Council Offices
Leisure	Steve Evans	Director of Community Services	Council Offices
Local Land Charges	Kate Berry	Head of Legal & Democratic Services	Council Offices
Planning	Peter Jackson	Director of Planning, Transportation & Strategic Environment	Council Offices
Social Services	Peter Murphy	Acting Director of Social Services	Council Offices
Technical Services	Alan Marshall	Head of Property Services	Council Offices
Trading Standards	Ken Latimer	Assistant Director – Environmental Services	Council Offices

On 1 April 1996, South Gloucestershire Council took over from Kingswood Borough Council, Northavon District Council and, in part, from Avon County Council.

Parish Councils in the authority's area: Acton Turville; Almondsbury; Alveston; Aust; Badminton; Bitton; Charfield; Cold Ashton; Cromhall; Dodington; Doynton; Dyrham & Hinton; Falfield; Frampton Cotterell; Hanham Abbots; Hawkesbury; Horton; Iron Acton; Mangotsfield; Marshfield; Oldbury-on-Severn; Oldland; Olveston; Pilning & Severn Beach; Pucklechurch; Rangeworthy; Rockhampton; Siston; Stoke Gifford; Tormarton; Tytherington; Westerleigh; Wick & Abson; Wickwar; Winterbourne.

Parish Meetings in the authority's area: Hill, Little Sodbury, Tortworth.

Town Councils in the authority's area: Bradley Stoke, Filton, Patchway; Sodbury; Thornbury, Yate.

SOUTHAMPTON CITY COUNCIL

www.southampton.gov.uk

Principal Office

Civic Centre, Civic Centre Road, Southampton, Hampshire SO14 7LY
Telephone: (023) 8022 3855

Legal Services
Southbrook Rise, 4/8 Millbrook Road East, Southampton SO15 1YG
Telephone: (023) 8022 3855; FAX: (023) 8023 3079; DX 115710 Southampton 17

Function	Chief Officer	Title	Location
Chief Executive	Mr Roynon	Chief Executive	Civic Centre
Education	Mr I Sandbrook	Executive Director of Lifelong Learning & Leisure	Civic Centre
Electoral Registration	Mr M Heath	Head of Legal Services & Solicitor to the Council	Civic Centre
Environmental Health	Mrs L Marsh	Acting Head of Environmental Services & Consumer Protection	Civic Centre
Finance	Mr T O'Rourke	Head of Financial Services	Civic Centre
Housing	Mr N Murphy	Executive Director	Civic Centre
Legal Services	Mr M Heath	Head of Legal Services & Solicitor to the Council	Civic Centre
Local Land Charges	Mr M Heath	Head of Legal Services & Solicitor to the Council	Civic Centre
Planning	Mrs L Brown	Executive Director of Development & Sustainability	Civic Centre
Purchasing & Supplies	Mr R Eyles	Head of Corporate Contracts	Sthbrook Rise
Social Services	Mr J Beer	Executive Director of Social Services	Civic Centre

Southampton City Council became a unitary authority on 1 April 1997.

Parish Councils & Parish Meetings in the authority's area: none.

Town Councils in the authority's area: none.

SOUTHEND-ON-SEA BOROUGH COUNCIL

www.southend.gov.uk

Principal Office
Civic Centre, Victoria Avenue, Southend-on-Sea, Essex SS2 6ER
Telephone: (01702) 215000; FAX: (01702) 215110; DX 2812 Southend-on-Sea

Function	Chief Officer	Title	Location
Chief Executive	Mr J K M Krawiec	Chief Executive & Town Clerk	Civic Centre
Education	Ms L O'Reilly	Director of Education & Lifelong Learning	Civic Centre
Electoral Registration	Mr J K M Krawiec	Chief Executive & Town Clerk	Civic Centre
Environmental Health	Mr D Watts	Director of Technical & Environmental Services	Civic Centre
Finance	Mr D Andrews	Borough Treasurer & Deputy Chief Executive	Civic Centre
Housing	Mr J Nawrockyi	Director of Social Care	Civic Centre
Legal Services	Mr J K M Krawiec	Chief Executive & Town Clerk	Civic Centre
Leisure	Mr J Dallaway	Director of Leisure, Culture & Amenity Services	Civic Centre
Local Land Charges	Mr J K M Krawiec	Chief Executive & Town Clerk	Civic Centre
Planning	Mr D Watts	Director of Technical & Environmental Services	Civic Centre
Social Services	Mr J Nawrockyi	Director of Social Care	Civic Centre
Technical Services	Mr D Watts	Director of Technical & Environmental Services	Civic Centre
Trading Standards	Mr D Watts	Director of Technical & Environmental Services	Civic Centre

Southend-on-Sea Borough Council became a unitary authority on 1 April 1998.

Parish Council in the authority's area: Leigh.

STOCKTON-ON-TEES BOROUGH COUNCIL

www.stockton.gov.uk

Principal Office
Municipal Buildings, PO Box 11, Church Road, Stockton-on-Tees, Cleveland TS18 1LD
Telephone: (01642) 393939; FAX: (01642) 393092; DX 60611 Stockton

Housing & Contract Services Department
Sun Street, Thornaby, Stockton-on-Tees, Cleveland TS17 6HB
Telephone: (01642) 393639; FAX: (01642) 393677

Trading Standards
16 Church Road, Stockton-on-Tees, Cleveland TS18 1TX
Telephone: (01642) 526560; FAX: (01642) 393092

Health & Social Care
Alma House, 6 Alma Street, Stockton-on-Tees, Cleveland TS18 2AP

Function	Chief Officer	Title	Location
Chief Executive	Mr George Garlick	Chief Executive	Municipal Bldgs
Education	Mr Stanley Bradford	Corporate Director of Education, Leisure & Cultural Services	Municipal Bldgs
Electoral Registration	Ms Janet Kitching	Electoral Registration Officer	Municipal Bldgs
Environmental Health	Mr Colin Snowdon	Environmental Health Unit Manager	Municipal Bldgs
Finance	Ms Julie Danks	Corporate Director of Finance	Municipal Bldgs
Housing	Mr Neil Schneider	Corporate Director of Service Stockton	Sun Street
Legal Services	Mr David Bond	Director of Law & Democracy	Municipal Bldgs
Leisure	Mr Kevin McAuley	Head of Leisure Services	Municipal Bldgs
Local Land Charges	Ms Judith Brown; Ms Tricia Pinder	Land Charges Officers	Municipal Bldgs
Planning	Mr Stephen Barker	Head of Planning & Environment	Municipal Bldgs
Social Services	Ms Ann Baxter	Corporate Director of Health & Social Care	Alma House
Technical Services	Mr Andy Edwards	Corporate Director of Development & Regeneration	Municipal Bldgs
Trading Standards	Mr David Kitching	Trading Standards & Licensing Manager	16 Church Road

Stockton-on-Tees Borough Council became a unitary authority on 1 April 1996. It took over from, in part, Cleveland County Council.

Town Councils in the authority's area: Thornaby, Yarm.

Parish Councils in the authority's area: Carlton, Castle Levington & Kirklevington, Egglescliffe, Elton, Grindon, Hilton, Long Newton, Maltby & Ingleby Barwick, Preston, Redmarshall, Stillington & Whitton, Wolviston,.

Parish Meetings in the authority's area: Aislaby, Newsham.

STOKE-ON-TRENT CITY COUNCIL

www.stoke.gov.uk

Principal Office
Civic Centre, Glebe Street, Stoke-on-Trent, Staffordshire ST4 1RN
Telephone: (01782) 234567; FAX: (01782) 232603; DX 21058 Stoke-on-Trent

Education Department
PO Box 758, Civic Centre, Glebe Street, Stoke-on-Trent, Staffordshire ST4 1RU
Telephone: (01782) 232014; FAX: (01782) 236102

Directorate of Regeneration & Community
Swift House, Glebe Street, Stoke-on-Trent, Staffordshire ST4 1HP
Telephone: (01782) 232823; FAX: (01782) 232872

Social Services Department
Civic Centre, Glebe Street, Stoke-on-Trent, Staffordshire ST4 1RT
Telephone: (01782) 235985; FAX: (1782) 235996/235920

Function	Chief Officer	Title	Location
Chief Executive	Dr Ita O'Donovan	Council Manager	Civic Centre
Education	Nigel Rigby	Director of Education & Lifelong Learning	Civic Centre
Electoral Registration	Mark Winstanley	City Secretary	Civic Centre
Environmental Health	Stephen Robinson	Director of Housing & Consumer Protection	Civic Centre
Finance	Paul Brindley	Director of Corporate Resources	Swann House
Housing	Stephen Robinson	Director of Housing & Consumer Protection	Civic Centre
Legal Services	Mark Winstanley	City Secretary	Civic Centre
Leisure	Nigel Rigby	Director of Education & Lifelong Learning	Civic Centre
Local Land Charges	Phillip Harper	Director of Urban Environment	Civic Centre
Planning	Phillip Harper	Director of Urban Environment	Civic Centre
Purchasing & Supplies	Paul Brindley	Director of Corporate Resources	Swann House
Social Services	Chris Brabbs	Director of Social Services	Civic Centre
Technical Services	Phillip Harper	Director of Urban Environment	Civic Centre
Trading Standards	Stephen Robinson	Director of Housing & Consumer Protection	Civic Centre

Stoke on Trent City Council became a unitary authority on 1 April 1997.

Parish Councils & Parish Meetings in the authority's area: none.

Town Councils in the authority's area: none.

SWINDON BOROUGH COUNCIL

www.swindon.gov.uk

Principal Office
Civic Offices, Euclid Street, Swindon, Wiltshire SN1 2JH
Telephone: (01793) 463000; FAX: (01793) 490420; DX 133055 Swindon 16

Function	Chief Officer	Title	Location
Chief Executive	Simon Birch	Chief Executive	Civic Offices
Education	Hilary Pitts	Director of Education	Civic Offices
Electoral Registration	Alan Winchcombe	Electoral Services Officer	Civic Offices
Environmental Health	Steve Harcourt	Acting Head of Development Services	Civic Offices
Finance	Paul Blacker	Acting Director of Finance	Civic Offices
Housing	Bernie Brannan	Director of Housing	Civic Offices
Legal Services	Stephen Taylor	Director of Law & Corporate Governance	Civic Offices
Leisure	Alan Greer	Head of Recreation Services	Civic Offices
Local Land Charges	Steve Harcourt	Acting Head of Development Services	Civic Offices
Planning	Steve Harcourt	Acting Head of Development Services	Civic Offices
Purchasing & Supplies	John Short	Director of Swindon Services	Civic Offices
Social Services	Keith Skerman	Director of Social Services	Civic Offices
Technical Services	John Stevenson	Head of Technical Services	Civic Offices
Trading Standards	Rob Taylor	Trading Standards Officer	Civic Offices

Swindon Borough Council (formerly Thamesdown Borough Council) became a unitary authority on 1 April 1997. It took over services previously provided in Thamesdown by Wiltshire County Council.

Parish Councils in the authority's area: Bishopstone; Blunsdon St Andrew; Castle Eaton; Chiseldon; Covingham; Hannington; Haydon Wick; Liddington; South Marston; Sparcells; Stanton Fitzwarren; Stratton St Margaret; Wanborough; Westlea; Wroughton.

Parish Meetings in the authority's area: Inglesham.

Town Councils in the authority's area: Highworth.

BOROUGH OF TELFORD & WREKIN

www.telford.gov.uk

Principal Office
Civic Offices, Telford, Shropshire TF3 4LD
Telephone: (01952) 202100; FAX: (01952) 291060; DX 28085 Telford 5

Housing, Health & Care and Leisure Services
Darby House, Lawn Central, Telford TF3 4JB
Telephone: (01952) 202100

Function	Chief Officer	Title	Location
Chief Executive	Michael Frater	Chief Executive	Civic Offices
Education	Christine Davies	Corporate Director: Education & Cultural Services	Civic Offices
Electoral Registration	Phil Griffiths	Electoral Registration Officer	Civic Offices
Environmental Health	Mike Atherton	Head of Consumer Services	Darby House
Finance	Steve Wellings	Corporate Director: Resources	Civic Offices
Housing	John Coughlan	Corporate Director: Housing, Health & Care	Darby House
Legal Services	Sue Kembrey	Head of Administration & Legal Services	Civic Offices
Leisure	Christine Davies	Corporate Director: Education & Cultural Services	Civic Offices
Local Land Charges	Sue Kembrey	Head of Administration & Legal Services	Civic Offices
Planning	Meredith Evans	Corporate Director: Environment & Economy	Civic Offices
Social Services	John Coughlan	Corporate Director: Housing, Health & Care	Darby House
Technical Services	Sander Kristel	Information Management & Technical Services	Civic Offices
Trading Standards	Mike Atherton	Head of Consumer Services	Darby House

The Borough of Telford & Wrekin received Borough status in May 2002.

Parish Councils in the authority's area: Chetwynd; Chetwynd Aston & Woodcote; Church Aston; Dawley Hamlets; Edgmond; Ercall Magna; The Gorge; Great Dawley; Hadley; Hollinswood & Randlay; Ketley; Kynnersley; Lawley & Overdale; Lilleshall & Donnington; Little Wenlock; Madeley; Rodington; St Georges & Priorslee; Stirchley & Brookside; Tibberton & Cherrington; Waters Upton; Wrockwardine; Wrockwardine Wood & Trench.

Parish Meetings in the authority's area: Bolas Magna; Cherrington; Eyton-upon-the-Weald Moors.

Town Councils in the authority's area: Newport; Oakengates; Wellington.

TELFORD & WREKIN COUNCIL
See now Borough of Telford & Wrekin.

THURROCK COUNCIL

www.thurrock.gov.uk

Principal Office
Civic Offices, New Road, Grays, Essex RM17 6SL
Telephone: (01375) 390000

Function	Chief Officer	Title	Location
Chief Executive	David White	Managing Director	Civic Offices
Education	Steve Beynon	Director of Education	Civic Offices
Environmental Health	Stephen Weigel	Director of Regeneration & Support Services	Civic Offices
Finance	Andrew Hardingham	Head of Finance	Civic Offices

| Housing | Christine Paley | Head of Housing & Social Care | Civic Offices |
| Social Services | Christine Paley | Head of Housing & Social Care | Civic Offices |

Thurrock Borough Council became a unitary authority on 1 April 1998.

Parish Councils & Parish Meetings in the authority's area: none.

Town Councils in the authority's area: none.

TORBAY COUNCIL

www.torbay.gov.uk

Principal Office
Town Hall, Castle Circus, Torquay, Devon TQ1 3DR
Telephone: (01803) 201201; FAX: (01803) 292866; DX 59006 Torquay 1

Education Services (LEA); Social Services
Oldway Mansion, Paignton TQ3 2TS
Telephone: (01803) 201201

Environment Services
Roebuck House, Abbey Road, Torquay TQ2 5TS
Telephone: (01803) 201201; FAX: (01803) 208756

Highways & Engineering Services
Union House, Union Street, Torquay TQ1 3TZ

Tourist Information Centre
The Tourist Centre, Vaughan Parade, Torquay TQ2 5JG
Telephone: 0906 680 1268 (calls charged at 25p/min); FAX: (01803) 214885

Function	Chief Officer	Title	Location
Chief Executive	Mr P Lucas	Interim Director of Paid Service	Town Hall
Education	Mr A Smith	Director of Education Services	Oldway Mansion
Environmental Health	Mrs F Hughes	Environmental Health & Consumer Protection Senior Group Manager	Roebuck House
Finance	Mr R Thorpe	Assistant Chief Executive	Town Hall
Legal Services	Mr B Norman	Assistant Chief Executive	Town Hall
Planning	Mr L Crump	Head of Development & Conservation Planning	Roebuck House
Social Services	Mrs J Wood	Director of Social Services	Oldway Mansion
Technical Services	Mr M Webley	Head of Highways & Engineering Services	Union House

Torbay Council became a unitary authority on 1 April 1998.

Parish Councils & Parish Meetings in the authority's area: none.

Town Councils in the authority's area: none.

WARRINGTON BOROUGH COUNCIL

www.warrington.gov.uk

Principal Office
Town Hall, Warrington WA1 1UH
Telephone: (01925) 444400; DX 17760 Warrington

Environment & Regeneration
Palmyra House, Palmyra Square North, Warrington WA1 1JN
Telephone: (01925) 442595

Education & Lifelong Learning
New Town House, Buttermarket Street, Warrington WA1 2NJ
Telephone: (01925) 442901; FAX: (01925) 442929

ENGLISH UNITARY AUTHORITIES

Corporate Resources
PO Box 13, Warrington WA1 1BN
Telephone: (01925) 442201; FAX: (01925) 231077/231091

Neighbourhood Services
Bank House, Sankey Street, Warrington
Telephone: (01925) 443001

Social Services
Bewsey Old School, Lockton Lane, Warrington WA5 5BF
Telephone: (01925) 444000; FAX: (01925) 444254

Function	Chief Officer	Title	Location
Chief Executive	Mr D Whitehead	Interim Chief Executive	Town Hall
Education	Mr M Roxbrough	Director of Education	New Town Hse
Electoral Registration	Mr Dave Pendleton	Democratic Services Manager	Town Hall
Environmental Health	Mr A Gilbert	Assistant Director	Palmyra Hse
Finance	Ms Yvonne Bottomley	Interim Director of Corporate Resources	PO Box 13
Housing	Mr P Mercer	Director of Golden Gates Housing	Bank House
Legal Services	Patricia Jervis	Head of Legal Services	New Town Hse
Local Land Charges	Bob Jones	Admin Services Manager	Town Hall
Planning	Mr J Earle	Assistant Director	New Town Hse
Purchasing & Supplies	Irene Maguire	Purchasing Officer	PO Box 13
Social Services	Pam Smith	Interim Director of Social Services	Bewsey Old Sch
Technical Services	Alan Stephenson	Director of Environment & Regeneration	New Town Hse
Trading Standards	Mr P Astley	Principal Trading Standards Officer	New Town Hse

Warrington Borough Council became a unitary authority on 1 April 1998.

Parish Councils in the authority's area: Appleton; Birchwood; Burtonwood; Croft; Cuerdley; Culcheth with Glazebury; Grappenhall; Great Sankey; Hatton; Lymm; Penketh; Poulton with Fearnhead; Rixton with Glazebrook; Stockton Heath; Stretton; Thelwall; Walton; Winwick; Woolston.

WEST BERKSHIRE DISTRICT COUNCIL

www.westberks.gov.uk

Principal Office
Council Offices, Market Street, Newbury, Berkshire RG14 5LD
Telephone: (01635) 42400; FAX: (01635) 519431; DX 30825 Newbury

Countryside & Environment
Council Offices, Faraday Road, Newbury RG14 2AF
Telephone: (01635) 42400

Highways Department
Faraday Road, Newbury RG14 2AF
Telephone: (01635) 42400

Social Services; Education; Culture & Youth
Avonbank House, West Street, Newbury RG14 1BZ
Telephone: (01635) 42400

Function	Chief Officer	Title	Location
Chief Executive	Jim Graham	Chief Executive	Market Street
Education	Richard Hubbard	Corporate Director, Children & Young People	Avonbank House
Environmental Health	John Ashworth	Corporate Director, Environment & Public Protection	Faraday Road

Finance	Nick Carter	Corporate Director, Strategy & Commissioning	Market Street
Housing	Margaret Goldie	Corporate Director, Community Care & Housing	Avonbank House
Planning	John Ashworth	Corporate Director, Environment & Public Protection	Faraday Road
Social Services	Margaret Goldie	Corporate Director, Community Care & Housing	Avonbank House
Trading Standards	John Ashworth	Corporate Director, Environment & Public Protection	Faraday Road

West Berkshire Council, formerly Newbury District Council, became a unitary authority on 1 April 1998.

Parish Councils in the authority's area: Aldermaston; Aldworth; Ashampstead; Basildon; Beech Hill; Beedon; Beenham; Boxford; Bradfield; Brightwalton; Brimpton; Bucklebury; Burghfield; Chaddleworth; Chieveley; Cold Ash; Compton; East Garston; East Ilsley; Enborne; Englefield; Frilsham; Great Shefford; Greenham; Hampstead Norreys; Hamstead Marshall; Hermitage; Inkpen; Kintbury; Lambourn; Leckhampstead; Midgham; Padworth; Pangbourne; Peasemore; Purley on Thames; Shaw-cum-Donnington; Speen; Stanford Dingley; Stratfield Mortimer; Streatley; Sulhamstead; Theale; Tidmarsh with Sulham; Tilehurst; Ufton Nervet; Welford; West Ilsley; Wokefield; Woolhampton; Yattendon.

Parish Meetings in the authority's area: Catmore; Farnborough; Fawley; West Woodhay; Winterbourne.

Town Councils in the authority's area: Hungerford; Newbury; Thatcham.

ROYAL BOROUGH OF WINDSOR & MAIDENHEAD

www.rbwm.gov.uk

Principal Office
Town Hall, St Ives Road, Maidenhead, Berkshire SL6 1RF
Telephone: (01628) 798888; FAX: (01628) 796408; DX 6422 Maidenhead 1

Education; Highways & Transportation; Finance;
Leisure and Cultural Services; Personnel
St Ives House and York Stream House, St Ives Road, Maidenhead SL6 1QS
Telephone: (01628) 798888; FAX: (01628) 796408

Planning (Windsor Area); Environmental Health Unit; Trading Standards Unit;
Social Services
York House, Sheet Street, Windsor SL4 1DD
Telephone: (01753) 810525; FAX: (01628) 796525

Function	Chief Officer	Title	Location
Chief Executive	Mr D C Lunn	Chief Executive	Town Hall
Education	Mr M Peckham	Director of Education	Town Hall
Electoral Registration	Mr L White	Head of Democratic Services	Town Hall
Environmental Health	Mr T Gould	Head of Environmental Services	York House
Finance	Mr J Taylor	Head of Finance	Town Hall
Housing	Mr C Thomas	Head of Housing Policy Unit	Town Hall
Legal Services	Miss D H Hills	Head of Central Services	Town Hall
Leisure	Mr D Oram	Director of Leisure, Cultural and Property Services	Town Hall
Local Land Charges	Mrs J Pringle	Senior Solicitor	Town Hall
Planning	Mrs S Holden	Director of Planning & Environment	St Ives House
Social Services	Mr J Gould	Director of Social Services	Town Hall
Technical Services	Mr S Brown	Head of Highways & Transportation	St Ives House
Trading Standards	Mr S Johnson	Trading Standards Manager	York House

ENGLISH UNITARY AUTHORITIES

The Royal Borough of Windsor & Maidenhead became a unitary authority on 1 April 1998.

Parish Councils in the authority's area: Bisham; Bray; Cookham; Cox Green; Datchet; Horton; Hurley; Old Windsor; Shottesbrooke; Sunningdale; Sunninghill; Waltham St Lawrence; White Waltham; Wraysbury.

Town Council in the authority's area: Eton.

WOKINGHAM DISTRICT COUNCIL

www.wokingham.gov.uk

Principal Office

Civic Offices, Shute End, Wokingham, Berkshire RG40 1BN
Telephone: (0118) 974 6000; FAX: (0118) 978 9078; DX 33506 Wokingham

Function	Chief Officer	Title	Location
Chief Executive	Mr Doug Patterson	Chief Executive	Council Offices
Education	Mr Vincent McDonnell	Interim Assistant Chief Executive	Council Offices
Electoral Registration	Mrs S Nelson-Wehrmeyer	Corporate Head of Legal & Democratic Services	Council Offices
Environmental Health	Mr Mark Moon	Corporate Head of Environment	Council Offices
Finance	Mr Graham Ebers	Corporate Head of Finance	Council Offices
Housing	Mr Keith Burns	Corporate Head of Community Wellbeing & Partnership	Council Offices
Legal Services	Mrs S Nelson-Wehrmeyer	Corporate Head of Legal & Democratic Services	Council Offices
Leisure	Mr Vincent McDonnell	Interim Assistant Chief Executive	Council Offices
Local Land Charges	Mrs S Nelson-Wehrmeyer	Corporate Head of Legal & Democratic Services	Council Offices
Planning	Ms Anna Cronin	Corporate Head of Planning	Council Offices
Purchasing & Supplies	Ms Charan Dhillon	Facilities Manager	Council Offices
Social Services	Mr John Beckerleg	Interim Director of Social Services	Council Offices
Technical Services	Mr Mark Moon	Corporate Head of Environment	Council Offices
Trading Standards	Mr Mark Moon	Corporate Head of Environment	Council Offices

Wokingham District Council became a unitary authority on 1 April 1998.

Parish Councils in the authority's area: Arborfield & Newland; Barkham; Charvil; Finchampstead; Hurst; Remenham; Ruscombe; Shinfield; Sonning; Swallowfield; Twyford; Wargrave; Winnersh; Wokingham Without.

Town Councils in the authority's area: Earley; Wokingham; Woodley.

CITY OF YORK COUNCIL

www.york.gov.uk

Principal Office
Guildhall, York YO1 9QN
Telephone: (01904) 613161

City Finance Centre
York YO1 7EW
Telephone: (01904) 613161

Educational Services
Mill House, North Street, York, YO1 6JD
Telephone: (01904) 613161

Environment & Development Services Department
9 St Leonard's Place, York YO1 7ET
Telephone: (01904) 613161

Housing
10–12 George Hudson Street, York
Telephone: (01904) 613161

Legal Services
2 Blake Street, York YO1 8QG
Telephone: (01904) 613161

Lifelong Learning & Leisure
Back Swinegate, York YO1 8ZD
Telephone: (01904) 613161

Trading Standards
De Grey House, Exhibition Square, York YO1 7HE
Telephone: (01904) 613161

Function	Chief Officer	Title	Location
Chief Executive	Mr David Atkinson	Chief Executive	Guildhall
Education	Mr Patrick Scott	Director of Education & Leisure	Mill House
Electoral Registration	Ms Elizabeth Ellis	Electoral & Civic Services Manager	Guildhall
Environmental Health	Mr Roy Templeman	Director of Environment & Development Services	St Leonard's Pl
Finance	Mr Simon Wiles	Director of Resources	City Finance Ctr
Housing	Mr Jim Crook	Director of Community Services	Geo Hudson St
Legal Services	Ms Suzan Hemingway	Head of Civic, Democratic & Legal Services	Guildhall
Leisure	Mr Charlie Croft	Assistant Director of Lifelong Learning & Leisure	Back Swinegate
Local Land Charges	Mr Peter Audin	Land Charges Manager	St Leonard's Pl
Planning	Mr Roy Templeman	Director of Environment & Development Services	St Leonard's Pl
Purchasing & Supplies	Mr Martin Gough	Procurement Adviser	City Finance Ctr
Social Services	Mr Jim Crook	Director of Community Services	Geo Hudson St
Trading Standards	Mr Colin Rumford	Head of Trading Standards	De Grey House

York City Council became a unitary authority on 1 April 1996, and became City of York Council.

Parish Councils in the authority's area: Acaster Malbis; Askham Bryan; Askham Richard; Bishopthorpe; Clifton Without; Copmanthorpe; Deighton; Dunnington; Earswick; Elvington; Fulford; Heslington; Hessay; Heworth Without; Holtby; Huntington; Kexby; Murton; Naburn; Nether Poppleton; New Earswick; Osbaldwick; Rawcliffe; Rufforth & Knapton; Skelton; Stockton-on-the-Forest; Strensall & Towthorpe; Upper Poppleton; Wheldrake; Wigginton.

Town Council in the authority's area: Haxby.

METROPOLITAN DISTRICT COUNCILS

BARNSLEY METROPOLITAN BOROUGH COUNCIL

www.barnsley.gov.uk

Principal Office
Town Hall, Barnsley, South Yorkshire S70 2TA
Telephone: (01226) 770770; FAX: (01226) 773305; DX 12266 Barnsley 1

Electoral Registration
18 Regent Street, Barnsley, South Yorkshire S70 2HG

Environment and Development Directorate
Central Offices, Kendray Street, Barnsley, South Yorkshire S70 2TN

Culture, Sport & Tourism – Development Directorate
Beevor Court, Pontefract Road, Barnsley, South Yorkshire S71 1HG
Telephone: (01226) 773601

Function	Chief Officer	Title	Location
Chief Executive	Mr P J Coppard	Chief Executive	Town Hall
Education	Mrs E Sutton	Executive Director, Education	Town Hall
Electoral Registration	Miss M Barrett	Senior Elections Assistant	Regent Street
Environmental Health	Mr M Hanson	Assistant Director, Environmental Health & Trading Standards	Central Offices
Finance	Mr S Pick	Executive Director, Financial Resources	Town Hall
Housing	[Vacant]	Executive Director, Housing & Property	Town Hall
Legal Services	Mr A E Frosdick	Borough Secretary	Town Hall
Leisure	Mr G Noble	Assistant Director, Culture, Sport & Tourism	Beevor Court
Local Land Charges	Mr A Maher	Assistant Borough Secretary	Town Hall
Planning	Ms R Middleton	Assistant Director, Planning & Transportation	Central Offices
Purchasing & Supplies	Mr G Stephenson	Corporate Commissioning & Procurement Officer	Town Hall
Social Services	Mr G Gatehouse	Executive Director, Social Services	Town Hall
Trading Standards	Mr M Hanson	Assistant Director, Environmental Health & Trading Standards	Central Offices

Parish Councils in the authority's area: Billingley; Brierley; Cawthorne; Dunford; Great Houghton; Gunthwaite & Ingbirchworth; Hunshelf; Langsett; Little Houghton; Oxspring; Shafton; Silkstone; Stainborough; Tankersley; Thurgoland; Wortley.

Parish Meetings in the authority's area: High Hoyland.

Town Council in the authority's area: Penistone.

BIRMINGHAM CITY COUNCIL

www.birmingham.gov.uk

Principal Office
The Council House, Victoria Square, Birmingham, West Midlands B1 1BB
Telephone: (0121) 303 9944

METROPOLITAN DISTRICT COUNCILS

Education Services
Education Offices, Margaret Street, Birmingham, West Midlands B3 3BU
Telephone: (0121) 203 2590; FAX: (0121) 303 1318

Housing Services; Social Care & Health Services
Louisa Ryland House, 44 Newhall Street, Birmingham, West Midlands B3 3PL
Telephone: (0121) 303 4125; FAX: (0121) 236 4833

Planning Services
12th Floor, Alpha Tower, Suffolk Street, Queensway, Birmingham B1 1TZ
Telephone: (0121) 303 1115; FAX: (0121) 303 1334

Function	Chief Officer	Title	Location
Chief Executive	Lin Homer	Chief Executive	Council House
Education	Tony Howell	Strategic Director of Learning & Culture	Education Offices
Finance	Stephen Hughes	Strategic Director of Resources	Council House
Housing	[Vacant]	Director of Housing	Louisa Ryland Hse
Planning	Emrys Jones	Chief Planning Officer	Alpha Tower
Social Services	Peter Hay	Strategic Director of Social Care & Health	Louisa Ryland Hse
Technical Services	David Pywell	Strategic Director of Development	Council House

Parish Councils & Parish Meetings in the authority's area: New Frankley.

Town Councils in the authority's area: none.

BOLTON METROPOLITAN BOROUGH COUNCIL

www.bolton.gov.uk

Principal Office
Town Hall, Bolton, Lancashire BL1 1RU
Telephone: (01204) 333333; FAX: (01204) 351060

Housing Department; Education & Culture Department
Paderborn House, Victoria Square North, Le Mans Crescent, Bolton BL1 1JW
Telephone: (01204) 333333

Social Services Department
Le Mans Crescent, Bolton BL1 1EU
Telephone: (01204) 333333

Commercial Services Department
Wellington House, Wellington Street, Bolton BL3 5DX
Telephone: (01204) 333333

Housing Department
1st Floor, Adelaide House, Adelaide Street, Bolton BL3 3NY

Function	Chief Officer	Title	Location
Chief Executive	Mr B Knight	Chief Executive	Town Hall
Education	Mrs M Blenkinsop	Director of Education & Culture	Paderborn Hse
Electoral Registration	Mr B Knight	Chief Executive	Town Hall
Environmental Health	Mr R Jefferson	Director of Environment	Town Hall
Finance	Mr S Arnfield	Director of Finance	Town Hall
Housing	Mr J Smethurst	Chief Housing Officer	Adelaide Hse
Legal Services	Mr P Wilson	Director of Central Services	Town Hall
Leisure	Mrs M Blenkinsop	Director of Education & Culture	Paderborn Hse
Local Land Charges	Mr P Wilson	Director of Central Services	Town Hall
Planning	Mr R Jefferson	Director of Environment	Town Hall
Purchasing & Supplies	Mrs M Blenkinsop	Director of Education & Culture	Paderborn Hse
Social Services	Mr A Robertson	Director of Social Services	Le Mans Cres

Technical Services	Mr A H Fisher	Director of Commercial Services	Wellington Hse
Trading Standards	Mr R Jefferson	Director of Environment	Town Hall

Parish Councils in the authority's area: none.

Town Councils in the authority's area: Blackrod; Horwich; Westhoughton.

CITY OF BRADFORD METROPOLITAN DISTRICT COUNCIL

www.bradford.gov.uk

Principal Office
City Hall, Bradford, West Yorkshire BD1 1HY
Telephone: (01274) 752111; FAX: (01274) 392718

Directorate of Education
Future's House, Bolling Road, Bradford, West Yorkshire BD4 7EB
Telephone: (01274) 752111; FAX: (01274) 390081

Directorate of Housing & Environmental Protection
Central House, Bradford, West Yorkshire BD1 1DJ
Telephone: (01274) 752111; FAX: (01274) 390076

Directorate of Social Services
Olicana House, Bradford, West Yorkshire BD1 5RE
Telephone: (01274) 752111; FAX: (01274) 390615

Function	Chief Officer	Title	Location
Chief Executive	Mr P Robinson	Interim Chief Executive	City Hall
Education	Mr P Green	Director (Education)	Future's House
Environmental Health	Mr R Wixey	Director	Central Hse
Social Services	Ms A O'Sullivan	Strategic Director (Social Services)	Olicana House

Parish Councils in the authority's area: Addingham; Cullingworth; Ilkley; Oxenhope; Silsden; Steeton-with-Eastburn.

Town Councils in the authority's area: Denholme; Keighley.

BURY METROPOLITAN BOROUGH COUNCIL

www.bury.gov.uk

Principal Office
Town Hall, Knowsley Street, Bury, Greater Manchester BL9 0SW
Telephone: (0161) 253 5000; FAX: (0161) 253 5119

Education & Culture
Athenaeum House, Market Street, Bury BL9 0BN
Telephone: (0161) 253 5000; FAX: (0161) 253 5653

Environment & Development Services
Craig House, Bank Street, Bury, Greater Manchester BL9 0DN
Telephone: (0161) 253 5000; FAX: (0161) 253 5759

Social Services, Health & Housing
Castle Buildings, Market Street, Bury, Greater Manchester BL9 0LT
Telephone: (0161) 253 5000; FAX: (0161) 253 6961

Function	Chief Officer	Title	Location
Chief Executive	Mr M Sanders	Chief Executive	Town Hall
Education	Mr H Williams	Director of Education & Culture	Athenaeum Hse
Electoral Registration	Mr W Rafferty	Elections & Land Charges Officer	Town Hall
Environmental Health	Mr P Allen	Director of Environment & Development Services	Craig House
Finance	Mr M A Owen	Director of Finance & E-Government	Town Hall
Housing	Ms E Ioannides	Director of Social Services, Health & Housing	Castle Buildings

Legal Services	Ms J Hammond	Director of Legal & Democratic Services	Town Hall
Local Land Charges	Mr W Rafferty	Elections & Land Charges Officer	Town Hall
Planning	Mr B Daniel	Chief Planning Officer	Craig House
Social Services	Ms E Ioannides	Director of Social Services, Health & Housing	Castle Buildings
Trading Standards	Mr A Freer	Borough Environmental Services Officer	Craig House

Parish Councils & Parish Meetings in the authority's area: none.

Town Councils in the authority's area: none.

CALDERDALE METROPOLITAN BOROUGH COUNCIL

www.calderdale.gov.uk

Principal Office
Town Hall, Halifax, West Yorkshire HX1 1UJ
Telephone: (01422) 357257; FAX: (01422) 393102

Schools & Children's Services; Environmental Health Services; Engineering Services; Housing Services; Planning Services
Northgate House, Northgate, Halifax, West Yorkshire HX1 1UN
Telephone: (01422) 357257

Finance Services
Princess Buildings, Halifax, West Yorkshire HX1 1TP
Telephone: (01422) 357257; FAX: (01422) 393533

Law & Administration Services
2nd Floor, Westgate House, Halifax, West Yorkshire HX1 1PF
Telephone: (01422) 357257; FAX: (01422) 393073

Leisure Services
1st Floor, Westgate House, Halifax, West Yorkshire HX1 1PF
Telephone: (01422) 359454; FAX: (01422) 342499

Social Services
1 Park Road, Halifax, West Yorkshire HX1 2TU
Telephone: (01422) 393800; FAX: (01422) 393815

Function	Chief Officer	Title	Location
Chief Executive	Mr P Sheehan	Chief Executive	Town Hall
Education	Ms C Gruen	Group Director, Schools & Childrens' Services	Town Hall
Electoral Registration	Mrs C Parkinson	Group Director, Corporate Services	Town Hall
Environmental Health	Mr P Lewer	Group Director, Health & Social Care	Town Hall
Finance	Mrs C Parkinson	Group Director, Corporate Services	Town Hall
Housing	Ms R Wheeler	Group Director, Community Services	Town Hall
Legal Services	Mrs C Parkinson	Group Director, Corporate Services	Town Hall
Leisure	Ms R Wheeler	Group Director, Community Services	Town Hall
Local Land Charges	Mrs C Parkinson	Group Director, Corporate Services	Town Hall
Planning	Ms J Waggott	Group Director, Regeneration & Development	Town Hall
Purchasing & Supplies	Mrs C Parkinson	Group Director, Corporate Services	Town Hall
Social Services	Mr P Lewer	Group Director, Health & Social Care	Town Hall
Technical Services	Ms J Waggott	Group Director, Regeneration & Development	Town Hall

Parish Councils in the authority's area: Blackshaw; Erringden; Heptonstall; Ripponden; Wadsworth.

Town Councils in the authority's area: Hebden Royd; Todmorden.

Neighbourhood Councils in the authority's area: Clifton; Sowerby Bridge.

COVENTRY CITY METROPOLITAN DISTRICT COUNCIL

www.coventry.gov.uk

Principal Office
The Council House, Earl Street, Coventry, West Midlands CV1 5RR
Telephone: (024) 7683 3333; DX 18868 Coventry 2

City Treasurer
First Floor, Christchurch House, Greyfriars Lane, Coventry CV1 2QL
Telephone: (024) 7683 3700; FAX: (024) 7683 3770

Environmental Services
Spire House, New Union Street, Coventry CV1 2PS
Telephone: (024) 7683 1800; FAX: (024) 7683 1970

Cultural Services
Spire House, New Union Street, Coventry CV1 2PS
Telephone: (024) 7683 2300; FAX: (024) 7683 2470

City Development
Seventh Floor, Civic Centre 4, Much Park Street, Coventry CV1 2PY
Telephone: (024) 7683 1200; FAX: (024) 7683 1257

Function	Chief Officer	Title	Location
Chief Executive	Stella Manzie	Chief Executive	Council House
Education	Roger Edwardson	Director of Education & Libraries	Council House
Electoral Registration	Val Clowes	Principal Officer	Council House
Finance	Angie Ridgwell	Director of Finance & ICT	C'stchurch Hse
Legal Services	Chris Hinde	City Secretary	Council House
Leisure	Tim Bryan	Head of Culture & Leisure	Spire House
Planning	Ted Hiscocks	Planning & Transportation Policy Team Manager	Civic Centre 4
Social Services	John Bolton	Director of Social Services & Housing	Council House
Technical Services	Keith Round	Client Services Manager	Spire House
Trading Standards	Clive Townend	Head of Trading Standards & Waste Services	Council House

Parish Councils in the authority's area: Allesley; Keresley.

DONCASTER METROPOLITAN BOROUGH COUNCIL

www.doncaster.gov.uk

Principal Office; Chief Executive's Department
2 Priory Place, Doncaster, South Yorkshire DN1 1BN
Telephone: (01302) 734000; FAX: (01302) 734040

Corporate Services
The Council House, College Road, Doncaster DN1 3QA
Telephone: (01302) 737686; FAX: (01302) 737923

Corporate Services
Copley House, College Road, Doncaster DN1 3EQ

Borough Strategy & Development
Danum House, St Sepulchre Gate, Doncaster DN1 1UB
Telephone: (01302) 734900; FAX: (01302) 734949

Education & Culture
The Council House, College Road, Doncaster DN1 3AD
Telephone: (01302) 737103; FAX: (01302) 737223

Neighbourhood Services
The Council House, College Road, Doncaster DN1 1RN
Telephone: (01302) 737500; FAX: (01302) 737510

METROPOLITAN DISTRICT COUNCILS

Social Services
The Council House, College Road, Doncaster DN1 3DA
Telephone: (01302) 737800; FAX: (01302) 737778

Neighbourhood Services
15 South Parade, Doncaster DN1 2DR
Telephone: (01302) 735400; FAX: (01302) 735136

Function	Chief Officer	Title	Location
Chief Executive	Mr D Marlow	Chief Executive	Priory Place
Education	Mr M Eales	Executive Director, Education & Culture	Council House
Electoral Registration	Mr P Evans	Head of Legal Services	Copley House
Environmental Health	Ms J Dean	Borough Strategy & Development	Council House
Finance	Mr J Pitt	Executive Director, Corporate Services	Council House
Housing	Mr I Stephenson	Neighbourhood Services	Council House
Legal Services	Mr P Evans	Head of Legal Services	Copley House
Leisure	Mr M Eales	Executive Director, Education & Culture	Council House
Local Land Charges	Mr G Bandy	Head of Financial Services	Council House
Planning	Ms J Dean	Borough Strategy & Development	Danum House
Social Services	Mr M Thomas	Executive Director, Social Services	Council House
Technical Services	Mr I Stephenson	Neighbourhood Services	Council House
Trading Standards	Mr R Grice	Chief Trading Standards Officer	Council House

Parish Councils in the authority's area: Adwick-on-Dearne; Armthorpe; Auckley; Austerfield; Barnburgh & Harlington; Barnby Dun-with-Kirk Sandall; Blaxton; Braithwell; Brodsworth; Burghwallis; Cantley-with-Branton; Clayton-with-Frickley; Conisbrough Parks; Denaby; Edenthorpe; Edlington; Finningley; Fishlake; Hampole & Skelbrook; Hickleton; High Melton; Hooton Pagnell; Loversall; Marr; Moss & District; Norton; Owston; Rossington; Sprotbrough; Stainton; Sykehouse; Thorpe-in-Balne; Wadworth; Warmsworth.

Parish Meetings in the authority's area: Cadeby.

Town Councils in the authority's area: Askern; Bawtry; Hatfield; Stainforth; Thorne; Tickhill.

DUDLEY METROPOLITAN BOROUGH COUNCIL
www.dudley.gov.uk

Principal Office
Council House, Priory Road, Dudley, West Midlands DY1 1HF
Telephone: (01384) 818181

Education Department
Westox House, 1 Trinity Road, Dudley
Telephone: (01384) 814201; FAX: (01384) 814216

Environment, Engineering & Transportation Department
The Council House, Mary Stevens Park, Norton, Stourbridge DY8 2AA
Telephone: (01384) 81442

Housing Department
2 St James's Road, Dudley
Telephone: (01384) 815001; FAX: (01384) 815167

Legal & Property Department; Directorate of Urban Environment
3 St James's Road, Dudley DY1 1HZ
Telephone: (01384) 815337 (Legal & Property); (01384) 814120 (Planning); (01384) 815521 (Leisure)

Social Services Department
Ednam House, St James's Road, Dudley DY1 3JJ
Telephone: (01384) 815801; FAX: (01384) 815865

METROPOLITAN DISTRICT COUNCILS

Function	Chief Officer	Title	Location
Chief Executive	Mr A Sparke	Chief Executive	Council House
Education	Mr J Freeman	Interim Director of Education	Westox House
Electoral Registration	Mr A Sparke	Chief Executive	Council House
Environmental Health	Mr J Millar	Acting Director of Urban Environment	Mary Stevens Pk
Finance	Mr M S Williams	Chief Finance Officer	Council House
Housing	Mr J Stringer	Chief Housing Officer	2 St James's Rd
Legal Services	Mr J Polychronakis	Chief Legal & Property Officer	3 St James's Rd
Leisure	Mr J Millar	Acting Director of Urban Environment	Mary Stevens Pk
Local Land Charges	Mr J Polychronakis	Chief Legal & Property Officer	3 St James's Rd
Planning	Mr J Millar	Acting Director of Urban Environment	Mary Stevens Pk
Purchasing & Supplies	Mr I Clarke	Head of Purchasing	Council House
Social Services	Ms L Warren	Director of Social Services	Ednam House
Technical Services	Mr M Williams	Assistant Director of Environmental Management	Mary Stevens Pk
Trading Standards	Mr J Millar	Acting Director of Urban Environment	Mary Stevens Pk

Parish Councils & Parish Meetings in the authority's area: none.

Town Councils in the authority's area: none.

GATESHEAD METROPOLITAN BOROUGH COUNCIL
See now Gateshead Council.

GATESHEAD COUNCIL

www.gateshead.gov.uk

Principal Office
Civic Centre, Regent Street, Gateshead, Tyne & Wear NE8 1HH
Telephone: (0191) 433 3000; FAX: (0191) 478 3495; DX 60308 Gateshead 1

Corporate Purchasing
Stonehills, Shields Rd, Pelaw, Gateshead NE10 0HW
Telephone: (0191) 438 5550

Function	Chief Officer	Title	Location
Chief Executive	Mr R Kelly	Chief Executive	Civic Centre
Education	Ms M Atkinson	Group Director of Learning and Culture	Civic Centre
Electoral Registration	Mr J Rew	Head of Corporate Administration	Civic Centre
Environmental Health	Mr J Robinson	Director of Regulatory Services	Civic Centre
Finance	Mr D Coates	Strategic Director of Finance and ICT	Civic Centre
Housing	Mr S Bramwell	Group Director of Community Based Services	Civic Centre
Legal Services	Mrs M Kesteven	Strategic Director of Legal and Corporate Services (Acting)	Civic Centre
Leisure	Mr D Bunce	Head of Leisure Activities	Civic Centre
Local Land Charges	Mr J Rew	Head of Corporate Administration	Civic Centre
Planning	Mr D Quinn	Group Director of Development and Enterprise	Civic Centre
Purchasing & Supplies	Ms A Tickner	Head of Corporate Purchasing	Stonehills
Social Services	Mr S Hart	Director of Social Services	Civic Centre
Trading Standards	Mr P Dowling	Head of Regulatory Services	Civic Centre

Parish Councils in the authority's area: Birtley; Lamesley.

METROPOLITAN DISTRICT COUNCILS

KIRKLEES METROPOLITAN COUNCIL

www.kirklees.gov.uk

Principal Office
Civic Centre 3, Market Street, Huddersfield HD1 1WG
Telephone: (01484) 221000; FAX: (01484) 221777; DX 710090 Huddersfield 8

Education Service; Social Services
Oldgate House, 2 Oldgate, Huddersfield HD1 6QW
Telephone (01484) 221000

Revenues & Benefits Service; Strategic Finance; Housing Services
Civic Centre 1, High Street, Huddersfield HD1 2YU
Telephone: (01484) 221000

Elections & Local Land Charges
49-51 Huddersfield Road, Huddersfield HD9 3ER
Telephone: (01484) 222403 FAX; (01484) 222450

Environmental Services
West Riding House, Manchester Road, Huddersfield HD1 3HH
Telephone: (01484) 221000; FAX: (01484) 226409

Design & Property Service
Kirkgate Buildings, Byram Street, Huddersfield HD1 1BY
Telephone: (01484) 226052; FAX: (01484) 226086

Culture & Leisure Services
The Stadium Business & Leisure Complex, Stadium Way, Huddersfield HD1 6PS
Telephone: (01484) 224002; FAX: (01484) 224014

Trading Standards West Yorkshire
PO Box 5, Nepshaw Lane South, Morley LS27 0QP
Telephone: (0113) 253 0241

Function	Chief Officer	Title	Location
Chief Executive	Tony Elson	Chief Executive	Civic Centre 3
Education	Gavin Tonkin	Director of Lifelong Learning	Oldgate House
Electoral Registration	Susan Hutson	Elections & Local Land Charges Officer	Huddersfield Rd
Environmental Health	Janet Russell	Director of Environment & Transport	West Riding Hse
Finance	Dick Hewitson	Director of Finance	Civic Centre 1
Housing	Tony Hood	Director of Housing	Civic Centre 1
Legal Services	John Emms	Solicitor to the Council	Civic Centre 3
Leisure	Alan Freeman	Head of Culture & Leisure Services	The Stadium
Local Land Charges	Susan Hutson	Elections & Local Land Charges Officer	Huddersfield Rd
Planning	Keith Faragher	Head of Planning Services	Civic Centre 3
Purchasing & Supplies	Caroline Giggal	Corporate Procurement Officer	Civic Centre 3
Social Services	Philip Cotterill	Director of Social Affairs & Health	Oldgate House
Technical Services	Andrew Howard	Head of Design & Property	Kirkgate Bldgs
Trading Standards	Martin Wood	Chief Trading Standards Officer	Nepshaw Lane

Parish Councils in the authority's area: Denby Dale; Holme Valley; Kirkburton.

Town Councils in the authority's area: Meltham; Mirfield.

METROPOLITAN DISTRICT COUNCILS

KNOWSLEY METROPOLITAN BOROUGH COUNCIL

www.knowsley.gov.uk

Principal Office
Municipal Buildings, Archway Road, Huyton, Knowsley,
Merseyside L36 9YU
Telephone: (0151) 489 6000

Education Department
Huyton Hey Road, Huyton, Knowsley L36 5YH
Telephone: (0151) 443 3231; FAX: (0151) 449 3852

Environmental Health Department
Kirkby Municipal Buildings, Cherry Field Drive, Kirkby L33
Telephone: (0151) 489 6000

Function	Chief Officer	Title	Location
Chief Executive	Steve Gallagher	Chief Executive	Municipal Bldgs
Education	Stephen Munby	Director of Education	Huyton Hey Rd
Electoral Registration	Jo Miller	Director of Corporate & Customer Services	Municipal Bldgs
Environmental Health	Neil Turner	Head of Environmental Health & Consumer Protection	Kirkby
Finance	Steve Houston	Director of Finance	Municipal Bldgs
Legal Services	Jo Miller	Director of Corporate & Customer Services	Municipal Bldgs
Leisure	John Bell	Director of Leisure & Community Services	Municipal Bldgs
Local Land Charges	Jo Miller	Director of Corporate & Customer Services	Municipal Bldgs
Planning	Graham Smith	Director of Regeneration & Development	Municipal Bldgs
Purchasing & Supplies	Steve Houston	Director of Finance	Municipal Bldgs
Social Services	Anita Marsland	Director of Social Services	Municipal Bldgs
Technical Services	Graham Smith	Director of Regeneration & Development	Municipal Bldgs
Trading Standards	Neil Turner	Head of Environmental Health & Consumer Protection	Kirkby

Parish Councils in the authority's area: Cronton; Knowsley; Tarbock.

Town Councils in the authority's area: Halewood; Prescot; Whiston.

LEEDS CITY COUNCIL

www.leeds.gov.uk

Principal Office
Civic Hall, Leeds, West Yorkshire LS1 1UR
Telephone: (0113) 234 8080

**Education Department; Planning and Environment Department;
Social Services Department**
Merrion House, 110 Merrion Street, Leeds LS2 8SH
Telephone: (0113) 234 8080

Housing and Environmental Health Department
Thoresby House, 2A Great George Street, Leeds LS2 8BB
Telephone: (0113) 234 8080; FAX: (0113) 224 3543

Leisure Services
The Town Hall, The Headrow, Leeds LS1 3AD
Telephone: (0113) 234 8080

Legal Services
40 Great George Street, Leeds LS1 3D

METROPOLITAN DISTRICT COUNCILS

Function	Chief Officer	Title	Location
Chief Executive	Mr P Rogerson	Chief Executive	Civic Hall
Education	Mr K Burton	Chief Education Officer	Civic Hall
Housing	Mr N Evans	Acting Director of Neighbourhoods & Housing	Thoresby House
Legal Services	Ms N Jackson	Director of Legal & Democratic Services	40 Great George St
Leisure	Mr J Davies	Director of Learning & Leisure	Town Hall
Planning	Mr J Lynch	Director of Planning & Environment	Merrion House
Social Services	Mr K Murray	Director of Social Services	Merrion House

Parish / Town Councils in the authority's area: Aberford & District; Allerton Bywater; Arthington; Bardsey cum Rigton; Barwick in Elmet & Scholes; Boston Spa; Bramham cum Oglethorpe; Bramhope & Carlton; Clifford; Collingham with Linton; Drighlington; East Keswick; Gildersome; Great & Little Preston; Harewood; Horsforth; Kippax; Ledsham; Ledston; Micklefield; Morley; Otley; Pool in Wharfedale; Scarcroft; Shadwell; Swillington; Thorner; Thorp Arch; Walton; Wetherby.

Parish Meetings in the authority's area: Austhorpe; Wothersome.

LIVERPOOL CITY COUNCIL

www.liverpool.gov.uk

Principal Office; Central Services and Resources
Municipal Buildings, Dale Street, Liverpool, L69 2DH
Telephone: (0151) 233 3000; FAX: (0151) 233 8770; Minicom: (0151) 225 3275

Education, Library and Sports Services
Renshaw Street, Liverpool L1 4NX
Telephone: (0151) 233 3000; FAX: (0151) 233 8770; Minicom: (0151) 225 3275

Regeneration
Kingsway House, Hatton Garden, Liverpool L69 2YR
Telephone: (0151) 233 3000; FAX: (0151) 233 8770; Minicom: (0151) 225 3275

Supported Living and Community Safety
Millennium House, 60 Victoria Street, Liverpool L1 6JH
Telephone: (0151) 233 3000; FAX: (0151) 233 8770; Minicom: (0151) 225 3275

Function	Chief Officer	Title	Location
Chief Executive	David Henshaw	Chief Executive	Municipal Bldgs
Education	Colin Hilton	Executive Director, Education, Library & Sports Services	Renshaw St
Electoral Registration	Phil Halsall	Executive Director, Resources	Municipal Bldgs
Environmental Health	Charlie Parker	Executive Director, Regeneration	Kingsway Hse
Finance	Phil Halsall	Executive Director, Resources	Municipal Bldgs
Housing	Charlie Parker	Executive Director, Regeneration	Kingsway Hse
Legal Services	Phil Halsall	Executive Director, Resources	Municipal Bldgs
Leisure	Colin Hilton	Executive Director, Education, Library & Sports Services	Renshaw St
Local Land Charges	Phil Halsall	Executive Director, Resources	Municipal Bldgs
Planning	Charlie Parker	Executive Director, Regeneration	Kingsway Hse
Purchasing & Supplies	Phil Halsall	Executive Director, Resources	Municipal Bldgs
Social Services	Tony Hunter	Executive Director, Supported Living & Community Safety	Millennium Hse
Trading Standards	Charlie Parker	Executive Director, Regeneration	Kingsway Hse

Parish Councils, Parish Meetings & Town Councils in the authority's area: none.

METROPOLITAN DISTRICT COUNCILS

MANCHESTER CITY COUNCIL

www.manchester.gov.uk

Principal Office
PO Box 532, Town Hall, Albert Square, Manchester M60 2LA
Telephone: (0161) 234 5000; FAX: (0161) 236 5909

Education Department
Overseas House, Quay Street, Manchester M3 3BB
Telephone: (0161) 234 5000

Manchester Leisure
Belle Vue Leisure Centre, Pink Bank Lane, Manchester M12 5GL
Telephone: (0161) 953 2450

Manchester City Galleries
Manchester City Art Gallery, Moseley Street, Manchester M2 3JL
Telephone: (0161) 235 8888

Operational Services Department
Hammerstone Road, Manchester M18 8EQ
Telephone: (0161) 954 9000

Function	Chief Officer	Title	Location
Chief Executive	H Bernstein	Chief Executive	Town Hall
Education	M Waters	Chief Education Officer	Overseas Hse
Electoral Registration	Ms M Slattery	Electoral Services Manager	Town Hall
Environmental Health	M Heather	Assistant Director of Environment & Development	Town Hall
Finance	R Paver	City Treasurer	Town Hall
Housing	S Rumbelow	Director of Housing	Town Hall
Legal Services	S Orrell	City Solicitor	Town Hall
Leisure	J Byrne	Head of Leisure	Belle Vue Leisure
Local Land Charges	S Orrell	City Solicitor	Town Hall
Planning	P Babb	Assistant Director of Environment & Development	Town Hall
Purchasing & Supplies	R Paver	City Treasurer	Town Hall
Social Services	P Newman	Director of Social Services	Town Hall
Technical Services	P North	Director of Works	Hammerstone Rd
Trading Standards	H Bernstein	Chief Executive	Town Hall

Parish Councils in the authority's area: Ringway.

NEWCASTLE CITY COUNCIL

www.newcastle.gov.uk

Principal Office
Civic Centre, Newcastle upon Tyne, Tyne & Wear NE99 2BN
Telephone: (0191) 232 8520; FAX: (0191) 211 4942

Neighbourhood Services Headquarters
Atkinson House, Cypress Avenue, Fenham, Newcastle upon Tyne, Tyne & Wear NE4 9JG
Telephone: (0191) 232 8520; FAX: (0191) 277 3686

Function	Chief Officer	Title	Location
Chief Executive	Mr Ian Stratford	Chief Executive	Civic Centre
Education	Mr Phillip Turner	Director of Education & Libraries	Civic Centre
Electoral Registration	Ms Deborah Frost	Electoral Services Manager	Civic Centre
Environmental Health	Mr Stephen Savage	Head of Public Health & Environmental Protection	Civic Centre
Finance	Mr Paul Woods	City Treasurer	Civic Centre

METROPOLITAN DISTRICT COUNCILS

Function	Chief Officer	Title	Location
Housing	Ms C Cunningham	Head of Strategic Housing	Civic Centre
Legal Services	Ms Valerie A Dodds	Head of Legal Services	Civic Centre
Leisure	Mr Ed Williams	General Manager of Leisure Services	Civic Centre
Local Land Charges	Mr Syd Bailey	Chief Conveyancer	Civic Centre
Planning	Mr John Miller	Head of Planning & Transportation	Civic Centre
Purchasing & Supplies	Mr Bill Potts	Head of Strategic Procurement	Civic Centre
Social Services	Mr Tom Dervin	Director of Social Services	Civic Centre
Technical Services	Mr Rob Nicols	General Manager of Street Services	Atkinson Hse
Trading Standards	Mr Stephen Savage	Head of Public Health & Environmental Protection	Civic Centre

Parish Councils in the authority's area: Blakelaw and North Fenham; Brunswick; Dinnington; Hazlerigg; North Gosforth; Woolsington.

NORTH TYNESIDE COUNCIL

www.northtyneside.gov.uk

Principal Office
Town Hall, Wallsend, Tyne & Wear NE28 7RR
Telephone: (0191) 200 6565; FAX: (0191) 200 7273

Strategic Services Directorate
Marine House, Norman Terrace, Willington Quay, Wallsend, Tyne & Wear NE28 6SU
Telephone: (0191) 200 1336; FAX: (0191) 200 6953

Social Services Directorate
Camden House, North Shields, Tyne & Wear NE30 1NW
Telephone: (0191) 200 6161; FAX: (0191) 200 5600

Education Services – Education and Cultural Services Directorate
Stephenson House, Stephenson Street, North Shields, Tyne & Wear NE30 1QA
Telephone: (0191) 200 5018; FAX: (0191) 200 5060

Cultural Services – Education and Cultural Services Directorate
7 Northumberland Square, North Shields, Tyne & Wear NE30 1QQ
Telephone: (0191) 200 5164; FAX: (0191) 200 5798

Function	Chief Officer	Title	Location
Chief Executive	Mr J Marsden	Chief Executive	Town Hall
Education	Ms G Alexander	Acting Director of Education & Cultural Services	Stephenson House
Electoral Registration	Mrs C Dunn	Head of Legal & Democratic Services	Marine House
Environmental Health	Mr K Wilson	Head of Environment	Station Road
Finance	Ms F Rooney	Head of Strategic Finance	Marine House
Housing	Mr P Tanney	Head of Housing	Station Road
Legal Services	Mrs C Dunn	Head of Legal & Democratic Services	Marine House
Leisure	Mr P Gowans	Head of Cultural Services	Northumberland Sq
Planning	Mr M Swales	Director of Environment, Regeneration & Housing	Station Road
Social Services	Mr J Phillipson	Director of Social Services	Camden House
Technical Services	Mr M Swales	Director of Environment, Regeneration & Housing	Station Road

Parish Councils & Parish Meetings in the authority's area: none.

Town Councils in the authority's area: none.

METROPOLITAN DISTRICT COUNCILS

OLDHAM METROPOLITAN BOROUGH COUNCIL

www.oldham.gov.uk

Principal Office
PO Box 160, Civic Centre, West Street, Oldham, Greater Manchester OL1 1UG
Telephone: (0161) 911 3000; FAX: (0161) 911 4700; DX 710000 Oldham

Environmental Services
Henshaw House, Cheapside, Oldham, Greater Manchester OL1 1NY

First Choice Homes, Oldham
1 Medtia Square, Phoenix Street, Oldham Greater Manchester OL1 1AN

Function	Chief Officer	Title	Location
Chief Executive	Andrew Kilburn	Chief Executive	Civic Centre
Education	Chris Berry	Executive Director (Education & Cultural Services)	Civic Centre
Electoral Registration	Aileen Johnson	Acting Assistant Chief Executive (Legal & Democratic Services)	Civic Centre
Environmental Health	John Hurst	Assistant Director (Environmental Protection)	Henshaw Hse
Finance	John Bland	Assistant Chief Executive (Finance, IT & Resources)	Civic Centre
Housing	Hugh Broadbent	Chief Executive (First Choice Homes, Oldham)	1 Medtia Square
Legal Services	Aileen Johnson	Acting Assistant Chief Executive (Legal & Democratic Services)	Civic Centre
Leisure	Chris Berry	Executive Director (Education & Cultural Services)	Civic Centre
Local Land Charges	Aileen Johnson	Acting Assistant Chief Executive (Legal & Democratic Services)	Civic Centre
Planning	Tom Flanagan	Executive Director (Environmental Services)	Henshaw Hse
Purchasing & Supplies	Paul Howarth	Strategic Finance Manager	Civic Centre
Social Services	Veronica Jackson	Executive Director (Social Services)	Civic Centre
Technical Services	Tom Flanagan	Executive Director (Environmental Services)	Henshaw Hse
Trading Standards	John Hurst	Assistant Director (Environmental Protection)	Henshaw Hse

Parish Councils in the authority's area: Saddleworth; Shaw & Crompton.

ROCHDALE METROPOLITAN BOROUGH COUNCIL

www.rochdale.gov.uk

Principal Office
PO Box 39, Municipal Offices, Smith Street, Rochdale OL16 1LQ
Telephone: (01706) 647474; FAX: (01706) 865450; DX 22831 Rochdale

Education Services; Community Services; Children, Schools & Families
Municipal Offices, Smith Street, Rochdale OL16 1LG
Telephone: (01706) 647474

Strategic Planning
PO Box 32, Telegraph House, Baillie Street, Rochdale OL16 1JH
Telephone: (01706) 647474; FAX: (01706) 864185

Environmental Health Services
PO Box 20, Electric House, Smith Street, Rochdale OL16 1YP
Telephone: (01706) 647474; FAX: (01706) 864686

Function	Chief Officer	Title	Location
Chief Executive	Mr R Ellis	Chief Executive	PO Box 39
Education	Mr T Piggott	Executive Director of Children, Schools & Families	Municipal Offices
Electoral Registration	Mr W J Lawley	Borough Solicitor	PO Box 39
Environmental Health	Mr S Beckwith	Executive Director of Strategic Development	Telegraph House
Finance	Ms M Barney	Executive Director of Resources	Municipal Offices
Legal Services	Mr W J Lawley	Borough Solicitor	PO Box 39
Leisure	Mr A Zuntz	Executive Director of Community Services	Municipal Offices
Local Land Charges	Mr W J Lawley	Borough Solicitor	PO Box 39
Planning	Mr J Patterson	Executive Director of Environmental Services	Electric House
Purchasing & Supplies	Mr J Winterbottom	Corporate Procurement Manager	Telegraph House
Social Services	Mr A Zuntz	Executive Director of Community Services	Municipal Offices
Trading Standards	Mr J Patterson	Executive Director of Environmental Services	Electric House

Parish Councils & Parish Meetings in the authority's area: none.

Town Councils in the authority's area: none.

ROTHERHAM METROPOLITAN BOROUGH COUNCIL

www.rotherham.gov.uk

Principal Office
Civic Building, Walker Place, Rotherham, South Yorkshire S65 1UF
Telephone: (01709) 382121; FAX: (01709) 822406; DX 12606 Rotherham

Chief Executive's Department
Eric Mann's Building, 45 Moorgate Street, Rotherham, South Yorkshire
Telephone: (01709) 822771; FAX: (01709) 822794

Education Department; Housing Services Department; Human Resources Department
Norfolk House, Walker Place, Rotherham S60 1QT
Telephone: (01709) 382121

Social Services Department
Crinoline House, Effingham Square, Rotherham S65 1AW
Telephone: (01709) 382121

Economic & Development Services Department
Bailey House, Rawmarsh Road, Rotherham S65 1AN
Telephone: (01709) 382121

Health & Consumer Affairs Department
Howard Building, College Lane, Rotheram S65 1AX
Telephone: (01709) 382121

Function	Chief Officer	Title	Location
Chief Executive	Mr M Cuff	Chief Executive	Eric Mann's Bldg
Education	Mr A Bedford	Acting Executive Director – Education, Culture & Leisure Services	Norfolk House
Electoral Registration	Mr J Walker	Chief Elections & Electoral Registration Officer	Civic Building
Environmental Health	Mr B Crosby	Head of Environmental Health	Howard Building
Finance	Ms C Mills	Executive Director – Resources	Civic Building
Housing	Mr T Cray	Executive Director – Housing & Environmental Services	Norfolk House
Legal Services	Mr T C Mumford	Head of Legal Services & Democratic Services	Civic Building

Leisure	Mr P Rogers	Strategic Leader, Culture, Leisure & Lifelong Learning	Norfolk House
Social Services	Mr J Gomersall	Executive Director – Social Services	Crinoline House
Trading Standards	Mr I Slack	Health & Commercial Standards Manager	Elm Bank House

Parish Councils in the authority's area: Anston; Aston-Cum-Aughton; Bramley; Brampton Bierlow; Brinsworth; Catcliffe; Dalton; Dinnington St John's; Firbeck; Harthill-with-Woodall; Laughton-en-le-Morthen; Letwell; Maltby; Orgreave; Ravenfield; Thorpe Salvin; Thrybergh; Thurcroft; Todwick; Treeton; Ulley; Wales; Wentworth; Whiston; Wickersley; Woodsetts.

Parish Meetings in the authority's area: Gildingwells; Hooton Levitt; Hooton Roberts.

ST HELENS METROPOLITAN BOROUGH COUNCIL

www.sthelens.gov.uk

Chief Executive's Department
Town Hall, Victoria Square, St Helens, Merseyside WA10 1HP
Telephone: (01744) 456000; FAX: (01744) 733337

Education & Leisure Services Department
Rivington Centre, Rivington Road, St Helens WA10 4ND
Telephone: (01744) 456000

Urban Regeneration Department; Environmental Protection Department
Wesley House, Corporation Street, St Helens WA10 1HF
Telephone: (01744) 456000

Social Services Department
The Gamble Institute, Victoria Square, St Helens WA10 1RN
Telephone: (01744) 456000

Function	Chief Officer	Title	Location
Chief Executive	Mrs Carole Hudson	Chief Executive	Town Hall
Education	Mrs Susan Richardson	Director of Education	Rivington Ctr
Electoral Registration	Mr Martin Hughes	Electoral Registration Officer	Town Hall
Environmental Health	Mr Steve Massey	Assistant Director, Environmental Protection	Wesley Hse
Finance	Mr Ian Roberts	Assistant Chief Executive, Finance	Town Hall
Housing	Mr Bob Hepworth	Director of Urban Regeneration & Housing	Wesley Hse
Legal Services	Mr Peter Blackburn	Assistant Chief Executive (Legal & Administrative Services)	Town Hall
Leisure	Mr David Pugh	Head of Recreation & Leisure	Rivington Ctr
Local Land Charges	Mr David Breeze	Land Charges Officer	Town Hall
Planning	Mr Bob Hepworth	Director of Urban Regeneration & Housing	Wesley Hse
Purchasing & Supplies	Mr Raymond Williams	Purchasing Manager	Wesley Hse
Social Services	Ms Sue Lightup	Director of Social Services	Gamble Inst
Trading Standards	Ms Jackie Baker	Chief Trading Standards Officer	Wesley Hse

Parish Councils in the authority's area: Billinge; Bold; Eccleston; Rainford; Rainhill; Seneley Green; Windle.

SALFORD CITY COUNCIL

www.salford.gov.uk

Principal Office
Chief Executive Directorate, Salford Civic Centre, Chorley Road, Swinton, Salford, Greater Manchester M27 5FJ
Telephone: (0161) 793 3401; FAX: (0161) 793 3435; DX 712100 Swinton 2

METROPOLITAN DISTRICT COUNCILS

Community & Social Services Directorate
Crompton House, 100 Chorley Road, Swinton, Salford M27 2BP
Telephone: (0161) 794 4711; FAX: (0161) 794 0197

Education and Leisure Directorate
Education Offices, Minerva House, Pendlebury Road, Swinton M27 4AX
Telephone: (0161) 778 0123

Environmental Services Directorate
Crompton House, 100 Chorley Road, Swinton, Salford M27 6ES
Telephone: (0161) 794 4711; FAX: (0161) 727 7162

Function	Chief Officer	Title	Location
Chief Executive	Mr J C Willis	Chief Executive	Civic Centre
Education	Mrs J Baker	Director of Education & Leisure	Minerva House
Electoral Registration	Mr P Daniels	Administrative Officer	Civic Centre
Environmental Health	Mr B Jassi	Director of Environmental Services	Crompton Hse
Finance	Mr J Spink	Head of Finance	Civic Centre
Legal Services	Mr A Eastwood	Head of Law & Administration	Civic Centre
Leisure	Mrs J Baker	Director of Education & Leisure	Minerva House
Local Land Charges	Mr I Sheard	Assistant Director (Legal Services)	Civic Centre
Planning	Mr M Sykes	Director of Development Services	Civic Centre
Purchasing & Supplies	Mr T Harrisson	Purchasing Manager	Civic Centre
Social Services	Mrs A Williams	Director of Community & Social Services	Crompton Hse
Technical Services	Mr M Sykes	Director of Development Services	Civic Centre
Trading Standards	Mr B Jassi	Director of Environmental Services	Crompton Hse

Parish Councils & Parish Meetings in the authority's area: none.

Town Councils in the authority's area: none.

SANDWELL METROPOLITAN BOROUGH COUNCIL

www.smbc.sandwell.gov.uk

Principal Office
Sandwell Council House, PO Box 2374, Oldbury, Warley, West Midlands B69 3DE
Telephone: (0121) 569 2200; FAX: (0121) 569 3100

Education & Community Services Department
PO Box 41, Shaftesbury House, 402 High Street, West Bromwich B70 9LT
Telephone: (0121) 525 7366

Housing Department
Development House, PO Box 42, Lonard Street, West Bromwich B70 8RU
Telephone: (0121) 569 5060

Social Services Department
1st Floor, Kingston House, 438 High Street, West Bromwich B70 9LD
Telephone: (0121) 569 5464

Function	Chief Officer	Title	Location
Chief Executive	Nigel Summers	Chief Executive	Sandwell Cl Hse
Education	Eric Griffiths	Executive Director of Education & Lifelong Learning	Shaftesbury Hse
Electoral Registration	Stephen Cork	Head of Democratic Services	Sandwell Cl Hse
Finance	Lynda Bateman	Director of Finance & Business Services	Sandwell Cl Hse
Housing	Steve Gregory; Brian Oakley	Executive Director of Urban Form; Executive Director of Direct & Support Services	Development Hse
Legal Services	Allison Fraser	Executive Director of Policy & Corporate Governance	Sandwell Cl Hse
Social Services	Angela Saganowska	Acting Executive Director of Social Inclusion & Health	Kingston House

Parish Councils & Parish Meetings in the authority's area: none.

Town Councils in the authority's area: none.

THE METROPOLITAN BOROUGH COUNCIL OF SEFTON

www.sefton.gov.uk

Principal Office
Town Hall, Lord Street, Southport, Merseyside PR8 1DA
Telephone: (01704) 533133; FAX: (0151) 934 2293

Finance Department; Technical Services Department; Environmental Protection Department
Balliol House, Balliol Road, Bootle L20 3AE
Telephone: (0151) 922 4040; FAX: (0151) 934 4579

Education Department
Town Hall, Oriel Road, Bootle L20 7AE
Telephone: (0151) 922 4040; FAX: (0151) 934 3349

Housing Department; Social Services Department
Merton House, Stanley Road, Bootle L20 3UU
Telephone: (0151) 922 4040

Leisure Services Department
Pavilion Buildings, 99-105 Lord Street, Southport PR8 1RJ
Telephone: (01704) 533133; FAX: (0151) 934 2370

Planning Department
Vermont House, 375 Standley Road, Bottle L203 RY
Telephone: (0151) 922 4040

Land Charges Department
Crown Buildings, 9/11 Eastbank Street, Southport PR8 1DL

Function	Chief Officer	Title	Location
Chief Executive	Mr G J Haywood	Chief Executive	Town Hall, Sthpt
Education	Mr M Dixon	Schools and Young People Director	Town Hall, Bootle
Electoral Registration	Mr J N Middlehurst	Electoral Services Officer	Town Hall, Sthpt
Environmental Health	Mr W Milburn	Environmental Protection Director	Balliol House
Finance	Mr A Yates	Finance Director	Balliol House
Housing	Mr R Williams	Housing Director	Merton House
Legal Services	Mrs C Elwood	Legal Director	Town Hall, Sthpt
Leisure	Mr G L Bayliss	Leisure Director	Pavilion Bldgs
Local Land Charges	Mrs M Kelly	Land Charges Supervisor	Crown Buildings
Planning	Mr R J Gibbons	Planning Director	Vermont House
Purchasing & Supplies	Mr D Worrall	Chief Purchasing Officer	Balliol House
Social Services	Mr C Barker	Social Services Director	Merton Hse
Technical Services	Mr P Williams	Technical Services Director	Balliol House
Trading Standards	Mr W Milburn	Environmental Protection Director	Balliol House

Parish Councils in the authority's area: Aintree Village; Formby; Hightown; Little Altcar; Ince Blundell; Lydiate; Melling; Sefton; Thornton.

Town Councils in the authority's area: Maghull.

SHEFFIELD CITY COUNCIL

www.sheffield.gov.uk

Principal Office
Town Hall, Sheffield, South Yorkshire S1 2HH
Telephone: (0114) 272 6444; FAX: (0114) 273 5003

Education Directorate
Derwent House, 150 Arundel Gate, Sheffield S1 2JY
Telephone: (0114) 272 6444; FAX: (0114) 273 6279

Environmental & Regulatory Services
Howden House, 1 Union Street, Sheffield S1 2FH
Telephone: (0114) 273 4643; FAX: (0114) 273 6281

Leisure Services
Central Library, Surrey Street, Sheffield S1 1XZ
Telephone: (0114) 272 6444; FAX: (0114) 273 5009

Social Services Directorate
Town Hall, Sheffield S1 2HH
Telephone: (0114) 273 4844; FAX: (0114) 273 4981

Corporate Finance
PO Box 1283, Town Hall, Sheffield, South Yorkshire S1 1UJ
Telephone: (0114) 273 4300; FAX: (0114) 273 5043

Function	Chief Officer	Title	Location
Chief Executive	Mr Bob Kerslake	Chief Executive	Town Hall
Education	Mr J Crossley-Holland	Executive Director	Town Hall
Electoral Registration	Mr Mark Webster	Head of Legal & Administrative Services	Town Hall
Environmental Health	Mr Gary McGrogan	Head of Environmental & Regulatory Services	Howden Hse
Finance	Ms Laraine Manley	Head of Corporate Finance	Corp Finance
Legal Services	Mr Mark Webster	Head of Legal & Administrative Services	Town Hall
Leisure	Mr Keith Crawshaw	Head of Leisure Services	Central Lib
Local Land Charges	Mr Mark Webster	Head of Legal & Administrative Services	Town Hall
Planning	Mr David Curtis	Head of Planning, Transport & Highways Service	Howden Hse
Purchasing & Supplies	Ms Lorraine Purcell	Head of Corporate Contracts Consultancy	Town Hall
Social Services	Ms Penny Thompson	Executive Director	Town Hall
Technical Services	Mr Ian Taylor	Assistant Head, Design & Project Management	Howden Hse
Trading Standards	Mr Gary McGrogan	Head of Environmental & Regulatory Services	Howden Hse

Parish Councils in the authority's area: Bradfield; Ecclesfield.

Town Councils in the authority's area: Stocksbridge.

SOLIHULL METROPOLITAN BOROUGH COUNCIL

www.solihull.gov.uk

Principal Office
PO Box 18, The Council House, Solihull, West Midlands B91 3QS
Telephone: (0121) 704 6000

Housing & Regeneration Department
Alcott House, Berwick Lane, Chelmsley Wood, Solihull B37 7RJ
Telephone: (0121) 704 6000

Function	Chief Officer	Title	Location
Chief Executive	Katherine Kerswell	Chief Executive	Council Hse
Education	Kevin Crompton	Corporate Director of Education & Children's Services	Council Hse
Electoral Registration	M Blamire-Brown	Solicitor to the Council	Council Hse

METROPOLITAN DISTRICT COUNCILS

Environmental Health	Dr Dennis Wilkes	Joint Director of Public Health	Council Hse
Finance	Clive Whereat	Corporate Director of Resources	Council Hse
Housing	Matt Cooney	Strategic Director of Housing Services	Alcott House
Legal Services	M Blamire-Brown	Solicitor to the Council	Council Hse
Leisure	Jeanette McGarry	Corporate Director of Community Services	Council Hse
Local Land Charges	Richard Honeysett	Strategic Director of Customer Services	Council Hse
Planning	Julian Wain	Strategic Director of Physical & Economic Regeneration	Council Hse
Purchasing & Supplies	Richard Honeysett	Strategic Director of Customer Services	Council Hse
Social Services	Michael Hake	Corporate Director of Social Care & Performance	Council Hse
Trading Standards	Michael Hake	Corporate Director of Social Care & Performance	Council Hse

Parish Councils in the authority's area: Balsall Common; Barston; Berkswell; Bickenhill; Castle Bromwich; Fordbridge; Hampton in Arden; Hockley Heath; Kingshurst; Meriden; Smith's Wood.

Town Councils in the authority's area: Chelmsley Wood.

SOUTH TYNESIDE METROPOLITAN BOROUGH COUNCIL

www.s-tyneside-mbc.gov.uk

Principal Office
Town Hall & Civic Offices, Westoe Road, South Shields, Tyne & Wear NE33 2RL
Telephone: (0191) 427 1717; FAX: (0191) 455 0208; DX 60850 South Shields 4

Neighbourhood Services
Middlefields Depot, Hudson Street, South Shields, Tyne & Wear NE34 0NT

Social Care & Health
Kelly House, Campbell Park Road, Hebburn NE31 2SW

Function	Chief Officer	Title	Location
Chief Executive	Irene Lucas	Chief Executive	Town Hall
Education	Barbara Hughes	Executive Director or Lifelong Learning & Leisure	Town Hall
Finance	Julie Alderson	Executive Director of Resources	Town Hall
Housing	Amanda Skelton	Executive Director of Neighbourhood Services	Middlefields Dep
Legal Services	Julie Alderson	Executive Director of Resources	Town Hall
Leisure	Barbara Hughes	Executive Director or Lifelong Learning & Leisure	Town Hall
Local Land Charges	Julie Alderson	Executive Director of Resources	Town Hall
Purchasing & Supplies	Julie Alderson	Executive Director of Resources	Town Hall
Social Services	Trevor Doughty	Executive Director of Social Care & Health	Kelly House

Parish Councils & Parish Meetings in the authority's area: none.

Town Councils in the authority's area: none.

STOCKPORT METROPOLITAN BOROUGH COUNCIL

www.stockport.gov.uk

Chief Executive's Services
Town Hall, Stockport SK1 3XE
Telephone: (0161) 480 4949; FAX: (0161) 477 9530; DX 22605 Stockport 2

METROPOLITAN DISTRICT COUNCILS

Education Services; Environment & Economic Development Services;
Finance & Property Services; Community Services
Stopford House, Piccadilly, Stockport SK1 3XE
Telephone: (0161) 480 4949

Environment & Economic Development Services
Hygarth House, 103 Wellington Road South, Stockport SK1 3TT
Telephone: (0161) 480 4949

Finance & Property Services
Burley House, Marriott Street, Stockport SK1 3PJ
Telephone: (0161) 474 5373; FAX: (0161) 474 5363

Social Services
Ponsonby House, Edward Street, Stockport SK1 3UR
Telephone: (0161) 474 4609; FAX: (0161) 474 7895

Stockport Direct Services; Finance & Property Services
Enterprise House, Bird Hall Lane, Cheadle Heath, Stockport SK3 0XS
Telephone: (0161) 480 4949; FAX: (0161) 474 5640

Function	Chief Officer	Title	Location
Chief Executive	Mr J Schultz	Chief Executive	Town Hall
Education	Mr E Blundell	Director for Education Services	Stopford Hse
Electoral Registration	Mr A Thompson	Civic & Electoral Services Manager	Town Hall
Environmental Health	Ms E McLean	Director of Environment & Economic Development Services	Hygarth House
Finance	Mr E J Lush	Director of Finance & Property Services	Stopford Hse
Housing	Ms H McHale	Assistant Director of Housing	Stopford Hse
Legal Services	Mr P Stonehouse	Council Solicitor & Secretary	Town Hall
Leisure	Mr G Lucas	Director of Community Services	Stopford Hse
Local Land Charges	Mr J Rimmer	Land Charges Manager	Town Hall
Planning	Mr S Lamb	Head of Development & Control	Hygarth House
Purchasing & Supplies	Mr G Leese	Corporate Purchasing Manager	Enterprise Hse
Social Services	Mr A Webb	Director of Social Services	Ponsonby Hse
Technical Services	Ms E McLean	Director of Environment & Economic Development Services	Hygarth House
Trading Standards	Mr D Cameron	Head of Commercial Services	Stopford Hse

Parish Councils & Parish Meetings in the authority's area: Offerton Estate.

Town Councils in the authority's area: none.

SUNDERLAND CITY COUNCIL

www.sunderland.gov.uk

Principal Office
Civic Centre, Sunderland, Tyne & Wear SR2 7DN
Telephone: (0191) 553 1000; FAX: (0191) 553 1020; DX 60729 Sunderland

Social Services Department
50 Fawcett Street, Sunderland SR1 1RF
Telephone: (0191) 553 7128; FAX: (0191) 553 7254

Community and Cultural Services
Jack Crawford House, Commercial Road, Sunderland SR2 8QR
Telephone: (0191) 553 7553; FAX: (0191) 553 7550

Function	Chief Officer	Title	Location
Chief Executive	Mr G Fitzgerald	Chief Executive	Civic Centre
Education	Ms B Comiskey	Director of Education	Civic Centre
Electoral Registration	Mr G Fitzgerald	Chief Executive	Civic Centre

Environmental Health	Mr P Dobson	Director of Community and Cultural Services	J Crawford Hse
Finance	Mr K Beardmore	City Treasurer	Civic Centre
Housing	Mr P Barrett	Director of Development and Regeneration	Civic Centre
Legal Services	Mr R C Rayner	City Solicitor	Civic Centre
Leisure	Mr P Dobson	Director of Community and Cultural Services	J Crawford Hse
Local Land Charges	Mr R C Rayner	City Solicitor	Civic Centre
Planning	Mr P Barrett	Director of Development and Regeneration	Civic Centre
Purchasing & Supplies	Mr K Beardmore	City Treasurer	Civic Centre
Social Services	Dr G Jones	Director of Social Services	50 Fawcett St
Trading Standards	Mr P Dobson	Director of Community and Cultural Services	J Crawford Hse

Town Councils in the authority's area: Hetton.

TAMESIDE METROPOLITAN BOROUGH COUNCIL

www.tameside.gov.uk

Principal Office

Council Offices, Wellington Road, Ashton under Lyne OL6 6DL
Telephone: (0161) 342 8355; FAX: (0161) 342 3115/3070

Function	Chief Officer	Title	Location
Chief Executive	Ms Janet Orchard	Chief Executive	Council Offices
Education	Mr Ian Smith	Executive Director, Lifelong Learning	Council Offices
Electoral Registration	Mr Ian Cochrane	Head of Democratic Services	Council Offices
Finance	Mr D Postlethwaite	Borough Treasurer	Council Offices
Housing	Mr H Davies	Assistant Executive Director, Housing & Regeneration	Council Offices
Legal Services	Ms Sandra Stewart	Borough Solicitor (Acting)	Council Offices
Leisure	Mr Jim Burns	Assistant Executive Director, Sustainable Community	Council Offices
Local Land Charges	Ms Judith Whittle	Senior Land Charges Officer	Council Offices
Planning	Mr Nigel Allen	Head of Planning	Council Offices
Purchasing & Supplies	Mr Malcolm Whitwood	Principal Purchasing Officer	Council Offices
Social Services	Mr Colin McKinless	Executive Director, Social Care & Health	Council Offices
Technical Services	Ms Alison Ashworth	Executive Director, Economy & Environment	Council Offices
Trading Standards	Mr David Meakin	Principal Trading Standards Officer	Council Offices

Parish Councils & Parish Meetings in the authority's area: none.

Town Councils in the authority's area: Mossley.

TRAFFORD METROPOLITAN BOROUGH COUNCIL

www.trafford.gov.uk

Principal Office

Trafford Town Hall, Talbot Road, Stretford, Trafford, Greater Manchester M32 0YT
Telephone: (0161) 912 1212; FAX: (0161) 912 4184

Function	Chief Officer	Title	Location
Chief Executive	Ms Carole Hassan	Chief Executive	Town Hall
Education	Mr C Pratt	Executive Director of Children & Young People's Services	Town Hall
Electoral Registration	Ms B Dunn	Head of Legal & Democratic Services	Town Hall

METROPOLITAN DISTRICT COUNCILS

Environmental Health	Mr P Harvey	Head of Public Protection	Town Hall
Finance	Mr I Duncan	Head of Finance	Town Hall
Housing	Mr M Khan	Head of Housing Strategy & Supporting People	Town Hall
Legal Services	Ms B Dunn	Head of Legal & Democratic Services	Town Hall
Leisure	Mrs A Saunders	Head of Sport & Leisure Development	Town Hall
Planning	Mr G Pickering	Strategic Director	Town Hall
Purchasing & Supplies	Mr I Duncan	Head of Finance	Town Hall
Social Services	M Cooney	Strategic Director Social Services	Town Hall
Technical Services	Mr G Pickering	Strategic Director	Town Hall
Trading Standards	Mr P Harvey	Head of Public Protection	Town Hall

Parish Councils in the authority's area: Carrington; Dunham Massey; Partington; Warburton.

WAKEFIELD METROPOLITAN DISTRICT COUNCIL

www.wakefield.gov.uk

Principal Office
Town Hall, Wood Street, Wakefield, West Yorkshire WF1 2HQ
Telephone: (01924) 306090; FAX: (01924) 305113

Education & Cultural Services
County Hall, Wood Street, Wakefield WF1 2QL
Telephone: (01924) 306090; FAX: (01924) 305632

Social Services & Health
8 St John's North, Wakefield WF1 3QA
Telephone: (01924) 307700; FAX: (01924) 307792

Environment Services
Newton Bar, Wakefield WF1 2TX
Telephone: (01924) 306090; FAX: (01924) 306690

Function	Chief Officer	Title	Location
Chief Executive	Mr J Foster, OBE	Chief Executive	Town Hall
Education	Mr J McLeod	Corporate Director of Education & Culture	Town Hall
Environmental Health	Mr I Stephenson	Corporate Director of Environmental Services	Newton Bar
Finance	Mr J Pitt	Corporate Director of Resources	Town Hall
Housing	Mr T Reeves	Deputy Chief Executive	Town Hall
Legal Services	Mr J Pitt	Corporate Director of Resources	Town Hall
Leisure	Mr T Reeves	Deputy Chief Executive	Town Hall
Local Land Charges	Mr J Pitt	Corporate Director of Resources	Town Hall
Planning	Mr T Reeves	Deputy Chief Executive	Town Hall
Social Services	Mrs E McHale	Corporate Director of Social Care & Health	8 St Johns Nth

Parish Councils in the authority's area: Ackworth; Badsworth; Crigglestone; Crofton; Darrington; East Hardwick; Featherstone; Havercroft-with-Cold Hiendley; Nostell; (Hessle and Hilltop, Huntwick with Foulby, Nostell and West Hardwick); Notton; Ryhill; Sharlston; Sitlington; South Hiendley; Thorpe Audlin; Upton & North Emsall; Walton; Warmfield-cum-Heath; West Bretton; Wintersett; Woolley.

Town Councils in the authority's area: Hemsworth; Normanton; South Elmsall; South Kirkby & Moorthorpe.

Community Councils in the authority's area: Horbury.

Community Associations in the authority's area: Kirkhamgate; Wrenthorpe.

METROPOLITAN DISTRICT COUNCILS

WALSALL METROPOLITAN BOROUGH COUNCIL

www.walsall.gov.uk

Principal Office
Civic Centre, Darwall Street, Walsall, West Midlands WS1 1TP
Telephone: (01922) 650000; FAX: (01922) 720885

Function	Chief Officer	Title	Location
Chief Executive	Mr H Bhogal	Chief Executive	Civic Centre
Education	Mr C Green	Director for Education & Community Services	Civic Centre
Electoral Registration	Lynne Burns	Chief Electoral Registration & Elections Officer	Civic Centre
Environmental Health	Mr Robert Hook	General Manager, Environmental Services	Civic Centre
Finance	Ms Carole Evans	Head of Finance	Civic Centre
Housing	Mrs Joanne Tyzzer	Director for Housing & Central Services	Civic Centre
Legal Services	Mr George Curran	Head of Legal Services	Civic Centre
Leisure	Mr Mike Somers	General Manager, Leisure & Community Services	Civic Centre
Local Land Charges	Ms Margaret Meade	Team Leader, Development & Operations, Searches & Land Charges	Civic Centre
Social Services	Mr D Phillips	Director for Social Services	Civic Centre
Trading Standards	Mr John Beavon	Divisional Trading Standards Officer	Civic Centre

Parish Councils & Parish Meetings in the authority's area: none.

Town Councils in the authority's area: none.

WIGAN METROPOLITAN BOROUGH COUNCIL

www.wiganmbc.gov.uk

Principal Office
Town Hall, Library Street, Wigan, Greater Manchester WN1 1YN
Telephone: (01942) 244991; FAX: (01942) 827451

Engineering Services Department; Planning and Development Department
Civic Buildings, New Market Street, Wigan WN1 1AZ
Telephone: (01942) 244991

Education Department
Gateway House, Standishgate, Wigan WN1 1AE
Telephone: (01942) 244991; FAX: (01942) 828811

Finance and IT Department
Civic Centre, Millgate, Wigan WN1 1YD
Telephone: (01942) 244991; FAX: (01942) 827454

Wigan & Leigh Housing Co. Ltd.
PO Box 48, 50 Millgate, Wigan WN1 1YR
Telephone: (01942) 244991; FAX: (01942) 828116

Wigan Leisure & Culture Trust
Indoor Sports Centre, Robin Park, Loire Drive, Wigan WN5 0UL
Telephone: (01942) 244991; FAX: (01942) 828540

Social Services Department
Civic Centre, Millgate, Wigan WN1 1AZ
Telephone: (01942) 244991; FAX: (01942) 827796

Function	Chief Officer	Title	Location
Chief Executive	Mr S M Jones	Chief Executive	Town Hall
Education	Mr G Rowney	Director of Education	Gateway Hse

METROPOLITAN DISTRICT COUNCILS

Electoral Registration	Mr B Hayes	Elections Administrator	Town Hall
Environmental Health	Mr R Saunders	Director of Environmental Health & Consumer Protection	Town Hall
Finance	Dr D Smith	Director of Finance & Information Technology	Civic Centre
Housing	Mr P Gee	Chief Executive, Wigan & Leigh Housing	50 Millgate
Legal Services	Mrs S D Lowe	Director of Legal Services	Town Hall
Leisure	Mr R Hill	Chief Executive, Wigan Leisure & Culture Trust	Sports Centre
Planning	Mr M Kimber	Director of Planning & Development	Civic Bldgs
Social Services	Mr B Walker	Director of Social Services	Civic Centre
Technical Services	Mr P Taylor	Director of Engineering Services	Civic Bldgs
Trading Standards	Mr R Saunders	Director of Environmental Health & Consumer Protection	Town Hall

Parish Councils in the authority's area: Haigh; Shevington.

METROPOLITAN BOROUGH OF WIRRAL

www.wirral.gov.uk

Principal Office
Town Hall, Brighton Street, Wallasey, Wirral, Merseyside CH44 8ED
Telephone (0151) 638 7070; FAX: (0151) 691 8468; DX 708630 Seacombe

Education & Engineering Services Department
Hamilton Building, Conway Street, Birkenhead, Wirral, Merseyside CH41 4FD
Telephone: (0151) 666 2121; FAX: (0151) 666 4207

Highways & Engineers Services Department
Town Hall, Civic Way, Bebington, Wirral, Merseyside CH63 7PT
Telephone: (0151) 643 9000; FAX: (0151) 643 7078

Finance Department
PO Box No 2, Treasury Buildings, Cleveland Street, Birkenhead, Wirral, Mersyeside CH41 6BU
Telephone: (0151) 647 7000; FAX: (0151) 666 1947

Housing & Environmental Protection Department
Westminster House, Hamilton Street, Birkenhead, Wirral, Merseyside CH41 5FN
Telephone: (0151) 647 2320; FAX: (0151) 666 5106

Planning & Economic Development Department
North Annexe, Municipal Offices, Brighton Street, Wallasey, Wirral. Merseyside CH44 8ED
Telephone: (0151) 691 8103; FAX: (0151) 691 8268

Social Services Department
Social Services Headquarters, Westminster House, Birkenhead, Wirral, Merseyside CH41 5FN
Telephone: (0151) 666 3600; FAX: (0151) 666 3603

Function	Chief Officer	Title	Location
Chief Executive	Stephen Maddox	Chief Executive	Wallasey Tn Hall
Education	Howard Cooper	Director of Education & Cultural Services	Hamilton Bldgs
Electoral Registration	Jo Miller	Borough Solicitor & Secretary	Wallasey Tn Hall
Environmental Health	Alan Stennard	Director of Housing & Environmental Protection	Westminster Hse
Finance	Ian Coleman	Director of Finance	Treasury Bldgs
Housing	Alan Stennard	Director of Housing & Environmental Protection	Westminster Hse
Legal Services	Jo Miller	Borough Solicitor & Secretary	Wallasey Tn Hall
Leisure	Howard Cooper	Director of Education & Cultural Services	Hamilton Bldgs

Local Land Charges	Jo Miller	Borough Solicitor & Secretary	Wallasey Tn Hall
Planning	James Wilkie	Director of Planning & Economic Development	North Annex
Social Services	Kevin Miller	Director of Social Services	Soc Services HQ
Technical Services	Dave Green	Director of Highways & Engineers Services	Bebington Tn Hall
Trading Standards	Alan Stennard	Director of Housing & Environmental Protection	Westminster Hse

Parish Councils & Parish Meetings in the authority's area: none.

Town Councils in the authority's area: none.

WOLVERHAMPTON CITY COUNCIL

www.wolverhampton.gov.uk

Principal Office
Civic Centre, St Peter's Square, Wolverhampton, West Midlands WV1 1SH
Telephone: (01902) 556556

Function	Chief Officer	Title	Location
Chief Executive	D B Anderson	Chief Executive	Civic Centre
Education	R Lockwood	Director for Lifelong Learning	Civic Centre
Electoral Registration	D J Plumb	Principal Elections Officer	Civic Centre
Environmental Health	N P Edwards	Chief Environmental Services Officer	Civic Centre
Finance	B Bailey	Director for Finance & Physical Resources	Civic Centre
Housing	I Gardner	Interim Chief Landlord Services Officer	Civic Centre
Legal Services	R Roberts	Director for Law & Resources	Civic Centre
Leisure	S Campbell	Chief Cultural Services Officer	Civic Centre
Local Land Charges	S Stephens	Chief Legal & Purchasing Officer	Civic Centre
Planning	C N Georghiou	Chief Planning Officer	Civic Centre
Purchasing & Supplies	J Jones	Group Manager, Purchasing	Civic Centre
Social Services	G Mason	Director for Social Care & Housing	Civic Centre
Technical Services	S P Boyes	Coordinating Director for Regeneration & Transportation	Civic Centre
Trading Standards	N P Edwards	Chief Environmental Services Officer	Civic Centre

Parish Councils & Parish Meetings in the authority's area: none.

Town Councils in the authority's area: none.

THE GREATER LONDON AUTHORITY, THE CORPORATION OF LONDON AND THE LONDON BOROUGHS

THE GREATER LONDON AUTHORITY

www.london.gov.uk

Principal Office
City Hall, The Queen's Walk, London SE1 2AA
Telephone: (020) 7983 4000; FAX: (020) 7983 4057; Minicom: (020) 7983 4458

Fire and Emergency Planning Authority (LFEPA)
20 Albert Embankment, London SE1 7SD
Telephone: (020) 7582 3811

London Development Agency (LDA)
Devon House, 58-60 St Katharine's Way, London E1W 1JX
Telephone: (020) 7680 2000

Metropolitan Police Authority (MPA)
10 Dean Farrar Street, London SW1H 0NY
Telephone: (020) 7202 0202

Transport for London (TfL)
Windsor House, 42-50 Victoria Street, London SW1H 0TL
Telephone: (020) 7941 4500

The Greater London Authority (GLA) assumed its responsibilities on 3 July 2000.

The eight main functions of the GLA are Transport, Policing, Fire and Emergency Planning, Economic Development, Planning, Culture, Environment and Health. The bodies above co-ordinate these functions.

THE CORPORATION OF LONDON

www.cityoflondon.gov.uk

Principal Office
PO Box 270, Guildhall, London EC2P 2EJ
Telephone: (020) 7606 3030; FAX: (020) 7332 1119; DX: 121780 Guildhall

Education Department
1 Bassishaw Highwalk, London EC2V 5DS
Telephone: (020) 7332 1750; FAX: (020) 7332 1621

Community Services Department
Milton Court, Moor Lane, London EC2Y 9BL
Telephone: (020) 7332 1224; FAX: (020) 7588 9173

Function	Chief Officer	Title	Location
Chief Executive	C Duffield	Town Clerk	Guildhall
Education	I Comfort	City Education Officer	1 Bassishaw H'walk
Electoral Registration	Miss N Edwards	Electoral Services Officer	Guildhall
Environmental Health	R Watson	Director of Environmental Services	Guildhall
Finance	P Derrick	Chamberlain	Guildhall

Housing	T Rogers	Director of Community Services	Guildhall
Legal Services	A J Colvin	Comptroller & City Solicitor	Guildhall
Local Land Charges	A C Johnson	Local Land Charges Officer	Guildhall
Planning	P W Rees	City Planning Officer	Guildhall
Purchasing & Supplies	G Dowding	Procurement Manager	Guildhall
Social Services	T Rogers	Director of Community Services	Milton Court
Technical Services	P Everett	Director of Technical Services	Guildhall
Trading Standards	B Aldridge	Director of Environmental Services	Guildhall

LONDON BOROUGH OF BARKING & DAGENHAM

www.lbbd.gov.uk

Principal Office
Civic Centre, Wood Lane, Dagenham, Essex RM10 7BN
Telephone: (020) 8592 4500; FAX: (020) 8227 2806

Development & Technical Services Department; Education Department; Legal Services
Town Hall, Barking, Essex IG11 7LU
Telephone: (020) 8592 4500; FAX: (020) 8227 3471 (Education);
FAX: (020) 8227 3129 (Leisure); FAX: (020) 8227 5705 (Legal)

Housing & Health Department
Roycraft House, Linton Road, Barking, Essex IG11 8HE
Telephone: (020) 8592 4500;

Legal Services
Town Hall, Barking, Essex IG11 7LU
Telephone: (020) 8592 4500; FAX: (020) 8227 3698

Function	Chief Officer	Title	Location
Chief Executive	Mr G Farrant	Chief Executive	Civic Centre
Education	Mr R Luxton	Director of Education, Arts & Libraries	Town Hall
Electoral Registration	Mrs N Clark	Borough Officer for Democratic & Legal Services	Roycraft House
Environmental Health	Mr D W Woods	Director of Housing & Health	Roycraft House
Finance	Mrs J Parker	Borough Finance Officer	Civic Centre
Housing	Mr D W Woods	Director of Housing & Health	Roycraft House
Legal Services	Mrs N Clark	Borough Officer for Democratic & Legal Services	Roycraft House
Leisure	Mr N Bolger	Director of Leisure & Environmental Services	Town Hall
Planning	Mr N Bolger	Director of Leisure & Environmental Services	Town Hall
Social Services	Mrs J Ross	Director of Social Services	Civic Centre
Technical Services	Mr N Bolger	Director of Leisure & Environmental Services	Town Hall
Trading Standards	Mr D W Woods	Director of Housing & Health	Roycraft House

LONDON BOROUGH OF BARNET

www.barnet.gov.uk

Principal Office
North London Business Park, Oakleigh Road South, London N11 1NP
Telephone: (020) 8359 2000; FAX: 0870 889 7453

Regeneration; Planning/Highways; Housing; Community Care; Environmental Services/Trading Standards
Barnet House, 1255 High Road, London N20 0EJ

Legal Services
The Town Hall, The Burroughs, Hendon, London NW4 4BG
Telephone: (020) 8359 2000; FAX: (020) 8359 2480

Function	Chief Officer	Title	Location
Chief Executive	Mr Leo Boland	Chief Executive	Nrth Lon Bus Pk
Education	Ms Gillian Palmer	Head of Education & Chief Education Officer	Nrth Lon Bus Pk
Electoral Registration	Mr Keith Porter	Principal Electoral Officer	Town Hall
Environmental Health	Mr Steve Presland	Head of Environmental & Neighbourhood Services	Nrth Lon Bus Pk
Finance	Mr Clive Medlam	Borough Treasurer	Nrth Lon Bus Pk
Housing	Ms Margaret McPeake	Head of Housing	Barnet House
Legal Services	Mr Jeff Lustig	Borough Solicitor	Town Hall
Local Land Charges	Mr Gareth Aspin	Principal Local Land Charges Officer	Town Hall
Planning	Mr Mike Freestone	Head of Planning, Highways & Design	Barnet House
Social Services	Mr Paul Fallon	Head of Children's Services & Director of Social Services	Barnet House
Trading Standards	Mr Dave Mosley	Chief Trading Standards Officer	Barnet House

BEXLEY LONDON BOROUGH

www.bexley.gov.uk

Principal Office
Bexley Civic Offices, Broadway, Bexleyheath, Kent DA6 7LB
Telephone: (020) 8303 7777; FAX: (020) 8301 2661; DX: 31807 Bexleyheath

Directorate of Education & Community Services
Hill View, Hill View Drive, Welling, Kent DA16 3RY
Telephone: (020) 8303 7777; FAX: (1081) 319 4302

Directorate of Environment & Regeneration Services
Wyncham House, 207 Longlands Road, Sidcup, Kent DA15 7JH
Telephone: (020) 8303 7777; FAX: (1081) 308 4897

Directorate of Environmental Health & Trading Standards
2A Hadlow Rd, Sidcup, Kent DA14 4AF
Telephone: (020) 8303 7777, FAX: (020) 8308 1300

Directorate of Highways & Amenities
Crayford Town Hall, 112 Crayford Road, Crayford, Kent DA1 4ER
Telephone: (020) 8303 7777

Function	Chief Officer	Title	Location
Chief Executive	Nick Johnson	Chief Executive	Civic Offices
Education	Deborah Absalom	Director of Education	Hill View
Electoral Registration	Julie Keith	Head of Democratic Services	Civic Offices
Environmental Health	Peter Ellershaw	Director of Environmental & Regeneration Services	Wyncham Hse
Finance	David Berry	Director of Finance & Business Services	Civic Offices
Housing	Simon Leftley	Director of Social Services & Housing	Hill View
Legal Services	Andrew Maughan	Head of Legal Services	Civic Offices
Leisure	Steve Wall	Assistant Director of Leisure & Property	Civic Offices
Planning	Peter Ellershaw	Director of Environmental & Regeneration Services	Wyncham Hse
Social Services	Simon Leftley	Director of Social Services & Housing	Hill View

Technical Services	Mike Frizoni	Assistant Director of Highways & Amenities	Crayford Tn Hall
Trading Standards	David Bryce-Smith	Assistant Director of Development & Public Protection	Wyncham Hse

LONDON BOROUGH OF BRENT

www.brent.gov.uk

Principal Office
Town Hall, Forty Lane, Wembley, Middlesex HA9 9HD
Telephone: (020) 8937 1234

Environmental Planning & Commissioning Department; Health, Safety & Licensing Department; Environmental Health; Streetcare; Transportation; Building Control Department; Area Planning Department
Brent House, 349-357 High Street, Wembley HA9 6BZ
Telephone: (020) 8937 5002 (Environmental Services); (020) 8937 5210 (Area Planning)

Housing Department; Social Services Department
Mahatma Gandhi House, 34 Wembley Hill Road, Wembley HA9 8AD
Telephone: (020) 8937 2341 (Housing); (020) 8937 4230 (Social Services)

Education, Arts & Libraries Department
Chesterfield House, 9 Park Lane, Wembley HA9 7RW
Telephone: (020) 8937 3130

Social Inclusion
Challenge House, 2 Bank Buildings, Harlesden NW10 4LX
Telephone: (020) 8937 6460

Trading Standards
Quality House, 249 Willesden Lane NW2 5JH
Telephone: (020) 8937 5555

Function	Chief Officer	Title	Location
Chief Executive	Gareth Daniel	Chief Executive	Town Hall
Education	John Christie	Director of Education	Chesterfield Hse
Electoral Registration	Sean O'Sullivan	Electoral Services Manager	Town Hall
Environmental Health	Derek Buck	Director of Environmental Health	Brent House
Finance	Duncan McLeod	Acting Director of Finance	Town Hall
Housing	Martin Cheeseman	Director of Housing	M Gandhi Hse
Legal Services	Terry Osborne	Solicitor to the Council	Town Hall
Leisure	Sue Harper	Assistant Director of Environment	Brent House
Planning	Chris Walker	Director of Planning Services	Brent House
Social Services	Jenny Goodall	Director of Social Services	M Gandhi Hse
Trading Standards	John Taylor	Director of Trading Standards Service	Quality House

BROMLEY COUNCIL

www.bromley.gov.uk

Principal Office
Bromley Civic Centre, Stockwell Close, Bromley, Kent BR1 3UH
Telephone: (020) 8464 3333; FAX: (020) 8290 0608

Community & Leisure Services Department
Central Library, High Street, Bromley BR1 1EX
Telephone: (020) 8460 9955; FAX: (020) 8313 9975

Function	Chief Officer	Title	Location
Chief Executive	Mr David Bartlett	Chief Executive	Civic Centre

Education	Mr Ken Davis	Director of Education & Libraries	Civic Centre
Environmental Health	Mr Gordon Hayward	Director of Environmental Services	Civic Centre
Finance	Mr Paul Dale	Borough Treasurer	Civic Centre
Legal Services	Mr Timothy Leader	Director of Legal & Democratic Services	Civic Centre
Social Services	Mr Terry Rich	Director of Social Services & Housing	Civic Centre

LONDON BOROUGH OF CAMDEN

www.camden.gov.uk

Chief Executive's Department
Town Hall, Judd Street, London WC1H 9JE
Telephone: (020) 7974 4444; DX: 2106 Euston

Education Department; Leisure & Community Services Department
The Crowndale Centre, 218-220 Eversholt Street, London NW1 1BD
Telephone: (020) 7974 1525; FAX: (020) 7974 1536

Environment Department; Financial Services Branch
Town Hall Extension, Argyle Street, London WC1H 8EQ (Environment)
WC1H 8NG (Financial Services)
Telephone: (020) 7974 4444

Housing Department
20 Mabledon Place, London WC1H 9BF
Telephone: (020) 7974 4444; FAX: (020) 7974 5946

Social Services Department
79 Camden Road, London NW1 9ES
Telephone: (020) 7974 6666; FAX: (020) 7974 6704

Information Technology
3-5 Cressy Road, Hampstead, London NW3 2ND
Telephone: (020) 7974 6879

Function	Chief Officer	Title	Location
Chief Executive	Mr B Litchfield	Acting Chief Executive	Town Hall
Electoral Registration	Ms A Paul	Head of Democratic Services	Town Hall
Environmental Health	Mr P Bishop	Director of Environment	Town Hall Extn
Finance	Mr J Mabey	Controller of Financial Services	Town Hall Extn
Housing	Mr N Litherland	Director of Housing	20 Mabledon Pl
Legal Services	Ms A Lowton	Borough Solicitor	Town Hall
Leisure	Mr N Graves	Head of Leisure & Community Services	Crowndale Ctre
Local Land Charges	Ms S Jackdeo	Chief Executive's Department	Town Hall
Planning	Mr T Jeffrey	Assistant Director (Planning)	Town Hall Extn
Purchasing & Supplies	Mr G Goodman	Chief Executive's Department	Town Hall Extn
Social Services	Ms J Held	Director of Social Services	79 Camden Rd
Technical Services	Mr G Evans	Head of ICT	Cressy Road
Trading Standards	Mr P Strange	Environment Department	Town Hall Extn

LONDON BOROUGH OF CROYDON

www.croydon.gov.uk

Principal Office
Taberner House, Park Lane, Croydon, Surrey CR9 3JS
Telephone: (020) 8686 4433; FAX: (020) 8760 0871; DX: 2630 Croydon

LONDON

Function	Chief Officer	Title	Location
Chief Executive	David Wechsler	Chief Executive	Taberner House
Education	Peter Wylie	Director of Education	Taberner House
Electoral Registration	Miles Smith	Director of Corporate Services	Taberner House
Environmental Health	Steve Halsey	Director of Environmental, Cultural & Sports Services	Taberner House
Finance	Roy Taylor	Acting Director of Finance & IT	Taberner House
Housing	Mike Davis	Director of Housing	Taberner House
Legal Services	Miles Smith	Director of Corporate Services	Taberner House
Leisure	Steve Halsey	Director of Environmental, Cultural & Sports Services	Taberner House
Local Land Charges	Miles Smith	Director of Corporate Services	Taberner House
Planning	Phillip Goodwin	Director of Planning & Transportation	Taberner House
Purchasing & Supplies	Miles Smith	Director of Corporate Services	Taberner House
Social Services	Hannah Miller	Director of Social Services	Taberner House
Technical Services	Steve Halsey	Director of Environmental, Cultural & Sports Services	Taberner House
Trading Standards	Steve Halsey	Director of Environmental, Cultural & Sports Services	Taberner House

EALING LONDON BOROUGH

www.ealing.gov.uk

Principal Office

Town Hall, New Broadway, Ealing, London W5 2BY
Telephone: (020) 8579 2424; FAX: (020) 8840 5574; DX: 5106 Ealing

Education Department; Social Services Department; Housing Department; Environment Group

Perceval House, 14/16 Uxbridge Road, Ealing, London W5 2HL
Telephone: (020) 8579 2424

Function	Chief Officer	Title	Location
Chief Executive	Ms G Guy	Chief Executive	Perceval Hse
Education	Ms C Whalley	Executive Director of Learning & Ambition	Perceval Hse
Electoral Registration	Ms J George	Head of Electoral Registration	Town Hall
Environmental Health	Mr T Dent	Assistant Director, Environmental Health & Trading Standards	Perceval Hse
Finance	Mr S Lawes	Executive Director of Corporate Resources	Perceval Hse
Housing	Ms S Gomer	Housing Director	Perceval Hse
Legal Services	[Vacant]	Director of Law & Democratic Services	Perceval Hse
Leisure	Mr P Hyman	Head of Leisure, Planning & Development	Perceval Hse
Local Land Charges	Mr N Rutherford	Assistant Director, Planning & Surveying Services	Perceval Hse
Planning	Mr N Rutherford	Assistant Director, Planning & Surveying Services	Perceval Hse
Trading Standards	Mr T Dent	Assistant Director, Environmental Health & Trading Standards	Perceval Hse

LONDON BOROUGH OF ENFIELD

www.enfield.gov.uk

Principal Office

Civic Centre, Silver Street, Enfield, Middlesex EN1 3XA
Telephone: (020) 8379 1000; FAX: (020) 8379 6458; DX: 90615 Enfield

Function	Chief Officer	Title	Location
Chief Executive	Rob Leak	Chief Executive	Civic Centre
Education	Peter Lewis	Director of Education, Children's Services & Leisure	Civic Centre
Electoral Registration	Philip Devonald	Assistant Director of Legal & Democratic	Civic Centre
Environmental Health	Mike Hainge	Assistant Director of Environmental Health & Regulation	Civic Centre
Finance	Mark McLaughlin	Director of Finance & Resources	Civic Centre
Housing	Donald Graham	Director of Community & Social Services	Civic Centre
Legal Services	Philip Devonald	Assistant Director of Legal & Democratic	Civic Centre
Leisure	Peter Lewis	Director of Education, Children's Services & Leisure	Civic Centre
Planning	Stephen Tapper	Assistant Director of Planning & Transportation	Civic Centre
Purchasing & Supplies	David Tullis	Assistant Director of Property & Procurement	Civic Centre
Social Services	Donald Graham	Director of Community & Social Services	Civic Centre
Technical Services	Stephen Tapper	Assistant Director of Planning & Transportation	Civic Centre

LONDON BOROUGH OF GREENWICH

www.greenwich.gov.uk

Housing Services; Strategic Planning
Peggy Middleton House, 50 Woolwich New Road, London SE18 6HQ
Telephone: (020) 8854 8888

Chief Executive
Town Hall, Wellington Street, Woolwich, London SE18 6PW
Telephone: (020) 8921 5001; FAX: (020) 8921 5943

Education Services; Public Services
Riverside House, Woolwich High Street, London SE18 6DF
Telephone: (020) 8854 8888

Social Services Department
Nelson House, Wellington Street, London SE18 6PY
Telephone: (020) 8854 8888; FAX: (020) 8921 3112

Function	Chief Officer	Title	Location
Chief Executive	Ms M Ney	Chief Executive	Town Hall
Education	Mr P Burnett	Director of Education Services	Riverside House
Electoral Registration	Mr S O'Hare	Electoral Services Manager	29-37 Wellington St
Environmental Health	Mr R Collingham	Assistant Director of Community & Enforcement Services	Riverside House
Finance	Mr C Perry	Chief Finance Officer	45-53 Wellington St
Housing	Mr R Thompson	Director of Housing Services	Peggy Middleton Hse
Legal Services	Mr R Power	Head of Legal Services	29-37 Wellington St
Leisure	G Singh-Kandola	Director of Public Services	Riverside House
Planning	Mr D McCollum	Director of Strategic Planning	Peggy Middleton Hse
Purchasing & Supplies	Mr J Dowers	Head of Corporate Procurement	Peggy Middleton Hse
Social Services	Mr J Nawrockyi	Director of Social Services	Nelson House
Trading Standards	Mr A Scott	Head of Commercial Services	Riverside House

LONDON BOROUGH OF HACKNEY

www.hackney.gov.uk

Principal Office
Town Hall, Mare Street, Hackney, London E8 1EA
Telephone: (020) 8356 5000; FAX: (020) 8356 2185

Directorate of Community & Environment
Maurice Bishop House, Reading Lane, Hackney, London E8 1HH
Telephone: (020) 8356 5000

Directorate of Housing
Christopher Addison House, 72 Wilton Way, London E8 1BJ
Telephone: (020) 8356 5000

Directorate of Social Services
205 Morning Lane, London E9 6JX
Telephone: (020) 8356 5000

The Learning Trust
1 Reading Lane, Hackney, London E8 1HH
Telephone: (020) 8820 7000

Function	Chief Officer	Title	Location
Chief Executive	Max Caller	Chief Executive	Town Hall
Education	Alan Wood	Chief Executive – The Learning Trust	1 Reading Ln
Environmental Health	Jon Judah	Director of Environment	Town Hall
Finance	Tim Shields	Acting Director of Finance	Town Hall
Housing	Steve Tucker	Director of Housing	C. Addison Hse
Legal Services	Claer Lloyd-Jones	Director of Law & Democratic Services	Town Hall
Leisure	Kim Wright	Director of Community & Leisure	M. Bishop Hse
Social Services	Mary Richardson	Director of Social Services	205 Morning Ln

LONDON BOROUGH OF HAMMERSMITH & FULHAM

www.lbhf.gov.uk

Principal Office
Hammersmith Town Hall, King Street, London W6 9JU
Telephone: (020) 8753 2001; FAX: (020) 8741 0307

Social Services Department
145 King Street, London W6 9XY
Telephone: (020) 8753 5001

Environment Department
Town Hall Extension, King Street, London W6
Telephone: (020) 8753 3001

Housing Department
Riverview House, Beaver Lane, Hammersmith, London W6 9AR
Telephone: (020) 8753 4001

Direct Services Department
4th Floor, Riverview House, Beaver Lane, Hammersmith, London W6 9AR
Telephone: (020) 8753 1157

Education Department
Cambridge House, Cambridge Grove, Hammersmith, London W6 0LE
Telephone: (020) 8753 3601

Function	Chief Officer	Title	Location
Chief Executive	Mr Geoff Alltimes	Managing Director	Town Hall
Education	Mr Sandy Adamson	Director of Education	Cambridge House

LONDON

Electoral Registration	Mr Steve Miller	Electoral Services Manager	Town Hall
Environmental Health	Mr Nigel Pallace	Director of Environment	Town Hall Extn
Finance	Ms Jane West	Director of Finance	Town Hall Extn
Housing	Ms Elaine Elkington	Director of Housing	Riverview House
Legal Services	Mr Michael Cogher	Head of Legal Services	Town Hall
Social Services	Mr James Reilly	Director of Social Services	145 King Street

HARINGEY LONDON BOROUGH

www.haringey.gov.uk
Principal Office
Civic Centre, High Road, London N22 8LE
Telephone: (020) 8489 0000

Corporate Services
Alexandra House, 10 Station Road, London N22 4TR
Telephone: (020) 8489 0000

Education Services
48 Station Road, London N22 4TY
Telephone: (020) 8489 0000

Housing & Social Services
40 Cumberland Road, London N22 4SG
Telephone: (020) 8489 0000

Environmental Services
639 High Road, London N17
Telephone: (020) 8489 0000

Function	Chief Officer	Title	Location
Chief Executive	Mr D Warwick	Chief Executive	Civic Centre
Environmental Health	Mr P Norton	Director of Environmental Services	639 High Road
Finance	Mr A Travers	Director of Finance	Alexandra Hse
Housing	Mr S Clark	Director of Housing	40 Cumberland Rd
Social Services	Ms A Bristow	Director of Social Services	40 Cumberland Rd

LONDON BOROUGH OF HARROW

www.harrow.gov.uk
Principal Office
Civic Centre, Station Road, Harrow, Middlesex HA1 2UJ
Telephone: (020) 8863 5611; FAX: (020) 8424 1557; DX: 30450 Harrow 3

Trading Standards Department (Brent & Harrow)
Quality House, 249 Willesden Lane, London NW2 5JH
Telephone: (020) 8937 5555; FAX: (020) 8937 5544

Function	Chief Officer	Title	Location
Chief Executive	Joyce Markham	Chief Executive	Civic Centre
Education	Paul Osburn	Executive Director (People First)	Civic Centre
Electoral Registration	Gerald Balabanoff	Borough Solicitor	Civic Centre
Environmental Health	Gareth Llywelyn-Roberts	Chief Environmental Health Officer	Civic Centre
Finance	Nick Bell	Executive Director (Business Connections)	Civic Centre
Housing	Michael Wright	Housing Manager/ALMO Project Manager	Civic Centre
Legal Services	Gerald Balabanoff	Borough Solicitor	Civic Centre

Leisure	Anna Robinson	Director of Strategy (Urban Living)	Civic Centre
Local Land Charges	Gerald Balabanoff	Borough Solicitor	Civic Centre
Planning	Graham Jones	Chief Planning Officer	Civic Centre
Purchasing & Supplies	Perry Scott	Procurement Manager	Civic Centre
Social Services	Nick Georgiou	Head of Community Care Services	Civic Centre
Technical Services	Brynn Hodgson	Director of Professional Services	Civic Centre
Trading Standards	John Taylor	Director of Trading Standards (Brent & Harrow)	Quality Hse

LONDON BOROUGH OF HAVERING

www.havering.gov.uk

Principal Office
Town Hall, Main Road, Romford, Essex RM1 3BD
Telephone: (01708) 434343; FAX: (01708) 432068

Building and Technical Services
The Whitworth Centre, Noak Hill Road, Harold Hill, Romford, Essex RM3 7YA
Telephone: (01708) 434343

Environmental Health; Planning
Mercury House, Mercury Gardens, Romford, Essex RM1 3SL
Telephone: (01708) 434343

Legal Services
Ballard Chambers, 26 High Street, Romford, Essex RM1 1HR
Telephone: (01708) 434343

Leisure Services
The Broxhill Centre, Broxhill Road, Harold Hill, Romford, Essex RM4 1XN
Telephone: (01708) 434343

Purchasing & Supplies
Mercury House, Mercury Gardens, Romford, Essex RM1 3SL
Telephone: (01708) 434343

Function	Chief Officer	Title	Location
Chief Executive	Stephen Evans	Chief Executive	Town Hall
Education	David MacLean	Acting Executive Director, Education	Town Hall
Electoral Registration	Sandra Cottle	Electoral Services Manager	Town Hall
Environmental Health	John Wade	Head of Environmental Health	Mercury House
Finance	Mike Stringer	Head of Financial Services	Town Hall
Housing	Mark Gaynor	Executive Director, Housing & Regeneration	Town Hall
Legal Services	Christine Dooley	Assistant Chief Executive, Legal & Democratic Services	Town Hall
Leisure	Julie Simpson	Head of Culture & Leisure Services	Whitworth Centre
Local Land Charges	Christine Dooley	Assistant Chief Executive, Legal & Democratic Services	Town Hall
Planning	Mike Day	Head of Planning	Mercury House
Purchasing & Supplies	Brian Hinchley	Business Development Manager	Mercury House
Social Services	Marilyn Richards	Executive Director, Social Services	Town Hall
Technical Services	Mike Robinson	Head of Strategic Planning & Technical Services	Mercury House
Trading Standards	Andrew McKenzie	Head of Environmental Management & Regulation	Mercury House

LONDON

LONDON BOROUGH OF HILLINGDON

www.hillingdon.gov.uk

Principal Office
Civic Centre, High Street, Uxbridge, Middlesex UB8 1UW
Telephone: (01895) 250111; FAX: (01895) 273636; DX: 45101 Uxbridge

Function	Chief Officer	Title	Location
Chief Executive	Mr D Leatham	Chief Executive	Civic Centre
Education	Mr P O'Hear	Corporate Director, Education, Youth & Leisure Services	Civic Centre
Electoral Registration	Mr M Liddiard	Electoral Services Manager	Civic Centre
Environmental Health	Mrs R Willis	Corporate Director of Environmental Services	Civic Centre
Finance	Mr C Neale	Director of Finance	Civic Centre
Housing	Ms P Lockley	Corporate Director of Housing Services	Civic Centre
Legal Services	Mr R Alagh	Borough Solicitor	Civic Centre
Leisure	Mr M Bhimani	Deputy Head of Youth & Leisure Services	Civic Centre
Planning	Ms J Palmer	Head of Planning & Transportation	Civic Centre
Social Services	Mr H Dunnachie	Director of Social Services	Civic Centre
Technical Services	Mr S Smith	Facilities Manager	Civic Centre
Trading Standards	Ms K Sparks	Head of Consumer Protection	Civic Centre

LONDON BOROUGH OF HOUNSLOW

www.hounslow.gov.uk

Principal Office
Civic Centre, Lampton Road, Hounslow, Middlesex TW3 4DN
Telephone: (020) 8583 2000; FAX: (020) 8583 2598; DX: 3505 Hounslow

Hounslow Homes (Housing ALMO)
St Catherine's House, 2 Hanworth Road, Feltham, Middlesex TW13 5AB
Telephone: (020) 8583 2000

Community Initiative Partnerships (Leisure Provider)
Treaty Centre, High Street, Hounslow TW3 1ES

Function	Chief Officer	Title	Location
Chief Executive	Mr M Gilks	Chief Executive	Civic Centre
Education	Mr B Garnett	Corporate Director of Lifelong Learning	Civic Centre
Electoral Registration	Mr A Rust	Deputy Returning Officer	Civic Centre
Environmental Health	Mr S Kamath	Head of Street Management & Public Protection	Civic Centre
Finance	Mr A Steele	Assistant Chief Executive, Borough Treasurer	Civic Centre
Housing	Ms B O'Shea	Head of Housing Strategy & Services	Civic Centre
Legal Services	Mr M J Smith	Assistant Chief Executive, Borough Solicitor	Civic Centre
Leisure	Mr J Rice	Chief Executive, Community Initiative Partnerships	Treaty Centre
Local Land Charges	Mr A Rust	Deputy Returning Officer	Civic Centre
Planning	Mr M Jordan	Borough Planning Officer	Civic Centre
Social Services	Ms S White	Corporate Director of Social Services & Health Partnerships	Civic Centre
Technical Services	Ms J Robson	Chief Technical Officer	St Catherine's

LONDON BOROUGH OF ISLINGTON

www.islington.gov.uk

Principal Office
Islington Town Hall, Upper Street, London N1 2UD
Telephone: (020) 7527 2000

Education Department
Laycock Street, London N1 1TH
Telephone: (020) 7527 5666

Environment & Conservation Department; Finance Department
Municipal Offices, PO Box 3333, 222 Upper Street, London N1 1YA
Telephone: (020) 7226 1234

Housing Department; Social Services Department
Highbury House, 5 Highbury Crescent, London N5 1RN
Telephone: (020) 7226 1234

Function	Chief Officer	Title	Location
Chief Executive	Helen Bailey	Chief Executive	Town Hall
Education	Mohammed Mehmet	Director of Education	Laycock Street
Electoral Registration	Iain Bowden	Manager Electoral Services	Town Hall
Environmental Health	Kevin O'Leary	Director of Environment & Conservation	Municipal Offices
Finance	David Cruickshank	Director of Finance & Property Services	Municipal Offices
Housing	Andy Jennings	Deputy Chief Executive	Town Hall
Legal Services	Louise Round	Director of Law & Public Services	Town Hall
Planning	Graham Loveland	Head of Planning & Transportation	Municipal Offices
Social Services	Paul Curran	Director of Social Services	Highbury House
Trading Standards	Richard Hill	Director of Customer Focus	Town Hall

THE ROYAL BOROUGH OF KENSINGTON & CHELSEA

www.rbkc.gov.uk

Principal Office
The Town Hall, Hornton Street, London W8 7NX
Telephone: (020) 7937 5464; FAX: (020) 7938 1445; DX: 84015 Kensington High Street 2

Environmental Services Department; Environmental Health, Waste Management & Leisure Department; Building Control Department
Council Offices, 37 Pembroke Road, London W8 6PW
Telephone: (020) 7937 5464; FAX: (020) 7341 5155

Function	Chief Officer	Title	Location
Chief Executive	Mr D Myers	Town Clerk & Chief Executive	Town Hall
Education	Ms J Griffin	Executive Director, Education, Libraries & Arts	Town Hall
Electoral Registration	Mr G Bishop	Director of Personnel & General Services	Town Hall
Environmental Health	Mr M Stroud	Executive Director, Environmental Services	Council Offices
Finance	Mrs S Beauchamp	Director of Finance & Information Systems	Town Hall
Housing	Mrs M Gibb	Executive Director, Housing & Social Services	Town Hall
Legal Services	Ms G Edila	Director of Law & Administration	Town Hall
Leisure	Mr N W Cook	Director of Waste Management & Leisure	Council Offices

Local Land Charges	Mr G Bishop	Director of Personnel & General Services	Town Hall
Planning	Mr M French	Executive Director, Planning & Conservation	Town Hall
Purchasing & Supplies	Mr G Bishop	Director of Personnel & General Services	Town Hall
Social Services	Mrs M Gibb	Executive Director, Housing & Social Services	Town Hall
Technical Services	Mr M Stroud	Executive Director, Environmental Services	Council Offices
Trading Standards	Mr P Morse	Director of Environmental Health	Council Offices

ROYAL BOROUGH OF KINGSTON UPON THAMES

www.kingston.gov.uk

Principal Office
Guildhall, Kingston upon Thames, Surrey KT1 1EU
Telephone: (020) 8546 2121

Community Services Department
Guildhall 1, Kingston upon Thames, Surrey KT1 1EU

**Education and Leisure Department; Finance Department;
Planning Department; Recycling and Waste Management Departments**
Guildhall 2, Kingston upon Thames, Surrey KT1 1EU

Function	Chief Officer	Title	Location
Chief Executive	Bruce McDonald	Chief Executive	Guildhall
Education	Patrick Leeson	Director of Education & Leisure	Guildhall 2
Electoral Registration	Andrew Bessant	Head of Democratic Services & Partnership	Guildhall
Environmental Health	Bob Smart	Borough Environmental Health Officer	Guildhall
Finance	Tony Knights	Director of Finance	Guildhall 2
Housing	Michael England	Head of Housing	Guildhall 1
Legal Services	Nick Bishop	Head of Legal Services	Guildhall
Leisure	Scott Herbertson	Assistant Director of Leisure & Lifelong Learning	Guildhall 2
Local Land Charges	Nick Bishop	Head of Legal Services	Guildhall
Planning	John Allen	Head of Planning & Development	Guildhall 2
Social Services	Roy Taylor, CBE	Director of Community Services	Guildhall
Technical Services	Tim Darwen	Head of Neighbourhood Services	Guildhall 2
Trading Standards	Ted Forsyth	Chief Trading Standards Officer	Guildhall

LONDON BOROUGH OF LAMBETH

www.lambeth.gov.uk

Principal Office
Lambeth Town Hall, Brixton Hill, London SW2 1RW
Telephone: (020) 8926 1000

Housing Services
Hambrook House, Porden Road, London SW2 1RP
Telephone: (020) 7926 3426; FAX: (020) 7926 3590

Social Services
Mary Seacole House, 91 Clapham High Street, London SW4 7TF
Telephone: (020) 7926 4788; FAX: (020) 7926 4783

Education Department
International House, Canterbury Crescent, London SW9 7QE
Telephone: (020) 7926 1000; FAX: (020) 7926 9843

Environment Department
2nd Floor, Blue Star House, 234-244 Stockwell Road, Brixton, London SW9 9SP

Finance & Corporate Services
Ninth Floor, International House, Canterbury Crescent, London SW9 7QE
Telephone: (020) 7926 9717; FAX: (020) 7926 9748

Planning Department
Acre House, Acre Lane, London SW2 5LL
Telephone: (020) 8926 1000

Regulatory Services
2 Herne Hill, London SE24 0AU

Function	Chief Officer	Title	Location
Chief Executive	Faith Boardman	Chief Executive	Town Hall
Education	Phyllis Dunipace	Executive Director of Education	International Hse
Electoral Registration	Len Lewis	Electoral Registration Officer	Town Hall
Environmental Health	David Evans	Assistant Director of Environment	Blue Star House
Finance	Richard Ennis	Executive Director of Finance	International Hse
Housing	Stewart Holton	Executive Director of Housing	Hambrook Hse
Legal Services	Ged Curran	Borough Solicitor	International Hse
Leisure	Grant Altken	Sport & Recreation Manager	Blue Star House
Local Land Charges	John Jolley	Land Charges Officer	Town Hall
Planning	Les Brown	Head of Planning	Acre House
Purchasing & Supplies	Mike Fogaty	Director of Business Development	Town Hall
Social Services	Andrew Webster	Executive Director of Social Services	M. Seacole Hse
Technical Services	Mike Fogaty	Director of Business Development	Town Hall
Trading Standards	Dave Bright	Regulatory Services	2 Herne Hill

LONDON BOROUGH OF LEWISHAM

www.lewisham.gov.uk

Principal Office
Lewisham Town Hall, Catford, London SE6 4RU
Telephone: (020) 8314 6000; FAX: (020) 8314 3000; DX: 139500 Lewisham 4

Education & Culture Directorate; Social Care & Health Directorate; Regeneration Directorate
Laurence House, Catford Road, London SE6 4SW
Telephone: (020) 8314 6000

Regeneration Directorate (Housing)
Capital House, Rushey Green, London SE6 4BA
Telephone: (020) 8314 6000; FAX: (020) 8314 3152

Function	Chief Officer	Title	Location
Chief Executive	Barry Quirk	Chief Executive	Town Hall
Education	Frankie Sulke	Executive Director of Education & Culture	Laurence Hse
Environmental Health	Patrick Hayes	Executive Director of Regeneration	Laurence Hse
Finance	Rob Whiteman	Executive Director of Resources	Town Hall
Housing	Patrick Hayes	Executive Director of Regeneration	Laurence Hse
Legal Services	Kath Nicholson	Head of Legal Services	Town Hall
Leisure	Patrick Hayes	Executive Director of Regeneration	Laurence Hse
Local Land Charges	Patrick Hayes	Executive Director of Regeneration	Laurence Hse
Planning	Patrick Hayes	Executive Director of Regeneration	Laurence Hse

Social Services	Zena Peatfield	Executive Director of Social Care & Health	Laurence Hse
Technical Services	Patrick Hayes	Executive Director of Regeneration	Laurence Hse
Trading Standards	Patrick Hayes	Executive Director of Regeneration	Laurence Hse

LONDON BOROUGH OF MERTON

www.merton.gov.uk

Principal Office

Merton Civic Centre, London Road, Morden, Surrey SM4 5DX
Telephone: (020) 8274 4901; FAX: (020) 8543 7126; DX: 41650 Morden

Function	Chief Officer	Title	Location
Chief Executive	Mr Ged Curran	Chief Executive	Civic Centre
Education	Ms Sue Evans	Director of Education, Leisure & Libraries	Civic Centre
Electoral Registration	Mr Michael Bentley	Electoral Services Manager	Civic Centre
Environmental Health	Mr Richard Rawes	Director of Environmental Services	Civic Centre
Finance	Mr Mike Parsons	Director of Financial Services	Civic Centre
Housing	Ms Rea Mattocks	Director of Housing & Social Services	Civic Centre
Legal Services	Mr Solomon Agutu	Acting Head of Legal Services	Civic Centre
Leisure	Ms Sue Evans	Director of Education, Leisure & Libraries	Civic Centre
Local Land Charges	Mr Solomon Agutu	Acting Head of Legal Services	Civic Centre
Planning	Mr Steve Clark	Head of Planning & Public Protection	Civic Centre
Social Services	Ms Rea Mattocks	Director of Housing & Social Services	Civic Centre
Technical Services	Gurmal Bansel	Head of I.T.	Civic Centre
Trading Standards	Mr Steve Clark	Head of Planning & Public Protection	Civic Centre

NEWHAM COUNCIL

www.newham.gov.uk

Principal Office
Newham Town Hall, East Ham, London E6 2RP
Telephone: (020) 8430 2000

Education Department; Social Services Department
Broadway House, 322 High Street, Stratford, London E15 1AJ
Telephone: (020) 8430 2000

Environment & Regeneration Department
25 Nelson Street, East Ham, London E6 6EH
Telephone: (020) 8430 2000

Culture & Community Department
292 Barking Road, London E6 3BA
Telephone: (020) 8430 2000

Housing Department
Bridge House, 320 High Street, Stratford, London E15 1EP
Telephone: (020) 8430 2000

Electoral Services Section
2–4 Nelson Street, East Ham, London E6 6EH
Telephone: (020) 8430 2000

LONDON

Consumer Protection Department
495 High Street North, London E12 6TH
Telephone: (020) 8430 2000

Environment & Planning Department
Town Hall Annexe, East Ham, London E6 2RP
Telephone: (020) 8430 2000

Environmental Health
Alice Billings House, 2–12 West Ham Lane, Stratford, London E15 4SF
Telephone: (020) 8430 2000

Function	Chief Officer	Title	Location
Chief Executive	Dave Burbage	Chief Executive	Town Hall
Education	Pauline Maddison	Director of Education	Broadway Hse
Electoral Registration	Mary Bradley	Electoral Services Manager	2–4 Nelson St
Environmental Health	Steve Miller	Head of Environmental & Commercial Standards	Alice Billings Hse
Finance	Bob Heaton	Director of Finance	Town Hall
Housing	Chris Wood	Director of Housing	Bridge House
Legal Services	Helen Sidwell	Head of Legal Services	Town Hall
Leisure	Norman Turner	Director of Culture & Community	292 Barking Rd
Local Land Charges	Viv Ramsey	Development & Building Control Manager	Town Hall Annexe
Planning	Malcolm Smith	Director of Environment & Regeneration	25 Nelson St
Purchasing & Supplies	David Robins	Strategic Procurement Manager	Town Hall
Social Services	Kathryn Hudson	Director of Social Services	Broadway Hse
Trading Standards	Ray Sweeting	Manager Trading Standards & Consumer Protection	495 High St Nth

LONDON BOROUGH OF REDBRIDGE

www.redbridge.gov.uk

Principal Office
PO Box 2, Town Hall, High Road, Ilford, Essex IG1 1DD
Telephone: (020) 8554 5000; FAX: (020) 8478 2356

Function	Chief Officer	Title	Location
Chief Executive	Roger Hampson	Chief Executive	Town Hall
Education	Edwina Grant	Director of Education, Leisure & Libraries	Town Hall
Finance	Geoff Pearce	Chief Finance Officer	Town Hall
Housing	Lisa Marston	Chief Housing Officer	Town Hall
Legal Services	Heidi Chottin	Chief Legal Officer	Town Hall
Leisure	Nigel Birch	Chief Leisure Officer	Town Hall
Planning	Paul Clark	Chief Planning Officer	Town Hall
Purchasing & Supplies	Tom Gayler	Chief Client & Purchasing Officer	Town Hall
Social Services	John Drew	Director of Social Services & Housing	Town Hall
Trading Standards	Ray Trendell	Chief Public Protection Officer	Town Hall

LONDON BOROUGH OF RICHMOND UPON THAMES

www.richmond.gov.uk

Principal Office
Civic Centre, 44 York Street, Twickenham, Middlesex TW1 3BZ
Telephone: (020) 8891 1411

Education Services Department; Legal Services Department;
Regal House, London Road, Twickenham, Middlesex TW1 3QB
Telephone: (020) 8891 7500 (Education Services); (020) 8891 7775 (Electoral Services);
(020) 8891 7774 (Local Land Charges); (020) 8891 7770 (Trading Standards)

Environmental & Operational Services Department
Central Depot, Langhorn Drive, Twickenham, Middlesex TW2 7SG
Telephone: (020) 8891 7359

Social Services
42 York Street, Twickenham, Middlesex TW1 3BW
Telephone: (020) 8891 7600

Function	Chief Officer	Title	Location
Chief Executive	Gillian Norton	Chief Executive	Civic Centre
Education	Anji Phillips	Chief Education Officer	Regal House
Electoral Registration	Judith Witt	Electoral Services Manager	Regal House
Environmental Health	David Streeter	Head of Environmental & Operational Services	Central Depot
Finance	Mark Maidment	Director of Finance	York Street
Housing	Jeff Jerome	Director of Social Services & Housing	York Street
Legal Services	Richard Mellor	Head of Legal Services	Regal House
Leisure	Anji Phillips	Director of Education & Leisure	Regal House
Local Land Charges	John Butcher	Land Charges Manager	Regal House
Planning	Philip Wealthy	Policy & Design;	
	Dave Barnes	Development Control;	
	Dave Batsford	Building Control	Civic Centre
Purchasing & Supplies	Andy Oakley	Corporate Purchasing Manager	Civic Centre
Social Services	Jeff Jerome	Director of Social Services & Housing	York Street
Technical Services	Trevor Pugh	Director of Environment	Civic Centre
Trading Standards	Martin Esom	Head of Environmental Protection & Customer Services	Central Depot

LONDON BOROUGH OF SOUTHWARK

www.southwark.gov.uk

Principal Office
Southwark Town Hall, Peckham Road, London SE5 8UB
Telephone: (020) 7525 5000

Education Department
John Smith House, Walworth Road, London SE17
Telephone: (020) 7525 5007

Electoral Services Department
Central House, Peckham Road, London, SE5
Telephone: (020) 7525 7694

Housing Department
Municipal Offices, 9 Larcom Street, London SE17 1RX
Telephone: (020) 7525 7845

Environment & Leisure Department
Chatelaine House, 186 Walworth Road, London SE17 1JJ

Regeneration Department
Council Offices, Chiltern House, Portland Street, London SE17 2ES
Telephone: (020) 7525 5507

Social Services Department
Mabel Goldwin House, 49 Grange Walk, London SE1 3DY
Telephone: (020) 7525 3793

Southwark Direct & Internal Services Department
19 Spa Road, London SE16 3QN
Telephone (202) 7525 3627

Trading Standards
Chaplin Centre, Thurlow Street, London SE17

Function	Chief Officer	Title	Location
Chief Executive	Mr R A Coomber	Chief Executive	Town Hall
Education	Dr Roger Smith	Strategic Director of Education & Culture	John Smith Hse
Electoral Registration	Ms Jane Ringham	Arbitration & Electoral Services	Central House
Environmental Health	Ms Gill Davies	Strategic Director of Environmental & Leisure	Chatelaine House
Housing	Mr Keith Broxup	Strategic Director of Housing	9 Larcom St
Legal Services	Ms Deborah Holmes	Borough Solicitor & Secretary	Town Hall
Leisure	Ms Gill Davies	Strategic Director of Environmental & Leisure	Chatelaine House
Local Land Charges	Mr Paul Horsnell	Local Land Charges Officer	Town Hall
Planning	Mr Paul Evans	Strategic Director of Regeneration	Chiltern House
Purchasing & Supplies	Ms Janet McMahon	Principal Procurement Officer	19 Spa Road
Social Services	Mr Chris Bull	Strategic Director of Social Services	Mabel Goldwin Hse
Trading Standards	Mr Tim England	Environmental Health & Trading Standards Officer	Chaplin Centre

LONDON BOROUGH OF SUTTON

www.sutton.gov.uk

Principal Office
Civic Offices, St Nicholas Way, Sutton, Surrey SM1 1EA
Telephone: (020) 8770 5000; FAX: (020) 8770 5404; DX: 56408 Sutton 1

Education Services Department
The Grove, Carshalton, Surrey SM5 3AL
Telephone: (020) 8770 6500; FAX: (020) 8770 6545

Environment & Leisure Department
24 Denmark Road, Carshalton, Surrey SM5 2JG
Telephone: (020) 8770 6100; FAX: (020) 8770 6112

Function	Chief Officer	Title	Location
Chief Executive	Joanna Simons	Chief Executive	Civic Offices
Education	Ian Birnbaum	Strategic Director of Learning for Life	The Grove
Electoral Registration	Fiona Ledden	Executive Head of Legal Services	Civic Offices
Environmental Health	Tom Jeffrey	Strategic Director of Environment & Leisure	24 Denmark Rd
Finance	Sue Higgins	Strategic Director of Finance & Information	Civic Offices
Housing	Ian Davey	Strategic Director of Community Services	Civic Offices
Legal Services	Fiona Ledden	Executive Head of Legal Services	Civic Offices
Leisure	Tom Jeffrey	Strategic Director of Environment & Leisure	24 Denmark Rd
Local Land Charges	Tom Jeffrey	Strategic Director of Environment & Leisure	24 Denmark Rd
Planning	Tom Jeffrey	Strategic Director of Environment & Leisure	24 Denmark Rd
Purchasing & Supplies	Tom Jeffrey	Strategic Director of Environment & Leisure	24 Denmark Rd
Social Services	Ian Davey	Strategic Director of Community Services	Civic Offices
Technical Services	Tom Jeffrey	Strategic Director of Environment & Leisure	24 Denmark Rd
Trading Standards	Tom Jeffrey	Strategic Director of Environment & Leisure	24 Denmark Rd

LONDON BOROUGH OF TOWER HAMLETS

www.towerhamlets.gov.uk

Principal Office
Mulberry Place, 5 Clove Crescent, London E14 2BG
Telephone: (020) 7364 5000; FAX: (020) 7364 4296

Customer Services Directorate
Council Offices, Southern Grove, London E3 4PN
Telephone: (020) 7364 5000

Housing Directorate
3 Millharbour, London E14 9XP
Telephone: (020) 7364 5000

Social Services Directorate
62 Roman Road, London E2 0PG
Telephone: (020) 7364 5000

Electoral Registration Office
1 Rushmead, Bethnal Green, London E2 6NE
Telephone: (020) 7364 3700/3772; FAX (020) 7364 3758

Planning Department
41-47 Bow Road, London E3 2BS
Telephone: (020) 7364 5367; FAX (020) 7364 5415

Function	Chief Officer	Title	Location
Chief Executive	Christine Gilbert	Chief Executive	Mulberry Place
Education	Stephen Grix	Corporate Director, Education	Mulberry Place
Electoral Registration	Terry Brown	Head of Electoral Registration	1 Rushmead
Environmental Health	David Farrell	Head of Environmental Protection	Southern Grove
Finance	Chris Perry	Head of Finance & Corporate Services	Mulberry Place
Housing	Sue Benjamins	Corporate Director, Housing	Millharbour
Legal Services	Helen Sidwell	Acting Borough Solicitor	Mulberry Place
Leisure	Ray Gerlach	Head of Arts, Leisure & Sports	Mulberry Place
Planning	Bryan Jones	Head of Built Environment	41-47 Bow Rd
Purchasing & Supplies	Kevin Rogers	Purchasing Manager	Mulberry Place
Social Services	Ian Wilson	Corporate Director, Social Services	62 Roman Rd
Trading Standards	Collin Perrins	Head of Trading Standards & Environmental Health (Commercial)	Southern Grove

LONDON BOROUGH OF WALTHAM FOREST

www.lbwf.gov.uk

Principal Office
Town Hall, Forest Road, London E17 4JF
Telephone: (020) 8496 3000; FAX: (020) 8527 8313

Education; Social Services
Leyton Municipal Offices, High Road, Leyton, London E10 5QJ
Telephone: (020) 8496 3000

Housing
Willow House, 869 Forest Road, London E17 4UH
Telephone: (020) 8496 3000

Legal Services; Arts & Leisure
Sycamore House, Forest Road, London E17 4SY
Telephone: (020) 8496 3000

LONDON

Planning Development
Chingford Municipal Offices, 16 The Ridgeway, London E4 6PS
Telephone: (020) 8496 3000

Consumer Protection Services
154 Blackhorse Road, London E17 6NW
Telephone: (020) 8496 3000; FAX: (020) 8521 9001

Highways & Services Department; Low Hall Manor Business Centre
30 South Access Road, London E17 8BS
Telephone: (020) 8496 3000; FAX: (020) 8496 2512

Function	Chief Officer	Title	Location
Chief Executive	Mr S White	Chief Executive	Town Hall
Education	Mr S Newland	Acting Executive Director, Life-long Learning Services	Town Hall
Electoral Registration	Ms J Goldsworthy	Electoral Services Manager	Town Hall
Environmental Health	Mr L Norton	Executive Director of Environmental Services	Ch'ford Mun Offs
Finance	Mr D O'Loan	Head of Strategic Finance	Town Hall
Housing	Mr J Wintour	Head of Housing	Willow House
Legal Services	Mr S Mistry	Head of Legal & Democratic Services	Town Hall
Leisure	Mr D Walton; Mr E O'Machail	Acting Heads of Leisure & Recreation Services	Sycamore House
Local Land Charges	Mr S Mistry	Head of Legal & Democratic Services	Sycamore House
Planning	Mr L Norton	Executive Director of Environmental Services	Ch'ford Mun Offs
Purchasing & Supplies	Mr H Swan	Corporate Procurement Manager	Town Hall
Social Services	Ms C Wilson	Head of Social Services	Leyton Mun Offs
Technical Services	Mr K Weir	Head of Street Services	Low Hall Manor
Trading Standards	Ms L Wacey	Head of Community Protection Services	Blackhorse Rd

WANDSWORTH LONDON BOROUGH

www.wandsworth.gov.uk

Principal Office
Town Hall, Wandsworth High Street, London SW18 2PU
Telephone: (020) 8871 6000; FAX: (020) 8871 7560

Environmental Services Division
78 Garratt Lane, London SW18 4DJ
Telephone: (020) 8871 6000; FAX: (020) 8871 6964

Frogmore Depot
Dormay Street, London SW18 1HA
Telephone: (020) 8871 6742; FAX: (020) 8871 6777

Housing Department
17/27 Garratt Lane, London SW18 4AE
Telephone: (020) 8871 6000

Function	Chief Officer	Title	Location
Chief Executive	G K Jones	Chief Executive & Director of Administration	Town Hall
Education	P Robinson	Director of Education	Town Hall
Electoral Registration	M Kennett	Registration Manager	Town Hall
Environmental Health	A Waren	Head of Environmental Services	78 Garratt Lane
Finance	H J S Heywood	Director of Finance	Town Hall
Housing	C J Buss	Director of Housing	17/27 Garratt Ln

Legal Services	M Walker	Borough Solicitor	Town Hall
Leisure	P Brennan	Director of Leisure & Amenity Services	Town Hall
Local Land Charges	I Renshaw	Local Land Charges Manager	Town Hall
Planning	R Erskine	Borough Planner	Town Hall
Purchasing & Supplies	C Tipper	Supplies Officer	Frogmore Depot
Social Services	P West	Director of Social Services	Town Hall
Technical Services	W Myers	Director of Technical Services	Town Hall
Trading Standards	A Waren	Head of Environmental Services	78 Garratt Lane

WESTMINSTER CITY COUNCIL

www.westminster.gov.uk

Principal Office

Westminster City Hall, 64 Victoria Street, London SW1E 6QP
Telephone: (020) 7641 6000; DX: 2310 Victoria

Function	Chief Officer	Title	Location
Chief Executive	Mr P Rogers	Chief Executive	City Hall
Education	Ms P Crawford	Director of Education	City Hall
Electoral Registration	Mr C Wilson	Director of Legal and Administrative Services	City Hall
Environmental Health	Mr J Duckworth	Director of Environment & Leisure	City Hall
Finance	Mr J Unsworth	Director of Finance	City Hall
Legal Services	Mr C Wilson	Director of Legal & Administrative Services	City Hall
Leisure	Mr J Duckworth	Director of Environment & Leisure	City Hall
Local Land Charges	Mr C Wilson	Director of Legal & Administrative Services	City Hall
Planning	Mr G Chard	Director of Planning & City Development	City Hall
Social Services	Mrs J Jones	Director of Social & Community Services	City Hall
Technical Services	Mr J Duckworth	Director of Environment & Leisure	City Hall
Trading Standards	Mr R Currie	Director of Community Protection	City Hall

COUNTY COUNCILS

AVON COUNTY COUNCIL

Avon County Council ceased to exist on 31 March 1996. Its functions were taken over by the following new unitary authorities: Bath & North East Somerset; Bristol City; North Somerset; South Gloucestershire.

BEDFORDSHIRE COUNTY COUNCIL

www.bedfordshire.gov.uk

Principal Office
County Hall, Cauldwell Street, Bedford MK42 9AP
Telephone: (01234) 363222; FAX: (01234) 228619

Function	Chief Officer	Title	Location
Chief Executive	Mr D Wilkinson	Chief Executive	County Hall
Education	Mr D Doran	Strategic Director (Education)	County Hall
Environment	Mr T Malynn	Strategic Director (Environment)	County Hall
Finance	Mr A R Brown	Chief Financial Officer	County Hall
Legal Services	Mr R D Wansbrough	County Solicitor	County Hall
Leisure	Mr K Ward	Head of Culture & Environment	County Hall
Planning	Mr S Potter	Head of Engineering Policy & Planning	County Hall
Social Services	Mr M Newsam	Strategic Director (Social Services)	County Hall
Trading Standards	Mr C Davies	Head of Trading Standards & Registration	County Hall

District/Borough Councils in Bedfordshire: Bedford; Mid Bedfordshire & South Bedfordshire.

Unitary authority in Bedfordshire: Luton.

BERKSHIRE COUNTY COUNCIL

Berkshire County Council ceased to exist on 31 March 1998. Its functions were taken over by the following new unitary authorities: Bracknell Forest; Reading; Slough; West Berkshire; Windsor & Maidenhead; Wokingham.

BUCKINGHAMSHIRE COUNTY COUNCIL

www.buckscc.gov.uk

Principal Office
County Hall, Aylesbury HP20 1UA
Telephone: (01296) 395000; FAX: (01296) 382611; DX 97405 Aylesbury 2

Function	Chief Officer	Title	Location
Chief Executive	Chris Williams	Chief Officer of the Council	County Hall
Education	Sue Imbriano	Strategic Manager of Schools	County Hall
Environment	Garry Emmerson	Strategic Manager of Planning & Transportation (Acting)	County Hall
Finance	[Vacant]	Head of Finance	County Hall
Legal Services	Ann Davies	Head of Legal Services	County Hall
Planning	Huw Jones	Head of Spatial Planning	County Hall
Social Services	Rita Lally	Director of Social Services	County Hall
Technical Services	Garry Emmerson	Strategic Manager of Planning & Transportation (Acting)	County Hall
Trading Standards	Phil Dart	Head of Trading Standards	County Hall

District/Borough Councils in Buckinghamshire: Aylesbury Vale; Chiltern; South Buckinghamshire; Wycombe.

Unitary authority in Buckinghamshire: Milton Keynes.

CAMBRIDGESHIRE COUNTY COUNCIL

www.cambridgeshire.gov.uk

Principal Office
Shire Hall, Castle Hill, Cambridge CB3 0AP
Telephone: (01223) 717111; FAX: (01223) 717201; DX 13870 Cambridge 9

Education, Libraries & Heritage Directorate; Environment & Transport Directorate; Social Services Directorate; Resources Directorate; Chief Executive's Department
Castle Court, Shire Hall, Castle Hill, Cambridge CB3 0AP
Telephone: (01223) 717111; FAX: (01223) 717201

Trading Standards
Hinchingbrooke Cottage, Brampton Road, Huntingdon, Cambs PE18 8NA
Telephone: (01480) 376060; FAX: (01480) 376070

Function	Chief Officer	Title	Location
Chief Executive	Mr I Stewart	Chief Executive	Shire Hall
Education	Mr A Baxter	Director of Education, Libraries & Heritage	Castle Court
Environment	Mr B Smith	Director of Environment & Transport	Castle Court
Finance	Mr M Parsons	Director of Resources	Shire Hall
Legal Services	Mrs J Postings	Head of Democratic, Legal & Registration Services	Shire Hall
Planning	Mr J Onslow	Assistant Director of Planning	Castle Court
Social Services	Mr E Robinson	Director of Social Services	Castle Court
Technical Services	Mr A Rowson	Head of Property & Procurement	Shire Hall
Trading Standards	Mr J Lawrance	Head of Trading Standards	Hinchingbrooke Cge

District/Borough Councils in Cambridgeshire: Cambridge City; East Cambridgeshire; Fenland; Huntingdonshire; South Cambridgeshire

Unitary authority in Cambridgeshire: Peterborough City.

CHESHIRE COUNTY COUNCIL

www.cheshire.gov.uk

Principal Office
County Hall, Chester, Cheshire CH1 1SF
Telephone: (01244) 602424; FAX: (01244) 603800

Environment Department; Trading Standards Department
Backford Hall, Backford, Chester, Cheshire CH1 6EA
Telephone: (01244) 602424

Function	Chief Officer	Title	Location
Chief Executive	Jeremy Taylor	Chief Executive	County Hall
Education	David Cracknell	Director of Education & Community	County Hall
Environment	Peter Cocker	Director of Environment	County Hall
Finance	Bill Tunnicliffe	County Finance Officer	County Hall
Legal Services	Gerry Budd	County Solicitor & Monitoring Officer	County Hall
Planning	Alan Thornley	County Planning Officer	Backford Hall
Social Services	John Weeks	Director of Social Services & Health	County Hall
Technical Services	Steve Hopson	County ICT Officer	County Hall
Trading Standards	Paul McGreary	County Trading Standards Officer	Backford Hall

COUNTY COUNCILS

District/Borough Councils in Cheshire: Chester; Congleton; Crewe & Nantwich; Ellesmere Port & Neston; Macclesfield; Vale Royal.

Unitary authorities in Cheshire: Halton; Warrington.

CLEVELAND COUNTY COUNCIL

Cleveland County Council ceased to exist on 31 March 1996. Its functions were taken over by the following new unitary authorities: Hartlepool; Middlesbrough; Redcar & Cleveland; Stockton-on-Tees.

CORNWALL COUNTY COUNCIL

www.cornwall.gov.uk

Principal Office
County Hall, Truro TR1 3AY
Telephone: (01872) 322000; FAX: (01872) 270340

Function	Chief Officer	Title	Location
Chief Executive	Peter Stethridge	Chief Executive	County Hall
Education	Geoff Aver	Director of Education, Arts & Libraries	County Hall
Finance	Frank Twyning	County Treasurer	County Hall
Legal Services	Ian Kennaway	County Solicitor	County Hall
Planning	Richard Fish	Director of Planning, Transportation & Estates	County Hall
Social Services	Dr Carol Tozer	Director of Social Services	County Hall
Trading Standards	David Phillips	Head of Trading Standards	County Hall

District/Borough Councils in Cornwall: Caradon; Carrick; Kerrier; North Cornwall; Penwith; Restormel.

CUMBRIA COUNTY COUNCIL

www.cumbria.gov.uk

Principal Office
The Courts, Carlisle CA3 8NA
Telephone: (01228) 606301; FAX: (01228) 606302

Cumbria Contract Services
Barras Lane, Dalston, Carlisle CA5 7ND
Telephone: (01228) 607730; FAX: (01228) 607605

Community, Economy & Environment
Citadel Chambers, Carlisle CA3 8SG
Telephone: (01228) 606700; FAX: (01228) 606715

Education Department
5 Portland Square, Carlisle CA1 1PU
Telephone: (01228) 606868; FAX: (01228) 606896

Legal Services Department
The Courts, English Street, Carlisle CA3 8LZ
Telephone: (01228) 607352; FAX: (01228) 607376

Social Services Department
15 Portland Square, Carlisle CA1 1QQ
Telephone: (01228) 607110; FAX: (01228) 607108

Trading Standards Department
County Offices, Kendal LA9 4RQ
Telephone: (01539) 773586; FAX: (01539) 773580

COUNTY COUNCILS

Function	Chief Officer	Title	Location
Chief Executive	John Harwood	Interim Chief Executive	The Courts
Education	Victoria Ashfield	Corporate Director of Education	5 Portland Sq
Environment	Ralph Howard	Corporate Director of Community, Economy & Environment	Citadel Chambers
Finance	Bob Mather	Senior Corporate Director of Finance	The Courts
Legal Services	Brian Walker	Head of Legal Services	The Courts
Leisure	Victoria Ashfield	Corporate Director of Education	5 Portland Sq
Planning	Shaun Gorman	Head of Environment	County Offices
Purchasing & Supplies	Clive Pickering	Interim Managing Director, Cumbria Contract Services	Barras Lane
Social Services	Stephen Wilds	Interim Corporate Director of Social Services	15 Portland Sq
Technical Services	Ralph Howard	Corporate Director of Community, Economy & Environment	Citadel Chambers
Trading Standards	Phil Ashcroft	Head of Trading Standards	County Offices

District/Borough Councils in Cumbria: Allerdale; Barrow-in-Furness; Carlisle; Copeland; Eden; South Lakeland.

DERBYSHIRE COUNTY COUNCIL

www.derbyshire.gov.uk

Principal Office
County Hall, Matlock DE4 3AG
Telephone: (01629) 580000; FAX: (01629) 585370

Function	Chief Officer	Title	Location
Chief Executive	Mr A R N Hodgson	Chief Executive	County Hall
Education	Mr R V Taylor	Chief Education Officer	County Hall
Environment	Mr D Harvey	Director of Environmental Services	County Hall
Finance	Mr P Swaby	County Treasurer	County Hall
Legal Services	Mr D W Tysoe	County Secretary	County Hall
Leisure	Mr M Molloy	Director of Cultural & Community Services	County Hall
Planning	Mr D Harvey	Director of Environmental Services	County Hall
Purchasing & Supplies	Mr G C Tommy	Director of Corporate Resources & Deputy Chief Executive	County Hall
Social Services	Mr B Buckley	Director of Social Services	County Hall
Technical Services	Mr A Beastall	County Property Officer	County Hall
Trading Standards	Mr M Molloy	Director of Cultural & Community Services	County Hall

District/Borough Councils in Derbyshire: Amber Valley; Bolsover; Chesterfield; Derbyshire Dales; Erewash; High Peak; North East Derbyshire; South Derbyshire.

Unitary authority in Derbyshire: Derby City.

DEVON COUNTY COUNCIL

www.devon.gov.uk

Principal Office
County Hall, Topsham Road, Exeter EX2 4QD
Telephone: (01392) 382000; FAX: (01392) 382286; DX 8345 Exeter

Function	Chief Officer	Title	Location
Chief Executive	Mr P Jenkinson	Chief Executive	County Hall
Education	Mr P Norrey	Director of Education, Arts & Libraries	County Hall
Environment	Mr E Chorlton	County Environment Director	County Hall
Finance	Mrs J Stanhope	Director of Resources	County Hall

Legal Services	Mr R Gash	County Solicitor	County Hall
Planning	Mr E Chorlton	County Environment Director	County Hall
Purchasing & Supplies	Mr P Dummett	Chief Purchasing Officer	County Hall
Social Services	Mr D Johnstone	Director of Social Services	County Hall
Trading Standards	Mr R Rivett	Head of Trading Standards & Consumer Protection	County Hall

District/Borough Councils in Devon: East Devon; Exeter; Mid Devon; North Devon; South Hams; Teignbridge; Torridge; West Devon.

Unitary authorities in Devon: Plymouth; Torbay.

DORSET COUNTY COUNCIL

www.dorset-cc.gov.uk

Principal Office
County Hall, Colliton Park, Dorchester DT1 1XJ
Telephone: (01305) 251000; FAX: (01305) 224839; DX 8716 Dorchester

Education Directorate; Environmental Services Directorate
Pullman Court, Station Approach, Weymouth Avenue, Dorhcester, Dorset
Telephone: (01305) 251000

Function	Chief Officer	Title	Location
Chief Executive	Mr D H Jenkins	Chief Executive	County Hall
Education	Mr D Goddard	Director of Education	County Hall
Environment	Mr M Butler	Director of Environmental Services	County Hall
Finance	Mr P Lewis	Director of Resources	County Hall
Legal Services	Mr J Mair	Head of Legal Services	County Hall
Planning	Mr A Price	Head of Planning	County Hall
Purchasing & Supplies	Mr A Ray	Contracts & Partnerships Manager	Pullman Court
Social Services	Mr S Pitt	Director of Social Services	County Hall
Technical Services	Mr M White	Head of Highways & Transportation	County Hall
Trading Standards	Mr W Jaggs	Head of Trading Standards	County Hall

District/Borough Councils in Dorset: Christchurch; East Dorset; North Dorset; Purbeck; West Dorset; Weymouth & Portland.

Unitary authorities in Dorset: Bournemouth; Poole.

DURHAM COUNTY COUNCIL

www.durham.gov.uk

Principal Office
County Hall, Durham DH1 5UL
Telephone: (0191) 383 3000; FAX: (0191) 383 4500; DX 722100 Durham 16

Function	Chief Officer	Title	Location
Chief Executive	Kingsley Smith	Chief Executive	County Hall
Education	Keith Mitchell	Director of Education	County Hall
Environment	Chris Tunstall	Deputy Chief Executive (Environment & Change Management)	County Hall
Finance	Stuart Crowe	County Treasurer	County Hall
Legal Services	Andrew North	Deputy Chief Executive (Corporate Services)	County Hall
Leisure	Patrick Conway	Director of Culture & Leisure	County Hall
Planning	Mark Lloyd	Deputy Chief Executive (Policy & Strategy)	County Hall
Social Services	Debbie Jones	Director of Social Care & Health	County Hall
Technical Services	Brian Tennant	Director of Service Direct	County Hall

District/Borough Councils in Durham: Chester-le-Street; Derwentside; Durham; Easington; Sedgefield; Teesdale; Wear Valley.

Unitary authority in Durham: Darlington.

EAST SUSSEX COUNTY COUNCIL

www.eastsussexcc.gov.uk

Chief Executive; Legal & Community Services Department
Pelham House, St Andrews Lane, Lewes BN7 1UN
Telephone: (01273) 481000; FAX: (01273) 473321; DX 50251 Lewes 2

Corporate Resources Directorate; Education Department;
Social Services Department; Transport & Environment Department
County Hall, St Anne's Crescent, Lewes BN7 1SW
Telephone: (01273) 481000; FAX: (01273) 481261

Trading Standards
St Mary's House, 52 St Leonards Road, Eastbourne, East Sussex, BN21 3UU
Telephone: (01323) 418200; FAX: (01323) 418227

Function	Chief Officer	Title	Location
Chief Executive	Mrs C Miller, CBE	Chief Executive	Pelham House
Education	Denise Stokoe	Director of Education	County Hall
Electoral Registration	H W H Cartwright	County Returning Officer	Pelham House
Environment	R Wilkins	Director of Transport & Environment	County Hall
Finance	S Nolan	Director of Corporate Resources	County Hall
Legal Services	Mr H W H Cartwright	Director of Legal & Community Services	Pelham House
Planning	R Wilkins	Director of Transport & Environment	County Hall
Purchasing & Supplies	S Nolan	Director of Corporate Resources	County Hall
Social Services	D Archibald	Director of Social Services	County Hall
Trading Standards	D Marshall	Head of Trading Standards	St Mary's House

District/Borough Councils in East Sussex: Eastbourne; Hastings; Lewes; Rother; Wealden.

Unitary authority in East Sussex: Brighton & Hove.

ESSEX COUNTY COUNCIL

www.essexcc.gov.uk

Principal Office
PO Box 11, County Hall, Chelmsford CM1 1LX
Telephone: (01245) 492211; FAX: (01245) 352710

Trading Standards Division
Beehive Lane, Chelmsford CM2 9SY
Telephone: (01245) 341800; FAX: (01245) 494616

Function	Chief Officer	Title	Location
Chief Executive	K W S Ashurst	Chief Executive	County Hall
Education	L Railton	Deputy Chief Executive – Learning & Social Care	County Hall
Finance	S O'Donell	Head of Finance	County Hall
Legal Services	P Thomson	Head of Legal Services	County Hall
Planning	M Burchell	Deputy Chief Executive – Planning & Environment	County Hall
Social Services	L Railton	Deputy Chief Executive – Learning & Social Care	County Hall
Trading Standards	M Hill	Head of Trading Standards	Beehive Lane

District/Borough Councils in Essex: Basildon; Braintree; Brentwood; Castle Point; Chelmsford; Colchester; Epping Forest; Harlow; Maldon; Rochford; Tendring; Uttlesford.

Unitary authorities in Essex: Southend-on-Sea; Thurrock.

GLOUCESTERSHIRE COUNTY COUNCIL

www.gloucestershire.gov.uk

Principal Office
Shire Hall, Westgate Street, Gloucester GL1 2TG
Telephone: (01452) 425000; FAX: (01452) 425850

Legal Services Department
Quayside House, Shire Hall, Gloucester GL1 2HY
Telephone: (01452) 425000; FAX: (01452) 425042

Leisure Department; Planning Department
Bearlands, Shire Hall, Gloucester GL1 2GH
Telephone: (01452) 425000; FAX: (01452) 425627

Trading Standards Department
Hillfield House, Denmark Road, Gloucester GL1 3LD
Telephone: (01452) 426201; FAX: (01452) 426274

Function	Chief Officer	Title	Location
Chief Executive	Joyce Redfearn	Chief Executive	Shire Hall
Education	Jo Davidson	Director of Education	Shire Hall
Environment	Peter Bungard	Director of Environment	Shire Hall
Finance	Bob Potter	Head of Financial Services	Shire Hall
Legal Services	Nigel Roberts	County Solicitor	Quayside Hse
Planning	Barry King	Head of Planning Services	Shire Hall
Purchasing & Supplies	Allan Wathan	Purchasing Officer	Shire Hall
Social Services	Margaret Sheather	Director of Social Services	Shire Hall
Trading Standards	Roger Marles	County Trading Standards Officer	Hillfield Hse

District/Borough Councils in Gloucestershire: Cheltenham; Cotswold; Forest of Dean; Gloucester; Stroud; Tewkesbury.

HAMPSHIRE COUNTY COUNCIL

www.hants.gov.uk

Principal Office
The Castle, Winchester SO23 8UJ
Telephone: (01962) 841841; FAX: (01962) 867273; DX 2510 Winchester

Recreation & Heritage
Mottisfont Court, High Street, Winchester SO23 8ZF
Telephone: (01962) 846007; FAX: (01962) 841565

Property, Business & Regulatory Services Department
Three Minsters House, 76 High Street, Winchester SO23 8UL
Telephone: (01962) 847826; FAX: (01962) 845144

Social Services Department
Trafalgar House, Trafalgar Street, Winchester SO23 8UQ
Telephone: (01962) 841841; FAX: (01962) 847159

Function	Chief Officer	Title	Location
Chief Executive	P C B Robertson	Chief Executive	The Castle
Education	A J Seber	County Education Officer	The Castle
Environment	A Quant	Director of Environment	The Castle

Finance	J C Pittam	County Treasurer	The Castle
Legal Services	P C B Robertson	Chief Executive	The Castle
Leisure	Y Ezra	Director of Recreation & Heritage	Mottisfont Court
Planning	A Quant	Director of Environment	The Castle
Purchasing & Supplies	A J Smith	Director of Property, Business & Regulatory Services	Three Minsters Hse
Social Services	N J T Butler	Director of Social Services	Trafalgar Hse
Technical Services	A Quant	Director of Environment	The Castle
Trading Standards	A J Smith	Director of Property, Business & Regulatory Services	Three Minsters Hse

District/Borough Councils in Hampshire: Basingstoke & Deane; East Hampshire; Eastleigh; Fareham; Gosport; Hart; Havant; New Forest; Rushmoor; Test Valley; Winchester.

Unitary authorities in Hampshire: Portsmouth City; Southampton City.

HEREFORD & WORCESTER COUNTY COUNCIL
See now Herefordshire Council, a unitary authority from 1 April 1998, and Worcestershire County Council.

HERTFORDSHIRE COUNTY COUNCIL

www.hertfordshire.org

Principal Office
County Hall, Hertford SG13 8DE
Telephone: (01992) 555555; FAX: (01992) 555643; DX 145781 Hertford 4

Community Information – Trading Standards
45 Grosvenor Road, St Albans AL1 3AW
Telephone: (01727) 813880; FAX: (01727) 813877

County Supplies & Contract Services
Mount Pleasant Lane, Hatfield AL9 5NR
Telephone: (01707) 281701; FAX: (01707) 281771

Function	Chief Officer	Title	Location
Chief Executive	Ms C Tapster	Acting Chief Executive	County Hall
Education	Mr J Harris	Director of Children, Schools & Families Services	County Hall
Environment	Mr J Wood	Director of Environment	County Hall
Finance	Mr C Sweeney	Finance Director, Corporate Services	County Hall
Legal Services	Mr A L Laycock	County Secretary	County Hall
Purchasing & Supplies	Mr S Gilbey	Head of County Supplies & Contract Services	Mt Pleasant Lane
Social Services	Ms S Pickup	Director of Adult Care Services	County Hall
Trading Standards	Mr I McLachlan	Head of Trading Standards	County Hall

District/Borough Councils in Hertfordshire: Broxbourne; Dacorum; East Hertfordshire; Hertsmere; North Hertfordshire; St Albans; Stevenage; Three Rivers; Watford; Welwyn Hatfield.

HUMBERSIDE COUNTY COUNCIL
Humberside County Council ceased to exist on 31 March 1996. Its functions were taken over by the following new unitary authorities: East Riding of Yorkshire; Kingston upon Hull; North East Lincolnshire; North Lincolnshire.

ISLE OF WIGHT COUNTY COUNCIL
The Isle of Wight Council became a unitary authority on 1 April 1995.

KENT COUNTY COUNCIL

www.kent.gov.uk

Principal Office
Sessions House, County Hall, Maidstone, Kent ME14 1XQ
Telephone: (01622) 671411

Education & Libraries; Highways; Planning; Economic Development; Social Services; Regulatory Services
Sessions and Invicta House, Maidstone, Kent ME14 1XQ (Sessions); ME14 1XX (Invicta)
Telephone: (01622) 671411

Commercial Services Department
Gibson Building, Gibson Drive, Kings Hill, West Malling, Kent ME19 4LZ
Telephone: (01622) 671411

Function	Chief Officer	Title	Location
Chief Executive	Mike Pitt	Chief Executive	Sessions House
Education	Graham Badman	Strategic Director – Education & Libraries	Sessions House
Finance	David Lewis	Strategic Director – Resources	Sessions House
Legal Services	Geoffrey Wild	County Secretary & Monitoring Officer	Sessions House
Planning	Pete Raine	Strategic Planning Director	Invicta House
Purchasing & Supplies	Kevin Harlock	County Commercial Services Officer	Gibson Building
Social Services	Peter Gilroy	Strategic Director, Social Services	Sessions House

District/Borough Councils in Kent: Ashford; Canterbury; Dartford; Dover; Gravesham; Maidstone; Sevenoaks; Shepway; Swale; Thanet; Tonbridge & Malling; Tunbridge Wells.

Unitary authority in Kent: Medway Council.

LANCASHIRE COUNTY COUNCIL

www.lancashire.gov.uk

Principal Office
County Hall, Preston PR1 8XJ
Telephone: (01772) 254868; FAX: (01772) 533506

Environment Directorate
PO Box 9, Guild House, Cross Street, Preston PR1 8RD
Telephone: (01772) 254868

Social Services Directorate
East Cliff, County Offices, East Cliff, Preston PR1 3EA
Telephone: (01772) 254868; FAX: (01772) 534255

Trading Standards Department
58-60 Guild Hall Street, Preston
Telephone: (01772) 533569

Function	Chief Officer	Title	Location
Chief Executive	Mr C J Trinick	Chief Executive	County Hall
Education	Mrs S Mulvany	Director of Education & Cultural Services	County Hall
Electoral Registration	Mr C J Trinick	Chief Executive	County Hall
Environment	Mr G Harding	Environment Director	Guild House
Finance	Mr J Edney	Director of Resources	County Hall
Legal Services	Mr C J Trinick	Chief Executive	County Hall
Planning	Mr G Harding	Environment Director	Guild House

| Social Services | Mr R Jones | Director of Social Services | East Cliff |
| Trading Standards | Mr J H Potts | Chief Trading Standards Officer | Guild Hall St |

District/Borough Councils in Lancashire: Burnley; Chorley; Fylde; Hyndburn; Lancaster; Pendle; Preston; Ribble Valley; Rossendale; South Ribble; West Lancashire; Wyre

Unitary authorities in Lancashire: Blackburn with Darwen; Blackpool.

LEICESTERSHIRE COUNTY COUNCIL

www.leics.gov.uk

Principal Office
County Hall, Glenfield, Leicester LE3 8RA
Telephone: (0116) 232 3232 FAX: (0116) 265 6260

Function	Chief Officer	Title	Location
Chief Executive	Mr J Sinnott	Chief Executive	County Hall
Education	Mrs J Strong	Director of Education	County Hall
Finance	Mr A D Youd	Director of Resources	County Hall
Legal Services	Mr D Morgan	Head of Legal Services	County Hall
Planning	Mr L Wojtulewicz	Group Manager – Planning	County Hall
Social Services	Mr A J Harrop	Director of Social Services	County Hall
Technical Services	Mr B Jamieson	Director of Highways, Transportation & Waste Management	County Hall
Trading Standards	Mr D Bull	Head of Regulatory Services	County Hall

District/Borough Councils in Leicestershire: Blaby; Charnwood; Harborough; Hinckley & Bosworth; Melton; North West Leicestershire; Oadby & Wigston.

Unitary authorities in Leicestershire: Leicester City; Rutland.

LINCOLNSHIRE COUNTY COUNCIL

www.lincolnshire.gov.uk

Principal Office
County Offices, Newland, Lincoln LN1 1YL
Telephone: (01522) 552222; FAX: (01522) 552323; DX 701680 Lincoln 5

Highways and Planning
City Hall, Beaumont Fee, Lincoln LN1 1DN
Telephone: (01522) 552222

Social Services
Orchard House, Orchard Street, Lincoln LN1 1YL
Telephone: (01522) 552222

Fire and Rescue Headquarters
South Park Avenue, Lincoln LN5 8EL

Function	Chief Officer	Title	Location
Chief Executive	David Bowles	Chief Executive	County Offices
Education	Dr Cheryle Berry	Director of Education and Cultural Services	County Offices
Finance	Pete Moore	County Treasurer	County Offices
Legal Services	Mrs Charlie Adan	County Secretary and Solicitor	County Offices
Planning	Richard Wills	Director of Highways and Planning	City Hall
Social Services	Matthew Bukowski	Director of Social Services	Orchard House
Technical Services	Richard Wills	Director of Highways and Planning	City Hall
Trading Standards	Peter Heafield	County Trading Standards Officer	County Offices

District/Borough Councils in Lincolnshire: Boston; East Lindsey; Lincoln; North Kesteven; South Holland; South Kesteven; West Lindsey.

COUNTY COUNCILS

NORFOLK COUNTY COUNCIL

www.norfolk.gov.uk

Principal Office
County Hall, Martineau Lane, Norwich NR1 2DH
Telephone: (01603) 222222; FAX: (01603) 222959

Function	Chief Officer	Title	Location
Chief Executive	Mr T Byles	Chief Executive	County Hall
Education	Dr B C Slater	Director of Education	County Hall
Electoral Registration	Mr I Lambert	Head of Democratic Services	County Hall
Finance	Mr R D Summers	Director of Finance	County Hall
Legal Services	Mr K Hounsome	Head of Law	County Hall
Planning	Mr S Ralph	Director of Planning & Transportation	County Hall
Social Services	Ms L Christensen	Director of Social Services	County Hall
Trading Standards	Mr S Holland	Head of Trading Standards	County Hall

District/Borough Councils in Norfolk: Breckland; Broadland; Great Yarmouth; King's Lynn & West Norfolk; North Norfolk; Norwich; South Norfolk.

NORTH YORKSHIRE COUNTY COUNCIL

www.northyorks.gov.uk

Principal Office
County Hall, Racecourse Lane, Northallerton DL7 8AD
Telephone: (01609) 780780; FAX: (01609) 780447; DX 69140 Northallerton 3

Function	Chief Officer	Title	Location
Chief Executive	Mr J Walker	Chief Executive	County Hall
Education	Miss C Welbourn	Director of Education	County Hall
Environment	Mr M O Moore	Director of Environmental Services	County Hall
Finance	Mr J S Moore	Chief Financial Services Officer	County Hall
Legal Services	Ms C Whitehead	Head of Legal Services	County Hall
Planning	Mr M O Moore	Director of Environmental Services	County Hall
Social Services	Ms R Archer	Director of Social Services	County Hall
Trading Standards	Mr S Pudney	Head of Trading Standards & Regulatory Services	County Hall

District/Borough Councils in North Yorkshire: Craven; Hambleton; Harrogate; Richmondshire; Ryedale; Scarborough; Selby.

NORTHAMPTONSHIRE COUNTY COUNCIL

www.northamptonshire.gov.uk

Principal Office
County Hall, Northampton NN1 1AN
Telephone: (01604) 236236; FAX: (01604) 236223; DX 12481 Northampton 1

Trading Standards Service
Wootton Hall Park, Northampton NN4 0GB
Telephone: (01604) 700900; FAX: (01604) 707901

Function	Chief Officer	Title	Location
Chief Executive	Mr P Gould	Chief Executive	County Hall
Education	Mr A Sortwell	Acting Corporate Director: Education Services	County Hall
Environment	Mr D Brennan	Director of Sustainability	County Hall
Finance	Mr J Neilson	Head of Strategic Finance	County Hall
Legal Services	Mr T Parker	Head of Legal Services	County Hall

COUNTY COUNCILS

Leisure	Mr M Charters	Director of Community Services	County Hall
Planning	Mr D Brennan	Director of Sustainability	County Hall
Social Services	Mr M Charters	Director of Community Services	County Hall
Trading Standards	Mr B Hall	Acting County Trading Standards Officer	Wootton Hall Pk

District/Borough Councils in Northamptonshire: Corby; Daventry; East Northamptonshire; Kettering; Northampton; South Northamptonshire; Wellingborough.

NORTHUMBERLAND COUNTY COUNCIL

www.northumberland.gov.uk

Principal Office
County Hall, Morpeth, Northumberland NE61 2EF
Telephone: (01670) 533000; FAX: (01670) 533013

Function	Chief Officer	Title	Location
Chief Executive	Mr M Henderson	Chief Executive	County Hall
Education	Mr B Edwards	Director of Education	County Hall
Environment	Mr H A Fawcett	Director of Environment	County Hall
Finance	Mr S Mason	Director of Finance	County Hall
Legal Services	Mr P Watts	Legal & Administrative Services Manager	County Hall
Planning	Mr H A Fawcett	Director of Environment	County Hall
Purchasing & Supplies	Mr A Ratcliffe	Head of Procurement	County Hall
Social Services	Mr G Hill	Director of Social Services	County Hall
Technical Services	Mr J Nicholson	Director of Operational Services	County Hall
Trading Standards	Mr M King	County Trading Standards Officer	County Hall

District/Borough Councils in Northumberland: Alnwick; Berwick-upon-Tweed; Blyth Valley; Castle Morpeth; Tynedale; Wansbeck.

NOTTINGHAMSHIRE COUNTY COUNCIL

www.nottscc.gov.uk

Principal Office
County Hall, West Bridgford, Nottingham NG2 7QP
Telephone: (0115) 982 3823; FAX: (0115) 981 7945

Environment Department
Trent Bridge House, Fox Road, West Bridgford, Nottingham NG2 6BJ
Telephone: (0115) 982 3823

County Supplies
Rolleston Drive, Arnold, Nottingham NG5 7JG
Telephone: (0115) 967 0015

Function	Chief Officer	Title	Location
Chief Executive	Roger Latham	Chief Executive	County Hall
Education	Pam Tulley	Director of Education	County Hall
Environment	Peter Webster	Director of Environment	Trent Bridge Hse
Finance	Athur Deakin	Director of Resources	County Hall
Legal Services	Elizabeth Bannett	Executive Head (Legal Services)	County Hall
Purchasing & Supplies	David Parr	County Supplies Officer	Rolleston Drive
Social Services	Stuart Brook	Director of Social Services	County Hall
Trading Standards	Richard Hodge	Assistant Director (Public Protection)	County Hall

District/Borough Councils in Nottinghamshire: Ashfield; Bassetlaw; Broxtowe; Gedling; Mansfield; Newark & Sherwood; Rushcliffe.

Unitary authority in Nottinghamshire: Nottingham City.

COUNTY COUNCILS

OXFORDSHIRE COUNTY COUNCIL

www.oxfordshire.gov.uk

Principal Office
County Hall, Oxford OX1 1ND
Telephone: (01865) 792422; FAX: (01865) 726155; DX 4310 Oxford

Education Department
Macclesfield House, Oxford OX1 1NA
Telephone: (01865) 815449; FAX: (01865) 791637

Environmental Services Department
Speedwell House, Speedwell Street, Oxford OX1 1NE
Telephone: (01865) 815700; FAX: (01865) 815085

Function	Chief Officer	Title	Location
Chief Executive	Dr Richard Shaw	Chief Executive	County Hall
Education	Keith Bartley	Director for Learning & Culture	Macclesfield Hse
Environment	Richard Dudding	Director for Environment & Economy	Speedwell Hse
Finance	John Jackson	Director for Resources	County Hall
Social Services	Charles Waddicor	Director for Social & Health Care	County Hall
Trading Standards	John Parry	Director for Community Safety	County Hall

District/Borough Councils in Oxfordshire: Cherwell; Oxford City; South Oxfordshire; Vale of White Horse; West Oxfordshire.

SHROPSHIRE COUNTY COUNCIL

www.shropshireonline.gov.uk

Principal Office
The Shirehall, Abbey Foregate, Shrewsbury SY2 6ND
Telephone: (01743) 251000; FAX: (01743) 360315; DX 702024 Shrewsbury

Function	Chief Officer	Title	Location
Chief Executive	Ms C Downs	Chief Executive	Shirehall
Education	Mrs L Nicholson	Corporate Director – Education Services	Shirehall
Environment	Mrs P Spencer	Corporate Director – Community & Environment	Shirehall
Finance	Ms L Rowley	Director of Resources	Shirehall
Legal Services	Miss C Porter	Head of Legal & Democratic Services	Shirehall
Planning	Ms A Wolstenholme	Assistant Director – Planning & Environment	Shirehall
Social Services	Mr J Collier	Corporate Director – Social Care & Health	Shirehall
Trading Standards	Mr D Walker	Chief Trading Standards Officer	Shirehall

District/Borough Councils in Shropshire: Bridgnorth; North Shropshire; Oswestry; Shrewsbury & Atcham; South Shropshire.

Unitary authority in Shropshire: Telford & Wrekin.

SOMERSET COUNTY COUNCIL

www.somerset.gov.uk

Principal Office
County Hall, Taunton TA1 4DY
Telephone: (01823) 355455 FAX: (01823) 355258; DX 122470 Taunton 7

Function	Chief Officer	Title	Location
Chief Executive	Mr A Jones	Chief Executive	County Hall
Education	J Rose	Acting Corporate Director (Lifelong Learning)	County Hall

Environment	N Farrow	Corporate Director (Economy, Transport & Environment)	County Hall
Environmental Health	Dr G Stephenson	County Community Protection Officer	County Hall
Finance	C N Bilsland	Corporate Director (Treasury)	County Hall
Legal Services	D Corry	County Solicitor	County Hall
Leisure	P Valentine	County Leisure Officer	County Hall
Planning	N Farrow	Corporate Director (Economy, Transport & Environment)	County Hall
Purchasing & Supplies	C N Bilsland	Corporate Director (Treasury)	County Hall
Social Services	D Gwyther	Acting Executive Director (Social Services)	County Hall
Technical Services	N Farrow	Corporate Director (Economy, Transport & Environment)	County Hall
Trading Standards	Dr G Stephenson	County Community Protection Officer	County Hall

District/Borough Councils in Somerset: Mendip; Sedgemoor; South Somerset; Taunton Deane; West Somerset.

STAFFORDSHIRE COUNTY COUNCIL

www.staffordshire.gov.uk

Principal Office
PO Box 11, County Buildings, Martin Street, Stafford ST16 2LH
Telephone: (01785) 223121; FAX: (01785) 215153; DX 712320 Stafford 5

Development Services Directorate
Riverway, Stafford ST16 3TJ
Telephone: (01785) 276519; FAX: (01785) 211279

Education and Lifelong Learning Directorate
County Education Offices, Tipping Street, Stafford ST16 2LE
Telephone: (01785) 278653; FAX: (01785) 278639

Social Care and Health Directorate
St Chad's Place, Stafford ST16 2NF

Resources Directorate
PO Box 11, Martin Street, Stafford ST16 2LH
Telephone: (01785) 223121; FAX: (01785) 215153

Function	Chief Officer	Title	Location
Chief Executive	N Pursey	Chief Executive	County Bldgs
Education	Mrs J Hawkins	Corporate Director (Education & Lifelong Learning)	Education Offices
Environment	R Hilton	Corporate Director (Development Services)	Riverway
Finance	B Roberts	Chief Finance Officer	Eastgate Street
Legal Services	O Pritchard-Jones	Corporate Director (Resources)	Martin Street
Planning	R Hilton	Corporate Director (Development Services)	Riverway
Social Services	R A Lake	Corporate Director (Social Care & Health)	St Chad's Pl
Technical Services	R Hilton	Corporate Director (Development Services)	Riverway
Trading Standards	R A Lake	Corporate Director (Social Care & Health)	St Chad's Pl

District/Borough Councils in Staffordshire: Cannock Chase; East Staffordshire; Lichfield; Newcastle-under-Lyme; South Staffordshire; Stafford; Staffordshire Moorlands; Tamworth.

Unitary authority in Staffordshire: Stoke-on-Trent.

SUFFOLK COUNTY COUNCIL

www.suffolkcc.gov.uk

Principal Office
Endeavour House, 8 Russell Road, Ipswich IP1 2BX
Telephone: (01473) 583000; FAX: (01473) 214549; DX 87951 Ipswich

Environment & Transport Directorate; Trading Standards;
Economic Development; Property; ICT
St Edmund House, County Hall, Ipswich IP4 1LZ

Resource Management Directorate; Procurement & Commissioning
St Giles House, County Hall, Rope Walk, Ipswich IP4 2JP

Education Directorate; Libraries & Heritage
St Andrew House, St Helens Court, Ipswich IP4 1LH

Social Care Directorate
St Paul House, County Hall, Rope Walk, Ipswich IP4 1LH

Function	Chief Officer	Title	Location
Chief Executive	Mike More	Chief Executive	Endeavour Hse
Education	David Thornton	Acting Director of Education	St Andrew Hse
Environment	Lucy Robinson	Director of Environment & Transport	St Edmund Hse
Finance	William Banks	Assistant Director of Resource Management (Finance)	St Giles House
Legal Services	Eric Whitfield	Assistant Director of Scrutiny & Monitoring	Endeavour Hse
Purchasing & Supplies	Nicol Thornton	Assistant Director of Resource Management (Procurement & Commissioning)	St Giles House
Social Services	Anthony Douglas	Director of Social Care	St Paul House
Trading Standards	Steve Greenfield	County Trading Standards Officer	St Edmund Hse

District/Borough Councils in Suffolk: Babergh; Forest Heath; Ipswich; Mid Suffolk; St Edmundsbury; Suffolk Coastal; Waveney.

SURREY COUNTY COUNCIL

www.surreycc.gov.uk

Principal Office
County Hall, Penrhyn Road, Kingston-upon-Thames, Surrey KT1 2DN
Telephone: (020) 8541 8800 FAX: (020) 8541 9005; DX 31509 Kingston upon Thames
Enquiries Telephone: 08456 009 009

Social Services HQ
AC Court, High Street, Thames Ditton KT7 0QA
Telephone: (020) 8541 8527; FAX: (020) 8541 8740
Enquiries Telephone: 08456 009 009

Surrey Trading Standards Services
Area Office 1, Bay Tree Avenue, Kingston Road, Leatherhead KT22 7SY
Telephone: (01372) 371700; FAX: (01372) 371704

Function	Chief Officer	Title	Location
Chief Executive	Mr Paul Coen	Chief Executive	County Hall
Education	Dr Paul Gray	Executive Director (Children & Young People)	County Hall
Environment	Mr Chris McCarthy	Executive Director (Sustainable Development)	County Hall
Finance	Mr Mike Taylor	Executive Director (Performance & Resources)	County Hall
Legal Services	Mrs Ann Charlton	County Solicitor	County Hall

COUNTY COUNCILS

Planning	Mr Roger Hargreaves	Head of Planning	County Hall
Purchasing & Supplies	Mr Andy Davies	Head of Procurement	County Hall
Social Services	Mr Alan Adams	Executive Director (Adults & Community Care)	AC Court
Trading Standards	Mr P Denard	County Trading Standards Officer	Area Office 1

District/Borough Councils in Surrey: Elmbridge; Epsom & Ewell; Guildford; Mole Valley; Reigate & Banstead; Runnymede; Spelthorne; Surrey Heath; Tandridge; Waverley; Woking.

WARWICKSHIRE COUNTY COUNCIL

www.warwickshire.gov.uk

Principal Office
Shire Hall, Warwick CV34 4RR
Telephone: (01926) 410410; FAX: (01926) 412326; DX 723362 Warwick 5

Education Department
22 Northgate Street, Warwick CV34 4SR
Telephone: (01926) 412114; FAX: (01926) 412886

Trading Standards Department
Old Budbrooke Road, Warwick CV35 7DP
Telephone: (01926) 410410; FAX: (01926) 414014

Department of Libraries & Heritage
Barrack Street, Warwick, Warwickshire CV34 4TH
Telephone: (01926) 412550; FAX: (01926) 412471

Function	Chief Officer	Title	Location
Chief Executive	Ian Caulfield	Chief Executive	Shire Hall
Education	Eric Wood	County Education Officer	22 Northgate St
Environment	John Deegan	Director of Planning, Transport & Economic Strategy	Shire Hall
Finance	David Clarke	County Treasurer	Shire Hall
Legal Services	David Carter	County Solicitor & Assistant Chief Executive	Shire Hall
Planning	John Deegan	Director of Planning, Transport & Economic Strategy	Shire Hall
Social Services	Marion Davies	Director of Social Care & Health	Shire Hall
Trading Standards	Noel Hunter	Director of Libraries, Heritage & Trading Standards	Barrack Street

District/Borough Councils in Warwickshire: North Warwickshire; Nuneaton & Bedworth; Rugby; Stratford-on-Avon; Warwick.

WEST SUSSEX COUNTY COUNCIL

www.westsussex.gov.uk

Principal Office
County Hall, West Street, Chichester PO19 1RQ
Telephone: (01243) 777100; FAX: (01243) 777952; DX 30330 Chichester

Property & Trading Standards Department
The Tannery, Westgate, Chichester PO19 3RJ
Telephone: (01243) 777100

Function	Chief Officer	Title	Location
Chief Executive	D P Rigg	Chief Executive	County Hall
Education	R Back	Director for Education & the Arts	County Hall
Environment	M Hammond	Director for Environment & Development	County Hall

Finance	Mrs H Kilpatrick	Director for Resources – County Treasurer	County Hall
Legal Services	M J Kendall	County Secretary	County Hall
Planning	M Hammond	Director for Environment & Development	County Hall
Social Services	J Dixon	Director for Social & Caring Services	County Hall
Technical Services	B Christie	Head of Information & Technology	County Hall
Trading Standards	P Bligh-Cheesman	County Trading Standards Officer	The Tannery

District/Borough Councils in West Sussex: Adur; Arun; Chichester; Crawley; Horsham; Mid Sussex; Worthing.

WILTSHIRE COUNTY COUNCIL

www.wiltshire.gov.uk

Principal Office
County Hall, Trowbridge BA14 8JN
Telephone: (01225) 713000; FAX: (01225) 713999; DX 116892 Trowbridge 3

Function	Chief Officer	Title	Location
Chief Executive	Dr K Robinson	Chief Executive	County Hall
Education	Mr B Wolfson	Director, Department for Children & Education	County Hall
Environment	Mr G Batten	Director of Environmental Services	County Hall
Finance	Mr M Prince	County Treasurer	County Hall
Legal Services	Mr S Gerrard	Solicitor to the Council	County Hall
Social Services	Dr R Jones	Director of Adult & Community Services	County Hall

District/Borough Councils in Wiltshire: Kennet; North Wiltshire; Salisbury; West Wiltshire.

Unitary authority in Wiltshire: Swindon

WORCESTERSHIRE COUNTY COUNCIL

www.worcestershire.gov.uk

Principal Office
County Hall, Spetchley Road, Worcester WR5 2NP
Telephone: (01905) 763763; FAX: (01905) 763000; DX 29941 Worcester 2

Trading Standards Department
28/30 Foregate Street, Worcester WR1 1DS
Telephone: (01905) 763763

Function	Chief Officer	Title	Location
Chief Executive	Rob Sykes	Chief Executive	County Hall
Education	Julien Kramer	Director of Educational Services	County Hall
Electoral Registration	Trevor Norton	Director of Corporate Services	County Hall
Environment	Richard Wigginton	Director of Environmental Services	County Hall
Finance	Mike Weaver	Director of Financial Services	County Hall
Legal Services	Simon Mallinson	Head of Legal Services	County Hall
Leisure	Richard Wigginton	Director of Environmental Services	County Hall
Planning	Mark Middleton	Head of Planning, Economy & Countryside Services	County Hall
Social Services	Jennie Bashforth	Director of Social Services	County Hall
Technical Services	Richard Wigginton	Director of Environmental Services	County Hall
Trading Standards	Clive Graham	Head of Trading Standards	Foregate St

District/Borough Councils in Worcestershire: Bromsgrove; Malvern Hills; Redditch; Worcester City; Wychavon; Wyre Forest

DISTRICT COUNCILS

ADUR DISTRICT COUNCIL

www.adurdc.gov.uk

Principal Office

Civic Centre, Ham Road, Shoreham-by-Sea, West Sussex BN43 6PR
Telephone: (01273) 263000; FAX: (01273) 454847; DX 59765 Shoreham-by-Sea

Leisure Services

Commerce Way, Lancing, West Sussex BN15 8TA
Telephone: (01273) 263000

Function	Chief Officer	Title	Location
Chief Executive	Mr I M Lowrie	Chief Executive	Civic Centre
Electoral Registration	Ms T Bryant	Elections & Land Charges Supervisor	Civic Centre
Environmental Health	Mr M Denwood	Head of Environmental Services	Civic Centre
Finance	Ms S Wheeler	Director of Corporate Services	Civic Centre
Housing	Mr P Latham	Corporate Director, Environment, Community & Housing Services	Civic Centre
Legal Services	Mr J Cook	Solicitor to the Council/Monitoring Officer	Civic Centre
Leisure	Mr B Newman	Corporate Director, Leisure & Direct Services	Commerce Way
Local Land Charges	Ms T Bryant	Elections & Land Charges Supervisor	Civic Centre
Planning	Mr W Boden	Corporate Director Strategy	Civic Centre
Technical Services	Mr D Porter	Head of Technical Services	Civic Centre

Parish Councils in the authority's area: Lancing; Sompting.

ALLERDALE BOROUGH COUNCIL

www.allerdale.gov.uk

Principal Office

Allerdale House, Workington, Cumbria CA14 3YJ
Telephone: (01900) 326333; FAX: (01900) 326346; DX 62861 Workington

Function	Chief Officer	Title	Location
Chief Executive	Mr P J Leonard	Chief Executive	Allerdale House
Electoral Registration	Ms H Cushin	Head of Democratic Services	Allerdale House
Environmental Health	Mr I Payne	Head of Environment	Allerdale House
Finance	Mrs C Carre	Director of Finance	Allerdale House
Legal Services	Mr N J Fardon	Borough Solicitor	Allerdale House
Leisure	Mr M Edwards	Leisure Services Manager	Allerdale House
Local Land Charges	Mr N J Fardon	Borough Solicitor	Allerdale House
Planning	Mr R Outhwaite	Planning Services Manager	Allerdale House

Parish Councils in the authority's area: Above Derwent; Aikton; Allhallows; Allonby; Bassenthwaite; Blennerhasset & Torpenhow; Blindbothel; Blindcrake; Boltons; Borrowdale; Bothel & Threapland; Bowness; Bridekirk; Brigham; Broughton; Bromfield; Broughton Moor; Buttermere; Caldbeck; Camerton; Crosscanonby; Dean; Dearham; Dundraw; Embleton & District; Gilcrux; Great Clifton; Greysouthen; Hayton & Mealo; Holme Abbey; Holme East Waver; Holme Low; Holme St Cuthbert; Ireby & Uldale; Kirkbampton; Kirkbride; Little Clifton; Lorton; Loweswater; Oughterside & Allerby; Papcastle; Plumbland; St John's, Castlerigg & Wythburn; Seaton; Sebergham; Thursby; Underskiddaw; Waverton; Westnewton; Westward; Winscales; Woodside.

DISTRICT COUNCILS

Parish Meetings in the authority's area: Bewaldeth & Snittlegarth.

Town Councils in the authority's area: Aspatria; Cockermouth; Keswick; Maryport; Silloth; Wigton; Workington.

ALNWICK DISTRICT COUNCIL

www.alnwick.gov.uk

Principal Office
Allerburn House, Alnwick, Northumberland NE66 1YY
Telephone: (01665) 510505; FAX: (01665) 605099

Housing Department
1 Clayport Street, Alnwick NE66 1LA
Telephone: (01665) 510505; FAX: (01665) 603312

Function	Chief Officer	Title	Location
Chief Executive	Mr B Batey	Chief Executive	Allerburn House
Finance	Mr M James	Director of Property and Resources	1 Clayport St
Housing	Mr M James	Director of Property and Resources	1 Clayport St
Legal Services	Mr T Farrell	Solicitor	Allerburn House
Planning	Mr P Gee	Director of Environment and Regeneration	Allerburn House
Technical Services	Mr P Gee	Director of Environment and Regeneration	Allerburn House

Parish Councils in the authority's area: Acklington; Alnham; Alnmouth; Alwinton; Biddlestone & Netherton; Brinkburn & Hesleyhurst; Cartington; Craster; Denwick; Edlingham; Eglingham; Elsdon; Embleton; Felton; Glanton; Harbottle; Hauxley; Hedgeley; Hepple; Lesbury; Longframlington; Longhoughton; Newton by the Sea; Newton on the Moor/Swarland; Nunnykirk; Rennington; Rothbury; Rothley & Hollinghill; Shilbottle; Snitter; Thropton; Togston; Warkworth; Whittingham & Callaly; Whitton & Tosson.

Town Councils in the authority's area: Alnwick; Amble.

AMBER VALLEY BOROUGH COUNCIL

www.ambervalley.gov.uk

Principal Office
Town Hall, Market Place, Ripley, Derbyshire DE5 3XE
Telephone: (01773) 570222; FAX: (01773) 841616

Function	Chief Officer	Title	Location
Chief Executive	Mr P M Carney	Chief Executive	Town Hall
Electoral Registration	Mr P M Carney	Chief Executive	Town Hall
Finance	Ms Sylvia Delahay	Executive Director of Financial Services	Town Hall
Legal Services	Mr P M Benski	Principal Solicitor	Town Hall
Leisure	Mr M D Calladine	Leisure Development Manager	Town Hall
Local Land Charges	Elaine Bonser	Local Land Charges Officer	Town Hall
Planning	Mr C Whysall	Director of Borough Development	Town Hall
Purchasing & Supplies	Mr J Grady	Assistant Chief Executive & Monitoring Officer	Town Hall

Parish Councils in the authority's area: Aldercar & Langley Mill; Alderwasley; Codnor; Crich; Denby; Dethick, Lea & Holloway; Duffield; Hazelwood; Holbrook; Horsley; Horsley Woodhouse; Idridgehay; Ironville; Kilburn; Kirk Langley; Mackworth; Mapperley; Pentrich; Quarndon; Shipley; Shottle & Postern; Smalley; Somercotes; South Wingfield; Swanwick; Turnditch & Windley; Weston Underwood.

Parish Meetings in the authority's area: Kedleston; Ravensdale Park.

Town Councils in the authority's area: Alfreton; Belper; Heanor & Loscoe; Ripley.

DISTRICT COUNCILS

ARUN DISTRICT COUNCIL

www.arun.gov.uk

Principal Office
Arun Civic Centre, Maltravers Road, Littlehampton, West Sussex BN17 5LF
Telephone: (01903) 737500; FAX: (01903) 730442; DX 57406 Littlehampton

Housing Department
Church Street, Littlehampton, West Sussex BN17 5EP
Telephone: (01903) 737500; FAX: (01903) 723431

Function	Chief Officer	Title	Location
Chief Executive	Ian Sumnall	Chief Executive & Strategy Director	Civic Centre
Electoral Registration	Liz Futcher	Head of Democratic Services	Civic Centre
Environmental Health	Paul Unsworth	Head of Environmental Health	Civic Centre
Finance	Alan Peach	Head of Financial Services	Civic Centre
Housing	Les Goodwin	Head of Housing Policy	Church Street
Legal Services	Wendy Ashenden-Bax	Solicitor to the Council	Civic Centre
Leisure	John Stride	Head of Leisure Services	Civic Centre
Local Land Charges	Christine Bardwell	Head of Land Charges	Civic Centre
Planning	Howard Cheadle	Head of Planning Services	Civic Centre
Purchasing & Supplies	Rupert Hatch	Procurement Manager	Civic Centre
Technical Services	David Green;	Head of Infrastructure Works & Engineering;	Civic Centre
	Nigel Horwill	Head of Surveying & Estates	Civic Centre

Parish Councils in the authority's area: Aldingbourne; Aldwick; Angmering; Barnham; Bersted; Clapham; Climping; East Preston; Eastergate; Felpham; Ferring; Findon; Ford; Kingston; Lyminster; Middleton-on-Sea; Pagham; Patching; Rustington; Slindon; Walberton; Yapton.

Parish Meetings in the authority's area: Burpham; Houghton; Madehurst; Poling; South Stoke; Warningcamp.

Town Councils in the authority's area: Arundel; Bognor Regis; Littlehampton.

ASHFIELD DISTRICT COUNCIL

www.ashfield-dc.gov.uk

Principal Office
Council Offices, Urban Road, Kirkby-in Ashfield, Nottingham NG17 8DA
Telephone: (01623) 450000; FAX: (01623) 457585

Function	Chief Officer	Title	Location
Chief Executive	Mr Alan Mellor	Chief Executive	Council Offices
Electoral Registration	Mr Philip Yendle	Solicitor to the Council & Head of Legal, Administration & Personnel Services	Council Offices
Environmental Health	Mr Bill Buckley	Head of Environmental Health & Control & Housing	Council Offices
Finance	Mrs Helen Woodhurst	Head of Financial Management	Council Offices
Legal Services	Mr Philip Yendle	Solicitor to the Council & Head of Legal, Administration & Personnel Services	Council Offices
Leisure	Mr Carl A Westby	Acting Head of Leisure Services	Council Offices
Local Land Charges	Mr Philip Yendle	Solicitor to the Council & Head of Legal, Administration & Personnel Services	Council Offices
Planning	Mr Peter Johnson	Head of Development Services	Council Offices
Purchasing & Supplies	Mr Philip Yendle	Solicitor to the Council & Head of Legal, Administration & Personnel Services	Council Offices
Technical Services	Mr Allen R Hunt	Head of Design & Construction Services	Council Offices

Parish Councils in the authority's area: Annesley; Selston.

ASHFORD BOROUGH COUNCIL

www.ashford.gov.uk

Principal Office

Civic Centre, Tannery Lane, Ashford, Kent TN23 1PL
Telephone: (01233) 637311; FAX: (01233) 645654; DX 30204 Ashford (Kent)

Function	Chief Officer	Title	Location
Chief Executive	Mr D Hill	Chief Executive	Civic Centre
Electoral Registration	Mr T Mortimer	Legal & Democratic Services Manager	Civic Centre
Environmental Health	Mr P Jackson	Head of Environmental Services	Civic Centre
Finance	Ms P Adams	Head of Finance	Civic Centre
Housing	Mrs T Kerly	Head of Housing Services	Civic Centre
Legal Services	Mr T Mortimer	Legal & Democratic Services Manager	Civic Centre
Leisure	Mr M Carty	Head of Cultural Services	Civic Centre
Local Land Charges	Mr T Mortimer	Legal & Democratic Services Manager	Civic Centre
Planning	Mr J Jory	Director of Development Services	Civic Centre
Technical Services	Mr D Oates	Property Services Manager	Civic Centre

Parish Councils in the authority's area: Aldington & Bonnington; Appledore; Bethersden; Biddenden; Bilsington; Boughton Aluph & Eastwell; Brabourne; Brook; Challock; Charing; Chilham; Egerton; Godmersham; Great Chart & Singleton; Hastingleigh; High Halden; Hothfield; Kenardington; Kingsnorth; Little Chart; Mersham & Sevington; Newenden; Orlestone; Pluckley; Rolvenden; Ruckinge; Shadoxhurst; Smarden; Smeeth; Stanhope; Stone-cum-Ebony; Tenterden; Warehorne; Westwell; Wittersham; Woodchurch; Wye & Hinxhill.

Parish Meetings in the authority's area: Crundale; Molash.

AYLESBURY VALE DISTRICT COUNCIL

www.aylesburyvaledc.gov.uk

Chief Executive's Department

Exchange Street, Aylesbury, Buckinghamshire HP20 1UB
Telephone: (01296) 585002; FAX: (01296) 336977; DX 4130 Aylesbury

Community Services Department

66 High Street, Aylesbury, Buckinghamshire HP20 1YN
Telephone: (01296) 585858; FAX: (01296) 585577

Corporate Resources Department

4 Great Western Street, Aylesbury, Buckinghamshire HP20 2TW
Telephone: (01296) 585858; FAX: (01296) 585585

Environment & Planning Department

4 Great Western Street, Aylesbury, Buckinghamshire HP20 2TW
Telephone: (01296) 585012; FAX: (01296) 585577

Function	Chief Officer	Title	Location
Chief Executive	Richard Carr	Chief Executive	Exchange Street
Electoral Registration	Richard Carr	Chief Executive	Exchange Street
Environmental Health	[Vacant]	Director of Community Services	66 High Street
Finance	Steve Watson	Director of Corporate Resources	66 High Street
Housing	[Vacant]	Director of Community Services	66 High Street
Legal Services	Steve Watson	Director of Corporate Resources	66 High Street
Leisure	[Vacant]	Director of Community Services	66 High Street
Local Land Charges	Steve Watson	Director of Corporate Resources	66 High Street
Planning	Norman Skedge	Director of Planning & Environment	4 Great Western St
Technical Services	Norman Skedge	Director of Planning & Environment	4 Great Western St

DISTRICT COUNCILS

Parish Councils in the authority's area: Adstock; Akeley; Ashendon; Aston Abbotts; Aston Clinton; Beachampton; Bierton-with-Broughton; Brill; Buckland; Charndon; Chearsley; Cheddington; Chilton; Coldharbour; Cublington; Cuddington; Dinton-with-Ford & Upton; Drayton Parslow; East Claydon; Edgcott; Edlesborough Northall & Dagnall; Gawcott-with-Lenborough; Granborough; Great Brickhill; Great Horwood; Grendon Underwood; Haddenham; Halton; Hardwick; Hillesden; Hulcott; Ickford; Ivinghoe; Leckhampstead; Lillingstone Dayrell with Luffield Abbey; Little Horwood; Long Crendon; Ludgershall; Maids Moreton; Marsh Gibbon; Marsworth; Mentmore; Middle Claydon; Mursley; Nash; Newton Longville; North Marston; Oakley; Oving; Padbury; Pitstone; Preston Bissett; Quainton; Radclive-cum-Chackmore; Shabbington; Slapton; Soulbury; Steeple Claydon; Stewkley; Stoke Hammond; Stoke Mandeville; Stone-with-Bishopstone & Hartwell; Stowe; Swanbourne; Thornborough; Tingewick; Turweston; Twyford; Waddesdon; Watermead; Weedon; Wendover; Westbury; Westcott; Weston Turville; Whaddon; Whitchurch; Wing; Wingrave-with-Rowsham; Worminghall.

Parish Meetings in the authority's area: Addington; Aston Sandford; Barton Harthshorn; Biddlesden; Boarstall; Chetwode; Creslow; Dorton; Drayton Beauchamp; Dunton; Fleet Marston; Foscote; Hoggeston; Hogshaw; Kingsey; Kingswood; Lillingstone Lovell; Nether Winchendon; Pitchcott; Poundon; Quarrendon; Shalstone; Thornton; Upper Winchendon; Water Stratford; Woodham; Wotton Underwood.

Town Councils in the authority's area: Aylesbury; Buckingham; Winslow.

BABERGH DISTRICT COUNCIL

www.babergh-south-suffolk.gov.uk

Principal Office

Council Offices, Corks Lane, Hadleigh, Ipswich, Suffolk IP7 6SJ
Telephone: (01473) 822801; FAX: (01473) 823594; DX 85055 Babergh

Function	Chief Officer	Title	Location
Chief Executive	Mrs P Rockall	Chief Executive	Council Offices
Electoral Registration	Mr R Amesbury	Electoral & Administrative Services Manager	Council Offices
Environmental Health	Mr M Firth	Head of Environmental Services	Council Offices
Finance	Mr G Kistner	Corporate Director	Council Offices
Housing	Mr C St John Foti	Head of Housing	Council Offices
Legal Services	Ms K Trickey	Head of Legal & Administrative Services	Council Offices
Leisure	Mr T Mutum	Head of Leisure & Community Services	Council Offices
Local Land Charges	Mr R Amesbury	Electoral & Administrative Services Manager	Council Offices
Planning	Mr M Hammond	Corporate Director	Council Offices
Purchasing & Supplies	Mrs D Williams	Head of Central & Office Services	Council Offices
Technical Services	Mr R Jones	Head of Technical Services	Council Offices

Parish Councils in the authority's area: Acton; Aldham; Alpheton; Assington; Belstead; Bentley; Bildeston; Boxford; Boxted; Brantham; Brent Eleigh; Brettenham; Bures St Mary; Burstall; Capel St Mary; Chattisham & Hintlesham; Chelmondiston; Chilton; Cockfield; Copdock & Washbrook; East Bergholt; Edwardstone; Elmsett; Freston; Glemsford; Great Cornard; Great Waldingfield; Groton; Harkstead; Hartest; Hitcham; Holbrook; Holton St Mary; Kersey; Kettlebaston; Lavenham; Lawshall; Layham; Leavenheath; Lindsey; Little Cornard; Little Waldingfield; Long Melford; Monks Eleigh; Nayland-with-Wissington; Nedging-with-Naughton; Newton; Pinewood; Polstead; Preston St Mary; Raydon; Semer; Shimpling; Shotley; Sproughton; Stanstead; Stoke by Nayland; Stratford St Mary; Stutton; Tattingstone; Thorpe Morieux; Wattisham; Wherstead; Woolverstone; Whatfield.

Parish Meetings in the authority's area: Arwarton; Chelsworth; Higham; Milden; Shelley; Somerton; Wenham Magna; Wenham Parva.

Town Councils in the authority's area: Hadleigh; Sudbury.

DISTRICT COUNCILS

BARROW-IN-FURNESS BOROUGH COUNCIL

www.barrowbc.gov.uk

Principal Office

Town Hall, Duke Street, Barrow-in-Furness, Cumbria LA14 2LD
Telephone: (01229) 894900; FAX: (01229) 894217; DX 63917 Barrow-in-Furness

Housing Department

Cavendish House, 78 Duke Street, Barrow-in-Furness LA14 1RR
Telephone: (01229) 894912; FAX: (01229) 894736

Leisure

The Park Leisure Centre, Greengate Street, Barrow-in-Furness LA14 9DT
Telephone: (01229) 871146; FAX: (01229) 430224

Function	Chief Officer	Title	Location
Chief Executive	Mr T O Campbell	Chief Executive	Town Hall
Electoral Registration	Mr N Anderton	Principal Administrator	Town Hall
Environmental Health	Mr G Ormondroyd	Chief Environmental Health Officer	Town Hall
Finance	Mr A McAdam	Director of Finance	Town Hall
Housing	Mr C Garnett	Housing Manager	Cavendish Hse
Legal Services	Mr A McAdam	Director of Finance	Town Hall
Leisure	Mrs M Wilson	Sports Contract Manager	Park Leisure Ctr
Local Land Charges	Mr S Warbrick	Director of Regeneration	Town Hall
Planning	Mr P Huck	Assistant Director of Regeneration	Town Hall
Purchasing & Supplies	Mr M Saleh	Assistant Director of Finance	Town Hall
Technical Services	Ms G Beckingham	Design Services Manager	Town Hall

Parish Councils in the authority's area: Askam & Ireleth; Lindal & Marton.

Town Councils in the authority's area: Dalton with Newton.

BASILDON DISTRICT COUNCIL

www.basildondistrict.com

Principal Office

The Basildon Centre, St Martin's Square, Basildon, Essex SS14 1DL
Telephone: (01268) 533333; FAX: (01268) 294350

Finance Department

Church Walk House, Church Walk, Basildon SS14 1YA
Telephone: (01268) 533333; FAX: (01268) 294662

Leisure Services Department

Barleylands Depot, Barleylands Road, Billericay CM11 2UF
Telephone: (01268) 294929; FAX: (01268) 533333

Function	Chief Officer	Title	Location
Chief Executive	John Robb	Chief Executive	Basildon Centre
Electoral Registration	Helen Chapman	Central Services Manager	Basildon Centre
Environmental Health	Richard Albon	Manager of Environmental Health Services	Basildon Centre
Finance	Mick Nice	Executive Director (Support Services)	Church Walk Hse
Housing	Bala Mahendran	Executive Director (Housing & Personal Services)	Basildon Centre
Legal Services	Lorraine Browne	Manager of Legal & Estates Service & Solicitor to the Council	Basildon Centre
Leisure	Roy Short	Manager of Leisure Services	Barleylands Dpt
Local Land Charges	Graeme Bloomer	Manager of Planning Services	Basildon Centre
Planning	Graeme Bloomer	Manager of Planning Services	Basildon Centre
Purchasing & Supplies	Peter Claus	Supplies Manager	Barleylands Dpt

Parish Councils & Parish Meetings in the authority's area: Great Burstead & South Green; Little Burstead; Ramsden Bellhouse; Ramsden Crays.

Town Councils in the authority's area: Billericay.

BASINGSTOKE & DEANE BOROUGH COUNCIL

www.basingstoke.gov.uk

Principal Office

Civic Offices, London Road, Basingstoke, Hampshire RG21 4AH
Telephone: (01256) 844844; FAX: (01256) 841945

Function	Chief Officer	Title	Location
Chief Executive	Mr G Holdcroft	Chief Executive	Civic Offices
Electoral Registration	Mrs E Cloke	Head of Electoral Services	Civic Offices
Environmental Health	Mr C Thomson	Head of Environmental Health, Licensing & Policy	Civic Offices
Finance	Mrs L George	Head of Financial Services	Civic Offices
Housing	Mrs D Luker	Head of Housing Services	Civic Offices
Legal Services	Mr C Guy	Head of Legal Services	Civic Offices
Leisure	Mr N Cole	Head of Leisure Services	Civic Offices
Local Land Charges	Mrs K Scobie	Head of Customer Services & Administration	Civic Offices
Planning	Mr R Thompson	Head of Planning & Transport	Civic Offices
Purchasing & Supplies	Mrs K Scobie	Head of Customer Services & Administration	Civic Offices
Technical Services	Mr R Thompson	Head of Planning & Transport	Civic Offices

Parish Councils in the authority's area: Ashford Hill with Headley; Ashmansworth; Baughurst; Bramley; Burghclere; Candovers; Chineham; Cliddesden; Dummer; East Woodhay; Ecchinswell, Sydmonton & Bishops Green; Ellisfield; Hannington; Hartley Wespall; Herriard; Highclere; Hurstbourne Priors; Kingsclere; Laverstoke & Freefolk; Mapledurwell & Up Nately; Monk Sherborne; Mortimer West End; Newnham; Newtown; North Waltham; Oakley & Deane; Old Basing; Overton; Pamber; Preston Candover & Nutley; St Mary Bourne; Sherborne St John; Sherfield on Loddon; Silchester; Steventon; Stratfield Saye; Upton Grey; Wootton St Lawrence.

Parish Meetings in the authority's area: Bradley; Farleigh Wallop; Litchfield & Woodcott; Popham; Stratfield Turgis; Tunworth; Weston Corbett & Weston Patrick; Winslade.

Town Councils in the authority's area: Tadley; Whitchurch.

BASSETLAW DISTRICT COUNCIL

www.bassetlaw.gov.uk

Principal Office

Queen's Buildings, Potter Street, Worksop, Notts S80 2AH
Telephone: (01909) 533533; FAX: (01909) 501758

Leisure & Amenity Services

West House, Carlton Forest, Hundred Acre Lane, Worksop S80 0TS
Telephone: (01909) 533489; FAX: (01909) 733769

Function	Chief Officer	Title	Location
Chief Executive	Mr James Molloy	Chief Executive	Queen's Bldgs
Electoral Registration	Ann Higgins	Principal Members Support Officer	Queen's Bldgs
Environmental Health	Chris Shaw	Head of Environment & Health Services	West House
Finance	John Brooks	Head of Financial Services	Queen's Bldgs
Housing	Bernard Coleman	Head of Housing & Technical Services	Queen's Bldgs

Legal Services	Sara Goodwin	Head of Legal & Scrutiny Services	Queen's Bldgs
Local Land Charges	Sara Goodwin	Head of Legal & Scrutiny Services	Queen's Bldgs
Planning	Jim Kehoe	Head of Planning Services	Queen's Bldgs
Purchasing & Supplies	Andy Burton	Head of Revenue Services	Queen's Bldgs
Technical Services	Bernard Coleman	Head of Housing & Technical Services	Queen's Bldgs

Parish Councils in the authority's area: Babworth; Barnby Moor; Beckingham-cum-Saundby; Blyth, Bothamsall; Carlton-in-Lindrick; Clarborough; Clayworth; Cuckney; Dunham-with-Ragnall & Fledborough; East Drayton; East Markham; Elkesley; Everton; Gamston, West Drayton & Eaton; Gringley-on-the Hill; Grove & Stokeham; Harworth/Bircoates; Hayton; Headon-cum-Upton; Hodsock; Holbeck & Welbeck; Laneham; Lound; Markham Clinton; Mattersey; Misson; Misterton; Nether Langwith; Normanton-on-Trent with Marnham; North Leverton with Habblesthorpe; North & South Wheatley; Oldcotes; Rampton; Ranskill; Rhodesia; Scrooby; Shireoaks; South Leverton; Sturton-le-Steeple; Styrrup-with-Oldcotes; Sutton; Torworth; Treswell with Cottam; Tuxford; Walkeringham; West Stockwith.

Parish Meetings in the authority's area: Askham; Bole; Carburton; Clumber & Hardwick; Darlton; Haughton; Norton; Scaftworth; Wallingwells; West Burton; Wiseton.

BATH CITY COUNCIL

Bath City Council was abolished on 31 March 1996; see now Bath & North East Somerset Council.

BEDFORD BOROUGH COUNCIL

www.bedford.gov.uk

Principal Office
Town Hall, Bedford, Bedfordshire MK40 1SJ
Telephone: (01234) 267422; FAX: (01234) 221606; DX 5600 Bedford

Function	Chief Officer	Title	Location
Chief Executive	Mr S E Field	Chief Executive & Director of Commercial Services	Town Hall
Electoral Registration	Mr M Hillier	Electoral Services Co-ordinator	Town Hall
Environmental Health	Mr G Johnston	Director of Environment & Community Strategies	Town Hall
Finance	Mr A Harris	Director of Finance & Corporate Strategy	Town Hall
Housing	Mr M Williams	Service Manager (Housing)	Town Hall
Legal Services	Mr T Fordham	Service Manager (Legal Services)	Town Hall
Leisure	Mr J Moore	Service Manager (Cultural Services)	Town Hall
Local Land Charges	Mrs M Kent	Chief Local Land Charges Officer	Town Hall
Planning	Mr D Bailey	Head of Planning Services	Town Hall
Technical Services	Mr D Logan	Head of Environment & Community Services	Town Hall

Parish Councils in the authority's area: Biddenham; Bletsoe; Bolnhurst & Keysoe; Bromham; Cardington; Carlton & Chellington; Clapham; Colmworth; Cople; Dean & Shelton; Eastcotts; Elstow; Felmersham & Radwell; Great Barford; Harrold; Kempston Rural; Knotting & Souldrop; Little Staughton; Melchbourne & Yielden; Milton Ernest; Oakley; Odell; Pavenham; Pertenhall & Swineshead; Podington; Ravensden; Renhold; Riseley; Roxton; Sharnbrook; Stagsden; Staploe; Stevington; Stewartby; Thurleigh; Turvey; Wilden; Willington; Wilshamstead; Wootton; Wymington.

Parish Meetings in the authority's area: Little Barford.

Town Councils in the authority's area: Kempston.

DISTRICT COUNCILS

BERWICK-UPON-TWEED BOROUGH COUNCIL

www.berwick-upon-tweed.gov.uk

Principal Office

Council Offices, Wallace Green, Berwick-upon-Tweed, Northumberland TD15 1ED
Telephone: (01289) 330044; FAX: (01289) 330540; DX 67798 Berwick-upon-Tweed

Function	Chief Officer	Title	Location
Chief Executive	Mrs J Pannell	Chief Executive	Council Offices
Electoral Registration	Miss J Turnbull	Committee Services Officer	Council Offices
Environmental Health	Mr R A Marriner	Borough Environmental Health Officer	Council Offices
Finance	Mr Richard Bell	Head of Finance	Council Offices
Housing	Ms H Bury	Borough Housing Officer	Council Offices
Legal Services	Mr W E Henry	Borough Solicitor	Council Offices
Leisure	Mr Tom Johnson	Sports Development Officer	Council Offices
Local Land Charges	Mrs V Herbert	Land Charges Assistant	Council Offices
Planning	Mr J Hayward	Principal Planning Officer	Council Offices
Technical Services	Mr C Budzynski	Borough Surveyor	Council Offices

Parish Councils in the authority's area: Adderstone with Lucker; Ancroft; Bamburgh; Beadnell; Belford; Bowsden; Branxton; Carham; Cheriotside; Cornhill-on-Tweed; Doddington; Duddo; Ellingham; Ford; Holy Island; Horncliffe; Ingram; Kirknewton; Kyloe; Lowick; Milfield; Norham; North Sunderland; Ord; Shoreswood; Tillside; Wooler.

BEVERLEY BOROUGH COUNCIL

Beverley Borough Council was abolished on 31 March 1996; see now the East Riding of Yorkshire Council.

BLABY DISTRICT COUNCIL

www.blaby.gov.uk

Principal Office

Council Offices, Desford Road, Narborough, Leicester LE19 2EP
Telephone: (0116) 275 0555; FAX: (0116) 275 0368; DX 706890 Narborough

Function	Chief Officer	Title	Location
Chief Executive	P Dolan	Chief Executive	Council Offices
Electoral Registration	K Johnston	Head of Admin & Legal Services	Council Offices
Environmental Health	S Beard	Head of Environmental Health Services	Council Offices
Finance	G Proctor	Head of Financial Services	Council Offices
Housing	E Mallon	Head of Housing Services	Council Offices
Legal Services	K Johnston	Head of Admin & Legal Services	Council Offices
Local Land Charges	K Johnston	Head of Admin & Legal Services	Council Offices
Planning	P Clarke	Head of Planning & Development Services	Council Offices
Purchasing & Supplies	K Johnston	Head of Admin & Legal Services	Council Offices

Parish Councils in the authority's area: Blaby; Cosby; Countesthorpe; Croft; Elmesthorpe; Enderby; Glenfield; Glen Parva; Huncote; Kilby; Kirby Muxloe; Leicester Forest East; Littlethorpe; Narborough; Sapcote; Sharnford; Stoney Stanton; Thurlaston; Whetstone.

Parish Meetings in the authority's area: Aston Flamville; Leicester Forest West; Lubbesthorpe; Potters Marston; Wigston Parva.

Town Councils in the authority's area: Braunstone.

BLACKBURN WITH DARWEN BOROUGH COUNCIL

Blackburn with Darwen Borough Council became a unitary authority on 1 April 1998.

DISTRICT COUNCILS

BLACKPOOL BOROUGH COUNCIL
Blackpool Borough Council became a unitary authority on 1 April 1998.

BLYTH VALLEY BOROUGH COUNCIL
www.blythvalley.gov.uk

Principal Office; Financial Services; Revenue Services
Civic Centre, Blyth, Northumberland NE24 2BX
Telephone: (01670) 542000; FAX: (01670) 542102

**Chief Executive; Corporate Support; Environment & Regeneration;
Housing Services; Planning & Environmental Protection; Technical Consultancy**
Council Offices, Avenue Road, Seaton Delaval, Whitley Bay NE25 0DX
Telephone: (01670) 542000; FAX: (01670) 542323

Leisure Services
Concordia, Forum Way, Cramlington, Northumberland NE23 6YB
Telephone: (01670) 717423; FAX: (01670) 590648

Legal & Democratic Services
Dinsdale House, Marine Terrace, Blyth NE24 2LN
Telephone: (01670) 542000; FAX: (01670) 542205

Function	Chief Officer	Title	Location
Chief Executive	Mr G Paul	Chief Executive	Council Offices
Electoral Registration	Mr G Paul	Chief Executive	Dinsdale Hse
Environmental Health	Mr S Robson	Head of Planning & Environmental Protection	Council Offices
Finance	Mr S Potts	Head of Financial Services	Civic Centre
Housing	Mrs P Walker	Head of Housing	Council Offices
Legal Services	Mr P Gascoigne	Head of Legal & Democratic Services	Dinsdale Hse
Leisure	Mr B Ledger	Head of Leisure Services	Concordia
Local Land Charges	Mr D Earl	Executive Director, Central & Protective Services	Dinsdale Hse
Planning	Mr S Robson	Head of Planning & Environmental Protection	Council Offices
Technical Services	Mr D Gray	Head of Technical Consultancy	Council Offices

Councils & Parish Meetings in the authority's area: none.

Town Councils in the authority's area: none.

BOLSOVER DISTRICT COUNCIL
www.bolsover.gov.uk

Principal Office
Sherwood Lodge, Bolsover, Derbyshire S44 6NF
Telephone: (01246) 240000; FAX: (01246) 242424

Function	Chief Officer	Title	Location
Chief Executive	Mr W Lumley	Acting Chief Executive	Sherwood Lodge
Electoral Registration	Mr W Lumley	Acting Chief Executive	Sherwood Lodge
Environmental Health	Mr S Bidwell	Chief Environmental Health & Housing Officer	Sherwood Lodge
Finance	Mr G Walker	Acting Treasurer	Sherwood Lodge
Housing	Mr S Bidwell	Chief Environmental Health & Housing Officer	Sherwood Lodge
Legal Services	Mrs S Sternberg	Solicitor to the Council	Sherwood Lodge
Leisure	Mr S Singleton	Leisure Services & Tourism Officer	Sherwood Lodge

Local Land Charges	Mr S Bidwell	Chief Environmental Health & Housing Officer	Sherwood Lodge
Planning	Mr G Clarke	Planning Services Manager	Sherwood Lodge
Purchasing & Supplies	Mr B Carnall	Technical Services Manager	Sherwood Lodge
Technical Services	Mr B Carnall	Technical Services Manager	Sherwood Lodge

Parish Councils in the authority's area: Ault Hucknall; Barlborough; Blackwell; Clowne; Elmton with Creswell; Glapwell; Pinxton; Pleasley; Scarcliffe; South Normanton; Tibshelf; Whitwell.

Town Councils in the authority's area: Old Bolsover; Shirebrook.

BOOTHFERRY BOROUGH COUNCIL

Boothferry Borough Council was abolished on 31 March 1996; see now the East Riding of Yorkshire Council.

BOSTON BOROUGH COUNCIL

www.boston.gov.uk

Principal Office

Municipal Buildings, West Street, Boston, Lincolnshire PE21 8QR
Telephone: (01205) 314200; FAX: (01205) 364604; DX 26823 Boston

Function	Chief Officer	Title	Location
Chief Executive	Ms N Bulbeck	Chief Executive	Municipal Bldgs
Electoral Registration	Ms N Bulbeck	Chief Executive	Municipal Bldgs
Environmental Health	Mr D McGregor	Director of Resources	Municipal Bldgs
Finance	Mr D McGregor	Director of Resources	Municipal Bldgs
Legal Services	Mr M Gallagher	Director of Development	Municipal Bldgs
Leisure	Mr M Gallagher	Director of Development	Municipal Bldgs
Local Land Charges	Mr D McGregor	Director of Resources	Municipal Bldgs
Planning	Mr M Gallagher	Director of Development	Municipal Bldgs
Purchasing & Supplies	Mr D McGregor	Director of Resources	Municipal Bldgs
Technical Services	Mr M Gallagher	Director of Development	Municipal Bldgs

Parish Councils in the authority's area: Algarkirk; Amber Hill; Benington; Bicker; Butterwick; Fishtoft; Fosdyke; Frampton; Freiston; Holland Fen with Brothertoft; Kirton; Leverton; Old Leake; Sutterton; Swineshead; Wigtoft; Wrangle; Wyberton.

BOURNEMOUTH BOROUGH COUNCIL

Bournemouth Borough Council became a unitary authority on 1 April 1997.

BRACKNELL FOREST BOROUGH COUNCIL

Bracknell Forest Borough Council became a unitary authority on 1 April 1998.

BRAINTREE DISTRICT COUNCIL

www.braintree.gov.uk

Principal Office

Causeway House, Braintree, Essex CM7 9HB
Telephone: (01376) 552525; FAX: (01376) 552626; DX 56210 Braintree

Function	Chief Officer	Title	Location
Chief Executive	Mr A Reid	Chief Executive	Causeway Hse
Electoral Registration	S Jolly	Electoral Officer	Causeway Hse
Environmental Health	P Tattersley	Operations Director	Causeway Hse
Finance	C Fleetham	Director of Finance	Causeway Hse
Housing	D Townshend	Housing Manager	Causeway Hse
Legal Services	P Dempsey	Head of Corporate Services	Causeway Hse
Leisure	Ms S Moutard	Community Services Manager	Causeway Hse

DISTRICT COUNCILS

Planning	P Crofts	Development Director	Causeway Hse
Purchasing & Supplies	J Wickes	Purchasing Manager	Causeway Hse
Technical Services	Mrs G Furlong	IT Client Manager	Causeway Hse

Parish Councils in the authority's area: Alphamstone & Lamarsh; Ashen; Belchamp Otten & Belchamp St Paul; Belchamp Walter; Birdbrook; Black Notley; Bradwell; Bulmer; Bures Hamlet; Castle Hedingham; Coggeshall; Colne Engaine; Cressing; Earls Colne; Fairstead; Feering; Finchingfield & Cornish Hall End; Foxearth & Liston; Gestingthorpe; Gosfield; Great Bardfield; Great Maplestead; Great Saling; Great Yeldham; Greenstead Green & Halstead Rural; Hatfield Peverel; Helions Bumpstead; The Hennys, Middleton & Twinstead; Kelvedon; Little Maplestead; Little Yeldham, Ovington & Tilbury Juxta Clare; Panfield; Pebmarsh; Pentlow; Rayne; Ridgewell; Rivenhall; Shalford; Sible Hedingham; Silver End; Stambourne; Steeple Bumpstead; Stisted; Sturmer; Toppesfield; Wethersfield; White Colne; White Notley & Faulkbourne; Wickham St Paul.

Parish Meetings in the authority's area: Bardfield Saling; Borley.

Town Councils in the authority's area: Halstead; Witham.

BRECKLAND DISTRICT COUNCIL
See now Breckland Council.

BRECKLAND COUNCIL
www.breckland.gov.uk
Principal Office
Elizabeth House, Walpole Loke, Dereham, Norfolk NR19 1EE
Telephone: (01362) 695333; FAX: (01362) 692582

Function	Chief Officer	Title	Location
Chief Executive	Mr R N Garnett	Chief Executive	Elizabeth Hse
Electoral Registration	Mr I Vargeson	Head of Electoral Registration	Elizabeth Hse
Environmental Health	Mr I Hayward	Portfolio Manager – Health & Housing	Elizabeth Hse
Finance	Mrs E Humphrey	Portfolio Manager – Finance	Elizabeth Hse
Housing	Mr I Hayward	Portfolio Manager – Health & Housing	Elizabeth Hse
Legal Services	Mr P Heard	Scrutiny & Standards Manager	Elizabeth Hse
Local Land Charges	Mr M Stokes	Portfolio Manager – Environment & Public Services	Elizabeth Hsel
Planning	Mr M Stokes	Portfolio Manager – Environment & Public Services	Elizabeth Hse
Purchasing & Supplies	Mr S Harris	Head of Facilities Management	Elizabeth Hse
Technical Services	Mr M Stokes	Portfolio Manager – Environment & Public Services	Elizabeth Hse

Parish Councils in the authority's area: Ashill; Banham; Bawdeswell; Beachamwell; Beeston with Bittering; Beetley; Besthorpe; Billingford; Bintree; Blo' Norton; Bradenham; Bridgham; Brisley; Buckenham Old; Buckenham New; Carbrooke; Caston; Cockley Cley; Colkirk; Cranworth; Croxton; Dunham; East Lexham; East Tuddenham; Elsing; Foulden; Foxley; Fransham; Garboldisham; Garvestone; Gooderstone; Great Cressingham; Great Dunham; Great Ellingham; Gressenhall; Griston; Guist; Hardingham; Harling; Hilborough; Hockering; Hockham; Holme Hale; Horningtoft; Kenninghall; Litcham; Little Cressingham; Little Dunham; Little Ellingham; Longham; Lyng; Mattishall; Merton; Mileham; Mundford; Narborough; Necton; New Buckenham; North Elmham; North Lopham; North Pickenham; North Tuddenham; Old Buckenham; Ovington; Oxborough; Quidenham; Rocklands; Roudham; Rougham; Saham Toney; Scarning; Scoulton; Shipdham; Shropharn; Snetterton; South Lopham; South Pickenham; Sparham; Sporle with Palgrave; Stanfield; Stow Bedon; Swanton Morley; Thompson; Tittleshall; Weasenham All Saints; Weasenham St Peter; Weeting with Broomhill; Wellingham; Wendling; Whinburgh; Whissonsett; Wretham; Yaxham.

Parish Meetings in the authority's area: Brettenham; Bylaugh; Cranwich; Didlington; Gateley; Hoe; Ickburgh; Kempstone; Kilverstone; Lexham; Lynford; Narford; Newton by Castle Acre; Riddlesworth; Southacre; Stanford; Sturston; Tottington; Twyford.

Town Councils in the authority's area: Attleborough; Dereham; Swaffham; Thetford; Watton.

DISTRICT COUNCILS

BRENTWOOD BOROUGH COUNCIL

www.brentwood-council.gov.uk

Principal Office
Town Hall, Ingrave Road, Brentwood, Essex CM15 8AY
Telephone: (01277) 261111; FAX: (01277) 260836; DX 5001 Brentwood

Function	Chief Officer	Title	Location
Chief Executive	R McLintock	Chief Executive & Town Clerk	Town Hall
Electoral Registration	J Stevens	Elections & Civic Functions Co-Ordinator	Town Hall
Environmental Health	S Bennett	Head of Environmental Health & Public Protection Services	Town Hall
Finance	Mrs S Keeble	Borough Treasurer	Town Hall
Housing	C P Wainman	Head of Housing & Welfare Services	Town Hall
Legal Services	B Keane	Deputy Town Clerk & Borough Solicitor	Town Hall
Leisure	J Glanville	Head of Community Services	Town Hall
Local Land Charges	B Keane	Deputy Town Clerk & Borough Solicitor	Town Hall
Planning	A Millard	Chief Planning Officer	Town Hall
Purchasing & Supplies	G Campbell	Central Services Co-ordinator	Town Hall
Technical Services	D Marchant	Deputy Chief Executive & Director of Environmental Services	Town Hall

Parish Councils in the authority's area: Blackmore, Hook End & Wyatts Green; Doddinghurst; Herongate & Ingrave; Ingatestone & Fryerning; Kelvedon Hatch; Mountnessing; Navestock; Stondon Massey; West Horndon.

BRIDGNORTH DISTRICT COUNCIL

www.bridgnorth-dc.gov.uk

Principal Office
Westgate, Bridgnorth, Shropshire WV16 5AA
Telephone: (01746) 713100; FAX: (01746) 764414; DX 23207 Bridgnorth

Works Department
Stanley Lane, Bridgnorth WV16 4SF
Telephone: (01746) 713100

Function	Chief Officer	Title	Location
Chief Executive	Mr J Harmeston	Chief Executive	Westgate
Electoral Registration	Mr J Harmeston	Chief Executive	Westgate
Environmental Health	Mr D Parish	Director of Operational Services	Stanley Lane
Finance	Mr A Martin	Director of Resources	Westgate
Housing	Mr D Parish	Director of Operational Services	Westgate
Legal Services	Mr A Martin	Director of Resources	Westgate
Leisure	Mr P Walker	Director of Development Services	Westgate
Local Land Charges	Mr A Martin	Director of Resources	Westgate
Planning	Mr P Walker	Director of Development Services	Westgate
Technical Services	Mr D Parish	Director of Operational Services	Stanley Lane

Parish Councils in the authority's area: Acton Round; Albrighton; Alveley/ Romsley; Astley Abbotts; Aston Botterell; Aston Eyre; Badger; Barrow; Beckbury; Billingsley; Boningale; Boscobel; Burwarton; Chelmarsh; Chetton; Claverley; Cleobury North; Deuxhill; Ditton Priors; Donington; Eardington; Easthope; Farlow; Glazeley; Highley; Kemberton; Kinlet; Middleton Scriven; Monkhopton; Morville; Neen Savage; Quatt Malvern; Rudge; Ryton; Sheriffhales; Shipton; Stockton; Stottesdon, Sidbury; Stanton Long; Sutton Maddock; Tasley; Tong; Upton Cressett; Worfield.

Parish Meetings in the authority's area: Neenton.

Town Councils in the authority's area: Bridgnorth; Broseley; Much Wenlock; Shifnal.

DISTRICT COUNCILS

BRIGHTON BOROUGH COUNCIL
Brighton Borough Council & Hove Borough Council became a single unitary authority on 1 April 1997.

BRISTOL CITY COUNCIL
Bristol City Council became a unitary authority on 1 April 1996.

BROADLAND DISTRICT COUNCIL

www.broadland.gov.uk

Principal Office
Thorpe Lodge, Yarmouth Road, Thorpe St Andrew, Norwich, Norfolk NR7 0DU
Telephone: (01603) 431133; FAX: (01603) 300087; DX 134740 Norwich 4

Function	Chief Officer	Title	Location
Chief Executive	Mr Colin Bland	Chief Executive	Thorpe Lodge
Electoral Registration	Mrs Ann Watkins	Electoral Services Manager	Thorpe Lodge
Environmental Health	Mr Andy Jarvis	Head of Environmental Services	Thorpe Lodge
Finance	Mr John Duvall	Head of Finance	Thorpe Lodge
Housing	Mr Anthony Oram	Head of Policy	Thorpe Lodge
Legal Services	Mrs Elisabeth Ashness	Head of Corporate Services & Monitoring Officer	Thorpe Lodge
Leisure	Mr Paul White	Head of Cultural Services	Thorpe Lodge
Local Land Charges	Mr Michael Derbyshire	Head of Planning	Thorpe Lodge
Planning	Mr Michael Derbyshire	Head of Planning	Thorpe Lodge
Purchasing & Supplies	Mr Martin Stephens	Central Services Manager	Thorpe Lodge
Technical Services	Mr Kevin Love	Head of Building Control Services	Thorpe Lodge

Parish Councils in the authority's area: Acle; Aylsham; Beighton; Blickling; Blofield; Brundall; Brampton; Burgh & Tuttington; Buxton with Lamas; Cantley; Cawston; Coltishall; Drayton; Felthorpe; Foulsham; Freethorpe; Frettenham; Great & Little Plumstead & Thorpe End; Great Witchingham; Hainford; Halvergate; Hellesdon; Hemblington; Hevingham; Honingham; Horsford; Horsham St Faith & Newton St Faith; Horstead with Stanninghall; Lingwood & Burlingham; Marsham; Old Catton; Oulton; Postwick; Rackheath; Reedham; Ringland; Salhouse; South Walsham; Spixworth; Sprowston; Stratton Strawless; Strumpshaw; Swannington with Alderford & Little Witchingham; Taverham; Thorpe St Andrew; Upton with Fishley; Weston Longville; Wood Dalling; Woodbastwick; Wroxham.

Parish Meetings in the authority's area: Attlebridge; Beeston St Andrew; Belaugh; Booton; Brandiston; Crostwick; Guestwick; Haveringland; Heydon; Morton on the Hill; Salle; Themelthorpe.

Town Councils in the authority's area: Aylsham; Reepham.

BROMSGROVE DISTRICT COUNCIL

www.bromsgrove.gov.uk

Principal Office
The Council House, Burcot Lane, Bromsgrove, Worcestershire B60 1AA
Telephone: (01527) 873232; FAX: (01527) 881414; DX 17279 Bromsgrove

Function	Chief Officer	Title	Location
Electoral Registration	Mr V Harrison	Head of Administrative Services	Council House
Environmental Health	Mr D R Williams	Director of Environmental Services	Council House
Finance	Mr J Charleson	Interim Director of Financial Services	Council House
Housing	Mr D Singh	Director of Housing Services	Council House
Legal Services	Mr R F Lewis	Corporate Director and District Secretary	Council House
Leisure	Mr R Hazlehurst	Director of Leisure Services	Council House

Local Land Charges	Mr V Harrison	Head of Administrative Services	Council House
Planning	Mr M Griffiths	Director of Planning Services	Council House
Purchasing & Supplies	Mr J Weir	Print Manager	Council House
Technical Services	Mr J Moody	Head of Community Safety & Engineering	Council House

Parish Councils in the authority's area: Alvechurch; Barnt Green; Belbroughton; Bentley Pauncefoot; Beoley; Bourneath; Catshill & North Marlbrook; Clent; Cofton Hackett; Dodford with Grafton; Finstall; Frankley; Hagley; Hunnington; Lickey & Blackwell; Lickey End; Romsley; Stoke Prior; Tutnall & Cobley; Wythall.

BROXBOURNE BOROUGH COUNCIL

www.broxbourne.gov.uk

Principal Office

Borough Offices, Bishops' College, Churchgate, Cheshunt, Waltham Cross, Herts EN8 9XQ
Telephone: (01992) 785555; FAX: (01992) 626917

Function	Chief Officer	Title	Location
Chief Executive	Mr M J Walker	Chief Executive Officer	Borough Offices
Electoral Registration	Mr M J Walker	Chief Executive Officer	Borough Offices
Environmental Health	Mr G Hirsch	Director of Environmental Services	Borough Offices
Finance	Mr M Hone	Director of Resources	Borough Offices
Housing	Mr J Giesen	Director of Housing	Borough Offices
Legal Services	Mr G Miles	Head of Legal Services	Borough Offices
Leisure	Mr J Fuller	Director of Leisure Services	Borough Offices
Local Land Charges	Mr M J Walker	Chief Executive Officer	Borough Offices
Planning	Mr G Hirsch	Director of Environmental Services	Borough Offices
Purchasing & Supplies	Mr M J Walker	Chief Executive Officer	Borough Offices
Technical Services	Mr G Hirsch	Director of Environmental Services	Borough Offices

Parish Councils & Parish Meetings in the authority's area: none.

Town Councils in the authority's area: none.

BROXTOWE BOROUGH COUNCIL

www.broxtowe.gov.uk

Principal Office

Council Offices, Foster Avenue, Beeston, Nottingham NG9 1AB
Telephone: (0115) 917 7777; FAX: (0115) 917 3131; DX 11663 Beeston

Chief Executive's Department; Directorate of Management Services

Town Hall, Foster Avenue, Beeston, Nottingham NG9 1AB
Telephone: (0115) 917 7777; FAX: (0115) 917 3030

Function	Chief Officer	Title	Location
Chief Executive	Mr M Brown	Chief Executive	Town Hall
Electoral Registration	Mr P D C Brown	Director of Legal & Admin Services	Council Offices
Environmental Health	Mr E J Czerniak	Director of Housing, Health & Leisure	Council Offices
Finance	Mr M Staley	Director of Finance	Council Offices
Housing	Mr E J Czerniak	Director of Housing, Health & Leisure	Council Offices
Legal Services	Mr P D C Brown	Director of Legal & Administrative Services	Council Offices
Leisure	Mr E J Czerniak	Director of Housing, Health & Leisure	Council Offices
Local Land Charges	Mr P D C Brown	Director of Legal & Administrative Services	Council Offices

Planning	Mr P Stone	Director of Planning & Community Development	Council Offices
Purchasing & Supplies	Mrs S Rodden	Assistant Director (Administration & Electoral Services)	Council Offices
Technical Services	Mr L McDonald	Acting Director of Technical & Works Services	Council Offices

Parish Councils in the authority's area: Awsworth; Brinsley; Cossall; Greasley; Nuthall; Trowell.

Town Councils in the authority's area: Eastwood; Kimberley; Stapleford.

BURNLEY BOROUGH COUNCIL

www.burnley.gov.uk

Principal Office
Town Hall, Manchester Road, Burnley, Lancashire BB11 1JA
Telephone: (01282) 425011; FAX: (01282) 438772

Community and Leisure Services; Development Department
Parker Lane Offices, Parker Lane, Burnley, Lancashire BB11 2DT
Telephone: (01282) 425011; FAX: (01282) 477266

Leisure Services
William Thompson Recreation Centre, Red Lion Street, Burnley, Lancashire BB11 2AE
Telephone: (01282) 425011; FAX: (01282) 664464

Function	Chief Officer	Title	Location
Chief Executive	Mrs G Taylor	Chief Executive	Town Hall
Electoral Registration	Mrs R Wynn	Head of Member Services	Town Hall
Environmental Health	Mr D Brown	Director of Environment	Parker Lane
Finance	Mr N Aves	Director of Resources	Town Hall
Legal Services	Mr N Aves	Director of Resources	Town Hall
Leisure	Mr M Cartledge	Director of Community Services	Parker Lane
Local Land Charges	Mr N Aves	Director of Resources	Town Hall
Planning	Mr D Brown	Director of Environment	Parker Lane
Technical Services	Mr D Brown	Director of Environment	Parker Lane

Parish Councils in the authority's area: Briercliffe; Cliviger; Dunnockshaw & Clowbridge; Habergham Eaves; Hapton; Ightenhill; Worsthorne-with-Hurstwood.

CAMBRIDGE CITY COUNCIL

www.cambridge.gov.uk

Principal Office
The Guildhall, Cambridge CB2 3QJ
Telephone: (01223) 457000; FAX: (01223) 457039; DX 5854 Cambridge

Community Services Department
Hobson House, 44 St Andrews Street, Cambridge CB2 3AS
Telephone: (01223) 457000; FAX: (01223) 457039

Finance Department; Personnel Department
10 Downing Street, Cambridge CB2 3DS
Telephone: (01223) 457000; FAX: (01223) 457039

Revenues Department; Environmental Health Department
Mandela House, 4 Regent Street, Cambridge CB2 1BY
Telephone: (01223) 457000; FAX: (01223) 457039

DISTRICT COUNCILS

Corn Exchange
Wheeler Street, Cambridge CB2 3QB
Telephone: (01223) 357851; FAX: (01223) 329074

Function	Chief Officer	Title	Location
Chief Executive	Mr R Hammond	Chief Executive	Guildhall
Environmental Health	Mr R Coey	Head of Environmental Health & Waste Strategy	Mandela Hse
Finance	Mr D Horspool	Director of Finance	10 Downing St
Housing	Mr D Poole	Director of Community Services	Hobson House
Legal Services	Mr S Pugh	Head of Legal and Democratic Services	Guildhall
Leisure	Mr N Cutting	Head of Arts & Entertainments	Corn Exchange
Planning	Mr P Studdert	Director of Environment & Planning	Guildhall

Parish Councils & Parish Meetings in the authority's area: none.

Town Councils in the authority's area: none.

CANNOCK CHASE DISTRICT COUNCIL

www.cannockchasedc.gov.uk

Principal Office
Civic Centre, PO Box 28, Beecroft Road, Cannock, Staffordshire WS11 1BG
Telephone: (01543) 462621; FAX: (01543) 462317; DX 16095 Cannock

Function	Chief Officer	Title	Location
Chief Executive	Mr S Brown	Chief Executive	Civic Centre
Electoral Registration	Mrs G Turner	Electoral Registration Officer	Civic Centre
Environmental Health	Mr S Shilvock	Head of Environmental Health	Civic Centre
Finance	Mr B Keane	Acting Head of Finance	Civic Centre
Housing	Mr I Tennant	Head of Housing	Civic Centre
Legal Services	Mrs A Kenny	Head of Legal	Civic Centre
Leisure	Ms K Bradford	Head of Leisure Services	Civic Centre
Planning	Mr P Garbett	Head, Planning Services	Civic Centre

Parish Councils in the authority's area: Brereton & Ravenhill; Bridgtown; Brindley Heath; Cannock Wood; Heath Hayes & Wimblebury; Hednesford; Norton Canes; Rugeley.

CANTERBURY CITY COUNCIL

www.canterbury.gov.uk

Principal Office
Military Road, Canterbury, Kent CT1 1YW
Telephone: (01227) 862000; FAX: (01227) 862020; DX 99713 Canterbury 3

Function	Chief Officer	Title	Location
Chief Executive	Mr C Carmichael	Chief Executive	Military Road
Electoral Registration	Mr C Carmichael	Chief Executive	Military Road
Finance	Mr J McDonald	Director of Corporate Services	Military Road
Housing	Ms V Coffey	Head of Housing & Community Development	Military Road
Legal Services	Mr M Ellender	Head of Legal & Democratic Services	Military Road
Local Land Charges	Mr David Reed	Director of Community & Environment Services	Military Road
Planning	Mr David Reed	Director of Community & Environment Services	Military Road
Purchasing & Supplies	Mr J McDonald	Director of Corporate Services	Military Road
Technical Services	Mr David Reed	Director of Community & Environment Services	Military Road

Parish Councils in the authority's area: Adisham; Barham; Bekesbourne with Patrixbourne; Bishopsbourne; Blean; Bridge; Chartham; Chestfield; Chislet; Hackington; Harbledown; Herne & Broomfield; Hoath; Ickham; Kingston; Littlebourne; Lower Hardres; Petham; Sturry; Thanington-Without; Upper Hardres; Waltham; Westbere; Wickhambreaux; Womenswold.

Town Councils in the authority's area: Fordwich.

CARADON DISTRICT COUNCIL

www.caradon.gov.uk

Principal Office

Luxstowe House, Liskeard, Cornwall PL14 3DZ
Telephone: (01579) 341000; FAX: (01579) 341001

Function	Chief Officer	Title	Location
Chief Executive	Mr Byron Davies	Chief Executive	Luxstowe Hse
Environmental Health	Mr Kevin Penny	Head of Housing & Environmental Services	Luxstowe Hse
Finance	Mrs Clare Glynn	Head of Financial Services	Luxstowe Hse
Housing	Mr Kevin Penny	Head of Housing & Environmental Services	Luxstowe Hse
Legal Services	Mrs Rita Diggens	Legal and Member Services Manager	Luxstowe Hse
Leisure	Mr S Besford-Foster	Head of Economic & Community Services	Luxstowe Hse
Planning	Mr Keith Rolfe	Head of Development & Building Control	Luxstowe Hse
Technical Services	Mr Jerry Masters	Head of Operations & Technical Services	Luxstowe Hse

Parish Councils in the authority's area: Antony; Botus Fleming; Calstock; Deviock; Dobwalls & Trewidland; Duloe; Landrake; Landulph; Lanreath; Lansallos; Lanteglos; Linkinhorne; Maker-with-Rame; Menheniot; Millbrook; Morval; Pelynt; Pillaton; Quethiock; St Cleer; St Dominic; St Germans; St Ive; St John; St Keyne; St Martin; St Mellion; St Neot; St Pinnock; St Veep; St Winnow; Sheviock; South Hill.

Parish Meetings in the authority's area: Boconnoc; Broadoak; Warleggan.

Town Councils in the authority's area: Callington; Liskeard; Looe; Saltash; Torpoint.

CARLISLE CITY COUNCIL

www.carlisle.gov.uk

Principal Office

Civic Centre, Carlisle, Cumbria CA3 8QG
Telephone: (01228) 817000; FAX: (01228) 817048; DX 63037 Carlisle

Function	Chief Officer	Title	Location
Chief Executive	P Stybelski	Town Clerk & Chief Executive	Civic Centre
Electoral Registration	P Stybelski	Town Clerk & Chief Executive	Civic Centre
Environmental Health	M Battersby	Head of Commercial & Technical Services	Civic Centre
Finance	A Brown	Head of Financial Services	Civic Centre
Housing	R Speirs	Head of Environmental Protection Services	Civic Centre
Legal Services	J M Egan	Head of Legal & Democratic Services	Civic Centre
Leisure	C Elliot	Head of Economic & Community Development Services	Civic Centre
Planning	M Battersby	Head of Commercial & Technical Services	Civic Centre
Purchasing & Supplies	M Battersby	Head of Commercial & Technical Services	Civic Centre
Technical Services	M Battersby	Head of Commercial & Technical Services	Civic Centre

DISTRICT COUNCILS

Parish Councils in the authority's area: Arthuret; Beaumont; Bewcastle; Brampton; Burgh-by-Sands; Burtholme; Carlatton; Castle Carrock; Cummersdale; Cumrew; Cumwhitton; Dalston; Denton Nether; Denton Upper; Farlam; Geltsdale; Hayton; Hethersgill; Irthington; Kingmoor; Kingwater; Kirkandrews; Kirklinton Middle; Midgeholme; Nicholforest; Orton; Rockcliffe; St Cuthbert Without; Scaleby; Solport; Stanwix Rural; Stapleton; Walton; Waterhead; Westlinton; Wetheral.

Parish Meetings in the authority's area: Askerton.

CARRICK DISTRICT COUNCIL

www.carrick.gov.uk

Principal Office
Carrick House, Pydar Street, Truro, Cornwall TR1 1EB
Telephone: (01872) 224400; FAX: (01872) 242104; DX 81232 Truro

Carrick Leisure Ltd.
Gyllyngdune Cottage, 41 Melvill Road, Falmouth TR11 4AR

Function	Chief Officer	Title	Location
Chief Executive	Mr J P Winskill	Chief Executive	Carrick Hse
Electoral Registration	Mr J P Winskill	Chief Executive	Carrick Hse
Environmental Health	Mr R Hooton	Head of Environmantal	Carrick Hse
Finance	Mr P West	Head of Finance	Carrick Hse
Housing	Ms F Turner	Head of Housing	Carrick Hse
Legal Services	Mrs D Hayes	Head of Legal & Democratic Services	Carrick Hse
Leisure	Mr A Horne	Managing Director (Carrick Leisure Ltd.)	Carrick Hse
Local Land Charges	Mrs D Hayes	Head of Legal & Democratic Services	Carrick Hse
Planning	Mr K Roberts	Head of Development	Carrick Hse
Purchasing & Supplies	Mrs J Kessell	Head of Human Resources	Carrick Hse
Technical Services	Mr B Dove	Head of ICT	Carrick Hse

Parish Councils in the authority's area: Chacewater; Cubert; Feock; Gerrans; Gwennap; Kea; Kenwyn; Ladock; Mylor; Perranarworthal; Perranzabuloe; Probus; Ruanlanihorne; St Agnes; St Allen; St Clement; St Erme; St Just in Roseland; St Michael Penkivel; St Newlyn East; Tregony; Veryan.

Parish Meetings in the authority's area: Cuby; Philleigh.

Town Councils in the authority's area: Falmouth; Penryn; Truro.

CASTLE MORPETH BOROUGH COUNCIL

www.castlemorpeth.gov.uk

Principal Office
Council Offices, The Kylins, Loansdean, Morpeth, Northumberland NE61 2EQ
Telephone: (01670) 535000; FAX: (01670) 535005

Function	Chief Officer	Title	Location
Chief Executive	Mr K Dunbar	Chief Executive	Council Offices
Finance	Mr B Scarr	Director of Resource & Property	Council Offices
Housing	[Vacant]	Housing Services Manager	Council Offices
Legal Services	Mrs S Row	Legal Services Manager	Council Offices
Leisure	Mr D Thompson	Assetts & Facilities Manager	Council Offices
Planning	Mr H Edmundson	Planning Services Manager	Council Offices
Purchasing & Supplies	Mrs J Brown	Business, Innovation & Procurement Manager	Council Offices

Parish Councils in the authority's area: Belsay; Capheaton; Cresswell; East Chevington; Ellington; Hartburn; Hebron; Heddon on the Wall; Hepscott; Longhirst; Longhorsley; Lynemouth; Matfen; Meldon; Mitford; Morpeth; Netherwitton; Pegswood; Ponteland; Stamfordham; Stannington; Thirston; Tritlington; Ulgham; Wallington; West Chevington; Whalton; Widdrington; Widdrington Station & Stobswood.

DISTRICT COUNCILS

CASTLE POINT BOROUGH COUNCIL

www.castlepoint.gov.uk

Principal Office
Council Offices, Kiln Road, Thundersley, Benfleet, Essex SS7 1TF
Telephone: (01268) 882200; FAX: (01268) 755332; DX 39603 Hadleigh

Purchasing & Supplies Department
The Farmhouse, Canvey Road, Canvey Island, Essex SS8 0QU
Telephone: (01268) 757103; FAX: (01268) 755527

Function	Chief Officer	Title	Location
Chief Executive	Mr B Rollinson	Chief Executive	Council Offices
Electoral Registration	John Riley	Corporate Policy & Electoral Officer	Council Offices
Environmental Health	Mr A R Longford	Director of Health & Housing	Council Offices
Finance	[Vacant]	Director of Central Services	Council Offices
Housing	Mr A R Longford	Director of Health & Housing	Council Offices
Legal Services	Mr A Smith	Head of Legal Services	Council Offices
Leisure	Mr T Galloway	Head of Leisure Services	Council Offices
Local Land Charges	Mr A Smith	Head of Legal Services	Council Offices
Planning	Mr I P Burchill	Director of Planning	Council Offices
Purchasing & Supplies	Mr J Jansen		The Farmhouse
Technical Services	Mr N Thomas	Director of Technical Services	Council Offices

Parish Councils & Parish Meetings in the authority's area: none.

Town Councils in the authority's area: none.

CHARNWOOD BOROUGH COUNCIL

www.charnwoodbc.gov.uk

Principal Office
Southfields Road, Loughborough, Leicestershire LE11 2TU
Telephone: (01509) 263151; FAX: (01509) 610626; DX 19628 Loughborough

Legal & Democratic Services Department
Macaulay House, 5 Cattlemarket, Loughborough LE11 2DH
Telephone: (01509) 263151; FAX: (01509) 211703

Loughborough Town Hall
Loughborough Town Hall, Market Place, Loughborough LE11 3EB

Function	Chief Officer	Title	Location
Chief Executive	Mr G Henshall	Acting Chief Executive	Sthfields Rd, LE11 2TR
Electoral Registration	Mr R Titterton	Administrative Officer	Macaulay Hse
Environmental Health	Mr R Fisk	Head of Environmental Services	Macaulay Hse
Finance	Mr I Geary	Head of Financial Services	Sthfields Rd, LE11 2TU
Housing	Mr J Foden	Head of Housing	Sthfields Rd, LE11 2TT
Legal Services	Mr J Bullock	Head of Legal & Democratic Services	Sthfields Rd, LE11 2TX
Leisure	Mr P Hogan	Head of Cultural Services	Loughborough Town Hall
Local Land Charges	Mr J Bullock	Head of Legal & Democratic Services	Sthfields Rd, LE11 2TX
Planning	Mr D Hankin	Head of Planning Services	Sthfields Rd, LE11 2TN
Purchasing & Supplies	Mr S Horner	Head of Information & Communication	Sthfields Rd, LE11 2TX
Technical Services	Mr P Rook	Head of Technical Services	Sthfields Rd, LE11 2TN

Parish Councils in the authority's area: Anstey; Barkby; Barrow-upon-Soar; Birstall; Burton-on-the-Wolds, Cotes & Prestweld; Cossington; East Goscote; Hathern; Hoton; Mountsorrel; Newtown Linford; Queniborough; Quorn; Rearsby; Rothley; Seagrave; Sileby; South Croxton;

Thrussington; Thurcaston & Cropston; Thurmaston; Walton-on-the-Wolds; Woodhouse; Wymeswold.

Parish Meetings in the authority's area: Beeby; Ratcliffe on the Wreake; Swithland; Ulverscroft; Wanlip.

Town Councils in the authority's area: Shepshed; Syston.

CHELMSFORD BOROUGH COUNCIL

www.chelmsfordbc.gov.uk

Principal Office

Civic Centre, Duke Street, Chelmsford, Essex CM1 1JE
Telephone: (01245) 606606; FAX: (01245) 606310

Function	Chief Officer	Title	Location
Chief Executive	Mr M Easteal	Chief Executive	Civic Centre
Electoral Registration	Mr A Battley	Democracy Team Manager	Civic Centre
Environmental Health	Mr S Martin	Head of Environmental Services	Civic Centre
Finance	Mr C Willetts	Head of Financial Services	Civic Centre
Housing	Mrs P Pennifold	Head of Strategic Housing	Civic Centre
Legal Services	Mrs S Deval	Head of Legal Services	Civic Centre
Leisure	Mr B Mella	Head of Leisure & Cultural Services	Civic Centre
Local Land Charges	Mrs S Deval	Head of Legal Services	Civic Centre
Planning	Mr D Green	Head of Planning	Civic Centre
Technical Services	Mr C Botfield	Head of Municipal Engineering Services	Civic Centre

Parish Councils in the authority's area: Boreham; Broomfield; Chignal; Danbury; East Hanningfield; Galleywood; Good Easter; Great Baddow; Great & Little Leighs; Great Waltham; Highwood; Little Baddow; Little Waltham; Margaretting; Pleshey; Rettendon; Roxwell; Runwell; Sandon; South Hanningfield; Springfield; Stock; West Hanningfield; Woodham Ferrers & Bicknacre; Writtle.

Parish Meetings in the authority's area: Mashbury.

Town Councils in the authority's area: South Woodham Ferrers.

CHELTENHAM BOROUGH COUNCIL

www.cheltenham.gov.uk

Principal Office

Municipal Offices, Promenade, Cheltenham, Gloucestershire GL50 1PP
Telephone: (01242) 262626; FAX: (01242) 264304; DX 7406 Cheltenham 1

Function	Chief Officer	Title	Location
Chief Executive	Mrs C Laird	Managing Director	Municipal Offices
Electoral Registration	Mr G Ford	Assistant Director (Legal & Democratic Services)	Municipal Offices
Environmental Health	Mr G Rowlinson	Assistant Director (Public Protection)	Municipal Offices
Finance	Mr D Perry	Group Director (Economic & Business Improvement)	Municipal Offices
Housing	Mr P Davies	Housing Manager	Municipal Offices
Legal Services	Mr G Ford	Assistant Director (Legal & Democratic Services)	Municipal Offices
Leisure	Mr C Huckle	Group Director (Social & Community)	Municipal Offices
Local Land Charges	Mr G Lewis	Assistant Director (Built Environment)	Municipal Offices
Planning	Mr G Lewis	Assistant Director (Built Environment)	Municipal Offices
Purchasing & Supplies	Mr T Byng	Head of Property & Asset Management	Municipal Offices
Technical Services	Mr M Ibbitson	Assistant Director (Information Communication Technology)	Municipal Offices

DISTRICT COUNCILS

Parish Councils in the authority's area: Charlton Kings; Leckhampton with Warden Hill; Prestbury; Swindon; Up Hatherly.

CHERWELL DISTRICT COUNCIL

www.cherwell-dc.gov.uk

Principal Office

Bodicote House, Bodicote, Banbury, Oxfordshire OX15 4AA

Telephone: (01295) 252535; FAX: (01295) 270028; DX 24224 Banbury

Function	Chief Officer	Title	Location
Chief Executive	G J Handley	Chief Executive	Bodicote Hse
Electoral Registration	P Rooke	Chief Administration Officer	Bodicote Hse
Environmental Health	Mrs E Edwards	Head of Environmental Services	Bodicote Hse
Finance	G Simcox	District Treasurer	Bodicote Hse
Housing	Mrs K Hindle	Head of Housing Services	Bodicote Hse
Legal Services	J Scarborough	Solicitor to the Council	Bodicote Hse
Leisure	D Ian Davies	Head of Leisure Services	Bodicote Hse
Local Land Charges	P Rooke	Chief Administration Officer	Bodicote Hse
Planning	A Jones	Head of Planning & Development Services	Bodicote Hse
Purchasing & Supplies	P Rooke	Chief Administration Officer	Bodicote Hse
Technical Services	D Marriott	Property & Technical Services Manager	Bodicote Hse

Parish Councils in the authority's area: Adderbury; Ambrosden; Ardley; Arncott; Barford St Michael & St John; Begbroke; Blackthorn; Bletchingdon; Bloxham; Bodicote; Bourton; Broughton; Bucknell; Caversfield; Charlton on Otmoor; Chesterton; Claydon with Clattercott; Cottisford; Cropredy; Deddington; Drayton; Duns Tew; Epwell; Finmere; Fringford; Fritwell; Gosford & Water Eaton; Hanwell; Hethe; Hook Norton; Horley; Hornton; Horton-cum-Studley; Islip; Kidlington; Kirtlington; Launton; Lower Heyford; Merton; Middleton Stoney; Milcombe; Mollington; North Newington; Piddington; Shenington with Alkerton; Shipton on Cherwell & Thrupp; Shutford; Sibford Ferris; Sibford Gower; Somerton; Souldern; South Newington; Steeple Aston; Stoke Lyne; Stratton Audley; Swalcliffe; Tadmarton; Upper Heyford; Wardington; Wendlebury; Weston on the Green; Wigginton; Wroxton; Yarnton.

Parish Meetings in the authority's area: Fencott & Murcott; Godington; Hampton Gay & Poyle; Hardwick with Tusmore; Middle Aston; Milton; Mixbury; Newton Purcell with Shelswell; Noke; North Aston; Oddington; Prescote.

Town Councils in the authority's area: Banbury; Bicester.

CHESTER CITY COUNCIL

www.chestercc.gov.uk

Principal Office

The Forum, Chester, Cheshire CH1 2HS

Telephone: (01244) 324324; FAX: (01244) 324338

Function	Chief Officer	Title	Location
Chief Executive	Paul Durham	Chief Executive	The Forum
Environmental Health	Mike East	Strategic Director (Community Services)	The Forum
Finance	Jim Cassin	Strategic Director (Resources)	The Forum
Housing	Andrew Farrall	Strategic Director (Development)	The Forum
Legal Services	Jim Cassin	Strategic Director (Resources)	The Forum
Leisure	Mike East	Strategic Director (Community Services)	The Forum
Local Land Charges	Andrew Farrall	Strategic Director (Development)	The Forum
Planning	Andrew Farrall	Strategic Director (Development)	The Forum

DISTRICT COUNCILS

Parish Councils in the authority's area: Aldford, Saighton & District; Ashton; Backford & District; Barrow; Beeston; Bickley; Broxton & District; Burwardsley; Capenhurst & Ledsham; Christleton; Churton; Clotton Hoofield; Coddington & District; Dodleston & District; Duddon; Dunham Hill & Hapsford; Eaton, Eccleston & Claverton; Elton; Farndon; Foulk Stapleford; Great Boughton; Guilden Sutton; Hampton, Edge & Larkton; Handley & District; Huntington; Huxley; Kelsall; Lea-by-Backford; Little Stanney & District; Littleton; Malpas; Mickle Trafford & District; Mollington; Mouldsworth; Poulton & Pulford; Puddington & District; Rowton; Saughall & Shotwick Park; Shocklach & District; Oviatt; Tarvin; Tattenhall & District; Thornton-le-Moors; Threapwood; Tilston; Tiverton; Upton-by-Chester; Waverton.

Parish Meetings in the authority's area: Agden; Chorlton; Cuddington; Tushingham, Bradley & Macefen.

CHESTERFIELD BOROUGH COUNCIL

www.chesterfield.gov.uk

Principal Office
Town Hall, Rose Hill, Chesterfield, Derbyshire S40 1LP
Telephone: (01246) 345345; FAX: (01246) 345252; DX 12356 Chesterfield

Function	Chief Officer	Title	Location
Chief Executive	Mr D R Shaw	Town Clerk & Chief Executive	Town Hall
Electoral Registration	Mr A Walls	Electoral Registration Officer	Town Hall
Environmental Health	Mr H Bowen	Corporate Director of Community Services	Town Hall
Finance	Mr R Earlam	Corporate Director of Resources	Town Hall
Housing	Mr H Bowen	Corporate Director of Community Services	Town Hall
Legal Services	Mr R Earlam	Corporate Director of Resources	Town Hall
Leisure	Mr H Bowen	Corporate Director of Community Services	Town Hall
Local Land Charges	Ms J Lines	Land Charges Clerk	Town Hall
Planning	Mr J Wrightson	Corporate Director of Regeneration	Town Hall

Parish Councils in the authority's area: Brimington.

Town Councils in the authority's area: Staveley.

CHESTER-LE-STREET DISTRICT COUNCIL

www.chester-le-street.gov.uk

Principal Office
Civic Centre, Newcastle Road, Chester-le-Street, Co Durham DH3 3UT
Telephone: (0191) 387 1919; FAX: (0191) 387 1583

Function	Chief Officer	Title	Location
Chief Executive	[Vacant]	Chief Executive	Civic Centre
Electoral Registration	Mr C Turnbull	Democratic Services Officer	Civic Centre
Environmental Health	Mr P Jenkins	Environmental Health Manager	Civic Centre
Finance	Mr D Shingleton	Director of Finance	Civic Centre
Housing	Mr B J O'Doherty	Housing Services Manager	Civic Centre
Legal Services	Mrs P Wilson	Legal & Democratic Services Manager	Civic Centre
Leisure	Mr I Simon	Leisure Services Manager	Civic Centre
Local Land Charges	Mrs P Wilson	Legal & Democratic Services Manager	Civic Centre
Planning	Mr T Watson	Planning Services Manager	Civic Centre
Purchasing & Supplies	Mr D Wright	Purchasing Officer	Civic Centre
Technical Services	Mr G Mansbridge	Economic Development Manager	Civic Centre

Parish Councils in the authority's area: Bournmoor; Edmondsley; Great Lumley; Kimblesworth & Plawsworth; Little Lumley; North Lodge; Ouston; Pelton; Sacriston; Urpeth; Waldridge.

DISTRICT COUNCILS

CHICHESTER DISTRICT COUNCIL

www.chichester.gov.uk

Principal Office

East Pallant House, East Pallant, Chichester, West Sussex PO19 1TY
Telephone: (01243) 785166; FAX: (01243) 776766; DX 30340 Chichester

Function	Chief Officer	Title	Location
Chief Executive	J S Marsland	Chief Executive	East Pallant Hse
Electoral Registration	G A Robertson	Head of Democratic Services	East Pallant Hse
Environmental Health	J Kingdon	Head of Environmental Health Services	East Pallant Hse
Finance	D Grove	District Treasurer	East Pallant Hse
Housing	A Jobling	Head of Community Services	East Pallant Hse
Legal Services	M J Kelley	District Solicitor	East Pallant Hse
Leisure	G Mayhew	Head of Cultural Services	East Pallant Hse
Local Land Charges	P Over	Head of Property Services	East Pallant Hse
Planning	A J Howes	Deputy Chief Executive (Environment and Economic Services)	East Pallant Hse
Purchasing & Supplies	G A Robertson	Head of Democratic Services	East Pallant Hse
Technical Services	P Over	Head of Property Services	East Pallant Hse

Parish Councils in the authority's area: Appledram; Bepton; Bignor; Birdham; Bosham; Boxgrove; Bury; Chidham; Cocking; Compton; Donnington; Duncton; Earnley; Easebourne; East Dean; East Lavington; East Wittering & Bracklesham; Ebernoe; Elsted & Treyford; Fernhurst; Fishbourne; Fittleworth; Funtington; Graffham; Harting; Heyshott; Hunston; Kirdford; Lavant; Linchmere; Lodsworth; Loxwood; Lurgashall; Milland; North Mundham; Northchapel; Oving; Petworth; Plaistow & Ifold; Rogate; Sidlesham; Singleton; Southbourne; Stedham with Iping; Stoughton; Sutton; Tangmere; Tillington; Trotton with Chithurst; West Dean; West Itchenor; West Lavington; West Wittering; Westbourne; Westhampnett; Wisborough Green; Woolbeding.

Parish Meetings in the authority's area: Barlavington; Eartham; Linch; Marden; Stopham; Upwaltham; West Thorney.

Town Councils in the authority's area: Chichester City; Midhurst; Selsey.

CHILTERN DISTRICT COUNCIL

www.chiltern.gov.uk

Principal Office

Council Offices, King George V Road, Amersham, Buckinghamshire HP6 5AW
Telephone: (01494) 729000; FAX: (01494) 586506; DX 50711 Amersham

Function	Chief Officer	Title	Location
Chief Executive	Mr A Goodrum	Chief Executive	Council Offices
Electoral Registration	Mr A Goodrum	Chief Executive	Council Offices
Environmental Health	Mrs G Gowing	Director of Planning & The Environment	Council Offices
Finance	Mr P Short	Director of Corporate Services	Council Offices
Housing	Mrs G Gowing	Director of Planning & The Environment	Council Offices
Legal Services	Mr H Patterson	Legal Manager	Council Offices
Local Land Charges	Mr H Patterson	Legal Manager	Council Offices
Planning	Mrs G Gowing	Director of Planning & The Environment	Council Offices

Parish Councils in the authority's area: Ashley Green; Chalfont St Giles; Chalfont St Peter; Chartridge; Chenies; Chesham Bois; Cholesbury cum St Leonards; Coleshill; Great Missenden; Latimer; The Lee; Little Missenden; Penn; Seer Green.

Town Councils in the authority's area: Amersham; Chesham.

CHORLEY BOROUGH COUNCIL

www.chorley.gov.uk

Principal Office

Town Hall, Market Street, Chorley, Lancashire PR7 1DP
Telephone: (01257) 515151; FAX: (01257) 515150

Financial Services; Housing Services

Civic Offices, Union Street, Chorley PR7 1AL
Telephone: (01257) 515151

Leisure Services

The Coach House, Duxbury Hall Road, Duxbury Park, Chorley PR7 4AT
Telephone: (01257) 515542; FAX: (01257) 515544

Policy & Community Services

Council Offices, Gillibrand Street, Chorley PR7 2EL
Telephone: (01257) 515151

Administrative Services

Bengal Street, Chorley PR7 1SA
Telephone: (01257) 515622; FAX: (01257) 515623

Function	Chief Officer	Title	Location
Chief Executive	Mr J W Davies	Chief Executive	Town Hall
Environmental Health	Mr J Lechmere	Head of Environmental Services	Civic Offices
Finance	Mr G Graham	Director of Finance	Civic Offices
Housing	Mr S Lomas	Head of Housing Services	Civic Offices
Legal Services	Mrs R Lyon	Director of Legal Services	Town Hall
Leisure	Mr D Jones	Head of Leisure Services	Coach House
Local Land Charges	Mrs R Lyon	Director of Legal Services	Town Hall
Planning	Mr A Croston	Head of Planning Services	Council Offices
Purchasing & Supplies	Mrs J Hinds	Central Buyer	Bengal Street

Parish Councils in the authority's area: Adlington; Anderton; Anglezarke; Astley Village; Bretherton; Brindle; Charnock Richard; Clayton-le-Woods; Coppull; Croston; Cuerden; Eccleston; Euxton; Heapey; Heath Charnock; Heskin; Hoghton Mawdesley; Rivington; Ulnes Walton; Wheelton; Whittle-le-Woods; Withnell.

CHRISTCHURCH BOROUGH COUNCIL

www.christchurch.gov.uk

Principal Office

Civic Offices, Christchurch, Dorset BH23 1AZ
Telephone: (01202) 495000; FAX: (01202) 482200

Function	Chief Officer	Title	Location
Chief Executive	M Turvey	Chief Executive & Town Clerk	Civic Offices
Electoral Registration	P Jones	Senior Administrative Officer	Civic Offices
Environmental Health	S Douglas-Beveridge	Environmental Health Manager	Civic Offices
Finance	K White	Director of Resources	Civic Offices
Housing	T Jaques	Head of Planning & Environmental Services	Civic Offices
Legal Services	D Fairbairn	Borough Solicitor	Civic Offices
Leisure	A Ottaway	Leisure Services Manager	Civic Offices
Local Land Charges	D Fairbairn	Borough Solicitor	Civic Offices
Planning	N Davies	Director of Planning & Environmental Services	Civic Offices
Purchasing & Supplies	R Morris	Head of Central Services	Civic Offices
Technical Services	P Barker	Head of Operations	Civic Offices

Parish Councils in the authority's area: Burton; Hurn.

DISTRICT COUNCILS

CLEETHORPES BOROUGH COUNCIL
Cleethorpes Borough Council was abolished on 31 March 1996; see now North East Lincolnshire Council.

COLCHESTER BOROUGH COUNCIL

www.colchester.gov.uk

Principal Office
PO Box 884, Town Hall, Colchester, Essex CO1 1FR
Telephone: (01206) 282222; FAX: (01206) 282288; DX 3612 Colchester 1

Function	Chief Officer	Title	Location
Chief Executive	Mrs A Hill	Chief Executive	Town Hall
Electoral Registration	Ms V Hemarpstead	Electoral Services Manager	Town Hall
Environmental Health	Ms N George	Head of Planning & Protection	Town Hall
Finance	Mr J Herbert	Head of Financial Services	Town Hall
Housing	Mr A Murray;	Housing Strategy Manager;	
	Mr P Adams	Head of Colchester Borough Homes	Town Hall
Legal Services	Mr A Weavers	Legal & Democratic Services Manager & Monitoring Officer	Town Hall
Leisure	Mr K Nicholson	Head of Leisure Services	Town Hall
Local Land Charges	Mr S Clarke	Head of Economic & Social Regeneration	Town Hall
Planning	Ms N George	Head of Planning & Protection	Town Hall
Purchasing & Supplies	Ms L Goodwin	Head of Democratic & Organisational Services	Town Hall
Technical Services	Mr J Simpson	Head of Street Services	Town Hall

Parish Councils in the authority's area: Abberton & Langenhoe; Aldham; Birch; Boxted; Chappel; Copford with Easthorpe; Dedham; East Donyland; East Mersea; Eight Ash Green; Fingringhoe; Fordham; Great Horkesley; Great Tey; Langham; Layer Breton; Layer de la Haye; Layer Marney; Little Horkesley; Marks Tey; Messing cum Inworth; Mount Bures; Stanway; Tiptree; Wakes Colne; West Bergholt; Winstree Hundred; Wormingford.

Town Councils in the authority's area: West Mersea; Wivenhoe.

CONGLETON BOROUGH COUNCIL

www.congleton.gov.uk

Sandbach Office
"Westfields", Middlewich Road, Sandbach, Cheshire CW11 1HZ
Telephone: (01270) 763231; FAX: (01270) 768460; DX 15658 Sandbach

Alsager Office
Council Offices, Lawton Road, Alsager, Stoke-on-Trent ST7 2AE
Telephone: (01270) 763231; FAX: (01270) 882463

Congleton Office
Municipal Offices, Market Square, Congleton CW12 1EX
Telephone: (01260) 274821; FAX: (01260) 280854

Function	Chief Officer	Title	Location
Chief Executive	Glyn Chambers	Chief Executive	Westfields
Electoral Registration	Nick Shatwell	Principal Electoral Services	Westfields
Environmental Health	John Gerring	Environmental Health Manager	Westfields
Finance	Donald Lowe	Head of Finance & Support Services Director	Municipal Offices
Housing	Robert Schaley	Housing Manager	Council Offices
Legal Services	Margaret Ingram	Head of Law & Administration	Westfields
Leisure	Bob Hardiker	Head of Local Services	Westfields
Local Land Charges	Margaret Ingram	Head of Law & Administration	Westfields

DISTRICT COUNCILS

| Planning | Geoff Allen | Head of Regulatory Services | Westfields |
| Technical Services | David Dingle | Public Services Director | Westfields |

Parish Councils in the authority's area: Arclid; Betchton; Bradwall; Brereton; Church Lawton; Cranage; Goostrey; Hassall; Holmes Chapel; Hulme Walfield; Moston; Newbold Astbury-cum-Moreton; Odd Rode; Smallwood; Somerford; Somerford Booths; Swettenham; Twemlow.

Town Councils in the authority's area: Alsager; Congleton; Holmes Chapel; Middlewich; Sandbach.

COPELAND BOROUGH COUNCIL

www.copelandbc.gov.uk

Principal Office

Council Offices, Catherine Street, Whitehaven, Cumbria CA28 7NY
Telephone: (01946) 852585; FAX: (01946) 852791; DX 62904 Whitehaven

Whitehaven Commercial Park

Whitehaven Commercial Park, Moresby Parks, Whitehaven, Cumbria CA28 8YD

Function	Chief Officer	Title	Location
Executive	Dr J Stanforth	General Manager	Council Offices
Electoral Registration	Mr M Jepson	Chief Legal Officer	Council Offices
Environmental Health	[Vacant]	Head of Development & Environment	Council Offices
Finance	Mrs M McDonald	Chief Finance Officer	Council Offices
Housing	Mr R Morgan	Chief Housing Officer	Council Offices
Legal Services	Mr M Jepson	Chief Legal Officer	Council Offices
Leisure	Mr P Sutton	Head of Leisure Services	Whitehaven
Local Land Charges	Mr M Jepson	Chief Legal Officer	Council Offices
Planning	Mr A Pomfret	Principal Planning Officer	Council Offices
Purchasing & Supplies	Mr J Parkinson	Purchasing Officer	Whitehaven
Technical Services	Mr C Lloyd	Head of Contracts, Projects & Valuation	Council Offices

Parish Councils in the authority's area: Arlecdon & Frizington; Bootle; Distington; Drigg & Carleton; Ennerdale & Kinniside; Eskdale; Gosforth; Haile & Wilton; Irton & Santon; Lamplugh; Lowca; Lowside Quarter; Millom Without; Moresby; Muncaster; Parton; Ponsonby; St Bees; St Bridget's Beckermet; St John's Beckermet; Seascale; Waberthwaite; Weddicar; Whicham.

Parish Meetings in the authority's area: Wasdale; Ulpha.

Town Councils in the authority's area: Cleator Moor; Egremont; Millom.

CORBY BOROUGH COUNCIL

www.corby.gov.uk

Principal Office

Grosvenor House, George Street, Corby, Northamptonshire NN17 1QB
Telephone: (01536) 402551; FAX: (01536) 400200

Function	Chief Officer	Title	Location
Chief Executive	Chris Mallender	Chief Executive	Grosvenor Hse
Electoral Registration	Tim Marren	Head of Service – Performance Management, E-Government & Scrutiny	Grosvenor Hse
Environmental Health	Carl Grimmer	Head of Service – Street Scene, Environment & Technical	Grosvenor Hse
Finance	Paul Hymers	Head of Service – Financial Services	Grosvenor Hse
Housing	Anthony Curren	Head of Service – Housing Services	Grosvenor Hse

Legal Services	Michelle Grove	Head of Service – Legal & Asset Management	Grosvenor Hse
Leisure	Chris Stephenson	Head of Service – Culture & Community	Grosvenor Hse
Local Land Charges	Michelle Grove	Head of Service – Legal & Asset Management	Grosvenor Hse
Planning	Norman Stronach	Head of Service – Planning & Economical Regeneration	Grosvenor Hse
Purchasing & Supplies	Paul Hymers	Head of Service – Financial Services	Grosvenor Hse
Technical Services	Carl Grimmer	Head of Service – Street Scene, Environment & Technical	Grosvenor Hse

Parish Councils in the authority's area: Cottingham; East Carlton; Gretton; Middleton; Rockingham; Stanion; Weldon.

COTSWOLD DISTRICT COUNCIL

www.cotswold.gov.uk

Principal Office
Trinity Road, Cirencester, Gloucestershire GL7 1PX
Telephone: (01285) 623000; FAX: (01285) 623906

Function	Chief Officer	Title	Location
Chief Executive	Mr R Austin	Chief Executive	Trinity Road
Electoral Registration	Mrs S Dalby	Electoral & Administration Officer	Trinity Road
Environmental Health	Mr A Grant	Corporate Director	Trinity Road
Finance	Mr R Austin	Chief Executive	Trinity Road
Housing	Mr A Grant	Corporate Director	Trinity Road
Legal Services	Mr J Ellis	Head of Legal Services	Trinity Road
Leisure	Mr A Grant	Corporate Director	Trinity Road
Local Land Charges	Cheryl Bellis	Land Charges Manager	Trinity Road
Planning	Mr K Cooper	Corporate Director	Trinity Road
Technical Services	Mr R Garner	IT Client Officer	Trinity Road

Parish Councils in the authority's area: Aldsworth; Ampney Crucis; Andoversford; Avening; Bagendon; Barrington; Baunton; Beverston; Bibury; Bledington; Blockley; Bourton-on-the-Hill; Bourton-on-the-Water; Boxwell with Leighterton; Brimpsfield; Broadwell; Chedworth; Cherington; Coates; Coberley; Cold Aston; Coln St Aldwyns; Coln St Dennis; Condicote; Cowley; Cutsdean; Daglingworth; Didmarton; Dowdeswell; Down Ampney; Driffield; The Duntisbournes; Eastleach; Ebrington; Elkstone; Evenlode; Great Rissington; Guiting Power; Hatherop; Kemble; Kempsford; Kingscote; Little Rissington; Long Newnton; Longborough; Lower Slaughter; Maugersbury; Meysey Hampton; Mickleton; Naunton; North Cerney; Oddington; Poulton; Preston; Quenington; Rendcomb; Rodmarton; Sapperton; Sevenhampton; Sherborne; Shipton Moyne; Shipton Oliffe; Siddington; Somerford Keynes; South Cerney; Southrop; Stow-on-the-Wold; Swell; Temple Guiting; Tetbury Upton; Todenham; Upper Slaughter; Weston-Sub-Edge; Westonbirt with Lasborough; Willersey; Winstone; Withington; Wyck Rissington.

Parish Meetings in the authority's area: Adlestrop; Ampney St Mary; Ampney St Peter; Ashley; Aston Subedge; Barnsley; Batsford; Clapton-on-the-Hill; Colesbourne; Compton Abdale; Donnington; Edgeworth; Farmington; Hampnett; Hazleton; Icomb; Notgrove; Ozleworth; Poole Keynes; Saintbury; Sezincote; Syde; Turkdean; Westcote; Whittington; Windrush; Winson; Yanworth.

Town Councils in the authority's area: Chipping Campden; Cirencester; Fairford; Lechlade; Moreton-in-Marsh; Northleach with Eastington; Tetbury.

CRAVEN DISTRICT COUNCIL

www.cravendc.gov.uk

Principal Office
Council Offices, Granville Street, Skipton, North Yorkshire BD23 1PS
Telephone: (01756) 700600; FAX: (01756) 700658; DX 21767 Skipton

Finance Unit
Town Hall, High Street, Skipton BD23 1AH
Telephone: (01756) 700600; FAX: (01756) 700657

Function	Chief Officer	Title	Location
Chief Executive	Gill Dixon	Chief Executive	Granville Street
Electoral Registration	Colin Iveson	Electoral Registration Officer	Granville Street
Finance	Vince Green	Head of Finance	Town Hall
Legal Services	[Vacant]	Head of Legal & Democratic Services	Granville Street
Leisure	[Vacant]	Head of Operational Services	Granville Street
Local Land Charges	Duncan Hartley	Head of Planning	Granville Street
Planning	Duncan Hartley	Head of Planning	Granville Street

Parish Councils in the authority's area: Appletreewick; Austwick; Bolton Abbey; Bradleys Both; Buckden; Burton-in-Lonsdale; Carleton; Clapham-cum-Newby; Coniston Cold; Cononley; Cowling; Draughton; Embsay with Eastby; Farnhill; Gargrave; Giggleswick; Glusburn; Grassington; Hebden; Hellifield; Horton-in-Ribblesdale; Ingleton; Kettlewell with Starbotton; Kirkby Malhamdale; Langcliffe; Linton; Long Preston; Lothersdale; Ribble Banks; Stainforth; Sutton-in-Craven; Thornton-in-Craven; Thornton-in-Lonsdale; Threshfield.

Parish Meetings in the authority's area: Airton; Arncliffe; Bank Newton; Barden; Beamsley; Bordley; Broughton; Burnsall; Calton; Conistone with Kilnsey; Cracoe; Elslack; Eshton; Flasby with Winterburn; Halton East; Halton Gill; Halton West; Hanlith; Hartlington; Hawkswick; Hazlewood with Storiths; Hetton; Kildwick; Kirkby Malham; Lawkland; Litton; Malham; Malham Moor; Martons Both; Nappa; Otterburn; Rathmell; Rylstone; Scosthrop; Stirton with Thorlby; Swinden; Thorpe; Wigglesworth.

Town Councils in the authority's area: Bentham; Settle; Skipton.

CRAWLEY BOROUGH COUNCIL

www.crawley.gov.uk

Principal Office
Town Hall, The Boulevard, Crawley, West Sussex RH10 1UZ
Telephone: (01293) 438000; FAX: (01293) 511803; Minicom: (01293) 405202; DX 57139 Crawley

Function	Chief Officer	Title	Location
Chief Executive	Mr M Coughlin	Chief Executive	Town Hall
Electoral Registration	Mr M Coughlin	Chief Executive	Town Hall
Environmental Health	Mr J I Redwood	Director of Environment & Housing	Town Hall
Finance	Mr D Covill	Director of Resources	Town Hall
Housing	Mr J I Redwood	Director of Environment & Housing	Town Hall
Legal Services	Mr D Covill	Director of Resources	Town Hall
Leisure	Mr J Thraves	Director of Community Services	Town Hall
Planning	Mr J I Redwood	Director of Environment & Housing	Town Hall
Purchasing & Supplies	Mr D Covill	Director of Resources	Town Hall
Technical Services	Mr J Thraves	Director of Community Services	Town Hall

Parish Councils & Parish Meetings in the authority's area: none.

Town Councils in the authority's area: none.

DISTRICT COUNCILS

CREWE & NANTWICH BOROUGH COUNCIL

www.crewe-nantwich.gov.uk

Principal Offices
Municipal Buildings, Earle Street, Crewe, Cheshire CW1 2BJ
Telephone: (01270) 537777; FAX: (01270) 537605

Delamere House, Delamere Street, Crewe CW1 2JZ
Telephone: (01270) 537777; FAX: (01270) 537756

Direct Services
Pyms Lane Depot, Crewe, Cheshire CW1 3PJ
Telephone: (01270) 537823; FAX: (01270) 537806

Function	Chief Officer	Title	Location
Chief Executive	A Wenham	Chief Executive	Municipal Bldgs
Environmental Health	D Cook	Environment and Development Director	Municipal Bldgs
Finance	J Cross	Treasury and Corporate Support Director	Delamere Hse
Housing	D Cook	Environment and Development Director	Municipal Bldgs
Legal Services	R Graham	Legal Director	Delamere Hse
Leisure	D Marren	Direct Services Director	Pyms Lane Dep
Planning	D Cook	Environment and Development Director	Municipal Bldgs

Parish Councils in the authority's area: Acton, Edleston & Henhull; Alpraham; Audlem; Barthomley; Bickerton & Egerton; Brindley & Faddiley; Buerton; Bulkeley & Ridley; Bunbury; Burland; Calveley; Cholmondeley & Chorley; Cholmondeston & Wettenhall; Church Minshull; Crewe Green; Dodcott-cum-Wilkesley; Doddington, Blakenhall, Bridgemere, Checkley-cum-Wrinehill, Hunsterston & Lea; Hankelow; Haslington; Hatherton & Walgherton; Haughton; Hough & Chorlton; Marbury-cum-Quoisley, Norbury & Wirswall; Minshull Vernon, Leighton & Woolstanwood; Nantwich; Newhall; Peckforton; Rope; Shavington-cum-Gresty; Sound, Austerson, Baddiley, Baddington, Broomhall & Coole Pilate; Spurstow; Stapeley & Batherton; Stoke & Hurleston; Wardle; Warmingham; Weston & Basford; Willaston; Wistaston; Worleston, Poole, Aston-Juxta-Mondrum; Wrenbury-cum-Frith; Wybunbury.

DACORUM BOROUGH COUNCIL

www.dacorum.gov.uk

Principal Office
Civic Centre, Marlowes, Hemel Hempstead, Hertfordshire HP1 1HH
Telephone: (01442) 228000; FAX: (01442) 228995; DX 8804 Hemel Hempstead

Function	Chief Officer	Title	Location
Chief Executive	Daniel Zammit	Chief Executive	Civic Centre
Electoral Registration	Michelle Evans-Riches	Member Services Manager	Civic Centre
Finance	Richard Micklewright	Head of Finance	Civic Centre
Housing	Colin Farrar	Head of Housing	Civic Centre
Legal Services	Steven Baker	Solicitor to the Council	Civic Centre
Leisure	[Vacant]	Head of Cultural Services	Civic Centre
Local Land Charges	Barbara Ansell		Civic Centre
Planning	Graham Winwright	Head of Planning & Regeneration	Civic Centre
Purchasing & Supplies	Ben Hosier		Civic Centre

Parish Councils in the authority's area: Aldbury; Bovingdon; Chipperfield; Flamstead; Flaunden; Great Gaddesden; Kings Langley; Little Gaddesden; Markyate; Nash Mills; Nettleden with Potten End; Northchurch; Tring Rural; Wigginton.

Town Councils in the authority's area: Berkhamsted; Tring.

DARLINGTON BOROUGH COUNCIL

Darlington Borough Council became a unitary authority on 1 April 1997.

DISTRICT COUNCILS

DARTFORD BOROUGH COUNCIL

www.dartford.gov.uk

Principal Office

Civic Centre, Home Gardens, Dartford, Kent DA1 1DR
Telephone: (01322) 343434; FAX: (01322) 343422

Function	Chief Officer	Title	Location
Electoral Registration	Mr Kenneth Lawrie	Cabinet Secretary	Civic Centre
Environmental Health	Mr Rob Scott	Director of Environment	Civic Centre
Finance	Mr Steve Brooks	Head of Finance & Human Resources	Civic Centre
Housing	Mr Rob Scott; Mr Chris Oliver	Director of Environment; Executive Director	Civic Centre Civic Centre
Legal Services	Ms Marie Kelly-Stone	Head of Legal Services	Civic Centre
Leisure	Mr Bob Penny	Recreation Services Manager	Civic Centre
Local Land Charges	Ms Marie Kelly-Stone	Head of Legal Services	Civic Centre
Planning	Mr Rob Scott	Director of Environment	Civic Centre
Purchasing & Supplies	Ms Catherine Snow	Financial Services Officer	Civic Centre
Technical Services	Ms Sheri Green	Director of Central Services	Civic Centre

Parish Councils in the authority's area: Bean; Darenth; Longfield & New Barn; Southfleet; Stone; Sutton-at-Hone & Hawley; Wilmington.

Town Councils in the authority's area: Swanscombe & Greenhithe.

DAVENTRY DISTRICT COUNCIL

www.daventrydc.gov.uk

Principal Office

Council Offices, Lodge Road, Daventry, Northamptonshire NN11 5AF
Telephone: (01327) 871100; FAX: (01327) 300011; DX 21965 Daventry

Function	Chief Officer	Title	Location
Chief Executive	Mr Stephen Atkinson	Chief Executive	Council Offices
Electoral Registration	Mr Dave Perry	Customer Services & ICT Manager	Council Offices
Environmental Health	Mr Mike Arnold	Environment & Recreation Manager	Council Offices
Finance	Mr Paul Hammond	Director of Finance & ICT	Council Offices
Housing	Mrs Hayley Davies	Housing Manager	Council Offices
Legal Services	Miss Mary Gallagher	Legal Services Officer	Council Offices
Leisure	Mr Mike Arnold	Environment & Recreation Manager	Council Offices
Local Land Charges	Mr Ossie Williams	Head of Personnel & Training	Council Offices
Planning	Mr Simon Bovey	Director of Public Protection	Council Offices
Technical Services	Mr Ian Vincent	Director of Corporate Assets & Development	Council Offices

Parish Councils in the authority's area: Arthingworth; Badby; Barby; Boughton; Braunston; Brington; Brixworth; Byfield; Church & Chapel Brampton; Clipston; Cold Ashby; Creaton; Crick; East Farndon; East Haddon; Everdon; Farthingstone; Flore; Great Oxendon; Guilsborough; Hannington; Harlestone; Holcot; Hollowell; Kilsby; Lamport; Lilbourne; Long Buckby; Maidwell with Draughton; Moulton; Naseby; Newnham; Norton; Old; Overstone; Pitsford; Preston Capes; Ravensthorpe; Scaldwell; Sibbertoft; Spratton; Stanford-on-Avon; Staverton; Stowe-ix-Churches; Teeton; Walgrave; Watford; Weedon Bec; Welford; Welton; West Haddon; Whilton; Woodford-cum-Membris; Yelvertoft.

Parish Meetings in the authority's area: Althorp; Ashby St Ledgers; Brockhall; Canons Ashby; Catesby; Charwelton; Clay Coton; Cottesbrooke; Dodford; Elkington; Fawsley; Haselbech; Hellidon; Holdenby; Kelmarsh; Marston Trussel; Sulby; Thornby; Winwick.

DERBY CITY COUNCIL

Derby City Council became a unitary authority on 1 April 1997.

DISTRICT COUNCILS

DERBYSHIRE DALES DISTRICT COUNCIL

www.derbyshiredales.gov.uk

Principal Office

Town Hall, Matlock, Derbyshire DE4 3NN

Telephone: (01629) 761100; FAX: (01629) 761148; DX 27259 Matlock

Function	Chief Officer	Title	Location
Chief Executive	Mr D Wheatcroft	Chief Executive	Town Hall
Electoral Registration	Mr D Wheatcroft	Chief Executive	Town Hall
Environmental Health	Mr J D Morris	Head of Community Services	Town Hall
Finance	Mr P Colledge	Finance Manager	Town Hall
Housing	Mr P Foley	Environmental Health Manager	Town Hall
Legal Services	Miss C Leddy	Head of Corporate Services	Town Hall
Leisure	Mr J D Morris	Head of Community Services	Town Hall
Local Land Charges	Miss C Leddy	Head of Corporate Services	Town Hall
Planning	Mr M D J Brooks	Head of Planning & Development Services	Town Hall
Technical Services	Mr M D J Brooks	Head of Planning & Development Services	Town Hall

Parish Councils in the authority's area: Alkmonton & Hungry Bentley; Ashford in the Water; Ballidon & Bradbourne; Baslow & Bubnell; Beeley; Birchover; Bonsall; Boylestone; Bradley; Bradwell; Brailsford; Brassington; Calver; Carsington & Hopton; Chelmorton; Clifton; Cromford; Cubley; Curbar; Doveridge; Eaton & Alsop & Newton Grange; Edlaston & Wyaston; Elton; Eyam; Fenny Bentley; Flagg; Great Longstone; Grindleford; Hartington Middle Quarter; Hartington Nether Quarter; Hartington Town Quarter; Hathersage; Hognaston; Hollington; Hucklow, Great Hucklow; Little Hucklow & Grindlow; Hulland Ward; Kirk Ireton; Kniveton; Litton; Longford; Mappleton; Marston Montgomery; Matlock Bath; Middleton & Smerrill; Middleton by Wirksworth; Monyash; Norbury & Roston; Northwood & Tinkersley; Offcote & Underwood; Osmaston & Yeldersley; Outseats; Over Haddon; Parwich; Rodsley & Yeaveley; Rowsley; Shirley; South Darley; Stanton in Peak; Stoney Middleton; Sudbury; Taddington; Tansley; Thorpe; Tideswell; Tissington; Winster; Youlgreave.

Parish Meetings in the authority's area: Aldwark; Atlow; Abney & Abney Grange, Highlow & Offerton; Biggin by Hulland; Blackwell in the Peak; Brushfield; Callow; Chatsworth; Edensor; Foolow; Froggatt; Gratton; Harthill; Hassop; Hazelbadge; Hulland; Ible; Ivonbrook Grange; Lea Hall; Little Longstone; Mercaston; Nether Haddon; Pilsley; Rowland; Sheldon; Snelston; Somersal Herbert; Wardlow; Wheston.

Town Councils in the authority's area: Ashbourne; Bakewell; Darley Dale; Matlock; Wirksworth.

DERWENTSIDE DISTRICT COUNCIL

www.derwentside.gov.uk

Principal Office

Civic Centre, Consett, Co Durham DH8 5JA

Telephone: (01207) 218000; FAX: (01207) 218200

Function	Chief Officer	Title	Location
Electoral Registration	Mr J A Thompson	Admin & Electoral Services Manager	Civic Centre
Environmental Health	Mr P Reynolds	Director of Environmental Services	Civic Centre
Finance	Mr A Smith	Director of Regulation & Resources	Civic Centre
Housing	Mr S Melvin	Director of Housing & Capital Works	Civic Centre
Legal Services	Mrs Y Donaldson	Head of Legal Services	Civic Centre
Leisure	Mr S Howell	Divisional Head of Leisure	Lamplight Arts
Local Land Charges	Mrs Y Donaldson	Head of Legal Services	Civic Centre
Planning	Mr P Reynolds	Director of Environmental Services	Civic Centre
Purchasing & Supplies	Mrs L A Gwillym	Admin & Electoral Services Officer	Civic Centre
Technical Services	Mr P Reynolds	Director of Environmental Services	Civic Centre

Parish Councils in the authority's area: Burnhope; Cornsay; Esh; Greencroft; Healeyfield; Hedleyhope; Lanchester; Muggleswick; Satley.

DOVER DISTRICT COUNCIL

www.dover.gov.uk

Principal Office

Council Offices, White Cliffs Business Park, Dover, Kent CT16 3PJ
Telephone: (01304) 821199; FAX: (01304) 872345; DX 6312 Dover

Function	Chief Officer	Title	Location
Chief Executive	Mr N Aziz	Managing Director	Council Offices
Electoral Registration	Mr D Blackburn	Democratic Services Manager	Council Offices
Environmental Health	Mrs L Golightly	Chief Environmental Health Officer	Council Offices
Finance	Mr P Julian	Head of Accountancy & S151 Officer	Council Offices
Housing	Mr B Ryan	Head of Housing	Council Offices
Legal Services	Mr J Horne	Head of Legal Services/Monitoring Officer	Council Offices
Leisure	Mr R Madge	Strategic Director (Community & Regeneration)	Council Offices
Local Land Charges	Mr D Blackburn	Democratic Services Manager	Council Offices
Planning	Mr R Madge	Strategic Director (Community & Regeneration)	Council Offices
Purchasing & Supplies	Mr P Wyles	Strategic Director (Resources)	Council Offices
Technical Services	Mr R Madge	Strategic Director (Community & Regeneration)	Council Offices

Parish Councils in the authority's area: Alkham; Ash; Aylesham; Capel-le-Ferne; Denton with Wootton; Eastry; Eythorne; Goodnestone; Great Mongeham; Guston; Hougham Without; Langdon; Lydden; Nonington; Northbourne; Preston; Ringwould with Kingsdown; Ripple; River; St Margaret's-at-Cliffe; Shepherdswell with Coldred; Sholden; Staple; Stourmouth; Sutton-by-Dover; Temple Ewell; Tilmanstone; Walmer; Whitfield; Wingham; Woodnesborough; Worth.

Town Councils in the authority's area: Sandwich; Deal; Dover.

DURHAM CITY COUNCIL

www.durhamcity.gov.uk

Chief Executive's Office

4 Saddler Street, Durham DH1 3NZ
Telephone: (0191) 386 6111; FAX: (0191) 386 0625; DX 60239 Durham

Community Services Department

17 Claypath, Durham DH1 1RG
Telephone: (0191) 386 6111; FAX: (0191) 386 2338
Unit 1, Damson Way, Dragonville Industrial Estate, Durham DH1 2YN
Telephone: (0191) 386 6111; FAX: (0191) 301 8678

Environmental Services Department

Byland Lodge, Hawthorn Terrace, Durham DH1 4TD
Telephone: (0191) 386 6111; FAX: (0191) 384 1529

Function	Chief Officer	Title	Location
Chief Executive	Mr B Spears	Chief Executive	4 Saddler St
Electoral Registration	Mr B Spears	Chief Exeucitve	4 Saddler St
Environmental Health	Mr J Jennings	Director of Environmental Services	Byland Lodge
Finance	Miss E Hall	Director of Corporate Finance	17 Claypath
Housing	Mr D Marrs	Director of Community Services	17 Claypath
Legal Services	Mrs L G Blackie	Director of Legal Services	4 Saddler St
Leisure	Mr D Marrs	Director of Community Services	Damson Way

Local Land Charges	Mrs L G Blackie	Director of Legal Services	4 Saddler St
Planning	Mr J Jennings	Director of Environmental Services	Byland Lodge
Purchasing & Supplies	Mr D Marrs	Director of Community Services	Damson Way
Technical Services	Mr J Jennings	Director of Environmental Services	Byland Lodge

Parish Councils in the authority's area: Bearpark; Belmont; Brancepeth; Brandon & Byshottles; Cassop cum Quarrington; Coxhoe; Croxdale & Hett; Framwellgate Moor; Kelloe; Pittington; Shadforth; Sherburn; Shincliffe; West Rainton; Witton Gilbert.

EASINGTON DISTRICT COUNCIL

www.easington.gov.uk

Principal Office
Council Offices, Seaside Lane, Easington, Peterlee, Co Durham SR8 3TN
Telephone: (0191) 527 0501; FAX: (0191) 527 0076

Function	Chief Officer	Title	Location
Chief Executive	Mr P Wilding	Chief Executive	Council Offices
Electoral Registration	Mr B Garside	Head of Democratic Services & Administration	Council Offices
Environmental Health	Mr K Parkinson	Environmental Health & Licensing Manager	Council Offices
Finance	Mr T Bell	Director of Finance & Corporate Services	Council Offices
Legal Services	Mr B Garside	Head of Democratic Services & Administration	Council Offices
Leisure	Ms J Johnson	Director of Regeneration & Development	Council Offices
Local Land Charges	Mr B Garside	Head of Democratic Services & Administration	Council Offices
Planning	Mr I Forster	Head of Planning & Building Control Services	Council Offices

Parish Councils in the authority's area: Blackhall; Castle Eden; Dalton-le-Dale; Easington Colliery; Easington Village; Haswell; Hawthorn; Horden; Hutton Henry; Murton; Sheraton; Shotton Colliery; South Hetton; Station Town; Thornley; Trimdon Station; Wheatley Hill; Wingate.

Town Councils in the authority's area: Peterlee; Seaham.

EAST CAMBRIDGESHIRE DISTRICT COUNCIL

www.eastcambs.gov.uk

Principal Office
The Grange, Nutholt Lane, Ely, Cambridgeshire CB7 4PL
Telephone: (01353) 665555/668833; FAX: (01353) 665240; DX 41001 Ely

Corporate Services
Babylon Bridge, Waterside, Ely, Cambridgeshire CB7 4AU

Function	Chief Officer	Title	Location
Chief Executive	Mr J Hill	Chief Executive	The Grange
Electoral Registration	Mrs J Human	Electoral Services Officer	The Grange
Environmental Health	Mr S Clements	Executive Director (Environmental Services)	The Grange
Finance	Mr A Colyer	Executive Director (Finance)	The Grange
Housing	Ms J Hollingworth	Principal Housing Officer	The Grange
Legal Services	Miss E Hoggart	Executive Director (Legal & Democratic Services)	The Grange
Leisure	Mr D Dixon	Cultural Services Team Leader	Babylon Bridge
Local Land Charges	Mrs P Holmes	Land Charges Officer	The Grange

Planning	Mr D Archer	Executive Director (Development Services)	The Grange
Purchasing & Supplies	Mr A Stevens	Facilities Manager	The Grange

Parish Councils in the authority's area: Ashley; Bottisham; Brinkley; Burrough Green; Burwell; Cheveley; Chippenham; Coveney; Dullingham; Ely; Fordham; Haddenham; Isleham; Kennett; Kirtling; Little Downham; Little Thetford; Littleport; Lode; Mepal; Reach; Snailwell; Soham; Stetchworth; Stretham; Sutton; Swaffham Bulbeck; Swaffham Prior; Wentworth; Westley Waterless; Wicken; Wiburton; Witcham; Witchford; Woodditton.

Town Councils in the authority's area: Ely City Council; Soham.

EAST DEVON DISTRICT COUNCIL

www.eastdevon.gov.uk

Principal Office
Knowle, Station Road, Sidmouth, Devon EX10 8HL
Telephone: (01395) 516551; FAX: (01395) 517507; DX 48705 Sidmouth

Function	Chief Officer	Title	Location
Chief Executive	Mr M R Williams	Chief Executive	Knowle
Electoral Registration	Mr M R Williams	Chief Executive	Knowle
Environmental Health	Mr P Jeffs	Corporate Director, Communities	Knowle
Finance	Mr D J Pearse	Corporate Director, Economy	Knowle
Housing	Mr P Jeffs	Corporate Director, Communities	Knowle
Legal Services	Mr M R Williams	Chief Executive	Knowle
Leisure	Mr P Jeffs	Corporate Director, Communities	Knowle
Local Land Charges	Mr K Hassan	Corporate Director, Environment	Knowle
Planning	Mr K Hassan	Corporate Director, Environment	Knowle
Technical Services	Mr K Hassan	Corporate Director, Environment	Knowle

Parish Councils in the authority's area: All Saints; Awliscombe; Axmouth; Aylesbeare; Beer; Bishops Clyst; Brampford Speke; Branscombe; Broadclyst; Broadhembury; Buckerell; Chardstock; Clyst Honiton; Clyst Hydon; Clyst St George; Colaton Raleigh; Colyton; Combpyne Rousdon; Cotleigh; Dalwood; Dunkeswell; East Budleigh with Bicton; Farringdon; Farway; Feniton; Gittisham; Hawkchurch; Kilmington; Luppitt; Lympstone; Membury; Monkton; Musbury; Newton Poppleford & Harpford; Northleigh; Offwell; Otterton; Payhembury; Plymtree; Poltimore; Rewe; Rockbeare; Shute; Southleigh; Stockland; Stoke Canon; Talaton; Uplyme; Upottery; Upton Pyne; Whimple; Widworthy; Woodbury; Yarcombe.

Parish Meetings in the authority's area: Clyst St Lawrence; Combe Raleigh; Huxham; Netherexe; Sheldon.

Town Councils in the authority's area: Axminster; Budleigh Salterton; Exmouth; Honiton; Ottery St Mary; Seaton; Sidmouth.

EAST DORSET DISTRICT COUNCIL

www.eastdorset.gov.uk

Principal Office
Council Offices, Furzehill, Wimborne, Dorset BH21 4HN
Telephone: (01202) 886201; FAX: (01202) 841390

Function	Chief Officer	Title	Location
Chief Executive	Mr A Breakwell	Chief Executive	Council Offices
Electoral Registration	Mrs S Griggs	Head of Central Policy & Performance	Council Offices
Environmental Health	Mr S L Duckett	Head of Health Services	Council Offices
Finance	Mr V Smith	Head of Financial Services	Council Offices
Housing	Mr K G Mallett	Head of Legal Services	Council Offices
Legal Services	Mr K G Mallett	Head of Legal Services	Council Offices
Leisure	Mr N Farmer	Head of Community Services	Council Offices

DISTRICT COUNCILS

Local Land Charges	Mr K G Mallett	Head of Legal Services	Council Offices
Planning	Mr M Hirsh	Head of Planning & Building Control	Council Offices
Purchasing & Supplies	Mrs S Griggs	Head of Central Policy & Performance	Council Offices
Technical Services	Mr L Cass	Head of Technical Services	Council Offices

Parish Councils in the authority's area: Alderholt; Colehill; Corfe Mullen; Cranborne & Edmondsham; Gussage St Michael; Holt; Knowlton; Pamphill & Shapwick; St Leonards & St Ives; Sixpenny Handley with Pentridge; Sturminster Marshall; Vale of Allen; West Moors; West Parley.

Town Councils in the authority's area: Ferndown; Wimborne Minster; Verwood.

EAST HAMPSHIRE DISTRICT COUNCIL

www.easthants.gov.uk

Principal Office
Penns Place, Petersfield, Hampshire GU31 4EX
Telephone: (01730) 266551; FAX: (01730) 267366; DX 100403 Petersfield

Function	Chief Officer	Title	Location
Chief Executive	Mr W Godfrey	Chief Executive	Penns Place
Electoral Registration	Ms T Stapleton	Electoral Registration Officer	Penns Place
Environmental Health	Mr M Reed	Head of Environmental Health	Penns Place
Finance	Mr B Price	Strategic Manager	Penns Place
Housing	Mrs J Potter	Head of Housing	Penns Place
Legal Services	Mr M Lawther	Head of Legal Services	Penns Place
Leisure	Mr A Ferrier	Head of Community	Penns Place
Local Land Charges	Mrs V Davidson	Land Charges Manager	Penns Place
Planning	Ms A Wood	Head of Planning Policy	Penns Place

Parish Councils in the authority's area: Bentley; Bentworth; Binsted; Bramshot & Liphook; Buriton; Chawton; Clanfield; East Meon; East Tisted; Farringdon; Four Marks; Froxfield; Froyle; Grayshott; Greatham; Hawkley; Headley; Horndean; Kingsley; Langrish; Lindford; Liss; Medstead; Newton Valence; Ropley; Rowlands Castle; Selborne; Shalden; Steep; Stroud; Wield; Worldham.

Parish Meetings in the authority's area: Colemore & Priors Dean; Lasham; West Tisted.

Town Councils in the authority's area: Alton; Petersfield; Whitehill.

EAST HERTFORDSHIRE DISTRICT COUNCIL

www.eastherts.gov.uk

Principal Office
Council Offices, The Causeway, Bishop's Stortford CM23 2EN
Telephone: (01279) 655261

Marketing and Operations Department
Wallfields, Pegs Lane, Hertford SG13 8EQ
Telephone: (01279) 655261

Function	Chief Officer	Title	Location
Chief Executive	Miranda Steward; Rachel Stopard	Executive Directors	Wallfields
Electoral Registration	Jeff Hughes	Head of Democratic Services	Council Offices
Environmental Health	Tracy Ferguson	Head of Environmental Health	Wallfields
Finance	Dave Tweedie	Assistant Director (Financial Services)	Council Offices
Housing	Will O'Neill	Head of Housing & Community Planning	Wallfields
Legal Services	Simon Drinkwater	Assistant Director (Law & Control)	Council Offices
Leisure	Martyn Dutfield	Head of Leisure	Wallfields

DISTRICT COUNCILS

Local Land Charges	Pam Archer	Head of Local Land Charges	Council Offices
Planning	Paul Rossington	Assistant Director (Development Control)	Wallfields
Purchasing & Supplies	Bryan Bye	Head of Internal Customer Services	Council Offices

Parish Councils in the authority's area: Albury; Anstey; Ardeley; Aspenden; Aston; Bayford; Bengeo Rural; Benington; Bramfield; Braughing; Brent Pelham/Meesden; Brickendon Liberty; Buckland; Cottered; Datchworth; Eastwick & Gilston; Furneux Pelham; Great Amwell; Great Munden; Hertford Heath; Hertingfordbury; High Wych; Hormead; Hunsdon; Little Berkhamsted; Little Hadham; Little Munden; Much Hadham; Standon; Stanstead Abbotts; Stanstead St Margarets; Stapleford; Stocking Pelham; Tewin; Thorley; Thundridge; Walkern; Wareside; Watton-at-Stone; Westmill; Widford; Wyddial.

Town Councils in the authority's area: Bishop's Stortford; Buntingford; Hertford; Sawbridgeworth; Ware.

EAST LINDSEY DISTRICT COUNCIL

www.e-lindsey.gov.uk

Principal Office

Tedder Hall, Manby Park, Louth, Lincolnshire LN11 8UP

Telephone: (01507) 601111; FAX: (01507) 600206

Function	Chief Officer	Title	Location
Chief Executive	Mr P Haigh	Chief Executive	Tedder Hall
Electoral Registration	Mr P Haigh	Chief Executive	Tedder Hall
Environmental Health	[Vacant]	Director of Environmental Services	Tedder Hall
Finance	Mr R Whetton	Director of Finance	Tedder Hall
Housing	[Vacant]	Director of Environmental Services	Tedder Hall
Legal Services	Mr P Haigh	Chief Executive	Tedder Hall
Leisure	Mr R A Suich	Head of Leisure & Tourism	Tedder Hall
Local Land Charges	Mr P Haigh	Chief Executive	Tedder Hall
Planning	Mr S Williamson	Director of Planning & Economic Development	Tedder Hall
Purchasing & Supplies	[Vacant]	Director of Environmental Services	Tedder Hall
Technical Services	Mr P Haigh	Chief Executive	Tedder Hall

Parish Councils in the authority's area: Aby with Greenfield; Addlethorpe; Alvingham; Anderby; Asterby; Baumber; Belchford; Benniworth; Bilsby, Farlesthorpe & Markby; Binbrook; Bolingbroke; Bratoft; Bucknall; Carrington; Chapel St Leonards; Claxby St Andrew; Coningsby; Covenham St Bartholomew; Covenham St Mary; Croft; Dalby; Donington on Bain; East Barkwith; East Keal; East Kirkby; Eastville; Elkington; Firsby; Fotherby; Friskney; Frithville; Fulletby; Fulstow; Gautby; Goulceby; Grainsby; Grainthorpe; Great Carlton; Great Steeping; Grimoldby; Hagworthingham; Hainton; Halton Holegate; Hannah cum Hagnaby; Haugh; Haugham; Hemingby; Hogsthorpe; Holton le Clay; Horsington; Hundleby; Huttoft; Ingoldmells; Irby in the Marsh; Kirkby on Bain; Langriville; Legbourne; Little Carlton; Little Cawthorpe; Little Steeping; Ludborough; Ludford (inc. East Wykeham), Maltby le Marsh; Manby; Mareham le Fen; Marshchapel; Midville; Minting; Mumby; New Leake; North Coates; North Somercotes; North Thoresby; Orby; Partney; Ranby; Revesby; Roughton; Saltfleetby; Scamblesby; Sibsey; Skidbrooke with Saltfleet Haven; South Cockerington; South Elkington; South Somercotes; South Thoresby; South Willingham; Stickford; Stickney; Swaby; Tathwell; Tattershall with Thorpe; Tattershall Thorpe; Tetford; Tetney; Theddlethorpe All Saints; Theddlethorpe St Helen; Thimbleby; Thornton le Fen; Thorpe St Peter; Toynton All Saints; Toynton St Peter; Tumby; Tupholme; Utterby; Waddingworth; Wainfleet St Mary; Waithe; Well; Welton le Marsh; West Ashby; West Barkwith; West Keal; Westville; Wildmore; Willoughtby with Sloothby; Withern with Stain; Woodhall Spa; Wragby.

Parish Meetings in the authority's area: Ashby with Scremby; Aswardby; Authorpe; Beesby with Saleby; Belleau; Brackenborough with Little Grimsby; Brinkhill; Burgh on Bain; Burwell; Calcethorpe with Kelstern; Candlesby with Gunby; Claxby with Moorby; Claythorpe; Conisholme; Cumberworth; Edlington with Wispington; Gayton le Marsh; Gayton le Wold; Great Sturton;

DISTRICT COUNCILS

Greetham with Somersby; Hallington; Haltham; Hammeringham; Harrington; Hatton; High Toynton; Keddington; Langton; Langton by Spilsby; Langton by Wragby; Low Toynton; Lusby with Winceby; Maidenwell; Mareham on the Hill; Market Stainton; Mavis Enderby; Muckton; North Cockerington; North Ormsby; Raithby; Raithby cum Maltby; Reston; Rigsby with Ailby; Sausthorpe; Scrivelsby; Skendleby; Sotby; South Ormsby cum Ketsby; Stenigot; Stewton; Stixwould & Woodhall; Strubby with Woodthorpe; Ulceby with Fordington; Walmsgate; Welton le Wold; West Fen; Wood Enderby; Wyham-cum-Cadeby; Yarburgh.

Town Councils in the authority's area: Alford; Burgh le Marsh; Horncastle; Louth; Mablethorpe & Sutton; Skegness; Spilsby; Wainfleet All Saints.

EAST NORTHAMPTONSHIRE COUNCIL

www.east-northamptonshire.gov.uk

Principal Office

East Northamptonshire House, Cedar Drive, Thrapston, Northants NN14 4LZ
Telephone: (01832) 742000; FAX: (01832) 734839; DX 701611 Thrapston

Function	Chief Officer	Title	Location
Chief Executive	Stephen Baker	Chief Executive	E. Northants Hse
Electoral Registration	Stephen Baker	Chief Executive	E. Northants Hse
Environmental Health	Russell Eacott	Director of Community Services	E. Northants Hse
Finance	Mark Lovell	Director of Corporate & Financial Services	E. Northants Hse
Housing	Russell Eacott	Director of Community Services	E. Northants Hse
Legal Services	Mark Lovell	Director of Corporate & Financial Services	E. Northants Hse
Leisure	Russell Eacott	Director of Community Services	E. Northants Hse
Local Land Charges	Russell Eacott	Director of Community Services	E. Northants Hse
Planning	Russell Eacott	Director of Community Services	E. Northants Hse
Purchasing & Supplies	Mark Lovell	Director of Corporate & Financial Services	E. Northants Hse
Technical Services	Russell Eacott	Director of Community Services	E. Northants Hse

Parish Councils in the authority's area: Aldwincle; Ashton; Barnwell; Benefield; Brigstock; Bulwick; Chelveston-cum-Caldecott; Collyweston; Deene & Deenethorpe; Denford; Duddington with Finshade; Easton on the Hill; Glapthorn; Great Addington; Hargrave; Harringworth; Hemington, Luddington, Thurning; Islip; Kings Cliffe; Lilford-cum-Wigsthorpe & Thorpe Achurch; Little Addington; Lowick & Slipton; Lutton; Nassington; Pilton, Stoke Doyle, Wadenhoe; Polebrook; Ringstead; Southwick; Stanwick; Sudborough; Titchmarsh; Twywell; Warmington; Woodford; Woodnewton; Yarwell.

Parish Meetings in the authority's area: Apethorpe; Blatherwycke; Clopton; Cotterstock; Fotheringhay; Laxton; Newton Bromswold; Tansor; Wakerley.

Town Councils in the authority's area: Higham Ferrers; Irthlingborough; Oundle; Raunds; Rushden; Thrapston.

EAST STAFFORDSHIRE BOROUGH COUNCIL

www.eaststaffsbc.gov.uk

Principal Office

Town Hall, Burton upon Trent, Staffordshire DE14 2EB
Telephone: (01283) 508000; FAX: (01283) 535412; DX 700331 Burton upon Trent 2

Midland Grain Warehouse Offices

Midland Grain Warehouse, Derby Street, Burton upon Trent, DE14 2JJ

Function	Chief Officer	Title	Location
Chief Executive	Mr F W Saunders	Chief Executive	Town Hall

Function	Chief Officer	Title	Location
Electoral Registration	Mr G Moss	Head of Resource & Financial Management	Town Hall
Environmental Health	Mr C Ward	Head of Health & Environment	Midland Grain
Finance	Mr G Moss	Head of Resource & Financial Management	Town Hall
Legal Services	Mr G Moss	Head of Resource & Financial Management	Town Hall
Leisure	Mr M Azam	Head of Regeneration & Leisure	Midland Grain
Local Land Charges	Mr A Wood	Head of Development Services	Midland Grain
Planning	Mr A Wood	Head of Development Services	Midland Grain

Parish Councils in the authority's area: Abbots Bromley; Anslow; Barton under Needwood; Blithfield; Branston; Croxden; Denstone; Draycott in the Clay; Dunstall; Ellastone; Hanbury; Hoar Cross; Kingstone; Leigh; Marchington; Mayfield; Newborough; Outwoods; Rocester; Rolleston on Dove; Stanton; Stretton; Tatenhill; Tutbury; Uttoxeter Rural; Wootton; Yoxall.

Parish Meetings in the authority's area: Okeover; Ramshorn; Wychnor.

Town Councils in the authority's area: Uttoxeter.

EAST YORKSHIRE BOROUGH COUNCIL

East Yorkshire Borough Council was abolished on 31 March 1996; see now the East Riding of Yorkshire Council.

EASTBOURNE BOROUGH COUNCIL

www.eastbourne.gov.uk

Principal Office

Town Hall, Grove Road, Eastbourne, East Sussex BN21 4UG
Telephone: (01323) 410000; FAX: (01323) 410322; DX 6921 Eastbourne

Finance and Corporate Services

Central Services Office, 1 Grove Road, Eastbourne BN21 4TW
Telephone: (01323) 410000; FAX: (01323) 415999

Planning; Regeneration, Amenities and Housing; Health and Community

68 Grove Road, Eastbourne BN21 1DF
Telephone: (01323) 410000; FAX: (01323) 415997

Tourism and Leisure

College Road, Eastbourne BN21 4JJ
Telephone: (01323) 410000; FAX: (01323) 638686

Function	Chief Officer	Title	Location
Chief Executive	Mr M Ray	Chief Executive	Town Hall
Electoral Registration	Mrs T Pannett	Electoral Services Manager	Town Hall
Environmental Health	Mr G Stevenson	Head of Environmental Health	68 Grove Road
Finance	Mr S McHugh	Director of Finance and Corporate Services	Cntrl Services
Housing	Mr N Fuller	Director of Housing, Health & Community Services	68 Grove Road
Legal Services	Mr M Freeman	Assistant Director of Audit & Legal Services	Town Hall
Leisure	Mr K Morrison	Assistant Director of Economy, Tourism & Planning	College Road
Local Land Charges	Mr M Reynard	Head of Legal Services	Town Hall
Planning	Mr T Cookson	Head of Planning	68 Grove Road
Technical Services	Mr N Kinnish	Director of Economy, Tourism & Environment	68 Grove Road

Parish Councils & Parish Meetings in the authority's area: none.

Town Councils in the authority's area: none.

DISTRICT COUNCILS

EASTLEIGH BOROUGH COUNCIL

www.eastleigh.gov.uk

Principal Office

Civic Offices, Leigh Road, Eastleigh, Hampshire SO50 9YN
Telephone: (023) 8068 8000; FAX: (023) 8064 3952; DX 122380 Eastleigh 2

Function	Chief Officer	Title	Location
Chief Executive	Chris Tapp	Chief Executive	Civic Offices
Electoral Registration	Sam Ward	Elections Officer	Civic Offices
Environmental Health	Paul Ruta	Head of Environmental Health	Civic Offices
Finance	Nick Tustian	Head of Finance	Civic Offices
Housing	Tony Hall	Head of Housing	Civic Offices
Legal Services	Richard Ward	Head of Legal Services	Civic Offices
Leisure	Phil Lomax;	Head of Countryside & Recreation Services;	
	Cheryl Butler	Head of Arts & Tourism	Civic Offices
Local Land Charges	Richard Ward	Head of Legal Services	Civic Offices
Planning	Colin Peters	Head of Development Control	Civic Offices
Purchasing & Supplies	Jennifer Filer	Facilities Manager	Civic Offices
Technical Services	Duncan McVey	Head of Engineering	Civic Offices

Parish Councils in the authority's area: Bishopstoke; Botley; Bursledon; Fair Oak & Horton Heath; Hamble-le-Rice; Hound; West End.

Town Council in the authority's area: Hedge End.

EDEN DISTRICT COUNCIL

www.eden.gov.uk/eden-dc

Principal Office

Town Hall, Penrith, Cumbria CA11 7QF
Telephone: (01768) 864671; FAX: (01768) 890470

Planning Department; Department of Technical Services

Mansion House, Friargate, Penrith CA11 7YG
Telephone: (01768) 864671; FAX: (01768) 890732

Function	Chief Officer	Title	Location
Chief Executive	Mr I W Bruce	Chief Executive	Town Hall
Electoral Registration	Mr I W Bruce	Chief Executive	Town Hall
Environmental Health	Mr S Huddart	Director of Technical Services	Mansion Hse
Finance	Mr D J Rawsthorn	Director of Finance	Town Hall
Housing	Mr S Huddart	Director of Technical Services	Mansion Hse
Legal Services	Mr P Foote	Director of Corporate & Legal Services	Town Hall
Leisure	Mr S Huddart	Director of Technical Services	Mansion Hse
Local Land Charges	Mr P Foote	Director of Corporate & Legal Services	Town Hall
Planning	Mr S Huddart	Director of Technical Services	Mansion Hse
Technical Services	Mr S Huddart	Director of Technical Services	Mansion Hse

Parish Councils in the authority's area: Ainstable; Alston Moor; Asby; Askham; Bampton; Bandleyside; Barton; Bolton; Brough; Brougham; Castle Sowerby; Catterlen; Clifton; Crosby Ravensworth; Culgaith; Dacre; Dufton; Glassonby; Great Salkeld; Great Strickland; Greystoke; Hesket; Hunsonby; Hutton; Kaber; Kirkby Thore; Kirkoswald; Langwathby; Lazonby; Long Marton; Lowther; Matterdale; Milburn; Morland; Mungrisdale; Murton; Musgrave; Orton; Ousby; Patterdale; Ravenstonedale; Shap; Skelton; Sockbridge & Tirril; Soulby; Stainmore; Tebay; Temple Sowerby; Threlkeld; Warcop; Yanwath & Eamont Bridge.

Parish Meetings in the authority's area: Brough Sowerby; Cliburn; Crackenthorpe; Crosby Garrett; Hartley; Helbeck; King's Meaburn; Little Strickland; Mallerstang; Martindale; Nateby; Newbiggin; Newby; Sleagill; Thrimby; Waitby; Wharton; Winton.

Town Councils in the authority's area: Appleby; Kirkby Stephen.

DISTRICT COUNCILS

ELLESMERE PORT & NESTON BOROUGH COUNCIL

www.epnbc.gov.uk

Principal Office
Council Offices, 4 Civic Way, Ellesmere Port, Cheshire CH65 0BE
Telephone: (0151) 356 6789; FAX: (0151) 355 4305

Works Department
Council Depot, Rossfield Road, Ellesmere Port CH65 3AW
Telephone: (0151) 356 6789

Function	Chief Officer	Title	Location
Chief Executive	Mr S Ewbank	Chief Executive & Town Clerk	Council Offices
Electoral Registration	Mr S Ewbank	Chief Executive & Town Clerk	Council Offices
Environmental Health	Mr M P Whittaker	Head of Environmental Health	Council Offices
Finance	Pamela J Williams	BoroughTreasurer	Council Offices
Housing	Mr R E Selby	Borough Housing Officer	Council Offices
Legal Services	Mr C Chapman	Borough Solicitor	Council Offices
Leisure	Mr P A Hearfield	Borough Community Leisure Officer	Council Offices
Local Land Charges	Mr C Chapman	Borough Solicitor	Council Offices
Planning	Mr T R Miller	Head of Planning Services	Council Offices
Purchasing & Supplies	Mr A Lodge	Works Department	Council Depot
Technical Services	Mrs J Williamson	Head of Technical Services	Council Offices

Parish Council in the authority's area: Ince.

ELMBRIDGE BOROUGH COUNCIL

www.elmbridge.gov.uk

Principal Office
Civic Centre, High Street, Esher, Surrey KT10 9SD
Telephone: (01372) 474474; FAX: (01372) 474972; DX 36302 Esher

Function	Chief Officer	Title	Location
Chief Executive	Mr M Lockwood	Chief Executive	Civic Centre
Electoral Registration	Mr R Williams	Electoral Services Manager	Civic Centre
Environmental Health	Mr D R Wiltshire	Director of Planning & Environmental Services	Civic Centre
Finance	Mr T Willington	Director of Finance & Corporate Services	Civic Centre
Housing	Barbara Spittle	Director of Community Services	Civic Centre
Legal Services	Frances Rutter	Borough Solicitor	Civic Centre
Leisure	Barbara Spittle	Director of Community Services	Civic Centre
Local Land Charges	Mrs C Goble	Land Charges Officer	Civic Centre
Planning	Mr D R Wiltshire	Director of Planning & Environmental Services	Civic Centre
Purchasing & Supplies	Tina Bailey	Civic Centre Manager	Civic Centre
Technical Services	Frances Pearce	Computer Services Manager	Civic Centre

Parish Council in the authority's area: Claygate.

Town Councils in the authority's area: none.

EPPING FOREST DISTRICT COUNCIL

www.eppingforestdc.gov.uk

Principal Office
Civic Offices, 323 High Street, Epping, Essex CM16 4BZ
Telephone: (01992) 564000; FAX: (01992) 578018

DISTRICT COUNCILS

Leisure Services Department
25 Hemnall Street, Epping CM16 4LX
Telephone: (01992) 564000

Function	Chief Officer	Title	Location
Chief Executive	Mr J Burgess	Chief Executive	Civic Offices
Electoral Registration	W Macleod	Senior Electoral Services Officer	Civic Offices
Environmental Health	Mr J Gilbert	Head of Environmental Services	Civic Offices
Finance	Robert Palmer	Finance Director	Civic Offices
Housing	Mr A Hall	Head of Housing Services	Civic Offices
Legal Services	Colleen O'Boyle	Head of Legal & Administrative Services	Civic Offices
Leisure	Derek MacNab	Head of Leisure Services	25 Hemnall St
Local Land Charges	Jill Dolder		Civic Offices
Planning	John Preston	Head of Planning Services	Civic Offices

Parish Councils in the authority's area: Abbess, Beauchamp & Berners Roding; Buckhurst Hill; Chigwell; Epping Upland; Fyfield; High Ongar; Lambourne; Matching; Moreton, Bobbingworth & The Lavers; Nazeing; North Weald Bassett; Ongar; Roydon; Sheering; Stanford Rivers; Stapleford Abbotts; Stapleford Tawney; Theydon Bois; Theydon Garnon; Theydon Mount; Willingale.

Town Councils in the authority's area: Epping; Loughton; Waltham Abbey.

EPSOM & EWELL BOROUGH COUNCIL

www.epsom-ewell.gov.uk

Principal Office
Town Hall, The Parade, Epsom, Surrey KT18 5BY
Telephone: (01372) 732000; FAX: (01372) 732720; DX 30713 Epsom

Function	Chief Officer	Title	Location
Chief Executive	Mr D J Smith	Chief Executive	Town Hall
Electoral Registration	Mrs A Macgregor	Head of Committee Services	Town Hall
Environmental Health	Mr R Woolston	Head of Regulatory Services	Town Hall
Finance	Mr J Turnbull	Director of Finance	Town Hall
Housing	Mr G Waters	Head of Venues, Housing and Personal Services	Town Hall
Legal Services	Mr T Smith	Chief Solicitor and Estates Services Manager	Town Hall
Local Land Charges	Mr D Grusty	Support Services Manager	Town Hall
Planning	Mr N Ide	Chief Planning Officer	Town Hall
Purchasing & Supplies	Mr A Forzani	Head of Procurement and Projects	Town Hall
Technical Services	Mr J Gransden	Head of Streetcare	Town Hall

Parish Councils & Parish Meetings in the authority's area: none.

Town Councils in the authority's area: none.

EREWASH BOROUGH COUNCIL

www.erewash.gov.uk

Principal Office
Town Hall, Ilkeston, Derbyshire DE7 5RP
Telephone: (0115) 907 2244; FAX: (0115) 907 1121; DX 10318 Ilkeston

Development Services Department; Leisure Services Department; Engineering Division; Architect's Division
Town Hall, Long Eaton, Nottingham NG10 1HU
Telephone: (0115) 907 2244; FAX: (0115) 907 2343

DISTRICT COUNCILS

Human Resources; Community Involvement Department; IT Section
Toll Bar House, 1 Derby Road, Ilkeston DE7 5FE
Telephone: (0115) 931 6000; FAX: (0115) 944 4544

Environmental Services Department & Environmental Health Division
Merlin House, Merlin Way, Ilkeston, Derbyshire DE7 4RA

Function	Chief Officer	Title	Location
Electoral Registration	Mr K M Spencer	Head of Administration	Town Hall, Ilkeston
Environmental Health	Dr S Holmes	Head of Environmental Services	Merlin House
Finance	[Vacant]	Head of Finance Services	Town Hall, Ilkeston
Legal Services	Mrs E Minnighan	Head of Legal Services	Town Hall, Ilkeston
Local Land Charges	Mrs V Adams		Town Hall, Ilkeston
Planning	Mr P Wigglesworth	Head of Development Services	Town Hall, L. Eaton
Purchasing & Supplies	Mrs J Soar	Office Manager	Town Hall, Ilkeston
Technical Services	Mr D Pycroft	Design Manager	Town Hall, L. Eaton

Parish Councils in the authority's area: Breadsall; Breaston; Dale Abbey; Draycott; Little Eaton; Morley; Ockbrook; Risley; Sandiacre; Sawley; Stanley; Stanton by Dale; West Hallam.

Town Councils in the authority's area: None.

EXETER CITY COUNCIL

www.exeter.gov.uk

Principal Office
Civic Centre, Paris Street, Exeter, Devon EX1 1JN
Telephone: (01392) 277888; FAX: (01392) 265265

Function	Chief Officer	Title	Location
Chief Executive	Philip Bostock	Chief Executive	Civic Centre
Electoral Registration	Philip Bostock	Chief Executive	Civic Centre
Environmental Health	Jayne Donovan	Head of Environmental Health	Civic Centre
Finance	Andrew Stark	Head of Treasury Services	Civic Centre
Housing	Rodney Lock	Head of Housing	Civic Centre
Legal Services	Baan Al-Khafaji	Head of Legal Services	Civic Centre
Leisure	Alan Caig	Head of Leisure & Museums	Civic Centre
Local Land Charges	David Prosser	Head of Estates Services	Civic Centre
Planning	Richard Short	Head of Planning Services	Civic Centre
Purchasing & Supplies	John Street	Head of General Services	Civic Centre
Technical Services	Bill Ricketts	Head of Technical Services	Civic Centre

Parish Councils & Parish Meetings in the authority's area: none.

Town Councils in the authority's area: none.

FAREHAM BOROUGH COUNCIL

www.fareham.gov.uk

Principal Office
Civic Offices, Civic Way, Fareham, Hampshire PO16 7PU
Telephone: (01329) 236100; FAX: (01329) 821770; DX 40814 Fareham

Function	Chief Officer	Title	Location
Chief Executive	Mr Alan Davies	Chief Executive Officer	Civic Offices
Electoral Registration	Mrs Barbara Wright	Head of Democratic Services	Civic Offices
Environmental Health	Mr Garry White	Chief Health & Regulatory Services Officer	Civic Offices
Finance	Mrs Carol Shaw	Director of Finance & Resources	Civic Offices
Housing	Mr David Blackburn	Director of Housing	Civic Offices
Legal Services	Ms Gina Bailey	Solicitor to the Council	Civic Offices

Leisure	Mr Jim Kettlewell	Director of Leisure & Environment	Civic Offices
Local Land Charges	Ms Gina Bailey	Solicitor to the Council	Civic Offices
Planning	Mr Jeff Williams	Director of Planning & Transportation;	
	Mr Alan Wells	Chief Development Control Officer	Civic Offices
Purchasing & Supplies	Ms Gina Bailey	Solicitor to the Council	Civic Offices
Technical Services	Mr Jeff Williams	Director of Planning & Transportation;	Civic Offices

Parish Councils & Parish Meetings in the authority's area: none.

Town Councils in the authority's area: none.

FENLAND DISTRICT COUNCIL

www.fenland.gov.uk

Principal Office

Fenland Hall, County Road, March, Cambridgeshire PE15 8NQ
Telephone: (01354) 654321; FAX: (01354) 622259; DX 30955 March

Function	*Chief Officer*	*Title*	*Location*
Chief Executive	T Pilsbury	Chief Executive	Fenland Hall
Electoral Registration	N Eighteen	Head of Democratic & Legal Services	Fenland Hall
Environmental Health	R Cassidy	Head of Environment & Health Services	Fenland Hall
Finance	M Taylor	Assistant Chief Executive (Finance)	Fenland Hall
Housing	T Mills	Head of Housing Services	Fenland Hall
Legal Services	N Eighteen	Head of Democratic & Legal Services	Fenland Hall
Leisure	[Vacant]	Head of Community Services	Fenland Hall
Local Land Charges	[Vacant]	Head of Planning Services	Fenland Hall
Planning	[Vacant]	Head of Planning Services	Fenland Hall
Purchasing & Supplies	M Taylor	Assistant Chief Executive (Finance)	Fenland Hall
Technical Services	G Garford	Head of Technical & Marine Services	Fenland Hall

Parish Councils in the authority's area: Benwick; Christchurch; Doddington; Elm; Gorefield; Leverington; Manea; Newton; Parson Drove; Tydd St Giles; Wimblington; Wisbech St Mary.

Town Councils in the authority's area: Chatteris; March; Whittlesey; Wisbech.

FOREST HEATH DISTRICT COUNCIL

www.forest-heath.gov.uk

Principal Office

District Offices, College Heath Road, Mildenhall, Suffolk IP28 7EY
Telephone: (01638) 719000; FAX: (01638) 716493

Function	*Chief Officer*	*Title*	*Location*
Chief Executive	David Burnip	Chief Executive	District Offices
Electoral Registration	Sarah King	Administration Manager	District Offices
Environmental Health	[Vacant]	Head of Environmental Services	District Offices
Finance	John Alexander	Strategic Director (Resources)	District Offices
Legal Services	Jonathan Reed	Legal Services Manager	District Offices
Leisure	Tony Bass	Head of Leisure Services	District Offices
Local Land Charges	Anna Wiseman	Land Charges Officer	District Offices
Planning	Nigel McCurdy	Head of Planning	District Offices

Parish Councils in the authority's area: Barton Mills; Beck Row, Holywell Row and Kenny Hill; Brandon; Dalham; Elveden; Eriswell; Exning; Freckenham; Gazeley; Herringswell; Icklingham; Kentford; Lakenheath; Mildenhall; Moulton; Newmarket; Red Lodge; Santon Downham; Tuddenham; Worlington.

Parish Meetings in the authority's area: Cavenham; Higham.

DISTRICT COUNCILS

FOREST OF DEAN DISTRICT COUNCIL

www.fdean.gov.uk

Principal Office

Council Offices, High Street, Coleford, Gloucestershire GL16 8HG
Telephone: (01594) 810000; FAX: (01594) 812590; Minicom: (01594) 812500; DX 94102 Coleford

Function	Chief Officer	Title	Location
Chief Executive	Mr T J Perrin	Chief Executive	Council Offices
Electoral Registration	Mr L J Harding	Head of Legal & Democratic Services	Council Offices
Environmental Health	Mr T J Perrin	Chief Executive	Council Offices
Finance	Mr D A Mathams	Director of Resources	Council Offices
Housing	Mr T J Perrin	Chief Executive	Council Offices
Legal Services	Mr L J Harding	Head of Legal & Democratic Services	Council Offices
Leisure	Mr T J Perrin	Chief Executive	Council Offices
Local Land Charges	Mr L J Harding	Head of Legal & Democratic Services	Council Offices
Planning	Mr S Hannaby	Head of Planning Services	Council Offices
Purchasing & Supplies	Mr D A Mattham	Director of Resources	Council Offices
Technical Services	Mr T J Perrin	Chief Executive	Council Offices

Parish Councils in the authority's area: Alvington; Awre; Aylburton; Blaisdon; Bromsberrow; Churcham; Corse; Drybrook; Dymock; English Bicknor; Gorsley & Kilcot; Hartpury; Hewelsfield & Brockweir; Huntley; Kempley; Littledean; Longhope; Lydbrook; Mitcheldean; Newland; Newnham; Pauntley; Redmarley; Ruardean; Rudford & Highleadon; Ruspidge & Soudley; St Briavels; Staunton (Glos); Staunton (Coleford); Taynton; Tibberton; Tidenham; Upleadon; West Dean; Westbury-on-Severn; Woolaston.

Parish Meetings in the authority's area: Oxenhall.

Town Councils in the authority's area: Cinderford; Coleford; Lydney; Newent.

FYLDE BOROUGH COUNCIL

www.fylde.gov.uk

Principal Office

Town Hall, Lytham St Annes, Lancashire FY8 1LW
Telephone: (01253) 658658; FAX: (01253) 713113

Environmental Services Department

Public Offices, 292 Clifton Drive South, Lytham St Annes FY8 1LH
Telephone: (01253) 724141; FAX: (01253) 713113

Planning Department

Council Offices, Derby Road, Wesham PR4 3AN
Telephone: (01772) 671488; FAX: (01772) 671401

Function	Chief Officer	Title	Location
Chief Executive	Mr K Lee	Chief Executive	Town Hall
Electoral Registration	Mr P Welsh	Electoral Registration Officer	Town Hall
Finance	Mr B White	Finance Business Unit	Town Hall
Housing	Mr D Wilkinson	Unit Manager – The Built Environment	Town Hall
Legal Services	Mr I Curtis	Unit Manager – Legal & Democratic Services	Town Hall
Leisure	Mr P Norris	Unit Manager – Cultural Services	Town Hall
Local Land Charges	Mr I Curtis	Unit Manager – Legal & Democratic Services	Town Hall
Planning	Mr D Wilkinson	Unit Manager – The Built Environment	Town Hall
Purchasing & Supplies	Mr A Oldfield	Unit Manager – Policy & Change Management	Town Hall
Technical Services	Mr D Jenkinson	Unit Manager – Streetscene Management	Town Hall

Parish Councils in the authority's area: Bryning with Warton; Elswick; Freckleton; Greenhalgh with Thistleton; Kirkham; Little Eccleston with Larbreck; Medlar with Wesham; Newton with Clifton; Ribby with Wrea; Singleton; Staining; Treales, Roseacre & Wharles; Weeton with Preese; Westby with Plumptons.

GEDLING BOROUGH COUNCIL

www.gedling.gov.uk

Principal Office
Civic Centre, Arnot Hill Park, Arnold, Nottingham NG5 6LU
Telephone: (0115) 901 3901; FAX: (0115) 901 3921

Leisure Services
Arnot Hill House, Arnot Hill Park, Arnold, Nottingham NG5 6LU

Function	Chief Officer	Title	Location
Electoral Registration	Mr P Murdock	Director of Community Services	Civic Centre
Environmental Health	Mr P Kanuritch	Director of Environment & Development	Civic Centre
Finance	Mr R A Hankin	Director of Resources	Civic Centre
Housing	Mrs L Clayton	Head of Housing Services	Civic Centre
Legal Services	Mr P Murdock	Director of Community Services	Civic Centre
Leisure	Mr K Tansley	Head of Leisure Services	Arnot Hill Hse
Local Land Charges	Mrs S Sale	Head of Legal & Administration	Civic Centre
Planning	Mr P Kanuritch	Director of Environment & Development	Civic Centre
Technical Services	Mr C Groves	Head of Engineering & Property	Civic Centre

Parish Councils in the authority's area: Bestwood St Albans; Burton Joyce; Calverton; Colwick; Lambley; Linby; Newstead; Papplewick; Ravenshead; Stoke Bardolph; Woodborough.

Town Councils in the authority's area: None.

GILLINGHAM BOROUGH COUNCIL
See Medway Council.

GLANFORD BOROUGH COUNCIL
Glanford Borough Council was abolished on 31 March 1996; see now North Lincolnshire Council.

GLOUCESTER CITY COUNCIL

www.gloucester.gov.uk

Principal Office
North Warehouse, The Docks, Gloucester GL1 2EP
Telephone: (01452) 522232; FAX: (01452) 396140; DX 7516 Gloucester 1

Function	Chief Officer	Title	Location
Chief Executive	Mr P Smith	Managing Director	North W'house
Electoral Registration	Mr A Webb	Resource Manager (Legal & Democratic Services)	North W'house
Environmental Health	Mr D Clegg	Director of Community Services	North W'house
Finance	Mr K Birtles	Director of Finance	North W'house
Housing	Mr D Clegg	Director of Community Services	North W'house
Leisure	Mr D Clegg	Director of Community Services	North W'house

Parish Councils in the authority's area: Quedgeley.

GOSPORT BOROUGH COUNCIL

www.gosport.gov.uk

Principal Office
Town Hall, High Street, Gosport, Hampshire PO12 1EB
Telephone: (023) 9258 4242; FAX: (023) 9251 1279

Function	Chief Officer	Title	Location
Chief Executive	Mr M Crocker	Chief Executive	Town Hall
Electoral Registration	Mr P Lister	Head of Electoral Services	Town Hall
Environmental Health	Mr I Lycett	Director of Development & Environment	Town Hall
Finance	Mr P Wilson	Borough Treasurer	Town Hall
Housing	Mr R Facey	Housing Services Manager	Town Hall
Legal Services	Ms L Edwards	Borough Solicitor	Town Hall
Leisure	Mr D Martin	Leisure & Amenities Manager	Town Hall
Local Land Charges	Sally Hall	Senior Land Charges Officer	Town Hall
Planning	Mr I Lycett	Director of Development & Environment	Town Hall
Purchasing & Supplies	Jan Sunley	Head of Central Services	Town Hall
Technical Services	Mr M Jeffery	Regulatory Services Manager	Town Hall

Parish Councils & Parish Meetings in the authority's area: none.

Town Councils in the authority's area: none.

GRAVESHAM BOROUGH COUNCIL

www.gravesham.gov.uk

Principal Office
Civic Centre, Windmill Street, Gravesend, Kent DA12 1AU
Telephone: (01474) 564422; FAX: (01474) 337453; DX 6804 Gravesend

**Environmental Services Division; Planning and Regeneration Services Department;
Engineering Services Department; Building Services Department;
Environment & Public Health Services Department**
Cygnet House, 132 Windmill Street, Gravesend DA12 1BQ
Telephone: (01474) 564422; FAX: (01474) 337546

Gravesham Services
Brookvale Depot, Springhead Road, Northfleet, Gravesend DA11 8HW
Telephone: (01474) 564422

Function	Chief Officer	Title	Location
Electoral Registration	Mrs S Whatmough	Head of Democratic Services	Civic Centre
Environmental Health	Mrs P Jefford	Head of Environmental & Public Health Services	Cygnet House
Finance	Mr W Williams	Head of Financial Services	Civic Centre
Housing	Mr A Chequers	Head of Housing Services	Civic Centre
Legal Services	Mr M Hayley	Head of Legal Services	Civic Centre
Leisure	Mr L Beven	Head of Leisure Services	Civic Centre
Local Land Charges	Mr M Hayley	Head of Legal Services	Civic Centre
Planning	Mr K Burbidge	Head of Planning & Regeneration Services	Cygnet House
Technical Services	Mr D Stone	Director of Gravesham Services	Brookvale Depot

Parish Councils in the authority's area: Cobham; Higham; Luddesdown; Meopham; Shorne; Vigo.

GREAT GRIMSBY BOROUGH COUNCIL
Great Grimsby Borough Council was abolished on 31 March 1996; see now North East Lincolnshire Council.

DISTRICT COUNCILS

GREAT YARMOUTH BOROUGH COUNCIL

www.great-yarmouth.gov.uk

Principal Office

Town Hall, Hall Quay, Great Yarmouth, Norfolk NR30 2QF

Telephone: (01493) 856100; FAX: (01493) 846221; DX 41121 Great Yarmouth

Function	Chief Officer	Title	Location
Chief Executive	Mr R W Packham	Chief Executive	Town Hall
Electoral Registration	Mr R W Packham	Chief Executive	Town Hall
Environmental Health	Mr M Barrow	Corporate Director (Environmental Policy)	Town Hall
Finance	Mr R W Packham	Chief Executive	Town Hall
Housing	Mr B Bergin	Corporate Director (Social Policy)	Town Hal
Legal Services	Mr R W Packham	Chief Executive	Town Hall
Leisure	Mr M Barrow	Corporate Director (Environmental Policy)	Town Hall
Local Land Charges	Mr J Woodcock	Corporate Director (Economic Policy)	Town Hall
Planning	Mr J Woodcock	Corporate Director (Economic Policy)	Town Hall
Technical Services	Mr M Barrow	Corporate Director (Environmental Policy)	Town Hall

Parish Councils in the authority's area: Belton with Browston; Bradwell; Burgh Castle; Caister-on-Sea; Filby; Fleggburgh; Fritton with St Olaves; Hemsby; Hopton-on-Sea; Martham; Mautby; Ormesby St Margaret with Scratby; Ormesby St Michael; Repps with Bastwick; Rollesby; Somerton; Stokesby; Thurne; West Caister; Winterton-on-Sea.

Parish Meetings in the authority's area: Ashby with Oby.

GUILDFORD BOROUGH COUNCIL

www.guildfordborough.gov.uk

Principal Office

Millmead House, Millmead, Guildford, Surrey GU2 4BB

Telephone: (01483) 505050; FAX: (01483) 444444; DX 2472 Guildford 1

Function	Chief Officer	Title	Location
Chief Executive	Mr D Williams	Chief Executive	Millmead Hse
Electoral Registration	Mr D Williams	Chief Executive	Millmead Hse
Environmental Health	Mr C Bell	Chief Environmental Health Officer	Millmead Hse
Finance	Mr M Paddock	Borough Treasurer	Millmead Hse
Housing	Mr A Maunders	Director of Housing & Health Services	Millmead Hse
Legal Services	Ms H Sutherland	Clerk & Solicitor	Millmead Hse
Leisure	Mr J Miles	Director of Leisure Services	Millmead Hse
Local Land Charges	Ms H Sutherland	Clerk & Solicitor	Millmead Hse
Planning	Mrs E Mitchell	Director of Environmental & Planning Services	Millmead Hse
Purchasing & Supplies	Mr M Paddock	Borough Treasurer	Millmead Hse

Parish Councils in the authority's area: Albury; Artington; Ash; Compton; East Clandon; East Horsley; Effingham; Normandy; Ockham; Pirbright; Puttenham; Ripley; St Martha; Seale & Sands; Send; Shackleford; Shalford; Shere; Tongham; Wanborough; West Clandon; West Horsley; Worplesdon.

Parish Meetings in the authority's area: Wisley.

HALTON BOROUGH COUNCIL

Halton Borough Council became a unitary authority on 1 April 1998.

HAMBLETON DISTRICT COUNCIL

www.hambleton.gov.uk

Principal Office
Civic Centre, Stone Cross, Northallerton, North Yorkshire DL6 2UU
Telephone: (01609) 779977; FAX: (01609) 767228; DX 61650 Northallerton 1

Function	Chief Officer	Title	Location
Chief Executive	Mr P Simpson	Chief Executive	Civic Centre
Electoral Registration	Mr P Simpson	Chief Executive	Civic Centre
Environmental Health	Mr S Quartermain	Director of Planning & Environmental Services	Civic Centre
Finance	Mr P Morton	Director of Resources	Civic Centre
Housing	Mr S Quartermain	Director of Planning & Environmental Services	Civic Centre
Legal Services	Mr P Simpson	Chief Executive	Civic Centre
Leisure	Mr S Quartermain	Director of Planning & Environmental Services	Civic Centre
Local Land Charges	Mr P Simpson	Chief Executive	Civic Centre
Planning	Mr S Quartermain	Director of Planning & Environmental Services	Civic Centre
Purchasing & Supplies	Mr P Morton	Director of Resources	Civic Centre
Technical Services	Mr S Quartermain	Director of Planning & Environmental Services	Civic Centre

Parish Councils in the authority's area: Ainderby Mires with Holtby; Aiskew; Aldwark; Alne; Appleton Wiske; Bagby; Balk; Bilsdale Midcable; Boltby; Borrowby; Brafferton; Brandsby-cum-Stearsby; Brompton; Burneston; Burrill with Cowling; Carlton; Carlton Miniott; Carthorpe; Clifton-on-Yore; Cotcliffe; Cowesby; Coxwold; Crakehall;' Crayke; Crosby; Dalton; Danby Wiske; East Cowton; East Harlsey; East Rounton; East Tanfield; Ellerbeck; Exelby, Leeming & Newton; Felixkirk; Flawith; Great Ayton; Great & Little Broughton; Great Smeaton; Hackforth; Helperby; High Worsall; Hornby; Howgrave; Huby; Husthwaite; Hutton Rudby; Hutton Sessay; Ingleby Arncliffe; Ingleby Greenhow; Kepwick; Kilburn High & Low; Kirby Knowle; Kirby Sigston; Kirby Wiske; Kirkby; Kirkby Fleetham with Fencote; Kirklington-cum-Upsland; Knayton with Brawith; Landmoth-cum-Catto; Langthorne; Lazenby; Linton-on-Ouse; Little Smeaton; Low Worsall; Maunby; Middleton-on-Leven; Morton-on-Swale; Nether Silton; Newby; Newby Wiske; Newsham with Breckenbrough; Newton-on-Ouse; Osmotherley; Over Silton; Pickhill with Roxby; Potto; Raskelf; Romanby; Rookwith; Rudby; Sandhutton; Scruton; Seamer; Sessay; Shipton; Sinderby; Skutterskelfe; Snape with Thorp; South Kilvington; South Otterington; Sowerby; Sowerby-under-Cotcliffe; Stillington; Stokesley; Sutton with Howgrave; Sutton-on-the-Forest; Sutton-under-Whitestonecliffe; Swainby with Allerthorpe; Theakston; Thimbleby; Thirkleby High & Low with Osgodby; Thirn; Thornton Watlass; Thornton-le-Beans; Thornton-le-Moor; Thornton-le-Street; Tollerton; Topcliffe; Upsall; Welbury; Well; West Harlsey; West Rounton; West Tanfield; Whorlton; Winton, Stank & Hallikeld; Youlton.

Parish Meetings in the authority's area: Ainderby Quernhow; Ainderby Steeple; Angram Grange; Beningbrough; Birdforth; Birkby; Carlton Husthwaite; Catton; Crathorne; Dalby-cum-Skewsby; Deighton; Easby; Eldmire with Crakehill; Faceby; Farlington; Fawdington; Firby; Gatenby; Girsby; Great Busby; Great Langton; Holme; Hood Grange; Howe; Hutton Bonville; Kildale; Killerby; Kiplin; Leake; Little Ayton; Little Busby; Little Langton; Marton-cum-Moxby; Myton-on-Swale; Newburgh; North Kilvington; North Otterington; Oulston; Over Dinsdale; Overton; Picton; Rand Grange; Sexhow; Skipton-on-Swale; South Cowton; Thirlby; Tholthorpe; Thormanby; Thornbrough; Thornton-on-the-Hill; Thrintoft; Warlaby; Whenby; Whitwell; Wildon Grange; Yafforth; Yearsley.

Town Councils in the authority's area: Bedale; Easingwold; Northallerton; Thirsk.

DISTRICT COUNCILS

HARBOROUGH DISTRICT COUNCIL

www.harborough.gov.uk

Principal Office
Council Offices, Adam & Eve Street, Market Harborough, Leicestershire LE16 7AG
Telephone: (01858) 821100; FAX: (01858) 821000; DX 27317 Market Harborough

Function	Chief Officer	Title	Location
Chief Executive	Mr M Wilson	Chief Executive	Council Offices
Electoral Registration	Mr N Burton	Electoral Services Officer	Council Offices
Environmental Health	Mr N Proudfoot;		
	Mr P Brailsford	Environmental Health Manager	Council Offices
Finance	Mrs V Heathcote	Finance Services Manager	Council Offices
Housing	Mrs A Ball	Housing Services Manager	Council Offices
Legal Services	Mr P McCourt	Head of Legal Services	Council Offices
Leisure	Mr C Holliday	Leisure & Community Development Manager	Council Offices
Local Land Charges	Mrs J Calvert	Land Charges Manager	Council Offices
Planning	Mr J Worley	Development Control Manager	Council Offices
Purchasing & Supplies	Mr P Rowbotham	Customer Services Manager	Council Offices
Technical Services	Mr B Coleman	Senior Engineer	Council Offices

Parish Councils in the authority's area: Arnesby; Ashby Magna; Billesdon; Bitteswell; Broughton Astley; Bruntingthorpe; Burton Overy; Claybrooke Magna; Claybrooke Parva; Cotesbach; Dunton Bassett; East Langton; Fleckney; Foxton; Gilmorton; Great Bowden; Great Easton; Great Glen; Hallaton; Houghton-on-the-Hill; Hungarton; Husbands Bosworth; Illston-on-the-Hill; Kibworth Beauchamp; Kibworth Harcourt; Kimcote & Walton; Knaptoft; Leire; Lubenham; Medbourne; Misterton with Walcote; North Kilworth; Scraptoft; Smeeton Westerby; South Kilworth; Stoughton; Swinford; Theddingworth; Thurnby; Tilton-on-the-Hill; Tugby Keythorpe; Tur Langton; Ullesthorpe; Willoughby Waterleys.

Parish Meetings in the authority's area: Allexton; Ashby Parva; Bittesby; Blaston; Bringhurst; Carlton Curlieu; Catthorpe; Cold Newton & Lowesby; Cranoe; Drayton & Neville Holt; East Norton; Frisby; Frolesworth; Gaulby; Glooston; Goadby; Gumley; Horninghold; Keyham; Kings Norton; Laughton; Little Stretton; Loddington with Launde; Marefield; Mowsley; Noseley; Owston; Peatling Magna; Peatling Parva; Rolleston; Saddington; Shangton; Shawell; Shearsby; Skeffington; Slawston; Stockerston; Stonton Wyville; Thorpe Langton; Welham; West Langton; Westrill & Starmore; Wistow & Newton Harcourt.

Town Councils in the authority's area: Lutterworth.

HARLOW DISTRICT COUNCIL

www.harlow.gov.uk

Principal Office
Civic Centre, The Water Gardens, Harlow, Essex CM20 1WG
Telephone: (01279) 446655; FAX: (01279) 446844

Purchasing & Supplies
Mead Park Depot, Riverway, Harlow, Essex CM20 2SE
Telephone: (01279) 446947; FAX: (01279) 446979

Function	Chief Officer	Title	Location
Chief Executive	Mr M Morley	Chief Executive	Civic Centre
Electoral Registration	Mr G Branchett	Executive Director of Resources	Civic Centre
Environmental Health	Mr M Pitt;		
	Mr P Anderson	Heads of Environmental Health	Civic Centre
Finance	Mr K Smith	Head of Finance	Civic Centre
Housing	[Vacant]	Executive Director for Housing	Civic Centre
Legal Services	Mr O Willcox	Legal Services Manager	Civic Centre
Leisure	[Vacant]	Head of Leisure	Civic Centre

Function	Chief Officer	Title	Location
Local Land Charges	Mr C Crake	Planning Policy Manager	Civic Centre
Planning	Mr C Crake	Planning Policy Manager	Civic Centre
Purchasing & Supplies	Mr G Drage	Supplies Manager	Mead Park Depot
Technical Services	Mr D Hirst;	Corporate Services Manager;	Civic Centre
	Ms C Harman	Development Systems Manager	Civic Centre

Parish Councils & Parish Meetings in the authority's area: none.

Town Councils in the authority's area: none.

HARROGATE BOROUGH COUNCIL

www.harrogate.gov.uk

Principal Office
Council Offices, Crescent Gardens, Harrogate, North Yorkshire HG1 2SG
Telephone: (01423) 500600; FAX: (01423) 556010; DX 11962 Harrogate

Health & Housing Department
Springfield House, Kings Road, Harrogate HG1 5NX
Telephone: (01423) 500600

Department of Leisure & Amenities
Brandreth House, St Lukes Avenue, Harrogate HG1 2AA
Telephone: (01423) 500600; FAX: (01423) 556710

Harrogate International Centre (Conference Centre)
Kings Road, Harrogate HG1 5LA
Telephone: (01423) 500500; FAX: (01423) 537210

Department of Technical Services
Knapping Mount, West Grove Road, Harrogate HG1 2AE
Telephone: (01423) 500600; FAX: (01423) 556510

Function	Chief Officer	Title	Location
Chief Executive	Mr P M Walsh	Chief Executive	Council Offices
Electoral Registration	Mrs K Birdsall	Senior Elections Officer	Council Offices
Environmental Health	Mr L Williamson	Director of Health & Housing	Springfield Hse
Finance	Mr J Sowden	Finance Director	Council Offices
Housing	Mr L Williamson	Director of Health & Housing	Springfield Hse
Legal Services	Miss F Hildred	Director of Administration	Council Offices
Leisure	Mr K V Douglas	Director of Leisure & Amenities	Brandreth Hse
Local Land Charges	Miss J Grainger		Council Offices
Planning	Mr T Richards	Head of Planning	Knapping Mount
Purchasing & Supplies	Mr R Firth		Council Offices
Technical Services	Mr J P Fitzgerald	Director of Technical Services	Knapping Mount

Parish Councils in the authority's area: Arkendale, Coneythorpe & Clareton; Asenby; Azerley & Winksley; Baldersby; Bewerley; Bilton-in-Ainsty with Bickerton; Birstwith; Bishop Monkton; Bishop Thornton & Warsill; Boroughbridge & Minskip; Burton Leonard; Cattal, Hunsingore & Great Ribston with Walshford; Clint-cum-Hamlets; Cundall with Leckby & Norton-le-Clay; Dacre; Dishforth; Fearby, Healey & District; Felliscliffe; Follifoot & Plompton; Fountains Abbey; Goldsborough & Flaxby; Grantley & Sawley, Eavestone & Skelding; Great Ouseburn; Green Hammerton; Grewelthorpe; Hampsthwaite; Hartwith-cum-Winsley; Haverah Park, Pannal & Beckwithshaw; Hewick & Hutton; High & Low Bishopside; Kearby with Netherby; Killinghall; Kirby Hill & District; Kirk Deighton; Kirk Hammerton; Kirkby Malzeard, Laverton; Kirkby Overblow; Knaresborough; Langthorpe; Little Ouseburn; Little Ribston & North Deighton; Littlethorpe; Long Marston; Lower Washburn; Markington with Wallerthwaite; Marton-cum-Grafton; Marton-le-Moor; Masham; Melmerby & Middleton; Menwith with Darley; Mid Wharfedale; Moor Monkton; Newall with Clifton; Nidd; North Rigton; North Stainley with Sleningford; Nun Monkton; Rainton with Newby; Ripon Successor; Roecliff & Westwicke; Scotton; Scriven; Sharow; Sicklinghall; Skelton; Spofforth with Stockeld; Staveley & Copgrove; Tockwith & Wilstrop; Upper Nidderdale; Washburn; Wath & Norton Conyers; Weeton; Whixley; Wighill.

Parish Meetings in the authority's area: Allerton Mauleverer with Hopperton; Brearton; Farnham; Ferrensby; Lower Dunsforth; Markenfield Hall; Ripley; South Stainley; Thornthwaite with Padside; Thornville; Thruscross; Walkingham Hill & Occaney.

Town Councils in the authority's area: Boroughbridge; Knaresborough; Pateley Bridge; Ripon.

HART DISTRICT COUNCIL

www.hart.gov.uk

Principal Office

Civic Offices, Harlington Way, Fleet, Hampshire GU51 4AE
Telephone: (01252) 622122; FAX: (01252) 626886

The Depot

Springwell Lane Depot, Springwell Lane, Hartley, Wintney, Hampshire
Telephone: (01252) 622122

Function	Chief Officer	Title	Location
Chief Executive	Jules Samuels	Chief Executive	Civic Offices
Electoral Registration	Tracy Cottee	Democratic Services Manager	Civic Offices
Environmental Health	Ron Percival	Head of Environmental Services	Civic Offices
Finance	David Skelton	Head of Finance	Civic Offices
Housing	[Vacant]	Housing Services Manager	Civic Offices
Legal Services	Charles Herbert	Solicitor to the Council & Monitoring Officer	Civic Offices
Leisure	Carol Peake	Head of Leisure & Cultural Services	Civic Offices
Local Land Charges	Rod Hursthouse	Principal Solicitor	Civic Offices
Planning	Ron Percival	Head of Environmental Services	Civic Offices
Purchasing & Supplies	Brian Daly	Office Services Manager	Civic Offices
Technical Services	Jim Pitkin;	Head of Technical Services;	Civic Offices;
	Phil Whiting	General Manager, Direct Services	Springwell Ln

Parish Councils in the authority's area: Bramshill; Crondall; Crookham Village; Dogmersfield; Eversley; Greywell; Hartley Wintney; Heckfield; Hook; Long Sutton; Mattingley; Odiham; Rotherwick; South Warnborough; Winchfield.

Town Councils in the authority's area: Blackwater & Hawley; Yateley.

HARTLEPOOL DISTRICT COUNCIL

Hartlepool became a unitary authority on 1 April 1996.

HASTINGS BOROUGH COUNCIL

www.hastings.gov.uk

Principal Office; Directorate of Finance

Town Hall, Queens Road, Hastings, East Sussex TN34 1QR
Telephone: (01424) 781066; FAX: (01424) 781743; DX 7055 Hastings

Leisure & Cultural Development Directorate;
Housing & Neighbourhood Renewal Directorate

No. 4 Robertson Terrace, Hastings, East Sussex TN34 1JE
Telephone: (01424) 781338; FAX: (01424) 781319 (Leisure); FAX: (01424) 781305 (Housing)

Regeneration & Planning Directorate

Aquila House, Breeds Place, Hastings, East Sussex TN34 3UY
Telephone: (01424) 781066; FAX: (01424) 781515

Environment & Safety Directorate

Century House, 100 Menzies Road, St Leonards on Sea TN38 9BB
Telephone: (01424) 781066; FAX: (01424) 783208

DISTRICT COUNCILS

Function	Chief Officer	Title	Location
Chief Executive	Mr R Mawford	Chief Executive	Town Hall
Electoral Registration	Mrs M Clarke	Scrutiny & Democratic Services Manager	Town Hall
Environmental Health	Mr R Homewood	Executive Director, Environment & Safety	Century House
Finance	Mr N Dart	Deputy Chief Executive & Director of Finance	Town Hall
Housing	Mr R Peters	Executive Director, Housing & Neighbourhood Renewal	Robertson Terrace
Legal Services	Mrs J Butters	Borough Solicitor	Town Hall
Leisure	Mr M Marsh	Executive Director, Leisure & Cultural Development	Robertson Terrace
Local Land Charges	Mr K Wood	Administrative Officer	Town Hall
Planning	Mr P Lewis	Borough Planning Officer	Century House

Parish Councils & Parish Meetings in the authority's area: none.

Town Councils in the authority's area: none.

HAVANT BOROUGH COUNCIL

www.havant.gov.uk

Principal Office

Civic Offices, Civic Centre Road, Havant, Hampshire PO9 2AX
Telephone: (023) 9247 4174; FAX: (023) 9248 0263; DX 50005 Havant

Function	Chief Officer	Title	Location
Chief Executive	Gwen Andrews	Managing Director	Civic Offices
Electoral Registration	Tim Slater	Head of Democratic Services	Civic Offices
Environmental Health	Frank Campbell	Director of Environmental Services	Civic Offices
Finance	Nigel Smith	Head of Resources	Civic Offices
Housing	Frank Campbell	Director of Environmental Services	Civic Offices
Legal Services	Tim Slater	Head of Democratic Services	Civic Offices
Leisure	David Bridges	Head of Community Services	Civic Offices
Local Land Charges	Jackie Batchelor	Acting Head of Planning & Development	Civic Offices
Planning	Frank Campbell	Director of Environmental Services	Civic Offices
Purchasing & Supplies	Nigel Smith	Head of Resources	Civic Offices
Technical Services	Alastair Norton	Head of Technical Services	Civic Offices

Parish Councils & Parish Meetings in the authority's area: none.

Town Councils in the authority's area: none.

HEREFORD CITY COUNCIL
Hereford City Council was abolished on 31 March 1998; see now The Herefordshire Council.

HERTSMERE BOROUGH COUNCIL

www.hertsmere.gov.uk

Principal Office

Civic Offices, Elstree Way, Borehamwood, Hertfordshire WD6 1WA
Telephone: (020) 8207 2277; FAX: (020) 8207 7441

Hertsmere Leisure

Suite 6, Bournehall House, Bournehall Road, Bushey, Hertfordshire WD23 3HP
Telephone: (020) 8386 4044

Function	Chief Officer	Title	Location
Chief Executive	Mr R Higgins	Head of Paid Service	Civic Offices

Electoral Registration	Ms B Foster	Head of Legal Services	Civic Offices
Environmental Health	Mr R Crooks	Head of Health & Housing	Civic Offices
Finance	Ms S Bijle	Head of Accountancy & Finance	Civic Offices
Housing	Mr M Knights	Head of Housing Services	Civic Offices
Legal Services	Ms B Foster	Head of Legal Services	Civic Offices
Leisure	Mr P Collins	Chief Executive (Hertsmere Leisure)	Bournehall Hse
Local Land Charges	Ms B Foster	Head of Legal Services	Civic Offices
Planning	Mr R Grove	Head of Planning	Civic Offices
Purchasing & Supplies	Ms M Earwood	Commercial Manager	Civic Offices
Technical Services	Mr E Casebourne	Interim Head of Technical Services	Civic Offices

Parish Councils in the authority's area: Aldenham; Ridge; Shenley.

Town Councils in the authority's area: Elstree & Borehamwood.

HIGH PEAK BOROUGH COUNCIL

www.highpeak.gov.uk

Principal Office
Council Offices, Hayfield Road, Chapel-en-le-Frith, High Peak SK23 0QJ
Telephone: 0845 129 7777; FAX: (01663) 751042

Finance; Environment and Health Services
Town Hall, Buxton, Derbyshire SK17 6EL
Telephone: 0845 129 7777; FAX: (01298) 27639

Housing, Regeneration and Leisure Services
Municipal Buildings, Glossop, Derbyshire SK13 8AF
Telephone: 0845 129 7777; FAX: (01457) 860290

Function	Chief Officer	Title	Location
Electoral Registration	Mr D Staden	Democratic Services Manager	Council Offices
Environmental Health	Mr A Leah	Head of Environment & Health	Town Hall
Finance	Mr D Johnson	Head of Finance	Town Hall
Housing	Ms S Cambridge	Chief Executive, High Peak Community Housing	Municipal Bldgs
Legal Services	Mrs R Stafford	Head of Legal & Democratic Services	Council Offices
Leisure	Mr R Hall	Head of Leisure	Municipal Bldgs
Local Land Charges	Mrs R Stafford	Head of Legal & Democratic Services	Council Offices
Planning	Mr I Shore	Development Control Manager	Municipal Bldgs
Purchasing & Supplies	Mrs B Barrett	Administration Manager	Council Offices

Parish Councils in the authority's area: Bamford with Thornhill; Castleton; Chapel-en-le-Frith; Charlesworth; Chinley, Buxworth & Brownside; Chisworth; Derwent & Hope Woodlands; Edale; Green Fairfield; Hartington Upper Quarter; Hayfield; Hope with Aston; New Mills; Peak Forest; Tintwistle; Whaley Bridge; Wormhill.

HINCKLEY & BOSWORTH BOROUGH COUNCIL

www.hinckley-bosworth.gov.uk

Principal Office
Council Offices, Argents Mead, Hinckley, Leicestershire LE10 1BZ
Telephone: (01455) 238141; FAX: (01455) 251172; DX 716429 Hinckley

Environmental Services Department; Law and Administration Department
Florence House, St Marys Road, Hinckley LE10 1EQ
Telephone: (01455) 238141

Function	Chief Officer	Title	Location
Chief Executive	Mr J Corry	Chief Executive	Council Offices
Electoral Registration	Mr J Corry	Chief Executive	Council Offices

Environmental Health	Mr T Prowse	Head of Environmental Services	Florence Hse
Finance	Ms J Penman	Head of Finance	Council Offices
Housing	Mr K G Bray	Head of Housing	Council Offices
Legal Services	Mr R M Tobin	Director of Resources	Council Offices
Leisure	Mr B Cullen	Head of Planning & Leisure	Council Offices
Local Land Charges	Mr R M Tobin	Director of Resources	Council Offices
Planning	Mr B Cullen	Head of Planning & Leisure	Council Offices

Parish Councils in the authority's area: Bagworth; Barlestone; Burbage; Cadeby; Carlton; Desford; Earl Shilton; Groby; Higham on the Hill; Market Bosworth; Markfield; Nailstone; Newbold-Verdon; Osbaston; Peckleton; Ratby; Shackerstone; Sheepy; Stanton-under-Bardon; Stoke Golding; Sutton Cheney; Twycross; Witherley.

Parish Meetings in the authority's area: none.

HOLDERNESS BOROUGH COUNCIL

Holderness Borough Council was abolished on 31 March 1996; see now East Riding of Yorkshire Council.

HORSHAM DISTRICT COUNCIL

www.horsham.gov.uk

Principal Office

Park House, North Street, Horsham, West Sussex RH12 1RL
Telephone: (01403) 215100; FAX: (01403) 262985; DX 57609 Horsham 6

Function	Chief Officer	Title	Location
Chief Executive	M J Pearson	Chief Executive	Park House
Electoral Registration	M J Wright	Head of Democratic Services & Community Strategy	Park House
Environmental Health	K C Feltham	Director of Environmental Services	Park House
Finance	A J Higgins	Director of Finance	Park House
Housing	Miss C J Antill	Head of Housing Services	Park House
Legal Services	I R Davison	Head of Legal Services	Park House
Leisure	C H Dier	Director of Leisure Services	Park House
Local Land Charges	G J Tucker	Plans Processing Officer	Park House
Planning	A W Stevens	Director of Planning	Park House
Technical Services	R E Skeet	Chief Technical Officer	Park House

Parish Councils in the authority's area: Amberley; Ashington; Ashurst; Billingshurst; Bramber; Broadbridge Heath; Coldwaltham; Colgate; Cowfold; Henfield; Itchingfield; Lower Beeding; North Horsham; Nuthurst; Parham; Pulborough; Rudgwick; Rusper; Shermanbury; Shipley; Slinfold; Southwater; Steyning; Storrington & Sullington; Thakeham; Upper Beeding; Warnham; Washington; West Chiltington; West Grinstead; Wiston; Woodmancote.

Neighbourhood Parish Councils in the authority's area: Denne; Forest & Riverside; Trafalgar.

HOVE BOROUGH COUNCIL

Brighton Borough Council & Hove Borough Council became a single unitary authority on 1 April 1997.

HUNTINGDONSHIRE DISTRICT COUNCIL

www.huntingdonshire.gov.uk

Principal Office

Pathfinder House, St Mary's Street, Huntingdon, Cambridgeshire PE29 3TN
Telephone: (01480) 388388; FAX: (01480) 388099; DX 80929 Huntingdon 1

Function	Chief Officer	Title	Location
Chief Executive	Mr D Monks	Chief Executive	Pathfinder Hse

DISTRICT COUNCILS

Electoral Registration	Mr P Watkins	Director of Central Services	Pathfinder Hse
Environmental Health	Mrs E Wilson	Director of Operational Services	Pathfinder Hse
Finance	Mr D Oliver	Director of Commerce & Technology	Pathfinder Hse
Housing	Mr S Plant	Head of Housing Services	Pathfinder Hse
Legal Services	Mr C Meadowcroft	Head of Legal & Estates	Pathfinder Hse
Leisure	Mr P Jones	Head of Community Services	Pathfinder Hse
Local Land Charges	Mr P Watkins	Director of Central Services	Pathfinder Hse
Planning	Mrs E Wilson	Director of Operational Services	Pathfinder Hse
Purchasing & Supplies	Mr R Lakin	Procurement Manager	Pathfinder Hse
Technical Services	Mrs E Wilson	Director of Operational Services	Pathfinder Hse

Parish Councils in the authority's area: Abbots Ripton; Abbotsley; Alconbury; Alconbury Weston; Alwalton; Barham & Woolley; Bluntisham; Brampton; Brington & Molesworth; Broughton; Buckden; Buckworth; Bury; Bythorn & Keyston; Catworth; Colne; Conington; Earith; Easton; Ellington; Elton; Eynesbury Hardwicke; Farcet; Fenstanton; Folksworth & Washingley; Glatton; Grafham; Great & Little Gidding; Great Gransden; Great Paxton; Great Staughton; Hail Weston; Hemingford Abbots; Hemingford Grey; Hilton; Holme; Holywell-cum-Needingworth; Houghton & Wyton; Kimbolton and Stonely; Kings Ripton; Leighton Bromswold; Little Paxton; Offord Cluny; Offord d'Arcy; Old Weston; Oldhurst; Perry; Pidley cum Fenton; St Neots Rural; Sawtry; Sibson-cum-Stibbington; Somersham; Southoe & Midloe; Spaldwick; Stilton; Stow Longa; Stukeleys; Tilbrook; Toseland; Upton & Coppingford; Upwood & The Raveleys; Warboys; Waresley; Wistow; Woodhurst; Woodwalton; Yaxley; Yelling.

Parish Meetings in the authority's area: Chesterton; Covington; Denton & Caldecote; Diddington; Haddon; Hamerton; Morborne; Steeple Gidding; Tetworth; Water Newton; Winwick.

Town Councils in the authority's area: Godmanchester; Huntingdon; Ramsey; St Ives; St Neots.

HYNDBURN BOROUGH COUNCIL

www.hyndburnbc.gov.uk

Principal Office
Council Offices, Scaitcliffe House, Ormerod Street, Accrington, Lancashire BB5 0PF
Telephone: (01254) 388111; FAX: (01254) 392597

Environmental Health Department; Housing Department
20 Cannon Street, Accrington BB5 1NJ
Telephone: (01254) 388111; FAX: (01254) 386711

Leisure Services
Town Hall, Broadway, Accrington BB5 1LA
Telephone: (01254) 388111; FAX: (01254) 380291

Works Services
Willows Lane Depot, Willows Lane, Accrington BB5 1LA
Telephone: (01254) 385021; FAX: (01254) 872250

Function	Chief Officer	Title	Location
Chief Executive	Mr D Welsby	Managing Director	Council Offices
Electoral Registration	Mr R Wilkinson	Senior Electoral Services Officer	Council Offices
Environmental Health	Mr S A Todd	Chief Environmental Services Officer	20 Cannon St
Finance	Mr J McIntyre	Chief Finance Officer	Council Offices
Housing	Mr K Bury	Director – Hyndburn Homes	20 Cannon St
Legal Services	Miss J Ellis	Head of Legal & Democratic Services	Council Offices
Leisure	Mr P Baron	Head of Leisure Services	Town Hall
Local Land Charges	Miss J Addison	Land Charges Officer	Council Offices
Planning	Mr B Lyons	Chief Planning & Transportation Officer	Council Offices
Purchasing & Supplies	Mr D Rydeheard	Assistant Services Manager	Council Offices
Technical Services	Mr J Schofield	Head of Transportation & Technical Services	Willows Lane Dep

Parish Council in the authority's area: Altham.

DISTRICT COUNCILS

IPSWICH BOROUGH COUNCIL

www.ipswich.gov.uk

Principal Office

Civic Centre, Civic Drive, Ipswich, Suffolk IP1 2EE
Telephone: (01473) 432000; FAX: (01473) 432522; DX 3225 Ipswich

Function	Chief Officer	Title	Location
Chief Executive	James Hehir	Chief Executive	Civic Centre
Electoral Registration	Brenda Welham-Clarke	Electoral Registration Officer	Civic Centre
Environmental Health	Concepta Palk	Environmental Services Manager	Civic Centre
Finance	Peter Matthews	Head of Financial Services	Civic Centre
Housing	Tracey Lee	Director	Civic Centre
Legal Services	[Vacant]	Head of Legal Services	Civic Centre
Leisure	Laurence Collins	Director	Civic Centre
Local Land Charges	Sally Boreham		Civic Centre
Planning	Laurence Collins	Director	Civic Centre
Purchasing & Supplies	Tracey Lee	Director	Civic Centre
Technical Services	[Vacant]	Borough Engineer	Civic Centre

Parish Councils & Parish Meetings in the authority's area: none.

Town Councils in the authority's area: none.

KENNET DISTRICT COUNCIL

www.kennet.gov.uk

Principal Office

Browfort, Bath Road, Devizes, Wiltshire SN10 2AT
Telephone: (01380) 724911; FAX: (01380) 729146; DX 42909 Devizes

Function	Chief Officer	Title	Location
Chief Executive	Mr M J Boden	Chief Executive	Browfort
Electoral Registration	Mr J Gale	Electoral Services Officer	Browfort
Environmental Health	Mrs M Bradley	Environmental Health & Protection Services Manager	Browfort
Finance	Mr F R Marshall	Director of Resources	Browfort
Housing	Mr P Cooper	Housing Services Manager	Browfort
Legal Services	Mrs M Memoli	Legal & Democratic Services Manager	Browfort
Leisure	Mr A Smith	Leisure Services Manager	Browfort
Local Land Charges	Mrs J Marsh	Local Land Charges Officer	Browfort
Purchasing & Supplies	Mrs S West	Procurement & Admin Manager	Browfort
Technical Services	Mr M Smith	Environment & Amenity Services Manager	Browfort

Parish Councils in the authority's area: Aldbourne; All Cannings; Alton; Avebury; Baydon; Beechingstoke; Berwick Bassett & Winterbourne Monkton; Bishops Cannings; Broad Hinton & Winterbourne Bassett; Bromham; Burbage; Charlton & Wilsford; Cheverell Magna; Cheverell Parva; Chilton Foliat; Chirton; Chute; Chute Forest; Collingbourne Ducis; Collingbourne Kingston; Easterton; Easton; Enford; Erlestoke; Etchilhampton; Everleigh; Fittleton; Froxfield; Fyfield & Overton; Grafton; Great Bedwyn; Ham; Little Bedwyn; Ludgershall; Manningford; Marden; Market Lavington; Marston; Mildenhall; Milton Lilbourne; Netheravon; North Newnton; Ogbourne St Andrew; Ogbourne St George; Patney; Pewsey; Potterne; Poulshot; Preshute; Ramsbury; Roundway; Rowde; Rushall; Savernake; Seend; Shalbourne; Stanton St Bernard; Stert; Tidworth; Upavon; Urchfont; West Lavington; Wilcot & Huish; Woodborough; Wootton Rivers; Worton.

Parish Meetings in the authority's area: Buttermere; East Kennett; Tidcombe & Fosbury.

Town Councils in the authority's area: Devizes; Marlborough.

DISTRICT COUNCILS

KERRIER DISTRICT COUNCIL

www.kerrier.gov.uk

Principal Office

Council Offices, Dolcoath Avenue, Camborne, Cornwall TR14 8SX
Telephone: (01209) 614000; FAX: (01209) 614491

Function	Chief Officer	Title	Location
Chief Executive	Mr B C Manning	Chief Executive	Council Offices
Electoral Registration	Mr N J Richards	Democratic Services Manager	Council Offices
Environmental Health	Mrs J Barlow	Head of Service (Housing & Environmental Health)	Council Offices
Finance	Mr N Tregenna	Chief Finance Officer (Acting)	Council Offices
Housing	Mrs J Barlow	Head of Service (Housing & Environmental Health)	Council Offices
Legal Services	Mr B E Davies	Head of Service (Legal)	Council Offices
Leisure	Mr R Grose	Head of Service (Regeneration)	Council Offices
Local Land Charges	Mr B E Davies	Head of Service (Legal)	Council Offices
Planning	Mr J Pender	Head of Service (Planning)	Council Offices
Purchasing & Supplies	Miss G Nettle	Senior Admin Assistant	Council Offices
Technical Services	Mr P Walsh	Head of Service (Environment & Engineering)	Council Offices

Parish Councils in the authority's area: Breage; Budock; Carharrack; Carn Brea; Constantine; Crowan; Cury; Germoe; Grade Ruan; Gunwalloe; Gweek; Illogan; Landewednack; Lanner; Mabe; Manaccan; Mawgan-in-Meneage; Mawnan; Mullion; Portreath; St Anthony; St Day; St Gluvias; St Keverne; St Martin; Sithney; Stithians; Wendron.

Town Councils in the authority's area: Camborne; Helston; Porthleven; Redruth.

KETTERING BOROUGH COUNCIL

www.kettering.gov.uk

Principal Office

Municipal Offices, Bowling Green Road, Kettering, Northamptonshire NN15 7QX
Telephone: (01536) 410333; FAX: (01536) 410795; DX 12816 Kettering

Function	Chief Officer	Title	Location
Chief Executive	Mr D Cook	Chief Executive	Municipal Offices
Electoral Registration	Mr I White	Head of Electoral Registration	Municipal Offices
Environmental Health	Mr S Isbister	Environmental Health Manager	Municipal Offices
Finance	Mr G Soulsby	Head of Finance & Strategic Development	Municipal Offices
Housing	Mr J Conway	Head of Housing Management	Municipal Offices
Legal Services	Mr J Eatough	Head of Legal & Democratic Services	Municipal Offices
Leisure	Mrs V Hitchman	Head of Community Services	Municipal Offices
Local Land Charges	Mrs M Deacon	Senior Land Charges Officer	Municipal Offices
Planning	Mrs C Harvey	Head of Development Services	Municipal Offices
Technical Services	Mr N Chapman	Transport & Engineering Manager	Municipal Offices
Purchasing & Supplies	Mr T Brown	Senior Administrator	Municipal Offices

Parish Councils in the authority's area: Ashley; Brampton; Braybrooke; Broughton; Cranford; Cransley; Dingley; Geddington, Newton & Little Oakley; Grafton Underwood; Harrington; Loddington; Pytchley; Rushton; Stoke Albany; Thorpe Malsor; Warkton; Weekley; Weston-by-Welland; Wilbarston.

Parish Meetings in the authority's area: Orton; Sutton Bassett.

Town Councils in the authority's area: Burton Latimer; Desborough; Rothwell.

KING'S LYNN & WEST NORFOLK BOROUGH COUNCIL

www.west-norfolk.gov.uk

Principal Office
Kings Court, Chapel Street, King's Lynn, Norfolk PE30 1EX
Telephone: (01553) 692722; FAX: (01553) 691663; DX 57825 King's Lynn

Function	Chief Officer	Title	Location
Chief Executive	Mr G Chilton	Chief Executive	Kings Court
Environmental Health	Mr T Hall	Corporate Director	Kings Court
Finance	Mr R Harding	Corporate Director	Kings Court
Housing	Mr T Hall	Corporate Director	Kings Court
Legal Services	Mr S Aley	Head of Legal & Democratic Services	Kings Court
Planning	Mr R High	Corporate Director	Kings Court
Purchasing & Supplies	Mr D Thomason	Head of Finance & ICT	Kings Court

Parish Councils in the authority's area: Barton Bendish; Bircham; Brancaster; Burnham Market; Burnham Overy; Burnham Thorpe; Castle Acre; Castle Rising; Clenchwarton; Congham; Crimplesham; Denver; Dersingham; Docking; Downham West; East Rudham; East Winch; Emneth; Feltwell; Fincham; Flitcham; Gayton; Great Massingham; Grimston; Harpley; Heacham; Hilgay; Hillington; Hockwold; Holme-next-Sea; Houghton; Ingoldisthorpe; Leziate; Little Massingham; Marham; Marshland St James; Methwold; Middleton; Nordelph; North Creake; North Runcton; North Wootton; Northwold; Outwell; Pentney; Ringstead; Roydon; Runcton Holme; Sandringham; Sedgeford; Shouldham; Snettisham; South Creake; South Wootton; Southery; Stanhoe; Stoke Ferry; Stow Bardolph; Syderstone; Terrington St Clement; Terrington St John; Thornham; Tilney All Saints; Tilney St Lawrence; Tottenhill; Upwell; Walpole; Walpole Cross Keys; Walpole Highway; Walsoken; Watlington; Welney; Wereham; West Acre; West Dereham; West Rudham; West Walton; West Winch; Wiggenhall St Germans; Wiggenhall St Mary Magdalen; Wimbotsham; Wormegay; Wretton.

Parish Meeetings in the authority's area: Anmer; Bagthorpe with Barmer; Barwick; Bawsey; Boughton; Burnham Norton; Choseley; East Walton; Fordham; Fring; Old Hunstanton; Ryston; Shernborne; Shouldham Thorpe; Stradsett; Titchwell.

Town Councils in the authority's area: Downham Market; Hunstanton.

KINGSTON UPON HULL CITY COUNCIL
Kingston upon Hull became a unitary authority on 1 April 1996.

KINGSWOOD BOROUGH COUNCIL
Kingswood Borough Council was abolished on 31 March 1995; see now South Gloucestershire Council.

LANCASTER CITY COUNCIL

www.lancaster.gov.uk

Principal Office
Town Hall, Lancaster LA1 1PJ
Telephone: (01524) 582000; FAX: (01524) 582161; DX 63531 Lancaster

Environmental Health Department; Leisure Department; Technical Services Department
Town Hall, Morecambe LA4 5AF
Telephone: (01524) 582000

Planning Department
Palatine Hall, Dalton Square, Lancaster LA1 1PW
Telephone: (01524) 582000

Function	Chief Officer	Title	Location
Chief Executive	Mr M Cullinan	Chief Executive	Town Hall, Lancaster
Electoral Registration	Mr M Cullinan	Chief Executive	Town Hall, Lancaster

DISTRICT COUNCILS

Environmental Health	Mrs S Lodge	Head of Health & Strategic Housing	Town Hall, M'cambe
Finance	Mr R Muckle	Corporate Director (Central Services)	Town Hall, Lancaster
Housing	Mr P Loker	Corporate Director (Community Services)	Town Hall, Lancaster
Legal Services	Mrs S Taylor	Head of Legal Services	Town Hall, Lancaster
Leisure	Mr W D Owen	Chief Leisure Officer	Town Hall, M'cambe
Local Land Charges	Mrs S Taylor	Head of Legal Services	Town Hall, Lancaster
Planning	Mr A Dobson	Head of Planning & Building Control	Palatine Hall
Purchasing & Supplies	Mrs G Noall	Acting Head of Administration Services	Town Hall, Lancaster
Technical Services	Mr J Robson	Head of Engineering	Town Hall, M'cambe

Parish Councils in the authority's area: Arkholme with Cawood; Bolton-le-Sands; Carnforth; Caton with Littledale; Claughton; Cockerham; Ellel; Gressingham; Halton with Aughton; Heaton with Oxcliffe; Hornby with Farleton; Ireby & Leck; Melling with Wrayton; Middleton; Nether Kellet; Over Kellet; Over Wyresdale; Overton; Quernmore; Scotforth; Silverdale; Slyne; Tatham; Thurnham; Warton; Wennington; Whittington; Wray with Wrayton; Yealand Conyers; Yealand Redmayne.

Parish Meetings in the authority's area: Borwick; Burrow with Burrow; Cantsfield; Priest Hutton; Roeburndale; Tunstall.

Neighbourhood Parish Councils in the authority's area: Heysham; Morecambe.

LANGBAURGH-ON-TEES BOROUGH COUNCIL
Langbaurgh-on-Tees Borough Council was abolished on 31 March 1996; see now Redcar & Cleveland Council.

LEICESTER CITY COUNCIL
Leicester City Council became a unitary authority on 1 April 1997.

LEOMINSTER DISTRICT COUNCIL
Leominster District Council was abolished on 31 March 1998; see now The Herefordshire Council.

LEWES DISTRICT COUNCIL
www.lewes.gov.uk
Principal Office
Lewes House, 32 High Street, Lewes, East Sussex BN7 2LX
Telephone: (01273) 471600; DX 3118 Lewes 1

Community Leisure
Downs Leisure Centre, Sutton Road, Seaford BN25 4QW
Telephone: (01323) 490011; FAX: (01323) 491531

Community Services
PO Box 2708, Southover House, Southover Road, Lewes BN7 1DY
Telephone: (01273) 471600; FAX: (01273) 484462

Finance Department
4 Fisher Street, Lewes BN7 2DQ
Telephone: (01273) 471600; FAX: (01273) 484090

Planning & Environmental Services
PO Box 2707, Southover House, Southover Road, Lewes BN7 1DW
Telephone: (01273) 471600; FAX: (01273) 484452

Personnel
Thebes Annexe, 32 High Street, Lewes, East Sussex BN7 2LX

Function	Chief Officer	Title	Location
Chief Executive	Mr J Crawford	Chief Executive	Lewes House
Electoral Registration	Mr A Batty	Head of Democratic Services	Lewes House
Environmental Health	Mr I Kedge	Head of Environmental Health	Southover Hse
Finance	Mr J Magness	Director of Finance & Community Services	Southover Hse
Housing	Mr M Keeping	Head of Housing Services	Southover Hse
Legal Services	Ms C Knight	District Solicitor	Lewes House
Leisure	Mr P Crowley	Head of Community Leisure	Leisure Centre
Local Land Charges	Ms C Knight	District Solicitor	Lewes House
Planning	Mr L Frost	Director of Planning & Environmental Services	Southover Hse
Technical Services	Mr J Clark	Head of IT Services	Thebes Annexe

Parish Councils in the authority's area: Barcombe; Chailey; Ditchling; East Chiltington; Falmer; Firle; Glynde & Beddingham; Hamsey; Kingston; Newick; Piddinghoe; Plumpton; Ringmer; Rodmell; South Heighton; Westmeston; Wivelsfield.

Parish Meetings in the authority's area: Iford; St Ann Without; St John Without; Southease; Streat; Tarring Neville.

Town Councils in the authority's area: Lewes; Newhaven; Peacehaven; Seaford; Telscombe.

LICHFIELD DISTRICT COUNCIL

www.lichfielddc.gov.uk

Principal Office

District Council House, Frog Lane, Lichfield, Staffordshire WS13 6YU
Telephone: (01543) 308000; FAX: (01543) 309899; Minicom: (01543) 308078

Depot

Vulcan Road, Lichfield, Staffordshire WS13 6RW

Function	Chief Officer	Title	Location
Chief Executive	Ms N A Dawes	Chief Executive	District Council Hse
Electoral Registration	Mr R K King	Corporate Director, Democratic & Legal Services	District Council Hse
Environmental Health	Ms H Spearey	Corporate Director, Health, Housing & Environmental Protection	District Council Hse
Finance	Mr I M Floyd	Deputy Chief Executive – Finance	District Council Hse
Housing	Ms H Spearey	Corporate Director, Health, Housing & Environmental Protection	District Council Hse
Legal Services	Mr R K King	Corporate Director, Democratic & Legal Services	District Council Hse
Leisure	Mrs S Smith	Deputy Chief Executive	District Council Hse
Local Land Charges	Mr R K King	Corporate Director, Democratic & Legal Services	District Council Hse
Planning	Mr I D Thompson	Corporate Director, Development Services	District Council Hse
Purchasing & Supplies	Mr R K King	Corporate Director, Democratic & Legal Services	District Council Hse
Technical Services	Ms R Plant	Corporate Director, Operational Services	Depot

Parish Councils in the authority's area: Alrewas & Fradley with Streethay; Armitage with Handsacre; Clifton Campville with Thorpe Constantine; Colton; Curborough & Elmhurst & Farewell & Chorley; Drayton Bassett; Edingale; Elford; Hammerwich; Hamstall Ridware; Harlaston; Hints & Canwell; Kings Bromley; Longdon; Mavesyn Ridware; Shenstone; Swinfen & Packington; Wall; Weeford; Whittington & Fisherwick; Wigginton & Hopwas.

Town Councils in the authority's area: Burntwood; Fazeley.

DISTRICT COUNCILS

City Council in the authority's area: Lichfield.

LINCOLN CITY COUNCIL

www.lincoln-info.org.uk

Principal Office
City Hall, Beaumont Fee, Lincoln LN1 1DD
Telephone: (01522) 881188; FAX: (01522) 521736

Function	Chief Officer	Title	Location
Chief Executive	Andrew Taylor	Chief Executive & Town Clerk	City Hall
Environmental Health	Keith J Laidler	Director of Development & Environmental Services	City Hall
Finance	Philip S Wright	Director of Resources	City Hall
Housing	John Bibby	Director of Housing & Community Services	City Hall
Legal Services	Anne Brown	Head of Legal Services	City Hall
Leisure	John Bibby	Director of Housing & Community Services	City Hall
Planning	Keith J Laidler	Director of Development & Environmental Services	City Hall

Parish Councils & Parish Meetings in the authority's area: none.

Town Councils in the authority's area: none.

LUTON BOROUGH COUNCIL
Luton Borough Council became a unitary authority on 1 April 1997.

MACCLESFIELD BOROUGH COUNCIL

www.macclesfield.gov.uk

Principal Office
Town Hall, Macclesfield, Cheshire SK10 1DX
Telephone: (01625) 500500; FAX: (01625) 504203; DX 25010 Macclesfield 2

Function	Chief Officer	Title	Location
Chief Executive	Mr D W Parr	Chief Executive	Town Hall
Electoral Registration	Mr D W Parr	Chief Executive	Town Hall
Environmental Health	Mrs E Alexander	Director (Environment)	Town Hall
Finance	Mrs C Booth	Chief Financial Officer	Town Hall
Legal Services	Mrs V J Horton	Director (Resources)	Town Hall
Leisure	Mrs H Oakley	Director (Community)	Town Hall
Local Land Charges	Mrs V J Horton	Director (Resources)	Town Hall
Planning	Mr P J Yates	Chief Planning Officer	Town Hall
Purchasing & Supplies	Mr D Naylor	Head of ECT	Town Hall
Technical Services	Mrs E Alexander	Director (Environment)	Town Hall

Parish Councils in the authority's area: Adlington; Alderley Edge; Ashley; Aston by Budworth; Bosley; Chelford; Chorley; Disley; Eaton; Gawsworth; Great Warford; Henbury; High Legh; Higher Hurdsfield; Kettleshulme; Little Warford; Lower Withington; Lyme Handley; Marton; Mere; Millington; Mobberley; Mottram St Andrew; Nether Alderley; North Rode; Ollerton with Marthall; Over Alderley; Peover Inferior; Pickmere; Plumley with Toft & Bexton; Pott Shrigley; Poynton with Worth; Prestbury; Rainow; Rostherne; Siddington; Snelson; Sutton; Tabley.

Parish Meetings in the authority's area: Agden; Little Bollington; Macclesfield Forest with Woldboarclough; Tatton; Wincle.

Town Councils in the authority's area: Bollington; Knutsford.

DISTRICT COUNCILS

MAIDSTONE BOROUGH COUNCIL

www.digitalmaidstone.co.uk

Principal Office
Council Offices, 13 Tonbridge Road, Maidstone, Kent ME16 8HG
Telephone: (01622) 602000; FAX: (01622) 602444; DX 4819 Maidstone

**Chief Executive's Department; Directorate of Customer and Civic Services;
Directorate of Corporate and Regulatory Services; Highways Management Unit**
London House, 5/11 London Road, Maidstone ME16 8HR
Telephone: (01622) 602000; FAX: (01622) 692246

Function	Chief Officer	Title	Location
Chief Executive	David Petford	Chief Executive	London House
Electoral Registration	Richard Snaith	Director of Customer & Civic Services	London House
Environmental Health	Keith Hatcher	Environmental Health and Building Surveying Manager	Council Offices
Finance	Derek Williamson	Assistant Director of Corporate Services	London House
Legal Services	Marita Jones	Head of Legal Services	London House
Leisure	Trevor Gasson	Director of Community Services	London House
Local Land Charges	Richard Snaith	Director of Customer & Civic Services	London House
Planning	Trevor Gasson	Director of Community Services	Council Offices

Parish Councils in the authority's area: Barming; Bearsted; Boughton Malherbe; Boughton Monchelsea; Boxley; Bredhurst; Broomfield & Kingswood; Chart Sutton; Collier Street; Coxheath; Detling; Downswood; East Farleigh; East Sutton; Harrietsham; Headcorn; Hollingbourne; Hunton; Langley; Leeds; Lenham; Linton; Loose; Marden; Nettlestead; Otham; Staplehurst; Stockbury; Sutton Valence; Teston; Thurnham; Tovil; Ulcombe; West Farleigh; Yalding.

Parish Meetings in the authority's area: Bicknor; Frinsted; Hucking; Otterden; Wichling; Wormshill.

MALDON DISTRICT COUNCIL

www.maldon.gov.uk

Principal Office
Princes Road, Maldon, Essex CM9 5DL
Telephone: (01621) 854477; FAX: (01621) 852575; DX 41264 Maldon

Function	Chief Officer	Title	Location
Electoral Registration	Ms L Elsegood	Elections Management Officer	Princes Road
Environmental Health	Mrs T Bragg	Head of Environment Services	Princes Road
Finance	Mr A Claydon	Chief Financial Services Officer	Princes Road
Housing	Mrs A Spencer	Chief Community Services Officer	Princes Road
Legal Services	Mr S Quelch	Solicitor	Princes Road
Leisure	Mrs A Spencer	Chief Community Services Officer	Princes Road
Local Land Charges	Mr S Quelch	Solicitor	Princes Road
Planning	Mr C Tokley	Chief Planning and Development Services Officer	Princes Road
Purchasing & Supplies	Mr R Holmes	Facilities Manager	Princes Road
Technical Services	Mr R Holmes	Facilities Manager	Princes Road

Parish Councils in the authority's area: Althorne; Asheldham & Dengie; Bradwell-on-Sea; Cold Norton; Goldhanger; Great Braxted; Great Totham; Heybridge; Langford & Ulting; Latchingdon; Little Braxted; Little Totham; The Maylands; Mundon; North Fambridge; Purleigh; St Lawrence; Southminster; Steeple; Stow Maries; Tillingham; Tollesbury; Tolleshunt D'Arcy; Tolleshunt Knights; Tolleshunt Major; Wickham Bishops; Woodham Mortimer with Hazeleigh; Woodham Walter.

Town Councils in the authority's area: Burnham on Crouch; Maldon.

MALVERN HILLS DISTRICT COUNCIL

www.malvernhills.gov.uk

Principal Office
The Council House, Avenue Road, Malvern, Worcestershire WR14 3AF
Telephone: (01684) 892700; FAX: (01684) 862473; DX 17608 Malvern

Planning Services
Brunel House, Portland Road, Malvern WR14 2TB
Telephone: (01684) 892700; FAX: (01684) 862499

Environmental Services; Housing, Revenues & Technical Services
Highlea, Church Street, Malvern, Worcestershire WR14 2AZ
Telephone: (01684) 892700; FAX: (01684) 862481

Financial Services; Customer Services
Portland House, Church Street, Malvern, Worcestershire WR14 2BA
Telephone: (01684) 892700; FAX: (01684) 862474

Function	Chief Officer	Title	Location
Chief Executive	Mr C J Bocock	Chief Executive	Council House
Electoral Registration	Mr D R Wood	Strategic Director Resources	Portland House
Environmental Health	Mr C Davis	Strategic Director Operational Services	Highlea
Finance	Mr D R Wood	Strategic Director Resources	Portland House
Housing	Mr C Davis	Strategic Director Operational Services	Highlea
Legal Services	Mr D R Wood	Strategic Director Resources	Portland House
Leisure	Mr C J Bocock	Chief Executive	Council House
Local Land Charges	Mr D R Wood	Strategic Director Resources	Portland House
Planning	Mr C Davis	Strategic Director Operational Services	Highlea
Purchasing & Supplies	Mr D R Wood	Strategic Director Resources	Portland House
Technical Services	Mr C Davis	Strategic Director Operational Services	Highlea

Parish Councils in the authority's area: Abberley; Alfrick & Lulsley; Astley & Dunley; Bayton; Berrow; Birtsmorton; Broadwas & Cotheridge; Bushley; Castlemorton; Clifton upon Teme; Earls Croome; Eastham; Eldersfield; Great Witley & Hillhampton; Grimley; Guarlford; Hallow; Hanley; Hanley Castle; Hill Croome; Holt; Kempsey; Kenswick & Wichenford; Knighton-on-Teme; Knightwick & Doddenham; Leigh & Bransford; Lindridge; Little Malvern & Welland; Little Witley; Longdon, Holdfast & Queenhill; Lower Broadheath; Lower Sapey; Madresfield; Malvern Wells; Mamble; Martley; Newland; Pendock; Pensax; Powick; Ripple; Rochford; Rushwick; Severn Stoke & Croome D'Abitot; Shelsley Beauchamp, Shelsley Kings & Shelsley Walsh; Shrawley; Stanford with Orleton; Stockton-on-Teme; Stoke Bliss, Kyre & Bockleton; Suckley; West Malvern.

Parish Meetings in the authority's area: none.

Town Councils in the authority's area: Malvern; Tenbury; Upton upon Severn.

MANSFIELD DISTRICT COUNCIL

www.mansfield-dc.gov.uk

Principal Office
Civic Centre, Chesterfield Road South, Mansfield, Nottinghamshire NG19 7BH
Telephone: (01623) 463463; FAX: (01623) 463900

Function	Chief Officer	Title	Location
Chief Executive	Mr R P Goad	Chief Executive	Civic Centre
Electoral Registration	Mr J R Burton	Solicitor to the Council and Monitoring Officer	Civic Centre
Environmental Health	Mr R D Smith	Head of Regulatory Services	Civic Centre

DISTRICT COUNCILS

Finance	Mr P Cook	Head of Finance	Civic Centre
Housing	Mr P Woollam	Head of Housing Services	Civic Centre
Legal Services	Mr J R Burton	Solicitor to the Council and Monitoring Officer	Civic Centre
Leisure	Mr M Farley	Head of Leisure and Technical Services	Civic Centre
Local Land Charges	Mr J R Burton	Solicitor to the Council and Monitoring Officer	Civic Centre
Planning	Mr R D Smith	Head of Regulatory Services	Civic Centre
Technical Services	Mr M Farley	Head of Leisure and Technical Services	Civic Centre

Parish Council in the authority's area: Warsop.

MEDINA DISTRICT COUNCIL
Medina District Council was abolished on 31 March 1995; see now Isle of Wight Council.

MELTON BOROUGH COUNCIL
www.melton.gov.uk
Principal Office
Council Offices, Nottingham Road, Melton Mowbray, Leicestershire LE13 0UL
Telephone: (01664) 502502; FAX: (01664) 410283; DX 722422 Melton Mowbray

Function	Chief Officer	Title	Location
Chief Executive	Mr J D Burbidge	Chief Executive	Council Offices
Electoral Registration	Mrs D Hudson	Head of Legal & Admin Services	Council Offices
Environmental Health	Mr P Evans	Head of Environmental Services	Council Offices
Finance	Mrs D Garton	Head of Financial Services	Council Offices
Housing	Mr H Rai	Head of Social & Economic Development	Council Offices
Legal Services	Mrs D Hudson	Head of Legal & Admin Services	Council Offices
Leisure	Mr H Rai	Head of Social & Economic Development	Council Offices
Local Land Charges	Mrs D Hudson	Head of Legal & Admin Services	Council Offices
Planning	Mr J Worley	Head of Physical Environment	Council Offices
Purchasing & Supplies	Mrs D Garton	Head of Financial Services	Council Offices
Technical Services	Mr C Stone	Head of ICT	Council Offices

Parish Councils in the authority's area: Ab Kettleby; Asfordby; Barkestone, Plungar & Redmile; Belvoir; Bottesford; Broughton & Old Dalby; Buckminster; Burton & Dalby; Clawson, Hose & Harby; Croxton Kerrial; Eaton; Freeby; Frisby & Kirby; Gaddesby; Garthorpe; Grimston; Hoby with Rotherby; Knossington & Cold Overton; Scalford; Somerby; Sproxton; Stathern; Twyford & Thorpe; Waltham; Wymondham.

MENDIP DISTRICT COUNCIL
www.mendip.gov.uk
Principal Office
Council Offices, Cannards Grave Road, Shepton Mallet, Somerset BA4 5BT
Telephone: (01749) 343399 FAX: (01749) 344050; DX 43001 Shepton Mallet

Function	Chief Officer	Title	Location
Chief Executive	Mr D Thomson	Chief Executive	Council Offs
Electoral Registration	Mr J Kilby	Elections Officer (Capita Managed Services)	Council Offs
Environmental Health	Mr C Uzzell	Business Manager – Planning & Environment	Council Offs
Finance	Mr P McKenzie	Corporate Financial Adviser	Council Offs
Housing	Mr M Williams	Business Manager – Community & Regeneration	Council Offs
Legal Services	Ms T Merrett	Solicitor (Merrett & Co)	Council Offs
Leisure	Mr M Williams	Business Manager – Community & Regeneration	Council Offs

DISTRICT COUNCILS

Local Land Charges	Ms C Marchant		Council Offs
Planning	Mr C Uzzell	Business Manager – Planning & Environment	Council Offs
Purchasing & Supplies	Ms M Scoble	Copy Shop Manager (Capita Managed Services)	Council Offs

Parish Councils in the authority's area: Ashwick; Baltonsborough; Batcombe; Beckington; Berkley; Binegar; Buckland Dinham; Butleigh; Chewton Mendip; Chilcompton; Coleford; Cranmore; Croscombe; Ditcheat; Doulting; East Pennard; Evercreech; Frome; Glastonbury; Godney; Great Elm; Hemington; Holcombe; Kilmersdon; Leigh on Mendip; Litton; Lydford-on-Fosse; Meare; Mells; North Wootton; Norton St Philip; Nunney; Pilton; Priddy; Rode; Rodney Stoke; St Cuthbert Out; Selwood; Shepton Mallet; Stoke St Michael; Ston Easton; Stratton on the Fosse; Street; Trudoxhill; Walton; Wanstrow; Wells; West Pennard; Westbury sub Mendip; Whatley; Witham Friary; Wookey.

Parish Meetings in the authority's area: Downhead; Emborough; Lamyatt; Lullington; Milton Clevedon; Pylle; Sharpham; Tellisford; Upton Noble; West Bradley.

MID BEDFORDSHIRE DISTRICT COUNCIL

www.midbeds.gov.uk

Principal Office

The Limes, 12 Dunstable Street, Ampthill, Bedfordshire MK45 2JU
Telephone: (01525) 402051/406464; FAX: (01525) 406288; DX 36903 Ampthill

Environmental Services Department; Housing Department

23 London Road, Biggleswade, Beds SG18 8ER
Telephone: (01767) 313137

Function	Chief Officer	Title	Location
Chief Executive	Mrs Jackie Salisbury	Chief Executive	The Limes
Electoral Registration	Mrs Barbara Morris	Head of Democratic & Legal Services	The Limes
Environmental Health	Mr Gary Alderson	Head of Environmental Services	23 London Rd
Finance	Mr David Sutherland	Head of Finance	The Limes
Legal Services	Mrs Barbara Morris	Head of Democratic & Legal Services	The Limes
Leisure	Mr Roy Waterfield	Head of Community Services, Leisure & Tourism	The Limes
Local Land Charges	Mrs Barbara Morris	Head of Democratic & Legal Services	The Limes
Planning	Mr Chris Valentine	Head of Planning Services	23 London Rd
Technical Services	Mr Clive Jones	Head of IT	The Limes

Parish Councils in the authority's area: Aspley Guise; Aspley Heath; Blunham; Brogborough; Campton; Chicksands; Clifton; Clophill; Cranfield; Dunton; Eversholt; Everton; Flitton & Greenfield; Gravenhurst; Harlington; Haynes; Henlow; Houghton Conquest; Hulcote & Salford; Husborne Crawley; Langford; Lidlington; Marston Moretaine; Maulden; Meppershall; Mogerhanger; Northill; Old Warden; Pulloxhill; Ridgmont; Shillington; Silsoe; Southill; Steppingley; Stondon; Sutton; Tempsford; Westoning; Woburn; Wrestlingworh & Cockayne Hatley.

Parish Meetings in the authority's area: Astwick; Battlesden; Edworth; Eyeworth; Millbrook; Milton Bryan; Potsgrove; Tingrith.

Town Councils in the authority's area: Ampthill; Arlesey; Biggleswade; Flitwick; Potton; Sandy; Shefford; Stotfold.

MID DEVON DISTRICT COUNCIL

www.middevon.gov.uk

Principal Office

Phoenix House, Phoenix Lane, Tiverton, Devon EX16 6PP
Telephone: (01884) 255255; FAX: (01884) 234318

Function	Chief Officer	Title	Location
Chief Executive	Paul Edwards	Chief Executive	Phoenix House
Electoral Registration	Ann House	Electoral Registration Assistant	Phoenix House
Environmental Health	Vivien Pring	Head of Environment Health	Phoenix House
Finance	John Foxworthy	Head of Finance & IT	Phoenix House
Housing	Martin Daly	Head of Housing	Phoenix House
Legal Services	Denise Rushton	Head of Legal & Personnel	Phoenix House
Leisure	Rob Kelley	Community Development Manager	Phoenix House
Local Land Charges	Maureen Sharland	Chief Local Land Charges Clerk	Phoenix House
Planning	Jonathan Guscott	Head of Planning	Phoenix House
Technical Services	Kevin Finan	Head of Operations	Phoenix House

Parish Councils in the authority's area: Bickleigh; Bordon Gate, Clayhanger, Hockworthy & Huntsham; Bow; Burlescombe; Chawleigh; Cheriton Bishop; Cheriton Fitzpaine; Clayhidon; Coldridge; Colebrooke; Copplestone; Crediton Hamlets; Cruwys Morchard; Culmstock; Down St Mary; Halberton; Hemyock; Hittisleigh; Holcombe Rogus; Kentisbeare; Lapford; Morchard Bishop; Morebath; Newton St Cyres; Nymet Rowland; Oakford; Poughill; Puddington; Sampford Peverell; Sandford; Shobrooke; Silverton; Stoodleigh; Templeton; Thelbridge; Thorverton; Uffculme; Uplowman; Washfield; Washford Pyne; Wembworthy; Willand.

Parish Meetings in the authority's area: Brushford; Butterleigh; Cadbury; Cadeleigh; Clannaborough; Eggesford; Kennerleigh; Stockleigh English; Stockleigh Pomeroy; Upton Hellions; Woolfardisworthy.

Town Councils in the authority's area: Bampton; Bradninch; Crediton; Cullompton; Tiverton.

MID SUFFOLK DISTRICT COUNCIL

www.midsuffolk.gov.uk

Principal Office

Council Offices, High Street, Needham Market, Ipswich, Suffolk IP6 8DL
Telephone: (01449) 720711; FAX: (01449) 721946

Function	Chief Officer	Title	Location
Chief Executive	A Good	Chief Executive	Council Offices
Electoral Registration	I Rickard	Head of Corporate Support	Council Offices
Environmental Health	D Ellis	Head of Environment & Planning	Council Offices
Finance	A Radford	Head of Financial Management	Council Offices
Housing	N Gowrley	Head of Housing	Council Offices
Legal Services	I Rickard	Head of Corporate Support	Council Offices
Leisure	C Fry	Head of Leisure & Amenities	Council Offices
Local Land Charges	I Rickard	Head of Corporate Support	Council Offices
Planning	D Ellis	Head of Environment & Planning	Council Offices
Purchasing & Supplies	I Rickard	Head of Corporate Support	Council Offices

Parish Councils in the authority's area: Ashbocking; Ashfield-cum-Thorpe; Bacton; Badwell Ash; Barham; Barking; Battisford; Bedfield; Bedingfield; Beyton; Botesdale; Bramford; Brome & Oakley; Brundish; Buxhall; Claydon & Whitton; Coddenham; Combs; Cotton; Creeting St Mary; Creeting St Peter; Crowfield; Debenham; Denham; Drinkstone; Earl Stonham; Elmswell; Felsham; Finningham; Framsden; Fressingfield; Gislingham; Gosbeck; Great Ashfield; Great Blakenham; Great Bricett; Great Finborough; Haughley; Helmingham; Hemingstone; Henley; Hessett; Hinderclay; Horham & Athelington; Hoxne; Laxfield; Little Blakenham; Mellis; Mendham; Mendlesham; Metfield; Mickfield; Monk Soham; Norton; Occold; Offton & Willisham; Old Newton with Dagworth & Gipping; Onehouse; Palgrave; Pettaugh; Rattlesden; Redgrave; Rickinghall; Ringshall; Somersham; Stoke Ash & Thwaite; Stonham Aspal; Stonham Parva; Stowlangtoft; Stowupland; Stradbroke; Stuston; Syleham; Thorndon; Thrandeston; Thurston; Tostock; Walsham-le-Willows; Wattisfield; Westhorpe; Wetherden; Wetheringsett-cum-Brockford; Weybread; Wickham Skeith; Wilby; Wingfield; Winston; Woolpit; Worlingworth; Wortham & Burgate; Wyverstone; Yaxley.

Parish Meetings in the authority's area: Akenham; Aspall; Badley; Baylham; Braiseworth; Flowton; Gedding; Harleston; Hunston; Kenton; Langham; Little Finborough; Nettlestead; Redlingfield; Rishangles; Shelland; Southolt; Tannington; Thornham Magna; Thornham Parva.

Town Councils in the authority's area: Eye; Needham Market; Stowmarket.

MID SUSSEX DISTRICT COUNCIL

www.midsussex.gov.uk

Principal Office

Oaklands, Oaklands Road, Haywards Heath, West Sussex RH16 1SS
Telephone: (01444) 458166; FAX: (01444) 450027; DX 300320 Haywards Heath 1

Function	Chief Officer	Title	Location
Chief Executive	Mr J Jory	Chief Executive	Oaklands
Electoral Registration	Mrs A M Halligey	Director of Resources	Oaklands
Environmental Health	Mr S J Morris	Director of Community Development	Oaklands
Finance	Mrs A M Halligey	Director of Resources	Oaklands
Housing	Mr S J Morris	Director of Community Development	Oaklands
Legal Services	Mrs A M Halligey	Director of Resources	Oaklands
Leisure	Mr J M Pegler	Director of Leisure & Property	Oaklands
Local Land Charges	Mr R Walker	Director of Environment	Oaklands
Planning	Mr R Walker,	Director of Environment	Oaklands
Purchasing & Supplies	Mrs A M Halligey	Director of Resources	Oaklands
Technical Services	Mrs A M Halligey	Director of Resources	Oaklands

Parish Councils in the authority's area: Albourne; Ardingly; Ashurst Wood; Balcombe; Bolney; Cuckfield; Cuckfield Rural; Fulking; Hassocks; Horsted Keynes; Hurstpierpoint & Sayers Common; Lindfield; Lindfield Rural; Poynings; Pyecombe; Slaugham; Turners Hill; Twineham; West Hoathly; Worth.

Parish Meetings in the authority's area: Newtimber.

Town Councils in the authority's area: Burgess Hill; East Grinstead; Haywards Heath.

MIDDLESBROUGH BOROUGH COUNCIL

Middlesbrough became a unitary authority on 1 April 1996.

MILTON KEYNES BOROUGH COUNCIL

Milton Keynes Borough Council became a unitary authority on 1 April 1997.

MOLE VALLEY DISTRICT COUNCIL

www.mole-valley.gov.uk

Principal Office

Pippbrook, Dorking, Surrey RH4 1SJ
Telephone: (01306) 885001; FAX: (01306) 876821; DX 57306 Dorking

Function	Chief Officer	Title	Location
Chief Executive	Mrs H Kerswell	Clerk & Chief Executive	Pippbrook
Electoral Registration	Mr R Burn	Solicitor	Pippbrook
Environmental Health	Mr M Wilkinson	Head of Environmental Health	Pippbrook
Finance	Mrs J Batchelor	Head of Finance	Pippbrook
Housing	[Vacant]	Head of Housing	Pippbrook
Legal Services	Mr R Burn	Solicitor	Pippbrook
Leisure	Mr J Cawdell	Head of Leisure	Pippbrook
Local Land Charges	Mr R Burn	Solicitor	Pippbrook
Planning	Mr C Smith	Head of Planning	Pippbrook
Purchasing & Supplies	Mr C Archer	Officer Support Manager	Pippbrook

Parish Councils in the authority's area: Abinger; Betchworth; Brockham; Buckland; Capel; Charlwood; Headley; Holmwood; Leigh; Mickleham; Newdigate; Ockley; Wotton.

NEW FOREST DISTRICT COUNCIL

www.nfdc.gov.uk

Principal Offices

Appletree Court, Lyndhurst, Hampshire SO43 7PA
Telephone: (023) 8028 5000; FAX: (023) 8028 5555; DX 123010 Lyndhurst 2

Town Hall, Avenue Road, Lymington, Hampshire SO41 9ZG
Telephone: (023) 8028 5000; FAX: (023) 8028 5626

Function	Chief Officer	Title	Location
Chief Executive	Mr D H Yates	Chief Executive	Appletree Court
Finance	Mr C P Malyon	Director of Resource	Town Hall
Housing	Mr N Gibbs	Director of Community Services	Appletree Court
Planning	Mr N Gibbs	Director of Community Services	Appletree Court
Technical Services	Mr C P Malyon	Director of Resource	Town Hall

Parish Councils in the authority's area: Ashurst & Colbury; Beaulieu; Boldre; Bramshaw; Bransgore; Breamore; Brockenhurst; Burley; Copythorne; Damerham; Denny Lodge; East Boldre; Ellingham, Harbridge & Ibsley; Exbury & Lepe; Fawley; Fordingbridge; Godshill; Hale; Hordle; Hyde; Hythe & Dibden; Lyndhurst; Marchwood; Martin; Milford-on-Sea; Minstead; Netley Marsh; Rockbourne; Sandleheath; Sopley; Sway; Woodgreen.

Town Councils in the authority's area: Lymington & Pennington; New Milton; Ringwood; Totton & Eling.

NEWARK & SHERWOOD DISTRICT COUNCIL

www.newark-sherwooddc.gov.uk

Principal Office

Kelham Hall, Newark, Nottinghamshire NG23 5QX
Telephone: (01636) 650000; FAX: (01636) 655233

Function	Chief Officer	Title	Location
Chief Executive	Mr R G Dix	Chief Executive	Kelham Hall
Electoral Registration	Mrs K White	Head of Legal & Democratic Services	Kelham Hall
Environmental Health	Mr P Robinson	Head of Environmental & Technical Services	Kelham Hall
Finance	Mr K Stedman	Strategic Director of Finance, Information Systems, Planning & Economic Regeneration	Kelham Hall
Housing	Mr S Palframan	Strategic Director (Operations)	Kelham Hall
Legal Services	Mrs K H Cole	Assistant Chief Executive	Kelham Hall
Leisure	Mr S Palframan	Strategic Director (Operations)	Kelham Hall
Local Land Charges	Mrs K White	Head of Legal & Democratic Services	Kelham Hall
Planning	Mr K Stedman	Strategic Director of Finance, Information Systems, Planning & Economic Regeneration	Kelham Hall
Technical Services	Mr P Robinson	Head of Environmental & Technical Services	Kelham Hall

Parish Councils in the authority's area: Alverton & Kilvington; Averham, Kelham & Staythorpe; Balderton; Barnby-in-the-Willows; Bathley; Bilsthorpe; Bleasby; Blidworth; Bulcote; Carlton-on-Trent; Caunton; Caythorpe; Clipstone; Coddington; Collingham; Eakring; East Stoke with Thorpe; Edingley; Edwinstowe; Elston; Epperstone; Farndon; Farnsfield; Fiskerton-cum-Morton; Gunthorpe; Halam; Harby; Hawton; Hoveringham; Kirklington; Kirton; Kneesall, Kersall & Ompton; Laxton & Moorhouse; Lowdham; North Clifton; North Muskham; Norwell; Ossington;

DISTRICT COUNCILS

Oxton; Perlethorpe-cum-Budby; Rainworth; Rolleston; Rufford; South Clifton; South Muskham; Spalford; Staunton; Sutton-on-Trent; Syerston; Thorney; Thurgarton; Upton; Walesby; Wellow; Weston; Wigsley; Winthorpe with Langford.

Parish Meetings in the authority's area: Besthorpe; Cotham; Cromwell; Egmanton; Girton & Meering; Gonalston; Grassthorpe; Halloughton; Hockerton; Holme; Lyndhurst; Maplebeck; South Scarle; Winkburn.

Town Councils in the authority's area: Boughton/Ollerton; Newark; Southwell.

NEWBURY DISTRICT COUNCIL

Newbury District Council became a unitary authority under the name West Berkshire Council on 1 April 1998.

NEWCASTLE-UNDER-LYME BOROUGH COUNCIL

www.newcastle-staffs.gov.uk
Principal Office
Civic Offices, Merrial Street, Newcastle-under-Lyme, Staffordshire ST5 2AG
Telephone: (01782) 717717; FAX: (01782) 711032; DX 20959 Newcastle-under-Lyme

Function	Chief Officer	Title	Location
Chief Executive	Felix Harley	Chief Executive	Civic Offices
Electoral Registration	Mrs Deborah Dimock	Head of Legal & Democratic Services	Civic Offices
Environmental Health	Alan Hudson	Head of Community Services	Civic Offices
Finance	Malcolm Crawford	Head of Financial Services	Civic Offices
Legal Services	Mrs Deborah Dimock	Head of Legal & Democratic Services	Civic Offices
Leisure	Alan Hudson	Head of Community Services	Civic Offices
Local Land Charges	Mrs Deborah Dimock	Head of Legal & Democratic Services	Civic Offices
Planning	Neale Clifton	Head of Regeneration & Planning	Civic Offices
Technical Services	Ian Jenkinson	Head of Technical & Amenity Services	Civic Offices

Parish Councils in the authority's area: Audley; Betley, Silverdale, Balterley & Wrinehill; Chapel & Hill Chorlton; Keele; Kidsgrove; Loggerheads; Madeley; Maer; Whitmore.

NORTH CORNWALL DISTRICT COUNCIL

www.ncdc.gov.uk
Principal Office
Council Offices, Higher Trenant Road, Wadebridge, Cornwall PL27 6TW
Telephone: (01208) 893333; FAX: (01208) 893255

Community Services Department
3/5 Barn Lane, Bodmin PL31 1LZ
Telephone: (01208) 893333; FAX: (01208) 265655

Council Offices, Trevanion Road, Wadebridge PL27 7NU
Telephone: (01208) 893333; FAX: (01208) 893455

Technical Services Department
Windwhistle House, Cooksland Road, Bodmin PL31 2RH
Telephone: (01208) 262800; FAX: (01208) 262810

Function	Chief Officer	Title	Location
Chief Executive	Mr D Brown	Chief Executive	Higher Trenant Rd
Electoral Registration	Mr D Brown	Chief Executive	Higher Trenant Rd

Function	Chief Officer	Title	Location
Environmental Health	Mr R Zorichak	Head of Environmental Health	Trevanion Rd
Finance	Mr D Pooley	Director of Finance	Higher Trenant Rd
Housing	Mr M Howell	Head of Housing Services	Trevanion Rd
Legal Services	Miss S Lloyd-Jones	Head of Legal Services	Higher Trenant Rd
Leisure	Mr S Blamey	Head of Leisure Services	Windwhistle Hse
Local Land Charges	Mr N Pendleton	Director of Community Services	3/5 Barn Lane
Planning	Mr N Pendleton	Director of Community Services	3/5 Barn Lane
Purchasing & Supplies	Mr D Pooley	Director of Finance	Higher Trenant Rd
Technical Services	Mr M Hall	Director of Technical Services	Windwhistle Hse

Parish Councils in the authority's area: Altarnun; Blisland; Boyton; Cardinham; Davidstow; Egloshayle; Egloskerry; Forrabury & Minster; Jacobstow; Kilkhampton; Lanhydrock; Lanivet; Launcells; Lawhitton; Lewannick; Lezant; Marhamchurch; Michaelstow; Morwenstow; North Hill; North Petherwin; North Tamerton; Otterham; Poundstock; St Breock; St Breward; St Endellion; St Ervan; St Eval; St Gennys; St Issey; St Juliot; St Kew; St Mabyn; St Merryn; St Minver Highlands; St Minver Lowlands; St Stephens Rural; St Teath; St Thomas Rural; St Tudy; South Petherwin; Stoke Climsland; Tintagel; Tremaine; Treneglos; Tresmeer; Warbstow; Week St Mary; Werrington; Whitstone; Withiel.

Parish Meetings in the authority's area: Advent; Helland; Laneast; Lesnewth; St Clether; Trevalga; Trewen.

Town Councils in the authority's area: Bodmin; Bude-Stratton; Camelford; Launceston; Padstow; Wadebridge.

NORTH DEVON DISTRICT COUNCIL

www.northdevon.gov.uk

Principal Office
Civic Centre, North Walk, Barnstaple, Devon EX31 1EA
Telephone: (01271) 327711; FAX: (01271) 388451

Function	Chief Officer	Title	Location
Chief Executive	John Sunderland	Chief Executive	Civic Centre
Electoral Registration	Don Pratt	Assistant Director (Member Services)	Civic Centre
Environmental Health	Jeremy Mann	Environment Manager	Civic Centre
Finance	Jeremy Stark	Accountancy Services Manager	Civic Centre
Housing	Barbara Venn	Housing Enabling Manager	Civic Centre
Legal Services	Julie Genge	Solicitor to the Council / Monitoring Officer	Civic Centre
Leisure	Robert Crabb	Sport & Recreation Manager	Civic Centre
Local Land Charges	Don Pratt	Assistant Director	Civic Centre
Planning	Malcolm Easton	Planning Manager	Civic Centre
Technical Services	Anne Cowley	Policy Performance & Information Manager	Civic Centre

Parish Councils in the authority's area: Arlington; Ashford; Atherington; Berrynarbor; Bishops Nympton; Bishops Tawton; Bratton Fleming; Braunton; Brayford; Brendon & Countisbury; Burrington; Chittlehamholt, Chittlehampton; Chulmleigh; Combe Martin; East & West Buckland; East Down; East Worlington; Filleigh; Fremington; Georgeham; Georgenympton & Queensnympton; Goodleigh; Heanton Punchardon; Horwood, Lovacott & Newton Tracey; Instow; Kentisbury & Trentishoe; Kings Nympton; Knowstone; Landkey; Marwood; Meshaw; Molland; Mortehoe; North Molton; Parracombe; Pilton West; Rackenford; Rose Ash; Satterleigh & Warkleigh; Shirwell; Swimbridge; Tawstock; West Down; Westleigh; Witheridge.

Parish Meetings in the authority's area: Bittadon; Challacombe; East Anstey; Loxhore; Mariansleigh; Martinhoe; Romansleigh; Stoke Rivers; Twitchen; West Anstey.

Town Councils in the authority's area: Barnstaple; Ilfracombe; Lynton & Lynmouth; South Molton.

DISTRICT COUNCILS

NORTH DORSET DISTRICT COUNCIL

www.north-dorset.gov.uk

Principal Office

Nordon, Salisbury Road, Blandford Forum, Dorset DT11 7LL
Telephone: (01258) 454111; FAX: (01258) 484007; DX 142922 Blandford Forum 2

Blandford Leisure Centre

Milldown Road, Blandford Forum, Dorset DT11 7DB
Telephone: (01258) 455556

Function	Chief Officer	Title	Location
Chief Executive	L Goodall	Chief Executive	Nordon
Electoral Registration	L Coffin	Electoral Services Officer	Nordon
Environmental Health	R Frost;	Food Safety Team Leader;	
	K Pitt-Kerby	Environmental Protection & Private Sector Housing Team Leader	Nordon
Finance	B Marshall	Finance Manager	Nordon
Housing	D Hardy	Policy Manager	Nordon
Legal Services	S Caundle	Legal Services Manager	Nordon
Leisure	T Whight	Leisure Manager	Blandford Leisure
Local Land Charges	E Upton	Senior Land Charges Clerk	Nordon
Planning	N Fagan	Development Control Manager	Nordon
Purchasing & Supplies	J Burgess	Facilities Team Leader	Nordon
Technical Services	B Bray;		
	M Coker	Principal Technical Officers	Nordon

Parish Councils in the authority's area: Anderson; Ashmore; Blandford St Mary; Bourton; Bryanston; Buckhorn Weston; Cann; Charlton Marshall; Chettle; Child Okeford; Compton Abbas; Durweston; East Orchard; East Stour; Farnham; Fontmell Magna; Hazelbury Bryan; Hilton; Hinton St Mary; Ibberton; Iwerne Courtney; Iwerne Minster; Iwerne Stepleton; Kington Magna; Lydlinch; Manston; Margaret Marsh; Marnhull; Melbury Abbas; Milborne St Andrew; Milton Abbas; Motcombe; Okeford Fitzpaine; Pimperne; Shillingstone; Spetisbury; Stour Provost; Stourpaine; Stourton Caundle; Sutton Waldron; Tarrant Crawford; Tarrant Gunville; Tarrant Hinton; Tarrant Keyneston; Tarrant Launceston; Tarrant Monkton; Tarrant Rawston; Tarrant Rushton; Todber; West Orchard; West Stour; Winterborne Houghton; Winterborne Kingston; Winterborne Stickland; Winterborne Whitechurch; Winterborne Zelston.

Parish Meetings in the authority's area: Fifehead Magdalen; Fifehead Neville; Glanvilles Wootton; Hammoon; Hanford; Langton Long; Mappowder; Pulham; Silton; Stoke Wake; Turnworth; Winterborne Clenston; Woolland.

Town Councils in the authority's area: Blandford Forum; Gillingham; Shaftesbury; Stalbridge; Sturminster Newton.

NORTH EAST DERBYSHIRE DISTRICT COUNCIL

www.ne-derbyshire.gov.uk

Principal Office

Council House, Saltergate, Chesterfield, Derbyshire S40 1LF
Telephone: (01246) 231111; FAX: (01246) 550213

Function	Chief Officer	Title	Location
Chief Executive	Mrs C A Gilby	Chief Executive	Council House
Environmental Health	Mr R Kirk	Head of Environmental Services	Council House
Finance	Mr M Goodwin	Head of Finance	Council House
Housing	Mr R Oliver	Head of Housing	Council House
Legal Services	Gyl Murphy	Head of Legal & Democratic Services	Council House
Leisure	Mr W Newton	Head of Leisure	Council House
Planning	Mr K Hill	Head of Planning & Development	Council House

Technical Services	Mr R Storrie	Head of Property & Technical Services	Council House

Parish Councils in the authority's area: Ashover; Barlow; Brackenfield; Brampton; Calow; Clay Cross; Eckington; Grassmoor, Hasland & Winsick; Heath; Holmesfield; Holmewood; Holymoorside & Walton; Killamarsh; Morton; North Wingfield; Pilsley; Shirland & Higham; Stretton; Sutton-cum-Duckmanton; Temple Normanton; Tupton; Unstone; Wessington; Wingerworth.

Town Councils in the authority's area: Dronfield.

NORTH HERTFORDSHIRE DISTRICT COUNCIL

www.north-herts.gov.uk

Principal Office
Council Offices, Gernon Road, Letchworth, Hertfordshire SG6 3JF
Telephone: (01462) 474000; FAX: (01462) 474227; DX 31317 Letchworth

Finance Department
Town Lodge, Gernon Road, Letchworth, Hertfordshire SG6 3HN

Function	Chief Officer	Title	Location
Chief Executive	John T Campbell	Chief Executive	Council Offices
Electoral Registration	David Miley		Council Offices
Environmental Health	Chris Evans	Chief Environmental Health Officer	Council Offices
Finance	Norma Atlay	Director of Finance	Town Lodge
Legal Services	Frances Bogie	Assistant Director, Legal	Council Offices
Leisure	Vaughan Watson	Assistant Director, Leisure	Council Offices
Local Land Charges	Frances Bogie	Assistant Director, Legal	Council Offices
Planning	David Scholes	Group Manager, Planning Services	Council Offices

Parish Councils in the authority's area: Ashwell; Barkway; Barley; Bygrave; Caldecote & Newnham; Clothall; Codicote; Graveley; Hexton; Hinxworth; Holwell; Ickleford; Kelshall; Kimpton; Kings Walden; Knebworth; Lilley; Newham; Nuthampstead; Offley with Cockernhoe; Pirton; Preston; Radwel; Reed; Rushden & Wallington; St Ippolyts; St Paul's Walden; Sandon; Therfield; Weston; Wymondley.

Parish Meetings in the authority's area: Clothall; Hexton; Kelshall; Langley; Nuthampstead; Radwell.

Town Councils in the authority's area: Royston.

NORTH KESTEVEN DISTRICT COUNCIL

www.n-kesteven.gov.uk

Principal Office
Kesteven Street, Sleaford, Lincolnshire NG34 7EF
Telephone: (01529) 414155; FAX: (01529) 413956; DX 26909 Sleaford

Function	Chief Officer	Title	Location
Chief Executive	Mrs R E Marlow	Chief Executive	Kesteven Street
Electoral Registration	Mr C N Robinson	Member Services Manager	Kesteven Street
Environmental Health	Mr S Archer	Head of Environmental Services	Kesteven Street
Finance	Mr A Thomas	Director of Central Services	Kesteven Street
Housing	Mr C Redshaw	Director of Housing & The Community	Kesteven Street
Legal Services	Mr M J Samson	Head of Legal & Member Services	Kesteven Street
Leisure	Mr C Redshaw	Director of Housing & The Community	Kesteven Street
Local Land Charges	Mr C N Robinson	Member Services Manager	Kesteven Street
Planning	Ms J Wells	Head of Economic & Community Services	Kesteven Street

Purchasing & Supplies	Mr K Bailey	Support Services Manager	Kesteven Street
Technical Services	[Vacant]	Estates Officer	Kesteven Street

Parish Councils in the authority's area: Anwick; Ashby-de-la-Launde & Bloxholm; Aubourn; Aurbourn Haddington & South Hykeham; Bassingham; Beckingham; Billinghay; Blankney; Bracebridge Heath; Branston & Mere; Brant Broughton & Stragglethorpe; Canwick; Carlton-le-Moorland; Chapel Hill; Coleby; Cranwell & Byard's Leap; Digby; Doddington & Whisby; Dogdyke; Dorrington; Dunston; Eagle & Swinethorpe; Ewerby & Evedon; Great Hale; Haddington; Harmston; Haverholme; Heckington; Heighington; Helpringham; Holdingham; Kirkby Green; Kirkby la Thorpe; Kirkstead Bridge; Leadenham; Leasingham; Martin; Metheringham; Morton; Navenby; Nocton; North Kyme; North Rauceby; North Scarle; Osbournby; Potterhanworth; Quarrington; Roxholm; Ruskington; Scopwick; Scott Willoughby; Scredington; Skellingthorpe; Skinnand; South Kyme; South Rauceby; Spanby; Swinderby; Tattershall Bridge; Temple Bruer with Temple High Grange; Thorpe Tilney; Thorpe-on-the-Hill; Timberland; Waddington; Walcott; Washingborough; Welbourn; Wellingore; Wilsford; Witham St. Hughes.

Parish Meetings in the authority's area: Asgarby & Howell; Aswarby & Swarby; Aunsby & Dembleby; Boothby Graffoe; Brauncewell; Burton Pedwardine; Culverthorpe & Kelby; Little Hale; Newton & Haceby; Norton Disney; Rowston; Silk Willoughby; Stapleford; Swaton; Threekingham; Thurlby; Walcot.

Town Councils in the authority's area: North Hykeham; Sleaford.

NORTH NORFOLK DISTRICT COUNCIL

www.northnorfolk.org

Principal Office
Council Offices, Holt Road, Cromer, Norfolk NR27 9EL
Telephone: (01263) 513811; FAX: (01263) 515042; DX 31008 Cromer

Function	Chief Officer	Title	Location
Chief Executive	Mr Philip Burton	Chief Executive	Council Offices
Electoral Registration	Mr Graham Bull	Corporate Director	Council Offices
Environmental Health	Mr Graham Bull	Corporate Director	Council Offices
Finance	Mr Philip Burton	Chief Executive	Council Offices
Housing	Mrs Ruth Langslow	Corporate Director	Council Offices
Legal Services	Mr Graham Bull	Corporate Director	Council Offices
Leisure	Mrs Ruth Langslow	Corporate Director	Council Offices
Local Land Charges	Mr Graham Bull	Corporate Director	Council Offices
Planning	Mrs Ruth Langslow	Corporate Director	Council Offices

Parish Councils in the authority's area: Alby with Thwaite; Aldborough; Antingham; Ashmanhaugh; Aylmerton; Baconsthorpe; Bacton; Bale; Banningham; Barney; Barsham; Barton Turf; Beeston Regis; Bessingham; Binham; Blakeney; Bodham; Bradfield; Briningham; Brinton; Briston; Brumstead; Calthorpe; Catfield; Cley; Cockthorpe; Colby; Corpusty; Crostwight; Dilham; Dunton; East Beckham; East Runton; East Ruston; Edgefield; Egmere; Erpingham; Felbrigg; Felmingham; Field Dalling; Fulmodestone; Gimingham; Great Snoring; Gresham; Gunthorpe; Gunton; Hanworth; Happisburgh; Helhoughton; Hempstead; Hempton; Hickling; High Kelling; Hindolveston; Hindringham; Holkham; Honing; Horning; Hoveton; Hunworth; Ingham; Ingworth; Irstead; Itteringham; Kelling; Kettlestone; Knapton; Langham; Lessingham; Letheringsett with Glandford; Little Barningham; Little Snoring; Ludham; Mannington; Matlaske; Melton Constable; Morston; Mundesley; Neatishead; Northrepps; Overstrand; Paston; Plumstead; Potter Heigham; Pudding Norton; Quarles; Raynham; Ridlington; Roughton; Ryburgh; Salthouse; Saxlingham; Saxthorpe; Scottow; Sculthorpe; Sea Palling; Sharrington; Shereford; Sidestrand; Skeyton; Sloley; Smallburgh; Southrepps; Stibbard; Stiffkey; Stody; Suffield; Sustead; Sutton; Swafield; Swanton Abbott; Swanton Novers; Tattersett; Testerton; Thornage; Thorpe Market; Thurgarton; Thursford; Toftrees; Trimingham; Trunch; Tunstead; Upper Sheringham; Walcott; Walsingham; Warham; West Beckham; West Runton; Weybourne; Wickmere; Wighton; Witton; Wiveton; Wood Norton; Worstead.

Parish Meetings in the authority's area: Horsey; Thurning; Westwick.

DISTRICT COUNCILS

Town Councils in the authority's area: Cromer; Fakenham; Holt; North Walsham; Sheringham; Stalham; Wells.

NORTH SHROPSHIRE DISTRICT COUNCIL

www.northshropshiredc.gov.uk

Principal Office
Edinburgh House, New Street, Wem, Shropshire SY4 5DB
Telephone: (01939) 232771; FAX: (01939) 238404; DX 27386 Wem

Function	Chief Officer	Title	Location
Chief Executive	Mr R J Hughes	Chief Executive & Director of Corporate Services	Edinburgh Hse
Electoral Registration	Mr K Reynolds	Senior Admin Officer	Edinburgh Hse
Environmental Health	Mr J Gibson	Head of Environmental Health	Edinburgh Hse
Finance	Mr J Hancock	Chief Finance Officer	Edinburgh Hse
Housing	Mr A Lewis	Chief Housing Officer	Edinburgh Hse
Legal Services	Mr R S C Owens	Head of Legal & Administrative Services	Edinburgh Hse
Leisure	Mrs C Ebben	Head of Leisure & Amenities	Edinburgh Hse
Local Land Charges	Miss L Batchelor	Clerical Assistant	Edinburgh Hse
Planning	Mr A D Venables	Director of Planning Services	Edinburgh Hse
Purchasing & Supplies	Mr P Appleton	Director of Community Services	Edinburgh Hse
Technical Services	Mr P Appleton	Director of Community Services	Edinburgh Hse

Parish Councils in the authority's area: Adderley; Baschurch; Cheswardine; Childs Ercall; Clive; Cockshutt-cum-Petton; Ellesmere Rural; Grinshill; Hadnall; Hinstock; Hodnet; Hordley; Ightfield; Loppington; Moreton Corbet & Lee Brockhurst; Moreton Saye; Myddle & Broughton; Norton in Hales; Prees; Shawbury; Stanton upon Hine Heath; Stoke upon Tern; Sutton upon Tern; Welshampton & Lyneal; Wem Rural; Weston under Redcastle; Whitchurch Rural; Whixall; Woore.

Town Councils in the authority's area: Ellesmere; Market Drayton; Wem; Whitchurch.

NORTH WARWICKSHIRE BOROUGH COUNCIL

www.northwarks.gov.uk

Principal Office
The Council House, South Street, Atherstone, Warwickshire CV9 1BD
Telephone: (01827) 715341; FAX: (01827) 719225; DX 23956 Atherstone

Chief Executive's Department; Housing Department; Environmental Health Department
Old Bank House, 129 Long Street, Atherstone CV9 1BQ
Telephone: (01827) 715341; FAX: (01827) 719430

Function	Chief Officer	Title	Location
Chief Executive	Mr J Hutchinson	Chief Executive	Old Bank Hse
Electoral Registration	Mr J Bird	Assistant Chief Executive	Council House
Environmental Health	Mr P Staveley	Assistant Director (Environment & Health)	Old Bank Hse
Finance	Mr C J Brewer	Director of Resources	Council House
Housing	Mr S Clark	Assistant Director (Housing)	Old Bank Hse
Legal Services	Mr P Oliver	Solicitor to the Council	Council House
Leisure	Mr S Powell	Assistant Director (Community Development)	Council House
Local Land Charges	Mr M Lambert	Assistant Director (Planning)	Council House
Planning	Mr M Lambert	Assistant Director (Planning)	Council House
Purchasing & Supplies	Mrs L Bird	Assistant Director (Informaton Services)	Council House
Technical Services	Mr I Sarson	Assistant Director (Leisure & Facilities)	Council House

DISTRICT COUNCILS

Parish Councils in the authority's area: Ansley; Arley; Astley; Austrey; Baddesley Ensor; Baxterley; Bentley/Merevale; Corley; Curdworth; Dordon; Fillongley; Grendon; Hartshill; Kingsbury; Lea Marston; Mancetter; Maxstoke; Middleton; Nether Whitacre; Newton Regis & Seckington; Over Whitacre; Polesworth; Shustoke; Shuttington; Water Orton; Wishaw & Moxhull.

Parish Meetings in the authority's area: Caldecote; Great Packington; Little Packington.

Town Councils in the authority's area: Atherstone; Coleshill.

NORTH WEST LEICESTERSHIRE DISTRICT COUNCIL

www.nwleics.gov.uk

Principal Office

Council Offices, Coalville, Leicestershire LE67 3FJ
Telephone: (01530) 454545; FAX: (01530) 454504; DX 23662 Coalville

Function	Chief Officer	Title	Location
Chief Executive	M J Diaper	Chief Executive	Council Offices
Electoral Registration	Mrs L Gill	Manager of Central Support	Council Offices
Environmental Health	B E Wolsey	Manager of Planning & Environment	Council Offices
Finance	Mrs L Gill	Manager of Central Support	Council Offices
Housing	D Swallow	Manager of Housing	Council Offices
Legal Services	J R Kirkham	Head of Legal Services	Council Offices
Leisure	D Halstead	Manager of Community Services	Council Offices
Local Land Charges	Mrs L Gill	Manager of Central Support	Council Offices
Planning	B E Wolsey	Manager of Planning & Environment	Council Offices
Technical Services	K Fairbrother	Manager of Technical & Contracting Support	Council Offices

Parish Councils in the authority's area: Appleby Magna; Belton; Breedon on the Hill; Castle Donington; Charley; Coleorton; Ellistown & Battleflat; Heather; Hemington; Ibstock; Kegworth; Lockington; Long Whatton; Measham; Oakthorpe & Donisthorpe; Osgathorpe; Packington; Ravenstone; Snarestone; Snibston; Swannington; Swepstone; Worthington.

Parish Meetings in the authority's area: Bardon; Chilcote; Isley cum Langley; Normanton le Heath; Staunton Harold; Stretton en le Field.

Town Councils in the authority's area: Ashby de la Zouch; Ashby Woulds.

NORTH WILTSHIRE DISTRICT COUNCIL

www.northwilts.gov.uk

Principal Office

Monkton Park, Chippenham, Wiltshire SN15 1ER
Telephone: (01249) 706111; FAX: (01249) 443152; DX 34208 Chippenham

Function	Chief Officer	Title	Location
Chief Executive	Mr Bob Marshall	Chief Executive	Monkton Pk
Environmental Health	Mr Nick Fenwick	Strategic Manager for Environmental Services	Monkton Pk
Finance	Mrs Sue Pangbourne	Strategic Manager for Corporate Services	Monkton Pk
Housing	Mrs Laurie Bell	Strategic Manager for Community & Renegeration	Monkton Pk
Legal Services	Mrs Sue Pangbourne	Strategic Manager for Corporate Services	Monkton Pk
Leisure	Mrs Laurie Bell	Strategic Manager for Community & Renegeration	Monkton Pk
Planning	Mr Alun Davies	Strategic Manager for Planning Services	Monkton Pk

Purchasing & Supplies Mr Nick Fenwick Strategic Manager for Environmental
Services Monkton Pk

Parish Councils in the authority's area: Ashton Keynes; Biddestone; Box; Bremhill; Brinkworth; Broad Town; Brokenborough; Calne Without; Castle Combe; Charlton; Cherhill; Chippenham Without; Christian Malford; Clyffe Pypard; Colerne; Compton Bassett; Crudwell; Dauntsey; Great Somerford; Grittleton; Hankerton; Heddington; Hilmarton; Hullavington; Kington Langley; Kington St Michael; Lacock; Langley Burrell; Latton; Lea & Cleverton; Leigh; Little Somerford; Luckington; Lydiard Millicent; Lydiard Tregoz; Lyneham & Bradenstoke; Minety; Nettleton; North Wraxall; Oaksey; Purton; St Paul Malmesbury Without; Seagry; Sherston; Stanton St Quintin; Sutton Benger; Tockenham; Yatton Keynell.

Parish Meetings in the authority's area: Braydon; Easton Grey; Marston Meysey; Norton & Foxley; Sopworth.

Town Councils in the authority's area: Chippenham; Calne; Corsham; Cricklade; Malmesbury; Wootton Bassett.

NORTHAMPTON BOROUGH COUNCIL

www.northampton.gov.uk

Principal Office
The Guildhall, St Giles Square, Northampton NN1 1DE
Telephone: (01604) 837837; FAX: (01604) 838729; DX 703139 Northampton 6

Development & Environment Services
Cliftonville House, Bedford Road, Northampton NN4 7NR
Telephone: (01604) 837837

Community Services
Westbridge Depot, St James Mill Road, Northampton NN5 5JW
Telephone: (01604) 837837; FAX: (01604) 838741

Function	Chief Officer	Title	Location
Chief Executive	Mr R J B Morris	Chief Executive & Town Clerk	The Guildhall
Electoral Registration	Mr R Thompson	Electoral Registrar	The Guildhall
Environmental Health	Mr S Elsey	Environmental Health Manager	Cliftonville Hse
Finance	Mr J Warlow	Director of Strategic Resources	The Guildhall
Housing	Mr A Farrell	Director of Housing & Business Services	The Guildhall
Legal Services	Mr P A Newham	Borough Solicitor	The Guildhall
Leisure	Mrs M Gill	Director of Community Services	Westbridge Dpt
Local Land Charges	Mr D Wilson	Head of Promotional & Property Services	The Guildhall
Planning	Mr D Alderson	Head of Planning, Transportation & Regeneration	Cliftonville Hse
Purchasing & Supplies	Mr A Foster	Head of Procurement	The Guildhall
Technical Services	Mr D Alderson	Head of Planning, Transportation & Regeneration	Cliftonville Hse

Parish Councils in the authority's area: Billing; Collingtree; Duston; Great Houghton; Hardingstone; Upton; Wootton.

NORTHAVON DISTRICT COUNCIL
Northavon District Council was abolished on 31 March 1996; see now South Gloucestershire Council.

DISTRICT COUNCILS

NORWICH CITY COUNCIL

www.norwich.gov.uk

Principal Office
City Hall, Norwich, Norfolk NR2 1NH
Telephone: (01603) 622233; FAX: (01603) 213000; DX 5278 Norwich

Development and Property Services
St Giles House, 27 St Giles Street, Norwich NR2 1UY
Telephone: (01603) 622233; FAX: (01603) 213548/213546

Function	Chief Officer	Title	Location
Chief Executive	Mrs A Seex	Chief Executive Officer	City Hall
Electoral Registration	Ms B Buttinger	Director of Organisational Development	City Hall
Environmental Health	Mr G Kasprzok	Head of Environmental Services	City Hall
Finance	Mr I Ambrose	Head of Financial Services	City Hall
Housing	Mr S Mudie	Director of Housing & Revenue Services	City Hall
Legal Services	Mr D Johnson	Head of Legal Services	City Hall
Leisure	Ms N Rotsos	Director of Culture	City Hall
Local Land Charges	Ms B Buttinger	Director of Organisational Development	City Hall
Planning	Mr P Allen	Director of Development	City Hall
Purchasing & Supplies	Mr I Ambrose	Head of Financial Services	City Hall
Technical Services	Mr P Allen;	Director of Development;	City Hall
	Mr M Butler	Head of Property Services	St Giles Hse

Parish Councils & Parish Meetings in the authority's area: none.

Town Councils in the authority's area: none.

NOTTINGHAM CITY COUNCIL
Nottingham City Council became a unitary authority on 1 April 1998.

NUNEATON & BEDWORTH BOROUGH COUNCIL

www.nuneatonandbedworth.gov.uk

Principal Office
Town Hall and Council House, Coton Road, Nuneaton, Warwickshire CV11 5AA
Telephone: (024) 7637 6376; FAX: (024) 7637 6574; DX 16458 Nuneaton

Function	Chief Officer	Title	Location
Chief Executive	Ms Christine Kerr	Chief Executive	Town Hall
Electoral Registration	Ms Christine Kerr	Chief Executive	Town Hall
Environmental Health	Mr Alan Franks	Director, Environmental Services	Town Hall
Finance	Mr Alan Davies	Director, Corporate Services	Town Hall
Housing	Mr Alan Davies	Director, Corporate Services	Town Hall
Legal Services	Mr Alan Davies	Director, Corporate Services	Town Hall
Leisure	Mr Alan Franks	Director, Environmental Services	Town Hall
Local Land Charges	Mr Alan Davies	Director, Corporate Services	Town Hall
Planning	Mr Alan Franks	Director, Environmental Services	Town Hall
Purchasing & Supplies	Ms Christine Kerr	Chief Executive	Town Hall

Parish Councils & Parish Meetings in the authority's area: none.

Town Councils in the authority's area: none.

OADBY & WIGSTON BOROUGH COUNCIL

www.oadby-wigston.gov.uk

Principal Office
Council Offices, Station Road, Wigston, Leicestershire LE18 2DR
Telephone: (0116) 288 8961; FAX: (0116) 288 7828

DISTRICT COUNCILS

Function	Chief Officer	Title	Location
Chief Executive	Mrs Ruth Hyde	Chief Executive	Council Offices
Electoral Registration	Mrs Ruth Hyde	Chief Executive	Council Offices
Environmental Health	Mr Stephen Bruce	Head of Environmental Health & Environment	Council Offices
Finance	Mrs Nicola Heap	Director of Resources	Council Offices
Housing	Mr Simon Folwell	Assistant Director (Housing)	Council Offices
Legal Services	Mr Stuart Sugarman	Head of Legal and Deputy Director of Resources	Council Offices
Leisure	Mrs Wendy Back	Director of Consumer Services	Council Offices
Local Land Charges	Mr Stuart Sugarman	Head of Legal and Deputy Director of Resources	Council Offices
Planning	Mr Martin Yardley	Assistant Director (Planning)	Council Offices
Purchasing & Supplies	Mr Stuart Sugarman	Head of Legal and Deputy Director of Resources	Council Offices
Technical Services	Mr Graham Norman	Head of Client Services & Contracts	Council Offices

Parish Councils & Parish Meetings in the authority's area: none.

Town Councils in the authority's area: none.

OSWESTRY BOROUGH COUNCIL

www.oswestrybc.gov.uk

Principal Office
Council Offices, Castle View, Oswestry, Shropshire SY11 1JR
Telephone: (01691) 671111; FAX: (01691) 677348; DX 26610 Oswestry

Function	Chief Officer	Title	Location
Chief Executive	Mr P F Shevlin	Chief Executive	Council Offices
Electoral Registration	Marilyn McCarron	Head of Administrative/Legal Services	Council Offices
Environmental Health	Mr H Jones	Head of Environmental Services	Council Offices
Finance	Mr T Durrell	Head of Financial Services	Council Offices
Housing	Mr T Lowry	Head of Housing Services	Council Offices
Legal Services	Marilyn McCarron	Head of Administrative/Legal Services	Council Offices
Leisure	Mr M Bamber	Head of Leisure Services	Council Offices
Local Land Charges	Marilyn McCarron	Head of Administrative/Legal Services	Council Offices
Planning	Mr B R Smith	Head of Development Services	Council Offices
Technical Services	Mr D Jones	Head of Technical Services	Council Offices

Parish Councils in the authority's area: Kinnerley; Knockin; Llanyblodwel; Llanymynech & Pant; Melverley; Oswestry Rural; Ruyton-xi-Towns; St Martins; Selattyn & Gobowen; West Felton; Weston Rhyn; Whittington.

Town Council in the authority's area: Oswestry.

OXFORD CITY COUNCIL

www.oxford.gov.uk

Principal Office
Town Hall, St Aldate's, Oxford OX1 1BX
Telephone: (01865) 249811; DX 4309 Oxford

Function	Chief Officer	Title	Location
Chief Executive	Mr N Gibson	Interim Chief Executive & Strategic Director – Housing, Health & Community	Town Hall
Electoral Registration	Mr M Luntley	Strategic Director – Finance & Corporate Services	Town Hall

DISTRICT COUNCILS

Environmental Health	Mr N Gibson	Interim Chief Executive & Strategic Director – Housing, Health & Community	Town Hall
Finance	Mr M Luntley	Strategic Director – Finance & Corporate Services	Town Hall
Housing	Mr N Gibson	Interim Chief Executive & Strategic Director – Housing, Health & Community	Town Hall
Legal Services	Mr M Luntley	Strategic Director – Finance & Corporate Services	Town Hall
Leisure	Ms S Cosgrove	Strategic Director – Physical Environment	Town Hall
Local Land Charges	Mr M Luntley	Strategic Director – Finance & Corporate Services	Town Hall
Planning	Ms S Cosgrove	Strategic Director – Physical Environment	Town Hall
Technical Services	Ms S Cosgrove	Strategic Director – Physical Environment	Town Hall

Parish Councils in the authority's area: Blackbird Leys; Littlemore; Old Marston; Risinghurst & Sandhills.

PENDLE BOROUGH COUNCIL

www.pendle.gov.uk

Principal Office
Town Hall, Market Street, Nelson, Lancashire BB9 7LG
Telephone: (01282) 661661; FAX: (01282) 661630; DX 14669 Nelson

Housing & Community Services; Urban Renewal Unit; Environmental Services
Colne Town Hall, Albert Road, Colne BB8 0AQ
Telephone: (01282) 661661; FAX: (01282) 661140

Accountancy & Audit Services; Information Services; Treasury Services
Elliott House, Market Square, Nelson BB9 7LP
Telephone: (01282) 661661; FAX: (01282) 661811

Highways, Engineering and Design Services
Booth Street, Nelson BB9 7PX
Telephone: (01282) 661661; FAX: (01282 661140

Pendle Leisure
Bank House, Albert Road, Colne BB8 0BP
Telephone: (01282) 661661; FAX: (01282) 661221

Function	Chief Officer	Title	Location
Chief Executive	Mr S Barnes	Chief Executive	Town Hall
Electoral Registration	Mr R Townson	Democratic & Legal Services Manager	Town Hall
Environmental Health	Mr T Mitton	Urban Renewal & Environmental Services Manager	Colne Town Hall
Finance	Mr T Morris	Financial Manager (Accountancy & Audit)	Elliott House
Housing	Mr I Broughton	Housing & Community Care Manager	Colne Town Hall
Legal Services	Mr R Townson	Democratic & Legal Services Manager	Town Hall
Leisure	Mr P Storey	Leisure Manager	Bank House
Local Land Charges	Mr R Townson	Democratic & Legal Services Manager	Town Hall
Planning	Mr A Wiggett	Planning & Building Control Manager	Town Hall
Technical Services	Mr P Atkinson	Highways, Engineering & Design Manager	Booth Street

Parish Councils in the authority's area: Barley with Wheatley Booth; Barrowford; Blacko; Bracewell & Brogden; Earby; Foulridge; Goldshaw Booth; Higham with West Close Booth; Kelbrook & Sough; Laneshaw Bridge; Old Laund Booth; Reedley Hallows; Roughlee Booth; Salterforth; Trawden Forest.

Town Councils in the authority's area: Barnoldswick; Brierfield.

PENWITH DISTRICT COUNCIL

www.penwith.gov.uk

Principal Office
The Council Offices, St Clare, Penzance, Cornwall TR18 3QW
Telephone: (01736) 362341; FAX: (01736) 336575; DX 144380 Penzance 3

Function	Chief Officer	Title	Location
Chief Executive	Mr J McKenna	Chief Executive	Council Offices
Electoral Registration	Mr P N Rylett	Head of Democratic Services	Council Offices
Environmental Health	Mr A Hampshire	Head of Housing and Environmental Services	Council Offices
Finance	Mr S P Hudson	Head of Financial Services	Council Offices
Housing	Mr A Hampshire	Head of Housing and Environmental Services	Council Offices
Legal Services	Mr W D Hooper	Head of Legal, Personnel & Estates	Council Offices
Leisure	Mrs C A Hill	Head of Regeneration, Tourism & Leisure	Council Offices
Local Land Charges	Mr W D Hooper	Head of Legal, Personnel & Estates	Council Offices
Planning	Mr R Harnett	Head of Planning and Building Control Services	Council Offices
Purchasing & Supplies	Mr S P Hudson	Head of Financial Services	Council Offices
Technical Services	Mr A Roberts	Head of Operational Services	Council Offices

Parish Councils in the authority's area: Gwinear-Gwithian; Ludgvan; Madron; Paul; Perranuthnoe; St Buryan; St Erth; St Hilary; St Levan; Sancreed; Sennen; Towednack; Zennor.

Parish Meetings in the authority's area: Morvah; St Michael's Mount.

Town Councils in the authority's area: Hayle; Marazion; Penzance; St Ives; St Just.

PETERBOROUGH CITY COUNCIL
Peterborough City Council became a unitary authority on 1 April 1998.

PLYMOUTH CITY COUNCIL
Plymouth City Council became a unitary authority on 1 April 1998.

POOLE BOROUGH COUNCIL
Poole Borough Council became a unitary authority on 1 April 1997.

PORTSMOUTH CITY COUNCIL
Portsmouth City Council became a unitary authority on 1 April 1997.

PRESTON BOROUGH COUNCIL
See now Preston City Council.

PRESTON CITY COUNCIL

www.preston.gov.uk

Principal Office
Town Hall, Preston, Lancashire PR1 2RL
Telephone: (01772) 906000; FAX: (01772) 906195

Leisure Services Department
Guild Hall, Preston PR1 1HT
Telephone: (01772) 203456; FAX: (01772) 881716

Function	Chief Officer	Title	Location
Chief Executive	Mr J Carr	Town Clerk & Chief Executive	Town Hall

DISTRICT COUNCILS

Function	Chief Officer	Title	Location
Electoral Registration	Mr M Thorpe	Head of Elections & Licensing	Town Hall
Environmental Health	Mr P Kuit	Director of Environmental Services	Town Hall
Finance	Mr B Hayes	Director of Finance & Property Services	Town Hall
Housing	Ms M Bailey; Mr T Miskell	Interim Directors of Housing & Direct Services	Town Hall
Legal Services	Mrs L Norris	Director of Corporate Services	Town Hall
Leisure	Mr S Jones	Director of Regeneration, Community & Leisure	Guild Hall
Local Land Charges	Ms B Heath	Acting Assistant Director of Legal & Administration	Town Hall
Planning	Mr P Davies	Assistant Director of Planning	Town Hall
Technical Services	Mr M Lovatt	Assistant Director, Works	Town Hall

Parish Councils in the authority's area: Barton; Broughton-in-Amounderness; Goosnargh; Grimsargh; Haighton; Lea; Whittingham; Woodplumpton.

PURBECK DISTRICT COUNCIL

www.purbeck.gov.uk

Principal Office
Westport House, Worgret Road, Wareham, Dorset BH20 4PP
Telephone: (01929) 556561; FAX: (01929) 552688

Function	Chief Officer	Title	Location
Chief Executive	P B Croft	Chief Executive	Westport House
Electoral Registration	P R Aston	Principal Administrative & Elections Officer	Westport House
Environmental Health	R Garwood	Environmental Services Manager	Westport House
Finance	F Williams	Financial Services Manager	Westport House
Housing	C Branch	Housing Services Manager	Westport House
Legal Services	G T Harding	Legal Services Manager	Westport House
Leisure	R C Whalley	Director of Community Services	Westport House
Local Land Charges	G T Harding	Legal Services Manager	Westport House
Planning	M Sturgess	Community Planning & Policy Manager	Westport House
Purchasing & Supplies	Mrs J Hall	Contracts Administration Officer	Westport House
Technical Services	[Vacant]	Principal Technical Officer	Westport House

Parish Councils in the authority's area: Affpuddle & Turnerspuddle; Arne; Bere Regis; Chaldon Herring; Church Knowle; Corfe Castle; East Lulworth; East Stoke; Langton Matravers; Lytchett Matravers; Morden; Moreton; Studland; Wareham St Martin; West Lulworth; Winfrith Newburgh; Wool; Worth Matravers.

Parish Meetings in the authority's area: Bloxworth; Coombe Keynes; East Holme; Kimmeridge; Steeple; Tyneham.

Town Councils in the authority's area: Lychett Minster & Upton; Swanage; Wareham.

READING BOROUGH COUNCIL
Reading Borough Council became a unitary authority on 1 April 1998.

REDDITCH BOROUGH COUNCIL

www.redditchbc.gov.uk

Principal Office
Town Hall, Alcester Street, Redditch, Worcestershire B98 8AH
Telephone: (01527) 64252; FAX: (01527) 65216; DX 19106 Redditch

Function	Chief Officer	Title	Location
Chief Executive	Mr Chris Smith	Borough Director	Town Hall

Electoral Registration	Mr Steve Skinner	Democratic Services Manager	Town Hall
Environmental Health	Mrs Sue Hanley	Director of Environment & Planning	Town Hall
Finance	Mr Chris Smith	Borough Director	Town Hall
Housing	Ms Jackie Smith	Acting Director of Housing	Town Hall
Legal Services	Ms Sue Mullins	Legal Services Manager	Town Hall
Leisure	Mr Paul Patten	Director of Culture & Development	Town Hall
Local Land Charges	Mr Steve Skinner	Democratic Services Manager	Town Hall
Planning	Mrs Sue Hanley	Director of Environment & Planning	Town Hall
Purchasing & Supplies	Mrs Teresa Kristunas	Financial Services Manager	Town Hall
Technical Services	Ms Jackie Smith	Acting Director of Housing	Town Hall

Parish Council in the authority's area: Feckenham.

REIGATE & BANSTEAD BOROUGH COUNCIL

www.reigate-banstead.gov.uk

Principal Office
Town Hall, Castlefield Road, Reigate, Surrey RH2 0SH
Telephone: (01737) 276000; DX 54102 Reigate 2

Earlswood Services
Earlswood Depot, Horley Road, Redhill RH1 6PN
Telephone: (01737) 276000

Function	Chief Officer	Title	Location
Chief Executive	Mr N Clifford	Chief Executive	Town Hall
Electoral Registration	Mr P Dungate	Electoral Services Officer	Town Hall
Environmental Health	Mr T Crowley	Director of Policy & Environment	Town Hall
Finance	Mr P McCallum	Director of Resources	Town Hall
Housing	Mr T Crowley	Director of Policy & Environment	Town Hall
Legal Services	Mrs A Coronel	Head of Legal & Property Services	Town Hall
Leisure	Mr G Cook	Director of Services to the Community	Town Hall
Local Land Charges	Mrs A Coronel	Head of Legal & Property Services	Town Hall
Planning	Mr M Harbottle	Head of Building & Development Services	Town Hall
Purchasing & Supplies	G Pratt	Materials Controller	Earlswood

Parish Councils in the authority's area: Salfords & Sidlow.

Town Councils in the authority's area: Horley.

RESTORMEL BOROUGH COUNCIL

www.restormel.gov.uk

Principal Office
39 Penwinnick Road, St Austell, Cornwall PL25 5DR
Telephone: (01726) 223300; FAX: (01726) 223301

Function	Chief Officer	Title	Location
Chief Executive	Mrs P Crowson	Chief Executive	Penwinnick Rd
Electoral Registration	Mr G Pinwell	Assistant Chief Executive	Penwinnick Rd
Environmental Health	Mr N Hibbett	Head of Environment & Health	Penwinnick Rd
Finance	Mr A Tremaine	Head of Financial Services	Penwinnick Rd
Housing	Mrs K Waters	Head of Economic & Community Development	Penwinnick Rd
Legal Services	Mr G Pinwell	Assistant Chief Executive	Penwinnick Rd
Leisure	Mr I Rigby	Head of Economic & Community Development	Penwinnick Rd
Local Land Charges	Mr P Mason	Head of Planning and Building Control	Penwinnick Rd
Planning	Mr P Mason	Head of Planning and Building Control	Penwinnick Rd

Technical Services   Mr R Thompson   Head of Operational Services   Penwinnick Rd

Parish Councils in the authority's area: Colan; Crantock; Grampound with Creed; Lanlivery; Luxulyan; Mawgan-in-Pydar; Mevagissey; Roche; St Dennis; St Enoder; St Ewe; St Goran; St Mewan; St Sampson; St Stephen-in-Brannel; St Wenn; Treverbyn; Tywardreath and Par.

Parish Meetings in the authority's area: St Michael Caerhays.

Town Councils in the authority's area: Fowey; Lostwithiel; Newquay; St Blaise; St Columb Major.

RIBBLE VALLEY BOROUGH COUNCIL

www.ribblevalley.gov.uk

Principal Office

Council Offices, Church Walk, Clitheroe, Lancashire BB7 2RA
Telephone: (01200) 425111; FAX: (01200) 414488; DX 15157 Clitheroe

Function	Chief Officer	Title	Location
Chief Executive	Mr D A G Morris	Chief Executive	Council Offices
Electoral Registration	Mr P F Timson	Director of Legal Services	Council Offices
Environmental Health	Mr J Russell	Environmental Health Manager	Council Offices
Finance	Mr M Scott	Director of Finance	Council Offices
Housing	Mrs C Grimshaw	Housing Manager	Council Offices
Legal Services	Mr P F Timson	Director of Legal Services	Council Offices
Leisure	Mr C Hughes	Leisure & Tourism Manager	Council Offices
Local Land Charges	Mrs M Smith	Legal and Administration Manager	Council Offices
Planning	Mr S Bailey	Chief Planning Officer	Council Offices
Technical Services	Mr J Heap	Director of Commercial Services	Council Offices

Parish Councils in the authority's area: Aighton, Bailey & Chaigley; Balderstone; Bashall Eaves & Mitton; Billington & Langho; Bolton-by-Bowland, Gisburn Forest & Sawley; Bowland Forest (Higher); Bowland Forest (Lower); Bowland with Leagram; Chatburn; Chipping; Clayton-le-Dale; Dutton; Gisburn; Grindleton; Hothersall; Mellor; Newton; Osbaldeston; Pendleton; Ramsgreave; Read; Ribchester; Rimington & Middop; Sabden; Salesbury; Simonstone; Slaidburn & Easington; Thornley with Wheatley; Waddington; West Bradford; Whalley; Wilpshire; Wiswell.

Parish Meetings in the authority's area: Dinckley; Downham; Horton; Mearley; Newsholme & Paythorne; Twiston; Worston.

Town Councils in the authority's area: Clitheroe; Longridge.

RICHMONDSHIRE DISTRICT COUNCIL

www.richmondshire.gov.uk

Principal Office

Swale House, Frenchgate, Richmond, North Yorkshire DL10 4JE
Telephone: (01748) 829100; FAX: (01748) 825071; DX 65047 Richmond NY

Environment Unit; Economic, Cultural & Leisure Unit

Friars Wynd, Richmond DL10 4RT
Telephone: (01748) 829100; FAX: (01748) 850897

Financial Unit; Housing Unit

Frenchgate House, Frenchgate, Richmond DL10 7AF
Telephone: (01748) 829100; FAX: (01748) 822257

Planning & Development Unit

Springwell House, Frenchgate, Richmond DL10 4JG
Telephone: (01748) 829100; FAX: (01748) 822535

DISTRICT COUNCILS

Contracting Services Unit
Gallowfields Depot, Gallowfields Trading Estate, Richmond DL10 4SY
Telephone: (01748) 829100; FAX: (01748) 822521

Function	Chief Officer	Title	Location
Chief Executive	Mr H Tabiner	Chief Executive	Swale House
Electoral Registration	Sandra Hullah	Electoral Services Officer	Swale House
Environmental Health	Mr M Garside	Manager, Environment Unit	Friars Wynd
Finance	Mr M Drydale	Manager, Financial Unit	Frenchgate Hse
Housing	Mr C Dales	Manager, Housing Unit	Frenchgate Hse
Legal Services	Mrs M Barry	Manager, Corporate Unit	Swale House
Leisure	Mr G Thompson	Manager, Leisure & Economic Development Unit	Friars Wynd
Local Land Charges	Mr P Earle	Planning & Development Unit Manager	Springwell Hse
Planning	Mr P Earle	Planning & Development Unit Manager	Springwell Hse
Purchasing & Supplies	Mr M Slee	Manager, Contracting Services	Gallowfields Depot
Technical Services	Mr P Earle	Planning & Development Unit Manager	Springwell Hse

Parish Councils in the authority's area: Aldbrough St John; Arkengarthdale; Askrigg; Aysgarth & District; Bainbridge; Barton; Bellerby; Brompton on Swale; Burton cum Walden; Carlton Town; Carperby cum Thoresby; Catterick; Constable Burton & Finghall; Croft on Tees; Dalton on Tees; East Witton; Ellerton on Swale; Eppleby; Gilling with Hartforth & Sedbury; Grinton; Harmby; Hawes & High Abbotside; Hipswell; Hudswell; Hunton; Manfield & Cliffe; Marrick; Melbecks; Melsonby; Middleton Tyas; Muker; Newsham; Newton le Willows; North Cowton; Patrick Brompton; Preston under Scar; Ravensworth; Redmire; Reeth, Fremington & Healaugh; St Martin's; Scorton; Scotton; Skeeby; Stanwick St John; Stapleton & Cleasby; Tunstall; West Witton.

Parish Meetings in the authority's area: Appleton East & West; Arrathorne; Aske; Bolton on Swale; Brough with St Giles; Caldbergh with East Scrafton; Caldwell; Carlton Highdale; Castle Bolton with East & West Bolton; Coverham with Agglethorpe; Dalton; Downholme, Walburn & New Forest; Easby; East & West Layton & Carkin; Ellerton Abbey; Forcett; Gayles; Hornby; Kirby Hill; Low Abbotside; Marske; Melmerby; Moulton; Newton Morrell; Spennithorne; Stainton; Thornton Steward; Uckerby; Wensley; West Scrafton; Whashton.

Town Councils in the authority's area: Colburn; Leyburn; Middleham; Richmond.

CITY OF ROCHESTER UPON MEDWAY COUNCIL
See Medway Council.

ROCHFORD DISTRICT COUNCIL

www.rochford.gov.uk

Principal Office
Council Offices, South Street, Rochford, Essex SS4 1BW
Telephone: (01702) 546366; FAX: (01702) 545737

Function	Chief Officer	Title	Location
Chief Executive	Mr P Warren	Chief Executive	Council Offices
Electoral Registration	Ms S Fowler	Head of Administrative & Member Services	Council Offices
Environmental Health	Mr G Woolhouse	Head of Housing, Health & Community Care	Council Offices
Finance	Mr R Crofts	Corporate Director (Finance & External Services)	Council Offices
Housing	Mr S Clarkson	Head of Housing, Health & Community Care	Council Offices

DISTRICT COUNCILS

Function	Chief Officer	Title	Location
Legal Services	Mr R J Honey	Corporate Director (Law, Planning & Administration)	Council Offices
Leisure	Mr R Crofts	Corporate Director (Finance & External Services)	Council Offices
Local Land Charges	Mr A Bugeja	Head of Legal Services	Council Offices
Planning	Mr S Scrutton	Head of Planning Services	Council Offices
Purchasing & Supplies	Ms S Fowler	Head of Administrative & Member Services	Council Offices
Technical Services	Mr D Timson	Property Maintenance & Highways Manager	Council Offices

Parish Councils in the authority's area: Ashingdon; Barling Magna; Canewdon; Foulness Island; Great Wakering; Hawkwell; Hockley; Hullbridge; Paglesham; Rawreth; Rochford; Stambridge; Sutton.

Town Councils in the authority's area: Rayleigh.

ROSSENDALE BOROUGH COUNCIL

www.rossendale.gov.uk

Principal Office
Town Hall, Lord Street, Rawtenstall, Rossendale, Lancashire BB4 7LZ
Telephone: (01706) 217777; FAX: (01706) 244504

Engineering & Planning Section
Stubbylee Hall, Bacup OL13 8DD
Telephone: (01706) 874333; FAX: (01706) 871618

Function	Chief Officer	Title	Location
Chief Executive	Mr O Williams	Chief Executive Officer	Town Hall
Electoral Registration	Mr O Williams	Chief Executive Officer	Town Hall
Environmental Health	Mr M Weston	Director of Corporate Support	Town Hall
Housing	Mrs L Hurrell	Director of Landlord Services	Town Hall
Legal Services	Mr M Weston	Director of Corporate Support	Town Hall
Leisure	Mrs G Bishop	Deputy Chief Executive	Town Hall
Planning	Mr M Weston	Director of Corporate Support	Town Hall

Town Council in the authority's area: Whitworth.

ROTHER DISTRICT COUNCIL

www.rother.gov.uk

Principal Office
Town Hall, Bexhill-on-Sea, East Sussex TN39 3JX
Telephone: (01424) 787878; FAX: (01424) 787879; DX 8103 Bexhill-on-Sea

Community Services Department
14 Beeching Road, Bexhill-on-Sea TN39 3LG
Telephone: (01424) 787500; FAX: (01424) 787520

Function	Chief Officer	Title	Location
Chief Executive	Mr D Stevens	Chief Executive	Town Hall
Electoral Registration	Mr D Stevens	Chief Executive	Town Hall
Environmental Health	Mr A Leonard	Director of Services	14 Beeching Rd
Finance	Dr P Ramewal	Director of Resources	Town Hall
Housing	Mr A Leonard	Director of Services	14 Beeching Rd
Legal Services	Dr P Ramewal	Director of Resources	Town Hall
Leisure	Mr A Leonard	Director of Services	14 Beeching Rd
Planning	Mr A Leonard	Director of Services	14 Beeching Rd
Technical Services	Mr A Leonard	Director of Services	14 Beeching Rd

DISTRICT COUNCILS

Parish Councils in the authority's area: Ashburnham & Penhurst; Beckley; Bodiam; Brede; Brightling; Burwash; Camber; Catsfield; Crowhurst; Dallington; Etchingham; Ewhurst; Fairlight; Guestling; Hurst Green; Icklesham; Iden; Mountfield; Northiam; Peasmarsh; Pett; Playden; Rye Foreign; Salehurst; Sedlescombe; Ticehurst; Udimore; Westfield; Whatlington.

Parish Meetings in the authority's area: East Guldeford.

Town Councils in the authority's area: Battle; Rye.

RUGBY BOROUGH COUNCIL

www.rugby.gov.uk

Principal Office
Town Hall, Evreux Way, Rugby, Warwickshire CV21 2LA
Telephone: (01788) 533533; FAX: (01788) 533577; DX 713161 Rugby 2

Housing & Environmental Health Department
PO Box 48, 'The Retreat', Newbold Road, Rugby CV21 2LG
Telephone: (01788) 533880; FAX: (01788) 533866

Function	Chief Officer	Title	Location
Chief Executive	Miss D M Colley	Chief Executive	Town Hall
Electoral Registration	Miss D M Colley	Chief Executive	Town Hall
Environmental Health	Mrs K Stone	Director of Housing & Environmental Health	The Retreat
Finance	Miss D M Colley	Chief Executive	Town Hall
Housing	Mrs K Stone	Director of Housing & Environmental Health	The Retreat
Legal Services	Mr A A Gabbitas	Director of Corporate Services	Town Hall
Leisure	Mr I Davis	Director of Technical Services	Town Hall
Local Land Charges	Mr A A Gabbitas	Director of Corporate Services	Town Hall
Planning	Mr I Davis	Director of Technical Services	Town Hall
Purchasing & Supplies	Mr A A Gabbitas	Director of Corporate Services	Town Hall
Technical Services	Mr I Davis	Director of Technical Services	Town Hall

Parish Councils in the authority's area: Ansty; Binley Woods; Birdingbury; Bourton & Draycote; Brandon & Bretford; Brinklow; Church Lawford; Churchover; Clifton upon Dunsmore; Combe Fields; Dunchurch; Easenhall; Frankton; Grandborough; Harborough Magna; Leamington Hastings; Long Lawford; Marton; Monks Kirby; Newton & Biggin; Pailton; Princethorpe; Ryton on Dunsmore; Shilton; Stretton under Fosse; Stretton-on-Dunsmore; Thurlaston; Willoughby; Withybrook; Wolfhampcote; Wolston; Wolvey.

Parish Meetings in the authority's area: Burton Hastings; Copston Magna; Cosford; Little Lawford; Newnham Regis; Stretton Baskerville; Wibtoft; Willey.

RUNNYMEDE BOROUGH COUNCIL

www.runnymede.gov.uk

Principal Office
Civic Offices, Station Road, Addlestone, Surrey KT15 2AH
Telephone: (01932) 838383; FAX: (01932) 855135; DX 46350 Addlestone

Function	Chief Officer	Title	Location
Chief Executive	Mr T N Williams	Chief Executive Officer	Civic Offices
Electoral Registration	Mr R Curtis	Elections Services Supervisor	Civic Offices
Finance	Mr S Cawthorne	Director of Finance	Civic Offices
Housing	Mrs D Blowers	Director of Housing & Community Services	Civic Offices
Legal Services	Mr A Pearson	Director of Administration & Leisure	Civic Offices
Leisure	Mr R Fleming	Head of Leisure Services	Civic Offices

DISTRICT COUNCILS

Local Land Charges	Mrs J Ryan	Land Charges Officer	Civic Offices
Planning	Mr P Sims	Director of Technical Services	Civic Offices
Technical Services	Mr P Sims	Director of Technical Services	Civic Offices

Parish Councils & Parish Meetings in the authority's area: none.

Town Councils in the authority's area: none.

RUSHCLIFFE BOROUGH COUNCIL

www.rushcliffe.gov.uk

Principal Office

Civic Centre, Pavilion Road, West Bridgford, Nottingham NG2 5FE
Telephone: (0115) 981 9911; FAX: (0115) 945 5882; DX 719907 West Bridgford

Function	Chief Officer	Title	Location
Chief Executive	Mr K Beaumont	Chief Executive	Civic Centre
Environmental Health	Ms T Blackwell	Head of Environmental Health	Civic Centre
Finance	Mr C Bullett	Borough Treasurer	Civic Centre
Legal Services	Mr P Cox	Borough Solicitor	Civic Centre
Leisure	Mr J Collinson	Borough Development Officer	Civic Centre
Local Land Charges	Mr J Collinson	Borough Development Officer	Civic Centre
Planning	Mr J Collinson	Borough Development Officer	Civic Centre

Parish Councils in the authority's area: Aslockton; Barton; Bradmore; Bunny; Car Colston; Clipson-on-the-Wolds; Colston Basset; Costock; Cotham; Cropwell Bishop; Cropwell Butler; East Bridgford; East Leake; Flawborough; Flintham; Granby-cum-Sutton; Hickling; Holme Pierrepont & Gamston; Keyworth; Kingston-on-Soar; Kinoulton; Langar-cum-Barnstone; Normanton-on-Soar; Normanton-on-the-Wolds; Orston; Plumtree; Radcliffe-on-Trent; Rempstone; Ruddington; Shelford & Newton; Stanford-on-Soar; Stanton-on-the-Wolds; Sutton Bonington; Tollerton; Upper Broughton; Whatton; Widmerpool; Willoughby-on-the-Wolds; Wysall & Thorpe-in-the-Glebe.

Parish Meetings in the authority's area: Elton; Hawksworth; Kneeton; Owthorpe; Ratcliffe-on-Soar; Saxondale; Scarrington; Screveton; Shelton; Sibthorpe; Thoroton; Thrumpton; Tithby & Wiverton; West Leake.

Town Councils in the authority's area: Bingham; Cotgrave.

RUSHMOOR BOROUGH COUNCIL

www.rushmoor.gov.uk

Principal Office

Council Offices, Farnborough Road, Farnborough, Hampshire GU14 7JU
Telephone: (01252) 398398; FAX: (01252) 524017; DX 122250 Farnborough 2

Function	Chief Officer	Title	Location
Chief Executive	J A Lloyd	Chief Executive	Council Offices
Electoral Registration	A E Colver	Head of Democratic Services	Council Offices
Environmental Health	J Edwards	Director of Environmental Services	Council Offices
Finance	D Taylor	Head of Financial Services	Council Offices
Housing	Ms A Whiteley	Head of Housing Services	Council Offices
Legal Services	Miss K Limmer	Solicitor to the Council	Council Offices
Leisure	P Amies	Head of Leisure Services	Council Offices
Local Land Charges	Mrs K Biggs	Land Charges Manager	Council Offices
Planning	K Holland	Head of Planning Services	Council Offices
Purchasing & Supplies	M McCarthy	Head of Administrative Services	Council Offices

Parish Councils & Parish Meetings in the authority's area: none.

Town Councils in the authority's area: none.

DISTRICT COUNCILS

RUTLAND DISTRICT COUNCIL
Rutland District Council became a unitary authority on 1 April 1997.

RYEDALE DISTRICT COUNCIL

www.ryedale.gov.uk

Principal Office
Ryedale House, Malton, North Yorkshire YO17 7HH
Telephone: (01653) 600666; FAX: (01653) 696801

Commercial Services Department
Ryedale Depot, Showfield Lane, Malton, North Yorkshire

Function	Chief Officer	Title	Location
Chief Executive	Mr H W Mosley	Chief Executive	Ryedale House
Electoral Registration	Mrs M Bell	Electoral Services & Local Land Charges Manager	Ryedale House
Environmental Health	Mr S Richmond	Environmental Health Manager	Ryedale House
Finance	Mr T Teasdale	Chief Financial Officer	Ryedale House
Housing	Mr R Etherington	Housing Services Manager	Ryedale House
Legal Services	Mr A Winship	Council Solicitor	Ryedale House
Leisure	Mr A Leeming	Economic Development Services Manager	Ryedale House
Local Land Charges	Mrs M Bell	Electoral Services & Local Land Charges Manager	Ryedale House
Planning	Mr G Housden	Development Control Manager	Ryedale House
Purchasing & Supplies	Mr H W Mosley	Chief Executive	Ryedale House
Technical Services	Mr J Davison	Manager of Commercial Services/ Assistant Chief Executive	Ryedale Depot

Parish Councils in the authority's area: Aislaby, Middleton & Wrelton; Allerston; Amotherby; Ampleforth; Appleton-le-Moors; Barton-le-Willows; Barugh; Beadlam; Birdsall; Bulmer; Burythorpe; Buttercrambe with Bossall; Byland with Wass & Oldstead; Claxton & Sand Hutton; Cropton; Ebberston & Yedingham; Farndale East; Flaxton; Foston & Thornton-le-Clay; Foxholes; Ganton; Gate Helmsley & Upper Helmsley; Gilling East, Cawton, Coulton & Grimstone; Habton; Harome; Hawnby; Heslerton; Hovingham & Scackleton; Hutton-le-Hole; Huttons Ambo; Kirby Grindalythe; Kirby Misperton; Leavening; Lillings Ambo; Lockton; Luttons; Nawton; Newton; Nunnington; Pockley; Rievaulx; Rillington; Rosedale East & West; Scagglethorpe; Scampston; Scrayingham; Settrington; Sherburn; Sheriff Hutton; Sinnington; Slingsby, South Holme & Fryton; Swinton; Terrington; Thixendale; Thornton-le-Dale; Warthill; Weaverthorpe; Welburn (Malton); Westow; Wharram; Whitwell-on-the-Hill & Crambe; Willerby; Wilton; Wintringham; Wombleton.

Parish Meetings in the authority's area: Acklam; Appleton-le-Street with Easthorpe; Barton-le-Street; Bransdale; Brawby; Broughton; Cold Kirby; Coneysthorpe; Edstone; Fadmoor; Farndale West; Gillamoor; Hartoft; Harton; Henderskelfe; Howsham; Langton; Lastingham; Levisham; Marishes; Marton; Normanby; Old Byland & Scawton; Oswaldkirk; Salton; Spaunton; Sproxton; Stonegrave; Thorpe Bassett; Welburn (Kirkbymoorside).

Town Councils in the authority's area: Helmsley; Kirkbymoorside; Malton; Norton-on-Derwent; Pickering.

ST ALBANS CITY & DISTRICT COUNCIL

www.stalbans.gov.uk

Principal Office
District Council Offices, Civic Centre, St Peter Street, St Albans, Hertfordshire AL1 3JE
Telephone: (01727) 866100; FAX: (01727) 843167; DX 6178 St Albans 1

Function	Chief Officer	Title	Location
Chief Executive	Mr P Lerner	Head of Paid Service	Council Offices

DISTRICT COUNCILS

Function	Chief Officer	Title	Location
Electoral Registration	Mr M Lovelady	Head of Legal and Democratic Services	Council Offices
Environmental Health	Mr M Ridley	Head of Environment and Health	Council Offices
Finance	Mr I Duffield	Head of Finance	Council Offices
Housing	Mrs K Dragovic	Head of Housing	Council Offices
Legal Services	Mr M Lovelady	Head of Legal and Democratic Services	Council Offices
Leisure	Mr K Tighe	Head of Leisure	Council Offices
Local Land Charges	Mr M Lovelady	Head of Legal and Democratic Services	Council Offices
Planning	Mr D Goodman	Head of Planning and Engineering Services	Council Offices
Purchasing & Supplies	Ms S Lambert	Buyer	Council Offices
Technical Services	Mr B Peers	Technical Services Manager	Council Offices

Parish Councils in the authority's area: Colney Heath; Harpenden Rural; London Colney; Redbourn; St Michael; St Stephen; Sandridge; Wheathampstead.

Town Councils in the authority's area: Harpenden.

ST EDMUNDSBURY BOROUGH COUNCIL

www.stedmundsbury.gov.uk

Principal Office
Borough Offices, Angel Hill, Bury St Edmunds, Suffolk IP33 1XB
Telephone: (01284) 763233; FAX: (01284) 757124; DX 57223 Bury St Edmunds

**Finance Department; Planning & Engineering; Waste Management;
Department of Construction Services & Works**
PO Box 122, St Edmundsbury House, Western Way, Bury St Edmunds IP33 3YS
Telephone: (01284) 763233; FAX: (01284) 757378

Function	Chief Officer	Title	Location
Chief Executive	Ms D Cadman	Chief Executive	Borough Offices
Electoral Registration	Miss J Bowes	Head of Legal & Democratic Services	Borough Offices
Environmental Health	Mr M Dawson	Corporate Director, Community	Borough Offices
Finance	Mr G Moore	Chief Finance Officer	St Edmundsbury
Housing	Mr M Dawson	Corporate Director, Community	Borough Offices
Legal Services	Miss J Bowes	Head of Legal & Democratic Services	Borough Offices
Leisure	Mr M Dawson	Corporate Director, Community	Borough Offices
Local Land Charges	Mr J Massey	Corporate Director, Economy & Environment	St Edmundsbury
Planning	Mr J Massey	Corporate Director, Economy & Environment	St Edmundsbury
Purchasing & Supplies	Mr C Brand	Corporate Director, Resources	Borough Offices
Technical Services	Mr J Massey	Corporate Director, Economy & Environment	St Edmundsbury

Parish Councils in the authority's area: Ampton; Bardwell; Barnham; Barningham; Barrow cum Denham; Bradfield Combust with Stanningfield; Bradfield St Clare; Bradfield St George; Brockley; Cavendish; Chedburgh; Chevington; Clare; Coney Weston; Cowlinge; Culford; Depden; Flempton cum Hargrave; Fornham All Saints; Fornham St Genevieve; Fornham St Martin; Great Barton; Great Bradley; Great Livermere; Great Thurlow; Great Whelnetham; Great Wratting; Hargrave; Hawkedon; Hawstead; Hepworth; Honington cum Sapiston; Hopton cum Knettishall; Horringer cum Ickworth; Hundon; Ingham; Ixworth; Ixworth Thorpe; Kedington; Lackford; Lidgate; Little Livermere; Little Thurlow; Little Whelnetham; Nowton; Ousden; Pakenham; Poslingford; Risby; Rushbrooke with Rougham; The Saxhams; Stansfield; Stanton; Stoke by Clare; Stradishall; Thelnetham; Timworth; Troston; West Stow; Westley; Whepstead; Wickhambrook; Withersfield; Wixoe; Wordwell.

DISTRICT COUNCILS

Parish Meetings in the authority's area: Barnadiston; Denston; Euston; Fakenham Magna; Little Bradley; Little Wratting; Market Weston; Rede.

SALISBURY DISTRICT COUNCIL

www.salisbury.gov.uk

Principal Office
Bourne Hill, Salisbury, Wiltshire SP1 3UZ
Telephone: (01722) 336272; DX 58026 Salisbury

Community Initiatives
16 Endless Street, Salisbury SP1 1DR
Telephone: (01722) 336272; FAX: (01722) 434632

Housing Department
26 Endless Street, Salisbury SP1 1DR
Telephone: (01722) 336272; FAX: (01722) 434530

Planning Department
61 Wyndham Road, Salisbury SP1 3AH
Telephone: (01722) 336272; FAX: (01722) 434520

Function	Chief Officer	Title	Location
Chief Executive	Mr R Sheard	Chief Executive	Bourne Hill
Electoral Registration	Mr S Agland	Head of Democratic Services	Bourne Hill
Environmental Health	Mr G Silver	Head of Environmental Services	Bourne Hill
Finance	Mrs J Bulgin	Head of Financial Services	Bourne Hill
Housing	Mr D Streek	Head of Housing Management	26 Endless St
Legal Services	Mr J Crawford	Legal and Property Services	Bourne Hill
Leisure	Ms L Waller	Head of Community Initiatives	16 Endless St
Local Land Charges	Mr J Crawford	Legal and Property Services	Bourne Hill
Planning	Mr E Teagle	Head of Forward Planning & Transportation	Wyndham Rd
Purchasing & Supplies	Mr Tony Beer	Best Value Officer	Bourne Hill

Parish Councils in the authority's area: Alderbury; Allington; Alvediston; Ansty; Barford St Martin; Berwick St James; Berwick St John; Berwick St Leonard; Bishopstone; Bowerchalke; Britford; Broadchalke; Bulford; Burcombe; Chicklade; Chilmark; Cholderton; Clarendon Park; Compton Chamberlayne; Coombe Bissett; Dinton; Donhead St Andrew; Donhead St Mary; Downton; Durnford; Durrington; East Knoyle; Ebbesbourne Wake; Figheldean; Firsdown; Fonthill Bishop; Fonthill Gifford; Fovant; Great Wishford; Grimstead; Hindon; Idmiston; Kilmington; Landford; Laverstock & Ford; Maiden Bradley; Mere; Milston; Netherhampton; Newton Tony; Odstock; Orcheston; Pitton & Farley; Quidhampton; Redlynch; Sedgehill & Semley; Shrewton; South Newton; Stapleford; Steeple Langford; Stourton with Gasper; Stratford Tony; Sutton Mandeville; Swallowcliffe; Teffont; Tilshead; Tisbury; Tollard Royal; West Dean; West Knoyle; West Tisbury; Whiteparish; Winterbourne; Winterbourne Stoke; Winterslow; Woodford; Wylye; Zeals.

Town Councils in the authority's area: Amesbury; Wilton.

SCARBOROUGH BOROUGH COUNCIL

www.scarborough.gov.uk

Principal Office
Town Hall, St Nicholas Street, Scarborough, North Yorkshire YO11 2HG
Telephone: (01723) 232323; FAX: (01723) 354979; DX 719230 Scarborough 5

Environmental Health & Housing Services
King Street, Scarborough, North Yorkshire YO11 1ND
Telephone: (01723) 232323

DISTRICT COUNCILS

Dean Road Depot
Dean Road Depot, Dean Road, Scarborough, North Yorkshire YO12 7QS
Telephone: (01723) 363865; FAX: (01723) 365340

Function	Chief Officer	Title	Location
Chief Executive	Mr J M Trebble	Chief Executive	Town Hall
Electoral Registration	Mr J M Trebble	Chief Executive	Town Hall
Environmental Health	Mr A Skelton	Head of Community Health & Environment	King Street
Finance	Mr P Cresswell	Head of Finance	Town Hall
Legal Services	Mr I Anderson	Head of Legal	Town Hall
Leisure	Mr S Hollingworth	Head of Tourism & Leisure	King Street
Local Land Charges	Mr I Anderson	Head of Legal	Town Hall
Planning	Mr G Somerville	Head of Planning	Town Hall
Purchasing & Supplies	Mr B Goulding	Head of Street Scene	Dean Road Dep
Technical Services	Mr G Price;	Head of Property;	
	Mr J Riby;	Head of Engineering & Procurement;	Town Hall
	Mr B Goulding	Head of Street Scene	Dean Road Dep

Parish Councils in the authority's area: Aislaby; Brompton by Sawdon; Burniston; Cayton; Cloughton; Danby Group (Commondale, Danby & Westerdale); East Ayton; Eastfield; Egton; Eskdaleside-cum-Ugglebarnby; Folkton; Fylingdales; Glaisdale; Goathland; Gristhorpe & Lebberston Group; Grosmont; Hackness & Harwood Dale Group (Broxa-cum-Troutsdale, Darncombe-cum-Langdale End, Silpho, Suffield-cum-Everley & Harwood Dale); Hawkser-cum-Stainsacre; Hinderwell; Hunmanby; Hutton Buscel; Irton; Lythe; Mickleby Group (Barnby, Ellerby & Mickleby); Muston; Newby & Scalby; Newholm-cum-Dunsley; Osgodby; Reighton; Roxby Group (Borrowby, Newton, Mulgrave & Roxby); Seamer; Snainton; Sneaton; Staintondale; Ugthorpe Group (Hutton Mulgrave & Ugthorpe); West Ayton; Wykeham.

Town Councils in the authority's area: Filey; Whitby.

SCUNTHORPE BOROUGH COUNCIL
Scunthorpe Borough Council was abolished on 31 March 1996; see now North Lincolnshire Council.

SEDGEFIELD BOROUGH COUNCIL

www.sedgefield.gov.uk

Principal Office
Council Offices, Spennymoor, Co Durham DL16 6JQ
Telephone: (01388) 816166; FAX: (01388) 817251

Function	Chief Officer	Title	Location
Chief Executive	Mr N Vaulks	Chief Executive	Council Offices
Electoral Registration	Mr J Stubbs	Principal Admin Officer	Council Offices
Environmental Health	Mr G Hall	Director of Neighbourhood Services	Council Offices
Finance	Mr B Allen	Director of Resources	Council Offices
Housing	Mr G Hall	Director of Neighbourhood Services	Council Offices
Legal Services	Mr D A Hall	Borough Solicitor	Council Offices
Leisure Services	Mr P K Ball	Head of Leisure Services	Council Offices
Local Land Charges	Mr D A Hall	Borough Solicitor	Council Offices
Planning	Mr C Walton	Acting Planning Manager	Council Offices
Technical Services	Mr G Lennon	Technical Services Manager	Council Offices

Parish Councils in the authority's area: Bishop Middleham; Chilton; Eldon; Fishburn; Middridge; Trimdon; West Cornforth; Windlestone.

Parish Meetings in the authority's area: Bradbury; Mordon.

Town Councils in the authority's area: Ferryhill; Great Aycliffe; Sedgefield; Shildon; Spennymoor.

DISTRICT COUNCILS

SEDGEMOOR DISTRICT COUNCIL

www.sedgemoor.gov.uk

Principal Office
Bridgwater House, King Square, Bridgwater, Somerset TA6 3AR
Telephone: (01278) 435435; FAX: (01278) 446412; DX 80619 Bridgwater

Housing and Property Management
Town Hall, High Street, Bridgwater, Somerset TA6 3AS
Telephone: (01278) 435435; FAX: (01278) 450558

Contract Services Department
Colley Lane Depot, Bridgwater TA6 5LB
Telephone: (01278) 435435; FAX: (01278) 455260

Function	Chief Officer	Title	Location
Chief Executive	Mr K Rickards	Chief Executive	Bridgwater Hse
Electoral Registration	Mrs C Facey	Electoral Services Officer	Bridgwater Hse
Finance	Mrs A Parsons	Head of Finance & Property	Bridgwater Hse
Housing	Mr P Taunton	Acting Head of Housing and Property Management	Town Hall
Legal Services	Mr C Spencer	Solicitor to the Council	Bridgwater Hse
Leisure	Mrs E Ford	Head of Toursim, Culture and Sport	Bridgwater Hse
Local Land Charges	Mrs D May	Land Charges Clerk	Bridgwater Hse
Planning	Mr S Atkinson	Head of Development Services	Bridgwater Hse
Purchasing & Supplies	Mrs S Hewlett	Procurement Officer	Bridgwater Hse

Parish Councils in the authority's area: Ashcott; Badgworth; Bawdrip; Berrow; Brean; Brent Knoll; Bridgwater Without; Broomfield; Burnham Without; Burtle; Cannington; Catcott; Chapel Allerton; Cheddar; Chedzoy; Chilton Polden; Chilton Trinity; Compton Bishop; Cossington; Durleigh; East Brent; East Huntspill; Edington; Enmore; Fiddington; Goathurst; Lympsham; Lyng; Mark; Middlezoy; Nether Stowey; Othery; Otterhampton; Over Stowey; Pawlett; Puriton; Shapwick; Shipham; Spaxton; Stawell; Thurloxton; Weare; Wedmore; Wembdon; West Huntspill; Westonzoyland; Woolavington.

Parish Meetings in the authority's area: Greinton; Moorlinch; Stockland Bristol.

Town Councils in the authority's area: Axbridge; Bridgwater; Burnham-on-Sea & Highbridge; North Petherton.

SELBY DISTRICT COUNCIL

www.selby.gov.uk

Principal Office
The Civic Centre, Portholme Road, Selby, North Yorkshire YO8 4SB
Telephone: (01757) 705101; FAX: (01757) 292020; DX 27408 Selby

Function	Chief Officer	Title	Location
Chief Executive	Mr M Connor	Chief Executive	Civic Centre
Electoral Registration	Mr R Besley	Electoral Services Officer	Civic Centre
Environmental Health	Mr S Martin	Head of Environment Services	Civic Centre
Finance	Mr Malcolm Kilner	District Treasurer	Civic Centre
Housing	Mr Steve Martin	Chief Housing Officer	Civic Centre
Legal Services	Mr P Devlin	Director of Legal & Planning Services	Civic Centre
Leisure	Mr R Griffiths	Leisure Services Manager	Civic Centre
Local Land Charges	Mrs B Neale	Land Charges Assistant	Civic Centre
Planning	Mr P Devlin	Director of Legal & Planning Services	Civic Centre

Parish Councils in the authority's area: Appleton Roebuck & Acaster Selby; Askham Bryan; Balne; Barkston Ash; Barlby/Osgodby; Barlow; Beal; Biggin; Bilbrough; Bolton Percy, Colton & Steeton; Brayton; Brotherton; Burn; Burton Salmon; Byram cum Sutton; Camblesforth; Carlton;

DISTRICT COUNCILS

Cawood; Chapel Haddlesey; Church Fenton; Cliffe; Drax; Eggborough; Escrick; Fairburn; Gateforth; Grimston, Kirkby Wharfe & Towton; Hambleton; Healaugh & Catterton; Heck; Hemingbrough; Hensall; Hillam; Huddleston with Newthorpe; Kelfield; Kellington; Kexby; Kirk Smeaton; Little Smeaton; Long Drax; Monk Fryston; Newland; Newton Kyme cum Toulston; North Duffield; Riccall; Ryther cum Ossendyke; Saxton cum Scarthingwell & Lead; Sherburn in Elmet; Skipwith; South Milford; Stillingfleet; Stutton with Hazlewood; Thorganby; Thorpe Willoughby; Ulleskelf; West Haddlesey; Whitley; Wistow; Womersley.

Parish Meetings in the authority's area: Birkin; Cridling Stubbs; Hirst Courtney; Little Fenton; Oxton; Stapleton; Temple Hirst; Walden Stubbs.

Town Councils in the authority's area: Selby; Tadcaster.

SEVENOAKS DISTRICT COUNCIL

www.sevenoaks.gov.uk

Principal Office

Council Offices, Argyle Road, Sevenoaks, Kent TN13 1HG
Telephone: (01732) 227000; FAX: (01732) 740693; DX 30006 Sevenoaks

Function	Chief Officer	Title	Location
Chief Executive	Mr R Hales	Chief Executive (w.e.f 2/6/03)	Council Offices
Electoral Registration	Mr I Bigwood	Electoral Registration Officer	Council Offices
Environmental Health	Mrs K Paterson	Director of Community Services	Council Offices
Finance	Mr D Williamson	Chief Financial Officer	Council Offices
Housing	Mrs K Paterson	Director of Community Services	Council Offices
Legal Services	Mrs C Nuttall	Chief Financial Officer	Council Offices
Leisure	Mrs K Paterson	Director of Community Services	Council Offices
Local Land Charges	Mr I Bigwood	Electoral Registration Officer	Council Offices
Planning	Mrs J Morgan	Strategic Services Director	Council Offices
Purchasing & Supplies	Mr H Jones	Chief Financial Officer	Council Offices
Technical Services	Mrs J Morgan	Strategic Services Director	Council Offices

Parish Councils in the authority's area: Ash-cum-Ridley; Brasted; Chevening; Chiddingstone; Cowden; Crockenhill; Dunton Green; Eynsford; Farningham; Fawkham; Halstead; Hartley; Hever; Horton Kirby; Kemsing; Knockholt; Leigh; Otford; Penshurst; Riverhead; Seal; Sevenoaks Weald; Shoreham; South Darenth; Sundridge; West Kingsdown; Westerham.

Town Councils in the authority's area: Edenbridge; Sevenoaks; Swanley.

SHEPWAY DISTRICT COUNCIL

www.shepwaydc.gov.uk

Principal Office

Civic Centre, Castle Hill Avenue, Folkestone, Kent CT20 2QY
Telephone: (01303) 850388; FAX: (01303) 245978; DX 4912 Folkestone

Function	Chief Officer	Title	Location
Chief Executive	Mr R J Thompson	Chief Executive	Civic Centre
Electoral Registration	Mr J Lund	Head of Administrative Services	Civic Centre
Environmental Health	Mr J Stack	Head of Planning, Environmental Health & Building Control Services	Civic Centre
Finance	Mr K Plowman	Head of Financial Services	Civic Centre
Housing	Mr K Cane	Head of Housing Services	Civic Centre
Legal Services	Mr P Wignall	Solicitor to the Council	Civic Centre
Leisure	Mr A Jarrett	Head of Partnerships & Regeneration	Civic Centre
Local Land Charges	Mr P Wignall	Solicitor to the Council	Civic Centre
Planning	Mr J Stack	Head of Planning, Environmental Health & Building Control Services	Civic Centre
Purchasing & Supplies	Mr J Lund	Head of Administrative Services	Civic Centre
Technical Services	Mr R Young	Head of Environment & Street Scene	Civic Centre

DISTRICT COUNCILS

Parish Councils in the authority's area: Brenzett; Brookland; Burmarsh; Dymchurch; Elham; Elmsted; Hawkinge; Ivychurch; Lyminge; Lympne; Newchurch; Newington; Postling; St Mary in the Marsh; Saltwood; Sandgate; Sellindge; Stanford; Stelling Minnis; Swingfield.

Parish Meetings in the authority's area: Acrise; Monks Horton; Old Romney; Paddlesworth; Snargate; Stowting.

Town Councils in the authority's area: Folkestone; Hythe; Lydd; New Romney.

SHREWSBURY & ATCHAM COUNCIL

www.shrewsbury-atcham.gov.uk

Principal Office

The Guildhall, Frankwell Quay, Shrewsbury, Shropshire SY3 8HQ
Telephone: (01743) 281000; FAX: (01743) 281040; DX 19723 Shrewsbury

Function	Chief Officer	Title	Location
Chief Executive	Mr R Hooper	Chief Executive	The Guildhall
Electoral Registration	Mr M Croston	Democratic & Legal Services Manager	The Guildhall
Environmental Health	Mr D Wraith	Environmental Health Manager	The Guildhall
Finance	Mr P Pennell	Head of Finance	The Guildhall
Legal Services	Mr M Croston	Democratic & Legal Services Manager	The Guildhall
Leisure	Mr A Wallin	Leisure Services Manager	The Guildhall
Local Land Charges	Mr M Croston	Democratic & Legal Services Manager	The Guildhall
Planning	Mr G Harrison;	Planning Policy Manager;	
	Mr P Fenwick	Development Control Manager	The Guildhall
Purchasing & Supplies	Mr G Trantham	Property Services Manager	The Guildhall
Technical Services	Mr E McGrath	Engineering Services Manager	The Guildhall

Parish Councils in the authority's area: Acton Burnell, Pitchford, Frodesley, Ruckley & Langley; Alberbury with Cardeston; All Stretton, Smethcott, Woolstaton; Astley; Atcham; Bayston Hill; Berrington; Bicton; Bomere Heath & District; Buildwas; Cardington; Church Preen, Hughley, Kenley; Church Pulverbatch; Condover; Cound; Cressage, Harley, Sheinton; Ford; Great Hanwood; Great Ness, Little Ness; Leebotwood, Longnor; Leighton & Eaton Constantine; Longden; Minsterley; Montford; Pontesbury; Uffington; Upton Magna; Westbury; Withington; Wollaston; Wroxeter & Uppington.

SLOUGH BOROUGH COUNCIL

Slough Borough Council became a unitary authority on 1 April 1988.

SOUTH BEDFORDSHIRE DISTRICT COUNCIL

www.southbeds.gov.uk

Principal Office

The District Offices, High Street North, Dunstable, Bedfordshire LU6 1LF
Telephone: (01582) 472222; FAX: (01582) 474009: DX 57012 Dunstable

Function	Chief Officer	Title	Location
Chief Executive	Mr J Ruddick	Chief Executive	District Offices
Environmental Health	Mr P Jones	CSM Environment	District Offices
Finance	Mr M Bensley	CSM Business Services	District Offices
Housing	Ms V Redican-Elliott	CSM Housing	District Offices
Legal Services	Mr A S Kang	CSM Legal & Democratic	District Offices
Leisure	Ms J Moakes	CSM Community & Leisure	District Offices
Local Land Charges	Mr A S Kang	CSM Legal & Democratic	District Offices
Planning	Mr J Hoad	CSM Planning & Economy	District Offices
Purchasing & Supplies	Mr D Tuffrey	CSM Public Financial Services	District Offices
Technical Services	Mr M Bensley	CSM Business Services	District Offices

DISTRICT COUNCILS

Parish Councils in the authority's area: Barton; Caddington; Chalgrave; Chalton; Eaton Bray; Eggington; Great Billington; Heath & Reach; Hockliffe; Hyde; Kensworth; Slip End; Stanbridge; Streatley; Studham; Sundon; Tilsworth; Toddington; Totternhoe; Whipsnade.

Town Councils in the authority's area: Dunstable; Houghton Regis; Leighton Linslade.

SOUTH BUCKS DISTRICT COUNCIL

www.southbucks.gov.uk

Principal Office
Council Offices, Windsor Road, Slough, Buckinghamshire SL1 2HN
Telephone: (01753) 533333; FAX: (01753) 529841; DX 42266 Slough West

Function	Chief Officer	Title	Location
Chief Executive	Mr C R Furness	Chief Executive	Council Offices
Electoral Registration	Mr C R Furness	Chief Executive	Council Offices
Environmental Health	Mr B Smith	Director of Services	Council Offices
Finance	Mr J Burness	Director of Resources	Council Offices
Housing	Mr B Smith	Director of Services	Council Offices
Legal Services	Mr J Burness	Director of Resources	Council Offices
Leisure	Mr B Smith	Director of Services	Council Offices
Local Land Charges	Mr J Burness	Director of Resources	Council Offices
Planning	Mr B Smith	Director of Services	Council Offices
Technical Services	Mr B Smith	Director of Services	Council Offices

Parish Councils in the authority's area: Burnham; Denham; Dorney; Farnham Royal; Fulmer; Gerrards Cross; Hedgerley; Iver; Stoke Poges; Taplow; Wexham.

Town Council in the authority's area: Beaconsfield.

SOUTH CAMBRIDGESHIRE DISTRICT COUNCIL

www.scambs.gov.uk

Principal Office
South Cambridgeshire Hall, 6010 Cambourne Business Park, Cambridge CB3 6EA
Telephone: (01223) 443000; FAX: (01223) 443149

Commercial Services
Dickerson Industrial Estate, Ely Road, Waterbeach, Cambridge CB5 9PG

Function	Chief Officer	Title	Location
Chief Executive	John S Ballantyne	Chief Executive	S Cambs Hall
Electoral Registration	John S Ballantyne	Chief Executive	S Cambs Hall
Environmental Health	S Hampson	Housing & Environment Services Director	S Cambs Hall
Finance	G J Harlock	Director of Finance & Resources	S Cambs Hall
Housing	S Hampson	Housing & Environment Services Director	S Cambs Hall
Legal Services	C J Taylor	Head of Legal Services	S Cambs Hall
Leisure	John S Ballantyne	Chief Executive	S Cambs Hall
Local Land Charges	C J Taylor	Head of Legal Services	S Cambs Hall
Planning	D B Hussell	Development Services Director	S Cambs Hall
Purchasing & Supplies	G J Harlock	Director of Finance & Resources	S Cambs Hall
Technical Services	S Hampson	Housing & Environment Services Director	S Cambs Hall

Parish Councils in the authority's area: Arrington; Babraham; Balsham; Bar Hill; Barrington; Barton; Bassingbourn cum Kneesworth; Bourn; Caldecote; Carlton; Castle Camps; Caxton; Comberton; Coton; Cottenham; Croxton; Croydon; Dry Drayton; Duxford; Elsworth; Eltisley; Fen Ditton; Fen Drayton; Fowlmere; Foxton; Fulbourn; Gamlingay; Girton; Grantchester; Graveley; Great Abington; Great & Little Chishill; Great & Little Eversden; Great Shelford; Great Wilbraham;

Guilden Morden; Hardwick; Harlton; Harston; Haslingfield; Hatley; Hauxton; Heydon; Hildersham; Hinxton; Histon; Horningsea; Horseheath; Ickleton; Impington; Kingston; Landbeach; Linton; Litlington; Little Abington; Little Gransden; Little Shelford; Little Wilbraham; Longstanton; Longstowe; Madingley; Melbourn; Meldreth; Milton; Newton; Oakington & Westwick; Orwell; Over; Pampisford; Papworth Everard; Rampton; Sawston; Shepreth; Shudy Camps; Stapleford; Steeple Morden; Stow cum Quy; Swavesey; Teversham; Thriplow; Toft; Waterbeach; West Wickham; West Wratting; Weston Colville; Whaddon; Whittlesford; Willingham; Wimpole.

Parish Meetings in the authority's area: Abington Pigotts; Bartlow; Boxworth; Childerley; Conington; Knapwell; Lolworth; Papworth St Agnes; Shingay cum Wendy; Tadlow.

SOUTH DERBYSHIRE DISTRICT COUNCIL

www.south-derbys.gov.uk

Principal Office
Civic Offices, Civic Way, Swadlincote, Derbyshire DE11 0AH
Telephone: (01283) 221000; FAX: (01283) 550128; DX 23912 Swadlincote

Function	Chief Officer	Title	Location
Chief Executive	Frank McArdle	Chief Executive	Civic Offices
Electoral Registration	Brenda Reed	Elections Officer	Civic Offices
Environmental Health	Mike Alflat	Director of Community Services	Civic Offices
Finance	Terry Neaves	Chief Finance Officer	Civic Offices
Housing	Mike Alflat	Director of Community Services	Civic Offices
Legal Services	Andrea McCaskie	Legal & Democratic Services Manager	Civic Offices
Leisure	Stuart Batchelor	Community & Leisure Development Manager	Civic Offices
Local Land Charges	Joyce Lambert	Land Charges Clerk	Civic Offices
Planning	John Birkett	Planning Services Manager	Civic Offices
Purchasing & Supplies	Terry Neaves	Chief Finance Officer	Civic Offices
Technical Services	[Vacant]	Technical Services Manager	Civic Offices

Parish Councils in the authority's area: Aston on Trent; Barrow on Trent; Bretby; Burnaston; Castle Gresley; Church Broughton; Coton in the Elms; Dalbury Lees; Eggington; Elvaston; Etwall; Findern; Foston & Scropton; Hartshorne; Hatton; Hilton; Linton; Melbourne; Netherseal; Newton Solney; Overseal; Repton; Rosliston; Shardlow & Great Wilne; Smisby; Stenson Fields; Ticknall; Walton on Trent; Weston on Trent; Willington; Woodville.

Parish Meetings in the authority's area: Ash; Barton Blount; Bearwardcote; Calke; Catton; Cauldwell; Drakelow; Foremark; Hoon; Ingleby; Lullington; Marston-on-Dove; Osleston & Thurvaston; Radbourne; Stanton-by-Bridge; Sutton-on-the-Hill; Swarkestone; Trusley; Twyford & Stenson.

SOUTH HAMS DISTRICT COUNCIL

www.southhams.gov.uk

Principal Office
Follaton House, Plymouth Road, Totnes, South Devon TQ9 5NE
Telephone: (01803) 861234; FAX: (01803) 866151; DX 300050 Totnes 2

Function	Chief Officer	Title	Location
Chief Executive	Ruth Bagley	Chief Executive	Follaton House
Electoral Registration	Graham Rowe	Chief of Legal & Property Services	Follaton House
Environmental Health	Alan Robinson	Chief Environment & Development Officer	Follaton House
Finance	Mark Seymour	Chief Finance & Administration Officer	Follaton House
Housing	Alan Robinson	Chief Environment & Development Officer	Follaton House

DISTRICT COUNCILS

Legal Services	Graham Rowe	Chief of Legal & Property Services	Follaton House
Leisure	Tony Eden	Chief Customer Operations Officer	Follaton House
Local Land Charges	Graham Rowe	Chief of Legal & Property Services	Follaton House
Planning	Alan Robinson	Chief Environment & Development Officer	Follaton House
Purchasing & Supplies	Mark Seymour	Chief Finance & Administration Officer	Follaton House
Technical Services	Tony Eden	Chief Customer Operations Officer	Follaton House

Parish Councils in the authority's area: Ashprington; Aveton Gifford; Berry Pomeroy; Bickleigh; Bigbury; Blackawton; Brixton; Buckfastleigh West; Buckland-tout-Saints; Charleton; Chivelstone; Churchstow; Cornwood; Cornworthy; Dartington; Dean Prior; Diptford; Dittisham; East Allington; East Portlemouth; Ermington; Frogmore & Sherford; Halwell & Moreleigh; Harberton; Holbeton; Holne; Kingston; Kingswear; Littlehempston; Loddiswell; Malborough; Marldon; Modbury; Newton & Noss; North Huish; Rattery; Ringmore; Shaugh Prior; Slapton; South Brent; South Huish; South Milton; South Pool; Sparkwell; Staverton; Stoke Fleming; Stoke Gabriel; Stokenham; Strete; Thurlestone; Ugborough; Wembury; West Alvington; Yealmpton.

Parish Meetings in the authority's area: Harford; Woodleigh.

Town Councils in the authority's area: Dartmouth; Ivybridge; Kingsbridge; Salcombe; Totnes.

SOUTH HEREFORDSHIRE DISTRICT COUNCIL

South Herefordshire District Council was abolished on 31 March 1988; see The Herefordshire Council.

SOUTH HOLLAND DISTRICT COUNCIL

www.sholland.gov.uk

Principal Office

Council Offices, Priory Road, Spalding, Lincolnshire PE11 2XE
Telephone: (01775) 761161; FAX: (01775) 711253

Function	Chief Officer	Title	Location
Chief Executive	T Huggins	Chief Executive	Council Offices
Electoral Registration	R E Atkins	Returning Officer	Council Offices
Environmental Health	M Dawson	Head of Environmental Health	Council Offices
Finance	E Jones	Head of Finance	Council Offices
Housing	J Craik	Head of Housing	Council Offices
Legal Services	J Scarsbrook	Head of Legal & Member Services	Council Offices
Leisure	S Starr	Head of Leisure & Tourism	Council Offices
Local Land Charges	S Williams	Head of Planning & Development	Council Offices
Planning	S Williams	Head of Planning & Development	Council Offices
Purchasing & Supplies	M Doherty	Head of Property	Council Offices
Technical Services	M Doherty	Head of Property	Council Offices

Parish Councils in the authority's area: Cowbit; Crowland; Deeping St Nicholas; Donington; Fleet; Gedney; Gedney Hill; Gosberton; Holbeach; Long Sutton; Lutton; Moulton; Pinchbeck; Quadring; Surfleet; Sutton St Edmund; Sutton St James; Tydd St Mary; Weston; Whaplode.

Town Councils in the authority's area: Sutton Bridge.

SOUTH KESTEVEN DISTRICT COUNCIL

www.skdc.com

Principal Office

Council Offices, St Peter's Hill, Grantham, Lincolnshire NG31 6PZ
Telephone: (01476) 406080; FAX: (01476) 406000; DX 27024 Grantham

DISTRICT COUNCILS

Function	Chief Officer	Title	Location
Chief Executive	Mr C Farmer	Chief Executive	Council Offices
Electoral Registration	Mr J Bishop	Head of Administration	Council Offices
Finance	Mr J Blair	Head of Financial Services	Council Offices
Legal Services	Mr N Goddard; Mrs L Youles	Solicitors to the Council	Council Offices
Leisure	Mr J Slater	Head of Cultural & Leisure Activities	Council Offices
Local Land Charges	Mr J Bishop	Head of Administration	Council Offices
Planning	Mr M Sibthorp	Head of Land Use Planning	Council Offices

Parish Councils in the authority's area: Allington; Ancaster; Aslackby & Laughton; Barkston & Syston; Barrowby; Baston; Belton & Manthorpe; Billingborough; Braceborough & Wilsthorpe; Carlby; Carlton Scroop & Normanton; Castle Bytham; Caythorpe; Claypole; Colsterworth, Gunby, Stainby; Corby Glen; Deeping St James; Denton; Dowsby; Edenham, Grimsthorpe, Elsthorpe, Scottlethorpe; Folkingham; Foston; Fulbeck; Great Gonerby; Great Ponton; Greatford; Haconby & Stainfield; Harlaxton; Heydour; Horbling; Hough on the Hill; Hougham; Ingoldsby; Irnham; Kirkby Underwood; Langtoft; Little Bytham; Little Ponton & Sproxton; Londonthorpe & Harrowby Without; Long Bennington; Marston; Morton & Hanthorpe; North Witham; Old Somerby; Pointon & Sempringham; Rippingale; Ropsley & District; Sedgebrook; Skillington; South Witham; Stoke Rochford & Easton; Stubton; Swayfield; Swinstead; Tallington; Thurlby; Toft, Lound & Manthorpe; Uffington; Welby; West Deeping; Westborough & Dry Doddington; Witham on the Hill; Woolsthorpe by Belvoir; Wyville cum Hungerton.

Parish Meetings in the authority's area: Barholm & Stowe; Bitchfield & Bassingthorpe; Boothby Pagnell; Braceby & Sapperton; Burton Coggles; Careby, Aunby & Holywell; Counthorpe & Creeton; Dunsby; Fenton, Honington; Lenton, Keisby & Osgodby; Pickworth.

Town Councils in the authority's area: Bourne; Market Deeping; Stamford.

Grantham Charter Trustees.

SOUTH LAKELAND DISTRICT COUNCIL

www.southlakeland.gov.uk

Principal Office
South Lakeland House, Lowther Street, Kendal, Cumbria LA9 4UQ
Telephone: (01539) 733333; FAX: (01539) 740300

Commercial Services Directorate
Canal Head Depot, Kendal LA9 7BY
Telephone: (01539) 733333; FAX: (01539) 740300

Function	Chief Officer	Title	Location
Chief Executive	Mr P J Cunliffe	Chief Executive	S Lakeland Hse
Electoral Registration	Mr P J Cunliffe	Chief Executive	S Lakeland Hse
Environmental Health	Mrs S Barton	Director of Strategy & Planning	S Lakeland Hse
Finance	Mr J Jones	Director of Finance	S Lakeland Hse
Housing	Mrs S Barton	Director of Strategy & Planning	S Lakeland Hse
Legal Services	Mr J Jones	Director of Finance	S Lakeland Hse
Leisure	Mr M Jones	Director of Customer Services	S Lakeland Hse
Local Land Charges	Mr J Jones	Director of Finance	S Lakeland Hse
Planning	Mrs S Barton	Director of Strategy & Planning	S Lakeland Hse
Purchasing & Supplies	Mr M Jones	Director of Customer Services	S Lakeland Hse
Technical Services	Mr M Jones	Director of Customer Services	S Lakeland Hse

Parish Councils in the authority's area: Aldingham; Allithwaite Upper; Arnside; Barbon; Beetham; Blawith & Subberthwaite; Broughton East; Burneside; Burton; Cartmel Fell; Casterton; Claife; Colton; Coniston; Crook; Crosthwaite & Lyth; Dent; Duddon; Egton with Newland; Mansriggs & Osmotherley; Garsdale; Haverthwaite; Hawkshead; Helsington; Heversham; Holme; Hugill; Hutton Roof; Kirkby Ireleth; Kirkby Lonsdale; Lakes; Levens; Lower Allithwaite; Lower Holker; Lowick; Lupton; Meathop; Milnthorpe; Natland; Nether Staveley; New Hutton; Old Hutton & Holmescales; Over Staveley; Pennington; Preston Patrick; Preston Richard; Satterthwaite;

Scalthwaiterigg; Sedbergh; Sedgwick; Skelsmergh; Skelwith; Stainton; Staveley-in-Cartmel; Torver; Underbarrow & Bradleyfield; Urswick; Windermere; Witherslack.

Parish Meetings in the authority's area: Docker; Fawcett Forest; Firbank; Grayrigg; Hincaster; Kentmere; Killington; Lambrigg; Longsleddale; Mansergh; Middleton; Whinfell; Whitwell & Selside.

Town Councils in the authority's area: Grange; Kendal; Ulverston.

SOUTH NORFOLK DISTRICT COUNCIL

www.south-norfolk.gov.uk

Principal Office

South Norfolk House, Swan Lane, Long Stratton, Norwich NR15 2XE
Telephone: (01508) 533633; FAX: (01508) 533695; DX 130080 Long Stratton 2

Function	Chief Officer	Title	Location
Chief Executive	Mr G Rivers	Chief Executive	S Norfolk Hse
Electoral Registration	Mr A Evans	Electoral Services Manager	S Norfolk Hse
Environmental Health	Mr D Osborne	Head of Environmental Services	S Norfolk Hse
Finance	Mr A Rasford	Head of Financial Services	S Norfolk Hse
Housing	Mr D Cork	Head of Strategic Housing	S Norfolk Hse
Legal Services	Mr S Shortman	Solicitor to the Council	S Norfolk Hse
Leisure	Ms A Andrews	Head of Leisure	S Norfolk Hse
Local Land Charges	Mrs A Hammond	Land Charges Officer	S Norfolk Hse
Planning	Mr J Tomlinson	Head of Planning	S Norfolk Hse
Technical Services	Mr C Dady	Head of Property & Facilities	S Norfolk Hse

Parish Councils in the authority's area: Alburgh; Aldeby; Alpington & Yelverton; Ashby St Mary; Ashwellthorpe; Aslacton; Barford & Wramplingham; Barnham Broom; Bawburgh; Bergh Apton; Bixley; Bracon Ash; Bramerton; Bressingham; Brockdish; Brooke; Broome; Bunwell; Burgh St Peter with Wheatacre; Burston & Shimpling; Caister St Edmund; Carleton Rode; Chedgrave; Claxton; Costessey; Cringleford; Denton; Deopham; Dickleburgh & Rushall; Ditchingham; Earsham; East Carleton & Ketteringham; Easton; Ellingham; Flordon; Forncett; Framingham Earl; Geldeston; Gillingham; Gissing; Great Melton; Great Moulton; Haddiscoe; Hales with Heckingham; Hempnall; Hethersett; Keswick & Intwood; Kimberley; Kirby Bedon; Kirby Cane; Langley with Hardley; Little Melton; Loddon; Long Stratton; Marlingford; Morley; Morningthorpe; Mulbarton; Mundham; Needham; Newton Flotman; Norton Subcourse; Poringland; Pulham Market; Pulham St Mary; Rockland St Mary & Hellington; Roydon; Runhall; Saxlingham Nethergate; Scole; Seething; Shelfanger; Shelton; Shotesham; Starston; Stoke Holy Cross; Surlingham; Swainsthorpe; Swardeston; Tacolneston; Tasburgh; Tharston & Hapton; Thurlton; Thurton; Tibenham; Tivetshall St Margaret & St Mary; Toft Monks; Topcroft; Trowse with Newton; Wacton; Wicklewood; Winfarthing; Woodton; Wortwell; Wreningham.

Parish Meetings in the authority's area: Bedingham; Carleton St Peter; Colney; Framingham Pigot; Haywood; Hedenham; Holverston; Howe; Kirstead; Raveningham; Sisland; Stockton; Thwaite.

Town Councils in the authority's area: Diss; Hingham; Redenhall with Harleston; Wymondham.

SOUTH NORTHAMPTONSHIRE COUNCIL

www.southnorthants.gov.uk

Principal Office

Council Offices, Springfields, Towcester, Northamptonshire NN12 6AE
Telephone: (01327) 322322; FAX: (01327) 322074; DX 16938 Towcester

Function	Chief Officer	Title	Location
Chief Executive	Rob Tinlin	Chief Executive	Council Offices

DISTRICT COUNCILS

Electoral Registration	Kevin Lane	Head of Corporate Support	Council Offices
Environmental Health	Andy Preston	Head of Environment	Council Offices
Finance	Martin Henry	Head of Finance	Council Offices
Housing	Chris Lambert	Head of Housing	Council Offices
Legal Services	Kevin Lane	Head of Corporate Support	Council Offices
Leisure	Ian Lindley	Head of Planning & Leisure	Council Offices
Local Land Charges	Kevin Lane	Head of Corporate Support	Council Offices
Planning	Ian Lindley	Head of Planning & Leisure	Council Offices
Purchasing & Supplies	Kevin Lane	Head of Corporate Support	Council Offices
Technical Services	Alex Lohman	Head of Property & Direct Services	Council Offices

Parish Councils in the authority's area: Abthorpe; Ashton; Aston-le-Walls; Aynho; Blakesley; Blisworth; Boddington; Brafield-on-the-Green; Bugbrooke; Castle Ashby; Chacombe; Chipping Warden; Cogenhoe & Whiston; Cold Higham; Cosgrove; Croughton; Culworth; Deanshanger; Denton; Evenley; Eydon; Farthinghoe; Gayton; Grange Park; Greatworth; Greens Norton; Hackleton; Harpole; Hartwell; Helmdon; Kings Sutton; Kislingbury; Litchborough; Little Houghton; Maidford; Marston St Lawrence; Middleton Cheney; Milton Malsor; Moreton Pinkney; Nether Heyford; Newbottle; Old Stratford; Overthorpe; Pattishall; Paulerspury; Potterspury; Quinton; Roade; Rothersthorpe; Shutlanger; Silverstone; Stoke Bruerne; Sulgrave; Syresham; Thorpe Mandeville; Tiffield; Wappenham; Weston & Weedon; Whittlebury; Wicken; Yardley Gobion; Yardley Hastings.

Parish Meetings in the authority's area: Adstone; Bradden; Courteenhall; Easton Neston; Edgcote; Grafton Regis; Hinton-in-the-Hedges; Radstone; Slapton; Thenford; Upper Heyford; Warkworth; Whitfield; Woodend.

Town Councils in the authority's area: Brackley; Towcester.

SOUTH OXFORDSHIRE DISTRICT COUNCIL

www.southoxon.gov.uk

Principal Office
Council Offices, Crowmarsh, Wallingford, Oxfordshire OX10 8HQ
Telephone: (01491) 823000

Function	Chief Officer	Title	Location
Chief Executive	David Buckle	Chief Executive	Council Offices
Electoral Registration	Steven Lake	Electoral Registration Officer	Council Offices
Environmental Health	Michael Jaques	Strategic Director	Council Offices
Finance	Michael Jaques	Strategic Director	Council Offices
Housing	David Hill	Strategic Director	Council Offices
Legal Services	Marie Ainsworth	Strategic Director	Council Offices
Leisure	David Hill	Strategic Director	Council Offices
Local Land Charges	Marie Ainsworth	Strategic Director	Council Offices
Planning	Marie Ainsworth	Strategic Director	Council Offices

Parish Councils in the authority's area: Aston Rowant; Aston Tirrold; Aston Upthorpe; The Baldons; Beckley & Stowood; Benson; Berinsfield; Berrick Salome; Binfield Heath; Bix & Assendon; Brightwell cum Sotwell; Chalgrove; Checkendon; Chinnor; Cholsey; Clifton Hampden; Crowmarsh; Cuddesdon & Denton; Culham; Dorchester; Drayton St Leonard; East Hagbourne; Ewelme; Eye & Dunsden; Forest Hill with Shotover; Garsington; Goring; Goring Heath; Great Haseley; Great Milton; Harpsden; Highmoor; Holton; Horspath; Ipsden; Kidmore End; Lewknor; Little Milton; Little Wittenham; Long Wittenham; Mapledurham; Marsh Baldon; Moulsford; Nettlebed; Newington; North Moreton; Nuffield; Nuneham Courtenay; Pishill with Stonor; Pyrton; Rotherfield Greys; Rotherfield Peppard; Sandford on Thames; Shiplake; Sonning Common; South Moreton; South Stoke; Stadhampton; Stanton St John; Stoke Row; Swyncombe; Sydenham; Tetsworth; Tiddington with Albury; Toot Baldon; Towersey; Waterperry with Thornley; Watlington; West Hagbourne; Wheatley; Whitchurch on Thames; Woodcote.

DISTRICT COUNCILS

Parish Meetings in the authority's area: Adwell; Brightwell Baldwin; Britwell Salome; Crowell; Cuxham with Easington; Elsfield; Shirburn; Stoke Talmage; Warborough; Waterstock; Wheatfield; Woodeaton.

Town Councils in the authority's area: Didcot; Henley on Thames; Thame; Wallingford.

SOUTH RIBBLE BOROUGH COUNCIL

www.southribble.gov.uk

Principal Office

Civic Centre, West Paddock, Leyland, Preston, Lancashire PR25 1DH
Telephone: (01772) 421491; FAX: (01772) 622287

Function	Chief Officer	Title	Location
Chief Executive	Ms J Hunter	Chief Executive	Civic Centre
Electoral Registration	Mr C Russell	Electoral Registration & Elections Officer	Civic Centre
Environmental Health	Ms D Johnson	Head of Public Health & Housing	Civic Centre
Finance	Mr M Nuttall	Corporate Director of Resources/ Deputy Chief Executive	Civic Centre
Housing	Ms J Bennett	Principal Housing Officer	Civic Centre
Legal Services	Mrs C J Parmenter	Legal Services Practice Manager & Solicitor	Civic Centre
Leisure	[Vacant]	Leisure & Commercial Services Manager	Civic Centre
Local Land Charges	Mrs C J Parmenter	Legal Services Practice Manager & Solicitor	Civic Centre
Planning	Mr J Dalton	Head of Planning & Regeneration	Civic Centre
Purchasing & Supplies	Mrs G Robinson	Office Services Manager	Civic Centre

Parish Councils in the authority's area: Farington; Hutton; Little Hoole; Longton; Much Hoole; Samlesbury & Cuerdale.

Town Council in the authority's area: Penwortham.

SOUTH SHROPSHIRE DISTRICT COUNCIL

www.southshropshire.gov.uk

Principal Office

Council Offices, Stone House, Corve Street, Ludlow, Shropshire SY8 1DG
Telephone: (01584) 813100; FAX: (01584) 813122; DX 709050 Ludlow 3

Function	Chief Officer	Title	Location
Chief Executive	G C Biggs	Chief Executive	Council Offices
Electoral Registration	G C Biggs	Chief Executive	Council Offices
Environmental Health	W N Jones	Director of Environment & Development	Council Offices
Finance	Ms L Chambers	Director of Central Services	Council Offices
Leisure	W N Jones	Director of Environment & Development	Council Offices
Legal Services	G C Biggs	Chief Executive	Council Offices
Local Land Charges	W N Jones	Director of Environment & Development	Council Offices
Planning	W N Jones	Director of Environment & Development	Council Offices
Technical Services	W N Jones	Director of Environment & Development	Council Offices

Parish Councils in the authority's area: Abdon; Ashford Carbonel; Bedstone & Bucknell; Bettws-y-Crwyn; Bitterley; Bromfield; Burford; Caynham; Chirbury with Brompton; Cleobury

DISTRICT COUNCILS

Mortimer; Clun; Clunbury; Clungunford; Coreley; Culmington; Diddlebury; East Hamlet; Eaton-under-Heywood & Hope Bowdler; Hopesay; Hopton Wafers; Llanfairwaterdine; Ludford; Lydbury North; Mainstone with Colebatch; Milson & Neen Sollars; Munslow; Myndtown, Norbury, Ratlinghope & Wentnor; Nash; Newcastle on Clun; Onibury; Richards Castle; Rushbury; Stanton Lacy; Stoke St Milborough & Hopton Cangeford; Wheathill; Wistanstow; Worthen with Shelve & Hope.

Parish Meetings in the authority's area: Acton Scott; Ashford Bowdler; Boraston; Clee St Margaret; Edgton; Greete; Hope Bagot; Hopton Castle; Lydham; More; Sibdon Carwood; Stowe; Whitton.

Town Councils in the authority's area: Bishop's Castle; Craven Arms; Ludlow; Church Stretton.

SOUTH SOMERSET DISTRICT COUNCIL

www.southsomerset.gov.uk

Principal Office
Council Offices, Brympton Way, Yeovil, Somerset BA20 2HT
Telephone: (01935) 462462; FAX: (01935) 462188

Langport Offices (Area North)
Council Offices, Old Kelways, Somerton Road, Langport TA10 9YE
Telephone: (01458) 257400; FAX: (01458) 257474

Petter's House Offices (Area South)
Petter's House, Petter's Way, Yeovil, Somerset BA20 1SH
Telephone: (01935) 462991; FAX: (01935) 404608

Function	Chief Officer	Title	Location
Chief Executive	Elaine Peters	Managing Director	Council Offices
Electoral Registration	Bob Gillis	Democratic Services Manager	Council Offices
Environmental Health	Alasdair Bell; Patrick Mackie; Laurence Willis	Environmental Health Managers	Council Offices
Finance	Bet Perrins	Strategic Director – Finance	Council Offices
Housing	Colin MacDonald	Housing Strategy Manager	Council Offices
Legal Services	Ian Clarke	Solicitor to the Council	Council Offices
Leisure	Martin Woods	Group Manager (Leisure and Culture)	Petter's House
Local Land Charges	Jackie Norman	Senior Local Land Charges Officer	Council Offices
Planning	Andy Foyne	Group Manager (Regeneration and Land Use)	Council Offices
Technical Services	Les Stringer; David Durrant	Technical Manager; Building Control Manager	Langport Offices; Petter's House

Parish Councils in the authority's area: Abbas & Templecombe; Alford; Aller; Ansford; Ash; Ashill; Babcary; Barrington; Barton St David; Barwick; Beercrocombe; Brewham; Broadway; Brympton; Buckland St Mary; Chaffcombe; Charlton Horethorne; Charlton Mackrell; Charlton Musgrove; Chilthorne Domer; Chiselborough; Combe St Nicholas; Compton Dundon; Corton Denham; Currey Rivel; Curry Mallet; Donyatt; Dowlish Wake; Drayton; East Chinnock; East Coker; Fivehead; Hambridge & Westport; Hardington Mandeville; Haselbury Plucknett; Henstridge; High Ham; Hinton St George; Holton; Horsington; Horton; Huish Episcopi; Ilchester; Ilton; Isle Abbotts; Keinton Mandeville; Kingsbury Episcopi; Kingsdon; Langport; Long Load; Long Sutton; Lopen; Lovington; Maperton; Marston Magna; Martock; Merriott; Milborne Port; Misterton; Montacute; Mudford; North Barrow; North Cadbury; North Cheriton; North Perrott; Norton-sub-Hamdon; Odcombe; Pen Selwood; Pitcombe; Pitney; Queen Camel; Rimpton; Seavington St Mary; Seavington St Michael; Shepton Beauchamp; Shepton Montague; Somerton; South Barrow; South Cadbury; South Petherton; Sparkford; Stocklinch; Stoke Trister; Stoke-sub-Hamdon; Tatworth & Forton; Tintinhull; Wayford; West Camel; West Chinnock; West Coker; West Crewkerne; Winsham; Yarlington; Yeovil Without; Yeovilton.

DISTRICT COUNCILS

Parish Meetings in the authority's area: Bratton Seymour; Chillington; Chilton Cantelo; Closworth; Compton Pauncefoot; Cricket St Thomas; Cucklington; Cudworth; Dinnington; Isle Brewers; Kingstone; Kingweston; Knowle St Giles; Limington; Muchelney; Puckington; Wambrook; Whitelackington; Whitestaunton.

Town Councils in the authority's area: Bruton; Castle Cary; Chard; Crewkerne; Ilminster; Wincanton; Yeovil.

SOUTH STAFFORDSHIRE COUNCIL

www.sstaffs.gov.uk

Principal Office
Council Offices, Codsall, South Staffordshire WV8 1PX
Telephone: (01902) 696000; FAX: (01902) 696800; DX 18036 Codsall

Function	Chief Officer	Title	Location
Chief Executive	Mr L T Barnfield	Chief Executive	Council Offices
Electoral Registration	Mr P Hardy	Head of Administrative Services	Council Offices
Environmental Health	Ken Walker	Head of Environmental Health (Commercial) Services	Council Offices
Finance	Mr P Holdcroft	Strategic Director (Finance)	Council Offices
Housing	Mr S Winterflood	Head of Strategic Development Services	Council Offices
Legal Services	Mr R Levesley	Strategic Director (Legal)	Council Offices
Leisure	Mr D Heywood	Head of Leisure Services	Council Offices
Local Land Charges	Mrs L Robinson	Head of Committee & Legal Services	Council Offices
Planning	Mr W G Meredith	Head of Development & Building Control Services	Council Offices
Purchasing & Supplies	Mr P Hardy	Head of Administrative Services	Council Offices
Technical Services	Mr B S Holland	Strategic Director (Technical)	Council Offices

Parish Councils in the authority's area: Acton Trussell & Teddesley Hay; Bednall; Bilbrook; Blymhill & Weston under Lizard; Bobbington; Brewood; Cheslyn Hay; Codsall; Coppenhall; Dunston; Enville; Essington; Featherstone; Great Wyrley; Hatherton; Hilton; Himley; Huntington; Kinver; Lapley Stretton & Wheaton Aston; Lower Penn; Pattingham & Patshull; Penkridge; Perton; Saredon; Shareshill; Swindon; Trysull & Seisdon; Wombourne.

SOUTH WIGHT DISTRICT COUNCIL
South Wight District Council was abolished on 31 March 1995; see now Isle of Wight Council.

SOUTHAMPTON CITY COUNCIL
Southampton City Council became a unitary authority on 1 April 1997.

SOUTHEND-ON-SEA BOROUGH COUNCIL
Southend-on-Sea Borough Council became a unitary authority on 1 April 1998.

SPELTHORNE BOROUGH COUNCIL

www.spelthorne.gov.uk

Principal Office
Council Offices, Knowle Green, Staines, Middlesex TW18 1XB
Telephone: (01784) 451499; FAX: (01784) 463356; DX 98044 Staines 2

Function	Chief Officer	Title	Location
Chief Executive	Karen Satterford	Chief Executive	Council Offices
Electoral Registration	Tim Kita	Head of Communications & Community Safety	Council Offices

Environmental Health	Karen Cregan	Head of Environmental Health & Building Control	Council Offices
Finance	Geoff Lewis	Head of Financial Services	Council Offices
Housing	Mike Peters	Head of Planning & Housing Strategy	Council Offices
Legal Services	Karen Whelan	Head of Legal Services	Council Offices
Leisure	Liz Borthwick	Head of Leisure Services	Council Offices
Local Land Charges	Dave Phillips	Head of Asset Management	Council Offices
Planning	Mike Peters	Head of Planning & Housing Strategy	Council Offices
Purchasing & Supplies	John Foggo	Head of Customer & Office Services	Council Offices
Tehnical Services	Phil Henley	Technical Services Manager	Council Offices

Parish Councils & Parish Meetings in the authority's area: none.

Town Councils in the authority's area: none.

STAFFORD BOROUGH COUNCIL

www.staffordbc.gov.uk

Principal Office

Civic Centre, Riverside, Stafford ST16 3AQ

Telephone: (01785) 619000; FAX: (01785) 619119; DX 723320 Stafford 7

Function	Chief Officer	Title	Location
Chief Executive	Mr D Rawlings	Chief Executive	Civic Centre
Electoral Registration	Mr A Welch	Head of Law & Administration	Civic Centre
Environmental Health	Mr R Ball	Head of Environmental & Health Services	Civic Centre
Finance	Mr M Vickers	Director of Central Services	Civic Centre
Housing	Mr D Hughes	Head of Housing Services	Civic Centre
Legal Services	Mr A Welch	Head of Law & Administration	Civic Centre
Leisure	Ms K Rickett	Head of Leisure Services	Civic Centre
Local Land Charges	Mr C Hindle	Head of Planning & Engineering	Civic Centre
Planning	Mr C Hindle	Head of Planning & Engineering	Civic Centre
Purchasing & Supplies	Ms C Rendell	Head of Technical Services	Civic Centre
Technical Services	Mr C Hindle	Head of Planning & Engineering	Civic Centre

Parish Councils in the authority's area: Adbaston; Barlaston; Berkswich; Bradley; Brocton; Castle Church; Chebsey; Church Eaton; Colwich; Creswell; Eccleshall; Forton; Fulford; Gnosall; Haughton; High Offley; Hilderstone; Hixon; Hopton & Coton; Ingestre with Tixall; Milwich; Norbury; Ranton; Salt & Enson; Sandon & Burston; Seighford; Standon; Stone Rural; Stowe-by-Chartley; Swynnerton; Weston with Gayton with Fradswell; Whitgreave.

Parish Meetings in the authority's area: Ellenhall; Marston.

Town Council in the authority's area: Stone.

STAFFORDSHIRE MOORLANDS DISTRICT COUNCIL

www.staffsmoorlands.gov.uk

Principal Office

Moorlands House, Stockwell Street, Leek, Staffordshire ST13 6HQ

Telephone: (01538) 483483; FAX: (01538) 483474; DX 16361 Leek

Function	Chief Officer	Title	Location
Chief Executive	Mr S Baker	Chief Executive Officer	Moorlands Hse
Electoral Registration	Mr M Trillo	Corporate Director	Moorlands Hse
Environmental Health	Mr J Berriman	Corporate Director	Moorlands Hse
Finance	Mr A Stokes	Corporate Director	Moorlands Hse
Housing	Mr A Stokes	Corporate Director	Moorlands Hse
Legal Services	Mr M Trillo	Corporate Director	Moorlands Hse

DISTRICT COUNCILS

Leisure	Mr J Berriman	Corporate Director	Moorlands Hse
Local Land Charges	Mr A Stokes	Corporate Director	Moorlands Hse
Planning	Mr J Berriman	Corporate Director	Moorlands Hse
Purchasing & Supplies	Mr A Stokes	Corporate Director	Moorlands Hse
Technical Services	Mr A Stokes	Corporate Director	Moorlands Hse

Parish Councils in the authority's area: Alstonefield; Alton; Bagnall; Bradnop; Brown Edge; Butterton; Caverswall; Checkley; Cheddleton; Consall; Cotton; Dilhorne; Draycott; Endon & Stanley; Farley; Fawfieldhead; Forsbrook; Grindon; Heathylee; Heaton; Hollinsclough; Horton; Ilam; Ipstones; Kingsley; Leekfrith; Longnor; Longsdon; Oakamoor; Onecote; Quarnford; Rushton; Sheen; Tittesworth; Warslow & Elkstones; Waterhouses; Werrington; Wetton.

Parish Meeting in the authority's area: Blore with Swinscoe.

Town Councils in the authority's area: Biddulph; Cheadle; Leek.

STEVENAGE BOROUGH COUNCIL

www.stevenage.gov.uk

Principal Office

Daneshill House, Danestrete, Stevenage, Hertfordshire SG1 1HN
Telephone: (01438) 242242; FAX: (01438) 740296; DX 6022 Stevenage 1

Function	Chief Officer	Title	Location
Chief Executive	Ian Paske	Chief Executive	Daneshill Hse
Electoral Registration	Ian Paske	Chief Executive	Daneshill Hse
Environmental Health	Nick Parry	Director of Environmental Services	Daneshill Hse
Finance	Scott Crudgington	Director of Resources	Daneshill Hse
Housing	Valerie Corrigan	Director of Community Services	Daneshill Hse
Legal Services	Bill Welch	Director of Resources	Daneshill Hse
Leisure	Valerie Corrigan	Director of Community Services	Daneshill Hse
Local Land Charges	Bill Welch	Director of Resources	Daneshill Hse
Planning	Nick Parry	Director of Environmental Services	Daneshill Hse
Purchasing & Supplies	Nick Parry	Director of Environmental Services	Daneshill Hse
Technical Services	Nick Parry	Director of Environmental Services	Daneshill Hse

Parish Councils & Parish Meetings in the authority's area: none.

Town Councils in the authority's area: none.

STOCKTON-ON-TEES BOROUGH COUNCIL
Stockton-on-Tees Borough Council became a unitary authority on 1 April 1996.

STOKE-ON-TRENT CITY COUNCIL
Stoke-on-Trent City Council became a unitary authority on 1 April 1997.

STRATFORD-ON-AVON DISTRICT COUNCIL

www.stratford.gov.uk

Principal Office

Elizabeth House, Church Street, Stratford-upon-Avon, Warwickshire CV37 6HX
Telephone: (01789) 267575; FAX: (01789) 260007; DX 700737 Stratford-on-Avon 2

Function	Chief Officer	Title	Location
Chief Executive	Paul Lankester	Chief Executive	Elizabeth Hse
Electoral Registration	Paul Lankester	Chief Executive	Elizabeth Hse
Environmental Health	David Nash	Corporate Director	Elizabeth Hse
Finance	Martin Henwood	Corporate Director	Elizabeth Hse
Housing	David Nash	Corporate Director	Elizabeth Hse
Legal Services	Martin Henwood	Corporate Director	Elizabeth Hse

DISTRICT COUNCILS

Leisure	Trevor Askew	Corporate Director	Elizabeth Hse
Local Land Charges	David Nash	Corporate Director	Elizabeth Hse
Planning	David Nash	Corporate Director	Elizabeth Hse
Purchasing & Supplies	Martin Henwood	Corporate Director	Elizabeth Hse
Technical Services	Trevor Askew	Corporate Director	Elizabeth Hse

Parish Councils in the authority's area: Admington; Alderminster; Arrow; Aston Cantlow; Avon Dassett; Barton-on-the-Heath; Bearley; Beaudesert & Henley-in-Arden; Bidford-on-Avon; Binton; Bishops Itchington; Brailes; Burton Dassett; Butlers Marston; Cherington & Stourton; Claverdon; Clifford Chambers; Combroke; Coughton; Dorsington; Ettington; Exhall; Farnborough; Fenny Compton; Gaydon; Great Alne; Great Wolford; Halford; Hampton Lucy; Harbury; Haselor; Ilmington; Kineton; Kinwarton; Ladbroke; Langley; Lighthorne; Little Compton; Long Compton; Long Itchington; Loxley; Luddington; Marston Sicca; Moreton Morrell; Morton Bagot, Oldberrow & Spernal; Napton-on-the-Hill; Newbold Pacey & Ashorne; Old Stratford & Drayton; Oxhill; Pillerton Hersey; Pillerton Priors; Preston-on-Stour; Priors Marston; Quinton; Radway; Ratley & Upton; Salford Priors; Sambourne; Shotteswell; Snitterfield; Stockton; Stourton; Stretton-on-Fosse; Studley; Tanworth-in-Arden; Temple Grafton; Tredington; Tysoe; Ufton; Ullenhall; Warmington; Welford-on-Avon; Wellesbourne; Whichford; Wixford; Wolverton; Wootton Wawen.

Parish Meetings in the authority's area: Atherstone-on-Stour; Barcheston & Willington; Billesley; Burmington; Chadshunt; Chapel Ascote; Charlecote; Chesterton & Kingston; Compton Verney; Compton Wynyates; Fulbrook; Hodnell & Wills Pastures; Honington; Idlicote; Little Wolford; Milcote; Preston Bagot; Priors Hardwick; Radbourne; Stoneton; Sutton-under-Brailes; Tidmington; Upper & Lower Shuckburgh; Watergall; Weethley; Weston-on-Avon; Whatcote; Whitchurch; Wormleighton.

Town Councils in the authority's area: Alcester; Shipston-on-Stour; Southam; Stratford-upon-Avon.

STROUD DISTRICT COUNCIL

www.stroud.gov.uk

Principal Office

Ebley Mill, Westward Road, Ebley, Stroud, Gloucestershire GL5 4UB
Telephone: (01453) 766321; FAX: (01453) 750932

Function	Chief Officer	Title	Location
Chief Executive	David Hagg	Chief Executive	Ebley Mill
Electoral Registration	M Rowan	Head of Legal Services	Ebley Mill
Environmental Health	K A May	Director of Housing & Environmental Services	Ebley Mill
Finance	M J Harwood	Director of Corporate Services	Ebley Mill
Housing	K A May	Director of Housing & Environmental Services	Ebley Mill
Legal Services	M Rowan	Head of Legal Services	Ebley Mill
Leisure	N Riglar	Head of Regeneration & Culture	Ebley Mill
Local Land Charges	M J Harwood	Director of Corporate Services	Ebley Mill
Planning	Barry Wyatt	Head of Development Services	Ebley Mill

Parish Councils in the authority's area: Alkington; Arlingham; Bisley-with-Lypiatt; Brookthorpe-with-Whaddon; Cainscross; Cam; Chalford; Coaley; Cranham; Eastington; Elmore; Frampton-on-Severn; Fretherne-with-Saul; Frocester; Ham & Stone; Hamfallow; Hardwicke; Harescombe; Haresfield; Hillesley & Tresham; Hinton; Horsley; Kings Stanley; Kingswood; Leonard Stanley; Longney; Minchinhampton; Miserden; North Nibley; Nympsfield; Painswick; Pitchcombe; Randwick; Rodborough; Slimbridge; Standish; Stinchcombe; Thrupp; Uley; Upton St Leonards; Whiteshill & Ruscombe; Whitminster; Woodchester.

Parish Meetings in the authority's area: Alderley; Moreton Valence; Owlpen.

Town Councils in the authority's area: Berkeley; Dursley; Nailsworth; Stonehouse; Stroud; Wotton-under-Edge.

DISTRICT COUNCILS

SUFFOLK COASTAL DISTRICT COUNCIL

www.suffolkcoastal.gov.uk

Principal Office
Melton Hill, Woodbridge, Suffolk IP12 1AU
Telephone: (01394) 383789; FAX: (01394) 385100; DX 41400 Woodbridge

Function	Chief Officer	Title	Location
Chief Executive	Mr J Gravenor	Chief Executive	Melton Hill
Electoral Registration	Mr J Gravenor	Chief Executive	Melton Hill
Environmental Health	Mr P Gore	Head of Environmental Health	Melton Hill
Finance	Mr P J Collicott	Director of Finance	Melton Hill
Housing	Mr M Eaton	Head of Housing	Melton Hill
Legal Services	Mrs H Slater	Solicitor	Melton Hill
Leisure	Mr T Osmanski	Head of Leisure & Tourism	Melton Hill
Local Land Charges	Mrs H Slater	Solicitor	Melton Hill
Planning	Mr J Schofield	Director of Development & Community Services	Melton Hill
Purchasing & Supplies	Mr J Gravenor	Chief Executive	Melton Hill
Technical Services	Mr D Ball	Director of Operational Services	Melton Hill

Parish Councils in the authority's area: Alderton; Aldringham; Badingham; Bawdsey; Benhall; Blaxhall; Blythburgh; Boyton; Bramfield; Brandeston; Bredfield; Brightwell; Bromeswell; Bruisyard; Bucklesham; Butley; Campsea Ashe; Capel St Andrew; Charsfield; Chediston; Clopton; Cookley; Cratfield; Cretingham; Culpho; Dallinghoo; Darsham; Dennington; Earl Soham; Easton; Eyke; Falkenham; Farnham; Foxhall; Friston; Gedgrave; Great Bealings; Great Glemham; Grundisburgh; Hacheston; Hasketon; Heveningham; Hollesley; Hoo; Huntingfield; Iken; Kelsale; Kettleburgh; Kirton; Knodishall; Letheringham; Levington with Stratton Hall; Linstead Magna; Linstead Parva; Little Bealings; Little Glemham; Marlesford; Martlesham; Melton; Middleton; Monewden; Nacton; Newbourne; Orford; Otley; Parham; Peasenhall; Pettistree; Playford; Purdis Farm; Rendlesham; Rendham; Rushmere St Andrew; Saxtead; Shottisham; Sibton; Snape; Sternfield; Stratford St Andrew; Sudbourne; Sutton; Sweffling; Swilland; Theberton; Thorington; Trimley St Martin; Trimley St Mary; Tuddenham St Martin; Tunstall; Ubbeston; Ufford; Walberswick; Waldringfield; Walpole; Wantisden; Wenhaston with Mells Hamlet; Westerfield; Westleton; Wickham Market; Witnesham; Yoxford.

Parish Meetings in the authority's area: Boulge; Burgh; Chillesford; Cransford; Debach; Dunwich; Hemley; Ramsholt.

Town Councils in the authority's area: Aldeburgh; Felixstowe; Framlingham; Kesgrave; Leiston-cum-Sizewell; Saxmundham; Woodbridge.

SURREY HEATH BOROUGH COUNCIL

www.surreyheath.gov.uk

Principal Office
Surrey Heath House, Knoll Road, Camberley, Surrey GU15 3RD
Telephone: (01276) 707100; FAX: (01276) 707177; DX 32722 Camberley

Function	Chief Officer	Title	Location
Chief Executive	Mr B R Catchpole	Chief Executive	Surrey Hth Hse
Electoral Registration	Ms Nicola Vooght	Elections Manager	Surrey Hth Hse
Finance	Mr C Allen	Director of Financial Services	Surrey Hth Hse
Housing	Mr R Collins	Assistant Chief Executive	Surrey Hth Hse
Legal Services	Mr R Ivory	Borough Solicitor	Surrey Hth Hse
Leisure	Mr J Silvester	Director of Planning & Community Service	Surrey Hth Hse
Local Land Charges	Mr R Ivory	Borough Solicitor	Surrey Hth Hse
Planning	Mr J Silvester	Director of Planning & Community Service	Surrey Hth Hse
Purchasing & Supplies	Mr R Collins	Assistant Chief Executive	Surrey Hth Hse

Technical Services	Mr D Thomson	Director of Environmental & Commercial Services	Surrey Hth Hse

Parish Councils in the authority's area: Bisley; Chobham; West End; Windlesham.

SWALE BOROUGH COUNCIL

www.swale.gov.uk

Principal Office
Swale House, East Street, Sittingbourne, Kent ME10 3HT
Telephone: (01795) 424341; FAX: (01795) 417217; DX 59900 Sittingbourne II

Function	Chief Officer	Title	Location
Chief Executive	Mr Chris Edwards	Chief Executive	Swale House
Electoral Registration	Mrs Bev Olds	Electoral Services Officer	Swale House
Environmental Health	Mr Mark Goldhawk	Environmental Service Manager	Swale House
Finance	Mr David Buckett	Financial Services Manager	Swale House
Housing	Mr Andy Kemp	Housing Services Manager	Swale House
Legal Services	Mr Duncan Milne	Chief Solicitor	Swale House
Leisure	Mrs Val Buckett	Recreation & Amenities Manager	Swale House
Local Land Charges	Mr David Stevens	Administration & Legal Services Manager	Swale House
Planning	Mr Ian Russell	Director of Development Services	Swale House
Purchasing & Supplies	Mr David Stevens	Administration & Legal Services Manager	Swale House
Technical Services	Mr Brian Planner	Engineering Services Manager	Swale House

Parish Councils in the authority's area: Bapchild; Bobbing; Borden; Boughton under Blean; Bredgar; Doddington; Dunkirk; Eastchurch; Eastling; Graveney with Goodnestone; Hartlip; Hernhill; Iwade; Leysdown; Lower Halstow; Luddenham; Lynsted; Milstead & Kingsdown; Newington; Newnham; Norton & Buckland; Oare; Ospringe; Rodmersham; Selling; Sheldwich, Badlesmere & Leaveland; Stalisfield; Teynham; Throwley; Tonge; Tunstall; Upchurch; Warden.

Town Councils in the authority's area: Faversham; Sheerness.

TAMWORTH BOROUGH COUNCIL

www.tamworth.gov.uk

Principal Office
Marmion House, Lichfield Street, Tamworth, Staffordshire B79 7BZ
Telephone: (01827) 709709; FAX: (01827) 709271; DX 709140 Tamworth 4

Function	Chief Officer	Title	Location
Chief Executive	David Weatherley	Chief Executive	Marmion Hse
Electoral Registration	Kevin Briggs	Democratic Services Manager	Marmion Hse
Environmental Health	Nick Thurston	Assistant Director (Environmental Management)	Marmion Hse
Finance	John Wheatley	Chief Finance Officer	Marmion Hse
Housing	Jason MacGilp	Corporate Director (Housing & Property Services)	Marmion Hse
Legal Services	Philip Lloyd-Williams	Solicitor to the Council	Marmion Hse
Leisure	Sue Finnigan	Assistant Director (Culture & Community)	Marmion Hse
Planning	Tim Clegg	Assistant Director (Planning & Regeneration)	Marmion Hse
Purchasing & Supplies	John Cromack	Assistant Director (Procurement)	Marmion Hse

Parish Councils & Parish Meetings in the authority's area: none.

Town Councils in the authority's area: none.

DISTRICT COUNCILS

TANDRIDGE DISTRICT COUNCIL

www.tandridge.gov.uk

Principal Office
Council Offices, Station Road East, Oxted, Surrey RH8 0BT
Telephone: (01883) 722000; FAX: (01883) 722015; DX 39359 Oxted

Function	Chief Officer	Title	Location
Chief Executive	Mr S Weigel	Chief Executive	Council Offices
Electoral Registration	Mr S Weigel	Chief Executive	Council Offices
Environmental Health	Mr B Evans	Director of Environmental Protection	Council Offices
Finance	Mr A Montgomery	Acting Chief Finance Officer	Council Offices
Housing	Mr R Woodward	Director of Community Services	Council Offices
Legal Services	Mr C Moore	Solicitor to the Council	Council Offices
Local Land Charges	Mr B Evans	Director of Environmental Protection	Council Offices
Planning	Mr B Evans	Director of Environmental Protection	Council Offices
Purchasing & Supplies	Mr A Montgomery	Acting Chief Finance Officer	Council Offices

Parish Councils in the authority's area: Bletchingley; Burstow; Chelsham & Farleigh; Crowhurst; Felbridge; Godstone; Horne; Limpsfield; Lingfield/Dormansland; Nutfield; Oxted; Tandridge; Tatsfield.

Parish Meeting in the authority's area: Titsey.

TAUNTON DEANE BOROUGH COUNCIL

www.tauntondeane.gov.uk

Principal Office
The Deane House, Belvedere Road, Taunton, Somerset TA1 1HE
Telephone: (01823) 356356; FAX: (01823) 356329

Depot
Priory Depot, Taunton TA1 2BB

Function	Chief Officer	Title	Location
Chief Executive	Stephen Fletcher	Chief Executive	Deane House
Electoral Registration	Craig Morse	Electoral Registration Officer	Deane House
Environmental Health	Peter Weaver	Chief Environmental Health Officer	Deane House
Finance	Shirlene Adam	Financial Services Manager	Deane House
Housing	Penny James	Director of Community Services	Deane House
Legal Services	Ian Taylor	Chief Solicitor	Deane House
Leisure	Karen Dyson	Community Leisure Manager	Deane House
Local Land Charges	Ian Taylor	Chief Solicitor	Deane House
Planning	Tom Noall	Chief Planning Officer	Deane House
Purchasing & Supplies	David Carpenter	Purchasing Officer	Priory Depot
Technical Services	Alan Hartridge	Director of Development	Deane House

Parish Councils in the authority's area: Ashbrittle; Bathealton; Bishops Hull; Bishops Lydeard; Bradford on Tone; Burrowbridge; Cheddon Fitzpaine; Chipstable; Churchstanton; Combe Florey; Comeytrowe; Corfe; Creech St Michael; Fitzhead; Halse; Hatch Beauchamp; Kingston St Mary; Langford Budville; Lydeard St Lawrence; Milverton; Neroche; North Curry; Norton Fitzwarren; Nynehead; Oake; Otterford; Pitminster; Ruishton; Sampford Arundel; Staplegrove; Stawley; Stoke St Gregory; Stoke St Mary; Trull; Wellington Without; West Bagborough; West Buckland; West Hatch; West Monkton; Wiveliscombe.

Parish Meetings in the authority's area: Ash Priors; Durston.

Town Council in the authority's area: Wellington.

DISTRICT COUNCILS

TEESDALE DISTRICT COUNCIL

www.teesdale.gov.uk

Principal Office
Teesdale House, Barnard Castle, Co Durham DL12 8EL
Telephone: (01833) 690000; FAX: (01833) 637269

Teesdale Leisure
Strathmore Road, Barnard Castle DL12 8DS
Telephone: (01833) 690400

Technical & Contracts Department
Council Depot, Stainton Grove, Barnard Castle DL12 8UU
Telephone: (01833) 637890

Function	Chief Officer	Title	Location
Chief Executive	Mr C M Anderson	Chief Executive	Teesdale Hse
Electoral Registration	Ms D Roberts	Senior Committee & Elections Officer	Teesdale Hse
Environmental Health	Mr C Tomlinson	Head of Streetcare	Teesdale Hse
Finance	Ms J Kellett	Head of Financial Services	Teesdale Hse
Housing	Mr P G Slack	Head of Housing	Teesdale Hse
Legal Services	Mrs A Rocks-Menon	Head of Legal & Licensing	Teesdale Hse
Leisure	Mr P Branch	Leisure Manager	Strathmore Rd
Local Land Charges	Miss S Porter	Legal & Local Land Charges Officer	Teesdale Hse
Planning	Mr Epfayle	Head of Planning	Teesdale Hse
Purchasing & Supplies	Mrs A Chrisp	Senior Administrative Officer	Teesdale Hse
Technical Services	Mr N O'Connor	Environmental Services Manager	Council Depot

Parish Councils in the authority's area: Bowes; Cockfield; Cotherstone; Eggleston; Etherley; Evenwood & Barony; Forest & Frith; Gainford; Hamsterley; Hunderthwaite; Ingleton; Lartington; Lunedale; Lynesack & Softley; Marwood; Mickleton; Middleton in Teesdale; Newbiggin-in-Teesdale; Ovington; Rokeby & Brignall; Romaldkirk; South Bedburn; Staindrop; Stainton & Streatham; Startforth; Whorlton & Westwick; Winston; Woodland.

Parish Meetings in the authority's area: Barforth; Barningham; Bolam; Boldron; Cleatlam; Eggleston Abbey; Gilmonby; Headlam; Hilton; Holwick; Hope Scargill; Huton Magna; Langleydale & Shotton; Langton; Morton Tinmouth; Raby & Keverstone; Wackerfield; Westwick; Wycliffe.

Town Council in the authority's area: Barnard Castle.

TEIGNBRIDGE DISTRICT COUNCIL

www.teignbridge.gov.uk

Principal Office
Forde House, Newton Abbot, Devon TQ12 4XX
Telephone: (01626) 361101; FAX: (01626) 215169; DX 121075 Newton Abbot 5

Function	Chief Officer	Title	Location
Chief Executive	Mr H M Davis	Chief Executive	Forde Hse
Electoral Registration	Mrs S Smith	Senior Admin/Electoral Services Officer	Forde Hse
Environmental Health	Mr B Hosford	Chief Environmental Health Officer	Forde Hse
Finance	Mr P Stabb	Director of Resources	Forde Hse
Legal Services	Mr S Barnes	Solicitor to the Council	Forde Hse
Leisure	Miss K Christie	Leisure & Tourism Officer	Forde Hse
Local Land Charges	Mr S Barnes	Solicitor to the Council	Forde Hse
Planning	Mr S Robinson	Head of Planning Services	Forde Hse
Purchasing & Supplies	Mr P Mason	Central Office Manager	Forde Hse
Technical Services	Mr B Gray	Director of Community Services	Forde Hse

Parish Councils in the authority's area: Abbotskerswell; Bickington; Bishopsteignton; Bridford; Broadhempston; Christow; Chudleigh; Coffinswell; Doddiscombsleigh; Dunchideock; Dunsford;

DISTRICT COUNCILS

Exminster; Haccombe-with-Coombe; Hennock; Holcombe Burnell; Ide; Ideford; Ilsington; Ipplepen; Kenn; Kenton; Kingskerswell; Kingsteignton; Lustleigh; Manaton; Moretonhampstead; North Bovey; Ogwell; Shaldon; Shillingford St George; Starcross; Stokeinteignhead; Tedburn St Mary; Teigngrace; Denbury & Torbryan; Whitestone; Widecombe-in-the-Moor.

Parish Meetings in the authority's area: Ashcombe; Ashton; Buckland-in-the-Moor; Mamhead; Powderham; Trusham; Woodland.

Town Councils in the authority's area: Ashburton; Bovey Tracey; Buckfastleigh; Dawlish; Newton Abbot; Teignmouth.

TENDRING DISTRICT COUNCIL

www.tendringdc.gov.uk

Principal Office
Town Hall, Station Road, Clacton-on-Sea, Essex CO15 1SE
Telephone: (01255) 425501; FAX: (01255) 253139; DX 34660 Clacton-on-Sea

Benefits & Revenues Services
88/90 Pier Avenue, Clacton-on-Sea CO15 1TN
Telephone: (01255) 425501; FAX: (01255) 254143

Legal & Administration Services; Community Services
Westleigh House, Carnarvon Road, Clacton-on-Sea CO15 6QF
Telephone: (01255) 425501; FAX: (01255) 255135

Planning & Building Services; Environmental Services
Council Offices, Weeley, Essex CO16 9AJ
Telephone: (01255) 425501; FAX: (01255) 256114

Function	Chief Officer	Title	Location
Chief Executive	Mr J Hawkins	Chief Executive	Town Hall
Electoral Registration	Miss S Walter-Browne	Head of Legal Services	Westleigh Hse
Environmental Health	Mr D Appleby	Head of Environmental Services	Council Offs, Weeley
Finance	Mr M King	Head of Financial Services	Town Hall
Housing	Mr D Whitehead	Head of Housing Services	Town Hall
Legal Services	Miss S Walter-Browne	Head of Legal & Services	Westleigh Hse
Leisure	Mr B Bennett	Head of Leisure Services	Town Hall
Local Land Charges	Miss S Walter-Browne	Head of Legal & Services	88/90 Pier Ave
Planning	[Vacant]	Head of Regeneration, Planning & Community Services	Council Offs, Weeley
Purchasing & Supplies	Mrs C Schleip	Head of Personnel & Management Services	Town Hall
Technical Services	Mr T Mackinlay	Head of Technical & Procurement Services	Town Hall

Parish Councils in the authority's area: Alresford; Ardleigh; Beaumont; Bradfield; Elmstead; Frating; Great Bentley; Great Bromley; Great Oakley; Lawford; Little Bentley; Little Bromley; Little Clacton; Little Oakley; Manningtree; Mistley; Ramsey & Parkeston; St Osyth; Tendring; Thorpe-le-Soken; Thorrington; Weeley; Wix; Wrabness.

Town Councils in the authority's area: Brightlingsea; Frinton & Walton; Harwich.

TEST VALLEY BOROUGH COUNCIL

www.testvalley.gov.uk

Principal Office
Council Offices, Beech Hurst, Weyhill Road, Andover, Hampshire SP10 3AJ
Telephone: (01264) 368000; FAX: (01264) 368099; Minicom: (01264) 368052;
DX 123080 Andover 6

DISTRICT COUNCILS

Environmental Health Department; Planning Department
Council Offices, Duttons Road, Romsey, Hampshire SO51 8XG
Telephone: (01794) 527700; FAX: (01794) 527723

Function	Chief Officer	Title	Location
Chief Executive	Mr R Tetstall	Chief Executive	Beech Hurst
Electoral Registration	Mr C Judd	Mayor's Assistant; Licensing & Electoral Registration Manager	Beech Hurst
Environmental Health	Ms L Taylor	Head of Environment & Health	Duttons Road
Finance	Mr R Carr	Head of Finance	Beech Hurst
Housing	Mr B Cowcher	Head of Housing	Beech Hurst
Legal Services	Mr M Mundy	Head of Legal Services	Beech Hurst
Leisure	Mr I McKie	Head of Leisure	Beech Hurst
Local Land Charges	Mr M Bunton	Land Charges Manager	Duttons Road
Planning	Mrs M Winter	Head of Planning	Duttons Road
Purchasing & Supplies	Mr D Harris	Administration Manager	Beech Hurst
Technical Services	Mr T Gilmour	Head of Technical Services	Beech Hurst

Parish Councils in the authority's area: Abbotts Ann; Ampfield; Amport; Appleshaw; Awbridge; Barton Stacey; Braishfield; Broughton; Bullington; Charlton; Chilbolton; Chilworth; East Dean; East Tytherley; Fyfield; Goodworth Clatford; Grateley; Houghton; Hurstbourne Tarrant; Kimpton; Kings Somborne; Lockerley; Longparish; Longstock; Melchet Park & Plaitford; Michelmersh; Monxton; Mottisfont; Nether Wallop; North Baddesley; Nursling & Rownhams; Over Wallop; Penton Grafton; Penton Mewsey; Quarley; Romsey Extra; Sherfield English; Shipton Bellinger; Smannell; Stockbridge; Tangley; Thruxton; Upper Clatford; Vernhams Dean; Wellow; West Tytherley; Wherwell.

Parish Meetings in the authority's area: Ashley; Bossington; Buckholt; Faccombe; Frenchmoor; Leckford; Linkenholt; Little Somborne.

Town Council in the authority's area: Romsey.

TEWKESBURY BOROUGH COUNCIL

www.tewkesburybc.gov.uk

Principal Office
Gloucester Road, Tewkesbury, Gloucestershire GL20 5TT
Telephone: (01684) 295010; FAX: (01684) 272039; DX 11406 Tewkesbury

Function	Chief Officer	Title	Location
Chief Executive	Mrs T B Turner	Chief Executive	Gloucester Rd
Electoral Registration	Miss S J Freckleton	Borough Solicitor	Gloucester Rd
Environmental Health	Mr J Kelly	Director of Community Services	Gloucester Rd
Finance	Mr P Antill	Director of Resources	Gloucester Rd
Housing	Mr J Kelly	Director of Community Services	Gloucester Rd
Legal Services	Miss S J Freckleton	Borough Solicitor	Gloucester Rd
Leisure	Mr J Kelly	Director of Community Services	Gloucester Rd
Local Land Charges	Miss S J Freckleton	Borough Solicitor	Gloucester Rd
Planning	Mr C J Shaw	Director of Planning Services	Gloucester Rd
Purchasing & Supplies	Mr P Antill	Director of Resources	Gloucester Rd
Technical Services	Mr J Kelly	Director of Community Services	Gloucester Rd

Parish Councils in the authority's area: Alderton; Ashchurch; Ashleworth; Badgeworth; Bishops Cleeve; Boddington; Brockworth; Buckland; Chaceley; Churchdown; Deerhurst; Down Hatherley; Dumbleton; Elmstone Hardwicke; Forthampton; Gotherington; Gretton; Highnam; Hucclecote; Innsworth; Leigh; Longford; Maisemore; Minsterworth; Norton; Sandhurst; Shurdington; Southam; Stanton; Stanway; Staverton; Stoke Orchard; Teddington; Tirley; Toddington; Twigworth; Twyning; Uckington; Woodmancote.

Parish Meetings in the authority's area: Great Witcombe; Hasfield; Hawling; Oxenton; Prescott; Snowshill; Sudeley; Walton Cardiff.

Town Councils in the authority's area: Tewkesbury; Winchcombe.

DISTRICT COUNCILS

THAMESDOWN BOROUGH COUNCIL

Thamesdown Borough Council became the unitary authority of Swindon on 1 April 1997.

THANET DISTRICT COUNCIL

www.thanet.gov.uk

Principal Office

PO Box 9, Council Offices, Cecil Street, Margate, Kent CT9 1XZ

Telephone: (01843) 577000; FAX: (01843) 290906; DX 30555 Margate

Function	Chief Officer	Title	Location
Chief Executive	Mr R Samuel	Chief Executive	Council Offices
Electoral Registration	Mr A King	Director of Finance	Council Offices
Environmental Health	Mr B Lear	Director of Community Services	Council Offices
Finance	Mr A King	Director of Finance	Council Offices
Housing	Mr B Lear	Director of Community Services	Council Offices
Legal Services	Mr S Davies	Director of Support Services	Council Offices
Leisure	Mr B Lear	Director of Community Services	Council Offices
Local Land Charges	Mr A King	Director of Finance	Council Offices
Planning	Mr R T Herron	Director of Planning Services	Council Offices
Purchasing & Supplies	Mr S Davies	Director of Community Services	Council Offices
Technical Services	Mr B Lear	Director of Community Services	Council Offices

Parish Councils in the authority's area: Acol; Birchington; Manston; Minster; Monkton; St Nicholas at Wade.

Town Council in the authority's area: Broadstairs & St Peters.

THREE RIVERS DISTRICT COUNCIL

www.3rivers.gov.uk

Principal Office

Three Rivers House, Northway, Rickmansworth, Hertfordshire WD3 1RL

Telephone: (01923) 776611; FAX: (01923) 896119; DX 38271 Rickmansworth

Function	Chief Officer	Title	Location
Chief Executive	Dr S Halls	Chief Executive	Three Rivers Hse
Electoral Registration	Mrs S Attard	Director of Strategic Services	Three Rivers Hse
Environmental Health	Mrs L Dallas	Director of Housing & Environment	Three Rivers Hse
Finance	Mr D Gardner	Director of Corporate Resources	Three Rivers Hse
Housing	Mrs L Dallas	Director of Housing & Environment	Three Rivers Hse
Legal Services	Mr D Gardner	Director of Corporate Resources	Three Rivers Hse
Leisure	Mr P Brooker	Director of Planning & Leisure	Three Rivers Hse
Local Land Charges	Mr P Brooker	Director of Planning & Leisure	Three Rivers Hse
Planning	Mr P Brooker	Director of Planning & Leisure	Three Rivers Hse

Parish Councils in the authority's area: Abbots Langley; Chorleywood; Croxley Green; Sarratt; Watford Rural.

THURROCK BOROUGH COUNCIL

Thurrock Borough Council became a unitary authority on 1 April 1998.

TONBRIDGE & MALLING BOROUGH COUNCIL

www.tmbc.gov.uk

Principal Office

Council Offices, Gibson Building, Gibson Drive, Kings Hill, West Malling, Kent ME19 4LZ
Telephone: (01732) 844522; FAX: (01732) 842170; DX 92854 West Malling

Function	Chief Officer	Title	Location
Chief Executive	David Hughes	Chief Executive	Council Offices
Electoral Registration	Roger Shapter	Principal Administrator	Council Offices
Environmental Health	John Batty	Director of Health & Housing	Council Offices
Finance	Sharon Shelton	Chief Finance Officer	Council Offices
Housing	John Batty	Director of Health & Housing	Council Offices
Legal Services	Duncan Robinson	Chief Solicitor	Council Offices
Leisure	Peter Wright	Director of Leisure	Council Offices
Local Land Charges	Duncan Robinson	Chief Solicitor	Council Offices
Planning	Steve Humphrey	Director of Planning & Engineering	Council Offices

Parish Councils in the authority's area: Addington; Aylesford; Birling; Borough Green; Burham; Ditton; East Malling & Larkfield; East Peckham; Hadlow; Hildenborough; Ightham; Kings Hill; Leybourne; Mereworth; Offham; Platt; Plaxtol; Ryarsh; Shipbourne; Snodland; Stansted; Trottiscliffe; Wateringbury; West Malling; West Peckham; Wouldham; Wrotham.

TORBAY BOROUGH COUNCIL

Torbay became a unitary authority on 1 April 1998.

TORRIDGE DISTRICT COUNCIL

www.torridge.gov.uk

Principal Office

Riverbank House, Bideford, Devon EX39 2QG
Telephone: (01237) 428700; FAX: (01237) 478849; DX 53606 Bideford

Financial Services Department

Bridge Buildings, Bideford EX39 2HT
Telephone: (01237) 428700; FAX: (01237) 424299

Housing & Environmental Services Department

Town Hall, Bideford EX39 2HS
Telephone: (01237) 428700; FAX: (01237) 474407

Function	Chief Officer	Title	Location
Chief Executive	Mr T J Smale	Chief Executive	Riverbank Hse
Electoral Registration	Mr T J Smale	Chief Executive	Riverbank Hse
Environmental Health	Mrs G L Bowering-Sheehan	Director of Housing & Environmental Services	Town Hall
Finance	Mrs J Wallace	Head of Financial Services	Bridge Bldings
Housing	Mrs G L Bowering-Sheehan	Director of Housing & Environmental Services	Town Hall
Legal Services	Mr J M Wyatt	District Secretary & Solicitor	Riverbank Hse
Leisure	Mrs V Saunders	Economic & Community Development Officer	Riverbank Hse
Local Land Charges	Mr J M Wyatt	District Secretary & Solicitor	Riverbank Hse
Planning	Mr D A Pinney	Director of Planning & Technical Services	Riverbank Hse
Technical Services	Mr D A Pinney	Director of Planning & Technical Services	Riverbank Hse

Parish Councils in the authority's area: Abbotsham; Alverdiscott & Huntshaw; Alwington; Ashreigney; Ashwater; Beaford; Black Torrington; Bradford & Cookbury; Bradworthy; Bridgerule; Broadwoodwidger; Buckland Brewer; Buckland Filleigh; Clawton; Clovelly; Dolton; East & West Putford; Frithelstock; Halwill; Hartland; High Bickington; Holsworthy Hamlets; Langtree; Little Torrington; Littleham & Landcross; Luffincott & Tetcott; Lundy Island; Merton; Milton Damerel; Monkleigh; Newton St Petrock; Pancrasweek; Parkham; Peters Marland; Petrockstowe; Pyworthy; Roborough; St Giles in the Wood; St Giles on the Heath & Northcott; Shebbear; Sheepwash; Sutcombe; Thornbury; Weare Giffard; Welcombe; Winkleigh; Woolfardisworthy; Yarnscombe.

Parish Meetings in the authority's area: Abbots Bickington; Bulkworthy; Dowland; Hollacombe; Huish; Virginstowe.

Town Councils in the authority's area: Bideford; Great Torrington; Holsworthy; Northam.

TUNBRIDGE WELLS BOROUGH COUNCIL

www.tunbridgewells.gov.uk

Principal Office
Town Hall, Royal Tunbridge Wells, Kent TN1 1RS
Telephone: (01892) 526121; FAX: (01892) 534227; DX 3929 Royal Tunbridge Wells

Function	Chief Officer	Title	Location
Chief Executive	Mr R J Stone	Chief Executive	Town Hall
Electoral Registration	Mr M Harris	Borough Secretary and Solicitor	Town Hall
Environmental Health	Ms D Stock	Head of Environmental Services	Town Hall
Finance	Mr G Levitt	Finance Director & Deputy Chief Executive	Town Hall
Housing	Ms C Beaumont	Head of Housing Services	Town Hall
Legal Services	Mr M Harris	Borough Secretary & Solicitor	Town Hall
Leisure	Mr N Bolton	Head of Leisure Services	Town Hall
Local Land Charges	Mr M Harris	Borough Secretary & Solicitor	Town Hall
Planning	Mr D Prentis	Head of Planning Services	Town Hall

Parish Councils in the authority's area: Benenden; Bidborough; Brenchley; Capel; Cranbrook; Frittenden; Goudhurst; Hawkhurst; Horsmonden; Lamberhurst; Pembury; Sandhurst; Speldhurst.

Town Councils in the authority's area: Paddock Wood; Southborough.

TYNEDALE DISTRICT COUNCIL

www.tynedale.gov.uk

Principal Office
Hexham House, Hexham, Northumberland NE46 3NH
Telephone: (01434) 652200; FAX: (01434) 652420; DX 63216 Hexham

Environmental Health & Housing Department; Leisure & Tourism Department
Prospect House, Hexham NE46 3NH
Telephone: (01434) 652200; FAX: (01434) 652423

Planning Department
Old Grammar School, Hallgates, Hexham NE46 3NH
Telephone: (01434) 652200; FAX: (01434) 652422

Contract & Technical Services Department
Tyne Mills Industrial Estate, Hexham
Telephone: (01434) 652200; FAX: (01434) 652424

Function	Chief Officer	Title	Location
Chief Executive	R J Robson	Chief Executive	Hexham House
Electoral Registration	Mr G C Pointer	Head of Legal Services	Hexham House
Environmental Health	Mr D Robinson	Chief Environmental Health & Housing Officer	Prospect House

DISTRICT COUNCILS

Finance	Mr J Copping	Chief Financial Officer	Hexham House
Housing	Mr D Robinson	Chief Environmental Health & Housing Officer	Prospect Hse
Legal Services	Mr G C Pointer	Head of Legal Services	Hexham House
Leisure	Ms L Turner	Chief Leisure & Tourism Officer	Prospect Hse
Local Land Charges	Mr G C Pointer	Head of Legal Services	Hexham House
Planning	Mrs H Winter	Chief Planning Officer	Old Grammar School
Technical Services	Mr I Douglas	Director of Contract & Technical Services	Tyne Mills

Parish Councils in the authority's area: Acomb; Allendale; Bardon Mill; Bavington; Bellingham; Birtley; Blanchland; Broomhaugh & Riding; Broomley & Stocksfield; Bywell; Chollerton; Coanwood; Corbridge; Corsenside; Falstone; Featherstone; Greenhead; Hartleyburn; Haydon; Healey; Hedley; Henshaw; Hexhamshire & District; Horsley; Humshaugh; Kielder; Kirkwhelpington; Knaresdale with Kirkhaugh; Melkridge; Newbrough; Otterburn; Ovingham; Ovington; Plenmeller with Whitfield; Rochester; Sandhoe; Shotley Low Quarter; Simonburn; Slaley; Tarset & Greystead; Thirlwall; Wall; Warden; Wark; West Allen; Whittington; Wylam.

Town Councils in the authority's area: Haltwhistle; Hexham; Prudhoe.

UTTLESFORD DISTRICT COUNCIL

www.uttlesford.gov.uk

Principal Office
Council Offices, London Road, Saffron Walden, Essex CB11 4ER
Telephone: (01799) 510510; FAX: (01799) 510550

Function	Chief Officer	Title	Location
Chief Executive	Mr A Bovaird	Chief Executive	London Rd
Electoral Registration	Mr P Snow	Electoral Services Officer	London Rd
Environmental Health	Mr R M Secker	Head of Environmental Services	London Rd
Finance	Mr J B Dickson	Director of Resources	London Rd
Housing	Mr R Chamberlain	Housing Services Manager	London Rd
Legal Services	Mr M Perry	Head of Legal Services	London Rd
Leisure	Mrs S McLagan	Head of Community & Leisure Services	London Rd
Local Land Charges	Mr M Perry	Head of Legal Services	London Rd
Planning	Mr J Mitchell	Head of Planning & Building Surveying	London Rd
Purchasing & Supplies	Mrs C Croft		London Rd

Parish Councils in the authority's area: Arkesden; Ashdon; Aythorpe Roding; Barnston; Berden; Birchanger; Broxted; Chrishall; Clavering; Debden; Elmdon & Wenden Lofts; Elsenham; Farnham; Felsted; Great Canfield; Great Chesterford; Great Easton; Great Hallingbury; Hadstock; Hatfield Broad Oak; Hatfield Heath; Hempstead; Henham; High Easter; High Roding; Langley; Leaden Roding; Little Bardfield; Little Canfield; Little Chesterford; Little Dunmow; Little Easton; Little Hallingbury; Littlebury; Manuden; Margaret Roding; Newport; Quendon & Rickling; Radwinter; The Sampfords; Sewards End; Stansted; Stebbing; Takeley; Thaxted; Ugley; Wenden Lofts; Wendens Ambo; White Roothing; Widdington; Wimbish.

Parish Meetings in the authority's area: Chickney; Lindsell; Strethall; Tilty; Wicken Bonhunt.

Town Councils in the authority's area: Great Dunmow; Saffron Walden.

VALE OF WHITE HORSE DISTRICT COUNCIL

www.whitehorsedc.gov.uk

Principal Office
The Abbey House, Abingdon, Oxfordshire OX14 3JE
Telephone: (01235) 520202; FAX: (01235) 554960; DX 35863 Abingdon

DISTRICT COUNCILS

Function	Chief Officer	Title	Location
Chief Executive	Terry Stock	Chief Executive	The Abbey Hse
Electoral Registration	David Quayle	Director of Support Services	The Abbey Hse
Environmental Health	John Rawling	Director of Environmental Services	The Abbey Hse
Finance	Sue Scane	Director of Corporate Resources	The Abbey Hse
Housing	Tim Sadler	Director of Social and Cultural Services	The Abbey Hse
Legal Services	David Quayle	Director of Support Services	The Abbey Hse
Leisure	Tim Sadler	Director of Social and Cultural Services	The Abbey Hse
Local Land Charges	David Quayle	Director of Support Services	The Abbey Hse
Planning	John Rawling	Director of Environmental Services	The Abbey Hse
Purchasing & Supplies	David Quayle	Director of Support Services	The Abbey Hse
Technical Services	David Quayle	Director of Support Services	The Abbey Hse

Parish Councils in the authority's area: Appleford-on-Thames; Appleton with Eaton; Ardington and Lockinge; Ashbury; Blewbury; Bourton; Buckland; Buscot; Charney Bassett; Childrey; Chilton; Coleshill; Cumnor; Drayton; East Challow; East Hanney; East Hendred; Fyfield & Tubney; Great Coxwell; Grove; Harwell; Hinton Waldrist; Kennington; Kingston Bagpuize with Southmoor; Kingston Lisle; Letcombe Regis; Little Coxwell; Longcot; Longworth; Marcham; Milton; North Hinksey; Radley; St Helen Without; Shrivenham; South Hinksey; Sparsholt; Stanford-in-the-Vale; Steventon; Sunningwell; Sutton Courtenay; Uffington; Upton; Watchfield; West Challow; West Hanney; West Hendred; Wootton.

Parish Meetings in the authority's area: Baulking; Besselsleigh; Compton Beauchamp; Denchworth; Eaton Hastings; Fernham; Frilford; Garford; Goosey; Hatford; Letcombe Bassett; Littleworth; Lyford; Pusey; Shellingford; Woolstone; Wytham.

Town Councils in the authority's area: Abingdon; Great Faringdon; Wantage.

VALE ROYAL BOROUGH COUNCIL

www.valeroyal.gov.uk

Principal Office

Wyvern House, The Drumber, Winsford, Cheshire CW7 1AH

Telephone: (01606) 862862; FAX: (01606) 862100; DX 722040 Winsford 2

Function	Chief Officer	Title	Location
Chief Executive	Anne Bingham-Holmes	Chief Executive	Wyvern Hse
Electoral Registration	Anne Bingham-Holmes	Chief Executive	Wyvern Hse
Environmental Health	Mr R Hallows	Director of Social and Community Services	Wyvern Hse
Finance	Mr N O'Neill	Director of Corporate and Economic Affairs	Wyvern Hse
Housing	Mr R Hallows	Director of Social and Community Services	Wyvern Hse
Legal Services	Mr N O'Neill	Director of Corporate and Economic Affairs	Wyvern Hse
Leisure	Mr R Hallows	Director of Social and Community Services	Wyvern Hse
Local Land Charges	Mr N O'Neill	Director of Corporate and Economic Affairs	Wyvern Hse
Planning	Mr R Hallows	Director of Social and Community Services	Wyvern Hse
Purchasing & Supplies	Mr N O'Neill	Director of Corporate and Economic Affairs	Wyvern Hse
Technical Services	Mr J Jeffrey	Director of Environment & Sustainability	Wyvern Hse

Parish Councils in the authority's area: Acton Bridge; Allostock; Alvanley; Anderton with Marbury; Antrobus; Aston; Barnton; Bostock; Byley; Comberbach; Crowton; Cuddington;

Darnhall; Davenham; Delamere; Dutton; Great Budworth; Hartford; Helsby; Kingsley; Lach Dennis; Little Budworth; Little Leigh; Lostock Gralam; Lower Peover; Manley; Marston; Moulton; Norley; Oakmere; Rudheath; Rushton; Sproston; Stanthorne; Sutton; Tarporley; Utkinton; Weaverham; Whitegate & Marton; Whitley; Wimboldsley; Wincham.

Town Councils in the authority's area: Frodsham; Northwich; Winsford.

WANSBECK DISTRICT COUNCIL

www.wansbeck.gov.uk

Chief Executive Office
Town Hall, Ashington, Northumberland NE63 8RX
Telephone: (01670) 532200; FAX: (01670) 520136

Corporate Services Department; Housing Services Department
Wansbeck Square, Ashington NE63 9XL
Telephone: (01670) 532200; FAX: (01670) 857743

Economic & Environment Services Department; Leisure Services Department
Bedlington Council Offices, Front Street, Bedlington NE22 5TU
Telephone: (01670) 530033; FAX: (01670) 530278

Contract Services Department
Stakeford Depot, East View, Stakeford, Choppington NE62 5TR
Telephone: (01670) 819802; FAX: (01670) 520457

Function	Chief Officer	Title	Location
Chief Executive	Mr R A Stephenson	Chief Executive	Town Hall
Electoral Registration	Mr K Crow	Electoral & Licensing Services Manager	Town Hall
Environmental Health	Mr N J Burden	Chief Economic & Environment Services Officer	Bedlington
Finance	Mr M Smith	Chief Financial Services Officer	Wansbeck Sq
Housing	Mr C Steel	Chief Housing Services Officer	Wansbeck Sq
Legal Services	Mrs C Forster	Solicitor & Monitoring Officer	Town Hall
Leisure	Mr C Mitchell	Chief Leisure Services Officer	Bedlington
Local Land Charges	Mr K Crow	Electoral & Licensing Services Manager	Town Hall
Planning	Mr N J Burden	Chief Economic & Environment Services Officer	Bedlington
Technical Services	Mr T Straker	Engineering Services Manager	Stakeford Depot

Parish Councils & Parish Meetings in the authority's area: none.

Town Councils in the authority's area: none.

WANSDYKE DISTRICT COUNCIL
Wansdyke District Council was abolished on 31 March 1996; see now Bath & North East Somerset Council.

WARRINGTON BOROUGH COUNCIL
Warrington Borough Council became a unitary authority on 1 April 1998.

WARWICK DISTRICT COUNCIL

www.warwickdc.gov.uk

Principal Office
Riverside House, Milverton Hill, Royal Leamington Spa, Warwickshire CV32 5HZ
Telephone: (01926) 450000; DX 29123 Leamington Spa 1

Function	Chief Officer	Title	Location
Chief Executive	Ms J M Barrett	Chief Executive	Riverside House
Electoral Registration	Ms G Friar	Electoral Administration	Riverside House
Finance	Mr A Dunnell	Head of Finance	Riverside House
Housing	Mr W Hunt	Head of Housing	Riverside House
Legal Services	Miss M S Stathe	Head of Legal Services	Riverside House
Leisure	Mr D Best	Head of Leisure & Amenities	Riverside House
Planning	Mr J Archer	Head of Planning & Engineering	Riverside House

Parish Councils in the authority's area: Baddesley Clinton; Baginton; Barford, Sherbourne & Wasperton; Beausale, Haseley, Honiley & Wroxall; Bishops Tachbrook; Bubbenhall; Budbrooke; Cubbington; Eathorpe, Hunningham, Offchurch, Wappenbury & Weston under Wetherley; Hatton; Lapworth; Leek Wootton & Guy's Cliffe; Norton Lindsey; Old Milverton & Blackdown; Radford Semele; Rowington; Shrewley; Stoneleigh & Ashow.

Town Councils in the authority's area: Kenilworth; Leamington Spa; Warwick; Whitnash.

WATFORD BOROUGH COUNCIL

www.watford.gov.uk

Principal Office
Town Hall, Watford, Hertfordshire WD17 3EX
Telephone: (01923) 226400; FAX: (01923) 226133; DX 4512 Watford 1

Function	Chief Officer	Title	Location
Electoral Registration	Mr Peter Lipman	Corporate Director	Town Hall
Environmental Health	Mr Alan Gough	Head of Environment, Health & Licensing	Town Hall
Finance	Mrs Janice Maule	Director of Finance	Town Hall
Housing	Ms Marian Harris	Head of Housing	Town Hall
Legal Services	Ms Carol Chen	Head of Legal Services	Town Hall
Leisure	Ms Kate Hall	Head of Leisure & Community Services	Town Hall
Local Land Charges	Ms Carol Chen	Head of Legal Services	Town Hall
Planning	Mr Chris Pagdin	Head of Planning & Development	Town Hall
Purchasing & Supplies	Mr Jago Durant	Print Manager	Town Hall
Technical Services	Mrs Alison Stainsby	Head of Technical Services	Town Hall

Parish Councils & Parish Meetings in the authority's area: none.

Town Councils in the authority's area: none.

WAVENEY DISTRICT COUNCIL

www.waveney.gov.uk

Principal Office; Corporate Governance Portfolio
Town Hall, High Street, Lowestoft, Suffolk NR32 1HS
Telephone: (01502) 562111; FAX: (01502) 589327; DX 41220 Lowestoft

Operations Portfolio
Town Hall, High Street, Lowestoft, Suffolk NR32 1HS
Telephone: (01502) 562111; FAX: (01502) 523310; DX 41220 Lowestoft

Regeneration and Environment Portfolio
Town Hall, High Street, Lowestoft, Suffolk NR32 1HS
Telephone: (01502) 562111; FAX: (01502) 514617; DX 41220 Lowestoft

Function	Chief Officer	Title	Location
Chief Executive	Mairi McLean	Chief Executive	Principal Office
Electoral Registration	Clive Olley	Corporate Director (Corporate Governance)	Corp Gov Portfol

DISTRICT COUNCILS

Environmental Health	Louise Jordan-Hall	Corporate Director (Regeneration & Environment)	Regen & Environ
Finance	Andrew Verney	Portfolio Manager (Finance & E-Government)	Operations Portfol
Housing	Simon Travis	Portfolio Manager (Housing & Social Inclusion)	Operations Portfol
Legal Services	Peter Cox	Portfolio Manager (Legal & Democratic)	Corp Gov Portfol
Planning	Louise Jordan-Hall	Corporate Director (Regeneration & Environment)	Regen & Environ
Purchasing & Supplies	Christine Gore	Corporate Director (Community & Operations)	Operations Portfol
Technical Services	Louise Jordan-Hall	Corporate Director (Regeneration & Environment)	Regen & Environ

Parish Councils in the authority's area: Ashby, Herringfleet & Somerleyton; Barnby; Barsham & Shipmeadow; Blundeston & Flixton (East); Blyford & Sotherton; Brampton with Stoven; Carlton Colville; Corton; Flixton (West), South Elmham St Cross & St Margaret; Frostenden, Uggeshall & South Cove; Gisleham; Henstead with Hulver Street; Holton; Homersfield (otherwise South Elmham St Mary); Ilketshall St Andrew; Ilketshall St Lawrence; Kessingland; Lound; Mettingham; Mutford; North Cove; Oulton; Reydon (inc. Easton Bavents); Ringsfield & Weston; Rumburgh; Shadingfield, Sotterley, Willingham & Ellough; South Elmham All Saints & St Nicholas, St Michael & St Peter; Spexhall; Wangford with Henham; Westhall; Weston; Wissett; Worlingham; Wrentham.

Parish Meetings in the authority's area: Benacre; Covehithe; Ilketshall St John; Ilketshall St Margaret; Redisham; Rushmere; South Elmham St James.

Town Councils in the authority's area: Beccles; Bungay; Halesworth; Southwold.

WAVERLEY BOROUGH COUNCIL

www.waverley.gov.uk

Principal Office

Council Offices, The Burys, Godalming, Surrey GU7 1HR
Telephone: (01483) 523333; FAX: (01483) 426337; DX 58303 Godalming 1

Function	Chief Officer	Title	Location
Chief Executive	Miss C L Pointer	Chief Executive	Council Offices
Electoral Registration	Mr R Pellow	Head of Committee & Member Services	Council Offices
Environmental Health	Mr P Maudsley	Director of Environment & Leisure	Council Offices
Finance	Mr P Wenham	Director of Finance	Council Offices
Housing	Mr D January	Director of Housing	Council Offices
Legal Services	Mrs S Whitmarsh	Head of Legal Services	Council Offices
Leisure	Mr P Maudsley	Director of Environment & Leisure	Council Offices
Local Land Charges	Mrs S Whitmarsh	Head of Legal Services	Council Offices
Planning	Mr S Thwaites	Director of Planning & Development	Council Offices
Technical Services	Mr P Maudsley	Director of Environment & Leisure	Council Offices

Parish Councils in the authority's area: Alfold; Bramley; Busbridge; Chiddingfold; Churt; Cranleigh; Dockenfield; Dunsfold; Elstead; Ewhurst; Frensham; Hambledon; Hascombe; Thursley; Tilford; Witley; Wonersh.

Parish Meeting in the authority's area: Peper Harow.

Town Councils in the authority's area: Farnham; Godalming; Haslemere.

DISTRICT COUNCILS

WEALDEN DISTRICT COUNCIL

www.wealden.gov.uk

Principal Office

Council Offices, Pine Grove, Crowborough, East Sussex TN6 1DH
Telephone: (01892) 653311; FAX: (01892) 602222; DX 36860 Crowborough

Finance Department; Housing Department; Environmental Health Department
Council Offices, Vicarage Lane, Hailsham BN27 2AX
Telephone: (01323) 442666; FAX: (01323) 443333

Function	Chief Officer	Title	Location
Chief Executive	Mr C Lant	Chief Executive	Pine Grove
Electoral Registration	Mr D Goodwin	Corporate Director of Corporate Services	Pine Grove
Environmental Health	Ms M C Deane	Corporate Director of Community Services	Vicarage Ln
Finance	Mr D Goodwin	Corporate Director of Corporate Services	Vicarage Ln
Housing	Ms M C Deane	Corporate Director of Community Services	Vicarage Ln
Legal Services	Mr D Goodwin	Corporate Director of Corporate Services	Pine Grove
Local Land Charges	Mr D Goodwin	Corporate Director of Corporate Services	Pine Grove
Planning	Ms Barakchizadeh	Corporate Director of Environmental Services	Pine Grove
Purchasing & Supplies	Mr M J Fleming	Corporate Director of Technical Services	Pine Grove
Technical Services	Mr M J Fleming	Corporate Director of Technical Services	Pine Grove

Parish Councils in the authority's area: Alfriston; Arlington; Berwick; Buxted; Chalvington with Ripe; Chiddingly; Cuckmere Valley; Danehill; East Dean & Friston; East Hoathly; Fletching; Forest Row; Framfield; Frant; Hadlow Down; Hartfield; Heathfield & Waldron; Hellingly; Herstmonceux; Hooe; Horam; Isfield; Laughton; Long Man; Maresfield; Mayfield & Five Ashes; Ninfield; Pevensey; Rotherfield; Wadhurst; Warbleton; Wartling; Westham; Willingdon & Jevington; Withyham.

Parish Meetings in the authority's area: Alciston; Little Horsted; Selmeston.

Town Councils in the authority's area: Crowborough; Hailsham; Polegate; Uckfield.

WEAR VALLEY DISTRICT COUNCIL

www.wearvalley.gov.uk

Principal Office

Civic Centre, Crook, Co Durham DL15 9ES
Telephone: (01388) 765555; FAX: (01388) 766660

Function	Chief Officer	Title	Location
Chief Executive	Mr I Phillips	Chief Executive	Civic Centre
Electoral Registration	Mr T Richardson	Senior Admin Assistant	Civic Centre
Environmental Health	Mr T Carver	Head of Public Protection	Civic Centre
Finance	Mr G Ridley	Director of Central Resources	Civic Centre
Housing	Mr M Laing	Director of Housing Services	Civic Centre
Leisure	Mr M Coleby	Acting Director of Community Services	Civic Centre
Legal Services	Mrs C Prest	Head of Legal Services	Civic Centre
Local Land Charges	Mrs A McCabe	Land Charges Officer	Civic Centre
Planning	Mr R M Hope	Director of Regeneration	Civic Centre

Parish Councils in the authority's area: Dene Valley, Stanhope; Witton Le Wear, Wolsingham, West Auckland.

Parish Meetings in the authority's area: Edmundbyers; Hunstanworth.

Town Council in the authority's area: Tow Law.

DISTRICT COUNCILS

WELLINGBOROUGH BOROUGH COUNCIL

www.wellingborough.gov.uk

Chief Executive's Department; Department of Technical & Leisure Services
Swanspool House, Wellingborough, Northamptonshire NN8 1BP
Telephone: (01933) 229777; FAX: (01933) 231540; DX 12865 Wellingborough

Department of Finance & IT Services;
Department of Housing & Community Development
Council Offices, Tithe Barn Road, Wellingborough NN8 1BN
Telephone: (01933) 229777; FAX: (01933) 273949

Department of Environmental Services
Croyland Abbey, Tithe Barn Road, Wellingborough NN8 1BJ
Telephone: (01933) 229777; FAX: (01933) 271574

Function	Chief Officer	Title	Location
Chief Executive	Mr A D W McArdle	Chief Executive	Swanspool Hse
Electoral Registration	Mrs B Lawrence	Head of Administration	Swanspool Hse
Environmental Health	Mrs L Martin-Bennison	Director of Environment & Economy	Croyland Abbey
Finance	Ms P Tunn	Director of Finance & Corporate Services	Tithe Barn Road
Housing	Mr J Hubbard	Director of Housing & Community Development	Tithe Barn Road
Legal Services	Miss L McShane	Head of Legal Services	Swanspool Hse
Local Land Charges	Mrs C Haybyrne		Swanspool Hse
Planning	Mr M Kilpin	Head of Development Control	Croyland Abbey
Purchasing & Supplies	Mr G Ward	Printing Office	Swanspool Hse
Technical Services	Mr R Entwistle	Director of Technical & Leisure Services	Swanspool Hse

Parish Councils in the authority's area: Bozeat; Earls Barton; Ecton; Finedon; Great Doddington; Grendon; Irchester; Isham; Little Harrowden; Mears Ashby; Orlingbury; Sywell; Wilby; Wollaston.

Parish Meetings in the authority's area: Easton Maudit; Hardwick; Great Harrowden; Strixton.

WELWYN HATFIELD DISTRICT COUNCIL

www.welhat.gov.uk

Principal Office
Council Offices, The Campus, Welwyn Garden City, Hertfordshire AL8 6AE
Telephone: (01707) 357000

Leisure Services Department
Campus West, The Campus, Welwyn Garden City AL8 6BX
Telephone: (01707) 357000; FAX: (01707) 357185

Function	Chief Officer	Title	Location
Chief Executive	Michel Saminaden	Chief Executive	Council Offices
Environmental Health	Chris Conway	Chief Planning & Environmental Health Officer	Council Offices
Finance	Bob Jewell	Chief Resources Officer	Council Offices
Housing	Darren Welsh	Chief Housing Strategy Officer	Council Offices
Legal Services	Bob Baldock	Chief Legal & Administrative Officer	Council Offices
Leisure	Richard Masters	Chief Leisure & Community Services Officer	Campus West
Local Land Charges	Bob Baldock	Chief Legal & Administrative Officer	Council Offices
Planning	Chris Conway	Chief Planning & Environmental Health Officer	Council Offices
Technical Services	Tony Ferrari	Chief Environmental Services Officer	Council Offices

DISTRICT COUNCILS

Parish Councils in the authority's area: Essendon; North Mymms; Northaw & Cuffley; Welwyn; Woolmer Green.

Parish Meetings in the authority's area: Ayot St Lawrence; Ayot St Peter.

Town Councils in the authority's area: Hatfield.

WEST DEVON BOROUGH COUNCIL

www.westdevon.gov.uk

Tavistock Office
Kilworthy Park, Drake Road, Tavistock, Devon PL19 0BZ
Telephone: (01822) 813600; FAX: (01822) 813634; DX 82405 Tavistock

Okehampton Office
Oaklands Drive, Okehampton, Devon EX20 1LH
Telephone: (01822) 813600; FAX: (01822) 813635

Function	Chief Officer	Title	Location
Chief Executive	Mr D J Incoll	Chief Executive	Tavistock
Electoral Registration	Tony Rose	Committee & Elections Officer	Tavistock
Environmental Health	Mr N Payne	Director for the Environment	Okehampton
Finance	Miss L J Halton	Director of Resources & Housing	Tavistock
Housing	Mrs M Playle	Housing Services Manager	Tavistock
Legal Services	Mrs C Bowen	Borough Solicitor	Tavistock
Leisure	Mr T Beavon	Economic & Leisure Development Manager	Tavistock
Local Land Charges	Mrs C Fryer	Land Charges Officer	Tavistock
Planning	Mr S Gill	Borough Planning Officer	Tavistock

Parish Councils in the authority's area: Beaworthy; Belstone; Bere Ferrers; Bratton Clovelly; Brentor; Bridestowe; Broadwoodkelly; Buckland Monachorum; Burrator Group; Chagford; Dartmoor Forest; Drewsteignton; Exbourne & Jacobstowe; Germansweek; Gulworthy; Highampton; Horrabridge; Iddesleigh; Inwardleigh; Kelly & Bradstone Group; Lamerton; Lewdown Group; Lifton; Lydford; Mary Tavy; Meeth; Milton Abbot Group; Monkokehampton; Northlew; Okehampton Hamlets; Peter Tavy; Plasterdown Group; Sampford Courtenay; Sourton; South Tawton; Spreyton; Sticklepath; Stowford; Sydenham Damerel; Throwleigh.

Parish Meetings in the authority's area: Bondleigh; Gidleigh.

Town Councils in the authority's area: Hatherleigh; North Tawton; Okehampton; Tavistock.

WEST DORSET DISTRICT COUNCIL

www.westdorset-dc.gov.uk

Principal Office
Stratton House, High West Street, Dorchester, Dorset DT1 1UZ
Telephone: (01305) 251010; FAX: (01305) 251481; DX 8724 Dorchester

Function	Chief Officer	Title	Location
Chief Executive	Mr D Clarke	Chief Executive	Stratton House
Electoral Registration	Mr M Hickman	Elections & Licensing Team Leader	Stratton House
Environmental Health	Mr M Grindle	Health & Housing Manager	Stratton House
Finance	Mr A Stuart	Finance Manager	Stratton House
Housing	Mr M Grindle	Health & Housing Manager	Stratton House
Legal Services	Mr A Muir	Legal Services Manager	Stratton House
Leisure	Mr N Thornley	Leisure & Tourism Manager	Stratton House
Local Land Charges	Mr D Mayne	Land Charges Officer	Stratton House
Planning	Mr J Greenslade	Development Services Manager	Stratton House

DISTRICT COUNCILS

Parish Councils in the authority's area: Abbotsbury; Allington; Alton Pancras; Athelhampton; Batcombe; Beer Hackett; Bettiscombe; Bincombe; Bishops Caundle; Bothenhampton & Walditch; Bradford Abbas; Bradford Peverell; Bradpole; Broadmayne; Broadwindsor; Buckland Newton; Burleston; Burstock; Burton Bradstock; Castleton; Cattistock; Cerne Abbas; Charminster; Charmouth; Chedington; Cheselbourne; Chetnole; Chideock; Chilfrome; Compton Valence; Corscombe; Crossways; Dewlish; East Chelborough; Evershot; Fleet; Folke; Frampton; Frome St Quintin; Goathill; Godmanstone; Halstock; Hermitage; Hilfield; Holnest; Holwell; Kingston Russell; Langton Herring; Leigh; Leweston; Lillington; Litton Cheney; Loders; Long Bredy; Longburton; Maiden Newton; Marshwood; Melbury Osmond; Minterne Magna; Mosterton; Nether Cerne; Nether Compton; Netherbury; North Poorton; Oborne; Osmington; Over Compton; Owermoigne; Piddlehinton; Piddletrenthide; Pilsdon; Portesham; Powerstock; Poyntington; Puddletown; Puncknowle; Purse Caundle; Ryme Intrinseca; Sandford Orcas; Seaborough; Shipton Gorge; South Perrott; Stanton St Gabriel; Stinsford; Stockwood; Stoke Abbott; Stratton; Sydling St Nicholas; Symondsbury; Thorncombe; Thornford; Tincleton; Toller Fratrum; Toller Porcorum; Tolpuddle; Trent; Up Cerne; Warmwell; West Chelborough; West Compton; West Knighton; West Stafford; Whitchurch Canonicorum; Whitcombe; Winterborne Came; Winterborne Herringston; Winterborne Monkton; Winterborne St Martin; Winterbourne Abbas; Winterbourne Steepleton; Woodsford; Wootton Fitzpaine; Wynford Eagle; Yetminster.

Parish Meetings in the authority's area: Askerswell; Catherston Leweston; Caundle Marsh; Chilcombe; Clifton Maybank; Frome Vauchurch; Haydon; Hooke; Littlebredy; Mapperton; Melbury Bubb; Melbury Sampford; Melcombe Horsey; North Wootton; Poxwell; Rampisham; Swyre; Wraxall.

Town Councils in the authority's area: Beaminster; Bridport; Chickerell; Dorchester; Lyme Regis; Sherborne.

WEST LANCASHIRE DISTRICT COUNCIL

www.westlancsdc.gov.uk

Principal Office
52 Derby Street, Ormskirk, Lancashire L39 2DF
Telephone: (01695) 577177; FAX: (01695) 585082

Housing & Health
Westec House, 52 Derby Street, Ormskirk L39 2DQ
Telephone: (01695) 577177

Function	Chief Officer	Title	Location
Chief Executive	Mr W J Taylor	Chief Executive	52 Derby St
Electoral Registration	Mr W J Taylor	Chief Executive	52 Derby St
Environmental Health	Mr D Tilleray	Executive Manager Environmental Services	Westec House
Finance	Mr J Gardener	Executive Manager Financial Services	52 Derby St
Housing	Mr R Livermore	Executive Manager Housing Services	Westec House
Legal Services	Mrs G L Rowe	Council Secretary and Solicitor	52 Derby St
Leisure	Mr P Barker	Executive Manager Leisure, Culture & Arts Services	52 Derby St
Local Land Charges	Mrs G L Rowe	Council Secretary and Solicitor	52 Derby St
Planning	Mr S Byron	Executive Manager Planning/ Development Services	52 Derby St
Purchasing & Supplies	Mr D Tilleray	Executive Manager Environmental Services	Westec House
Technical Services	Mr S Byron	Executive Manager Planning/ Development Services	52 Derby St

Parish Councils in the authority's area: Aughton; Bickerstaffe; Burscough; Dalton; Downholland; Great Altcar; Halsall; Hesketh with Becconsall; Hilldale; Lathom; Newburgh; North Meols; Parbold; Rufford; Scarisbrick; Simonswood; Tarleton; Up Holland; Wrightington.

Parish Meeting in the authority's area: Bispham.

DISTRICT COUNCILS

WEST LINDSEY DISTRICT COUNCIL

www.west-lindsey.gov.uk

Principal Office

The Guildhall, Gainsborough, Lincolnshire DN21 2DH
Telephone: (01427) 676676; FAX: (01427) 810622; DX 27214 Gainsborough

Directorate of Customer Services

26 Spital Terrace, Gainsborough DN21 2HG
Telephone: (01427) 676676; FAX: (01427) 810623

Directorate of Community Services

11/13 Cross Street, Gainsborough DN21 2AX
Telephone: (01427) 676676; FAX: (01427) 811579

Function	Chief Officer	Title	Location
Chief Executive	Mr R W Nelsey	Chief Executive	Guildhall
Electoral Registration	Mr R R Vine	Assistant Chief Executive	Guildhall
Environmental Health	Mr J Nicholson	Head of Environment Services	Cross Street
Finance	[Vacant]	Head of Financial Services	Guildhall
Housing	Ms R M North	Head of Community Services	Guildhall
Legal Services	Mr R R Vine	Assistant Chief Executive	Guildhall
Leisure	Ms R M North	Head of Community Services	Guildhall
Local Land Charges	Ms R M North	Head of Community Services	Guildhall
Planning	Mr G Martin	Head of Planning Services	Spital Terrace
Purchasing & Supplies	Mrs A Allport	Head of Support Services	Guildhall
Technical Services	Mr C Godley	Property Services Manager	Guildhall

Parish Councils in the authority's area: Bardney; Barlings (Langworth); Bigby; Bishop Norton; Blyton; Brattleby; Burton; Cammeringham; Cherry Willingham; Claxby; Corringham; Dunholme; East Stockwith; Faldingworth; Fenton; Fiskerton; Glentham; Glentworth; Grasby; Great Limber; Greetwell; Hackthorn & Cold Hanworth; Hemswell; Hemswell Cliff; Ingham; Keelby; Kettlethorpe & Laughterton; Kexby; Knaith; Langworth; Laughton; Lea; Marton & Gate Burton; Middle Rasen; Morton; Nettleham; Newton-on-Trent; Normanby-by-Spital; North Kelsey; Northorpe; Osgodby; Owersby; Owmby-by-Spital; Reepham; Riseholme; Rothwell; Saxilby; Scampton; Scothern; Scotter; Scotton; Snitterby; South Kelsey; Stainton-le-Vale; Stow; Sturton-by-Stow; Sudbrooke; Swallow; Tealby; Toft Newton; Torksey; Upton; Waddingham; Walesby; Welton; Wickenby; Willingham; Willoughton.

Parish Meetings in the authority's area: Aisthorpe; Apley; Blyborough; Brampton; Broadholme; Brocklesby; Broxholme; Bullington; Buslingthorpe; Cabourne; Caenby; East Ferry; Fillingham; Friesthorpe; Fulnetby; Goltho; Grange-de-Lings; Grayingham; Hardwick; Harpswell; Heapham; Holton-cum-Beckering; Holton-le-Moor; Kirmond-le-Mire; Legsby; Linwood; Lissington; Normanby-le-Wold; North Carlton; North Willingham; Pilham; Rand; Riby; Saxby; Searby-cum-Owmby; Sixhills; Snarford; Snelland; Somerby; South Carlton; Springthorpe; Swinhope; Thonock; Thoresway; Thorganby; Thorpe-le-Fallows; Walkerith; West Firsby; West Rasen; Wildsworth.

Town Councils in the authority's area: Caistor; Gainsborough; Market Rasen.

WEST OXFORDSHIRE DISTRICT COUNCIL

www.westoxon.gov.uk

Principal Office

Council Offices, Woodgreen, Witney, Oxfordshire OX28 1NB
Telephone: (01993) 861000; FAX: (01993) 861450

Environmental Services; Housing Services

Elmfield, New Yatt Road, Witney, Oxfordshire OX28 1PB
Telephone: (01993) 861000

Function	Chief Officer	Title	Location
Chief Executive	Mr G Bonner	Chief Executive	Woodgreen

DISTRICT COUNCILS

Electoral Registration	Mr K Butler	Head of Administrative Services	Woodgreen
Environmental Health	Ms C James	Strategic Director (Environment)	Elmfield
Finance	Mr V Allison	Strategic Director (Resources)	Woodgreen
Legal Services	Ms C Redzikowska	Head of Legal Services	Woodgreen
Leisure	Mr M Prosser	Head of Cultural Services	Woodgreen
Local Land Charges	Mr G O'Brien	Land Charges Supervisor	Elmfield
Planning	Mr A Tucker	Strategic Director (Development)	Elmfield
Technical Services	Ms G Davis;	Head of Environmental Policy & Development;	
	Mr L Wilks	Head of Street Scene	Woodgreen

Parish Councils in the authority's area: Alvescot; Ascott under Wychwood; Asthal; Aston, Cote, Shifford & Chimney; Bampton; Black Bourton; Bladon; Brize Norton; Cassington; Chadlington; Churchill & Sarsden; Clanfield; Combe; Crawley; Curbridge & Lew; Ducklington; Enstone; Eynsham; Filkins & Broughton Poggs; Finstock; Freeland; Fulbrook; Great Tew; Hailey; Hanborough; Kingham; Langford; Leafield; Milton under Wychwood; Minster Lovell; North Leigh; Northmoor; Over Norton; Ramsden; Rollright; Salford; Sandford St Martin; Shilton; Shipton under Wychwood; South Leigh; Spelsbury; Standlake; Stanton Harcourt; Steeple Barton; Stonesfield; Swerford; Swinbrook & Widford; Tackley; Wootton.

Parish Meetings in the authority's area: Blenheim; Broadwell; Bruern; Chastleton; Chilson; Cornbury & Wychwood; Cornwell; Fawler; Fifield; Glympton; Grafton & Radcot; Hardwick with Yelford; Heythrop; Holwell; Idbury; Kelmscott; Kencot; Kiddington with Asterleigh; Little Faringdon; Little Tew; Lyneham; Rousham; Taynton; Westcot Barton; Westwell; Worton.

Town Councils in the authority's area: Burford; Carterton; Charlbury; Chipping Norton; Witney; Woodstock.

WEST SOMERSET DISTRICT COUNCIL

www.westsomerset.gov.uk

Williton Office
20 Fore Street, Williton, Taunton, Somerset TA4 4QA
Telephone: (01643) 703704; FAX: (01984) 633022; DX 117701 Williton

Minehead Office
37 Blenheim Road, Minehead TA24 5PS
Telephone: (01643) 703704

Function	Chief Officer	Title	Location
Chief Executive	Mr T Howes	Chief Executive	Williton
Electoral Registration	Mrs E Day	Electoral Services Officer	Williton
Environmental Health	Mr I Timms	Environmental Health & Licensing Manager .	Williton
Finance	Mr R Latham	Deputy Chief Executive	Williton
Housing	Mr M Ali	Housing Manager	Minehead
Leisure	Mr N Hutchinson	Leisure Development Officer	Williton
Local Land Charges	Mrs J Evans	Land Charges Clerk	Williton
Planning	Mr G Symons	Planning Manager	Williton
Purchasing & Supplies	Mrs J Grieve	Reprographics Assistant	Williton
Technical Services	Mr S Watts	Liveability Manager	Williton

Parish Councils in the authority's area: Bicknoller; Brompton Ralph; Brompton Regis; Brushford; Carhampton; Clatworthy; Crowcombe; Cutcombe; Dunster; East Quantoxhead; Elworthy; Exford; Exmoor; Exton; Holford; Huish Champflower; Kilve; Luccombe; Luxborough; Monksilver; Nettlecombe; Oare; Old Cleeve; Porlock; Sampford Brett; Selworthy & Minehead Without; Skilgate; Stogumber; Stogursey; Stringston; Timberscombe; Treborough; Upton; West Quantoxhead; Williton; Winsford; Withycombe; Withypool & Hawkridge; Wootton Courtenay.

Town Councils in the authority's area: Dulverton; Minehead; Watchet.

DISTRICT COUNCILS

WEST WILTSHIRE DISTRICT COUNCIL

www.westwiltshire.gov.uk

Principal Office

Council Offices, Bradley Road, Trowbridge, Wiltshire BA14 0RD
Telephone: (01225) 776655; FAX: (01225) 770316; DX 116891 Trowbridge 3

Function	Chief Officer	Title	Location
Chief Executive	Mr A Pate	Chief Executive	Council Offices
Electoral Registration	Mr P Woodcock	Corporate Officer (Democratic Services)	Council Offices
Environmental Health	Mr T Darsley	Corporate Officer (Policy)	Council Offices
Housing	Mr T Darsley	Corporate Officer (Policy)	Council Offices
Legal Services	Mr P Woodcock	Corporate Officer (Democratic Services)	Council Offices
Leisure	Mr P Woodcock	Corporate Officer (Democratic Services)	Council Offices
Local Land Charges	Mr P Woodcock	Corporate Officer (Democratic Services)	Council Offices
Planning	Mr T Darsley	Corporate Officer (Policy)	Council Offices

Parish Councils in the authority's area: Atworth; Boyton; Bratton; Broughton Gifford; Chapmanslade; Chitterne; Codford; Corsley; Coulston; Dilton Marsh; Edington; Great Hinton; Heytesbury; Heywood; Hilperton; Holt; Horningsham; Imber; Keevil; Knook; Limpley Stoke; Longbridge Deverill; Melksham Without; Monkton Farleigh; North Bradley; Semington; South Wraxall; Southwick; Staverton; Steeple Ashton; Stockton; Sutton Veny; Upper Deverills; Upton Lovell; Upton Scudamore; West Ashton; Westwood; Wingfield; Winsley.

Parish Meetings in the authority's area: Bishopstrow; Bulkington; Norton Bavant; Sherrington.

Town Councils in the authority's area: Bradford on Avon; Melksham; Trowbridge; Warminster; Westbury.

WEYMOUTH & PORTLAND BOROUGH COUNCIL

www.weymouth.gov.uk

Principal Office

Council Offices, North Quay, Weymouth, Dorset DT4 8TA
Telephone: (01305) 761222; FAX: (01305) 760971

Function	Chief Officer	Title	Location
Chief Executive	Mr T Grainger	Chief Executive & Director of Policy	Council Offices
Electoral Registration	Mr I Locke	Director of Community Services	Council Offices
Environmental Health	Mr R Burgess	Director of Environmental Services	Council Offices
Finance	Mr J Vaughan	Finance Manager	Council Offices
Housing	Mrs J Evans	Housing Advice Manager	Council Offices
Legal Services	Ms J Earns	Legal Services Manager	Council Offices
Leisure	Mr I Locke	Director of Community Services	Council Offices
Local Land Charges	Mr I Locke	Director of Community Services	Council Offices
Planning	Mr R Burgess	Director of Environmental Services	Council Offices
Technical Services	Mr R Burgess	Director of Environmental Services	Council Offices

Town Council in the authority's area: Portland.

WINCHESTER CITY COUNCIL

www.winchester.gov.uk

Principal Office

City Offices, Colebrook Street, Winchester, Hampshire SO23 9LJ
Telephone: (01962) 840222; FAX: (01962) 841365; DX 120400 Winchester 5

Planning Department

Avalon House, Chesil Street, Winchester, Hampshire SO23 0HU

Function	Chief Officer	Title	Location
Chief Executive	Mr S Eden	Chief Executive	City Offices

Electoral Registration	Mr S Whetnall	City Secretary & Solicitor	City Offices
Environmental Health	Mr R Merrett	Director of Health & Housing	City Offices
Finance	Ms S Boden	Director of Finance	City Offices
Housing	Mr R Merrett	Director of Health & Housing	City Offices
Legal Services	Mr S Whetnall	City Secretary & Solicitor	City Offices
Leisure	Mr S Tilbury	Director of Community Services	City Offices
Local Land Charges	Mr S Whetnall	City Secretary & Solicitor	City Offices
Planning	Mr R Cooper	Director of Development Services	Avalon House
Purchasing & Supplies	Ms S Boden	Director of Finance	City Offices

Parish Councils in the authority's area: Badger Farm; Bighton; Bishops Sutton; Bishops Waltham; Boarhunt; Bramdean & Hinton Ampner; Cheriton; Colden Common; Compton & Shawford; Corhampton & Meonstoke; Crawley; Curdridge; Denmead; Droxford; Durley; Hambledon; Headbourne Worthy; Hursley; Itchen Stoke & Ovington; Itchen Valley; Kilmeston; Kingsworthy; Littleton & Harestock; Micheldever; Northington; Old Alresford; Olivers Battery; Otterbourne; Owslebury; Shedfield; Soberton; South Wonston; Southwick & Widley; Sparsholt; Swanmore; Tichborne; Twyford; Upham; West Meon; Whiteley; Wickham; Wonston.

Parish Meetings in the authority's area: Beauworth; Chilcomb; Exton; Warnford.

Town Councils in the authority's area: New Alresford.

ROYAL BOROUGH OF WINDSOR & MAIDENHEAD

The Royal Borough of Windsor & Maidenhead became a unitary authority on 1 April 1998.

WOKING BOROUGH COUNCIL

www.woking.gov.uk

Principal Office

Civic Offices, Gloucester Square, Woking, Surrey GU21 6YL
Telephone: (01483) 755855; FAX: (01483) 768746; DX 2931 Woking

Function	Chief Officer	Title	Location
Chief Executive	Mr P Russell	Chief Executive	Civic Offices
Electoral Registration	Mr P Russell	Chief Executive	Civic Offices
Environmental Health	Mr C Fairlamb	Borough Planning Officer	Civic Offices
Finance	Mr S Bonsor	Head of Resources	Civic Offices
Housing	Ms J Chapman	Head of Housing Services	Civic Offices
Legal Services	Mr A Harrison	Borough Secretary	Civic Offices
Leisure	Ms S Barham	Head of Community Services	Civic Offices
Local Land Charges	Mr R Lee	Head of Customer Services	Civic Offices
Planning	Mr C Fairlamb	Borough Planning Officer	Civic Offices
Purchasing & Supplies	Mr A Harrison	Borough Secretary	Civic Offices

Parish Councils & Parish Meetings in the authority's area: Byfleet.

Town Councils in the authority's area: none.

WOKINGHAM DISTRICT COUNCIL

Wokingham District Council became a unitary authority on 1 April 1998.

WOODSPRING DISTRICT COUNCIL

Woodspring District Council was abolished on 31 March 1996; see now North Somerset District Council.

DISTRICT COUNCILS

WORCESTER CITY COUNCIL

www.cityofworcester.gov.uk

Principal Office
Guildhall, Worcester WR1 2EY
Telephone: (01905) 723471; FAX: (01905) 722028; DX 716287 Worcester

Department of Community Services; Department of Development Services
Farrier House, Farrier Street, Worcester WR1 3BH
Telephone: (01905) 723471

Orchard House, Farrier Street, Worcester WR1 3BW
Telephone: (01905) 723471; FAX: (01905) 722350

Function	Chief Officer	Title	Location
Chief Executive	Mr D T Wareing	Chief Executive	Guildhall
Environmental Health	Mr M Gillies	Head of Environmental Health	Farrier House
Finance	Mr G Lucas	Head of Finance	Guildhall
Housing	Mr I Harkess	Housing Services	Farrier House
Legal Services	Miss D Porter	Head of Legal & Democratic Services	Guildhall
Leisure	Mr A Stuttard	Head of Community Services	Orchard House
Local Land Charges	Miss D Porter	Head of Legal & Democratic Services	Guildhall
Planning	Mr S McNidder	Head of Development Services	Farrier House
Technical Services	Mr S McNidder	Head of Development Services	Farrier House

Parish Councils in the authority's area: St Peter the Great County; Warndon.

WORTHING BOROUGH COUNCIL

www.worthing.gov.uk

Chief Executive's Department; Resources Department; Services Department
Town Hall, Chapel Road, Worthing, West Sussex BN11 1HA
Telephone: (01903) 239999; FAX: (01903) 236552

Housing Services; Services Department
Portland House, Richmond Road, Worthing BN11 1HH
Telephone: (01903) 239999; FAX: (01903) 207035

Function	Chief Officer	Title	Location
Chief Executive	Miss S Grady	Chief Executive	Town Hall
Electoral Registration	Mr P Collington	Assistant Director (Democratic Services & Scrutiny)	Town Hall
Environmental Health	Mr H Smith	Assistant Director (Health & Housing Services)	Portland House
Finance	Mr Smith	Director of Resources	Town Hall
Legal Services	Mr B Johnson	Assistant Director (Legal Services)	Town Hall
Leisure	Mr J Thorpe	Assistant Director (Leisure & Cultural Services)	Town Hall
Local Land Charges	Mr B Johnson	Assistant Director (Legal Services)	Town Hall
Planning	Mr T Everitt	Director of Services	Portland House
Purchasing & Supplies	Mr P Collington	Assistant Director (Democratic Services & Scrutiny)	Town Hall
Technical Services	Mr C Harrison	Assistant Director (Property Services)	Portland House

Parish Councils & Parish Meetings in the authority's area: none.

Town Councils in the authority's area: none.

DISTRICT COUNCILS

THE WREKIN DISTRICT COUNCIL

The Wrekin District Council became a unitary authority on 1 April 1998; see Telford & Wrekin Council.

WYCHAVON DISTRICT COUNCIL

www.wychavon.gov.uk

Principal Office

Civic Centre, Queen Elizabeth Drive, Pershore, Worcestershire WR10 1PT
Telephone: (01386) 565000; FAX: (01386) 561091; DX 25934 Pershore

Function	Chief Officer	Title	Location
Chief Executive	Mr Jack Hegarty	Managing Director	Civic Centre
Environmental Health	Mr Steve Jorden	Head of Environmental Services	Civic Centre
Finance	Mrs Sonia Rees	Head of Resources	Civic Centre
Housing	Mrs Liz Dyde	Head of Housing & Revenues	Civic Centre
Legal Services	Mr Ian Marshall	Head of Legal Services	Civic Centre
Leisure	Mr Brian Norfolk	Head of Corporate Projects	Civic Centre
Planning	Mrs Gill Collin	Head of Planning	Civic Centre

Parish Councils in the authority's area: Abbots Morton; Aldington; Ashton under Hill; Aston Somerville; Badsey; Beckford; Besford; Birlingham; Bishampton; Bradley; Bredon; Bredons Norton; Bretforton; Bricklehampton; Broadway; Charlton; Childswickham; Church Lench; Cleeve Prior; Conderton; Cookhill; Cropthorne; Crowle; Defford; Dodderhill; Dormston; Doverdale; Drakes Broughton & Wadborough; Eckington; Elmbridge; Elmley Castle; Elmley Lovett; Fladbury; Flyford Flavell; Grafton Flyford; Great Comberton; Hadzor; Hampton Lovett; Hanbury; Hartlebury; Harvington; Hill & Moor; Himbleton; Hindlip, Martin Hussingtree & Salwarpe; Hinton on the Green; Honeybourne; Huddington; Inkberrow; Kemerton; Kington; Little Comberton; Naunton Beauchamp; Netherton; North Claines; North & Middle Littleton; North Piddle; Norton & Lenchwick; Norton Juxta Kempsey; Oddingley; Offenham; Ombersley; Overbury; Pebworth; Peopleton; Pinvin; Pirton; Rous Lench; Sedgeberrow; South Littleton; Stock; Stoulton; Strensham; Throckmorton; Tibberton; Upton Snodsbury; Upton Warren; Westwood; Whittington; Wick; Wickhamford; Wyre Piddle.

Parish Meetings in the authority's area: Abberton; Bickmarsh; Bredicot; Broughton Hackett; Churchill; Spetchley; White Ladies Aston.

Town Councils in the authority's area: Droitwich Spa; Evesham; Pershore.

WYCOMBE DISTRICT COUNCIL

www.wycombe.gov.uk

Principal Office

Queen Victoria Road, High Wycombe, Buckinghamshire HP11 1BB
Telephone: (01494) 461000; FAX: (01494) 461292; DX 4411 High Wycombe

Function	Chief Officer	Title	Location
Chief Executive	Mr Richard J Cummins	Chief Executive & Director of Finance	Qn Victoria Rd
Electoral Registration	Ms Julie Mills	Electoral Services Manager	Qn Victoria Rd
Environmental Health	Mrs Caroline Hughes	Head of Environmental Services	Qn Victoria Rd
Finance	Mr John Piddington	Head of Financial Services	Qn Victoria Rd
Housing	Mr Ian Westgate	Director of Community & Housing	Qn Victoria Rd
Legal Services	Mr David Dongray	District Solicitor	Qn Victoria Rd
Local Land Charges	Ms Julie Mills	Electoral Services Manager	Qn Victoria Rd
Planning	Mr Chris Swanwick	Director of Planning & Major Projects	Qn Victoria Rd
Purchasing & Supplies	Mr Simon Blackett	Purchasing Officer	Qn Victoria Rd
Technical Services	Mr Steve Bramhill	Head of Information Systems	Qn Victoria Rd

DISTRICT COUNCILS

Parish Councils in the authority's area: Bledlow-cum-Saunderton; Bradenham; Chepping Wycombe; Downley; Ellesborough; Fawley; Great & Little Hampden; Great & Little Kimble; Great Marlow; Hambleden; Hazlemere; Hedsor; Hughenden; Ibstone; Lacey Green; Lane End; Little Marlow; Longwick-cum-Ilmer; Medmenham; Piddington & Wheeler End; Radnage; Stokenchurch; Turville; West Wycombe; Wooburn.

Town Councils in the authority's area: Marlow; Princes Risborough.

High Wycombe Charter Trustees.

WYRE BOROUGH COUNCIL

www.wyrebc.gov.uk

Principal Office
Civic Centre, Breck Road, Poulton-le-Fylde, Lancashire FY6 7PU
Telephone: (01253) 891000; FAX: (01253) 899000

Function	Chief Officer	Title	Location
Chief Executive ·	J Corry	Managing Director	Civic Centre
Environmental Health	R Atkinson;	Divisional Manager (Commercial);	Civic Centre
	N Bailey	Divisional Manager (Environmental Protection)	Civic Centre
Finance	B Parsonage	Treasurer	Civic Centre
Housing	S Sylvester	Housing Services Manager	Civic Centre
Legal Services	E O'Connor	Legal Services Manager	Civic Centre
Leisure	T Pridmore	Head of Leisure and Cultural Services	Civic Centre
Local Land Charges	E O'Connor	Legal Services Manager	Civic Centre
Planning	[Vacant]	Divisional Manager (Planning)	Civic Centre
Purchasing & Supplies	L Wright	Office Services Manager	Civic Centre

Parish Councils in the authority's area: Barnacre with Bonds; Bilsborrow; Bleasdale; Cabus; Catterall; Claughton-on-Brock; Forton; Great Eccleston; Hambleton; Inskip with Sowerby; Kirkland; Myerscough; Nateby; Nether Wyresdale; Out Rawcliffe; Pilling; Stalmine with Staynall; Upper Rawcliffe with Tarnacre; Winmarleigh.

Town Councils in the authority's area: Garstang; Preesall.

WYRE FOREST DISTRICT COUNCIL

www.wyreforestdc.gov.uk

Principal Office
Civic Centre, Stourport-on-Severn, Worcestershire DY13 8UJ
Telephone: (01562) 820505; FAX: (01299) 879688

**Financial Services; Planning, Health & Environment Services;
Housing & Environmental Health**
Duke House, Clensmore Street, Kidderminster DY10 2JX

Cultural, Leisure & Commercial Services
Green Street, Kidderminster DY10 1HA
Telephone: (01562) 820505; FAX: (01562) 829027

Function	Chief Officer	Title	Location
Chief Executive	Mr W Delin	Chief Executive	Civic Centre
Electoral Registration	Mr A Pilgrim	Principal Elections Officer	Civic Centre
Environmental Health	Mr M Parker	Head of Planning, Health & Environment	Duke House
Finance	Mr K Bannister	Head of Financial Services	Duke House
Housing	Mr T Rice	Housing Services Manager	Duke House
Legal Services	Miss C Caygill	Head of Legal & Democratic Services	Civic Centre

DISTRICT COUNCILS

Leisure	Mr A W Dickens	Head of Cultural, Leisure & Commercial Services	Green Street
Local Land Charges	Mrs N Green		Civic Centre
Planning	Mr M Parker	Head of Planning, Health & Environment	Duke House

Parish Councils in the authority's area: Broome; Chaddesley Corbett; Churchill & Blakedown; Kidderminster Foreign; Rock; Rushock; Stone; Upper Arley; Wolverley & Cookley.

Parish Meeting in the authority's area: Ribbesford.

Town Councils in the authority's area: Bewdley; Stourport-on-Severn.

Kidderminster Charter Trustees.

YORK CITY COUNCIL

York City Council became a unitary authority on 1 April 1996.

WALES

ABERCONWY BOROUGH COUNCIL
See now Conwy County Borough Council.

ALYN & DEESIDE DISTRICT COUNCIL
See now Flintshire County Council.

ISLE OF ANGLESEY COUNTY COUNCIL

www.ynysmon.gov.uk

Principal Office
Swyddfa'r Sir, Llangefni, Anglesey LL77 7TW
Telephone: (01248) 750057; FAX: (01248) 750839

Function	Chief Officer	Title	Location
Chief Executive	Geraint F Edwards	Managing Director	Llangefni
Education	Richard Parry Jones	Corporate Director – Education & Leisure	Llangefni
Electoral Registration	Geraint F Edwards	Managing Director	Llangefni
Environmental Health	Arthur W Owen	Corporate Director – Planning & Environment	Llangefni
Finance	David G Elis-Williams	Corporate Director – Finance	Llangefni
Housing	Byron Williams	Corporate Director – Housing & Social Services	Llangefni
Legal Services	Julie Openshaw	Director of Legal Services	Llangefni
Leisure	Richard Parry Jones	Corporate Director – Education & Leisure	Llangefni
Local Land Charges	Geraint F Edwards	Managing Director	Llangefni
Planning	Arthur W Owen	Corporate Director – Planning & Environment	Llangefni
Social Services	Byron Williams	Corporate Director – Housing & Social Services	Llangefni
Technical Services	Dewi Rowlands	Corporate Director – Highways, Transportation & Property	Llangefni
Trading Standards	Arthur W Owen	Corporate Director – Planning & Environment	Llangefni

On 1 April 1996, Isle of Anglesey County Council took over from Ynys Môn/Isle of Anglesey Borough Council.

Community Councils in the authority's area: Aberffraw; Bodedern; Bodffordd; Bodorgan; Bryngwran; Cwm Cadnant; Cylch-y-Garn; Llanbadrig; Llanddaniel Fab; Llanddona; Llanddyfnan; Llaneilian; Llannerchy-y-Medd; Llaneugrad; Llanfachraeth; Llanfaelog; Llanfaethlu; Llanfair-Mathafarn-Eithaf; Llanfairpwll; Llanfair-yn-Neubwll; Llanfihangelesceifiog; Llangoed; Llangristiolus; Llanidan; Mechell; Moelfre; Penmynydd; Pentraeth; Rhoscolyn; Rhosybol; Rhosyr; Trearddur; Tref Alaw; Trewalchmai; Valley.

Town Councils in the authority's area: Amlwch; Beaumaris; Holyhead; Llangefni; Menai Bridge.

ARFON BOROUGH COUNCIL
See now Gwynedd County Council.

WALES

BLAENAU GWENT BOROUGH COUNCIL
See now Blaenau Gwent County Borough Council; Monmouthshire County Council.

COUNTY BOROUGH OF BLAENAU GWENT

www.blaenau-gwent.gov.uk

Principal Office
Municipal Offices, Civic Centre, Ebbw Vale, Gwent NP23 6XB
Telephone: (01495) 350555; FAX: (01495) 301255; DX 43956 Ebbw Vale

Community Services Department
Central Depot, Barleyfield Way, Nantyglo, Gwent NP23 4YF
Telephone: (01495) 311556; FAX: (01495) 312357

Regeneration Department
Business Resource Centre, Tredegar, Gwent NP22 3AA
Telephone: (01495) 355701; FAX: (01495) 355783

Lifelong Learning and Strategic Partnerships
Victoria House, Victoria Business Park, Ebbw Vale, Gwent NP23 6ER
Telephone: (01495) 355335; FAX: (01495) 355495

Function	Chief Officer	Title	Location
Chief Executive	R Morrison	Chief Executive	Municipal Offices
Education	J Pearce	Director of Lifelong Learning & Strategic Partnerships	Victoria House
Electoral Registration	S A Bosson	Chief Policy Officer	Municipal Offices
Finance	D Waggett	Director of Resources	Municipal Offices
Legal Services	D John	Chief Legal Officer	Municipal Offices
Leisure	J Parsons	Director of Community Services	Central Depot
Local Land Charges	D John	Chief Legal Officer	Municipal Offices
Social Services	M Murphy	Deputy Director of Social Services	Municipal Offices
Technical Services	J Parsons	Director of Community Services	Central Depot

On 1 April 1996, Blaenau Gwent County Borough Council took over from Blaenau Gwent Borough Council, excluding the community of Llanelly.

Community Councils in the authority's area: Abertillery & Llanhilleth.

Town Councils in the authority's area: Brynmawr; Nantyglo & Blaina; Tredegar.

BRECKNOCK BOROUGH COUNCIL
See now Powys County Council.

BRIDGEND COUNTY BOROUGH COUNCIL

www.bridgend.gov.uk

Principal Office
Civic Offices, Angel Street, Bridgend, CF31 4WB
Telephone: (01656) 643643

Directorate of Personal Services;
Directorate of Education, Leisure & Community Services
Sunnyside, Sunnyside Road, Bridgend CF31 4WB
Telephone: (01656) 642200

Function	Chief Officer	Title	Location
Chief Executive	Mr I K Lewis	Chief Executive Officer	Civic Offices
Education	Mr D Matthews	Director of Education, Leisure & Community Services	Sunnyside
Electoral Registration	Mr I K Lewis	Chief Executive Officer	Civic Offices
Environmental Health	Mr R Jones	Director of Environmental & Planning Services	Civic Offices

Finance	Mr L James	Director of Corporate Services	Civic Offices
Housing	Mr J McKirdle	Head of Service, Housing & Community Wellbeing	Civic Offices
Legal Services	Mr A Jolley	Head of Legal Services	Civic Offices
Leisure	Mr M Shephard	Assistant Director of Education, Leisure & Community Services	Sunnyside
Local Land Charges	Mr A Jolley	Head of Legal Services	Civic Offices
Planning	Mr R Jones	Director of Environmental & Planning Services	Civic Offices
Purchasing & Supplies	Mr L James	Director of Corporate Services	Civic Offices
Social Services	Mr A Garthwaite	Director of Personal Services	Sunnyside
Technical Services	Mr R Fletcher	Assistant Director of Architectural & Technical Services	Civic Offices
Trading Standards	Mr M Stoddart	Assistant Director of Public Protection	Civic Offices

On 1 April 1996, Bridgend County Borough Council succeeded Ogwr Borough Council, but excluding the communities of Wick, St Bride's Major and Ewenny.

Community Councils in the authority's area: Brackla; Cefn Cribwr; Coity Higher; Cornelly; Coychurch Higher; Coychurch Lower; Garw Valley; Laleston; Llangynwyd Lower; Llangynwyd Middle; Merthyr Mawr; Newcastle Higher; Ogmore Valley; Pyle; St Brides Minor; Ynsawdre.

Town Councils in the authority's area: Bridgend; Maesteg; Pencoed; Porthcawl.

CAERNARFONSHIRE & MERIONETHSHIRE COUNTY COUNCIL
See now Gwynedd County Council.

CAERPHILLY COUNTY BOROUGH COUNCIL
www.caerphilly.gov.uk
Principal Office
Council Offices, Nelson Road, Tredomen, Ystrad Mynach, Hengoed CF82 7WF
Telephone: (01443) 815588

Directorate of the Environment
Council Offices, Pontllanfraith, Blackwood NP12 2YW
Telephone: (01495) 226622

Directorate of Social Services
Council Offices, Hawtin Road, Gellihaf, Blackwood NP12 2PZ
Telephone: (01443) 815588

Directorate of Education
Council Offices, Ystrad Mynach, Hengoed CF82 7EP
Telephone: (01443) 815588

Procurement Services
Tir-y-Berth Depot, New Road, Hengoed
Telephone: (01443) 863160

Function	Chief Officer	Title	Location
Chief Executive	Mr Malgwyn Davies	Chief Executive	Nelson Road
Education	Mr David Hopkins	Director of Education & Leisure	Ystrad Mynach
Electoral Registration	Mr Bob Screen	Electoral Services Manager	Nelson Road
Housing	Mr Cris Davies	Chief Housing Officer	Pontllanfraith
Legal Services	Mr Daniel Perkins	Head of Legal Services	Nelson Road
Leisure	Mr Peter Gomer	Head of Leisure	Ystrad Mynach
Local Land Charges	Mr Roger Webb	Director of the Environment	Pontllanfraith
Planning	Mr Pat Mears	Chief Planning Officer	Pontllanfraith
Purchasing & Supplies	Ms Liz Lucas	Head of Procurement	Tir-y-Berth Dep
Social Services	Mr Jo Howsam	Director of Social Services	Hawtin Road

| Technical Services | Mr Roger Webb | Director of the Environment | Pontllanfraith |
| Trading Standards | Mr Steve Delehaye | Chief Trading Standards Officer | Pontllanfraith |

On 1 April 1996, Caerphilly County Borough Council took over from Islwyn Borough Council and Rhymney Valley District Council, and, in part, from Gwent and Mid Glamorgan County Councils.

Community Councils in the authority's area: Aber Valley; Bedwas; Crumlin; Darren Valley; Gelligaer; Llanbradach; Machen; Maesycwmmer; Nelson; New Tredegar; Newbridge; Penyrheol; Rhymney; Risca; Rudry; Van; Ystrad Mynach.

Town Councils in the authority's area: Bargoed; Blackwood; Caerphilly.

CARDIFF CITY COUNCIL
See now Cardiff County Council.

CARDIFF COUNTY COUNCIL

www.cardiff.gov.uk

Principal Office
Cardiff County Hall, Atlantic Wharf, Cardiff CF10 4UW
Telephone: (029) 2087 2000; FAX: (029) 2087 2020

Function	Chief Officer	Title	Location
Chief Executive	Byron Davies	Chief Executive	County Hall
Education	Hugh Knight	Chief Schools Services Officer	County Hall
Electoral Registration	Peter Woodward	Principal Officer	County Hall
Environmental Health	Malcolm Evans	Chief Regulatory Officer	County Hall
Finance	Phillip Higgins	Corporate Manager	County Hall
Housing	Sarah McGill	Chief Housing, Advice & Benefits Officer	County Hall
Legal Services	[Vacant]	Corporate Manager	County Hall
Leisure	Trevor Gough	Chief Leisure and Lifelong Learning Officer	County Hall
Local Land Charges	Stephanie King-Davies	Chief Legal Services Officer	County Hall
Planning	Tony Riches	Chief Strategic Planning & Neighbourhood Renewal Officer	County Hall
Purchasing & Supplies	Christine Salter	Chief Financial Services Officer	County Hall
Social Services	Maria Michael; Margaret Evans	Chief Childrens Services Officer; Chief Adult Services Officer	County Hall
Trading Standards	Malcolm Evans	Chief Regulatory Officer	County Hall

On 1 April 1996, City & County of Cardiff Council took over from Cardiff City Council and, in part, from South Glamorgan County Council.

Community Councils in the authority's area: Lisvane; Old St Mellons; Pentyrch; Radyr & Morganstown; St Fagans; Tongwynlais.

CARMARTHEN DISTRICT COUNCIL
See now Carmarthenshire County Council.

CARMARTHENSHIRE COUNTY COUNCIL

www.carmarthenshire.gov.uk

Principal Office
County Hall, Carmarthen SA31 1JP
Telephone: (01267) 234567

Recreation & Leisure Department
Ty'r Nant, Trostre, Llanelli SA14 9UT
Telephone: (01554) 747510

Function	Chief Officer	Title	Location
Chief Executive	Mr Mark James	Chief Executive	County Hall
Education	Mr Alun Davies	Director of Education & Leisure	County Hall
Electoral Registration	Mr Peter Jones	Head of Statutory Services	County Hall
Environmental Health	Mr Philip Davies	Head of Public Protection	County Hall
Finance	Mr Roger Jones	Director of Resources	County Hall
Housing	Mr Bruce McLernon	Director of Social Care & Housing	County Hall
Legal Services	Ms Lyn Thomas	Head of Legal Services	County Hall
Leisure	Mr Colin James	Head of Recreation & Leisure	Ty'r Nant
Local Land Charges	Ms Lyn Thomas	Head of Legal Services	County Hall
Planning	Mr Eifion Bowen	Head of Planning Services	County Hall
Purchasing & Supplies	Mr Clive Boyles	Head of Corporate Finance	County Hall
Social Services	Mr Bruce McLernon	Director of Social Care & Housing	County Hall
Technical Services	Mr Richard Workman	Director of Technical Services	County Hall
Trading Standards	Mr Philip Davies	Head of Public Protection	County Hall

On 1 April 1996, Carmarthenshire County Council took over from Carmarthen District Council, Dinefwr Borough Council, Llanelli Borough Council and the Eastern division of Dyfed County Council.

Community Councils in the authority's area: Abergwili; Abernant; Betws; Bronwydd; Cenarth; Cilycwm; Cilymaenllwyd; Clynderwen; Cynwyl Elfed; Cynwyl Gaeo; Dyffrn Cennen; Eglwys Gymyn; Gorslas; Henllanfallteg; Llanarthne; Llanboidy; Llanddarog; Llanddeusant; Llanddowror; Llandybie; Llandyfaelog; Llanedi; Llanegwad; Llanfair-ar-y-bryn; Llanfihangel Aberbythych; Llanfihangel-ar-Arth; Llanfihangel-Rhos-y-Corn; Llanfynydd; Llangadog; Llangain; Llangathen; Llangeler; Llangennech; Llangynnwr; Llangyndeyrn; Llangynin; Llangynog; Llanllawddog; Llanllwni; Llan-non; Llanpumsaint; Llansadwrn; Llansawel; Llansteffan; Llanwinio; Llanwrda; Llanybydder; Llanycrwys; Manordeilo & Salem; Meidrim; Myddfai; Newchurch & Merthyr; Pencarreg; Pendine; Pontyberem; Quarter Bach; St Clears; St Ishmael; Talley; Trelech a'r Betws; Trimsaran.

Town Councils in the authority's area: Ammanford; Carmarthen; Cwmamman; Kidwelly; Laugharne; Llandeilo; Llandovery; Llanelli; Llanelli Rural; Newcastle Emlyn ; Pembrey & Burry Port; Whitland.

CEREDIGION COUNTY COUNCIL

www.ceredigion.gov.uk

Principal Office
Neuadd Cyngor Ceredigion, Penmorfa, Aberaeron, Ceredigion SA46 0PA
Telephone: (01545) 570881; FAX: (01545) 572009; DX 92401 Aberaeron

Education & Community Services Department
Swyddfa'r Sir, Marine Terrace, Aberystwyth SY23 2DE
Telephone: (01970) 633655; FAX: (01970) 633663

Finance Department
Town Hall, Queen's Road, Aberystwyth SY23 2EB
Telephone: (01970) 617911; FAX: (01970) 633109

Highways, Property & Works Department
County Hall, Aberaeron SA46 0AT
Telephone: (01545) 570881; FAX: (01545) 571089

Function	Chief Officer	Title	Location
Chief Executive	Mr Owen Watkin	Chief Executive	Penmorfa
Education	Mr Roger Williams	Director of Education & Community Services	Swyddfa´r Sir
Electoral Registration	Mr Owen Watkin	Chief Executive	Penmorfa
Environmental Health	Mr Bryan Thomas	Director of Environmental Services & Housing	Penmorfa
Finance	Mr Gwyn Jones	Director of Finance	Town Hall
Housing	Mr Bryan Thomas	Director of Environmental Services & Housing	Penmorfa

Function	Chief Officer	Title	Location
Legal Services	Miss Bronwen Morgan	Director of Corporate & Legal Services	Penmorfa
Leisure	Mr Roger Williams	Director of Education & Community Services	Swyddfa'r Sir
Local Land Charges	Miss Bronwen Morgan	Director of Corporate & Legal Services	Penmorfa
Planning	Mr Bryan Thomas	Director of Environmental Services & Housing	Penmorfa
Social Services	Mr Parry Davies	Director of Social Services	Penmorfa
Technical Services	Mr Huw Morgan	Director of Highways, Property & Works	County Hall
Trading Standards	Mr Bryan Thomas	Director of Environmental Services & Housing	Penmorfa

On 1 April 1996, Ceredigion County Council took over from Ceredigion District Council.

Community Councils in the authority's area: Aberporth; Beulah; Blaenrheidol; Borth; Ceulanamaesmawr; Ciliau Aeron; Dyffryn Arth; Faenor; Genau'r Glyn; Henfynyw; Llanarth; Llanbadarn Fawr; Llancynfelin; Llanddewi Brefi; Llandyfriog; Llandysiliogogo; Llandysul; Llanfair Clydogau; Llanfarian; Llanfihangel Ystrad; Llangeitho; Llangoedmor; Llangrannog; Llangwyryfon; Llangybi; Llanilar; Llanllwchaiarn; Llanrhystud; Llansantffraed; Llanwenog; Llanwnen; Lledrod; Melindwr; Nantcwnlle; Penbryn; Pontarfynach; Tirymynach; Trawsgoed; Trefeurig; Tregaron; Troedyraur; Y Ferwig; Ysbyty Ystwyth; Ysgubor Y Coed; Ystrad Fflur; Ystrad Meurig.

Town Councils in the authority's area: Aberaeron; Aberystwyth; Aberteifi/Cardigan; Llanbedr Pont Steffan/ Lampeter; Cei Newydd/New Quay.

CEREDIGION DISTRICT COUNCIL
See now Ceredigion County Council.

CLWYD COUNTY COUNCIL
See now Conwy County Borough Council; Denbighshire County Council; Flintshire County Council; Powys County Council; Wrexham County Borough Council.

COLWYN BOROUGH COUNCIL
See now Conwy County Borough Council.

CONWY COUNTY BOROUGH COUNCIL

www.conwy.gov.uk
Principal Office
Bodlondeb, Conwy LL32 8DU
Telephone: (01492) 574000; FAX: (01492) 592114; DX 24628 Conwy

Education Department; Leisure Services
Government Buildings, Dinerth Road, Rhos-on-Sea LL28 4UL
Telephone: (01492) 574000; FAX: (01492) 541311

Environmental Health Department; Planning Department; Trading Standards Department
Civic Offices, Colwyn Bay LL29 8AR
Telephone: (01492) 574000; FAX: (01492) 512637

Housing Department
Mochdre Offices, Conway Road, Mochdre, Colwyn Bay LL29 8AR
Telephone: (01492) 574000; FAX: (01492) 574227

Social Services Department
Builder Street, Llandudno LL30 1DA
Telephone: (01492) 574000; FAX: (01492) 874739

Function	Chief Officer	Title	Location
Chief Executive	Mr C D Barker	Chief Executive	Bodlondeb
Education	Mr E Williams	Corporate Director of Lifelong Learning	Gov. Bldgs

Electoral Registration	Mr R Evans	Corporate Director of Performance	Bodlondeb
Environmental Health	Mr C Phillips	Chief Environmental Regulation Officer	Civic Offices
Finance	Mr K Finch	Director of Finance & Resources	Bodlondeb
Housing	Mr A Bowden	Chief Housing Officer	Mochdre Offs
Legal Services	Mr R Evans	Corporate Director of Performance	Bodlondeb
Leisure	Mr P Frost	Assistant Director of Leisure	Gov. Bldgs
Local Land Charges	Mr R Evans	Corporate Director of Performance	Bodlondeb
Planning	Mr C D Baker	Chief Executive	Bodlondeb
Purchasing & Supplies	Mr R Evans	Corporate Director of Performance	Bodlondeb
Social Services	Ms B E Jones	Director of Social Care & Housing	Builder Street
Technical Services	Mr B Bond	Assistant Director of Environmental Services	Civic Offices
Trading Standards	Mr C Phillips	Chief Environmental Regulation Officer	Civic Offices

On 1 April 1996, Conwy County Borough Council took over from Aberconwy and Colwyn Borough Councils, but excluding (from Colwyn) the communities of Cefnmeiriadog and Trefnant.

Community Councils in the authority's area: Betws-y-Coed; Betws-yn-Rhos; Bro Garmon; Bro Machno; Caerhun; Capel Curig; Cerrigydrudion; Dolgarrog; Dolwyddelan; Eglwysbach; Henryd; Llanddoged a Maenan; Llanddulas & Rhyd-y-Foel; Llanfairtalhaiarn; Llanfihangel Glyn Myfyr; Llangernyw; Llangwm; Llannefydd; Llansanffraid Glan Conwy; Llansannan; Llysfaen; Mochdre; Pentrefoelas; Trefriw; Ysbyty Ifan.

Town Councils in the authority's area: Abergele; Bay of Colwyn; Conwy; Llandudno; Llanfairfechan; Llanrwst; Penmaenmawr; Towyn & Kinmel Bay.

CYNON VALLEY BOROUGH COUNCIL
See now Rhondda, Cynon, Taff County Borough Council.

DELYN BOROUGH COUNCIL
See now Flintshire County Council.

DENBIGHSHIRE COUNTY COUNCIL
www.denbighshire.gov.uk

Principal Office
Council Offices, Wynnstay Road, Ruthin, Denbighshire LL15 1YN
Telephone: (01824) 706000; FAX: (01824) 707446

Lifelong Learning
Caledfryn, Smithfield Road, Denbigh, Denbighshire LL16 3RJ
Telephone: (01824) 706777; FAX: (01824) 706710

County Clerk
Russell House, Churton Road, Rhyl, Denbighshire LL18 3DP
Telephone: (01824) 706374; FAX: (01824) 706389

Environment
Trem Clwyd, Canol y Dre, Ruthin Denbighshire LL15 1QA
Telephone: (01824) 708111; FAX: (01824) 708015

Personal Services
Tŷ Nant, Nant Hall Road, Prestatyn LL19 9LG
Telephone: (01824) 706655; FAX: (01824) 706660

Resources
Council Offices, Wynnstay Road, Ruthin, Denbighshire LL15 1YN
Telephone: (01824) 706000; FAX: (01824) 706045

Function	Chief Officer	Title	Location
Chief Executive	Mr I Miller	Chief Executive	Ruthin
Education	Mrs S Bowen	Corporate Director: Lifelong Learning	Ruthin

WALES

Function	Chief Officer	Title	Location
Electoral Registration	Mr I K Hearle	County Clerk	Rhyl
Environment	Mr I Prys Jones	Corporate Director: Environment	Trem Clwyd
Environmental Health	Mr G Boase	Head of Planning & Public Protection	Ruthin
Finance	Mr A Evans	Corporate Director: Resources	Ruthin
Housing	Ms S Ellis	Corporate Director: Personal Services	Ruthin
Legal Services	Mr I K Hearle	County Clerk	Rhyl
Leisure	Mrs S Bowen	Corporate Director: Lifelong Learning	Ruthin
Local Land Charges	Mr I K Hearle	County Clerk	Rhyl
Planning	Mr I Prys Jones	Corporate Director: Environment	Trem Clwyd
Social Services	Ms S Ellis	Corporate Director: Personal Services	Ruthin
Technical Services	Mr I Prys Jones	Corporate Director: Environment	Trem Clwyd
Trading Standards	Mr G Boase	Head of Planning & Public Protection	Ruthin

On 1 April 1996, Denbighshire County Council took over from Rhuddlan Borough Council and, from Glyndwr District Council, the communities of Aberwheeler, Cynwyd, Llandrillo, Henllan, Denbigh, Llandyrnog, Llangynhafal, Llanynys, Llanrhaeadr-yng-Nghinmeirch, Nantglyn, Cyffylliog, Ruthin, Llanbedr Dyffryn Clwyd, Llanferres, Clocaenog, Efenechtyd, Llandegla, Llanfair Dyffryn Clwyd, Llanarmon-yn-Ial, Llanelidan, Derwen, Betws Gwerfil Goch, Gwyddelwern, Bryneglwys, Corwen & Llangollen; and, from Colwyn Borough Council, the communities of Trefnant and Cefnmeiriadog.

Community Councils in the authority's area: Aberwheeler; Betws Gwerfil Goch; Bodfari; Bryneglwys; Cefn Meiriadog; Clocaenog; Corwen; Cyffylliog; Cynwyd; Derwen; Dyserth; Efenechtyd; Gwyddelwern; Henllan; Llanarmon Yn Ial; Llanbedr DC; Llandegla; Llandrillo; Llandyrnog; Llanelidan; Llanfair DC; Llanferres; Llangynhafal; Llanrhaeadr Y C; Llantysilio; Llanynys; Nantglyn; Trefnant; Tremeirchion, Cwm & Waen.

Town Councils in the authority's area: Bodelwyddan; Denbigh; Llangollen; Ruthin; Prestatyn; Rhuddlan; Rhyl; St Asaph.

DINEFWR BOROUGH COUNCIL
See now Carmarthenshire County Council.

DWYFOR DISTRICT COUNCIL
See now Gwynedd County Council.

DYFED COUNTY COUNCIL
See now Carmarthenshire, Ceredigion and Pembrokeshire County Councils.

FLINTSHIRE COUNTY COUNCIL
www.flintshire.gov.uk

Principal Office
County Hall, Mold, Flintshire CH7 6NB
Telephone: (01352) 752121; FAX: (01352) 758240; DX 708590 Mold 4

Community and Housing
County Offices, Chapel Street, Flint CH6 5WS
Telephone: (01352) 752121; FAX: (01352) 758240

Function	Chief Officer	Title	Location
Chief Executive	Philip McGreevy	Chief Executive	County Hall
Education	John Clutton	Director of Education & Children's Services and Recreation	County Hall
Electoral Registration	Andrew Loveridge	County Secretary	County Hall
Environmental Health	Chris Kay	Director of Transportation, Planning & Environment	County Hall
Finance	Lynne Blake	County Treasurer	County Hall
Housing	Steve Partner	Director of Community & Housing	County Offices

WALES

Function	Chief Officer	Title	Location
Legal Services	Andrew Loveridge	County Secretary	County Hall
Leisure	John Clutton	Director of Education & Children's Services and Recreation	County Hall
Local Land Charges	Andrew Loveridge	County Secretary	County Hall
Planning	Chris Kay	Director of Transportation, Planning & Environment	County Hall
Purchasing & Supplies	Philip McGreevy	Chief Executive	County Hall
Social Services	Susan Lewis	Director of Adult Social Care	County Hall
Technical Services	Steve Partner	Director of Community & Housing	County Offices
Trading Standards	Steve Partner	Director of Community & Housing	County Offices

On 1 April 1996, Flintshire County Council took over from Alyn & Deeside District Council and Delyn Borough Council, and, in part, from Clwyd County Council.

Community Councils in the authority's area: Argoed; Bagillt; Broughton & Bretton; Brynford; Cilcain; Gwernaffield; Gwernymynydd; Halkyn; Hawarden; Higher Kinnerton; Hope; Leeswood; Llanasa; Llanfynydd; Mostyn; Nannerch; Nercwys; Northop; Northop Hall; Penyffordd; Queensferry; Trelawnyd & Gwaenysgor; Treuddyn; Whitford; Ysceifiog.

Town Councils in the authority's area: Buckley; Caerwys; Connah's Quay; Flint; Holywell; Mold; Saltney; Sealand; Shotton.

GLYNDWR DISTRICT COUNCIL
See now Denbighshire County Council; Powys County Council; Wrexham County Borough Council.

GWENT COUNTY COUNCIL
See now Blaenau Gwent County Borough Council; Caerphilly County Borough Council; Monmouthshire County Council; Newport County Borough Council; Torfaen County Borough Council.

CYNGOR GWYNEDD COUNCIL

www.gwynedd.gov.uk

Principal Office

Council Offices, Shirehall Street, Caernarfon, Gwynedd LL55 1SH
Telephone: (01286) 672255; FAX: (01286) 673993

Function	Chief Officer	Title	Location
Chief Executive	Harry Thomas	Chief Executive	Council Offices
Education	Dr Gwynne Jones	Head of Schools	Council Offices
Electoral Registration	Dilys Ann Phillips	Head of Administration & Public Protection	Council Offices
Environmental Health	Dilys Ann Phillips	Head of Administration & Public Protection	Council Offices
Finance	Dafydd Lewis Edwards	Head of Finance	Council Offices
Housing	Ffrancon Williams	Head of Housing	Council Offices
Legal Services	Dilys Ann Phillips	Head of Administration & Public Protection	Council Offices
Leisure	Rhys Wyn Parri	Head of Lifelong Learning Services	Council Offices
Local Land Charges	Dilys Ann Phillips	Head of Administration & Public Protection	Council Offices
Planning	Iwan Evans	Head of Planning & Transportation	Council Offices
Purchasing & Supplies	Geraint George	Head of Policy & Performance	Council Offices
Social Services	Glyn Hughes	Head of Social Services	Council Offices
Technical Services	Huw Williams	Head of Gwynedd Consultancy	Council Offices
Trading Standards	Dilys Ann Phillips	Head of Administration & Public Protection	Council Offices

WALES

Community Councils in the authority's area: Aberdaron; Aberdyfi; Abergwyngregyn; Abermaw; Arthog; Beddgelert; Bethesda; Betws Garmon; Bontnewydd; Botwnnog; Brithdir & Llanfachreth; Bryncrug; Buan; Clynnog; Corris; Dolbenmaen; Dyffryn Ardudwy; Ganllwyd; Harlech; Llanaelhaearn; Llanbedr; Llanbedrog; Llanberis; Llanddeiniolen; Llandderfel; Llandwrog; Llandygai; Llanegryn; Llanelltyd; Llanengan; Llanfair; Llanfihangel-y-Pennant; Llanfrothen; Llangelynin; Llangywer; Llanllechid; Llanllyfni; Llannor; Llanrug; Llanuwchllyn; Llanwnda; Llanycil; Llanystumdwy; Maentwrog; Mawddwy; Nefyn; Pennal; Penrhyndeudraeth; Pentir; Pistyll; Talsarnau; Trawsfynydd; Tudweiliog; Waunfawr; Y Felinheli.

Town Councils in the authority's area: Bala; Caernarfon; Criccieth; Dolgellau; Ffestiniog; Porthmadog; Pwllheli; Tywyn.

City Council in the authority's area: Bangor.

ISLE OF ANGLESEY BOROUGH COUNCIL
See now Isle of Anglesey County Council.

ISLWYN BOROUGH COUNCIL
See now Caerphilly County Borough Council.

LLANELLI BOROUGH COUNCIL
See now Carmarthenshire County Council.

LLIW VALLEY BOROUGH COUNCIL
See now Neath Port Talbot County Borough Council; City & County of Swansea.

MEIRIONNYDD DISTRICT COUNCIL
See now Gwynedd County Council.

MERTHYR TYDFIL BOROUGH COUNCIL
See now Merthyr Tydfil County Borough Council.

MERTHYR TYDFIL COUNTY BOROUGH COUNCIL
www.merthyr.gov.uk

Principal Office; Finance Department
Civic Centre, Castle Street, Merthyr Tydfil CF47 8AN
Telephone: (01685) 725000

Integrated Childrens' Services; Adults, Families and Life-Long Learning; Legal Services
Ty Keir Hardie, Riverside Court, Avenue de Clichy, Merthyr Tydfil
Telephone: (01685) 725000

Function	Chief Officer	Title	Location
Chief Executive	Alastair Neil	Chief Executive	Civic Centre
Electoral Registration	Gareth Chapman	Director of Customer Corporate Services	Civic Centre
Education	Vernon Morgan	Director of Integrated Childrens' Services	Ty Kier Hardie
Environmental Health	Gary Thomas	Director of Customer Community Services	Civic Centre
Finance	Hugh O'Sullivan	Chief Officer: Finance, Audit & Risk Management	Civic Centre
Housing	Gary Thomas	Director of Customer Community Services	Civic Centre
Legal Services	Gareth Chapman	Director of Customer Corporate Services	Civic Centre
Leisure	Gary Thomas	Director of Customer Community Services	Civic Centre

Local Land Charges	Gareth Chapman	Director of Customer Corporate Services	Civic Centre
Planning	Gareth Chapman	Director of Customer Corporate Services	Civic Centre
Purchasing & Supplies	Hugh O'Sullivan	Chief Officer: Finance, Audit & Risk Management	Civic Centre
Social Services	Giovanni Isingrini	Director of Adults, Families & Life-Long Learning	Ty Kier Hardie
Technical Services	Gary Thomas	Director of Customer Community Services	Civic Centre
Trading Standards	Gareth Chapman	Director of Customer Corporate Services	Civic Centre

On 1 April 1996, Merthyr Tydfil County Borough Council took over from Merthyr Tydfil Borough Council.

Community Councils in the authority's area: Bedlinog.

MID GLAMORGAN COUNTY COUNCIL

See now Bridgend County Borough Council; Cardiff County Council; Caerphilly County Borough Council; Merthyr Tydfil County Borough Council; Rhondda, Cynon, Taff County Borough Council and Vale of Glamorgan County Borough Council.

MONMOUTH BOROUGH COUNCIL

See now Monmouthshire County Council

MONMOUTHSHIRE COUNTY COUNCIL

www.monmouthshire.gov.uk

Principal Office
County Hall, Cwmbran, South Wales NP44 2XH
Telephone: (01633) 644644; FAX: (01633) 644666

Function	Chief Officer	Title	Location
Chief Executive	[Vacant]	Chief Executive	County Hall
Education	Phil Cooke	Corporate Director (Lifelong Learning & Leisure Directorate)	County Hall
Electoral Registration	Murray Andrews	Head of Local Democracy and Legal Services	County Hall
Environmental Health	Jeff Martin	Corporate Director (Environment Directorate)	County Hall
Finance	Steve Greenslade	Corporate Director (Resources and Customer Services)	County Hall
Housing	Colin Berg	Corporate Director (Social and Housing Services Directorate)	County Hall
Legal Services	Murray Andrews	Head of Local Democracy and Legal Services	County Hall
Leisure	Phil Cooke	Corporate Director (Lifelong Learning & Leisure Directorate)	County Hall
Local Land Charges	Brenda Chandler	Land Charges Officer	County Hall
Planning	George Ashworth	Head of Planning	County Hall
Social Services	Colin Berg	Corporate Director (Social and Housing Services Directorate)	County Hall
Trading Standards	Phil Glanville	Trading Standards Manager	County Hall

On 1 April 1996, Monmouthshire County Council took over from Monmouth Borough Council and, from Blaenau Gwent Borough Council, the community of Llanelly.

Community Councils in the authority's area: Caerwent; Crucorney; Devauden; Goetre Fawr; Grosmont; Gwehelog Fawr; Llanarth; Llanbadoc; Llanelly; Llanfoist Fawr; Llangattock-Vibon-Avel;

Llangwm; Llangybi; Llanhennock; Llanover; Llantilio Crossenny; Llantilio Pertholey; Llantrisant Fawr; Magor with Undy; Mathern; Mitchel Troy; Portskewett; Raglan; Rogiet; St Arvans; Shirenewton; Tintern; Trellech United.

Town Councils in the authority's area: Abergavenny; Caldicot; Chepstow; Monmouth; Usk.

MONTGOMERYSHIRE DISTRICT COUNCIL
See now Powys County Council

NEATH PORT TALBOT COUNTY BOROUGH COUNCIL
www.neath-porttalbot.gov.uk

Principal Office
Civic Centre, Port Talbot, SA13 1PJ
Telephone: (01639) 763333; FAX: (01639) 763444

Environmental & Consumer Services Department
Civic Centre, Neath, SA11 3QZ
Telephone: (01639) 763333; FAX: (01639) 764000

Technical Services
Civic Centre, Penllergaer, Swansea SA4 9GH
Telephone: (01639) 763333; FAX: (01792) 512717

Function	Chief Officer	Title	Location
Chief Executive	Mr K R Sawyers	Chief Executive	Port Talbot
Education	Mr K Napieralla	Director of Education, Leisure & Lifelong Learning	Port Talbot
Electoral Registration	Mr K R Sawyers	Chief Executive	Port Talbot
Environmental Health	Mr G A I Jenkins	Director of Environment & Consumer Services	Neath
Finance	Mr D W Davies	Director of Finance & Corporate Services	Port Talbot
Housing	Mr Robert Rees	Head of Housing	Port Talbot
Legal Services	Mrs C A John	Head of Legal Services	Port Talbot
Leisure	Mr R Ward	Head of Lifelong Learning, Culture & Leisure	Port Talbot
Local Land Charges	Mrs C A John	Head of Legal Services	Port Talbot
Planning	Mr G White	Head of Planning	Neath
Purchasing & Supplies	Mr W Watson	Director of Technical Services	Penllergaer
Social Services	Mr C Preece	Director of Social Services & Housing	Port Talbot
Technical Services	Mr W Watson	Director of Technical Services	Penllergaer
Trading Standards	Steve Bolchover	Head of Trading Standards	Neath

On 1 April 1996, Neath Port Talbot County Borough Council took over from Neath Borough Council, Port Talbot Borough Council and, from Lliw Valley Borough Council, the communities of Pontardawe, Gwaun-Cae-Gurwen, Cwmllynfell, Ystalyfera and Cilybebyll.

Community Councils in the authority's area: Blaengwrach; Blaenhonddan; Cilybebyll; Clyne; Coedffranc; Crynant; Cwmllynfell; Dyffryn Clydach; Gwaun-cae-Gurwen; Onllwyn; Pelenna; Pontardawe; Resolven; Seven Sisters; Tonna; Ystalyfera.

Town Councils in the authority's area: Briton Ferry; Glynneath; Neath.

NEATH BOROUGH COUNCIL
See now Neath Port Talbot County Borough Council.

NEWPORT BOROUGH COUNCIL
See now Newport County Borough Council.

NEWPORT COUNTY BOROUGH COUNCIL

See now Newport City Council.

NEWPORT CITY COUNCIL

www.newport.gov.uk

Principal Office

Civic Centre, Newport, South Wales NP20 4UR
Telephone: (01633) 656656; FAX: (01633) 244721; DX 33238 Newport

Function	Chief Officer	Title	Location
Chief Executive	Mr Chris Freegard	Managing Director	Civic Centre
Education	Mr David Griffiths	Head of Resourcing, Support & Co-ordination	Civic Centre
Electoral Registration	Mr Greg Ashurst	Head of Law & Standards	Civic Centre
Environmental Health	Mr Steve Davison	Head of Public Protection & Environmental Services	Civic Centre
Finance	Mrs Joyce Steven	Head of Finance & Scrutiny	Civic Centre
Housing	Mr Robert Lynbeck	Head of Housing & Area Regeneration	Civic Centre
Legal Services	Mr Greg Ashurst	Head of Law & Standards	Civic Centre
Leisure	Mr Iain Varah	Head of Continuing Learning & Leisure	Civic Centre
Local Land Charges	Mr Greg Ashurst	Head of Law & Standards	Civic Centre
Planning	Mr Stewart Wild	Head of Planning & Economic Regeneration	Civic Centre
Purchasing & Supplies	Mr Andrew McManus	Head of Information Systems & Communications	Civic Centre
Social Services	Mr Ellis Williams	Head of Resource & Strategy	Civic Centre
Technical Services	Mr Brian Kemp	Head of Engineering & Construction	Civic Centre
Trading Standards	Mr Steven Davison	Head of Public Protection & Environmental Services	Civic Centre

On 1 April 1996, Newport County Borough Council (Newport City Council as of 21 May 2002) took over from Newport Borough Council, and, in part, from Gwent County Council.

Community Councils in the authority's area: Bishton; Coedkernew; Goldcliff; Graig; Langstone; Llanvaches; Llanwern; Marshfield; Michaelstone-y-Fedw; Nash; Penhow; Redwick; Rogerstone; Wentloog.

OGWR BOROUGH COUNCIL

See now Bridgend County Borough Council; Vale of Glamorgan County Borough Council.

PEMBROKESHIRE COUNTY COUNCIL

www.pembrokeshire.gov.uk

Principal Office

County Hall, Haverfordwest, Pembrokeshire SA61 1TP
Telephone: (01437) 764551

Function	Chief Officer	Title	Location
Chief Executive	Mr Bryn Parry-Jones	Chief Executive	County Hall
Education	Gerson Davies	Director of Education & Community Services	County Hall
Electoral Registration	Glynne Morgan	Elections Manager	County Hall
Environmental Health	Alan Bennett	Head of Public Protection	County Hall
Finance	Mark Lewis	Director of Finance & Leisure	County Hall
Housing	Jon Skone	Director of Social Care & Housing	County Hall
Legal Services	Huw James	Director of Support & Cultural Services	County Hall

Leisure	Mark Lewis	Director of Finance & Leisure	County Hall
Local Land Charges	Huw Miller	Head of Legal & Committee Services	County Hall
Planning	David Lawrence	Head of Planning	County Hall
Purchasing & Supplies	Paul Ashley-Jones	Procurement Manager	County Hall
Social Services	Jon Skone	Director of Social Care & Housing	County Hall
Technical Services	Huw Roberts	Director of Transportation & Environment	County Hall
Trading Standards	Alan Bennett	Head of Public Protection	County Hall

On 1 April 1996, Pembrokeshire County Council took over from Preseli Pembrokeshire and South Pembrokeshire District Councils, together with Caldey Island and St Margaret's Island.

Community Councils in the authority's area: Ambleston; Amroth; Angle; Boncath; Brawdy; Burton; Camrose; Carew; Castlemartin; Cilgerran; Clydau; Cosheston; Crymych; Cwm Gwaun; Dale; Dinas Cross; East Williamston; Eglwyswrw; Freystrop; Havens, The; Hayscastle; Herbrandston; Hook; Hundleton; Jeffreyston; Johnston; Kilgetty/Begelly; Lampeter Velfrey; Lamphey; Letterston; Llanddewi Velfrey; Llandissilio West; Llangwm; Llanrhian; Llanstadwell; Llawhaden; Maenclochog; Manorbier; Manordeifi; Marloes & St Brides; Martletwy; Mathry; Merlins Bridge; Mynachlogddu; Nevern; New Moat; Nolton & Roch; Penally; Pencaer; Puncheston; Rosemarket; Rudbaxton; St Dogmaels; St Florence; St Ishmaels; St Mary-Out-Liberty; Saundersfoot; Scleddau; Slebech; Solva; Spittal; Stackpole; Templeton; Tiers Cross; Trecwn; Uzmaston & Boulston; Walwyns Castle; Wiston; Wolfscastle.

Town Councils in the authority's area: Fishguard & Goodwick; Haverfordwest; Milford Haven; Narberth; Newport; Neyland; Pembroke; Pembroke Dock; St David's & Cathedral Close; Tenby.

PORT TALBOT BOROUGH COUNCIL
See now Neath Port Talbot County Borough Council.

POWYS COUNTY COUNCIL

www.powys.gov.uk

Principal Office
Powys County Hall, Llandrindod Wells, Powys LD1 5LG
Telephone: (01597) 826000; FAX: (01597) 826230

Community Services
Neuadd Brycheiniog, Cambrian Way, Brecon, Powys LD3 7HR
Telephone: (01597) 826000; FAX: (01874) 615781

Economic and Community Regeneration
St John's Offices, Five Ways, Llandrindod Wells, Powys LD1 5ES
Telephone: (01597) 826000; FAX: (01597) 827575

Function	Chief Officer	Title	Location
Chief Executive	Mr J Patterson	Acting Chief Executive	County Hall
Electoral Registration	Mr J Patterson	Acting Chief Executive	County Hall
Education	Mr M J Barker	Group Director for Children, Families & Lifelong Learning	County Hall
Finance	Mr J Patterson	Acting Chief Executive	County Hall
Housing	Mr P Robson	Director for Community Services & Director of Social Services	Neuadd Brycheiniog
Legal Services	Mr J Patterson	Acting Chief Executive	County Hall
Leisure	Mr G Davey	Group Director for Economic & Community Regeneration	St John's Offices
Local Land Charges	Mr J Patterson	Acting Chief Executive	County Hall
Planning	Mr G Davey	Group Director for Economic & Community Regeneration	St John's Offices
Purchasing & Supplies	Mr J Patterson	Acting Chief Executive	County Hall

Social Services	Mr P Robson	Director for Community Services & Director of Social Services	Neuadd Brycheiniog
Technical Services	Mr J Owen	Group Director for Technical & Local Services	County Hall
Trading Standards	Mr P Robson	Director for Community Services & Director of Social Services	Neuadd Brycheiniog

On 1 April 1996, Powys County Council took over from Brecknock Borough Council, Montgomeryshire District Council and Radnorshire District Council, together with, from Glyndwr District Council, the communities of Llanrhaeadr-ym-Mochnant, Llansilin and Llangedwyn.

Community Councils in the authority's area: Abbeycwmhir; Aberedw; Aberhafesp; Banwy; Bausley with Criggion; Beguildy; Berriew; Bettws; Brecon; Bronllys; Cadfarch; Caersws; Carno; Carreghofa; Castle Caereinion; Churchstoke; Cilmery; Clyro; Cray; Crickhowell; Disserth & Trecoed; Duhonw; Dwyriw; Erwood; Felinfach; Forden; Gladestry; Glantwymyn; Glasbury; Glascwm; Glyn Tarrell; Guilsfield; Gwernyfed; Honddu Isaf; Kerry; Llanafanawr; Llanbadarn Fawr; Llanbadarn Fynydd; Llanbister; Llanbrynmair; Llanddew; Llanddewi Ystradenny; Llandinam; Llandrinio; Llandysilio; Llandyssil; Llanelwedd; Llanerfyl; Llanfechain; Llanfihangel; Llanfihangel Cwmdu with Bwlch & Cathedine; Llanfihangel Rhydithon; Llanfrynach; Llangammarch; Llangattock; Llangedwyn; Llangorse; Llangunllo; Llangurig; Llangynidr; Llangyniew; Llangynog; Llanidloes Without; Llanigon; Llanrhaeadr; Llanrhaeadr-ym-Mochnant; Llansantffraid; Llansilin; Llanwddyn; Llanwrthwl; Llanyre; Llywel; Maescar; Manafon; Meifod; Merthyr Cynog; Mochdre; Nantmel; New Radnor; Newtown & Llanllwchaiarn; Old Radnor; Painscastle; Pen-y-Bont Fawr; Penybont & Llandegley; St Harmon; Talybont-on-Usk; Tawe Uchaf; Trallong; Trefeglwys; Treflys; Tregynon; Trewern; Vale of Grwyney; Whitton; Yscir; Ystradfellte; Ystradgynlais.

Town Councils in the authority's area: Builth Wells; Knighton; Hay; Llandrindod Wells; Llanfair Caereinion; Llanfyllin; Llanidloes; Llanwrtyd Wells; Machynlleth; Montgomery; Talgarth; Presteigne & Norton; Rhayader; Welshpool.

PRESELI PEMBROKESHIRE DISTRICT COUNCIL
See now Pembrokeshire County Council.

RADNORSHIRE DISTRICT COUNCIL
See now Powys County Council

RHONDDA BOROUGH COUNCIL
See now Rhondda, Cynon, Taff County Borough Council.

RHONDDA, CYNON, TAFF COUNTY BOROUGH COUNCIL

www.rhondda-cynon-taff.gov.uk

Principal Office
The Pavilions, Cambrian Park, Clydach Vale CF40 2XX
Telephone: (01443) 424000

Education Department & Children's Services Group
Ty Trevithick, Abercynon, Mountain Ash CF45 4UQ
Telephone: (01443) 744000

Public Health & Protection Services Department
Ty Elai, Dinas Isaf Industrial Estate, Williamstown CF40 1NY
Telephone: (01443) 442100

Transportation & Building Control Department
Sardis House, Sardis Road, Pontypridd CF37 1DU
Telephone: (01443) 494700

Environmental Services
Liwyncastan, Library Road, Pontypridd CF37 2YA
Telephone: (01443) 400563

Function	Chief Officer	Title	Location
Chief Executive	Mr K Ryley	Chief Executive	The Pavilions
Education	Mr D Jones	Group Director of Education & Childrens Services	The Pavilions
Electoral Registration	Mr P Lucas	County Borough Legal & Democratic Services Officer	The Pavilions
Environmental Health	Mr D Bishop	Group Director of Environmental Services	The Pavilions
Finance	Mr K Griffiths	Group Director of Corporate Services	The Pavilions
Housing	Mr J Griffiths	Divisional Director of Community Housing	The Pavilions
Legal Services	Mr P Lucas	County Borough Legal & Democratic Services Officer	The Pavilions
Leisure	Mr L Lewis	Divisional Director of Public Health	Ty Elai
Local Land Charges	Mr P Lucas	County Borough Legal & Democratic Services Officer	The Pavilions
Planning	Mr D Sherrard	Divisional Director of Transportation & Building Control	Sardis House
Purchasing & Supplies	Mr P Lucas	County Borough Legal & Democratic Services Officer	The Pavilions
Social Services	Ms S Halls	Divisional Director of Childrens Services	The Pavilions
Technical Services	Mr G Jones	Divisional Director of Environmental Services	Liwyncastan
Trading Standards	Mrs A Jones	Acting Divisional Director of Public Health & Protection	Ty Elai

On 1 April 1996, Rhondda, Cynon, Taff County Borough Council took over from Cynon Valley, Rhondda and Taff Ely District Councils, but excluding, from Taff-Ely District Council, the community of Pentyrch; and, in part, from Mid Glamorgan County Council.

Community Councils in the authority's area: Gilfach Goch; Hirwaun; Llanharan; Llanharry; Llantrisant; Llantwit Fardre; Pontyclun; Rhigos; Taffs Well; Tonyrefail; Ynysbwl.

Town Councils in the authority's area: Pontypridd.

RHUDDLAN BOROUGH COUNCIL
See now Denbighshire County Council.

RHYMNEY VALLEY DISTRICT COUNCIL
See now Caerphilly County Borough Council.

SOUTH GLAMORGAN COUNTY COUNCIL
See now Cardiff County Council; Vale of Glamorgan Council.

SOUTH PEMBROKESHIRE DISTRICT COUNCIL
See now Pembrokeshire County Council.

SWANSEA CITY COUNCIL
See now City & County of Swansea.

CITY & COUNTY OF SWANSEA

www.swansea.gov.uk

Principal Office
County Hall, Swansea SA1 3SN
Telephone: (01792) 636000

Culture and Recreation Department; Development Department; Housing Department; Environment and Health Department
The Guildhall, Swansea SA1 4PE
Telephone: (01792) 636000

Function	Chief Officer	Title	Location
Chief Executive	Mr Tim Thorogood	Chief Executive	County Hall
Education	Mr Richard Parry	Strategic Director of Education	County Hall
Electoral Registration	Ms Julie James	Assistant Chief Executive	County Hall
Environmental Health	Mrs Reena Owen	Strategic Director of Envronment	Guildhall
Finance	Mr Bob Carter	Deputy Chief Executive	County Hall
Housing	Mr Hugh Gardner	Strategic Director of Social Services & Housing	Guildhall
Legal Services	Ms Julie James	Assistant Chief Executive	County Hall
Leisure	Mr Dave Evans	Strategic Director of Regeneration	Guildhall
Planning	Mrs Reena Owen	Strategic Director of Envronment	Guildhall
Purchasing & Supplies	Mr Bob Carter	Deputy Chief Executive	County Hall
Social Services	Mr Hugh Gardner	Strategic Director of Social Services & Housing	Guildhall
Technical Services	Mrs Reena Owen	Strategic Director of Envronment	Guildhall
Trading Standards	Mrs Reena Owen	Strategic Director of Envronment	Guildhall

On 1 April 1996, The City & County of Swansea took over from the Western area of West Glamorgan County Council, Swansea City Council and from Lliw Valley District Council, the communities of Gowerton, Llwchwr, Gorseinon, Grovesend, Pontarddulais, Mawr, Pontlliw, Penllergaer, Llangyfelach and Clydach.

Community Councils in the authority's area: Bishopston; Clydach; Dunvant; Gorseinon; Gowerton; Grovesend; Ilston; Killay; Llangennith; Llangyfelach; Llanrhidian Higher; Llanrhidian Lower; Llwchwr; Mawr; Mumbles; Penllergaer; Pennard; Penrice; Pontarddulais; Pontlliw; Port Eynon; Reynoldston; Rhossili; Upper Killay.

TAFF ELY BOROUGH COUNCIL

See now Cardiff County Council; Rhondda, Cynon, Taff County Borough Council.

TORFAEN BOROUGH COUNCIL

See now Torfaen County Borough Council.

TORFAEN COUNTY BOROUGH COUNCIL

www.torfaen.gov.uk

Principal Office

Civic Centre, Pontypool, Gwent NP4 6YB

Telephone: (01495) 762200; FAX: (01495) 755513; DX 44257 Pontypool

**Education Department; For the Environment;
Social Services Department**

County Hall, Croesyceilog, Cwmbran NP44 2WN

Telephone: (01495) 762200

Function	Chief Officer	Title	Location
Chief Executive	Ms Meg Holborow	Chief Executive	Civic Centre
Education	Mr Michael de Val	Director of Education	County Hall
Electoral Registration	Mr Duncan Forbes	County Borough Solicitor & Electoral Registration Officer	Civic Centre
Environmental Health	Mr Andy Fretter	Director for the Environment	County Hall
Finance	Mr Philip Nash	Director of Finance	Civic Centre
Housing	Mr David Burnell	Director of Housing	Civic Centre
Legal Services	Mr Duncan Forbes	County Borough Solicitor & Electoral Registration Officer	Civic Centre
Leisure	Mr David Congreve	Head of Leisure, Youth & Culture	Civic Centre
Social Services	Mr Gary Birch	Director of Social Services	County Hall

On 1 April 1996, Torfaen County Borough Council became a unitary authority.

WALES

Community Councils in the authority's area: Pontypool; Ponthir; Cwmbran; Henllys; Llanyrafon & Croesyceiliog.

Town Councils in the authority's area: Blaenavon.

VALE OF GLAMORGAN BOROUGH COUNCIL
See now The Vale of Glamorgan Council.

THE VALE OF GLAMORGAN COUNCIL
www.valeofglamorgan.gov.uk
Principal Office
Civic Offices, Holton Road, Barry CF63 4RU
Telephone: (01446) 700111; FAX: (01446) 421479; DX 38553 Barry

Economic Development; Planning and Transportation;
Leisure and Community Services
The Dock Offices, Subway Road, Barry CF63 4RT
Telephone: (01446) 704600; FAX: (01446) 421392

Function	Chief Officer	Title	Location
Chief Executive	J M Evans	Chief Executive	Civic Offices
Education	B Jeffreys	Director of Learning & Development	Civic Offices
Electoral Registration	I Hutchinson	Electoral Registration Officer	Civic Offices
Environmental Health	P H Evans	Director of Legal and Regulatory	Civic Offices
Finance	S Davies	Director of Finance, ICT & Property	Civic Offices
Housing	J Cawley	Director of Community Services	The Dock Offices
Legal Services	P H Evans	Director of Legal and Regulatory	Civic Offices
Leisure	R Quick	Director of Environmental & Economic Regeneration	The Dock Offices
Planning	R Quick	Director of Environmental & Economic Regeneration	The Dock Offices
Purchasing & Supplies	R Malcolm	Procurement Officer	Civic Offices
Social Services	J Cawley	Director of Community Services	The Dock Offices
Technical Services	B Morgan	Head of ICT	Civic Offices
Trading Standards	P H Evans	Director of Legal and Regulatory	Civic Offices

On 1 April 1996, The Vale of Glamorgan Council took over from the Vale of Glamorgan Borough Council, and, from Ogwr District Council, the communities of Wick, St Bride's Major and Ewenny (part).

Community Councils in the authority's area: Colwinston; Dinas Powys; Ewenny; Llancarfan; Llandough; Llandow; Llanfair; Llangan; Llanmaes; Michaelston; Pendoylan; Penllyn; Peterston-Super-Ely; St Athan; St Bride's Major; St Donats; St Georges & St Bride's-Super-Ely; St Nicholas & Bonvilston; Sully; Welsh St Donats; Wenvoe; Wick.Town Councils in the authority's area: Barry; Cowbridge & Llanblethian; Llantwit Major; Penarth.

WEST GLAMORGAN COUNTY COUNCIL
See now Neath Port Talbot County Borough Council; City & County of Swansea.

WREXHAM COUNTY BOROUGH COUNCIL
www.wrexham.gov.uk
Principal Office
The Guildhall, Wrexham LL11 1AY
Telephone: (01978) 292000; DX 26672 Wrexham

Education & Leisure Services Department
Ty Henblas, Henblas Square, Wrexham
Telephone: (01978) 297420; FAX: (01978) 297422

Environmental Services Department
Crown Buildings, Chester Street, Wrexham
Telephone: (01978) 297001; FAX: (01978) 297003

Housing Department; Planning Department
Lambpit Street, Wrexham
Telephone: (01978) 292500; FAX: (01978) 292502

Social Services Department
2nd Floor, Crown Buildings, Chester Street, Wrexham
Telephone: (01978) 298010; FAX: (01978) 298029

Technical Services Department
Old Library, Queen's Square, Wrexham LL11 1AU
Telephone: (01978) 292300

Trading Standards Department
Ruthin Road, Wrexham
Telephone: (01978) 292045; FAX: (01978) 290961

Function	Chief Officer	Title	Location
Chief Executive	I Garner	Chief Executive	Guildhall
Education	M Lloyd Jones	Chief Education Officer	Ty Henblas
Electoral Registration	G Coventry	Support Services Manager	Guildhall
Environmental Health	J Bradbury	Chief Community Services Officer	Crown Buildings
Finance	M Scholes	Director of Finance & Information Services	Guildhall
Housing	P Calland	Chief Housing Officer	Lambpit Street
Legal Services	T Coxon	Chief Legal & Administration Officer	Guildhall
Leisure	A Watkin	Chief Leisure, Libraries & Culture Officer	Ty Henblas
Local Land Charges	G Pilmoor	Land Charges/Claims Manager	Guildhall
Planning	L Isted	Chief Planning Officer	Lambpit Street
Social Services	A Figiel	Chief Social Services Officer	Crown Buildings
Technical Services	C Allingham	Principal Technical Support Officer	Old Library
Trading Standards	M Dean	Trading Standards Manager	Ruthin Road

On 1 April 1996, Wrexham County Borough Council took over from Wrexham Maelor Borough Council and, from Glyndwr District Council, the communities of Chirk, Glyntraian, Llansantffraid Glyn Ceriog and Ceiriog Ucha. In April 1997 the Council incorporated the Llangollen Rural areas of Froncysyllte, Garth and Trevor.

Community Councils in the authority's area: Abenbury; Acton; Bangor Is y Coed; Bronington; Broughton; Brymbo; Caia Park; Cefn; Ceiriog Ucha; Chirk; Coedpoeth; Erbistock; Esclusham; Glyntraian; Gresford; Gwersyllt; Hanmer; Holt; Isycoed; Llangollen Rural; Llansantffraid Glyn Ceiriog; Llay; Maelor South; Marchwiel; Minera; Offa; Overton; Penycae; Rhosddu; Rhosllanerchrugog; Rossett; Ruabon; Sesswick; Willington; Worthenbury.

WREXHAM MAELOR BOROUGH COUNCIL
See now Wrexham County Borough Council.

YNYS MON/ISLE OF ANGLESEY BOROUGH COUNCIL
See now Isle of Anglesey County Council.

SCOTLAND

ABERDEEN CITY COUNCIL

www.aberdeencity.gov.uk

Principal Office
Town House, Broad Street, Aberdeen AB10 1FY
Telephone: (01224) 522000; DX AB 52 Aberdeen

**Office of the Chief Executive; Environment and Infrastructure;
City Development; Finance and ICT; Personnel and Organisational Development;
Neighbourhood Services (South and Central)**
St Nicholas House, Broad Street, Aberdeen AB10 1GU
Telephone: (01224) 522000

Learning and Leisure
Summerhill Education Centre, Stronsay Drive, Aberdeen AB15 6JA
Telephone: (01224) 208626; FAX: (01224) 208674

Grampian Valuation Joint Board
Woodhill House, Westburn Road, Aberdeen AB16 5GE
Telephone: (01224) 664848; FAX: (01224) 664361

Function	Chief Officer	Title	Location
Chief Executive	Douglas Paterson	Chief Executive	Town House
Assessor	Alex McConnochie	Assessor	Woodhill House
Education	John Stodter	Corporate Director for Learning & Leisure	Summerhill
Environmental Health	Ian Livingstone	Head of Environmental Policy & Protective Services	St Nicholas Hse
Finance	Gordon Edwards	Corporate Director for Finance & ICT	Town House
Housing	Mike Scott	Corporate Director for Community Services	St Nicholas Hse
Legal Services	Crawford J Langley	Corporate Director for Legal & Democratic	Town House
Leisure	John Stodter	Corporate Director for Learning & Leisure	Summerhill
Planning	Bob Reid	Head of Physical Development	St Nicholas Hse
Purchasing & Supplies	Crawford J Langley	Corporate Director for Legal & Democratic	Town House
Technical Services	Donald Murdoch	Corporate Director for City Development	St Nicholas Hse
Trading Standards	Ian Livingstone	Head of Environmental Policy & Protective Services	St Nicholas Hse

On 1 April 1996, Aberdeen City Council took over from Aberdeen District Council.

Community Councils in the authority's area: Ashley & Broomhill; Braeside & Mannofield; Bridge of Don; Bucksburn & Newhills; Castlehill/Pittodrie; Cove & Altens; Culter; Cults; Bieldside & Milltimber; Ferryhill; Garthdee; George Street; Kingswells; Mastrick/Sheddocksley; Nigg; Old Aberdeen; Queen's Cross/Harlaw; Rosemount & Mile End; Seaton, Linksfield & Pittodrie; Tillydrone; Torry; West Don.

ABERDEEN DISTRICT COUNCIL
See now Aberdeen City Council

SCOTLAND

ABERDEENSHIRE COUNCIL

www.aberdeenshire.gov.uk

Principal Office
Woodhill House, Westburn Road, Aberdeen AB16 5GB
Telephone: (01467) 620981

Grampian Valuation Joint Board
Woodhill House, Westburn Road, Aberdeen AB16 5GE
Telephone: (01224) 664848; FAX: (01224) 664361

Function	Chief Officer	Title	Location
Chief Executive	Alan Campbell	Chief Executive	Woodhill Hse
Assessor	Alex McConnochie	Assessor	Woodhill Hse
Education	Hamish Vernal	Director of Education & Recreation	Woodhill Hse
Environmental Health	Eric Melrose	Director of Planning & Environmental Services	Woodhill Hse
Finance	Charles Armstrong	Director of Finance	Woodhill Hse
Housing	Colin Mackenzie	Director of Housing & Social Work	Woodhill Hse
Legal Services	Neil McDowall	Director of Law & Administration	Woodhill Hse
Leisure	Hamish Vernal	Director of Education & Recreation	Woodhill Hse
Planning	Eric Melrose	Director of Planning Environmental Services	Woodhill Hse
Purchasing & Supplies	Craig Innes	Purchasing Manager	Woodhill Hse
Social Services	Colin Mackenzie	Director of Housing & Social Work	Woodhill Hse
Technical Services	Iain Gabriel	Director of Transportation & Infrastructure	Woodhill Hse
Trading Standards	Eric Melrose	Director of Planning & Environmental Services	Woodhill Hse

On 1 April 1996, Aberdeenshire Council took over from Banff & Buchan, Gordon and Kincardine & Deeside District Councils.

Community Councils in the authority's area: Aberdour-Tyrie; Aberchirder-Marnoch; Alvah-Forglen; Arbuthnott; Auchterless Inverkeithny; Ballater & Crathie; Banchory; Banff-Macduff; Belhelvie; Benholm & Johnshaven; Boddam & District; Braemar; Catterline Kinneff & Dunnottar; Cluny Midmar & Monymusk; Collieston; Cornhill-Ordiquhill; Crathes, Drumoak & Durris; Cromar; Cruden; Deer; Donside; Echt & Skene; Ellon; Feughdee West; Fintray & Kinellar; Fordyce-Sandend & District; Foveran; Fraserburgh; Fyvie Rothie Monquhitter; Garioch; Gourdon; Huntly; Invercairn; Inverurie; Kemnay; King Edward-Gamrie; Kintore & District; Longside & District; Lumphanan; Mearns; Meldrum & Bourtie; Methlick; Mid-Deeside; Mintlaw & District; New Pitsligo; Newmachar; Newtonhill, Muchalls, Cammachmore; North Kincardine Rural; Peterhead; Portlethen & District; Portsoy & District; Rathen & District; Rosehearty; Royal Burgh of Inverbervie; Sandhaven, Pitullie; St Cyrus; St Fergus/Crimmond/ Lonmay; Stonehaven & District; Strathbogie; Strichen; Tarves; Tap o' Noth; Torphins; Turriff & District; Udny; West Garioch; Westhill & District; Whitehills & District; Ythan.

ANGUS COUNCIL

www.angus.gov.uk

Principal Office
The Cross, Forfar, Angus DD8 1BX
Telephone: (01307) 461460; FAX: (01307) 461874

Environmental & Consumer Protection Department
Municipal Buildings, Castle Street, Forfar DD8 3AF
Telephone: (01307) 461460; FAX: (01307) 467185

SCOTLAND

Law & Administration Department; Finance Department; Planning & Transport Department
St James House, St James Road, Forfar DD8 2AF
Telephone: (01307) 461460

Contract Services Department; Personnel Services; Education Department; Housing Department; Leisure Services Department; Roads Department; Social Work Department
County Buildings, Market Street, Forfar DD8 3LG
Telephone: (01307) 461460

Property Services Department
Ravenswood, New Road, Forfar DD8 2ZG
Telephone: (01307) 473800; FAX: (01307) 466773

The Tayside Valuation Joint Board
Nethergate Centre, 35 Yeaman Shore, Dundee DD1 4BU
Telephone: (01382) 315603; FAX: (01382) 315600

Function	Chief Officer	Title	Location
Chief Executive	Mr A B Watson	Chief Executive	The Cross
Assessor	Mr N Clark Low	Assessor	Nethergate Centre
Education	Mr J Anderson	Director of Education	County Buildings
Environmental Health	Mr S Heggie	Director of Environmental & Consumer Protection	Municipal Bldgs
Finance	Mr D Sawers	Director of Finance	St James House
Housing	Mr R Ashton	Director of Housing	County Buildings
Legal Services	Ms C Coull	Director of Law & Administration	St James House
Leisure	Mr J Zimny	Director of Leisure Services	County Buildings
Planning	Mr A Anderson	Director of Planning & Transport	St James House
Social Services	Dr R Peat	Director of Social Work & Health Liaison	County Buildings
Technical Services	Mr M Lunny	Director of Property Services	Ravenswood
Trading Standards	Mr S Heggie	Director of Environmental & Consumer Protection	Municipal Bldgs

On 1 April 1996, Angus Council took over from Angus District Council, Tayside Regional Council; and, in part, from Dundee District Council.

Community Councils in the authority's area: Aberlemno; Arbroath; Auchterhouse; Brechin; Carnoustie; Ferryden & Craig; Forfar; Fowlis, Liff & Balruddery; Friockheim; Glamis; Hillside, Dun & Logie Pert; Inverarity; Inveresk; Inverkeillor & District; Kirriemuir; Kirriemuir & Landward East; Kirriemuir Landward West; Letham & District; Lunanhead; Lundie, Muirhead & Birkhill; Monifieth; Monikie & Newbigging; Montrose; Murroes & Wellbank; Newtyle & Eassie; Strathmartine; Tealing.

ANGUS DISTRICT COUNCIL
See now Angus Council.

ANNANDALE & ESKDALE DISTRICT COUNCIL
See now Dumfries & Galloway Council.

ARGYLL AND BUTE COUNCIL

www.argyll-bute.gov.uk

Principal Office
Kilmory, Lochgilphead, Argyll PA31 8RT
Telephone: (01546) 602127; FAX: (01546) 604138

Education Department
Argyll House, Alexandra Parade, Dunoon PA23 8AJ
Telephone: (01369) 704000; FAX: (01369) 702944

The Dunbartonshire and Argyll & Bute Valuation Joint Board
235 Dumbarton Road, Clydebank G81 4XJ
Telephone: (0141) 562 1200; FAX: (0141) 562 1255

Function	Chief Officer	Title	Location
Chief Executive	James McLellan	Chief Executive	Kilmory
Assessor	David C Thomson	Assessor	Dumbarton Rd
Education	Douglas Hendry	Director of Community Services	Kilmory
Environmental Health	George Harper	Director of Development Services	Kilmory
Housing	Douglas Hendry	Director of Community Services	Kilmory
Legal Services	Nigel Stewart	Director of Corporate Services	Kilmory

On 1 April 1996, Argyll and Bute Council took over from Argyll and Bute District Council.

Community Councils in the authority's area: Appin; Archattan; Ardentinny; Ardrishaig; Arrochar & Tarbet; Avich & Kilchrenan; Bute; Cairndow; Cambeltown; Cardross; Colgrain; Colintraive & Glendaruel; Colonsay; Connel; Cove & Kilcreggan; Craignish; Dunadd; Dunbeg; Dunoon; East Kintyre; Furnace; Garelochhead; Gigha; Glenorhcy & Innishael; Helensburgh; Hunter's Quay; Inveraray; Isle of Coll; Isle of Iona; Isle of Mull; Isle of Tiree; Jura; Kerrera; Kilchoman & Portnahaven; Kildalton; Kilfinan; Kilkarrow & Kelmeny; Kilmore; Kilmun; Kilninver & Kilmelford; Laggan; Lismore; Lochgilphead; Lochgoil; Luing; Luss & Arden; North Knapdale; Oban; Rhu & Shandon; Roseneath & Clynder; Sandbank; Seil; South Cowal; South Knapdale; Southend; Strachur; Tarbert & Skipness; Taynuilt; West Kintyre; West Loch Fyne.

ARGYLL & BUTE DISTRICT COUNCIL
See now Argyll and Bute Council.

BADENOCK & STRATHSPEY DISTRICT COUNCIL
See now The Highland Council.

BANFF & BUCHAN DISTRICT COUNCIL
See now Aberdeenshire Council.

BEARSDEN & MILNGAVIE DISTRICT COUNCIL
See now East Dunbartonshire Council.

BERWICKSHIRE DISTRICT COUNCIL
See now Scottish Borders Council.

BORDERS REGIONAL COUNCIL
See now Scottish Borders Council.

CAITHNESS DISTRICT COUNCIL
See now The Highland Council.

CENTRAL REGIONAL COUNCIL
See now the Clackmannanshire Council; Falkirk Council; Stirling Council.

CLACKMANNAN DISTRICT COUNCIL
See now the Clackmannanshire Council.

CLACKMANNANSHIRE COUNCIL

www.clacksweb.org.uk

Principal Office
Greenfield, Alloa, Clackmannanshire FK10 2AD
Telephone: (01259) 450000; FAX: (01259) 452010

Design & Property Department; Education & Community Services Department; Housing & Social Work Department; Technical Services Department
Lime Tree House, Alloa FK10 1EX
Telephone: (01259) 450000

The Central Scotland Valuation Board
Hillside House, Laurelhill, Stirling FK7 9QJ
Telephone: (01786) 892200; FAX: (01786) 892255

Function	Chief Officer	Title	Location
Chief Executive	Mr K Bloomer	Chief Executive	Greenfield
Assessor	Mr K D Scott	Assessor	Hillside House
Education	Mr D Jones	Director of Services to People	Lime Tree Hse
Environmental Health	Mr G Dallas	Director of Development & Environmental Services	Lime Tree Hse
Finance	Mr M Wilson	Head of Corporate Accountancy	Greenfield
Housing	Mr D Jones	Director of Services to People	Lime Tree Hse
Legal Services	Ms J McGuire	Head of Administration & Legal	Greenfield
Leisure	Mr D Jones	Director of Services to People	Lime Tree Hse
Planning	Mr G Dallas	Director of Development & Environmental Services	Lime Tree Hse
Social Services	Mr D Jones	Director of Services to People	Lime Tree Hse
Technical Services	Mr G Stewart	Head of Design & Property	Lime Tree Hse
Trading Standards	Mr E McAuslane	Head of Environment Services	Lime Tree Hse

On 1 April 1996, Clackmannanshire Council took over from Clackmannan District Council and Central Regional Council.

Community Councils in the authority's area: Alloa Central; Alloa West; Alva; Clackmannan; Dollar; Menstrie; Muckhart; Tillicoultry; Tullibody, Cambus & Glenochil.

CLYDEBANK DISTRICT COUNCIL
See now West Dunbartonshire Council.

CLYDESDALE DISTRICT COUNCIL
See now South Lanarkshire Council.

COMHAIRLE NAN EILEAN SIAR
(formerly Western Isles Council)

www.cne-siar.gov.uk

Principal Office
Council Offices, Sandwick Road, Stornoway, Isle of Lewis HS1 2BW
Telephone: (01851) 703773; FAX: (01851) 705349

The Highland & Western Isles Valuation Joint Board
Moray House, 16/18 Bank Street, Inverness IV1 1QY
Telephone: (01463) 703340; FAX: (01463) 703301

Function	Chief Officer	Title	Location
Chief Executive	Mr B Howat	Chief Executive	Council Offices
Assessor	Mr D Gillespie	Assessor & Electoral Registration Office	Moray House
Education	Mr M MacLeod	Director of Education	Council Offices

Environmental Health	Mr M Gold	Director of Sustainable Communities	Council Offices
Finance	Mr R W Bennie	Director of Finance	Council Offices
Housing	Mr A Lamont	Director of Housing	Council Offices
Legal Services	Ms H A Froud	Director of Corporate Services	Council Offices
Leisure	Mr W Houston	Head of Leisure & Learning	Council Offices
Local Land Charges	Ms H A Froud	Director of Corporate Services	Council Offices
Planning	Mr M Gold	Director of Sustainable Communities	Council Offices
Purchasing & Supplies	Mr Ian Cockburn		Council Offices
Social Services	Mr M Smith	Director of Social Work	Council Offices
Technical Services	Mr M Murray	Director of Technical Services	Council Offices
Trading Standards	Mr H Miller	Head of Health & Community Services	Council Offices

Community Councils in the authority's area: Airidhantium; Back; Benbecula; Bernera; Berneray; Bornish; Breasclete; Carloway; Castlebay; Eriskay; Lochdar; Kinloch; Laxdale; Lochboisdale; Ness; Northbay; North Harris; North Tolsta; North Uist; Pairc; Point; Sandwick; Scalpay; Shawbost; South Harris; Tong; Uig.

CUMBERNAULD & KILSYTH DISTRICT COUNCIL
See now North Lanarkshire Council.

CUMNOCK & DOON VALLEY DISTRICT COUNCIL
See now East Ayrshire Council.

CUNNINGHAME DISTRICT COUNCIL
See now North Ayrshire Council.

DUMBARTON DISTRICT COUNCIL
See now West Dunbartonshire Council.

DUMFRIES & GALLOWAY COUNCIL
www.dumgal.gov.uk

Principal Office
Council Offices, English Street, Dumfries DG1 2DD
Telephone: (01387) 260543

Education and Community Services
30 Edinburgh Road, Dumfries DG1 1NW
Telephone: (01387) 260000; FAX (01387) 260632

Assessors Department
27 Moffat Road, Dumfries DG1 1NB
Telephone: (01387) 260605; FAX: (01387) 260632

Planning and Environment Services
Militia House, English Street, Dumfries DG1 2HR

Finance Department
Carruthers House, Dumfries DG1 2HP

Housing Services
Carmont House, Bankend Road, Crichton, Dumfries DG1 1DZ
Telephone: (01387) 260000; FAX: (01387) 245139

Legal Services
Council Offices, Buccleuch Street, Dumfries DG1 2AD
Telephone: (01387) 260000; FAX: (01387) 267225

Adult and Children's Services (Social Work)
Grierson House, The Crichton, Bankend Road, Dumfries DG1 4ZH
Telephone: (01387) 260928; FAX: (01387) 260924

Trading Standards Department
1 Newall Terrace, Dumfries DG1 1LN

Function	Chief Officer	Title	Location
Chief Executive	Philip Jones	Chief Executive	English Street
Assessor	Alan Henry	Assessor & Electoral Registration Officer	Moffat Road
Education	Fraser Sanderson	Corporate Director for Education & Community Services	Edinburgh Road
Environment	Peter Bulmer	Corporate Director for Planning & Environment Services	Militia House
Finance	Julian Cowie	Director for Finance	Carruthers House
Leisure	Stewart Atkinson	Group Manager – Community Services	118 English St
Planning	Peter Bulmer	Corporate Director for Planning & Environment Services	Militia House
Social Services	Beth Smith	Chief Social Work Officer	Grierson House

On 1 April 1996, Dumfries & Galloway Council took over from Dumfries & Galloway Regional Council, comprising Annandale & Eskdale, Nithsdale, Stewartry and Wigtown District Councils.

Community Councils in the authority's area: Ae; Auchencairn; Auldgirth & District; Balmaclellan; Balmaghie; Beeswing; Borgue; Brydekirk & District; Buittle Parish; Caerlaverock; Cairnryan; Canonbie & District; Carronbridge; Carsphairn; Castle Douglas; Closeburn; Colvend & Southwick; Cree Valley; Crossmichael & District; Cummertrees & Cummertrees West; Dalbeattie; Dalry; Dalton & Carrutherstown; Dundrennan; Dunscore; Eastriggs Dornock & Creca; Eskdalemuir; Gatehouse of Fleet; Glencairn; Gretna & Rigg; Heathhall; Hoddom & Ecclefechan; Holywood & Newbridge; Irongray; Isle of Whithorn; Johnstone; Keir; Kelton; Kirkbean; Kirkcolm; Kirkconnel & Kelloholm; Kirkcowan; Kirkgunzeon; Kirkmabreck; Kirkmahoe & Locharbriggs; Kirkmaiden; Kirkpatrick Durham, Corsock & Parton; Kirkpatrick Fleming & District; Kirkpatrick Juxta; Kirtle & Eaglesfield; Langholm Ewes & Westerkirk; Lincluden; Lochrutton; Lochside & Woodlands; Lockerbie & District; Loreburn; Middlebie & Waterbeck; Moffat & District; Mouswald; New Abbey; New Luce; Ochtrelure & Belmont; Old Luce; Penpont; Port William & District; Portpatrick; Royal Burgh of Annan; Royal Burgh of Kirkcudbright & District; Royal Burgh of Lochmaben & District; Royal Burgh of New Galloway & Kells Parish; Royal Burgh of Sanquhar & District; Royal Burgh of Wigtown & District; Royal Burgh of Whithorn & District; Royal Four Towns; Ruthwell & Clarencefield; Ryedale; Southerness; Springfield & Gretna Green; Stoneykirk; Terregles; Thornhill; Tinwald Parish; Tongland; Torthorwald; Troqueer Landward; Twynholm; Tynron; Urr; Wamphray; Wanlockhead.

DUMFRIES & GALLOWAY REGIONAL COUNCIL
See now Dumfries & Galloway Council

DUNDEE CITY COUNCIL

www.dundeecity.gov.uk

Principal Office
21 City Square, Dundee DD1 3BY
Telephone: (01382) 434000; FAX: (01382) 434666; LP 38 Dundee

Dundee Contract Services
353 Clepington Road, Dundee DD3 8PL
Telephone: (01382) 434729; FAX: (01382) 434777

Economic Development Department
3 City Square, Dundee DD1 3BA
Telephone: (01382) 434251; FAX: (01382) 434650

Education Department; Finance Department; Leisure & Arts Department; Planning and Transportation Department; Social Work Department; Architects Department
Tayside House, 28 Crichton Street, Dundee DD1 3RZ

Waste Management
Marchbanks, 34 Harefield Road, Dundee DD2 3JW
Telephone: (01382) 432777; FAX: (01382) 432746

Housing Department
1 Shore Terrace, Dundee DD1 3AH
Telephone: (01382) 434538; FAX (01382) 434942

Communities Department
Podium Block, Tayside House, 28 Chrichton Street, Dundee DD1 3RZ
Telephone: (01382) 433924; FAX: (01382) 433871

Personnel and Management Services Department
8 City Square, Dundee DD1 3BG
Telephone: (01382) 434438; FAX: (01382) 434614

Environmental Health & Trading Standards Department
296 Strathmore Avenue, Dundee DD3 6SH
Telephone: (01382) 436260; FAX: (01382) 436283

The Tayside Valuation Joint Board
Nethergate Centre, 35 Yeaman Shore, Dundee DD1 4BU
Telephone: (01382) 315603; FAX: (01382) 315600

Function	Chief Officer	Title	Location
Chief Executive	Mr A Stephen	Chief Executive	21 City Square
Assessor	Mr N Clark Low	Assessor	Nethergate Cntr
Education	Ms A Wilson	Director of Education	Tayside House
Environmental Health	Mr A Oswald	Head of Environmental Health & Trading Standards	Strathmore Ave
Finance	Mr D Dorward	Assistant Chief Executive	Tayside House
Housing	Mrs E Zwirlein	Director of Housing	1 Shore Terrace
Leisure	Mr S Grimmond	Director of Leisure & Arts	Tayside House
Planning	Mr M P Galloway	Director of Planning & Transport	Tayside House
Social Services	Mr A Baird	Director of Social Work	Tayside House
Trading Standards	Mr K Daly	Trading Standards Manager	Strathmore Ave

On 1 April 1996, Dundee City Council took over from the City of Dundee District Council and Tayside Regional Council (Dundee only).

Community Councils in the authority's area: Ancrum/Blackness; Ardler/Blackshade; Broughty Ferry; Caird; Charleston; City Centre/Harlow; Craigiebank and District; Douglas, Angus, and Craigie; Downfield and Brackens; Fintry; Hilltown & District; Kirkton; Lochee; Mid Craigie/Linlathen; Menzieshill; Rockwell/Fairmuir; Stobswell & District; West End; Whitfield.

DUNFERMLINE DISTRICT COUNCIL
See now Fife Council.

EAST AYRSHIRE COUNCIL

www.east-ayrshire.gov.uk

Principal Office
Council Headquarters, London Road, Kilmarnock KA3 7BU
Telephone: (01563) 576000; FAX: (01563) 576500

Finance Department
Council Offices, Greenholm Street, Kilmarnock KA1 4DL
Telephone: (01563) 576300; FAX: (01563) 576390

Planning & Building Control Department
Council Offices, Croft Street, Kilmarnock
Telephone: (01563) 576767; FAX: (01563) 576774

Social Work Department
Council Offices, Civic Centre, Kilmarnock KA1 1BY
Telephone: (01563) 576920; FAX: (01563) 576690

Trading Standards Department
14 London Road, Kilmarnock KA3 7AS
Telephone: (01563) 554380; FAX: (01563) 554379

The Ayrshire Valuation Joint Board
9 Wellington Square, Ayr KA7 1HL
Telephone: (01292) 612221; FAX: (01292) 612673

Function	Chief Officer	Title	Location
Chief Executive	[Vacant]	Chief Executive	Council HQ
Assessor	William Sommerville	Assessor & Electoral Registration Officer	Wellington Sq
Education	John Mulgrew	Director of Educational & Social Services	Council HQ
Environmental Health	John Crawford	Head of Protective Services	Council HQ
Finance	Alex McPhee	Head of Finance	Greenholm St
Housing	Chris McAleavey	Head of Housing	Civic Centre
Legal Services	David Mitchell	Head of Administrative & Legal Services	Council HQ
Leisure	John Griffiths	Head of Leisure Services	Council HQ
Local Land Charges	David Mitchell	Head of Administrative & Legal Services	Council HQ
Planning	Allan Neish	Head of Planning & Building Control	Croft Street
Social Services	Jackie Donnelly	Head of Social Work	Civic Centre
Technical Services	Jim Lavery	Director of Development & Property Services	Civic Centre
Trading Standards	Joe Donnelly	Principal Officer of Trading Standards	14 London Rd

On 1 April 1996, East Ayrshire Council took over from Cumnock & Doon Valley and Kilmarnock & Loudoun District Councils, and, in part, from Strathclyde Regional Council.

Community Councils in the authority's area: Auchinleck; Bellfield; Bonnyton; Catrine; Crosshouse; Cumnock & District; Cumnock Landward; Dalmellington; Dalrymple; Darvel & District; The Dean; Drongan; Dunlop & Lugton; Fenwick; Galston; Gatehead; Grange/Howard; Hurlford; Kilmaurs; Knockentiber; Lugar & Logan; Mauchline; Moscow & Waterside; Muirkirk; New Cumnock; New Farm Loch; Newmilns & Greenholm; Ochiltree; North West; Patna; Piersland-Bentinck; Riccarton; Shortlees; Sorn; Stewarton & District.

EAST DUNBARTONSHIRE COUNCIL
www.eastdunbarton.gov.uk

Principal Office
Tom Johnston House, Civic Way, Kirkintilloch, G66 4TJ
Telephone: (0141) 578 8000

Education Department
Boclair House, 100 Milngavie Road, Dearsden G61 2TQ
Telephone: (0141) 578 8000

Environmental & Consumer Services
2 Grange Avenue, Milngavie, Glasgow G62 8AQ
Telephone: (0141) 578 8000; FAX: (0141) 578 8823

Leisure Services
Broomhill Leisure Industrial Estate, Kilsyth Road, Kilsyth, Kirkintilloch G66 1TF
Telephone: (0141) 574 5555

Partnership & Planning
The Triangle, Kirkintilloch Road, Bishopbriggs, Glasgow G64 2TR
Telephone: (0141) 578 8000; FAX: (0141) 578 8575

Social Services Department
Wm Patrick Library, 2/4 West High Street, Kirkintilloch, Glasgow G66 1AP
Telephone: (0141) 775 9000; FAX: (0141) 578 3444

The Dunbartonshire and Argyll & Bute Valuation Joint Board
235 Dumbarton Road, Clydebank G81 4XJ
Telephone: (0141) 562 1200; FAX: (0141) 562 1255

Function	Chief Officer	Title	Location
Chief Executive	[Vacant]	Chief Executive	T. Johnston Hse
Assessor	David C Thomson	Assessor	Dumbarton Rd
Education	John Simmons	Head of Education	Boclair Hse
Environmental Health	Hugh Sheridan	Head of Environmental Services	2 Grange Ave
Finance	Karen Mitchell	Accounting & Budgeting Manager	T. Johnston Hse
Housing	Kenny Simpson	Head of Housing & Home Support	T. Johnston Hse
Legal Services	Diane Campbell	Head of Legal & Administration	T. Johnston Hse
Leisure	Mark Grant	Commercial Manager, Sports Development	Broomhill
Planning	Alan Sim	Head of Partnership & Planning	The Triangle
Social Services	Sue Bruce	Strategic Director of Community	T. Johnston Hse
Technical Services	George Thom	Director of Development & Environment	T. Johnston Hse
Trading Standards	Gavin Kenny	Consumer Services Manager	Whitegates

On 1 April 1996, East Dunbartonshire Council took over from Bearsden & Milngavie District Council.

Community Councils in the authority's area: Balmore; Bearsden; Bishopbriggs; Kirkintilloch; Lennoxtown; Lenzie; Milngavie; Milton of Campsie; Torrance; Twechar.

EAST KILBRIDE DISTRICT COUNCIL
See now South Lanarkshire Council.

EAST LOTHIAN COUNCIL

www.eastlothian.gov.uk

Principal Office
John Muir House, Haddington, East Lothian EH41 3HA
Telephone: (01620) 827827; FAX: (01620) 827888; DX 734 Haddington

Department of Social Work & Housing
9-11 Lodge Street, Haddington, East Lothian EH41 3DX
Telephone: (01620) 826600; FAX: (01620) 824295

The Lothian Valuation Joint Board
PO Box 467, Chesser House, 500 Gorgie Road, Edinburgh EH11 3YJ
Telephone: (0131) 469 5589; FAX: (0131) 469 5599

Function	Chief Officer	Title	Location
Chief Executive	John Lindsay	Chief Executive	John Muir Hse
Assessor	John E Cardwell	Assessor & Electoral Registration Officer	Chesser House
Education	Alan Blackie	Director of Education & Community Services	John Muir Hse
Environmental Health	Roy Hannah	Director of Environment & Technical Services	John Muir Hse
Finance	Alex McCrorie	Director of Finance & Information Technology	John Muir Hse
Housing	Bruce Walker	Director of Social Work & Housing	9-11 Lodge St
Legal Services	Keith MacConnachie	Council Solicitor	John Muir Hse
Leisure	Alan Blackie	Director of Education & Community Services	John Muir Hse
Local Land Charges	Roy Hannah	Director of Environment & Technical Services	John Muir Hse
Planning	Roy Hannah	Director of Environment & Technical Services	John Muir Hse
Purchasing & Supplies	Billy Hislop	Purchasing Manager	John Muir Hse

Social Services	Bruce Walker	Director of Social Work & Housing	9-11 Lodge St
Technical Services	Roy Hannah	Director of Environment & Technical Services	John Muir Hse
Trading Standards	Roy Hannah	Director of Environment & Technical Services	John Muir Hse

On 1 April 1996, East Lothian Council took over from East Lothian District Council and, in part, from Lothian Regional Council.

Community Councils in the authority's area: Cockenzie & Port Seton; Dunbar; Dunpender; East Lammermuir; Garvald & Morham; Gifford; Gullane & Area; Haddington & Area; Humbie, East & West Saltoun & Bolton; Longniddry; Macmerry & Gladsmuir; Musselburgh & Inveresk; North Berwick; Ormiston; Pencaitland; Prestonpans; Tranent & Elphinstone; Wallyford & Whitecraig; West Barns.

EAST LOTHIAN DISTRICT COUNCIL
See now East Lothian Council.

EAST RENFREWSHIRE COUNCIL
www.eastrenfrewshire.gov.uk

Principal Office
Council Headquarters, Eastwood Park, Rouken Glen Road, Giffnock,
East Renfrewshire G46 6UG
Telephone: (0141) 577 3000; FAX: (0141) 620 0884

Education Department
Barrhead Council Offices, 211 Main Street, Barrhead G78 1SY

Housing & Commercial Operations Department
Capelrig House, Capelrig Road, Newton Mearns G77 6LA

The Renfrewshire Valuation Joint Board
The Robertson Centre, 16 Glasgow Road, Paisley PA1 3QF
Telephone: (0141) 842 5922; FAX: (0141) 842 5929

Function	Chief Officer	Title	Location
Chief Executive	Peter W Daniels	Chief Executive	Council HQ
Assessor	Edward Duffy	Assessor & Electoral Registration Officer	Robertson Cntr
Education	John Wilson	Director of Education	Barrhead Cl Offs
Environmental Health	Andrew Cahill	Director of Environment	Council HQ
Finance	David Dippie	Director of Finance	Council HQ
Housing	Bob Russell	Director of Housing & Commercial Operations	Capelrig House
Legal Services	Jeff Hawkins	Director of Central Services	Council HQ
Leisure	Ann Saunders	Director of Community & Leisure	Council HQ
Planning	Andrew Cahill	Director of Environment	Council HQ
Purchasing & Supplies	Jim Livingstone	Purchasing & Procurement Manager	Council HQ
Social Services	George Hunter	Director of Social Work	Council HQ
Technical Services	Jeff Hawkins	Director of Central Services	Council HQ
Trading Standards	Andrew Cahill	Director of Environment	Council HQ

On 1 April 1996, East Renfrewshire Council took over from Eastwood and Renfrew District Councils.

Community Councils in the authority's area: Barrhead; Busby; Clarkston; Eaglesham; Giffnock; Linn; Mearns; Neilston; Stamperland/Netherlee; Thornliebank; Uplawmoor.

SCOTLAND

EASTWOOD DISTRICT COUNCIL
See now East Renfrewshire Council.

THE CITY OF EDINBURGH COUNCIL
www.edinburgh.gov.uk

Principal Office
Council Headquarters, Wellington Court, Waterloo Place, Edinburgh EH1 3EG
Telephone: (0131) 200 2000

City Development Department
1 Cockburn Street, Edinburgh EH1 1BJ
Telephone: (0131) 529 3595

Environmental & Consumer Services Department
Chesser House, 500 Gorgie Road, Edinburgh EH11 3YJ
Telephone: (0131) 529 3030

Culture and Leisure Department; Housing Department
23-25 Waterloo Place, Edinburgh EH1 3BH
Telephone: (0131) 200 2000

Social Work Department
Shrubhill House, 7 Shrub Place, Edinburgh EH7 4PD
Telephone: (0131) 554 4301

Legal Services
City Chambers, High Street, Edinburgh EH1 1YJ

The Lothian Valuation Joint Board
PO Box 467, Chesser House, 500 Gorgie Road, Edinburgh EH11 3YJ
Telephone: (0131) 469 5589; FAX: (0131) 469 5599

Function	Chief Officer	Title	Location
Chief Executive	Tom Aitchison	Chief Executive	Council HQ
Assessor	John E Cardwell	Assessor & Electoral Registration Officer	Chesser House
Education	Roy Jobson	Director of Education	Council HQ
Environmental Health	Mike Drewry	Director of Environment & Consumer Services	Chesser House
Finance	Donald McGougan	Director of Finance	Council HQ
Housing	Mark Turley	Director of Housing	23 Waterloo Pl
Legal Services	Gill Lindsay	Council Solicitor	City Chambers
Leisure	Herbert Coutts	Director of Recreation	23 Waterloo Pl
Planning	Andrew Holmes	Director of City Development	1 Cockburn St
Social Services	Roy Jobson	Acting Director of Social Work	Council HQ
Trading Standards	Mike Drewry	Director of Environment & Consumer Services	Chesser House

On 1 April 1996, The City of Edinburgh Council took over from the City of Edinburgh District Council and, in part, from the Lothian Regional Council.

ETTRICK & LAUDERDALE DISTRICT COUNCIL
See now Scottish Borders Council.

FALKIRK COUNCIL
www.falkirk.gov.uk

Principal Office
Municipal Buildings, Falkirk FK1 5RS
Telephone: (01324) 506070; FAX: (01324) 506071

SCOTLAND

Community Services
Kilns House, Falkirk FK1 5SA
Telephone: (01324) 506170; FAX: (01324) 506171

Education Services
McLaren House, Marchmont Avenue, Polmont, Falkirk FK2 0NZ
Telephone: (01324) 506600; FAX: (01324) 506601

Housing Services
Denny Town House, Glasgow Road, Denny FK6 5DL
Telephone: (01324) 504000; FAX: (01324) 504001

Social Work Services
Brockville, Falkirk FK1 5RW
Telephone: (01324) 506400; FAX: (01324) 506401

Development Services
Abbotsford House, David's Loan, Bainsford, Falkirk FK2 7YZ
Telephone: (01324) 504950; FAX: (01324) 504850

The Central Scotland Valuation Board
Hillside House, Laurelhill, Stirling FK7 9QJ
Telephone: (01786) 892200; FAX: (01786) 892255

Function	Chief Officer	Title	Location
Chief Executive	Mary Pitcaithly	Chief Executive	Municipal Bldgs
Assessor	Kenneth D Scott	Assessor	Hillside House
Education	Dr Graeme Young	Director of Education Services	McLaren House
Environmental Health	Rhona Geisler	Director of Development Services	Abbotsford Hse
Finance	Alex Jannetta	Director of Finance	Municipal Bldgs
Housing	Janet Birks	Director of Housing & Social Work Services	Brockville
Legal Services	Elizabeth S Morton	Director of Law & Administration	Municipal Bldgs
Leisure	Maureen Campbell	Head of Leisure Services	Kilns House
Planning	Rhona Geisler	Director of Development Services	Abbotsford Hse
Purchasing & Supplies	Stuart Ritchie	Director of Corporate & Commercial Services	Municipal Bldgs
Social Services	Janet Birks	Director of Housing & Social Work Services	Brockville
Technical Services	Rhona Geisler	Director of Development Services	Abbotsford Hse
Trading Standards	Rhona Geisler	Director of Development Services	Abbotsford Hse

On 1 April 1996, Falkirk Council took over from Falkirk District Council and, in part, from Central Regional Council.

Community Councils in the authority's area: Airth Parish; Avonbridge & Standburn; Banknock, Haggs & Longcroft; Blackness Area; Bo'ness; Brightons; Camelon & District, Carronshore; Denny & District; Falkirk Central; Falkirk South; Grahamston; Grangemouth; Langless, Bainsford & New Carron; Larbert & Stenhousemuir; Lower Braes; Polmont; Reddingmuirhead & Wallacestone; Shieldhill & California; Slammanan & Limerigg.

FALKIRK DISTRICT COUNCIL
See now Falkirk Council.

FIFE COUNCIL

www.fifedirect.org.uk

Principal Office
Fife House, North Street, Glenrothes, Fife KY7 5LT
Telephone: (01592) 414141; DX 561501 Glenrothes

SCOTLAND

Community Services Department; Education Department;
Competitive & Technical Strategy Department
Rothesay House, North Street, Glenrothes KY7 5PN
Telephone: (01592) 414141

Housing Department
Unicorn House, Fakland Gate, Glenrothes KY7 5PD
Telephone: (01592) 414141

Assessor's Department
Kingdom House, Kingdom Avenue, Glenrothes KY7 5LY
Telephone: (01592) 413183; FAX: (01592) 413194

Function	Chief Officer	Title	Location
Chief Executive	Douglas Sinclair	Chief Executive	Fife House
Education	Roger Stewart	Head of Education	Rothesay Hse
Assessor	James Harris	Assessor & Electoral Registration Officer	Kingdom Hse
Environmental Health	Stuart Nichol	Strategic Manager of Environment & Development Services	Fife House
Finance	Brian Lawrie	Head of Finance & Asset Management	Fife House
Housing	Alan Davidson	Head of Housing	Unicorn House
Legal Services	Harry Tait	Head of Law & Administration	Fife House
Leisure	David Somerville	Head of Community Services	Rothesay Hse
Planning	Keith Winter	Head of Development Services	Fife House
Purchasing & Supplies	John McHugh	Head of Service Support	Kingdom Hse
Social Services	Stephen Moore	Head of Social Work	Fife House
Technical Services	John McHugh	Head of Service Support	Kingdom Hse
Trading Standards	Neil Edwards	Head of Trading Standards	Kingdom Hse

On 1 April 1996, Fife Council took over from Fife Regional Council, and Dunfermline, Kirkcaldy and North East Fife District Councils.

Community Councils in the authority's area: Abbeyview; Abdie & Dunbog; Aberdour; Auchtermuchty & Strathmiglo; Auchtertool; Balmerino, Kilmany & Logie; Balmullo; Bellyeoman; Benarty; Blairhall; Boarhills & Dunino; Burntisland; Cairneyhill; Cameron; Cardenden & Kinglassie; Carnbee & Arncroach; Carnock & Gowkhall; Central Dunfermline; Ceres & District; Charlestown, Limekilns & Pattiesmuir; Colinsburgh & Kilconquhar; Collessie; Cowdenbeath; Crail & District; Creich & Flisk; Crombie; Crossford; Crossgates & Mossgreen; Culross; Cults; Dairsie; Dalgety Bay & Hillend; Dunnikier; East Wemyss & McDuff; Elie & the Royal Burgh of Earlsferry; Falkland & Newton of Falkland; Freuchie; Giffordtown & District; Guardbridge; High Valleyfield; Inverkeithing; Izatt Avenue & Netherton; Kelty; Kemback, Pitscottie & Blebo; Kettle; Kincardine; Kinghorn; Kingsbarns; Kingseat; Kirkcaldy West; Largo Area; Largoward & District; Leslie; Leuchars; Leven; Lochgelly; Low Valleyfield; Lumphinnans; Markinch; Methilhill; Milton & Coaltown of Balgonie; Monimail; Moonzie; Newburgh; Newport, Wormit & Forgan; North Glenrothes; North Queensferry; Oakley & Comrie; Pitcorthie; Pitteuchar, Stenton & Finglassie; Rosyth; Royal Burgh of Cupar & District; Royal Burgh of Kilrenny, Anstruther & District; Royal Burgh of Ladybank & District; Royal Burgh of Pittenweem & District; Royal Burgh of St Andrews; St Monans; Saline & Steelend; Springfield; Star of Markinch; Strathkinness; Tayport Ferryport-on-Craig; Thornton; Torryburn & Newmills; Touch & Garvock; Townhill; West Wemyss.

FIFE REGIONAL COUNCIL
See now Fife Council.

GLASGOW CITY COUNCIL

www.glasgow.gov.uk

Principal Office
City Chambers, George Square, Glasgow G2 1DU
Telephone: (0141) 287 2000; FAX: (0141) 287 5666

SCOTLAND

Cultural & Leisure Services
20 Trongate, Glasgow G1 5ES
Telephone: (0141) 287 4350; FAX: (0141) 287 5918

Development & Regeneration Services
229 George Street, Glasgow G1 1QU
Telephone: (0141) 287 8555; FAX: (0141) 287 8444

Education; Social Work
Nye Bevan House, 20 India Street, Glasgow G2 4PF
Telephone: (0141) 287 2000

Environmental Protection Services
231 George Street, Glasgow G1 1RX
Telephone: (0141) 287 2000

Financial Services
City Chambers, 285 George Street, Glasgow G2 1DU
Telephone: (0141) 287 3837; FAX: (0141) 287 3917

Assessor and Electoral Registration
Charlotte House, 78 Queen Street, Glasgow G1 3DR
Telephone: (0141) 287 7547; FAX (0141) 287 7529

Function	Chief Officer	Title	Location
Chief Executive	George Black	Chief Executive	City Chambers
Assessor	William Jonhston	Assessor & Electoral Registration Officer	Charlotte House
Education	Ronnie O'Connor	Director of Education	Nye Bevan Hse
Environmental Health	Robert O'Neill	Director of Environmental Protection Services	231 George St
Finance	Lynn Brown	Director of Financial Services	City Chambers
Legal Services	Ian Drummond	Solicitor to the Council/Monitoring Officer	City Chambers
Leisure	Bridget McConnell	Director of Cultural & Leisure Services	20 Trongate
Planning	Rodger McConnell	Director of Development & Regeneration Services	229 George St
Social Services	David Comley	Director, Social Work Services	Nye Bevan Hse
Technical Services	Willie Martin	Head of Technical Services & Project Management	229 George St
Trading Standards	Ian Wilson	Head of Consumer & Trading Standards	231 George St

On 1 April 1996, the City of Glasgow Council took over from the City of Glasgow District Council.

Community Councils in the authority's area: Anderston; Arden, Carnwadric, Kennishead & Old Darnley; Baillieston; Balgrayhill; Blairdardie, Old Drumchapel; Brockburn; Broomhill; Broomhouse; Calton, Bridgeton; Carmyle; Carmunnock; Cathcart & District; Claythorn; Corkerhill; Dalmarnock; Darnley Estate; Dennistoun; Drumchapel; Drumoyne; Dumbreck; Garnethill; Garrowhill; Gartcraig; Germiston; Govan; Govan East; Hillhead; Hillington; Hurlet; Hutchesontown; Ibrox Cessnock; Jordanhill; Kelvindale; Kelvin North; Kelvinside; Kings Park & Croftfoot; Kinning Park; Knightswood; Knightswood/North Templar; Laurieston; Levern District; Mansewood & Hillpark; Merchant City; Milton; Molendinar; Mosspark; Mount Florida; Mount Vernon; Newlands & Auldhouse; Oatlands; Parkhouse; Partick; Pollok; Pollok (North); Pollockshaws/Eastwood; Pollokshields; Possilpark; Ruchill; Scotstoun; Simshill/Old Cathcart; Springboig; Springburn Central; Swinton; Thornwood; Toryglen; Townhead; Trongate; Wallacewell; Waverley; Wellhouse; Whiteinch; Woodlands & Park; Woodside; Yoker South; Yorkhill/Kelvingrove.

GORDON DISTRICT COUNCIL
See now Aberdeenshire Council.

SCOTLAND

GRAMPIAN REGIONAL COUNCIL
See now Aberdeen City Council; Aberdeenshire Council; The Moray Council.

HAMILTON DISTRICT COUNCIL
See now South Lanarkshire Council.

THE HIGHLAND COUNCIL
www.highland.gov.uk

Principal Office
Council Buildings, Glenurquhart Road, Inverness IV3 5NX
Telephone: (01463) 702000; FAX: (01463) 702111

Procurement Unit
Town House, High Street, Inverness IV1 1JJ
Telephone: (01463) 702143; FAX: (01463) 724223

The Highland & Western Isles Valuation Joint Board
Moray House, 16/18 Bank Street, Inverness IV1 1QY
Telephone: (01463) 703340; FAX: (01463) 703301

Function	Chief Officer	Title	Location
Chief Executive	Mr A D McCourt	Chief Executive	Council Buildings
Assessor	Mr D Gillespie	Assessor and Electoral Registration Officer	Moray House
Education	Mr B Robertson	Director of Education, Culture & Sport	Council Buildings
Environmental Health	Ms M McLauchlan	Director of Transport, Environmental & Community Services	Council Buildings
Finance	Mr A Geddes	Director of Finance	Council Buildings
Housing	Mr G W Fisher	Director of Housing	Council Buildings
Legal Services	Mr M McRae	Head of Legal Services	Council Buildings
Leisure	Mr B Robertson	Director of Education, Culture & Sport	Council Buildings
Local Land Charges	Mr A Dodds	Director of Corporate Services	Council Buildings
Planning	Mr J Rennilson	Director of Planning & Development	Council Buildings
Purchasing & Supplies	Mr A Gould	Procurement Manager	Town House
Social Services	Ms H Dempster	Director of Social Work	Council Buildings
Technical Services	Dr A Coutts	Director of Property & Architectural Services	Council Buildings

On 1 April 1996, The Highland Council took over from Highland Regional Council, comprising Badenoch & Strathspey, Caithness, Inverness, Lochaber, Nairn, Ross & Cromarty, Skye & Lochalsh and Sutherland District Councils.

Community Councils in the authority's area: Acharacle; Achmore & Stromeferry; Alness; Applecross; Ardersier & Petty; Ardgour; Ardross; Arisaig; Assynt; Auldearn; Aultbea; Aviemore & District; Avoch & Killen; Balintore & Hilton; Ballachulish & Glencoe; Ballifeary; Balloch; Beauly; Berriedale & Dunbeath; Bettyhill, Strathnaver & Altnaharra; Boat of Garten; Bower; Braes; Broadford & Strath; Brora; Caithness West; Caol; Carrbridge & Vicinity; Castletown; Cawdor & West Nairnshire; Coigach; Conon Bridge; Contin; Creich; Cromarty & District; Cromdale & Advie; Crown; Croy; Culcabock & Drakies; Dalneigh & Columba; Dalwhinnie; Dingwall; Dores & Essich; Dornie & District; Dornoch Area; Dulnain Bridge; Dunvegan & District; Durness; Duror & Kentallen; East Nairn; Edderton; Fearn; Ferintosh; Fortrose & Rosemarkie; Fort William; Fort Augustus/Glenmoriston; Gairloch; Garve & District; Glendale; Glenelg & Arnisdale; Glenfinnan; Glengarry; Glenurquhart; Golspie; Grantown-on-Spey; Halkirk; Helmsdale; Hilton & Milton of Culcabock; Holm; Inver; Invergordon; Inverlochy & Torlundy; Inverness West; Killearnan; Kilmallie; Kilmorack; Kilmuir Easter; Kilmuir; Kiltarlity; Kiltearn; Kincardine & Croick; Kincraig & Vicinity; Kingussie; Kinlochbervie; Kinlochleven; Kirkhill/Bunchrew; Knockbain; Kyle; Kyleakin &

Kylerhea; Laggan; Lairg; Latheron & Lybster; Lochalsh & Lochlong; Lochardil & Drummond; Lochbroom; Lochcarron; Lochduich; Mallaig; Marybank, Scatwell & Strathconon; Maryburgh; Melvich; Merkinch; Minginish; Morar; Morvern; Muir of Ord; Muirtown; Nairn River; Nairn West; Nether Lochaber; Nethybridge & Vicinity; Newtonmore Area; Nigg & Shandwick; Plockton & District; Portree; Raasay; Resolis; Rogart; Saltburn & Westwood; Sconser; Scorie; Shieldaig; Sinclair Bay; Skeabost & District; Sleat; Small Isles; Smithton/Culloden; Spean Bridge/Roy Bridge/Achnacarry; Staffin; Strathdearn; Stratherrick & Foyers; Strathglass; Strathnairn; Strathpeffer; Strathy & Armadale; Struan; Sunart; Tain; Tarbat; Thurso; Tongue; Torridon & Kinlochewe; Uig; Waternish; Watten; West Nairnshire; Wester Lochewe; Western Ardnamurchan; Westhill; Wick.

HIGHLAND REGIONAL COUNCIL
See now The Highland Council

INVERCLYDE COUNCIL

www.inverclyde.gov.uk

Inverclyde Council Municipal Buildings, Greenock PA15 1LY
Telephone: (01475) 717171; FAX: (01475) 712010

Environmental Services
Old Library Buildings, Wallace Place, Greenock PA15 1LZ
Telephone: (01475) 717171

Leisure Services
Highholm Centre, Highholm Avenue, Port Glasgow PA14 5JN
Telephone: (01475) 717171

Property Services
Cathcart House, Cathcart Square, Greenock PA15 1LS
Telephone: (01475) 717171

Trading Standards
40 West Stewart Street, Greenock PA15 1YA
Telephone: (01475) 717171

The Renfrewshire Valuation Joint Board
The Robertson Centre, 16 Glasgow Road, Paisley PA1 3QF
Telephone: (0141) 842 5922; FAX: (0141) 842 5929

Function	Chief Officer	Title	Location
Chief Executive	Robert Cleary	Chief Executive	Municipal Bldgs
Assessor	Edward Duffy	Assessor & Electoral Registration Officer	Robertson Centre
Education	Bernard McLeary	Director (Education Services)	Municipal Bldgs
Environmental Health	John Arthur	Head of Environment & Consumer Services	Old Library Bldgs
Finance	Caroline Williamson	Director of Finance Services	Municipal Bldgs
Housing	Tom Keenan	Director of Social Work & Housing Services	Old Library Bldgs
Legal Services	Elaine Paterson	Director (Legal & Support Services)	Municipal Bldgs
Leisure	Richard Kenney	Head of Leisure & Community Support Services	Highholm Centre
Local Land Charges	Elaine Paterson	Director (Legal & Support Services)	Municipal Bldgs
Planning	Fraser Williamson	Head of Planning Services	Municipal Bldgs
Purchasing & Supplies	Alan Puckrin	Head of Financial Service	Municipal Bldgs
Social Services	Tom Keenan	Director of Social Work & Housing Services	Old Library Bldgs
Technical Services	Dennis Stoddart	Head of Property Services	Cathcart House

SCOTLAND

On 1 April 1996, Inverclyde Council took over from Inverclyde District Council.

Community Councils in the authority's area: Auchmountain; Bow Farm; Braeside/Branchton; Cardwell Bay; Cartsdyke; Gibshill/Weir Street; Greenock (Larkfield); Greenock Central; Grieve Road/Fancy Farm; Hole Farm; Inverkip; Kilmacolm; Old Gourock; Port Glasgow (Central West); Port Glasgow (Lower East); Port Glasgow (Upper East); Port Glasgow (Upper West); Upper Gourock; Wemyss Bay.

INVERCLYDE DISTRICT COUNCIL
See now Inverclyde Council.

INVERNESS DISTRICT COUNCIL
See now The Highland Council.

KILMARNOCK & LOUDOUN DISTRICT COUNCIL
See now East Ayrshire Council.

KINCARDINE & DEESIDE DISTRICT COUNCIL
See now Aberdeenshire Council.

KIRKCALDY DISTRICT COUNCIL
See now Fife Council.

KYLE & CARRICK DISTRICT COUNCIL
See now South Ayrshire Council.

LOCHABER DISTRICT COUNCIL
See now The Highland Council.

LOTHIAN DISTRICT COUNCIL
See now City of Edinburgh Council; Midlothian Council; West Lothian Council.

LOTHIAN REGIONAL COUNCIL
See now City of Edinburgh Council; East Lothian Council; West Lothian Council.

MIDLOTHIAN COUNCIL
www.midlothian.gov.uk

Executive Services; Strategic Services; Corporate Services
Midlothian House, Buccleuch Street, Dalkeith, Midlothian EH22 1DJ
Telephone: (0131) 270 7500; FAX: (0131) 271 3050

Education Services; Community Services
Fairfield House, 8 Lothian Road, Dalkeith, Midlothian EH22 3AA
Telephone: (0131) 270 7500; FAX: (0131) 271 3050

The Lothian Valuation Joint Board
PO Box 467, Chesser House, 500 Gorgie Road, Edinburgh EH11 3YJ
Telephone: (0131) 469 5589; FAX: (0131) 469 5599

Function	Chief Officer	Title	Location
Chief Executive	Trevor Muir	Chief Executive	Midlothian Hse
Assessor	John E Cardwell	Assessor & Electoral Registration Officer	Chesser House
Education	Donald MacKay	Director, Education	Fairfield House
Environmental Health	Graeme Marwick	Director, Community Services	Fairfield House
Finance	Ian Jackson	Director, Finance	Midlothian Hse
Housing	Tom Ogilvie	Head of Revenues & Housing Management	Fairfield House

Legal Services	Norman Grieve	Head of Law & Administration	Midlothian Hse
Leisure	Graeme Marwick	Director, Community Services	Fairfield House
Planning	John Allan	Director of Strategic Services	Midlothian Hse
Social Services	Malcolm McEwan	Chief Social Work Officer	Fairfield House
Trading Standards	Graeme Marwick	Director, Community Services	Fairfield House

On 1 April 1996, Midlothian Council took over from Midlothian District Council.

Community Councils in the authority's area: Bonnyrigg & Lasswade; Dalkeith; Damhead; Danderhall & District; Eskbank & Newbattle; Howgate; Loanhead & District; Mayfield/ Easthouses; Moorfoot; Newtongrange; Penicuik; Rosewell & District; Roslin & Bilston; Tynewater.

MIDLOTHIAN DISTRICT COUNCIL
See now Midlothian Council.

MONKLANDS DISTRICT COUNCIL
See now North Lanarkshire Council.

THE MORAY COUNCIL

www.moray.org

Principal Office
High Street, Elgin, Moray IV30 1BX
Telephone: (01343) 543451; FAX: (01343) 540183

Education Department
High Street, Elgin, Moray IV30 1BX
Telephone: (01343) 563134

Community Services Department; Housing Department
High Street, Elgin, Moray IV30 1BX
Telephone: (01343) 563530; FAX: (01343) 563521

Trading Standards Department
232 High Street, Elgin, Moray IV30 1BA
Telephone: (01343) 554610

Grampian Valuation Joint Board
Woodhill House, Westburn Road, Aberdeen AB16 5GE
Telephone: (01224) 664848; FAX: (01224) 664361

Function	Chief Officer	Title	Location
Chief Executive	Alastair Keddie	Chief Executive	High Street
Assessor	Alex McConnochie	Assessor	Woodhill Hse
Education	Donald Duncan	Director of Educational Services	High Street
Environmental Health	Donnie Mackay	Environmental Health Manager	High Street
Finance	Mark Palmer	Chief Financial Officer	High Street
Housing	Jill Stewart	Chief Housing Officer	High Street
Legal Services	Roddy Burns	Chief Legal Officer	High Street
Leisure	Eric Scarbrough	Head of Educational Support Service	High Street
Local Land Charges	John Black	Head of Estates Services	High Street
Planning	Bob Stewart	Director of Environmental Services	High Street
Social Services	Mike Martin	Director of Community Services	High Street
Trading Standards	Peter Adamson	Trading Standards Manager	232 High St

On 1 April 1996, Moray Council took over from Moray District Council.

Community Councils in the authority's area: Buckie; Burghead, Cummingston & Roseisle; Dyke Landward; Elgin; Findhorn & Kinloss; Findochty; Forres; Heldon; Keith; Lennox; Lossiemouth; Portknockie; Rathven & Arradoul; Strathisla.

SCOTLAND

MORAY DISTRICT COUNCIL
See now The Moray Council.

MOTHERWELL DISTRICT COUNCIL
See now North Lanarkshire Council.

NAIRN DISTRICT COUNCIL
See now The Highland Council.

NITHSDALE DISTRICT COUNCIL
See now Dumfries & Galloway Council.

NORTH AYRSHIRE COUNCIL

www.north-ayrshire.gov.uk

Headquarters
Cunninghame House, Irvine KA12 8EE
Telephone: (01294) 324100

Social Services
Elliott House, Kilwinning Road, Irvine KA12 8TB
Telephone: (01294) 317700

North Ayrshire Leisure Ltd.
Galt House, 31 Bank Street, Irvine KA12 0AJ

The Ayrshire Valuation Joint Board
9 Wellington Square, Ayr KA7 1HL
Telephone: (01292) 612221; FAX: (01292) 612673

Function	Chief Officer	Title	Location
Chief Executive	Mr Bernard Devine	Chief Executive	Cunninghame Hse
Assessor	Mr William Sommerville	Assessor & Electoral Registration Officer	Wellington Square
Education	Mr John Travers	Corporate Director (Educational Services)	Cunninghame Hse
Environmental Health	Mr Ian Mackay	Assistant Chief Executive (Legal & Protective)	Cunninghame Hse
Finance	Mr Alasdair J Herbert	Assistant Chief Executive (Finance)	Cunninghame Hse
Housing	Mr Tom Orr	Corporate Director (Property Services)	Cunninghame Hse
Legal Services	Mr Ian Mackay	Assistant Chief Executive (Legal & Protective)	Cunninghame Hse
Leisure	Mr Frank Keddilty	Chief Executive (North Ayrshire Leisure Ltd.)	Galt House
Planning	Mr Ian Mackay	Assistant Chief Executive (Legal & Protective)	Cunninghame Hse
Social Services	Ms Bernadette Docherty	Corporate Director (Social Services)	Elliott House
Technical Services	Mr Tom Orr	Corporate Director (Property Services)	Cunninghame Hse
Trading Standards	Mr Ian Mackay	Assistant Chief Executive (Legal & Protective)	Cunninghame Hse

On 1 April 1996, North Ayrshire Council took over from Cunninghame District Council.

Community Councils in the authority's area: Ardrossan; Arran; Beith; Cumbrae; Dalry; Fairlie; Girdle Toll & Bourtreehill; Irvine; Kilbirnie & Glengarnock; Kilwinning; Largs; Skelmorlie; Stevenston; West Kilbride.

SCOTLAND

NORTH EAST FIFE DISTRICT COUNCIL

See now Fife Council.

NORTH LANARKSHIRE COUNCIL

www.northlan.gov.uk

Principal Office
PO Box 14, Civic Centre, Motherwell ML1 1TW
Telephone: (01698) 302222; FAX: (01698) 275125; DX 571700 Motherwell 2

Education Department
Municipal Buildings, Kildonan Street, Coatbridge ML5 3BT
Telephone: (01236) 812222; FAX: (01236) 812247

Housing and Property Services Department
Municipal Buildings, Kildonan Street, Coatbridge ML5 3NG
Telephone: (01236) 812222; FAX: (01236) 812502

Community Services Department
Buchanan Business Park, Stepps G33 6HR
Telephone: (0141) 304 1800; FAX: (0141) 304 1839

Planning & Environment Department
Fleming House, Tryst Road, Cumbernauld G67 1JW
Telephone: (01236) 616200; FAX: (01236) 616206

Social Work Department
Scott House, 73-77 Merry Street, Motherwell ML1 1JE
Telephone: (01698) 332000; FAX: (01698) 332095

The Lanarkshire Valuation Joint Board
North Stand, Cadzow Avenue, Hamilton ML3 0LU
Telephone: (01698) 476000; FAX: (01698) 476010

Function	Chief Officer	Title	Location
Chief Executive	Mr G Whitefield	Chief Executive	Civic Centre
Assessor	Mr M A Lithgow	Assessor & Electoral Registration Officer	North Stand
Education	Mr M O'Neill	Director of Education	Municipal Bldgs
Environmental Health	Mr D Porch	Director of Planning & Environment	Fleming House
Finance	Mr A Crichton	Director of Finance	Civic Centre
Housing	Mr T McKenzie	Director of Housing & Property Services	Municipal Bldgs
Legal Services	Mr J O'Hagan	Director of Administration	Civic Centre
Leisure	Mr P Jukes	Director of Community Services	Buchanan Bus Pk
Planning	Mr D Porch	Director of Planning & Environment	Fleming House
Purchasing & Supplies	Mr A Crichton	Director of Finance	Civic Centre
Social Services	Mr J Dickie	Director of Social Work	Scott House
Technical Services	Mr T McKenzie	Director of Housing & Property Services	Municipal Bldgs
Trading Standards	Mr D Porch	Director of Planning & Environment	Fleming House

On 1 April 1996, North Lanarkshire Council took over from Cumbernauld & Kilsyth, Monklands and Motherwell District Councils.

Community Councils in the authority's area: Abronhill & Arns; Allanton & Hartwood; Auchinloch; Balloch & Eastfield; Banton & Kelvinhead; Bargeddie; Bellshill; Blackwood & Craiglinn; Blairhill; Cairnhill; Calder; Calderbank; Caldercruix; Calder Valley; Cambusnethan; Carbrain & Hillcrest; Carfin; Carrickstone; Castlecary; Central Wishaw; Chapelhall; Chapelside; Chryston; Clarkston; Cleland; Cliftonville; Coatdyke; Coltness; Condorrat; Craigmarloch; Craigneuk; Croy; Dullatur; Forgewood; Gartcosh; Gartlea; Gartness; Glenboig; Glencairn; Glenmavis; Golfhill, Burnfoot & Commonside; Greenfaulds & Luggiebank; Greengairs; Harthill &

SCOTLAND

Eastfield; Holehills, Rawyards & Thrashbush; Holytown; Kildrum; Kilsyth; Kirkwood; Kirkshaws; Ladywell; Langloan; Longriggend; Monkland Glen; Moodiesburn; Mossend; Muirhouse & Flemington; Netherton & Gowkthrapple; New Stevenston; Newarthill; Newmains & District; North Calder (Craigneuk, Dunrobin, Petersburn etc); North Motherwell; Old Monkland; Overtown & Waterloo; Plains; Queenzieburn; Salsburgh; Seafar & Ravenswood; Shawhead; Shotts; Stepps & District; Sunnyside; Tannochside; Townhead; Westerwood; Westfield: Whifflet; Winhall; Village.

ORKNEY ISLANDS COUNCIL

www.orkney.gov.uk

Principal Office
Council Offices, School Place, Kirkwall, Orkney KW15 1NY
Telephone: (01856) 873535; FAX: (01856) 874615

The Orkney & Shetland Valuation Joint Board
8 Albert Street, Kirkwall, Orkney KW15 1HP
Telephone: (01856) 876222; FAX: (01856) 870949

Function	Chief Officer	Title	Location
Chief Executive	A Buchan	Chief Executive	Council Offices
Assessor	D M Leslie	Assessor & Electoral Registration Officer	Albert Street
Education	W L Manson	Director of Education & Recreation Services	Council Offices
Environmental Health	V Cameron	Principal Environmental Health Officer	Council Offices
Finance	A Tait	Director of Finance & Housing	Council Offices
Housing	J T Richards	Assistant Director	Council Offices
Legal Services	D Thompson	Principal Legal Officer	Council Offices
Planning	J Baster	Director of Development & Protective Services	Council Offices
Social Services	H Garland	Director of Community Social Services	Council Offices
Technical Services	B Thomson	Director of Technical Services	Council Offices
Trading Standards	I Watt	Head of Protective Services	Council Offices

Community Councils in the authority's area: Birsay; Eday; Evie & Rendall; Firth & Sunnybrae; Flotta; Graemsay, Hoy & Walls; Harray & Stenness; Holm & Wideford; Kirkwall; North Ronaldsay; Orphir & Scapa; Papa Westray; Rousay, Egilsay & Wyre; Sanday; Sandwick; Shapinsay; South Ronaldsay & Burray; St Andrews & Deerness; Stromness; Stronsay; Westray.

PERTH & KINROSS COUNCIL

www.pkc.gov.uk

Principal Office; Chief Executive's Service; Corporate Services
2 High Street, Perth PH1 5PH
Telephone: (01738) 475000; FAX: (01738) 475710

Housing & Community Care; Education & Children's Services; Planning, Transportation Services; Environment Services
Pullar House, 35 Kinnoull Street, Perth PH1 5GD

Care Together
Moncrieffe Ward, Perth Royal Infirmary, Perth PH1 1NX
Telephone: (01738) 473115; FAX: (01738) 473113

The Tayside Valuation Joint Board
Nethergate Centre, 35 Yeaman Shore, Dundee DD1 4BU
Telephone: (01382) 316603; FAX: (01382) 315600

Function	Chief Officer	Title	Location
Chief Executive	Ms Bernadette Malone	Chief Executive	2 High Street
Education	Mr George Waddell	Acting Director of Education & Children's Services	Pullar House

Function	Chief Officer	Title	Location
Assessor	Mr N Clark Low	Assessor	Nethergate Cntr
Environmental Health	Mr John Milne	Executive Director of Environment Services	Pullar House
Finance	Mr Roddy McArthur	Executive Director of Corporate Services	2 High Street
Housing	Mr Dave Roberts	Executive Director of Housing & Community Care	Pullar House
Legal Services	Mr Ian Innes	Head of Legal Services	2 High Street
Leisure	Mr Peter Bing	Executive Manager (Perth & Kinross Leisure)	2 High Street
Local Land Charges	Mr Dave Roberts	Executive Director of Housing & Community Care	Pullar House
Planning	Mr Jim Irons	Executive Director of Planning & Transportation	Pullar House
Purchasing & Supplies	Mr Ian Hall	Administrative Services Manager	2 High Street
Social Services	Mr Dave Roberts	Executive Director of Housing & Community Care	Pullar House
Technical Services	Mr Jim Irons	Executive Director of Planning & Transportation	Pullar House
Trading Standards	Mr Sandy Nicoll	Trading Standards Manager	Pullar House

On 1 April 1996, Perth & Kinross Council took over from Perth & Kinross District Council.

Community councils in the authority's area: Aberfeldy; Abernethy; Alyth; Auchterarder & District; Auchtergaven; Blackford; Blair Atholl & Struan; Blairgowrie & Rattray; Braco & Greenloaning; Bridgend, Gannochy & Kinnoull; Burrelton & District; Central; Cleish & Blairadam; Comrie & District; Coupar Angus, Ardler & Bendochy; Crieff; Dull & Weem; Dunkeld & Birnam; Dunning; Earn; East Strathearn; Errol; Fossoway; Friarton & Craigie; Glenfarg; Glenlyon & Loch Tay; Inchture; Invergowrie & Gingoodie; Kenmore & District; Kettins; Killiecrankie & Fincastle; Kinross; Longforgan; Meigle; Methven; Mid Atholl, Strathtay & Grandtully; Milnathort; Mount Blair; Muthill & Tullibardine; Pitlochry & Moulin; Portmoak; Rannoch & Tummel; St Fillans; Scone & District; Spittalfield & District; Stanley; Tulloch; Viewlands; West Carse.

PERTH & KINROSS DISTRICT COUNCIL

See now Perth & Kinross Council.

RENFREW DISTRICT COUNCIL

See now East Renfrewshire Council; Renfrewshire Council.

RENFREWSHIRE COUNCIL

www.renfrewshire.gov.uk

Chief Executive's Department; Corporate Services Department; Social Work Department
North Building, Cotton Street, Paisley, Renfrewshire PA1 1TR
Telephone: (0141) 842 5000; FAX: (0141) 840 3335

Education & Leisure Services Department; Environmental Services Department; Finance & Information Technology Department; Planning & Transport Department; Housing & Property Services Department
South Building, Cotton Street, Paisley PA1 1LQ
Telephone: (0141) 842 5000; FAX: (0141) 840 3335

The Renfrewshire Valuation Joint Board
The Robertson Centre, 16 Glasgow Road, Paisley PA1 3QF
Telephone: (0141) 842 5922; FAX: (0141) 842 5929

Function	Chief Officer	Title	Location
Chief Executive	Thomas Scholes	Chief Executive	North Building
Assessor	Edward Duffy	Assessor & Electoral Registration Officer	Robertson Cntr

Function	Chief Officer	Title	Location
Education	Shelagh Rae	Director of Education & Leisure Services	South Building
Environmental Health	Bernard Forteath	Director of Environmental Services	South Building
Finance	William Hughes	Director of Finance & Information Technology	South Building
Housing	Michael Bailey	Director of Housing & Property Services	South Building
Legal Services	Margaret Quinn	Director of Corporate Services	North Building
Leisure	Shelagh Rae	Director of Education & Leisure Services	South Building
Local Land Charges	Margaret Quinn	Director of Corporate Services	North Building
Planning	Ian Snodgrass	Director of Planning & Transport	South Building
Purchasing & Supplies	William Hughes	Director of Finance & Information Technology	South Building
Social Services	David Crawford	Director of Social Work	North Building
Technical Services	Michael Bailey	Director of Housing & Property Services	South Building
Trading Standards	Bernard Forteath	Director of Environmental Services	South Building

On 1 April 1996, Renfrewshire Council took over from Renfrew District Council and, in part, from Strathclyde Regional Council.

Community Councils in the authority's area: Bishopton; Bridge of Weir; Brookfield; Elderslie; Erskine; Gallowhill; Glenburn; Hawkead & Lochfield; Houston; Howwood; Hunterhill; Inchinnan; Johnstone; Kilbarchan; Langbank; Linwood; Lochwinnoch; Paisley East End; Paisley West & Central; Ralston; Renfrew.

ROSS & CROMARTY DISTRICT COUNCIL
See now The Highland Council.

ROXBURGH DISTRICT COUNCIL
See now Scottish Borders Council.

SCOTTISH BORDERS COUNCIL

www.scotborders.gov.uk

Principal Office
Council Headquarters, Newtown St Boswells, Melrose TD6 0SA
Telephone: (01835) 824000; FAX: (01835) 825001

Consumer & Trading Standards Department
St Dunstan's, Melrose, Roxburghshire TD6 9RU
Telephone: (01896) 823922; FAX: (01896) 823924

Assessors Department
Scott House, Sprouston Road, Newtown St Boswells, Melrose TD6 0QD
Telephone: (01835) 825100; FAX: (01835) 825101

Function	Chief Officer	Title	Location
Chief Executive	Mr D Hume	Chief Executive	Council HQ
Education	Mr G Rodger	Director of Education and Lifelong Learning	Council HQ
Assessor	Mr L Walker	Assessor & Electoral Registration Officer	Scott House
Environmental Health	Mrs F Stuart	Acting Director of Lifelong Care	Council HQ
Finance	Mr J I Campbell	Director of Corporate Resources	Council HQ
Legal Services	Mr I Wilkie	Head of Legal Services	Council HQ
Leisure	Mrs F Stuart	Acting Director of Lifelong Care	Council HQ
Planning	Mr P Gregory	Director of Environmental Planning and Economic Development	Council HQ

Purchasing & Supplies	[Vacant]	Central Purchasing Officer	Council HQ
Social Services	Mrs F Stuart	Acting Director of Lifelong Care	Council HQ
Technical Services	Mr W A Lillico	Director of Transport and Environmental Standards	Council HQ
Trading Standards	Mr J Sharratt	Chief Trading Standards Officer	St Dunstan's

On 1 April 1996, Scottish Borders Council took over from Borders Regional Council, and the former Berwickshire, Ettrick & Lauderdale; Roxburgh and Tweeddale District Councils.

Community Councils in the authority's area: Abbey St Bathans, Bunkle & Preston; Ancrum; Ayton; Bowden; Burnfoot; Burnmouth; Carlops; Chirnside; Clovenfords & District; Cockburnspath; Coldingham; Coldstream; Crailing & Eckford; Cranshaws & Longformacus; Denholm & District; Duns; Earlston; Eddleston; Ednam, Stichill & Berrymoss; Edrom, Allanton & Whitsome; Ettrick & Yarrow; Eyemouth; Floors, Makerstoun, Nenthorn & Smailholm; Foulden, Mordington & Lamberton; Galashiels & Langlee; Gavinton, Fogo & Polworth; Gordon & Westruther; Grantshouse; Greenlaw & Hume; Hawick; Heiton & Roxburgh; Heriot; Hobkirk; Innerleithen, Traquair & Glen; Jed Valley; Jedburgh; Kalewater; Kelso; Lamancha, Newlands & Kirkurd; Lanton; Lauderdale; Leitholm, Eccles & Birgham; Lilliesleaf, Ashkirk & Midlem; Manor, Stobo & Lyne; Melrose & District; Newcastleton; Newtown St Boswells; Oxnam; Oxton & Channelkirk; Paxton & Hutton; Peebles & District; Reston & Auchencrow; St Abbs; St Boswells; Selkirk & District; Skirling; Southdean; Sprouston; Stow & Fountainhall; Swinton & Ladykirk; Tweedbank; Upper Teviotdale & Borthwick Water; Upper Tweed; Walkerburn & District; West Linton; Yetholm.

SHETLAND ISLANDS COUNCIL

www.shetland.gov.uk

Principal Office
Town Hall, Lerwick, Shetland ZE1 0HB
Telephone: (01595) 744505; FAX: (01595) 744509

Community Services
Hayfield House, Hayfield Lane, Lerwick ZE1 0QD
Telephone: (01595) 744000; FAX: (01595) 692810

Infrastructure Services
Grantfield, Lerwick ZE1 0NT
Telephone: (01595) 744800/744866; FAX: (01595) 695887

Finance Services
Montfield, Burgh Road, Lerwick ZE1 0TY
Telephone: (01595) 744681; FAX: (01595) 744667

Housing Services
Fort Road, Lerwick ZE1 0LW
Telephone: (01595) 744360; FAX: (01595) 744395

Legal Services
Hayfield House, Lerwick ZE1 0QD
Telephone: (01595) 744058; FAX: (01595) 744083

Legal and Administration Services
4 Market Street, Lerwick ZE1 0JN
Telephone: (01595) 744550; FAX: (01795) 744585

Social Work
Quendale House, 31 Commercial Street, Lerwick ZE1 0AN
Telephone: (01595) 744300; FAX: (01595) 744321

The Orkney & Shetland Valuation Joint Board
8 Albert Street, Kirkwall, Orkney KW15 1HP
Telephone: (01856) 876222; FAX: (01856) 870949

SCOTLAND

Function	Chief Officer	Title	Location
Chief Executive	Morgan Goodlad	Chief Executive	Town Hall
Assessor	Duncan M Leslie	Assessor & Electoral Registration Officer	Albert Street
Education	Jacqui Watt	Executive Director	Hayfield House
Environmental Health	Graham Spall	Executive Director	Grantfield
Finance	Graham Johnston	Head of Finance	Montfield
Housing	Chris Medley	Head of Housing	Fort Road
Legal Services	Jan Riise	Head of Legal & Administration	4 Market Street
Leisure	Neil Watt	Sport & Leisure Services Manager	Hayfield House
Planning	Alastair Hamilton	Head of Planning	Grantfield
Social Services	Christine Ferguson	Community Care Manager	Quendale House
Technical Services	Graham Spall	Executive Director	Breiwick House
Trading Standards	David Marsh	Trading Standards Manager	Grantfield

Community Councils in the authority's area: Aithsting & Sandsting; Bressay; Burra & Trondra; Delting; Dunrossness; Fetlar; Gulberwick, Quarff & Cunningsburgh; Lerwick; Nesting & Lunnasting; Northmavine; Sandness & Walls; Sandwick; Scalloway; Unst; Whalsay & Skerries; Whiteness, Weisdale & Tingwall; Yell.

SKYE & LOCKALSH DISTRICT COUNCIL
See now The Highland Council.

SOUTH AYRSHIRE COUNCIL

www.south-ayrshire.gov.uk

Principal Office
County Buildings, Wellington Square, Ayr KA7 1DR
Telephone: (01292) 612000; FAX: (01292) 612143; DX AY 47 Ayr

The Ayrshire Valuation Joint Board
9 Wellington Square, Ayr KA7 1HL
Telephone: (01292) 612221; FAX: (01292) 612673

Function	Chief Officer	Title	Location
Chief Executive	Tom Curtis	Chief Executive	County Bldgs
Assessor	William Somerville	Assessor & Electoral Registration Officer	Wellington Sq
Education	Mike McCabe	Director of Education, Culture & Lifelong Learning	County Bldgs
Environmental Health	Graham Peterkin	Director of Development, Safety & Regulation	County Bldgs
Finance	Eileen Howat	Head of Financial Services	County Bldgs
Housing	Elaine Noad	Director of Social Work, Housing & Health	County Bldgs
Legal Services	Graham Peterkin	Director of Development, Safety & Regulation	County Bldgs
Leisure	Ronnie Sheed	Director of Environment, Land & Property	County Bldgs
Local Land Charges	Ronnie Sheed	Director of Environment, Land & Property	County Bldgs
Planning	Graham Peterkin	Director of Development, Safety & Regulation	County Bldgs
Purchasing & Supplies	Ronnie Sheed	Director of Environment, Land & Property	County Bldgs
Social Services	Elaine Noad	Director of Social Work, Housing & Health	County Bldgs
Technical Services	Ronnie Sheed	Director of Environment, Land & Property	County Bldgs
Trading Standards	Graham Peterkin	Director of Development, Safety & Regulation	County Bldgs

On 1 April 1996, South Ayrshire Council took over from Kyle & Carrick District Council and from Strathclyde Regional Council.

Community Councils in the authority's area: Alloway & Doonfoot; Annbank, Mossblown & St Quivox; Ballantrae; Barr; Barrhill; Belmont & Kincaidson; Colmonell & Lendalfoot; Coylton; Craigie; Crosshill, Straiton & Kirkmichael; Dailly; Dundonald; Dunure; Fort & Seafield; Loans; Maidens & Kirkoswald; Maybole; Monkton; Newton & Heathfield; Pinwherry; Prestwick South; Symington; Troon.

SOUTH LANARKSHIRE COUNCIL

www.southlanarkshire.gov.uk

Principal Office
Headquarters, Council Offices, Almada Street, Hamilton ML3 0AA
Telephone: (01698) 454444; FAX: (01698) 454275

Trading Standards Department
North Stand, Cadzow Avenue, Hamilton ML3 0LU
Telephone: (01698) 476291

The Lanarkshire Valuation Joint Board
North Stand, Cadzow Avenue, Hamilton ML3 0LU
Telephone: (01698) 476000; FAX: (01698) 476010

South Lanarkshire Leisure Ltd. (Sports Trust)
North Stand, Cadzow Avenue, Hamilton ML3 0LU
Telephone: (01698) 476154

Function	Chief Officer	Title	Location
Chief Executive	Michael Docherty	Chief Executive	Council Offices
Assessor	Mr M A Lithgow	Assessor & Electoral Registration Officer	North Stand
Education	Maggi Allan	Executive Director of Education Resources	Council Offices
Environmental Health	Robert Howe	Head of Environmental Services	Council Offices
Finance	Archibald Strang	Executive Director of Finance & Information Technology Resources	Council Offices
Housing	Stewart Gilchrist	Executive Director of Housing & Technical Resources	Council Offices
Legal Services	Sandra Dickson	Head of Legal Services	Council Offices
Leisure	Hugh Waters	South Lanarkshire Leisure Ltd. (Sports Trust)	North Stand
Local Land Charges	Bob Darrocott	Head of Planning, Building Control & Estates	Council Offices
Planning	Bob Darrocott	Head of Planning, Building Control & Estates	Council Offices
Social Services	Sandy Cameron	Executive Director of Social Work Resources	Council Offices
Technical Services	Stewart Gilchrist	Executive Director of Housing & Technical Resources	Council Offices
Trading Standards	Peter Sherry	Consumer & Trading Standards Manager	North Stand

On 1 April 1996, South Lanarkshire Council took over from Clydesdale, Hamilton and East Kilbride District Councils, and incorporated the Rutherglen and Cambuslang parts of Glasgow.

STEWARTRY DISTRICT COUNCIL
See now Dumfries & Galloway Council.

STIRLING COUNCIL
www.stirling.gov.uk
Principal Office
Viewforth, Stirling FK8 2ET
Telephone: (01786) 443322; FAX: (01786) 443078

Environmental Operations Department
Municipal Buildings, Corn Exchange, Stirling FK8 2HX
Telephone: (01786) 432170

The Central Scotland Valuation Board
Hillside House, Laurelhill, Stirling FK7 9QJ
Telephone: (01786) 892200; FAX: (01786) 892255

Function	Chief Officer	Title	Location
Chief Executive	Keith Yates	Chief Executive	Viewforth
Assessor	Kenneth D Scott	Assessor	Hillside House
Education	Gordon Jeyes	Director of Children's Services	Viewforth
Environmental Health	Ian Kelly	Head of Environmental Operations	Viewforth
Finance	Willie Watson	Head of Resource Management	Viewforth
Housing	Val Rooney	Head of Housing Services	Viewforth
Legal Services	Peter Broadfoot	Chief Solicitor	Viewforth
Leisure	Des Friel	Head of Sport, Leisure & Youth	Viewforth
Planning	Mick Stewart	Head of Planning & Environmental Strategy	Viewforth
Purchasing & Supplies	Don MacMillan	Procurement Officer	Viewforth
Social Services	Irene Cavanagh	Head of Community Care (Adult)/ Chief Social Work Officer	Viewforth
Technical Services	Arthur Nicholls	Director of Technical Services	Viewforth
Trading Standards	Neil Chalmers	Service Manager	Municipal Bldgs

On 1 April 1996, Stirling Council took over from Stirling District Council and Central Regional Council.

Community Councils in the authority's area: Arnprior; Balfron; Balquhidder; Bannockburn; Borestone; Bridge of Allan; Broomridge; Buchanan; Buchlyvie; Callander; Cambusbarron; Cambuskenneth; Causewayhead; Cornton; Cowie; Craigs; Croftamie; Drymen; Dunblane; Fintry; Gargunnock; Gartmore; Killearn; Killin; Kilmadock; Kings Park; Kippen; Logie; Mercat Cross; Plean; Polmaise; Port of Menteith; Raploch; Riverside; Strathard; Strathblane; Strathfillan; Thornhill & Blairdrummond; Torbrex; Trossachs.

STIRLING DISTRICT COUNCIL
See now Stirling Council.

STRATHCLYDE REGIONAL COUNCIL
See now Argyll & Bute Council; City of Glasgow Council; East Ayrshire Council; East Dunbartonshire Council; East Renfrewshire Council; Renfrewshire Council; South Ayrshire Council; South Lanarkshire Council; West Dunbartonshire Council.

STRATHKELVIN DISTRICT COUNCIL
See now North Lanarkshire Council.

SUTHERLAND DISTRICT COUNCIL
See now The Highland Council.

TAYSIDE REGIONAL COUNCIL
See now Angus Council; Dundee City Council; Perth & Kinross Council.

SCOTLAND

TWEEDDALE DISTRICT COUNCIL
See now Scottish Borders Council.

WEST DUNBARTONSHIRE COUNCIL

www.wdcweb.info

Principal Offices
Council Offices, Garshake Road, Dumbarton G82 3PU
Telephone: (01389) 737000; FAX: (01389) 737070

Council Offices, Rosbery Place, Clydebank G81 1TG
Telephone: (01389) 737000; FAX: (01389) 737070

The Dunbartonshire and Argyll & Bute Valuation Joint Board
235 Dumbarton Road, Clydebank G81 4XJ
Telephone: (0141) 562 1200; FAX: (0141) 562 1255

Function	Chief Officer	Title	Location
Chief Executive	Tim Huntingford	Chief Executive	Garshake Road
Assessor	David C Thomson	Assessor	Dumbarton Road
Education	Ian McMurdo	Director of Education & Cultural Services	Garshake Road
Environmental Health	Dan Henderson	Director of Economic Planning & Environmental Services	Rosebery Place
Finance	Eric Walker	Director of Corporate Services	Garshake Road
Housing	Alexis Jay	Director of Social Work & Housing	Garshake Road
Legal Services	Eric Walker	Director of Corporate Services	Garshake Road
Leisure	David MacMillan	Director of Commercial & Technical Services	Garshake Road
Planning	Dan Henderson	Director of Economic Planning & Environmental Services	Rosebery Place
Purchasing & Supplies	David MacMillan	Director of Commercial & Technical Services	Garshake Road
Social Services	Alexis Jay	Director of Social Work & Housing	Garshake Road
Technical Services	David MacMillan	Director of Commercial & Technical Services	Garshake Road
Trading Standards	Dan Henderson	Director of Economic Planning & Environmental Services	Rosebery Place

On 1 April 1996, West Dunbartonshire Council took over from Clydebank and Dumbarton District Councils and Strathclyde Regional Council.

Community Councils in the authority's area: Balloch & Haldane; Bonhill & Dalmonach; Bowling & Milton; Dumbarton East & Central; Dumbarton North; Dumbarton West; Kilmaronock; Old Kilpatrick; Parkhall, North Kilbowie & Central; Silverton & Overtoun.

WEST LOTHIAN COUNCIL

www.westlothian.org.uk

Principal Office
West Lothian House, Almondvale Boulevard, Livingston EH54 6QG
Telephone: (01506) 777000

Commercial Services
Contracts House, Whitehill Industrial Estate, Bathgate, West Lothian EH48 2HA
Telephone: (01506) 776555; FAX: (01506) 776568

Construction Services
Ogilvie House, Ogilvie Way, Livingston EH54 8HL
Telephone: (01506) 777497; FAX: (01506) 777495

SCOTLAND

SCOTLAND

Education Services
Lindsay House, South Bridge Street, Bathgate EH48 1TT
Telephone: (01506) 776000

Environmental & Protective Services
County Buildings, High Street, Linlithgow EH49 7EZ
Telephone: (01506) 775200; FAX: (01506) 775255

The Lothian Valuation Joint Board
PO Box 467, Chesser House, 500 Gorgie Road, Edinburgh EH11 3YJ
Telephone: (0131) 469 5589; FAX: (0131) 469 5599

Function	Chief Officer	Title	Location
Chief Executive	Mr A Linkston	Chief Executive	W Lothian Hse
Assessor	Mr J E Cardwell	Assessor & Electoral Registration Officer	Chesser House
Education	Mrs K Reid	Director of Education & Cultural Services	Lindsay House
Environmental Health	Mr A Blake	Environmental Health & Trading Standards Manager	County Bldgs
Finance	Mr A Logan	Finance Manager	W Lothian Hse
Housing	Mr M Armstrong	Head of Housing & Customer Services	W Lothian Hse
Legal Services	Ms G McCann	Chief Solicitor	W Lothian Hse
Leisure	Mr C Raeburn	Leisure & Sports Manager	Lindsay House
Local Land Charges	Mr R Hartland	Development & Building Control Manager	County Bldgs
Planning	Mr R Hartland	Development & Building Control Manager	County Bldgs
Purchasing & Supplies	Mr N Gubby	Commercial Manager	Contracts Hse
Social Services	Mr Grahame Blair	Head of Social Policy	W Lothian Hse
Technical Services	Mr B Plummer	Head of Construction Design	Ogilvie House
Trading Standards	Mr A Blake	Environmental Health & Trading Standards Manager	County Bldgs

On 1 April 1996, West Lothian Council took over from West Lothian District Council.

Community Councils in the authority's area: Addiewell/Loganlea; Armadale; Bathgate; Bellsquarry; Blackburn; Blackridge; Boghall; Breich; Bridgend; Broxburn; Dechmont; Dedridge; East Calder & Wilkieston; Ecclesmachan/Threemiletown; Eliburn; Fauldhouse; Greenrigg; Howden; Kirknewton; Knightsridge; Ladywell; Linlithgow Bridge; Linlithgow; Mid Calder; Murieston; Newton & District; Polbeth; Pumpherston; Seafield; Stoneyburn; Torphichen; Uphall; Uphall Station; West Calder & Harburn; Westfield; Whitburn; Winchburgh.

WEST LOTHIAN DISTRICT COUNCIL
See now West Lothian Council.

WESTERN ISLES COUNCIL
See now Comhairle Nan Eilean Siar.

WIGTOWN DISTRICT COUNCIL
See now Dumfries & Galloway Council.

NORTHERN IRELAND

ANTRIM BOROUGH COUNCIL

www.antrim.gov.uk

Principal Office
The Steeple, Antrim, Co Antrim BT41 1BJ
Telephone: (028) 9446 3113; FAX: (028) 9446 4469

Function	Chief Officer	Title	Location
Chief Executive	Mr D McCammick	Chief Executive	The Steeple
Environmental Health	Mr J R Quinn	Director of Environmental Services	The Steeple
Finance	Mr N P Cauwood	Director of Corporate Services	The Steeple
Leisure	Miss G Girvan	Director of Development & Leisure	The Steeple
Technical Services	Mr J R Quinn	Director of Environmental Services	The Steeple

ARDS BOROUGH COUNCIL

www.ards-council.gov.uk

Principal Office
2 Church Street, Newtownards, Co Down BT23 4AP
Telephone: (028) 9182 4000; FAX: (028) 9181 9628

Function	Chief Officer	Title	Location
Chief Executive	Mr David Fallows	Town Clerk & Chief Executive	2 Church Street
Environmental Health	Mr John Rea	Director of Environmental Services	2 Church Street
Finance	Mr David Clarke	Director of Corporate Services	2 Church Street
Leisure	Mr Archie Walls	Director of Leisure Services	2 Church Street

ARMAGH CITY AND DISTRICT COUNCIL

www.armagh.gov.uk

Principal Office
Council Offices, The Palace Demesne, Armagh, Co Armagh BT60 4EL
Telephone: (028) 3752 9600; FAX: (028) 3752 9601

Function	Chief Officer	Title	Location
Chief Executive	Mr V Brownlees	Clerk & Chief Executive	Council Offices
Environmental Health	Mr W J Briggs	Strategic Director of Environment, Health & Recreation	Council Offices
Finance	Mr D McCammick	Strategic Director of Corporate Services	Council Offices
Legal Services	Mr D McCammick	Strategic Director of Corporate Services	Council Offices
Leisure	Mr W J Briggs	Strategic Director of Environment, Health & Recreation	Council Offices
Purchasing & Supplies	Miss C Halligan	Purchasing Officer	Council Offices
Technical Services	Mr W J Briggs	Strategic Director of Environment, Health & Recreation	Council Offices
Trading Standards	Mr W J Briggs	Strategic Director of Environment, Health & Recreation	Council Offices

NORTHERN IRELAND

BALLYMENA BOROUGH COUNCIL

www.ballymena.gov.uk

Principal Office
"Ardeevin", 80 Galgorm Road, Ballymena, Co Antrim BT42 1AB
Telephone: (028) 2566 0300; FAX: (028) 2566 0400

Function	Chief Officer	Title	Location
Chief Executive	Mr M Rankin	Town Clerk & Chief Executive	Ardeevin
Environmental Health	Mr A Kinghorn	Director of Environmental Health	Ardeevin
Finance	Mr V Benson	Director of Finance & IT Services	Ardeevin
Leisure	Mr R McBride	Director of Development, Leisure	Ardeevin

BALLYMONEY BOROUGH COUNCIL

www.ballymoney.gov.uk

Principal Office
Riada House, 14 Charles Street, Ballymoney, Co Antrim BT53 6DZ
Telephone: (028) 2766 0200; FAX: (028) 2766 0222

Function	Chief Officer	Title	Location
Chief Executive	J P Dempsey	Chief Executive & Town Clerk	Riada Hse
Environmental Health	J C Michael	Director of Health & Environmental Services	Riada Hse
Finance	Mrs I McCleery	Director of Financial & Administrative Services	Riada Hse
Leisure	W J Paul	Director of Leisure & Amenities	Riada Hse

BANBRIDGE DISTRICT COUNCIL

www.banbridge.gov.uk

Principal Office
Council Offices, Downshire Road, Banbridge, Co Down BT32 3JY
Telephone: (028) 4066 0600; FAX: (028) 4066 0601

Function	Chief Officer	Title	Location
Chief Executive	Robert Gilmore	Chief Executive	Council Offices
Environmental Health	Kenneth Forbes	Director of Environmental Services	Council Offices
Finance	Pat Cumiskey	Director of Corporate Services	Council Offices
Leisure	Michael Reith	Director of Leisure Services	Council Offices

BELFAST CITY COUNCIL

www.belfastcity.gov.uk

Principal Office
City Hall, Donegall Square, Belfast BT1 5GS
Telephone: (028) 9032 0202; FAX: (028) 9027 0232

**Client Services; Development; Human Resources;
Health & Environment Services**
Cecil Ward Building, 4-10 Linen Hall Street, Belfast BT2 8BP
Telephone: (028) 9032 0202

Function	Chief Officer	Title	Location
Chief Executive	Mr P McNaney	Chief Executive	City Hall
Environmental Health	Mr W Francey	Director of Health & Environmental Services	Cecil Ward
Finance	Mr T Salmon	Director of Corporate Services	City Hall
Legal Services	Mr C Quigley	Director of Legal Services	City Hall

Leisure	Mr M Elder	Director of Client Services	Cecil Ward
Purchasing & Supplies	Ms H Louden	Director of Contract Services	Cecil Ward

CARRICKFERGUS BOROUGH COUNCIL

www.carrickfergus.org

Principal Office
Town Hall, Carrickfergus, Co Antrim BT38 7DL
Telephone: (028) 9335 1604; FAX: (028) 9336 6676

Building Services Department; Environmental Services Department
Heritage Plaza, Antrim Street, Carrickfergus BT38 7DG
Telephone: (028) 9335 1604

Development Services Department
The Waterfront Administration Building, 3 Rodgers Quay, Carrickfergus BT38 8BE
Telephone: (028) 9336 6666; FAX: (028) 9335 0505

Function	Chief Officer	Title	Location
Chief Executive	Mr A Cardwell	Town Clerk & Chief Executive	Town Hall
Environmental Health	Mr A Barkley	Director of Environmental Services	Heritage Plaza
Purchasing & Supplies	Mr I Eagleson	Director of Support Services	Town Hall
Technical Services	Mr J McCormick	Director of Development Services	The Waterfront

CASTLEREAGH BOROUGH COUNCIL

www.castlereagh.gov.uk

Principal Office
Bradford Court, Upper Galwally, Castlereagh BT8 6RB
Telephone: (028) 9049 4500; FAX: (028) 9049 4515

Function	Chief Officer	Title	Location
Chief Executive	Mr Adrian Donaldson	Chief Executive	Bradford Court
Environmental Health	Mr Edwin Campbell	Director of Technical Services	Bradford Court
Finance	Mr Edward Patterson	Director of Finance & Leisure Services	Bradford Court
Leisure	Mr Edward Patterson	Director of Finance & Leisure Services	Bradford Court
Technical Services	Mr Edwin Campbell	Director of Technical Services	Bradford Court

COLERAINE BOROUGH COUNCIL

www.colerainebc.gov.uk

Principal Office
Cloonavin, 66 Portstewart Road, Coleraine, Co Londonderry BT52 1EY
Telephone: (028) 7034 7034; FAX: (028) 7034 7026

Function	Chief Officer	Title	Location
Chief Executive	Mr H W T Moore	Town Clerk & Chief Executive	Cloonavin
Environmental Health	Mr K Doherty	Director of Environmental Health	Cloonavin
Finance	Mr D Bell	Director of Corporate Services	Cloonavin
Leisure	Mr J E Curry	Director of Leisure Services	Cloonavin
Technical Services	Mr D Wreath	Director of Technical Services	Cloonavin

NORTHERN IRELAND

COOKSTOWN DISTRICT COUNCIL

www.cookstown.gov.uk

Principal Office
12 Burn Road, Cookstown, Co Tyrone BT80 8DT
Telephone: (028) 8676 2205; FAX: (028) 8676 4360

Leisure Centre
Fountain Road, Cookstown, Co Tyrone
Telephone: (028) 8676 3853

Function	Chief Officer	Title	Location
Chief Executive	M J McGuckin	Clerk/Chief Executive	12 Burn Road
Environmental Health	M Kelso	Director of Environmental Health	12 Burn Road
Leisure	[Vacant]	Leisure Services Manager	Fountain Road
Technical Services	D Duncan	Director of Operational Services	12 Burn Road

CRAIGAVON BOROUGH COUNCIL

www.craigavon.gov.uk

Principal Office
Civic Centre, PO Box 66, Lakeview Road, Craigavon, Co Armagh BT64 1AL
Telephone: (028) 3831 2400; FAX: (028) 3831 2444

Function	Chief Officer	Title	Location
Chief Executive	F Ruck	Chief Executive	Civic Centre
Environmental Health	Mrs L Crawford	Director of Environmental Services	Civic Centre
Finance	D A Pepper	Director of Finance & Corporate Services	Civic Centre
Leisure	R Millar	Director of Leisure Services	Civic Centre
Technical Services	T Graham	Head of Technical Services	Civic Centre
Trading Standards	C Kerr	Head of Environmental Health	Civic Centre

DERRY CITY COUNCIL

www.derrycity.gov.uk

Principal Office
98 Strand Road, Derry, Co Londonderry BT48 7NN
Telephone: (028) 7136 5151; FAX: (028) 7136 8536

Function	Chief Officer	Title	Location
Chief Executive	Mr A McGurk	Town Clerk & Chief Executive	98 Strand Rd
Environmental Health	Mr J Meehan	Chief Environmental Health Officer & Deputy Chief Executive	98 Strand Rd
Finance	Mr J Campbell	City Treasurer	98 Strand Rd
Legal Services	Mr D J McMahon	City Secretary & Solicitor	98 Strand Rd
Leisure	Mr J Sanderson	Director of Recreation & Leisure	98 Strand Rd
Technical Services	Mr J Kelpie	City Engineer	98 Strand Rd

DOWN DISTRICT COUNCIL

www.downdc.gov.uk

Principal Office
24 Strangford Rd, Downpatrick, Co Down BT30 6SR
Telephone: (028) 4461 0800; FAX: (028) 4461 0801

Function	Chief Officer	Title	Location
Chief Executive	Mr John McGrillen	Clerk & Chief Executive	24 Strangford Rd
Environmental Health	Mr Tony McCrory	Principal Environmental Engineer	24 Strangford Rd

Finance	Mr Norman Stewart	Director of Corporate Services	24 Strangford Rd
Leisure	Mr Frank Cunningham	Director of Recreation & Technical Services	24 Strangford Rd
Purchasing & Supplies	Mr Norman Stewart	Director of Corporate Services	24 Strangford Rd
Technical Services	Mr Frank Cunningham	Director of Recreation & Technical Services	24 Strangford Rd

DUNGANNON AND SOUTH TYRONE BOROUGH COUNCIL

www.dungannon.gov.uk

Principal Office
Council Offices, Circular Road, Dungannon, Co Tyrone BT71 6DT
Telephone: (028) 8772 0300; FAX: (028) 8772 0368

Works Depot
Coalisland Road, Dungannon, Co Tyrone

Function	Chief Officer	Title	Location
Chief Executive	Mr W J Beattie	Chief Executive	Council Offices
Environmental Health	Mr A Burke	Director of Environmental Health	Council Offices
Finance	Mrs P Kerr	Head of Finance	Council Offices
Leisure	Mr I Frazer	Director of Development	Council Offices
Purchasing & Supplies	Mrs P Kerr	Head of Finance	Council Offices
Technical Services	Mr R McMinn	Director of Technical Services	Works Depot
Trading Standards	Mr A Burke	Director of Environmental Health	Council Offices

FERMANAGH DISTRICT COUNCIL

www.fermanagh.gov.uk

Principal Office
Town Hall, Enniskillen, Co Fermanagh BT74 7BA
Telephone: (028) 6632 5050; FAX: (028) 6632 2024

Contract Services
Killyvilly Works Depot, Tempo Road, Enniskillen BT74 6HR

Function	Chief Officer	Title	Location
Chief Executive	Mr R Connor	Chief Executive	Town Hall
Environmental Health	Mr R Forde	Director of Environmental Health	Town Hall
Finance	Mr B Hegarty	Director of Finance & Information Technology	Town Hall
Leisure	Mr R Gibson	Director of Environmental Services	Town Hall
Technical Services	Mr G Knox	Director of Technical Services	Killyvilly Depot

LARNE BOROUGH COUNCIL

www.larne.gov.uk

Principal Office
Smiley Buildings, Victoria Road, Larne, Co Antrim BT40 1RU
Telephone: (028) 2827 2313; FAX: (028) 2826 0660

Function	Chief Officer	Title	Location
Chief Executive	Mr C McGarry	Chief Executive	Smiley Buildings
Environmental Health	Mr M Crum	Director of Environmental Services	Smiley Buildings
Finance	Mr T Clarke	Director of Corporate Services	Smiley Buildings
Leisure	Mrs G McGahey	Director of Building Services	Smiley Buildings
Purchasing & Supplies	Mr T Clarke	Director of Corporate Services	Smiley Buildings
Technical Services	Mrs G McGahey	Director of Building Services	Smiley Buildings

LIMAVADY BOROUGH COUNCIL

www.limavady.org

Principal Office

Council Offices, 7 Connell Street, Limavady, Co Londonderry BT49 0HA
Telephone: (028) 7772 2226; FAX: (028) 7772 2010

Function	Chief Officer	Title	Location
Chief Executive	Mr J K Stevenson	Town Clerk & Chief Executive	Council Offices
Environmental Health	Mr N Crawford	Chief Environmental Health Officer	Council Offices
Finance	Mr E McCotter	Chief Finance & Administration Officer	Council Offices
Leisure	Mr S McGregor	Chief Recreation/Tourist Officer	Council Offices
Technical Services	Mr V Wallace	Chief Technical Services Officer	Council Offices

LISBURN CITY COUNCIL

www.lisburncity.gov.uk

Principal Office

Island Civic Centre, The Island, Lisburn BT27 4RL
Telephone: (028) 9250 9250; FAX: (028) 9250 9285

Function	Chief Officer	Title	Location
Chief Executive	Mr N Davidson	Chief Executive	Island Civic Centre
Environmental Health	Mr C McClintock	Director of Environmental Services	Island Civic Centre
Finance	Mr D Briggs	Director of Corporate Services	Island Civic Centre
Leisure	Mr J Rose	Director of Leisure Services	Island Civic Centre
Purchasing & Supplies	Mr D Briggs	Director of Corporate Services	Island Civic Centre
Technical Services	Mr C McClintock	Director of Environmental Services	Island Civic Centre

MAGHERAFELT DISTRICT COUNCIL

www.magherafelt.gov.uk

Principal Office

50 Ballyronan Road, Magherafelt, Co Londonderry BT45 6EN
Telephone: (028) 7939 7979; FAX: (028) 7939 7980

Function	Chief Officer	Title	Location
Chief Executive	Mr J McLaughlin	Chief Executive	Ballyronan Rd
Environmental Health	Mr C W Burrows	Director of Environmental Health	Ballyronan Rd
Finance	Mr J J Tohill	Director of Finance & Administration	Ballyronan Rd
Legal Services	Mr J J Tohill	Director of Finance & Administration	Ballyronan Rd
Leisure	Mr T J Johnson	Director of Operations	Ballyronan Rd
Purchasing & Supplies	Mr J J Tohill	Director of Finance & Administration	Ballyronan Rd
Technical Services	Mr T J Johnson	Director of Operations	Ballyronan Rd
Trading Standards	Mr C W Burrows	Director of Environmental Health	Ballyronan Rd

MOYLE DISTRICT COUNCIL

www.moyle-council.org

Principal Office

Sheskburn House, 7 Mary Street, Ballycastle, Co Antrim BT54 6QH
Telephone: (028) 2076 2225; FAX: (028) 2076 2515

Function	Chief Officer	Title	Location
Chief Executive	Mr R G Lewis	Clerk & Chief Executive	Sheskburn Hse
Environmental Health	Mr P Mawdsley	Director of District Services	Sheskburn Hse

Function	Chief Officer	Title	Location
Finance	Mrs M Quinn	Director of Finance & Administration	Sheskburn Hse
Leisure	Mr P Mawdsley	Director of District Services	Sheskburn Hse
Purchasing & Supplies	Mrs M Quinn	Director of Finance & Administration	Sheskburn Hse
Technical Services	Mr P Mawdsley	Director of District Services	Sheskburn Hse

NEWRY & MOURNE DISTRICT COUNCIL

www.newryandmourne.gov.uk

Principal Office

District Council Offices, O'Hagan House, Monaghan Row, Newry, Co Down BS35 8DL
Telephone: (028) 3031 3031; FAX: (028) 3031 3077

District Services Department; Direct Services Organisation

District Council Offices, Haughey House, Unit 19, Rampart Road,
Greenbank Industrial Estate, Newry
Telephone: (028) 3031 3233; FAX: (028) 3031 3299

Function	Chief Officer	Title	Location
Chief Executive	Mr T McCall	Clerk & Chief Executive	O'Hagan Hse
Environmental Health	Mr H O'Neill	Director of Environmental Health	O'Hagan Hse
Finance	Mr R Dowey	Director of Finance	O'Hagan Hse
Leisure	Mr G McGivern	Director of District Development	Haughey Hse
Technical Services	Mr J McCorry	Director of Technical & Leisure Services	Haughey Hse

NEWTOWNABBEY BOROUGH COUNCIL

www.newtownabbey.gov.uk

Principal Office

Mossley Mill, Newtownabbey, Co Antrim BT36 5QA
Telephone: (028) 9034 0000; FAX: (028) 9034 0200

Function	Chief Officer	Title	Location
Chief Executive	N Dunn	Chief Executive	Mossley Mill
Environmental Health	R Cameron	Acting Head of Environmental Health	Mossley Mill
Finance	P McCabe	Head of Financial Services	Mossley Mill
Leisure	H Brady	Head of Development Services	Mossley Mill
Purchasing & Supplies	N Willis	Head of Administration & Human Resources	Mossley Mill
Technical Services	H Kelly	Head of Contract Services	Mossley Mill

NORTH DOWN BOROUGH COUNCIL

www.northdown.gov.uk

Principal Office

Town Hall, The Castle, Bangor, Co Down BT20 4BT
Telephone: (028) 9127 0371; FAX: (028) 9127 1370

Function	Chief Officer	Title	Location
Chief Executive	Mr T Polley	Chief Executive	Town Hall
Environmental Health	Mr G Yarr	Director of Environmental Services	Town Hall
Finance	Mr K Webb	Director of Corporate Services	Town Hall
Leisure	Mr S Reid		Town Hall
Technical Services	Mr J Snodden	Director of Amenities & Technical Services	Town Hall

OMAGH DISTRICT COUNCIL

www.omagh.gov.uk

Principal Office
The Grange, Mountjoy Road, Omagh, Co Tyrone BT79 7BL
Telephone: (028) 8224 5321; FAX: (028) 8224 3888

Leisure Complex
Old Mountfield Road, Omagh, Co Tyrone BT79 7EG
Telephone: (028) 8224 6711; FAX: (028) 8225 1926

Environmental Health
Lisnamallard House, Old Mountfield Road, Omagh, Co Tyrone BT79 7EG
Telephone: (028) 8224 5321; FAX: (028) 8224 8086

Function	Chief Officer	Title	Location
Chief Executive	Mr Danny McSorley	Clerk & Chief Executive	The Grange
Environmental Health	Mr Gerry Harte	Chief Environmental Health Officer	Lisnamallard Hse
Finance	Joan McCaffrey	Chief Finance Officer	The Grange
Purchasing & Supplies	Joan McCaffrey	Chief Finance Officer	The Grange
Technical Services	Mr Kevin O'Gara	Chief Client Services Officer	The Grange
Trading Standards	Mr Gerry Harte	Chief Environmental Health Officer	Lisnamallard Hse

STRABANE DISTRICT COUNCIL

www.strabanedc.org.uk

Principal Office
47 Derry Road, Strabane, Co Tyrone BT82 8DY
Telephone: (028) 7138 2204; FAX: (028) 7138 2264

Function	Chief Officer	Title	Location
Chief Executive	Mr P Faithfull	Clerk & Chief Executive	47 Derry Road
Environmental Health	Mr P P Cosgrove	Chief Environmental Health Officer	47 Derry Road
Finance	Mrs M Henebery	Head of Finance	47 Derry Road
Leisure	Mrs K MacFarland	Head of Culture, Arts & Leisure	47 Derry Road
Technical Services	Mr M Scott	Chief Technical Services Officer	47 Derry Road

GAZETTEER

The purpose of the Gazetteer is to identify the local authorities into which particular places fall. It lists parishes, towns, villages, hamlets and other geographical areas, showing the relevant local authority in each case.

A Chill, Highland Cl
Ab Kettleby, Melton BC
Abbas Combe, S Somerset DC
Abberley, Malvern Hills DC
Abberton, Colchester BC
Abberton, Wychavon DC
Abberwick, Alnwick DC
Abbess Roding, Epping Forest DC
Abbey Dore, Herefordshire Cl
Abbey St Bathans, Scottish Borders Cl
Abbeycwmhir, Powys CC
Abbeydale, Sheffield City
Abbeystead, Lancaster City
Abbeytown, Allerdale BC
Abbots Bickington, Torridge DC
Abbots Bromley, E Staffs BC
Abbots Langley, Three Rivers DC
Abbots Leigh, N Somerset DC
Abbots Morton, Wychavon DC
Abbots Ripton, Huntingdonshire DC
Abbots Salford, Stratford/Avon DC
Abbotsbury, W Dorset DC
Abbotsham, Torridge DC
Abbotskerswell, Teignbridge DC
Abbotsley, Huntingdonshire DC
Abbotswood, Test Valley BC
Abbotts Ann, Test Valley BC
Abdon, S Shropshire DC
Abenbury, Wrexham CBC
Aber Valley, Caerphilly CBC
Aberaeron, Ceredigion CC
Aberarder, Highland Cl
Aberavon, Neath Port Talbot CBC
Abercanaid, Merthyr Tydfil CBC
Aberchalder, Highland Cl
Aberchirder, Aberdeenshire Cl
Abercregan, Neath Port Talbot CBC
Abercrombie, Fife Cl
Aberdare, Rhondda Cynon Taff CBC
Aberdaron, Gwynedd CC
Aberdeen, Aberdeen City
Aberdour, Aberdeenshire Cl
Aberdour, Fife Cl
Aberdulais, Neath Port Talbot CBC

Aberdyfi, Gwynedd CC
Aberedw, Powys CC
Aberfan, Merthyr Tydfil CBC
Aberfeldy, Perth/Kinross Cl
Aberffraw, Isle of Anglesey CC
Aberford, Leeds City
Aberfoyle, Stirling Cl
Abergavenny, Monmouthshire CC
Abergele, Conwy CBC
Abergwili, Carmarthenshire CC
Abergwynfi, Neath Port Talbot CBC
Abergwyngregyn, Gwynedd CC
Aberhafesp, Powys CC
Aberkenfig, Bridgend CBC
Aberlady, E Lothian Cl
Aberlemnoe, Angus Cl
Aberlour, Moray Cl
Abermaw, Gwynedd CC
Abernant, Carmarthenshire CC
Abernethy, Perth/Kinross Cl
Aberporth, Ceredigion CC
Abersoch, Gwynedd CC
Abersychan, Torfaen CBC
Aberteifi, Ceredigion CC
Abertillery, Blaenau Gwent CBC
Aberwheeler, Denbighshire CC
Aberystwyth, Ceredigion CC
Abingdon, Vale of White Horse DC
Abinger, Mole Valley DC
Abinger Bottom, Mole Valley DC
Abinger Common, Mole Valley DC
Abinger Hammer, Mole Valley DC
Abington, Cotswold DC
Abington, S Lanarkshire Cl
Abington Pigotts, S Cambs DC
Abney, Derbys Dales DC
Above Derwent, Allerdale BC
Aboyne, Aberdeenshire Cl
Abram, Wigan MBC
Abriachan, Highland Cl
Abridge, Epping Forest DC
Abson, S Glos Cl
Abthorpe, S Northants Cl
Aby, E Lindsey DC
Acarsaid, Highland Cl
Acaster Malbis, City of York Cl
Acaster Selby, Selby DC
Accrington, Hyndburn BC

Achachork, Highland Cl
Achan Todhair, Highland Cl
Achaphubuil, Highland Cl
Acharacle, Highland Cl
Achargary, Highland Cl
Achavandra Muir, Highland Cl
Achfary, Highland Cl
Achfrish, Highland Cl
Achgarve, Highland Cl
Achiemore, Highland Cl
Achiltibuie, Highland Cl
Achina, Highland Cl
Achinahuagh, Highland Cl
Achindarroch, Highland Cl
Achininver, Highland Cl
Achintee, Highland Cl
Achintraid, Highland Cl
Achluachrach, Highland Cl
Achlyness, Highland Cl
Achmelvich, Highland Cl
Achmore, Highland Cl
Achnacarnin, Highland Cl
Achnacarry, Highland Cl
Achnacloich, Highland Cl
Achnaha, Highland Cl
Achnahanat, Highland Cl
Achnahannet, Highland Cl
Achnairn, Highland Cl
Achnasheen, Highland Cl
Achosnich, Highland Cl
Achreamie, Highland Cl
Achriesgill, Highland Cl
Achrimsdale, Highland Cl
Achtalean, Highland Cl
Achterneed, Highland Cl
Achtoty, Highland Cl
Achuvoldrach, Highland Cl
Ackergill, Highland Cl
Acklam, Ryedale DC
Ackleton, Bridgnorth DC
Acklington, Alnwick DC
Ackton, Wakefield MDC
Ackworth, Wakefield MDC
Acle, Broadland DC
Acocks Green, Birmingham City
Acol, Thanet DC
Acomb, Tynedale DC
Aconbury, Herefordshire Cl
Acre, Rossendale BC
Acrise, Shepway DC
Acton, Babergh DC

Acton, Crewe/Nantwich BC
Acton, Ealing LBC
Acton, Purbeck DC
Acton, S Shropshire DC
Acton, Wrexham CBC
Acton Beauchamp, Herefordshire
    CI
Acton Bridge, Vale Royal BC
Acton Burnell,
    Shrewsbury/Atcham CI
Acton Pigott, Shrewsbury/Atcham
    CI
Acton Round, Bridgnorth DC
Acton Scott, S Shropshire DC
Acton Trussell, S Staffs CI
Acton Turville, S Glos CI
Adamsdown, Cardiff CC
Adamthwaite, Eden DC
Adbaston, Stafford BC
Adderbury, Cherwell DC
Adderley, N Shropshire DC
Adderstone, Berwick-u-Tweed BC
Addiewell, W Lothian CI
Addingham, Bradford MDC
Addington, Aylesbury Vale DC
Addington, Croydon LBC
Addington, Tonbridge/Malling BC
Addlestone, Runnymede BC
Addlethorpe, E Lindsey DC
Adeney, Telford/Wrekin BC
Adforton, Herefordshire CI
Adisham, Canterbury City
Adlestrop, Cotswold DC
Adlingfleet, E Riding of Yks
Adlington, Chorley BC
Adlington, Macclesfield BC
Admington, Stratford/Avon DC
Adsdean, Chichester DC
Adstock, Aylesbury Vale DC
Adstone, S Northants CI
Advent, N Cornwall DC
Advie, Highland CI
Adwell, S Oxon DC
Adwick le Street, Doncaster MBC
Adwick on Dearne, Doncaster
    MBC
Ae, Dumfries/Galloway CI
Affetside, Bury MBC
Affpuddle, Purbeck DC
Agden, Chester City
Agden, Macclesfield BC
Agglethorpe, Richmondshire DC
Aghadowey, Coleraine BC
Aghalee, Lisburn City
Aighton, Ribble Valley BC
Aiketgate, Eden DC
Aikton, Allerdale BC
Ailby, E Lindsey DC
Ailstone, Stratford/Avon DC
Ailsworth, Peterborough City

Aimes Green, Epping Forest DC
Ainderby Mires, Hambleton DC
Ainderby Quernhow, Hambleton
    DC
Ainderby Steeple, Hambleton DC
Aingers Green, Tendring DC
Ainstable, Eden DC
Ainsworth, Bury MBC
Aintree, Sefton MBC
Aird, Highland CI
Aird of Sleat, Highland CI
Airdens, Highland CI
Airdrie, N Lanarkshire CI
Airdtorrisdale, Highland CI
Airidhantuim, Comhairle Nan
    Eilean Siar
Airmyn, E Riding of Yks
Airor, Highland CI
Airth, Falkirk CI
Airton, Craven DC
Aisby, W Lindsey DC
Aiskew, Hambleton DC
Aislaby, Ryedale DC
Aislaby, Scarborough BC
Aisthorpe, W Lindsey DC
Aithsting, Shetland Is CI
Akebar, Richmondshire DC
Akeld, Berwick-u-Tweed BC
Akeley, Aylesbury Vale DC
Akenham, Mid Suffolk DC
Alberbury, Shrewsbury/Atcham CI
Albourne, Mid Sussex DC
Albrighton, Bridgnorth DC
Albrighton, Shrewsbury/Atcham
    CI
Alburgh, S Norfolk DC
Albury, E Herts DC
Albury, Guildford BC
Albury, S Oxon DC
Alby Hill, N Norfolk DC
Alcaig, Highland CI
Alcaston, S Shropshire DC
Alcester, Stratford/Avon DC
Alcester Health, Stratford/Avon
    DC
Alciston, Wealden DC
Alcombe, W Somerset DC
Alconbury, Huntingdonshire DC
Alconbury Weston,
    Huntingdonshire DC
Aldborough, Harrogate BC
Aldborough, N Norfolk DC
Aldbourne, Kennet DC
Aldbrough, E Riding of Yks
Aldbrough St John,
    Richmondshire DC
Aldbury, Dacorum BC
Aldeburgh, Suffolk C'I DC
Aldeby, S Norfolk DC
Aldenham, Hertsmere BC

Alderbury, Salisbury DC
Aldercar, Amber Valley BC
Alderford, Broadland DC
Alderholt, E Dorset DC
Alderley, Stroud DC
Alderley Edge, Macclesfield BC
Aldermaston, W Berks DC
Alderminster, Stratford/Avon DC
Alderney, Poole BC
Aldersey, Chester City
Aldershot, Rushmoor BC
Alderton, N Shropshire DC
Alderton, S Northants CI
Alderton, Suffolk C'I DC
Alderton, Tewkesbury BC
Alderwasley, Amber Valley BC
Aldfield, Harrogate BC
Aldford, Chester City
Aldham, Babergh DC
Aldham, Colchester BC
Aldingbourne, Arun DC
Aldingham, S Lakeland DC
Aldington, Ashford BC
Aldington, Wychavon DC
Aldington Frith, Ashford BC
Aldreth, E Cambs DC
Aldridge (part), Lichfield DC
Aldringham, Suffolk C'I DC
Aldsworth, Chichester DC
Aldsworth, Cotswold DC
Aldwark, Derbys Dales DC
Aldwark, Hambleton DC
Aldwick, Arun DC
Aldwincle, E Northants CI
Aldworth, W Berks DC
Alexandra Park, Haringey LBC
Alexandria, W Dunbartonshire CI
Alfington, E Devon DC
Alfold, Waverley BC
Alfold (part), Chichester DC
Alford, Aberdeenshire CI
Alford, E Lindsey DC
Alford, S Somerset DC
Alfreton, Amber Valley BC
Alfrick, Malvern Hills DC
Alfriston, Wealden DC
Algarkirk, Boston BC
Alhampton, Mendip DC
Alisary, Highland CI
Alkborough, N Lincs CI
Alkerton, Cherwell DC
Alkham, Dover DC
Alkington, N Shropshire DC
Alkington, Stroud DC
Alkmonton, Derbys Dales DC
All Cannings, Kennet DC
All Saints, E Devon DC
All Saints South Elmham,
    Waveney DC

All Stretton, Shrewsbury/Atcham CI
Allandale, Falkirk CI
Allanton, N Lanarkshire CI
Allanton, Scottish Borders CI
Allanton, S Lanarkshire CI
Allendale, Tynedale DC
Allens Green, E Herts DC
Allensmore, Herefordshire CI
Aller, S Somerset DC
Allerby, Allerdale BC
Allerford, W Somerset DC
Allerston, Ryedale DC
Allerthorpe, E Riding of Yks
Allerthorpe, Hambleton DC
Allerton, Liverpool City
Allerton Bywater, Leeds City
Allerton Mauleverer, Harrogate BC
Allesley, Coventry City MDC
Allestree, Derby City
Allexton, Harborough DC
Allgreave, Macclesfield BC
Allhallows, Allerdale BC
Allhallows, Medway CI
Alligin Shias, Highland CI
Allimore Green, Stafford BC
Allington, Kennet DC
Allington, Salisbury DC
Allington, S Kesteven DC
Allington, W Dorset DC
Allithwaite, S Lakeland DC
Alloa, Clackmannanshire CI
Allonby, Allerdale BC
Allostock, Vale Royal BC
Alloway, S Ayrshire CI
Alltour, Highland CI
Alltsigh, Highland CI
Alltwen, Neath Port Talbot CBC
Allweston, W Dorset DC
Allwood Green, Mid Suffolk DC
Almeley, Herefordshire CI
Almer, E Dorset DC
Almington, Newcastle-u-Lyme BC
Almodington, Chichester DC
Almondbury, Kirklees MC
Almondsbury, S Glos CI
Alne, Hambleton DC
Alne End, Stratford/Avon DC
Alness, Highland CI
Alnessferry, Highland CI
Alnham, Alnwick DC
Alnmouth, Alnwick DC
Alnwick, Alnwick DC
Alperton, Brent LBC
Alphamstone, Braintree DC
Alpheton, Babergh DC
Alpington, S Norfolk DC
Alport, Derbys Dales DC
Alpraham, Crewe/Nantwich BC

Alresford, Tendring DC
Alresford, Winchester City
Alrewas, Lichfield DC
Alsager, Congleton BC
Alscote Park, Stratford/Avon DC
Alsop en le Dale, Derbys Dales DC
Alston, Eden DC
Alstone, Tewkesbury BC
Alstonefield, Staffs Moorlands DC
Altarnun, N Cornwall DC
Altass, Highland CI
Altcar, Sefton MBC
Altens, Aberdeen City
Altham, Hyndburn BC
Althorne, Maldon DC
Althorp, Daventry DC
Althorpe, N Lincs CI
Altmore, Dungannon & S Tyrone BC
Altnabreac, Highland CI
Altnaharra, Highland CI
Altofts, Wakefield MDC
Alton, E Hants DC
Alton, Kennet DC
Alton, N E Derbys DC
Alton, Staffs Moorlands DC
Alton Pancras, W Dorset DC
Alton Priors, Kennet DC
Alton Towers, Staffs Moorlands DC
Altrincham, Trafford MBC
Alva, Clackmannanshire CI
Alvah, Aberdeenshire CI
Alvanley, Vale Royal BC
Alvaston, Derby City
Alvechurch, Bromsgrove DC
Alvediston, Salisbury DC
Alveley, Bridgnorth DC
Alverdiscott, Torridge DC
Alverstone, Isle of Wight CI
Alverton, Newark/Sherwood DC
Alvescot, W Oxon DC
Alveston, S Glos CI
Alveston, Stratford/Avon DC
Alveston Hill, Stratford/Avon DC
Alvie, Highland CI
Alvingham, E Lindsey DC
Alvington, Forest of Dean DC
Alwalton, Huntingdonshire DC
Alwington, Torridge DC
Alwinton, Alnwick DC
Alyth, Perth/Kinross CI
Amatnatua, Highland CI
Amber Hill, Boston BC
Ambergate, Amber Valley BC
Amberley, Horsham DC
Amberley, Stroud DC
Ambersham, Chichester DC
Amble, Alnwick DC

Amblecote, Dudley MBC
Ambleside, S Lakeland DC
Ambleston, Pembrokeshire CC
Ambrosden, Cherwell DC
Amcotts, N Lincs CI
Amersham, Chiltern DC
Amesbury, Salisbury DC
Ameysford, E Dorset DC
Amington, Tamworth BC
Amlwch, Isle of Anglesey CC
Ammanford, Carmarthenshire CC
Amotherby, Ryedale DC
Ampfield, Test Valley BC
Ampleforth, Ryedale DC
Ampney Crucis, Cotswold DC
Ampney St Mary, Cotswold DC
Ampney St Peter, Cotswold DC
Amport, Test Valley BC
Ampthill, Mid Beds DC
Ampton, St Edmundsbury BC
Amroth, Pembrokeshire CC
Anagach, Highland CI
Anaheilt, Highland CI
Anancaun, Highland CI
Ancaster, S Kesteven DC
Anchor, S Shropshire DC
Ancroft, Berwick-u-Tweed BC
Ancrum, Dundee City
Ancrum, Scottish Borders CI
Ancton, Arun DC
Anderby, E Lindsey DC
Anderson, N Dorset DC
Anderston, Glasgow City
Anderton, Chorley BC
Anderton, Vale Royal BC
Andover, Test Valley BC
Andoversford, Cotswold DC
Angel, The, Islington LBC
Angerton, S Lakeland DC
Angle, Pembrokeshire CC
Anglezarke, Chorley BC
Angmering, Arun DC
Angram, Harrogate BC
Angram, Richmondshire DC
Angram Grange, Hambleton DC
Anlaby, E Riding of Yks
Anmer, King's Lynn/W Norfolk BC
Annahilt, Lisburn City
Annalong, Newry/Mourne DC
Annan, Dumfries/Galloway CI
Annaside, Copeland BC
Annat, Highland CI
Annbank, S Ayrshire CI
Annesley Woodhouse, Ashfield DC
Annet, Isles of Scilly CI
Annfield Plain, Derwentside DC
Annishader, Highland CI
Annscroft, Shrewsbury/Atcham CI
Ansford, S Somerset DC

Ansley, N Warks BC
Anslow, E Staffs BC
Anstey, Charnwood DC
Anstey, E Herts DC
Anston, Rotherham MBC
Anstruther, Fife Cl
Ansty, Mid Sussex DC
Ansty, Rugby BC
Ansty, Salisbury DC
Anthill Common, Winchester City
Anthorn, Allerdale BC
Antingham, N Norfolk DC
Antony, Caradon DC
Antrim, Antrim BC
Antrobus, Vale Royal BC
Anwick, N Kesteven DC
Aonachan, Highland Cl
Apethorpe, E Northants Cl
Apley, W Lindsey DC
Appersett, Richmondshire DC
Appin, Argyll/Bute Cl
Appleby, N Lincs Cl
Appleby in Westmorland, Eden
    DC
Appleby Magna, N W Leics DC
Applecross, Highland Cl
Appledore, Ashford BC
Appledore, Mid Devon DC
Appledore, Torridge DC
Appledram, Chichester DC
Appleford-on-Thames, Vale of
    White Horse DC
Appleshaw, Test Valley BC
Applethwaite, Allerdale BC
Appleton, Vale of White Horse
    DC
Appleton, Warrington BC
Appleton le Moors, Ryedale DC
Appleton le Street, Ryedale DC
Appleton Roebuck, Selby DC
Appleton West, Richmondshire
    DC
Appleton Wiske, Hambleton DC
Appletreewick, Craven DC
Appley Bridge, W Lancs DC
Apse Heath, Isle of Wight Cl
Arabella, Highland Cl
Arborfield, Wokingham DC
Arbourthorne, Sheffield City
Arbroath, Angus Cl
Arbuthnott, Aberdeenshire Cl
Archattan, Argyll/Bute Cl
Archdeacon Newton, Darlington
    BC
Arclid, Congleton BC
Ardachu, Highland Cl
Ardaneaskan, Highland Cl
Ardarroch, Highland Cl
Ardchronie, Highland Cl
Ardeley, E Herts DC

Ardelve, Highland Cl
Arden, Argyll/Bute Cl
Arden, Glasgow City
Ardendrain, Highland Cl
Ardens Grafton, Stratford/Avon
    DC
Ardentinny, Argyll/Bute Cl
Ardersier, Highland Cl
Ardery, Highland Cl
Ardgay, Highland Cl
Ardgayhill, Highland Cl
Ardglass, Down DC
Ardgour, Highland Cl
Ardharnich, Highland Cl
Ardheslaig, Highland Cl
Ardindrean, Highland Cl
Ardingly, Mid Sussex DC
Ardington, Vale of White Horse
    DC
Ardleigh, Tendring DC
Ardler, Perth/Kinross Cl
Ardley, Cherwell DC
Ardlui, Argyll/Bute Cl
Ardmair, Highland Cl
Ardmolich, Highland Cl
Ardmore, Highland Cl
Ardnaff, Highland Cl
Ardnagoine, Highland Cl
Ardnagrask, Highland Cl
Ardnastang, Highland Cl
Ardrishaig, Argyll/Bute Cl
Ardroag, Highland Cl
Ardross, Highland Cl
Ardrossan, N Ayrshire Cl
Ardshealach, Highland Cl
Ardsley, Barnsley MBC
Ardtoe, Highland Cl
Ardullie, Highland Cl
Ardvannie, Highland Cl
Ardvassar, Highland Cl
Ardverikie, Highland Cl
Arean, Highland Cl
Argoed, Flintshire CC
Argos Hill, Wealden DC
Argyll, Argyll/Bute Cl
Arinacrinachd, Highland Cl
Arisaig, Highland Cl
Ariundle, Highland Cl
Arivegaig, Highland Cl
Arkendale, Harrogate BC
Arkengarthdale, Richmondshire
    DC
Arkesden, Uttlesford DC
Arkholme, Lancaster City
Arkley, Barnet LBC
Arksey, Doncaster MBC
Arlecdon, Copeland BC
Arlescote, Stratford/Avon DC
Arlesey, Mid Beds DC
Arleston, Telford/Wrekin BC

Arley, Macclesfield BC
Arley, N Warks BC
Arlingham, Stroud DC
Arlington, Cotswold DC
Arlington, N Devon DC
Arlington, Wealden DC
Armadale, Highland Cl
Armadale, W Lothian Cl
Armagh, Armagh City/DC
Armathwaite, Eden DC
Arminghall, S Norfolk DC
Armitage, Lichfield DC
Armoy, Moyle DC
Armscote, Stratford/Avon DC
Armthorpe, Doncaster MBC
Arncliffe, Craven DC
Arncott, Cherwell DC
Arncroach, Fife Cl
Arne, Purbeck DC
Arnesby, Harborough DC
Arnish, Highland Cl
Arnold, Gedling BC
Arnprior, Stirling Cl
Arnside, S Lakeland DC
Arpafeelie, Highland Cl
Arradoul, Moray Cl
Arram, E Riding of Yks
Arran, Isle of, N Ayrshire Cl
Arrathorne, Richmondshire DC
Arreton, Isle of Wight Cl
Arrington, S Cambs DC
Arrochar, Argyll/Bute Cl
Arrow, Stratford/Avon DC
Artafallie, Highland Cl
Arthington, Leeds City
Arthingworth, Daventry DC
Arthog, Gwynedd CC
Arthuret, Carlisle City
Articlave, Coleraine BC
Artigarvan, Strabane DC
Artington, Guildford BC
Arundel, Arun DC
Asby, Copeland BC
Asby, Eden DC
Ascot, Windsor/Maidenhead RB
Ascott, Stratford/Avon DC
Ascott under Wychwood, W Oxon
    DC
Asenby, Harrogate BC
Asfordby, Melton BC
Asgarby, E Lindsey DC
Asgarby, N Kesteven DC
Ash, Dover DC
Ash, Guildford BC
Ash, S Derbys DC
Ash, S Somerset DC
Ash cum Ridley, Sevenoaks DC
Ash Magna, N Shropshire DC
Ash Priors, Taunton Deane BC
Ash Street, Babergh DC

Ash Thomas, Mid Devon DC
Ashaig, Highland Cl
Ashampstead, W Berks DC
Ashbocking, Mid Suffolk DC
Ashbourne, Derbys Dales DC
Ashbrittle, Taunton Deane BC
Ashburnham, Rother DC
Ashburton, Teignbridge DC
Ashbury, Vale of White Horse DC
Ashbury, W Devon BC
Ashby, Gt Yarmouth BC
Ashby, N Lincs Cl
Ashby, Waveney DC
Ashby by Partney, E Lindsey DC
Ashby cum Fenby, N E Lincs Cl
Ashby de la Launde, N Kesteven
  DC
Ashby de la Zouch, N W Leics
  DC
Ashby Folville, Melton BC
Ashby Magna, Harborough DC
Ashby Parkland, N Lincs Cl
Ashby Parva, Harborough DC
Ashby St Ledgers, Daventry DC
Ashby St Mary, S Norfolk DC
Ashby Woulds, N W Leics DC
Ashchurch, Tewkesbury BC
Ashcombe, Teignbridge DC
Ashcott, Sedgemoor DC
Ashdon, Uttlesford DC
Asheldham, Maldon DC
Ashen, Braintree DC
Ashendon, Aylesbury Vale DC
Asheridge, Chiltern DC
Ashfield cum Thorpe, Mid Suffolk
  DC
Ashfield Green, Mid Suffolk DC
Ashford, Ashford BC
Ashford, N Devon DC
Ashford, Spelthorne BC
Ashford Bowdler, S Shropshire
  DC
Ashford Carbonel, S Shropshire
  DC
Ashford Hill, Basingstoke/Deane
  BC
Ashford in the Water, Derbys
  Dales DC
Ashgate, Chesterfield BC
Ashgill, S Lanarkshire Cl
Ashill, Breckland Cl
Ashill, S Somerset DC
Ashingdon, Rochford DC
Ashington, Horsham DC
Ashington, Wansbeck DC
Ashkirk, Scottish Borders Cl
Ashleworth, Tewkesbury BC
Ashley, Aberdeen City
Ashley, Cotswold DC
Ashley, E Cambs DC

Ashley, Kettering BC
Ashley, Macclesfield BC
Ashley, Test Valley BC
Ashley Green, Chiltern DC
Ashley Heath, E Dorset DC
Ashmanhaugh, N Norfolk DC
Ashmansworth,
  Basingstoke/Deane BC
Ashmore, N Dorset DC
Ashorne, Stratford/Avon DC
Ashorne Hill, Stratford/Avon DC
Ashover, N E Derbys DC
Ashow, Warwick DC
Ashperton, Herefordshire Cl
Ashprington, S Hams DC
Ashreigney, Torridge DC
Ashtead, Mole Valley DC
Ashton, Chester City
Ashton, E Northants Cl
Ashton, Herefordshire Cl
Ashton, Kerrier DC
Ashton, S Northants Cl
Ashton, Teignbridge DC
Ashton in Makerfield, Wigan MBC
Ashton Keynes, N Wilts DC
Ashton on Mersey, Trafford MBC
Ashton under Hill, Wychavon DC
Ashton under Lyne, Tameside
  MBC
Ashurst, Horsham DC
Ashurst, New Forest DC
Ashurst Wood, Mid Sussex DC
Ashwater, Torridge DC
Ashwell, N Herts DC
Ashwell, Rutland CC
Ashwellthorpe, S Norfolk DC
Ashwick, Mendip DC
Ashwicken, King's Lynn/W
  Norfolk BC
Ashwood, S Staffs Cl
Askam in Furness, Barrow-in-
  Furness DC
Aske, Richmondshire DC
Askern, Doncaster MBC
Askerswell, W Dorset DC
Askerton, Carlisle City
Askett, Wycombe DC
Askham, Bassetlaw DC
Askham, Eden DC
Askham Bryan, Selby DC
Askham Richard, City of York Cl
Askrigg, Richmondshire DC
Askwith, Harrogate BC
Aslackby, S Kesteven DC
Aslacton, S Norfolk DC
Aslockton, Rushcliffe BC
Aspall, Mid Suffolk DC
Aspatria, Allerdale BC
Aspenden, E Herts DC
Aspley Guise, Mid Beds DC

Aspley Heath, Mid Beds DC
Aspley Heath, Stratford/Avon DC
Aspull, Wigan MBC
Asselby, E Riding of Yks
Assendon, S Oxon DC
Assington, Babergh DC
Astbury, Congleton BC
Astcote, S Northants Cl
Asterby, E Lindsey DC
Asterleigh, W Oxon DC
Asterley, Shrewsbury/Atcham Cl
Asterton, S Shropshire DC
Asthal, W Oxon DC
Asthall Leigh, W Oxon DC
Astley, Malvern Hills DC
Astley, N Warks BC
Astley, Shrewsbury/Atcham Cl
Astley, Wigan MBC
Astley Abbotts, Bridgnorth DC
Astley Village, Chorley BC
Aston, Birmingham City
Aston, Crewe/Nantwich BC
Aston, E Herts DC
Aston, High Peak BC
Aston, Newcastle-u-Lyme BC
Aston, N Shropshire DC
Aston, Rotherham MBC
Aston, Telford/Wrekin BC
Aston, Vale Royal BC
Aston, W Oxon DC
Aston Abbotts, Aylesbury Vale
  DC
Aston Botterell, Bridgnorth DC
Aston by Budworth, Macclesfield
  BC
Aston by Stone, Stafford BC
Aston Cantlow, Stratford/Avon
  DC
Aston Clinton, Aylesbury Vale DC
Aston End, E Herts DC
Aston Eyre, Bridgnorth DC
Aston Fields, Bromsgrove DC
Aston Flamville, Blaby DC
Aston Ingham, Herefordshire Cl
Aston Juxta Mondrum,
  Crewe/Nantwich BC
Aston le Walls, S Northants Cl
Aston Magna, Cotswold DC
Aston Munslow, S Shropshire DC
Aston on Clun, S Shropshire DC
Aston on Trent, S Derbys DC
Aston Rowant, S Oxon DC
Aston Sandford, Aylesbury Vale
  DC
Aston Somerville, Wychavon DC
Aston Subedge, Cotswold DC
Aston Tirrold, S Oxon DC
Aston Upthorpe, S Oxon DC
Astwell, S Northants Cl
Astwick, Mid Beds DC

Astwood, Milton Keynes Cl
Astwood Bank, Redditch BC
Aswarby, W Somerset DC
Aswardby, E Lindsey DC
Atcham, Shrewsbury/Atcham Cl
Athelhampton, W Dorset DC
Athelington, Mid Suffolk DC
Athelstaneford, E Lothian Cl
Atherington, N Devon DC
Atherstone, N Warks BC
Atherstone on Stour,
   Stratford/Avon DC
Atherton, Wigan MBC
Atlow, Derbys Dales DC
Attadale, Highland Cl
Attercliffe, Sheffield City
Attical, Newry/Mourne DC
Attingham, Shrewsbury/Atcham
   Cl
Attleborough, Breckland Cl
Attleborough, Nuneaton/Bedworth
   BC
Attlebridge, Broadland DC
Atwick, E Riding of Yks
Atworth, W Wilts DC
Aubourn, N Kesteven DC
Auchenblae, Aberdeenshire Cl
Auchencairn, Dumfries/Galloway
   Cl
Auchencrow, Scottish Borders Cl
Auchengray, S Lanarkshire Cl
Auchenheath, S Lanarkshire Cl
Auchertyre, Highland Cl
Auchindour, Aberdeenshire Cl
Auchinleck, E Ayrshire Cl
Auchinloch, N Lanarkshire Cl
Auchterarder, Perth/Kinross Cl
Auchtercairn, Highland Cl
Auchterderran, Fife Cl
Auchtergaven, Perth/Kinross Cl
Auchterhouse, Angus Cl
Auchterless, Aberdeenshire Cl
Auchtermuchty, Fife Cl
Auchtertool, Fife Cl
Auckley, Doncaster MBC
Audenshaw, Tameside MBC
Audlem, Crewe/Nantwich BC
Audley, Newcastle-u-Lyme BC
Augher, Dungannon & S Tyrone
   BC
Aughnacloy, Dungannon & S
   Tyrone BC
Aughton, E Riding of Yks
Aughton, Lancaster City
Aughton, Rotherham MBC
Aughton, W Lancs DC
August Hill, Stratford/Avon DC
Auldearn, Highland Cl
Auldgirth, Dumfries/Galloway Cl
Auldhouse, Glasgow City

Auldhouse, S Lanarkshire Cl
Ault Hucknall, Bolsover DC
Aultbea, Highland Cl
Aultiphurst, Highland Cl
Aultivullin, Highland Cl
Aultvaich, Highland Cl
Aunby, S Kesteven DC
Aunsby, N Kesteven DC
Aust, S Glos Cl
Austerfield, Doncaster MBC
Austerson, Crewe/Nantwich BC
Austhorpe, Leeds City
Austrey, N Warks BC
Austwick, Craven DC
Authorpe, E Lindsey DC
Avebury, Kennet DC
Aveley, Thurrock BC
Avenbury, Herefordshire Cl
Avening, Cotswold DC
Averham, Newark/Sherwood DC
Aveton Gifford, S Hams DC
Avich, Argyll/Bute Cl
Aviemore, Highland Cl
Aville Vale, W Somerset DC
Avington, W Berks DC
Avoch, Highland Cl
Avon, New Forest DC
Avon Dassett, Stratford/Avon DC
Avonbridge, Falkirk Cl
Avondale Road, Torfaen CBC
Avonmouth, Bristol City
Avonwick, S Hams DC
Awbridge, Test Valley BC
Awliscombe, E Devon DC
Awre, Forest of Dean DC
Awsworth, Broxtowe BC
Axbridge, Sedgemoor DC
Axford, Basingstoke/Deane BC
Axford, Kennet DC
Axminster, E Devon DC
Axmouth, E Devon DC
Aylburton, Forest of Dean DC
Aylesbeare, E Devon DC
Aylesbury, Aylesbury Vale DC
Aylesby, N E Lincs Cl
Aylesford, Tonbridge/Malling BC
Aylesham, Dover DC
Aylestone, Leicester City
Aylmerton, N Norfolk DC
Aylsham, Broadland DC
Aylton, Herefordshire Cl
Aymestrey, Herefordshire Cl
Aynho, S Northants Cl
Ayot St Lawrence, Welwyn
   Hatfield DC
Ayot St Peter, Welwyn Hatfield
   DC
Ayr, S Ayrshire Cl
Aysgarth, Richmondshire DC
Ayside, S Lakeland DC

Ayston, Rutland CC
Aythorpe Roding, Uttlesford DC
Ayton, Scottish Borders Cl
Azerley, Harrogate BC

Babbacombe, Torbay Cl
Babbinswood, Oswestry BC
Babcary, S Somerset DC
Babraham, S Cambs DC
Babworth, Bassetlaw DC
Bache, Chester City
Backbarrow, S Lakeland DC
Backford, Chester City
Backies, Highland Cl
Backmoor, Sheffield City
Backwell, N Somerset DC
Backworth, N Tyneside Cl
Baconsthorpe, N Norfolk DC
Bacton, Herefordshire Cl
Bacton, Mid Suffolk DC
Bacton, N Norfolk DC
Bacup, Rossendale BC
Badachonacher, Highland Cl
Badbury, Swindon DC
Badby, Daventry DC
Badcall, Highland Cl
Badcaul, Highland Cl
Baddesley Clinton, Warwick DC
Baddesley Ensor, N Warks BC
Baddidarach, Highland Cl
Baddiley, Crewe/Nantwich BC
Baddington, Crewe/Nantwich BC
Badenscallie, Highland Cl
Badger, Bridgnorth DC
Badger Farm, Winchester City
Badgers Mount, Sevenoaks DC
Badgeworth, Tewkesbury BC
Badgworth, Sedgemoor DC
Badicaul, Highland Cl
Badingham, Suffolk C'l DC
Badlesmere, Swale BC
Badley, Mid Suffolk DC
Badluarach, Highland Cl
Badminton, S Glos Cl
Badnaban, Highland Cl
Badnagie, Highland Cl
Badninish, Highland Cl
Badrallach, Highland Cl
Badsey, Wychavon DC
Badsworth, Wakefield MDC
Badwell Ash, Mid Suffolk DC
Bagby, Hambleton DC
Bagendon, Cotswold DC
Bagillt, Flintshire CC
Baginton, Warwick DC
Baglan, Neath Port Talbot CBC
Baglan Bay, Neath Port Talbot
   CBC
Bagley, N Shropshire DC
Bagnall, Staffs Moorlands DC

Bagshot, Surrey Heath BC
Bagthorpe, Ashfield DC
Bagthorpe, King's Lynn/W Norfolk BC
Bagworth, Hinckley/Bosworth BC
Baildon, Bradford MDC
Bailetonach, Highland CI
Bailey, Ribble Valley BC
Baillieston, Glasgow City
Bainbridge, Richmondshire DC
Bainsford, Falkirk CI
Bainton, E Riding of Yks
Bainton, Peterborough City
Bakers End, E Herts DC
Bakewell, Derbys Dales DC
Bala, Gwynedd CC
Balavil, Highland CI
Balbeg, Highland CI
Balblair, Highland CI
Balchladich, Highland CI
Balchraggan, Highland CI
Balchrick, Highland CI
Balcombe, Mid Sussex DC
Baldernock, E Dunbartonshire CI
Baldersby, Harrogate BC
Balderstone, Ribble Valley BC
Balderton, Newark/Sherwood DC
Baldhu, Carrick DC
Baldingstone, Bury MBC
Baldock, N Herts DC
Baldwin's Gate, Newcastle-u-Lyme BC
Bale, N Norfolk DC
Balerno, Edinburgh City
Balfron, Stirling CI
Balgowan, Highland CI
Balgown, Highland CI
Balgrayhill, Glasgow City
Balgunearie, Highland CI
Balgunloune, Highland CI
Balham, Wandsworth LBC
Balintore, Highland CI
Balintraid, Highland CI
Balk, Hambleton DC
Balkholme, E Riding of Yks
Ballachulish, Highland CI
Ballantrae, S Ayrshire CI
Ballater, Aberdeenshire CI
Balleigh, Highland CI
Ballidon, Derbys Dales DC
Ballifeary, Highland CI
Ballinderry, Lisburn City
Ballinger, Chiltern DC
Ballingham, Herefordshire CI
Ballingry, Fife CI
Ballintoy, Moyle DC
Balloan, Highland CI
Balloch, Highland CI
Balloch, W Dunbartonshire CI
Balls Cross, Chichester DC

Ballycastle, Moyle DC
Ballyclare, Newtownabbey BC
Ballydonegan, Limavady BC
Ballyeaston, Newtownabbey BC
Ballygawley, Dungannon & S Tyrone BC
Ballygowan, Lisburn City
Ballyhanna, Limavady BC
Ballykelly, Limavady BC
Ballylesson, Lisburn City
Ballylintagh, Coleraine BC
Ballymartin, Newry/Mourne DC
Ballymena, Ballymena BC
Ballymoney, Ballymoney BC
Ballynahinch, Down DC
Ballyness, Limavady BC
Ballynure, Newtownabbey BC
Ballyrobert, Newtownabbey BC
Ballyroney, Banbridge DC
Ballyward, Banbridge DC
Balmacara, Highland CI
Balmacqueen, Highland CI
Balmaghie, Dumfries/Galloway CI
Balmalcolm, Fife CI
Balmeanach, Highland CI
Balmedie, Aberdeenshire CI
Balmerino, Fife CI
Balmnaclellan, Dumfries/Galloway CI
Balmore, E Dunbartonshire CI
Balmore, Highland CI
Balnabruach, Highland CI
Balnabruich, Highland CI
Balnacoil, Highland CI
Balnacra, Highland CI
Balnadelson, Highland CI
Balnain, Highland CI
Balnakeil, Highland CI
Balnakeil Craft Village, Highland CI
Balnaknock, Highland CI
Balnamore, Ballymoney BC
Balnapaling, Highland CI
Balne, Selby DC
Balquhidder, Stirling CI
Balruddery, Angus CI
Balsall Common, Solihull MBC
Balscote, Cherwell DC
Balsham, S Cambs DC
Balterley, Newcastle-u-Lyme BC
Baltonsborough, Mendip DC
Balvraid, Highland CI
Bamber Bridge, S Ribble BC
Bamburgh, Berwick-u-Tweed BC
Bamford, High Peak BC
Bampton, Eden DC
Bampton, Mid Devon DC
Bampton, W Oxon DC
Banavie, Highland CI
Banbridge, Banbridge DC

Banbury, Cherwell DC
Banchory, Aberdeenshire CI
Banchory Devenick, Aberdeenshire CI
Banchory Ternan, Aberdeenshire CI
Bancroft, Milton Keynes CI
Bancroft Park, Milton Keynes CI
Bandleyside, Eden DC
Banff, Aberdeenshire CI
Bangor, Gwynedd CC
Bangor, N Down BC
Bangor Is y Coed, Wrexham CBC
Banham, Breckland CI
Bank Newton, Craven DC
Bankhead, Aberdeen City
Banknock, Falkirk CI
Banks, Carlisle City
Banks, W Lancs DC
Bannercross, Sheffield City
Banningham, N Norfolk DC
Bannockburn, Stirling CI
Banstead, Reigate/Banstead BC
Bantham, S Hams DC
Banton, N Lanarkshire CI
Banwell, N Somerset DC
Banwen, Neath Port Talbot CBC
Banwy, Powys CC
Bapchild, Swale BC
Bar Hill, S Cambs DC
Baramore, Highland CI
Barassie, S Ayrshire CI
Barbaraville, Highland CI
Barbon, S Lakeland DC
Barbridge, Crewe/Nantwich BC
Barby, Daventry DC
Barcheston, Stratford/Avon DC
Barcombe, Lewes DC
Barden, Craven DC
Bardfield Saling, Braintree DC
Bardney, W Lindsey DC
Bardon, N W Leics DC
Bardon Mill, Tynedale DC
Bardowie, E Dunbartonshire CI
Bardsea, S Lakeland DC
Bardsey cum Rigton, Leeds City
Bardsley, Oldham MBC
Bardwell, St Edmundsbury BC
Barford, S Norfolk DC
Barford, Warwick DC
Barford St John, Cherwell DC
Barford St Martin, Salisbury DC
Barford St Michael, Cherwell DC
Barfordon, Warwick DC
Barforth, Teesdale DC
Barfrestone, Dover DC
Bargate, Southampton City
Bargeddie, N Lanarkshire CI
Bargoed, Caerphilly CBC
Barham, Brent LBC

Barham, Canterbury City
Barham, Huntingdonshire DC
Barham, Mid Suffolk DC
Barholm, S Kesteven DC
Barkby, Charnwood DC
Barkby Thorpe, Charnwood DC
Barkestone le Vale, Melton BC
Barkham, Wokingham DC
Barking, Barking/Dagenham LBC
Barking, Mid Suffolk DC
Barkingside, Redbridge LBC
Barkisland, Calderdale MBC
Barkston, S Kesteven DC
Barkston Ash, Selby DC
Barkway, N Herts DC
Barlaston, Stafford BC
Barlavington, Chichester DC
Barlborough, Bolsover DC
Barlby, Selby DC
Barlestone, Hinckley/Bosworth
    BC
Barley, N Herts DC
Barley, Pendle BC
Barleythorpe, Rutland CC
Barling, Rochford DC
Barling Magna, Rochford DC
Barlings (Langworth), W Lindsey
    DC
Barlow, N E Derbys DC
Barlow, Selby DC
Barmby Moor, E Riding of Yks
Barmby on the Marsh, E Riding of
    Yks
Barmer, King's Lynn/W Norfolk
    BC
Barming, Maidstone BC
Barmouth, Gwynedd CC
Barmpton, Darlington BC
Barmston, E Riding of Yks
Barnack, Peterborough City
Barnacre, Wyre BC
Barnadiston, St Edmundsbury BC
Barnard Castle, Teesdale DC
Barnard Gate, W Oxon DC
Barnburgh, Doncaster MBC
Barnby, Waveney DC
Barnby (East/West), Scarborough
    BC
Barnby Dun, Doncaster MBC
Barnby in the Willows,
    Newark/Sherwood DC
Barnby Moor, Bassetlaw DC
Barnehurst, Bexley LBC
Barnes, Richmond upon Thames
    LBC
Barnet, Barnet LBC
Barnetby le Wold, N Lincs Cl
Barney, N Norfolk DC
Barnham, Arun DC
Barnham, St Edmundsbury BC

Barnham Broom, S Norfolk DC
Barnhill, Brent LBC
Barningham, St Edmundsbury BC
Barningham, Teesdale DC
Barnmoor Green, Stratford/Avon
    DC
Barnoldby le Beck, N E Lincs Cl
Barnoldswick, Pendle BC
Barns Green, Horsham DC
Barnsbury, Islington LBC
Barnsley, Barnsley MBC
Barnsley, Cotswold DC
Barnstaple, N Devon DC
Barnston, Uttlesford DC
Barnston, Wirral MBC
Barnstone, Rushcliffe BC
Barnt Green, Bromsgrove DC
Barnton, Vale Royal BC
Barnwell, E Northants Cl
Barony, Teesdale DC
Barr, S Ayrshire Cl
Barra, Comhairle Nan Eilean Siar
Barras, Eden DC
Barrasford, Tynedale DC
Barrhead, E Renfrewshire Cl
Barrhill, S Ayrshire Cl
Barrington, Cotswold DC
Barrington, S Cambs DC
Barrington, S Somerset DC
Barripper, Kerrier DC
Barrmill, N Ayrshire Cl
Barrow, Bridgnorth DC
Barrow, Chester City
Barrow, Ribble Valley BC
Barrow, Rutland CC
Barrow Bridge, Bolton MBC
Barrow Burn, Alnwick DC
Barrow cum Denham, St
    Edmundsbury BC
Barrow Gurney, N Somerset DC
Barrow Hill, Chesterfield BC
Barrow-in-Furness, Barrow-in-
    Furness BC
Barrow on Humber, N Lincs Cl
Barrow on Trent, S Derbys DC
Barrow upon Soar, Charnwood
    DC
Barrowby, S Kesteven DC
Barrowden, Rutland CC
Barrowford, Pendle BC
Barry, Vale of Glamorgan Cl
Barsby, Melton BC
Barsham, N Norfolk DC
Barsham, Waveney DC
Barston, Solihull MBC
Bartestree, Herefordshire Cl
Barthomley, Crewe/Nantwich BC
Bartley, New Forest DC
Bartley Green, Birmingham City
Bartlow, S Cambs DC

Barton, Chester City
Barton, Cotswold DC
Barton, Eden DC
Barton, Preston City
Barton, Richmondshire DC
Barton, Rushcliffe BC
Barton, S Cambs DC
Barton, Stratford/Avon DC
Barton, Torbay Cl
Barton Bendish, King's Lynn/W
    Norfolk BC
Barton Blount, S Derbys DC
Barton Harthshorn, Aylesbury
    Vale DC
Barton in the Beans,
    Hinckley/Bosworth BC
Barton le Clay, S Beds DC
Barton le Street, Ryedale DC
Barton le Willows, Ryedale DC
Barton Mills, Forest Heath DC
Barton Moss, Salford City
Barton on Humber, N Lincs Cl
Barton on Sea, New Forest DC
Barton on the Heath,
    Stratford/Avon DC
Barton St David, S Somerset DC
Barton Seagrave, Kettering BC
Barton Stacey, Test Valley BC
Barton Turf, N Norfolk DC
Barton under Needwood, E Staffs
    BC
Barugh, Ryedale DC
Barway, E Cambs DC
Barwell, Hinckley/Bosworth BC
Barwick, King's Lynn/W Norfolk
    BC
Barwick, S Somerset DC
Barwick Ford, E Herts DC
Barwick in Elmet, Leeds City
Baschurch, N Shropshire DC
Bascote, Stratford/Avon DC
Bascote Heath, Stratford/Avon
    DC
Basegreen, Sheffield City
Basford, Crewe/Nantwich BC
Basford Green, Staffs Moorlands
    DC
Bashall Eaves, Ribble Valley BC
Bashley, New Forest DC
Basildon, Basildon DC
Basildon, W Berks DC
Basingstoke, Basingstoke/Deane
    BC
Baslow, Derbys Dales DC
Bassenthwaite, Allerdale BC
Bassett, Southampton City
Bassingbourn, S Cambs DC
Bassingfield, Rushcliffe BC
Bassingham, N Kesteven DC
Bassingthorpe, S Kesteven DC

Baston, S Kesteven DC
Bastwick, Gt Yarmouth BC
Batchmere, Chichester DC
Batcombe, Mendip DC
Batcombe, W Dorset DC
Bate Heath, Macclesfield BC
Batemoor, Sheffield City
Bath, Bath/N E Somerset Cl
Bathampton, Bath/N E Somerset Cl
Bathealton, Taunton Deane BC
Batheaston, Bath/N E Somerset Cl
Batherton, Crewe/Nantwich BC
Bathford, Bath/N E Somerset Cl
Bathgate, W Lothian Cl
Bathley, Newark/Sherwood DC
Batley, Kirklees MC
Batsford, Cotswold DC
Battersby, Hambleton DC
Battersea, Wandsworth LBC
Battisford, Mid Suffolk DC
Battisford Tye, Mid Suffolk DC
Battle, Rother DC
Battlefield, Glasgow City
Battlefield, Shrewsbury/Atcham Cl
Battleflat, N W Leics DC
Battlesbridge, Rochford DC
Battlesden, Mid Beds DC
Battleton, W Somerset DC
Battramsley, New Forest DC
Baughurst, Basingstoke/Deane BC
Baulking, Vale of White Horse DC
Baumber, E Lindsey DC
Baunton, Cotswold DC
Bausley, Powys CC
Bavington, Tynedale DC
Bawburgh, S Norfolk DC
Bawdeswell, Breckland Cl
Bawdrip, Sedgemoor DC
Bawdsey, Suffolk C'l DC
Bawsey, King's Lynn/W Norfolk BC
Bawtry, Doncaster MBC
Baxenden, Hyndburn BC
Baxterley, N Warks BC
Bay, Highland Cl
Baycliff, S Lakeland DC
Baydon, Kennet DC
Bayford, E Herts DC
Baylham, Mid Suffolk DC
Bayston Hill, Shrewsbury/Atcham Cl
Bayswater, Westminster City
Beachampton, Aylesbury Vale DC
Beachamwell, Breckland Cl
Beachy Head, Eastbourne BC

Beaconsfield, S Bucks DC
Beadlam, Ryedale DC
Beadnell, Berwick-u-Tweed BC
Beaford, Torridge DC
Beal, Berwick-u-Tweed BC
Beal, Selby DC
Beaminster, W Dorset DC
Beamish, Chester-le-Street DC
Beamish (part), Derwentside DC
Beamond End, Chiltern DC
Beamsley, Craven DC
Bean, Dartford BC
Beanhill, Milton Keynes Cl
Beanley, Alnwick DC
Beard, High Peak BC
Beare Green, Mole Valley DC
Bearley, Stratford/Avon DC
Bearley Cross, Stratford/Avon DC
Bearpark, Durham City
Bearsbridge, Tynedale DC
Bearsden, E Dunbartonshire Cl
Bearsted, Maidstone BC
Bearwardcote, S Derbys DC
Bearwood, Poole BC
Bearwood, Sandwell MBC
Beauchamp, Epping Forest DC
Beauchamp Roding, Epping Forest DC
Beauchief, Sheffield City
Beaudesert, Stratford/Avon DC
Beaulieu, New Forest DC
Beauly, Highland Cl
Beaumaris, Isle of Anglesey CC
Beaumont, Carlisle City
Beaumont, Tendring DC
Beaumont Chase, Rutland CC
Beausale, Warwick DC
Beauworth, Winchester City
Beaworthy, W Devon BC
Bebington, Wirral MBC
Beccles, Waveney DC
Beck Foot, S Lakeland DC
Beck Hole, Scarborough BC
Beck Row, Forest Heath DC
Beck Side, S Lakeland DC
Beckbury, Bridgnorth DC
Beckenham, Bromley LBC
Beckermet, Copeland BC
Beckermonds, Craven DC
Beckfoot, Allerdale BC
Beckfoot, Copeland BC
Beckford, Wychavon DC
Beckhampton, Kennet DC
Beckingham, Bassetlaw DC
Beckingham, N Kesteven DC
Beckington, Mendip DC
Beckley, Rother DC
Beckley, S Oxon DC
Beckton, Newham LBC
Beckwithshaw, Harrogate BC

Bedale, Hambleton DC
Bedburn, Teesdale DC
Beddgelert, Gwynedd CC
Beddingham, Lewes DC
Beddington, Sutton LBC
Bedfield, Mid Suffolk DC
Bedfont, Hounslow LBC
Bedford, Bedford BC
Bedham, Chichester DC
Bedhampton, Havant BC
Bedingfield, Mid Suffolk DC
Bedingham, S Norfolk DC
Bedlington, Wansbeck DC
Bedlinog, Merthyr Tydfil CBC
Bednall, S Staffs Cl
Bedstone, S Shropshire DC
Bedwas, Caerphilly CBC
Bedworth, Nuneaton/Bedworth BC
Beeby, Charnwood DC
Beech, E Hants DC
Beech, Stafford BC
Beech Hill, W Berks DC
Beechingstoke, Kennet DC
Beechwood, Highland Cl
Beedon, W Berks DC
Beeford, E Riding of Yks
Beeley, Derbys Dales DC
Beelsby, N E Lincs Cl
Beenham, W Berks DC
Beer, E Devon DC
Beer Hackett, W Dorset DC
Beercrocombe, S Somerset DC
Beesands, S Hams DC
Beesby in the Marsh, E Lindsey DC
Beeston, Breckland Cl
Beeston, Broxtowe BC
Beeston, Chester City
Beeston, Leeds City
Beeston Regis, N Norfolk DC
Beeston St Andrew, Broadland DC
Beeswing, Dumfries/Galloway Cl
Beetham, S Lakeland DC
Beetley, Breckland Cl
Begbroke, Cherwell DC
Begdale, Fenland DC
Begelly, Pembrokeshire CC
Beguildy, Powys CC
Beighton, Broadland DC
Beighton, Sheffield City
Beith, N Ayrshire Cl
Bekesbourne, Canterbury City
Belaugh, Broadland DC
Belbroughton, Bromsgrove DC
Belchamp Otten, Braintree DC
Belchamp St Paul, Braintree DC
Belchamp Walter, Braintree DC
Belchford, E Lindsey DC

Belfast, Belfast City
Belford, Berwick-u-Tweed BC
Belgrave, Tamworth BC
Belgravia, Westminster City
Belhelvie, Aberdeenshire Cl
Bell Busk, Craven DC
Bell Green, Coventry City MDC
Bell Vale, Chichester DC
Bellaghy, Magherafelt DC
Bellarena, Limavady BC
Belleau, E Lindsey DC
Bellerby, Richmondshire DC
Bellingdon, Chiltern DC
Bellingham, Lewisham LBC
Bellingham, Tynedale DC
Bells Yew Green, Wealden DC
Bellsbank, E Ayrshire Cl
Bellshill, Berwick-u-Tweed BC
Bellshill, N Lanarkshire Cl
Belmont, Blackburn with Darwen BC
Belmont, Dumfries/Galloway Cl
Belmont, Durham City
Belmont, Sutton LBC
Belowda, Restormel BC
Belper, Amber Valley BC
Belsay, Castle Morpeth BC
Belstead, Babergh DC
Belstone, W Devon BC
Belthorn, Hyndburn BC
Beltinge, Canterbury City
Beltoft, N Lincs Cl
Belton, Gt Yarmouth BC
Belton, N Lincs Cl
Belton, N W Leics DC
Belton, Rutland CC
Belton, S Kesteven DC
Belvedere, Bexley LBC
Belvoir, Melton BC
Bembridge, Isle of Wight Cl
Bempton, E Riding of Yks
Benacre, Waveney DC
Benbecula, Comhairle Nan Eilean Siar
Benbradagh, Limavady BC
Benburb, Dungannon & S Tyrone BC
Bendish, N Herts DC
Bendochy, Perth/Kinross Cl
Benefield, E Northants Cl
Benenden, Tunbridge Wells BC
Benfleet, Castle Point BC
Bengeo Rural, E Herts DC
Benhall, Suffolk C'l DC
Benholm, Aberdeenshire Cl
Beningbrough, Hambleton DC
Benington, Boston BC
Benington, E Herts DC
Bennacott, N Cornwall DC
Benniworth, E Lindsey DC

Benover, Maidstone BC
Benson, S Oxon DC
Benthall, Bridgnorth DC
Bentham, Craven DC
Bentham, Tewkesbury BC
Bentley, Babergh DC
Bentley, E Hants DC
Bentley, E Riding of Yks
Bentley Heath, Solihull MBC
Bentley Merevale, N Warks BC
Bentley Pauncefoot, Bromsgrove DC
Bents Green, Sheffield City
Bentworth, E Hants DC
Benvie, Angus Cl
Benwell, Newcastle City
Benwick, Fenland DC
Beobridge, Bridgnorth DC
Beoley, Bromsgrove DC
Beoraidbeg, Highland Cl
Bepton, Chichester DC
Beragh, Omagh DC
Berden, Uttlesford DC
Bere Alston, W Devon BC
Bere Ferrers, W Devon BC
Bere Regis, Purbeck DC
Berepper, Kerrier DC
Bergh Apton, S Norfolk DC
Berinsfield, S Oxon DC
Berkeley, Stroud DC
Berkhamsted, Dacorum BC
Berkley, Mendip DC
Berkswell, Solihull MBC
Berkswich, Stafford BC
Bermondsey, Southwark LBC
Bernera, Comhairle Nan Eilean Siar
Berneray, Comhairle Nan Eilean Siar
Berners Roding, Epping Forest DC
Bernisdale, Highland Cl
Berrick Salome, S Oxon DC
Berriedale, Highland Cl
Berrier, Eden DC
Berriew, Powys CC
Berringdon, Berwick-u-Tweed BC
Berrington, Shrewsbury/Atcham Cl
Berrow, Malvern Hills DC
Berrow, Sedgemoor DC
Berry Hill, Forest of Dean DC
Berry Pomeroy, S Hams DC
Berrymoss, Scottish Borders Cl
Berrynarbor, N Devon DC
Bersted, Arun DC
Bervie, Aberdeenshire Cl
Berwick, Wealden DC
Berwick Bassett, Kennet DC
Berwick Hill, Castle Morpeth BC

Berwick St James, Salisbury DC
Berwick St John, Salisbury DC
Berwick St Leonard, Salisbury DC
Berwick-upon-Tweed, Berwick-u-Tweed BC
Besford, Wychavon DC
Bessacarr, Doncaster MBC
Bessbrook, Newry/Mourne DC
Besselsleigh, Vale of White Horse DC
Besses o' th' Barn, Bury MBC
Bessingham, N Norfolk DC
Besthorpe, Breckland Cl
Besthorpe, Newark/Sherwood DC
Bestwood St Albans, Gedling BC
Beswick, E Riding of Yks
Betchton, Congleton BC
Betchworth, Mole Valley DC
Bethersden, Ashford BC
Bethesda, Gwynedd CC
Bethnal Green, Tower Hamlets LBC
Betley, Newcastle-u-Lyme BC
Betsham, Dartford BC
Betteshanger, Dover DC
Bettiscombe, W Dorset DC
Betton, N Shropshire DC
Bettws, Powys CC
Bettws y Crwyn, S Shropshire DC
Bettyhill, Highland Cl
Betws, Carmarthenshire CC
Betws Garmon, Gwynedd CC
Betws Gwerfil Goch, Denbighshire CC
Betws y Coed, Conwy CBC
Betws yn Rhos, Conwy CBC
Beulah, Ceredigion CC
Bevercotes, Bassetlaw DC
Beverley, E Riding of Yks
Beverston, Cotswold DC
Bewaldeth, Allerdale BC
Bewcastle, Carlisle City
Bewdley, Wyre Forest DC
Bewerley, Harrogate BC
Bewholme, E Riding of Yks
Bexhill, Rother DC
Bexley, Bexley LBC
Bexley Hill, Chichester DC
Bexleyheath, Bexley LBC
Bexton, Macclesfield BC
Bexwell, King's Lynn/W Norfolk BC
Beyton, Mid Suffolk DC
Bibury, Cotswold DC
Bicester, Cherwell DC
Bickenhill, Solihull MBC
Bicker, Boston BC
Bickerstaffe, W Lancs DC
Bickerton, Crewe/Nantwich BC
Bickerton, Harrogate BC

Bickford, S Staffs Cl
Bickington, Teignbridge DC
Bickleigh, Mid Devon DC
Bickleigh, S Hams DC
Bickley, Bromley LBC
Bickley, Chester City
Bickmarsh, Wychavon DC
Bicknacre, Chelmsford BC
Bicknoller, W Somerset DC
Bicknor, Maidstone BC
Bickton, New Forest DC
Bicton, E Devon DC
Bicton, Shrewsbury/Atcham Cl
Bicton, S Shropshire DC
Bidborough, Tunbridge Wells BC
Biddenden, Ashford BC
Biddenham, Bedford BC
Biddestone, N Wilts DC
Biddlesden, Aylesbury Vale DC
Biddlestone, Alnwick DC
Biddulph, Staffs Moorlands DC
Bideford, Torridge DC
Bidford on Avon, Stratford/Avon DC
Bidston, Wirral MBC
Bielby, E Riding of Yks
Bieldside, Aberdeen City
Bierley, Isle of Wight Cl
Bierton, Aylesbury Vale DC
Big Sand, Highland Cl
Bigbury, S Hams DC
Bigby, W Lindsey DC
Biggar, Barrow-in-Furness BC
Biggar, S Lanarkshire Cl
Biggin, Rugby BC
Biggin, Selby DC
Biggin by Hartington, Derbys Dales DC
Biggin by Hulland, Derbys Dales DC
Biggin Hill, Bromley LBC
Biggleswade, Mid Beds DC
Bighton, Winchester City
Bignor, Chichester DC
Bigrigg, Copeland BC
Bilberry, Restormel BC
Bilbrook, S Staffs Cl
Bilbrough, Selby DC
Bilbster, Highland Cl
Bilbster Mains, Highland Cl
Bildeston, Babergh DC
Billericay, Basildon DC
Billesdon, Harborough DC
Billesley, Birmingham City
Billesley, Stratford/Avon DC
Billing, Northampton BC
Billingborough, S Kesteven DC
Billinge, St Helens MBC
Billingford, Breckland Cl
Billingford, S Norfolk DC

Billingham, Stockton-on-Tees BC
Billinghay, N Kesteven DC
Billingley, Barnsley MBC
Billingshurst, Horsham DC
Billingsley, Bridgnorth DC
Billington, Ribble Valley BC
Billington, S Beds DC
Billsmoor Park, Alnwick DC
Billy Row, Wear Valley DC
Bilsborrow, Wyre BC
Bilsby, E Lindsey DC
Bilsdale Midcable, Hambleton DC
Bilsington, Ashford BC
Bilsthorpe, Newark/Sherwood DC
Bilston, Midlothian Cl
Bilston, Wolverhampton MBC
Bilstone, Hinckley/Bosworth BC
Bilton, Alnwick DC
Bilton, E Riding of Yks
Bilton, Harrogate BC
Binbrook, E Lindsey DC
Bincombe, W Dorset DC
Bindal, Highland Cl
Binderton, Chichester DC
Binegar, Mendip DC
Binfield, Bracknell Forest BC
Binfield Heath, S Oxon DC
Bingfield, Tynedale DC
Bingham, Rushcliffe BC
Bingley, Bradford MDC
Binham, N Norfolk DC
Binley, Basingstoke/Deane BC
Binley, Coventry City MDC
Binley Woods, Rugby BC
Binstead, Isle of Wight Cl
Binsted, E Hants DC
Binton, Stratford/Avon DC
Bintree, Breckland Cl
Binweston, S Shropshire DC
Birch, Colchester BC
Birch Green, E Herts DC
Birch Vale, High Peak BC
Bircham Newton, King's Lynn/W Norfolk BC
Bircham Tofts, King's Lynn/W Norfolk BC
Birchanger, E Herts DC
Birchanger, Uttlesford DC
Birchen, Highland Cl
Birchington, Thanet DC
Birchover, Derbys Dales DC
Birchwood, Lincoln City
Birchwood, Warrington BC
Bircotes, Bassetlaw DC
Birdbrook, Braintree DC
Birdforth, Hambleton DC
Birdham, Chichester DC
Birdholme, Chesterfield BC
Birdingbury, Rugby BC
Birdsall, Ryedale DC

Birdwell, Barnsley MBC
Birdwood, Forest of Dean DC
Birgham, Scottish Borders Cl
Birkby, Hambleton DC
Birkby, Kirklees MC
Birkdale, Sefton MBC
Birkenhead, Wirral MBC
Birkenshaw, Kirklees MC
Birkhill, Angus Cl
Birkin, Selby DC
Birley, Herefordshire Cl
Birley, Sheffield City
Birley Carr, Sheffield City
Birley Edge, Sheffield City
Birling, Alnwick DC
Birling, Tonbridge/Malling BC
Birlingham, Wychavon DC
Birmingham, Birmingham City
Birnam, Perth/Kinross Cl
Birsay, Orkney Is Cl
Birse, Aberdeenshire Cl
Birstall, Charnwood DC
Birstall, Kirklees MC
Birstwith, Harrogate BC
Birtley, Gateshead Cl
Birtley, Tynedale DC
Birtsmorton, Malvern Hills DC
Bisbrooke, Rutland CC
Bisham, Windsor/Maidenhead RB
Bishampton, Wychavon DC
Bishop Auckland, Wear Valley DC
Bishop Burton, E Riding of Yks
Bishop Kinkell, Highland Cl
Bishop Middleham, Sedgefield BC
Bishop Monkton, Harrogate BC
Bishop Norton, W Lindsey DC
Bishop Sutton, Bath/N E Somerset Cl
Bishop Thornton, Harrogate BC
Bishop Wilton, E Riding of Yks
Bishop's Castle, S Shropshire DC
Bishop's Frome, Herefordshire Cl
Bishop's Offley, Stafford BC
Bishop's Stortford, E Herts DC
Bishop's Wood, S Staffs Cl
Bishopbriggs, E Dunbartonshire Cl
Bishopdale, Richmondshire DC
Bishops Bowl, Stratford/Avon DC
Bishops Cannings, Kennet DC
Bishops Caundle, W Dorset DC
Bishops Cleeve, Tewkesbury BC
Bishops Green, Basingstoke/Dean BC
Bishops Hull, Taunton Deane BC
Bishops Itchington, Stratford/Avon DC

Bishops Lydeard, Taunton Deane BC
Bishops Nympton, N Devon DC
Bishops Sutton, Winchester City
Bishops Tachbrook, Warwick DC
Bishops Tawton, N Devon DC
Bishops Waltham, Winchester City
Bishopsbourne, Canterbury City
Bishopsgarth, Stockton-on-Tees BC
Bishopsteignton, Teignbridge DC
Bishopstoke, Eastleigh BC
Bishopston, Swansea C&C
Bishopstone, Aylesbury Vale DC
Bishopstone, Herefordshire CI
Bishopstone, Salisbury DC
Bishopstone, Swindon BC
Bishopstrow, W Wilts DC
Bishopsworth, N Somerset DC
Bishopthorpe, City of York CI
Bishopton, Darlington BC
Bishopton, Renfrewshire CI
Bishopton, Stratford/Avon DC
Bishopton Hill, Stratford/Avon DC
Bishton, Newport City CI
Bisley, Stroud DC
Bisley, Surrey Heath BC
Bispham, W Lancs DC
Bissoe, Carrick DC
Bitchfield, S Kesteven DC
Bittadon, N Devon DC
Bittaford, S Hams DC
Bittering, Breckland CI
Bitterley, S Shropshire DC
Bitterne, Southampton City
Bitterne Park, Southampton City
Bittesby, Harborough DC
Bitteswell, Harborough DC
Bitton, S Glos CI
Bix, S Oxon DC
Bixley, S Norfolk DC
Blaby, Blaby DC
Black Bourton, W Oxon DC
Black Dog, Mid Devon DC
Black Marsh, S Shropshire DC
Black Notley, Braintree DC
Black Park, Highland CI
Black Torrington, Torridge DC
Blackawton, S Hams DC
Blackbird Leys, Oxford City
Blackborough End, King's Lynn/W Norfolk BC
Blackboys, Wealden DC
Blackbrook, Amber Valley BC
Blackburn, Aberdeenshire CI
Blackburn, Blackburn with Darwen BC
Blackburn, W Lothian CI
Blackden Heath, Congleton BC

Blackdown, Chichester DC
Blackdown, Warwick DC
Blackdown, W Dorset DC
Blackfen, Bexley LBC
Blackfold, Highland CI
Blackford, Carlisle City
Blackford, Perth/Kinross CI
Blackfordby, N W Leics DC
Blackfriars, Salford City
Blackgang, Isle of Wight CI
Blackhall, Easington DC
Blackham, Wealden DC
Blackheath, Sandwell MBC
Blackhill, Derwentside DC
Blackhill, Highland CI
Blackley, Manchester City
Blackmill, Bridgend CBC
Blackmoor, E Hants DC
Blackmore, Brentwood BC
Blackmore End, Braintree DC
Blackness, Dundee City
Blackness, Falkirk CI
Blacknest, E Hants DC
Blacko, Pendle BC
Blackpool, Blackpool BC
Blackridge, W Lothian CI
Blackrod, Bolton MBC
Blackshaw, Calderdale MBC
Blackshaw Moor, Staffs Moorlands DC
Blackstone, Horsham DC
Blackthorn, Cherwell DC
Blacktoft, E Riding of Yks
Blackwater, Carrick DC
Blackwater, Hart DC
Blackwater, Isle of Wight CI
Blackwaterfoot, N Ayrshire CI
Blackwell, Bolsover DC
Blackwell, Bromsgrove DC
Blackwell, Stratford/Avon DC
Blackwell in the Peak, Derbys Dales DC
Blackwood, Caerphilly CBC
Blackwood, S Lanarkshire CI
Bladon, W Oxon DC
Blaenavon, Torfaen CBC
Blaengarw, Bridgend CBC
Blaengwrach, Neath Port Talbot CBC
Blaengwynfi, Neath Port Talbot CBC
Blaenhonddan, Neath Port Talbot CBC
Blaenrheidol, Ceredigion CC
Blagdon, N Somerset DC
Blagdon, Torbay CI
Blaich, Highland CI
Blain, Highland CI
Blaina, Blaenau Gwent CBC
Blair Atholl, Perth/Kinross CI

Blairadam, Perth/Kinross CI
Blairdardie, Glasgow City
Blairgowrie, Perth/Kinross CI
Blairhall, Fife CI
Blairmore, Argyll/Bute CI
Blairmore, Highland CI
Blairninich, Highland CI
Blaisdon, Forest of Dean DC
Blakebrook, Wyre Forest DC
Blakedown, Wyre Forest DC
Blakelands, Milton Keynes CI
Blakelaw, Newcastle City
Blakemere, Herefordshire CI
Blakeney, Forest of Dean DC
Blakeney, N Norfolk DC
Blakenhall, Crewe/Nantwich BC
Blakenhall, Wolverhampton MBC
Blakesley, S Northants CI
Blanchland, Tynedale DC
Blandford Forum, N Dorset DC
Blandford St Mary, N Dorset DC
Blandy, Highland CI
Blankney, N Kesteven DC
Blantyre, S Lanarkshire CI
Blarmachfoldach, Highland CI
Blarnalearoch, Highland CI
Blaston, Harborough DC
Blatherwycke, E Northants CI
Blawith, S Lakeland DC
Blaxhall, Suffolk CI DC
Blaxton, Doncaster MBC
Blaydon, Gateshead CI
Bleadon, N Somerset DC
Blean, Canterbury City
Bleasby, Newark/Sherwood DC
Bleasdale, Wyre BC
Bleatarn, Eden DC
Bledington, Cotswold DC
Bledlow, Wycombe DC
Bledlow Ridge, Wycombe DC
Blencarn, Eden DC
Blencogo, Allerdale BC
Blencow, Eden DC
Blendworth, E Hants DC
Blenheim, W Oxon DC
Blennerhasset, Allerdale BC
Bletchingdon, Cherwell DC
Bletchingley, Tandridge DC
Bletchley, Milton Keynes CI
Bletchley, N Shropshire DC
Bletsoe, Bedford BC
Blewbury, Vale of White Horse DC
Blickling, Broadland DC
Blidworth, Newark/Sherwood DC
Blindbothel, Allerdale BC
Blindburn, Alnwick DC
Blindcrake, Allerdale BC
Blindley Heath, Tandridge DC
Blisland, N Cornwall DC

Bliss Gate, Wyre Forest DC
Blissford, New Forest DC
Blisworth, S Northants Cl
Blithfield, E Staffs BC
Blo' Norton, Breckland Cl
Blockley, Cotswold DC
Bloemfontein, Derwentside DC
Blofield, Broadland DC
Bloomsbury, Camden LBC
Blore, Staffs Moorlands DC
Bloxham, Cherwell DC
Bloxholm, N Kesteven DC
Bloxwich, Walsall MBC
Bloxworth, Purbeck DC
Blubberhouses, Harrogate BC
Blue Bridge, Milton Keynes Cl
Blue Hall, Stockton-on-Tees BC
Blundellsands, Sefton MBC
Blundeston, Waveney DC
Blunham, Mid Beds DC
Blunsdon St Andrew, Swindon
    BC
Bluntisham, Huntingdonshire DC
Blunts Green, Stratford/Avon DC
Blyborough, W Lindsey DC
Blyford, Waveney DC
Blymhill, S Staffs Cl
Blyth, Bassetlaw DC
Blyth, Blyth Valley BC
Blythburgh, Suffolk C'l DC
Blyton, W Lindsey DC
Bo'ness, Falkirk Cl
Boardmills, Lisburn City
Boarhills, Fife Cl
Boarhunt, Winchester City
Boarshead, Wealden DC
Boarstall, Aylesbury Vale DC
Boasley Cross, W Devon BC
Boat of Garten, Highland Cl
Bobbing, Swale BC
Bobbington, Bridgnorth DC
Bobbington, S Staffs Cl
Bobbingworth, Epping Forest DC
Bocaddon, Caradon DC
Bocking, Braintree DC
Bocking Churchstreet, Braintree
    DC
Boconnoc, Caradon DC
Boddam, Aberdeenshire Cl
Boddington, Tewkesbury BC
Bodedern, Isle of Anglesey CC
Bodelwyddan, Denbighshire CC
Bodenham, Herefordshire Cl
Bodfari, Denbighshire CC
Bodffordd, Isle of Anglesey CC
Bodham, N Norfolk DC
Bodiam, Rother DC
Bodicote, Cherwell DC
Bodmin, N Cornwall DC
Bodney, Breckland Cl

Bodorgan, Isle of Anglesey CC
Bogallen, Highland Cl
Boghall, W Lothian Cl
Bognor Regis, Arun DC
Bohenie, Highland Cl
Bohuntine, Highland Cl
Bohuntinville, Highland Cl
Bojewyan, Penwith DC
Bolam, Teesdale DC
Bolbeck Park, Milton Keynes Cl
Bold, St Helens MBC
Boldon, S Tyneside MBC
Boldon Colliery, S Tyneside MBC
Boldre, New Forest DC
Boldron, Teesdale DC
Bole, Bassetlaw DC
Bolehill, Derbys Dales DC
Bolie, Limavady BC
Bolingbroke, E Lindsey DC
Bolingey, Carrick DC
Bollington, Macclesfield BC
Bolney, Mid Sussex DC
Bolnhurst, Bedford BC
Bolsterstone, Sheffield City
Bolstone, Herefordshire Cl
Boltby, Hambleton DC
Bolton, Alnwick DC
Bolton, Bolton MBC
Bolton, E Lothian Cl
Bolton, E Riding of Yks
Bolton, Eden DC
Bolton Abbey, Craven DC
Bolton by Bowland, Ribble Valley
    BC
Bolton le Sands, Lancaster City
Bolton on Swale, Richmondshire
    DC
Bolton Percy, Selby DC
Bolton upon Dearne, Barnsley
    MBC
Boltonfellend, Carlisle City
Boltongate, Allerdale BC
Boltons, Allerdale BC
Bolventor, N Cornwall DC
Bomere Heath,
    Shrewsbury/Atcham Cl
Bonar Bridge, Highland Cl
Bonby, N Lincs Cl
Boncath, Pembrokeshire CC
Bondleigh, W Devon BC
Bonds, Wyre BC
Bonehill, Lichfield DC
Bonehill, Tamworth BC
Bonhill, W Dunbartonshire Cl
Boningale, Bridgnorth DC
Bonkyl, Scottish Borders Cl
Bonnavoulin, Highland Cl
Bonnington, Ashford BC
Bonnybridge, Falkirk Cl
Bonnyrigg, Midlothian Cl

Bonsall, Derbys Dales DC
Bontnewydd, Gwynedd CC
Bonvilston, Vale of Glamorgan Cl
Booker, Wycombe DC
Bookham, Mole Valley DC
Booley, N Shropshire DC
Boothby Graffoe, N Kesteven DC
Boothby Pagnell, S Kesteven DC
Boothstown, Salford City
Bootle, Copeland BC
Bootle, Sefton MBC
Booton, Broadland DC
Boraston, S Shropshire DC
Borden, Swale BC
Borden Village, Chichester DC
Bordley, Craven DC
Bordon Camp, E Hants DC
Bordon Gate, Mid Devon DC
Bordon Hill, Stratford/Avon DC
Boreham, Chelmsford BC
Boreham Street, Wealden DC
Borehamwood, Hertsmere BC
Borgie, Highland Cl
Borgue, Dumfries/Galloway Cl
Borgue, Highland Cl
Borley, Braintree DC
Borley Green, Mid Suffolk DC
Bornesketaig, Highland Cl
Bornish, Comhairle Nan Eilean
    Siar
Borough Fen, Peterborough City
Borough Green,
    Tonbridge/Malling BC
Boroughbridge, Harrogate BC
Borreraig, Highland Cl
Borrodale, Highland Cl
Borrowash, Erewash BC
Borrowby, Hambleton DC
Borrowby, Scarborough BC
Borrowdale, Allerdale BC
Borrowston, Highland Cl
Borth, Ceredigion CC
Borthwick Water, Scottish
    Borders Cl
Borve, Highland Cl
Borwick, Lancaster City
Bosavern, Penwith DC
Bosbury, Herefordshire Cl
Boscastle, N Cornwall DC
Boscobel, Bridgnorth DC
Boscombe, Bournemouth BC
Boscombe, Salisbury DC
Bosham, Chichester DC
Boskednan, Penwith DC
Bosley, Macclesfield BC
Bossall, Ryedale DC
Bossiney, N Cornwall DC
Bossingham, Canterbury City
Bossington, Test Valley BC
Bostock, Vale Royal BC

Boston, Boston BC
Boston Spa, Leeds City
Boswinger, Restormel BC
Botallack, Penwith DC
Botcheston, Hinckley/Bosworth
    BC
Botesdale, Mid Suffolk DC
Bothamsall, Bassetlaw DC
Bothel, Allerdale BC
Bothenhampton, W Dorset DC
Bothwell, S Lanarkshire CI
Botley, Chiltern DC
Botley, Eastleigh BC
Botley, Vale of White Horse DC
Bottacks, Highland CI
Bottesford, Melton BC
Bottesford, N Lincs CI
Bottisham, E Cambs DC
Bottomcraig, Fife CI
Botus Fleming, Caradon DC
Botwnnog, Gwynedd CC
Boughton, Daventry DC
Boughton, King's Lynn/W Norfolk
    BC
Boughton, Newark/Sherwood DC
Boughton Aluph, Ashford BC
Boughton Lees, Ashford BC
Boughton Malherbe, Maidstone
    BC
Boughton Monchelsea,
    Maidstone BC
Boughton under Blean, Swale BC
Boulby, Redcar/Cleveland BC
Bouldon, S Shropshire DC
Boulge, Suffolk C'l DC
Boulmer, Alnwick DC
Boulston, Pembrokeshire CC
Boultham, Lincoln City
Bourn, S Cambs DC
Bourne, Chichester DC
Bourne, S Kesteven DC
Bourne Valley, Poole BC
Bournes Green, Stroud DC
Bournheath, Bromsgrove DC
Bournmoor, Chester-le-Street DC
Bournmoor, Sunderland City
Bournville, Birmingham City
Bourtie, Aberdeenshire CI
Bourton, Bridgnorth DC
Bourton, Cherwell DC
Bourton, N Dorset DC
Bourton, Vale of White Horse DC
Bourton on Dunsmore, Rugby BC
Bourton on the Hill, Cotswold DC
Bourton on the Water, Cotswold
    DC
Bourton St Georges, N Somerset
    DC
Bourton Westwood, Bridgnorth
    DC

Bovevagh, Limavady BC
Bovey Tracey, Teignbridge DC
Boviel, Limavady BC
Bovingdon, Dacorum BC
Bovingdon Green, Wycombe DC
Bovington, Purbeck DC
Bow, Mid Devon DC
Bow, Tower Hamlets LBC
Bow Brickhill, Milton Keynes CI
Bow of Fife, Fife CI
Bowbank, Teesdale DC
Bowburn, Durham City
Bowden, Scottish Borders CI
Bowderdale, Eden DC
Bowdon, Trafford MBC
Bower, Highland CI
Bowerchalke, Salisbury DC
Bowermadden, Highland CI
Bowes, Teesdale DC
Bowhill, Fife CI
Bowland, Ribble Valley BC
Bowland Bridge, S Lakeland DC
Bowland Forest, Ribble Valley BC
Bowlhead Green, Waverley BC
Bowling, W Dunbartonshire CI
Bowmanstead, S Lakeland DC
Bowmar, Clackmannanshire CI
Bowmore, Argyll/Bute CI
Bowness on Solway, Allerdale BC
Bowness on Windermere, S
    Lakeland DC
Bowsden, Berwick-u-Tweed BC
Box, N Wilts DC
Box Hill, Mole Valley DC
Boxford, Babergh DC
Boxford, W Berks DC
Boxgrove, Chichester DC
Boxley, Maidstone BC
Boxted, Babergh DC
Boxted, Colchester BC
Boxwell, Cotswold DC
Boxworth, S Cambs DC
Boylestone, Derbys Dales DC
Boyndie, Aberdeenshire CI
Boynton, E Riding of Yks
Boythorpe, Chesterfield BC
Boyton, N Cornwall DC
Boyton, Suffolk C'l DC
Boyton, W Wilts DC
Bozeat, Wellingborough BC
Brabling Green, Suffolk C'l DC
Brabourne, Ashford BC
Bracadale, Highland CI
Braceborough, S Kesteven DC
Bracebridge, Lincoln City
Bracebridge Heath, N Kesteven
    DC
Braceby, S Kesteven DC
Bracewell, Pendle BC
Brackenborough, E Lindsey DC

Brackenfield, N E Derbys DC
Brackens, Dundee City
Brackla, Bridgend CBC
Bracklesham, Chichester DC
Brackley, S Northants CI
Bracknell, Bracknell Forest BC
Braco, Perth/Kinross CI
Bracon Ash, S Norfolk DC
Bracora, Highland CI
Bracorina, Highland CI
Bradbourne, Derbys Dales DC
Bradbury, Sedgefield BC
Bradden, S Northants CI
Bradenham, Breckland CI
Bradenham, Wycombe DC
Bradenstoke, N Wilts DC
Bradfield, N Norfolk DC
Bradfield, Sheffield City
Bradfield, Tendring DC
Bradfield, W Berks DC
Bradfield Combust, St
    Edmundsbury BC
Bradfield Green, Crewe/Nantwich
    BC
Bradfield St Clare, St
    Edmundsbury BC
Bradfield St George, St
    Edmundsbury BC
Bradford, Berwick-u-Tweed BC
Bradford, Bradford MDC
Bradford, Torridge DC
Bradford Abbas, W Dorset DC
Bradford on Avon, W Wilts DC
Bradford on Tone, Taunton
    Deane BC
Bradford Peverell, W Dorset DC
Brading, Isle of Wight CI
Bradley, Basingstoke/Deane BC
Bradley, Chester City
Bradley, Derbys Dales DC
Bradley, N E Lincs CI
Bradley, Stafford BC
Bradley, Staffs Moorlands DC
Bradley, Wychavon DC
Bradley Fold, Bury MBC
Bradley Stoke, S Glos CI
Bradleyfield, S Lakeland DC
Bradleys Both, Craven DC
Bradmore, Rushcliffe BC
Bradninch, Mid Devon DC
Bradnop, Staffs Moorlands DC
Bradpole, W Dorset DC
Bradshaw, Bolton MBC
Bradstone, W Devon BC
Bradville, Milton Keynes CI
Bradwall, Congleton BC
Bradway, Sheffield City
Bradwell, Braintree DC
Bradwell, Derbys Dales DC
Bradwell, Gt Yarmouth BC

Bradwell, Milton Keynes CI
Bradwell Abbey, Milton Keynes CI
Bradwell Common, Milton Keynes CI
Bradwell Grove, W Oxon DC
Bradwell on Sea, Maldon DC
Bradwell Waterside, Maldon DC
Bradworthy, Torridge DC
Brae of Achnahaird, Highland CI
Braefindon, Highland CI
Braehead, S Ayrshire CI
Braemar, Aberdeenshire CI
Braemore, Highland CI
Braes of Ullapool, Highland CI
Braeside, Aberdeen City
Brafferton, Darlington BC
Brafferton, Hambleton DC
Brafield on the Green, S Northants CI
Bragbury End, E Herts DC
Braggington, Stratford/Avon DC
Braidly, Richmondshire DC
Braidwood, S Lanarkshire CI
Brailes, Stratford/Avon DC
Brailsford, Derbys Dales DC
Braintree, Braintree DC
Braiseworth, Mid Suffolk DC
Braishfield, Test Valley BC
Braithwaite, Allerdale BC
Braithwaite, Doncaster MBC
Braithwell, Doncaster MBC
Bramber, Horsham DC
Bramcote, Broxtowe BC
Bramdean, Winchester City
Bramerton, S Norfolk DC
Bramfield, E Herts DC
Bramfield, Suffolk C'l DC
Bramford, Mid Suffolk DC
Bramhall, Stockport MBC
Bramham cum Oglethorpe, Leeds City
Bramhope, Leeds City
Bramley, Basingstoke/Deane BC
Bramley, Rotherham MBC
Bramley, Waverley BC
Brampford Speke, E Devon DC
Brampton, Barnsley MBC
Brampton, Broadland DC
Brampton, Carlisle City
Brampton, Eden DC
Brampton, Huntingdonshire DC
Brampton, N E Derbys DC
Brampton, Waveney DC
Brampton, W Lindsey DC
Brampton Abbotts, Herefordshire CI
Brampton Ash, Kettering BC
Brampton Bierlow, Rotherham MBC
Brampton Bryan, Herefordshire CI

Bramshall, E Staffs BC
Bramshaw, New Forest DC
Bramshill, Hart DC
Bramshot, E Hants DC
Bran End, Uttlesford DC
Branault, Highland CI
Brancaster, King's Lynn/W Norfolk BC
Brancepeth, Durham City
Brandesburton, E Riding of Yks
Brandeston, Suffolk C'l DC
Brandiston, Broadland DC
Brandon, Berwick-u-Tweed BC
Brandon, Durham City
Brandon, Forest Heath DC
Brandon, Rugby BC
Brandon, S Kesteven DC
Brandon Parva, S Norfolk DC
Brands Hatch, Sevenoaks DC
Brandsby, Hambleton DC
Brandsby cum Stearsby, Hambleton DC
Brandwood, Birmingham City
Brane, Penwith DC
Branksome Park, Poole BC
Branscombe, E Devon DC
Bransdale, Ryedale DC
Bransford, Malvern Hills DC
Bransgore, New Forest DC
Bransholme, Kingston upon Hull City
Branston, E Staffs BC
Branston, N Kesteven DC
Branstone, Isle of Wight CI
Brant Broughton, N Kesteven DC
Brant Fell, S Lakeland DC
Brantham, Babergh DC
Branthwaite, Allerdale BC
Brantingham, E Riding of Yks
Branton, Berwick-u-Tweed BC
Branton, Doncaster MBC
Brasside, Durham City
Brassington, Derbys Dales DC
Brasted, Sevenoaks DC
Bratoft, E Lindsey DC
Brattleby, W Lindsey DC
Bratton, W Wilts DC
Bratton Clovelly, W Devon BC
Bratton Fleming, N Devon DC
Bratton Seymour, S Somerset DC
Braughing, E Herts DC
Brauncewell, N Kesteven DC
Braunston, Daventry DC
Braunston, Rutland CC
Braunstone, Blaby DC
Braunton, N Devon DC
Brawby, Ryedale DC
Brawdy, Pembrokeshire CC
Brawith, Hambleton DC
Bray, Windsor/Maidenhead RB

Braybrooke, Kettering BC
Braydon, N Wilts DC
Brayford, N Devon DC
Braystones, Copeland BC
Brayton, Selby DC
Brazacott, N Cornwall DC
Breachwood Green, N Herts DC
Breadsall, Derby City
Breadsall, Erewash BC
Breadstone, Stroud DC
Breage, Kerrier DC
Bream, Forest of Dean DC
Breamore, New Forest DC
Brean, Sedgemoor DC
Brearton, Harrogate BC
Breasclete, Comhairle Nan Eilean Siar
Breaston, Erewash BC
Brechin, Angus CI
Breckenbrough, Hambleton DC
Breckles, Breckland CI
Breckrey, Highland CI
Brecon, Powys CC
Bredbury, Stockport MBC
Brede, Rother DC
Bredenbury, Herefordshire CI
Bredfield, Suffolk C'l DC
Bredgar, Swale BC
Bredhurst, Maidstone BC
Bredicot, Wychavon DC
Bredon, Wychavon DC
Bredons Norton, Wychavon DC
Bredwardine, Herefordshire CI
Breedon on the Hill, N W Leics DC
Breich, W Lothian CI
Breighton, E Riding of Yks
Breinton, Herefordshire CI
Bremhill, N Wilts DC
Brenachie, Highland CI
Brenchley, Tunbridge Wells BC
Brendon, N Devon DC
Brent Eleigh, Babergh DC
Brent Knoll, Sedgemoor DC
Brent Pelham, E Herts DC
Brentford, Hounslow LBC
Brentor, W Devon BC
Brentwater, Brent LBC
Brentwood, Brentwood BC
Brenzett, Shepway DC
Brereton, Cannock Chase DC
Brereton, Congleton BC
Bressay, Shetland Is CI
Bressingham, S Norfolk DC
Bretby, S Derbys DC
Bretford, Rugby BC
Bretforton, Wychavon DC
Bretherton, Chorley BC
Brettenham, Babergh DC
Brettenham, Breckland CI

Bretton, Peterborough City
Brewham, S Somerset DC
Brewood, S Staffs Cl
Briantspuddle, Purbeck DC
Brickendon, E Herts DC
Bricket Wood, St Albans City/DC
Bricklehampton, Wychavon DC
Bridekirk, Allerdale BC
Bridestowe, W Devon BC
Bridford, Teignbridge DC
Bridge, Canterbury City
Bridge of Allan, Stirling Cl
Bridge of Don, Aberdeen City
Bridge of Orchy, Argyll/Bute Cl
Bridge of Weir, Renfrewshire Cl
Bridge Sollers, Herefordshire Cl
Bridge Street, Babergh DC
Bridge Trafford, Chester City
Bridgefoot, Allerdale BC
Bridgemere, Crewe/Nantwich BC
Bridgemont, High Peak BC
Bridgend, Argyll/Bute Cl
Bridgend, Bridgend CBC
Bridgend, Eden DC
Bridgend, Perth/Kinross Cl
Bridgend, W Lothian Cl
Bridgerule, Torridge DC
Bridgeton, Glasgow City
Bridgetown, S Hams DC
Bridgetown, Stratford/Avon DC
Bridgetown, W Somerset DC
Bridgham, Breckland Cl
Bridgnorth, Bridgnorth DC
Bridgtown, Cannock Chase DC
Bridgwater, Sedgemoor DC
Bridlington, E Riding of Yks
Bridport, W Dorset DC
Bridstow, Herefordshire Cl
Briercliffe, Burnley BC
Brierfield, Pendle BC
Brierley, Barnsley MBC
Brierley, Forest of Dean DC
Brierley Green, High Peak BC
Brierton, Hartlepool BC
Brigg, N Lincs Cl
Briggsworth, Scarborough BC
Brigham, Allerdale BC
Brigham, E Riding of Yks
Brighouse, Calderdale MBC
Brighstone, Isle of Wight Cl
Brighthampton, W Oxon DC
Brightling, Rother DC
Brightlingsea, Tendring DC
Brighton, Brighton/Hove Cl
Brighton, Restormel BC
Brightons, Falkirk Cl
Brightside, Sheffield City
Brightwalton, W Berks DC
Brightwell, S Oxon DC
Brightwell, Suffolk C'l DC

Brightwell Baldwin, S Oxon DC
Brightwell cum Sotwell, S Oxon DC
Brignall, Teesdale DC
Brigsley, N E Lincs Cl
Brigsteer, S Lakeland DC
Brigstock, E Northants Cl
Brill, Aylesbury Vale DC
Brilley, Herefordshire Cl
Brimfield, Herefordshire Cl
Brimington, Chesterfield BC
Brimpsfield, Cotswold DC
Brimpton, W Berks DC
Brincliffe, Sheffield City
Brind, E Riding of Yks
Brindle, Chorley BC
Brindley, Crewe/Nantwich BC
Brindley Heath, Cannock Chase DC
Brineton, S Staffs Cl
Bringhurst, Harborough DC
Brington, Daventry DC
Brington, Huntingdonshire DC
Briningham, N Norfolk DC
Brinkburn, Alnwick DC
Brinkhill, E Lindsey DC
Brinkley, E Cambs DC
Brinklow, Rugby BC
Brinkworth, N Wilts DC
Brinscall, Chorley BC
Brinsley, Broxtowe BC
Brinsop, Herefordshire Cl
Brinsworth, Rotherham MBC
Brinton, N Norfolk DC
Brisley, Breckland Cl
Brislington, Bristol City
Bristol, Bristol City
Briston, N Norfolk DC
Britford, Salisbury DC
Brithdir, Gwynedd CC
Briton Ferry, Neath Port Talbot CBC
Britwell, Slough BC
Britwell Salome, S Oxon DC
Brixham, Torbay Cl
Brixton, Lambeth LBC
Brixton, S Hams DC
Brixworth, Daventry DC
Brize Norton, W Oxon DC
Bro Garmon, Conwy CBC
Bro Machno, Conwy CBC
Broad Blunsdon, Swindon BC
Broad Campden, Cotswold DC
Broad Chalke, Salisbury DC
Broad Green, Malvern Hills DC
Broad Haven, Highland Cl
Broad Hinton, Kennet DC
Broad Lanes, Bridgnorth DC
Broad Layings, Basingstoke/Deane BC

Broad Marston, Wychavon DC
Broad Oak, Bridgnorth DC
Broad Oak, Canterbury City
Broad Town, N Wilts DC
Broadbridge, Chichester DC
Broadbridge Heath, Horsham DC
Broadclyst, E Devon DC
Broadford, Highland Cl
Broadford Bridge, Horsham DC
Broadham Green, Tandridge DC
Broadheath, Malvern Hills DC
Broadheath, Trafford MBC
Broadhembury, E Devon DC
Broadhempston, Teignbridge DC
Broadholme, W Lindsey DC
Broadley, Rochdale MBC
Broadley Common, Epping Forest DC
Broadmayne, W Dorset DC
Broadmere, Basingstoke/Deane BC
Broadmoor, Mole Valley DC
Broadoak, Caradon DC
Broadstairs, Thanet DC
Broadstone, Poole BC
Broadstone, S Shropshire DC
Broadwas, Malvern Hills DC
Broadwath, Carlisle City
Broadway, E Staffs BC
Broadway, S Somerset DC
Broadway, Wychavon DC
Broadwell, Cotswold DC
Broadwell, Forest of Dean DC
Broadwell, Rugby BC
Broadwell, W Oxon DC
Broadwindsor, W Dorset DC
Broadwoodkelly, W Devon BC
Broadwoodwidger, Torridge DC
Brobury, Herefordshire Cl
Brochel, Highland Cl
Brockbridge, Winchester City
Brockburn, Glasgow City
Brockdish, S Norfolk DC
Brockenhurst, New Forest DC
Brockhall, Daventry DC
Brockhall/Old Langho, Ribble Valley BC
Brockham, Mole Valley DC
Brockhampton (nr Fownhope), Herefordshire Cl
Brockhampton (nr Whitbourne), Herefordshire Cl
Brockholes, Kirklees MC
Brocklesby, W Lindsey DC
Brockley, N Somerset DC
Brockley, St Edmundsbury BC
Brockton, S Shropshire DC
Brockton Much Wenlock, Bridgnorth DC

Brockton Sotton Maddock,
    Bridgnorth DC
Brockweir, Forest of Dean DC
Brockwood Park, Winchester City
Brockworth, Tewkesbury BC
Brocton, Stafford BC
Brodick, N Ayrshire CI
Brodsworth, Doncaster MBC
Brogaig, Highland CI
Brogborough, Mid Beds DC
Brogden, Pendle BC
Broken Cross, Macclesfield BC
Broken Cross, Vale Royal BC
Brokenborough, N Wilts DC
Bromborough, Wirral MBC
Brome, Mid Suffolk DC
Bromeswell, Suffolk C'l DC
Bromfield, Allerdale BC
Bromfield, S Shropshire DC
Bromham, Bedford BC
Bromham, Kennet DC
Bromley, Bromley LBC
Bromley Green, Ashford BC
Brompton, Hambleton DC
Brompton, S Shropshire DC
Brompton by Sawdon,
    Scarborough BC
Brompton on Swale,
    Richmondshire DC
Brompton Ralph, W Somerset DC
Brompton Regis, W Somerset DC
Bromsberrow, Forest of Dean DC
Bromsgrove, Bromsgrove DC
Bromson Hill, Stratford/Avon DC
Bromyard, Herefordshire CI
Brondesbury Park, Brent LBC
Bronington, Wrexham CBC
Bronllys, Powys CC
Bronwydd, Carmarthenshire CC
Brook, Ashford BC
Brook, Isle of Wight CI
Brook, New Forest DC
Brook, Test Valley BC
Brook Street, Brentwood BC
Brooke, Rutland CC
Brooke, S Norfolk DC
Brookfield, Renfrewshire CI
Brookhouse, Lancaster City
Brookhouse Green, Congleton
    BC
Brookland, Shepway DC
Brookmans Park, Welwyn
    Hatfield DC
Brookside, Telford/Wrekin BC
Brookthorpe, Stroud DC
Brookwood, Woking BC
Broom, Mid Beds DC
Broom, Stratford/Avon DC
Broom Hill, E Dorset DC
Broome, S Norfolk DC

Broome, S Shropshire DC
Broome, Wyre Forest DC
Broomfield, Canterbury City
Broomfield, Chelmsford BC
Broomfield, Maidstone BC
Broomfield, Sedgemoor DC
Broomfleet, E Riding of Yks
Broomhall, Crewe/Nantwich BC
Broomhaugh, Tynedale DC
Broomhill, Aberdeen City
Broomhill, Breckland CI
Broomhill, Cannock Chase DC
Broomhill, Castle Morpeth BC
Broomhill, Glasgow City
Broomhill, Sheffield City
Broomhill, Highland CI
Broomhouse, Glasgow City
Broomley, Tynedale DC
Broompark, Durham City
Broomy Lodge, New Forest DC
Brora, Highland CI
Broseley, Bridgnorth DC
Brothertoft, Boston BC
Brotherton, Selby DC
Brotton, Redcar/Cleveland BC
Brough, E Riding of Yks
Brough, Eden DC
Brough, High Peak BC
Brough, Newark/Sherwood DC
Brough, Richmondshire DC
Brough Sowerby, Eden DC
Broughall, N Shropshire DC
Brougham, Eden DC
Broughton, Allerdale BC
Broughton, Aylesbury Vale DC
Broughton, Bridgnorth DC
Broughton, Cherwell DC
Broughton, Craven DC
Broughton, Flintshire CC
Broughton, Huntingdonshire DC
Broughton, Melton BC
Broughton, Milton Keynes CI
Broughton, N Lincs CI
Broughton, N Shropshire DC
Broughton, Ryedale DC
Broughton, Salford City
Broughton, Test Valley BC
Broughton, Wrexham CBC
Broughton Astley, Harborough
    DC
Broughton Beck, S Lakeland DC
Broughton Gifford, W Wilts DC
Broughton Hackett, Wychavon
    DC
Broughton in Amounderness,
    Preston City
Broughton in Furness, S
    Lakeland DC
Broughton Mills, S Lakeland DC
Broughton Moor, Allerdale BC

Broughton Poggs, W Oxon DC
Broughton Pytchley, Kettering BC
Broughty Ferry, Dundee City
Brown Candover,
    Basingstoke/Deane BC
Brown Edge, Staffs Moorlands
    DC
Brownhills (part), Lichfield DC
Brownlow Heath, Congleton BC
Browns Green, Stratford/Avon DC
Browns Wood, Milton Keynes CI
Brownside, High Peak BC
Browsholme, Ribble Valley BC
Browston, Gt Yarmouth BC
Broxa cum Troutsdale,
    Scarborough BC
Broxbourne, Broxbourne BC
Broxburn, W Lothian CI
Broxholme, W Lindsey DC
Broxted, Uttlesford DC
Broxton, Chester City
Bruan, Highland CI
Bruera, Chester City
Bruern, W Oxon DC
Bruisyard, Suffolk C'l DC
Brumby, N Lincs CI
Brumstead, N Norfolk DC
Brund, Staffs Moorlands DC
Brundall, Broadland DC
Brundish, Mid Suffolk DC
Brunery, Highland CI
Brunswick, Newcastle City
Bruntingthorpe, Harborough DC
Brunton, Alnwick DC
Brunton, Fife CI
Brushfield, Derbys Dales DC
Brushford, W Somerset DC
Bruton, S Somerset DC
Bryanston, N Dorset DC
Brydekirk, Dumfries/Galloway CI
Bryher, Isles of Scilly CI
Brymbo, Wrexham CBC
Brympton, S Somerset DC
Bryn, Neath Port Talbot CBC
Bryn, S Shropshire DC
Bryn, Wigan MBC
Bryn Rhyd yr Arian, Conwy CBC
Bryn y maen, Conwy CBC
Bryncethin, Bridgend CBC
Bryncoch, Neath Port Talbot CBC
Bryncrug, Gwynedd CC
Bryneglwys, Denbighshire CC
Brynford, Flintshire CC
Bryngwran, Isle of Anglesey CC
Bryning, Fylde BC
Brynmawr, Blaenau Gwent CBC
Brynwern, Torfaen CBC
Bualintur, Highland CI
Buan, Gwynedd CC
Bubbenhall, Warwick DC

Bubnell, Derbys Dales DC
Bubwith, E Riding of Yks
Buchlyvie, Stirling CI
Buckabank, Carlisle City
Buckden, Craven DC
Buckden, Huntingdonshire DC
Buckenham, Breckland CI
Buckerell, E Devon DC
Buckfastleigh, S Hams DC
Buckfastleigh, Teignbridge DC
Buckhaven, Fife CI
Buckholt, Test Valley BC
Buckhorn Weston, N Dorset DC
Buckhurst Hill, Epping Forest DC
Buckie, Moray CI
Buckingham, Aylesbury Vale DC
Buckland, Aylesbury Vale DC
Buckland, Dover DC
Buckland, E Herts DC
Buckland, Mole Valley DC
Buckland, Swale BC
Buckland, Tewkesbury BC
Buckland, Vale of White Horse
    DC
Buckland Brewer, Torridge DC
Buckland Common, Chiltern DC
Buckland Dinham, Mendip DC
Buckland Filleigh, Torridge DC
Buckland in the Moor,
    Teignbridge DC
Buckland Monachorum, W Devon
    BC
Buckland Newton, W Dorset DC
Buckland St Mary, S Somerset
    DC
Buckland-tout-Saints, S Hams DC
Bucklebury, W Berks DC
Bucklers Hard, New Forest DC
Bucklesham, Suffolk C'I DC
Buckley, Flintshire CC
Buckley Hill, Stratford/Avon DC
Bucklow Hill, Macclesfield BC
Buckminster, Melton BC
Bucknall, E Lindsey DC
Bucknall, Stoke-on-Trent City
Bucknell, Cherwell DC
Bucknell, S Shropshire DC
Bucks Cross, Torridge DC
Bucks Green, Horsham DC
Bucks Hill, Three Rivers DC
Bucks Horn Oak, E Hants DC
Bucks Mills, Torridge DC
Bucksburn, Aberdeen City
Buckton, Berwick-u-Tweed BC
Buckton, Herefordshire CI
Buckworth, Huntingdonshire DC
Budborough (part), Lichfield DC
Budbrooke, Warwick DC
Budby, Newark/Sherwood DC
Bude, N Cornwall DC

Budle, Berwick-u-Tweed BC
Budleigh Salterton, E Devon DC
Budock Water, Kerrier DC
Budshead, Plymouth City
Buerton, Crewe/Nantwich BC
Bugbrooke, S Northants CI
Bugle, Restormel BC
Bugthorpe, E Riding of Yks
Buildwas, Shrewsbury/Atcham CI
Builth Wells, Powys CC
Buittle, Dumfries/Galloway CI
Bulcote, Newark/Sherwood DC
Buldoo, Highland CI
Bulford, Salisbury DC
Bulkeley, Crewe/Nantwich BC
Bulkington, Nuneaton/Bedworth
    BC
Bulkington, W Wilts DC
Bulkworthy, Torridge DC
Bullbridge, Amber Valley BC
Bullington, Test Valley BC
Bullington, W Lindsey DC
Bulmer, Braintree DC
Bulmer, Ryedale DC
Bulphan, Thurrock BC
Bulwell, Nottingham City
Bulwick, E Northants CI
Bumbles Green, Epping Forest
    DC
Bunacaimb, Highland CI
Bunarkaig, Highland CI
Bunbury, Crewe/Nantwich BC
Bunchrew, Highland CI
Bundalloch, Highland CI
Bungay, Waveney DC
Bunkegivie, Highland CI
Bunkers Hill, Stratford/Avon DC
Bunloit, Highland CI
Bunny, Rushcliffe BC
Bunree, Highland CI
Buntingford, E Herts DC
Bunwell, S Norfolk DC
Burbage, High Peak BC
Burbage, Hinckley/Bosworth BC
Burbage, Kennet DC
Burchett's Green,
    Windsor/Maidenhead RB
Burcombe, Salisbury DC
Burcot, S Oxon DC
Bures, Babergh DC
Bures, Braintree DC
Bures St Mary, Babergh DC
Burford, S Shropshire DC
Burford, W Oxon DC
Burgate, Mid Suffolk DC
Burgess Hill, Mid Sussex DC
Burgh, Broadland DC
Burgh, Suffolk C'I DC
Burgh by Sands, Carlisle City
Burgh Castle, Gt Yarmouth BC

Burgh Heath, Reigate/Banstead
    BC
Burgh le Marsh, E Lindsey DC
Burgh on Bain, E Lindsey DC
Burgh St Margaret, Gt Yarmouth
    BC
Burgh St Peter, S Norfolk DC
Burghclere, Basingstoke/Deane
    BC
Burghead, Moray CI
Burghfield, W Berks DC
Burghfield Common, W Berks DC
Burghfield Hill, W Berks DC
Burghill, Herefordshire CI
Burghwallis, Doncaster MBC
Burham, Tonbridge/Malling BC
Buriton, E Hants DC
Buriton, N Shropshire DC
Burland, Crewe/Nantwich BC
Burlawn, N Cornwall DC
Burlescombe, Mid Devon DC
Burleston, W Dorset DC
Burley, New Forest DC
Burley, Rutland CC
Burley in Wharfedale, Bradford
    MDC
Burlingham, Broadland DC
Burmarsh, Shepway DC
Burmington, Stratford/Avon DC
Burn, Selby DC
Burnage, Manchester City
Burnaston, S Derbys DC
Burnbank, S Lanarkshire CI
Burnby, E Riding of Yks
Burncross, Sheffield City
Burneside, S Lakeland DC
Burneston, Hambleton DC
Burnfoot, Limavady BC
Burnfoot, Scottish Borders CI
Burnham, N Lincs CI
Burnham, S Bucks DC
Burnham Beeches, S Bucks DC
Burnham Deepdale, King's
    Lynn/W Norfolk BC
Burnham Green, E Herts DC
Burnham Market, King's Lynn/W
    Norfolk BC
Burnham Norton, King's Lynn/W
    Norfolk BC
Burnham on Crouch, Maldon DC
Burnham on Sea, Sedgemoor DC
Burnham Overy, King's Lynn/W
    Norfolk BC
Burnham Thorpe, King's Lynn/W
    Norfolk BC
Burnham Without, Sedgemoor
    DC
Burnhope, Derwentside DC
Burniston, Scarborough BC
Burnley, Burnley BC

Burnmouth, Scottish Borders Cl
Burnopfield, Derwentside DC
Burnsall, Craven DC
Burnside, Fife Cl
Burnside, S Lanarkshire Cl
Burnt Oak, Barnet LBC
Burnt Yates, Harrogate BC
Burntisland, Fife Cl
Burntwood, Lichfield DC
Burpham, Arun DC
Burra, Shetland Is Cl
Burradon, Alnwick DC
Burradon, N Tyneside Cl
Burras, Kerrier DC
Burray, Orkney Is Cl
Burrelton, Perth/Kinross Cl
Burren, Newry/Mourne DC
Burrigill, Highland Cl
Burrill, Hambleton DC
Burringham, N Lincs Cl
Burrington, Herefordshire Cl
Burrington, N Devon DC
Burrington, N Somerset DC
Burrough Green, E Cambs DC
Burrowbridge, Taunton Deane BC
Burrowhill, Surrey Heath BC
Burry Port, Carmarthenshire CC
Burscough, W Lancs DC
Bursea, E Riding of Yks
Burshill, E Riding of Yks
Bursledon, Eastleigh BC
Burslem, Stoke-on-Trent City
Burstall, Babergh DC
Burstock, W Dorset DC
Burston, S Norfolk DC
Burston, Stafford BC
Burstow, Tandridge DC
Burstwick, E Riding of Yks
Burtersett, Richmondshire DC
Burtholme, Carlisle City
Burtle, Sedgemoor DC
Burton, Berwick-u-Tweed BC
Burton, Chester City
Burton, Chichester DC
Burton, Christchurch BC
Burton, E Staffs BC
Burton, Ellesmere Port/Neston BC
Burton, Pembrokeshire CC
Burton, W Lindsey DC
Burton Agnes, E Riding of Yks
Burton Bradstock, W Dorset DC
Burton Coggles, S Kesteven DC
Burton Constable, E Riding of Yks
Burton cum Walden, Richmondshire DC
Burton Dassett, Stratford/Avon DC
Burton Fleming, E Riding of Yks

Burton Green, Warwick DC
Burton Hastings, Rugby BC
Burton in Kendal, S Lakeland DC
Burton in Lonsdale, Craven DC
Burton Joyce, Gedling BC
Burton Latimer, Kettering BC
Burton Lazars, Melton BC
Burton Leonard, Harrogate BC
Burton on Stather, N Lincs Cl
Burton on the Wolds, Charnwood DC
Burton Overy, Harborough DC
Burton Pedwardine, N Kesteven DC
Burton Pidsea, E Riding of Yks
Burton Salmon, Selby DC
Burton upon Trent, E Staffs BC
Burtonwood, Warrington BC
Burwardsley, Chester City
Burwarton, Bridgnorth DC
Burwash, Rother DC
Burwell, E Cambs DC
Burwell, E Lindsey DC
Bury, Bury MBC
Bury, Chichester DC
Bury, Huntingdonshire DC
Bury Green, E Herts DC
Bury Park, Luton BC
Bury St Edmunds, St Edmundsbury BC
Burythorpe, Ryedale DC
Busbridge, Waverley BC
Busby, E Renfrewshire Cl
Busby, S Lanarkshire Cl
Buscot, Vale of White Horse DC
Bush End, Uttlesford DC
Bush Hill Park, Enfield LBC
Bushbury, Wolverhampton MBC
Bushey, Hertsmere BC
Bushley, Malvern Hills DC
Bushmills, Moyle DC
Buslingthorpe, W Lindsey DC
Butcher's Pasture, Uttlesford DC
Butcombe, N Somerset DC
Bute, Argyll/Bute Cl
Butetown, Cardiff CC
Butleigh Wootton, Mendip DC
Butlers Marston, Stratford/Avon DC
Butley, Suffolk C'l DC
Butsfield, Derwentside DC
Butterburn, Carlisle City
Buttercrambe, Ryedale DC
Butterknowle, Teesdale DC
Butterleigh, Mid Devon DC
Buttermere, Allerdale BC
Buttermere, Kennet DC
Buttershaw, Bradford MDC
Butterton, Staffs Moorlands DC
Butterwick, Boston BC

Butterwick, N Lincs Cl
Butterwick, Ryedale DC
Buttsole, Dover DC
Buxhall, Mid Suffolk DC
Buxted, Wealden DC
Buxton, Broadland DC
Buxton, High Peak BC
Buxworth, High Peak BC
Bwlch, Powys CC
Byard's Leap, N Kesteven DC
Byers Green, Sedgefield BC
Byfield, Daventry DC
Byfleet, Woking BC
Byford, Herefordshire Cl
Bygrave, N Herts DC
Byker, Newcastle City
Byland, Ryedale DC
Bylaugh, Breckland Cl
Bylchau, Conwy CBC
Byley, Vale Royal BC
Byram cum Sutton, Selby DC
Byrness, Tynedale DC
Byshottles, Durham City
Bythorn, Huntingdonshire DC
Byton, Herefordshire Cl
Bywell, Tynedale DC
Byworth, Chichester DC

Cabourne, W Lindsey DC
Cabrich, Highland Cl
Cabus, Wyre BC
Cadbury, Mid Devon DC
Caddington, S Beds DC
Cade Street, Wealden DC
Cadeby, Doncaster MBC
Cadeby, Hinckley/Bosworth BC
Cadfarch, Powys CC
Cadgwith, Kerrier DC
Cadishead, Salford City
Cadley, Kennet DC
Cadmore End, Wycombe DC
Cadnam, New Forest DC
Cadney, N Lincs Cl
Cadoxton, Neath Port Talbot CBC
Caenby, W Lindsey DC
Caerau, Bridgend CBC
Caerau, Cardiff CC
Caerhun, Conwy CBC
Caerlaverock, Dumfries/Galloway Cl
Caernarfon, Gwynedd CC
Caerphilly, Caerphilly CBC
Caersws, Powys CC
Caerwent, Monmouthshire CC
Caerwys, Flintshire CC
Caia Park, Wrexham CBC
Cainscross, Stroud DC
Cairnbulg, Aberdeenshire Cl
Cairndow, Argyll/Bute Cl
Cairneyhill, Fife Cl

Cairnie, Aberdeenshire CI
Cairnryan, Dumfries/Galloway CI
Caister on Sea, Gt Yarmouth BC
Caister St Edmund, S Norfolk DC
Caistor, W Lindsey DC
Caistron, Alnwick DC
Calbourne, Isle of Wight CI
Calcethorpe, E Lindsey DC
Caldbeck, Allerdale BC
Caldbergh, Richmondshire DC
Caldecote, Huntingdonshire DC
Caldecote, N Herts DC
Caldecote, N Warks BC
Caldecote, S Cambs DC
Caldecote, S Northants CI
Caldecott, Chester City
Caldecott, E Northants CI
Caldecott, Rutland CC
Caldecotte, Milton Keynes CI
Calder Bridge, Copeland BC
Calder Mains, Highland CI
Calder Vale, Wyre BC
Calderbank, N Lanarkshire CI
Calderbrook, Rochdale MBC
Caldercruix, N Lanarkshire CI
Caldey Island, Pembrokeshire CC
Caldicot, Monmouthshire CC
Caldwell, Richmondshire DC
Caldwell, S Derbys DC
Caldy, Wirral MBC
Caledon, Dungannon & S Tyrone
    BC
Calf Heath, S Staffs CI
California, Falkirk CI
California, Gt Yarmouth BC
Calke, S Derbys DC
Callaly, Alnwick DC
Callander, Stirling CI
Callaughton, Bridgnorth DC
Callestick, Carrick DC
Calligarry, Highland CI
Callington, Caradon DC
Callow, Herefordshire CI
Callow End, Malvern Hills DC
Callow Hill, Wyre Forest DC
Calmore, New Forest DC
Calmsden, Cotswold DC
Calne, N Wilts DC
Calne Without, N Wilts DC
Calow, N E Derbys DC
Calstock, Caradon DC
Calthorpe, N Norfolk DC
Calthwaite, Eden DC
Calton, Craven DC
Calton, Glasgow City
Calton, Staffs Moorlands DC
Calveley, Crewe/Nantwich BC
Calver, Derbys Dales DC
Calverhall, N Shropshire DC
Calverleigh, Mid Devon DC

Calverley, Leeds City
Calvert, Aylesbury Vale DC
Calverton, Gedling BC
Calverton, Milton Keynes CI
Cam, Stroud DC
Camaghael, Highland CI
Camasnacroise, Highland CI
Camastianavaig, Highland CI
Camault Muir, Highland CI
Camber, Rother DC
Camberley, Surrey Heath BC
Camberwell, Southwark LBC
Camblesforth, Selby DC
Cambo, Castle Morpeth BC
Cambois, Wansbeck DC
Camborne, Kerrier DC
Cambridge, Cambridge City
Cambus, Clackmannanshire CI
Cambuslang, S Lanarkshire CI
Camden, Camden LBC
Cameley, Bath/N E Somerset CI
Camelford, N Cornwall DC
Camelon, Falkirk CI
Camelsdale, Chichester DC
Camerton, Allerdale BC
Camerton, Bath/N E Somerset CI
Camlachie, Glasgow City
Cammeringham, W Lindsey DC
Camore, Highland CI
Camowen, Omagh DC
Camp Hill, Nuneaton/Bedworth
    BC
Campbeltown, Argyll/Bute CI
Camphill, Glasgow City
Campsall, Doncaster MBC
Campsey Ash, Suffolk C'l DC
Campsie Glen, E Dunbartonshire
    CI
Campton, Mid Beds DC
Camrose, Pembrokeshire CC
Camus Croise, Highland CI
Camusnagaul, Highland CI
Camusteel, Highland CI
Camusterrach, Highland CI
Canada Common, Test Valley BC
Candlesby, E Lindsey DC
Cane End, S Oxon DC
Canewdon, Rochford DC
Canford Cliffs, Poole BC
Canford Heath, Poole BC
Canford Magna, Poole BC
Canisbay, Highland CI
Canley, Coventry City MDC
Cann, N Dorset DC
Cannich, Highland CI
Canning Town, Newham LBC
Cannington, Sedgemoor DC
Cannock, Cannock Chase DC
Cannock Wood, Cannock Chase
    DC

Canon Bridge, Herefordshire CI
Canon Bridge, Highland CI
Canon Pyon, Herefordshire CI
Canonbie, Dumfries/Galloway CI
Canonbury, Islington LBC
Canons Ashby, Daventry DC
Canons Park, Harrow LBC
Canonstown, Penwith DC
Canterbury, Canterbury City
Cantley, Broadland DC
Cantley, Doncaster MBC
Canton, Cardiff CC
Cantraywood, Highland CI
Cantsfield, Lancaster City
Canvey Island, Castle Point BC
Canwell, Lichfield DC
Canwick, N Kesteven DC
Canworthy Water, N Cornwall DC
Caol, Highland CI
Capel, Mole Valley DC
Capel, Tunbridge Wells BC
Capel Curig, Conwy CBC
Capel Garmon, Conwy CBC
Capel le Ferne, Dover DC
Capel St Andrew, Suffolk C'l DC
Capel St Mary, Babergh DC
Capelulo, Conwy CBC
Capenhurst, Chester City
Capernwray, Lancaster City
Capheaton, Castle Morpeth BC
Capstone, Medway CI
Car Colston, Rushcliffe BC
Carbis Bay, Penwith DC
Carbost, Highland CI
Carbrook, Sheffield City
Carbrooke, Breckland CI
Carburton, Bassetlaw DC
Carclew, Carrick DC
Carcroft, Doncaster MBC
Carden, Chester City
Cardenden, Fife CI
Cardeston, Shrewsbury/Atcham
    CI
Cardigan, Ceredigion CC
Cardington, Bedford BC
Cardington, Shrewsbury/Atcham
    CI
Cardinham, N Cornwall DC
Cardross, Argyll/Bute CI
Cardurnock, Allerdale BC
Careby, S Kesteven DC
Carew, Pembrokeshire CC
Carfin, N Lanarkshire CI
Cargo, Carlisle City
Carham, Berwick-u-Tweed BC
Carhampton, W Somerset DC
Carharrack, Kerrier DC
Carisbrooke, Isle of Wight CI
Cark, S Lakeland DC
Carkin, Richmondshire DC

Carland Cross, Carrick DC
Carlatton, Carlisle City
Carlby, S Kesteven DC
Carlecotes, Barnsley MBC
Carleton, Copeland BC
Carleton, Craven DC
Carleton, Wyre BC
Carleton Forehoe, S Norfolk DC
Carleton Rode, S Norfolk DC
Carleton St Peter, S Norfolk DC
Carlingcott, Bath/N E Somerset CI
Carlisle, Carlisle City
Carlops, Scottish Borders CI
Carloway, Comhairle Nan Eilean Siar
Carlton, Barnsley MBC
Carlton, Bedford BC
Carlton, Brent LBC
Carlton, Gedling BC
Carlton, Hambleton DC
Carlton, Hinckley/Bosworth BC
Carlton, Leeds City
Carlton, Richmondshire DC
Carlton, Ryedale DC
Carlton, Selby DC
Carlton, S Cambs DC
Carlton, Stockton-on-Tees BC
Carlton, Suffolk C'l DC
Carlton Colville, Waveney DC
Carlton Curlieu, Harborough DC
Carlton Highdale, Richmondshire DC
Carlton Husthwaite, Hambleton DC
Carlton in Lindrick, Bassetlaw DC
Carlton le Moorland, N Kesteven DC
Carlton Miniott, Hambleton DC
Carlton on Trent, Newark/Sherwood DC
Carlton Scroop, S Kesteven DC
Carluke, S Lanarkshire CI
Carmarthen, Carmarthenshire CC
Carmunnock, Glasgow City
Carmyle, Glasgow City
Carn, Limavady BC
Carn Brea, Kerrier DC
Carn Towan, Penwith DC
Carnaby, E Riding of Yks
Carnach, Highland CI
Carnachuin, Highland CI
Carnachy, Highland CI
Carnanbane, Limavady BC
Carnbee, Fife CI
Carne, Carrick DC
Carnedd Moel Siabod, Conwy CBC
Carnforth, Lancaster City
Carnlough, Larne BC

Carnmoney, Newtownabbey BC
Carno, Powys CC
Carnock, Fife CI
Carnon Downs, Carrick DC
Carnoustie, Angus CI
Carnwadric, Glasgow City
Carnwath, S Lanarkshire CI
Carnyorth, Penwith DC
Caroy, Highland CI
Carperby, Richmondshire DC
Carpley Green, Richmondshire DC
Carr Vale, Bolsover DC
Carradale, Argyll/Bute CI
Carrbridge, Highland CI
Carreghofa, Powys CC
Carrick, Limavady BC
Carrickfergus, Carrickfergus BC
Carrington, E Lindsey DC
Carrington, Trafford MBC
Carron, Falkirk CI
Carronbridge, Dumfries/Galloway CI
Carronshore, Falkirk CI
Carrshield, Tynedale DC
Carrutherstown, Dumfries/Galloway CI
Carrville, Durham City
Carrydoo, Limavady BC
Carryduff, Castlereagh BC
Carshalton, Sutton LBC
Carshalton Beeches, Sutton LBC
Carsick, Sheffield City
Carsington, Derbys Dales DC
Carsphairn, Dumfries/Galloway CI
Carstairs, S Lanarkshire CI
Carswell Marsh, Vale of White Horse DC
Carter's Clay, Test Valley BC
Carterton, W Oxon DC
Carterway Heads, Tynedale DC
Carthew, Restormel BC
Carthorpe, Hambleton DC
Cartington, Alnwick DC
Cartmel, S Lakeland DC
Cartmel Fell, S Lakeland DC
Cashel, Limavady BC
Cashmoor, E Dorset DC
Cassington, W Oxon DC
Cassop cum Quarrington, Durham City
Castallack, Penwith DC
Castell y bwch, Torfaen CBC
Casterton, S Lakeland DC
Castle Acre, King's Lynn/W Norfolk BC
Castle Ashby, S Northants CI
Castle Bolton, Richmondshire DC
Castle Bromwich, Solihull MBC
Castle Bytham, S Kesteven DC

Castle Caereinion, Powys CC
Castle Camps, S Cambs DC
Castle Carrock, Carlisle City
Castle Cary, S Somerset DC
Castle Church, Stafford BC
Castle Combe, N Wilts DC
Castle Donington, N W Leics DC
Castle Douglas, Dumfries/Galloway CI
Castle Eaton, Swindon BC
Castle Eden, Easington DC
Castle Frome, Herefordshire CI
Castle Gresley, S Derbys DC
Castle Hedingham, Braintree DC
Castle Kennedy, Dumfries/Galloway CI
Castle Rising, King's Lynn/W Norfolk BC
Castle Sowerby, Eden DC
Castlebay, Comhairle Nan Eilean Siar
Castlecary, N Lanarkshire CI
Castlecaulfield, Dungannon & S Tyrone BC
Castledawson, Magherafelt DC
Castlederg, Strabane DC
Castleford, Wakefield MDC
Castlehill, Aberdeen City
Castlemartin, Pembrokeshire CC
Castlemorton, Malvern Hills DC
Castlerock, Coleraine BC
Castleside, Derwentside DC
Castlethorpe, Milton Keynes CI
Castleton, High Peak BC
Castleton, Rochdale MBC
Castleton, Scarborough BC
Castleton, W Dorset DC
Castletown, Sunderland City
Castletown, Highland CI
Castlewellan, Down DC
Caston, Breckland CI
Castor, Peterborough City
Catchgate, Derwentside DC
Catchory, Highland CI
Catcliffe, Rotherham MBC
Catcott, Sedgemoor DC
Caterham on the Hill, Tandridge DC
Caterham Valley, Tandridge DC
Catesby, Daventry DC
Catfield, N Norfolk DC
Catford, Lewisham LBC
Catforth, Preston City
Cathays, Cardiff CC
Cathcart, Glasgow City
Cathedine, Powys CC
Catherington, E Hants DC
Catherston Leweston, W Dorset DC
Catlodge, Highland CI

Catlowdy, Carlisle City
Catmore, W Berks DC
Caton, Lancaster City
Catrine, E Ayrshire CI
Catsfield, Rother DC
Catshill, Bromsgrove DC
Cattal, Harrogate BC
Catterall, Wyre BC
Catterick, Richmondshire DC
Catterlen, Eden DC
Catterline, Aberdeenshire CI
Catterton, Selby DC
Catthorpe, Harborough DC
Cattistock, W Dorset DC
Catton, E Riding of Yks
Catton, Hambleton DC
Catton, S Derbys DC
Catton, Tynedale DC
Catwick, E Riding of Yks
Catworth, Huntingdonshire DC
Caudworthy Park, N Cornwall DC
Caughall, Chester City
Caukwell, E Lindsey DC
Caulcott, Cherwell DC
Cauldon, Staffs Moorlands DC
Caundle Marsh, W Dorset DC
Caunton, Newark/Sherwood DC
Causewayhead, Stirling
Causey Park, Castle Morpeth BC
Cautley, S Lakeland DC
Cavendish, St Edmundsbury BC
Cavenham, Forest Heath DC
Caversfield, Cherwell DC
Caverswall, Staffs Moorlands DC
Cawdor, Highland CI
Cawood, Selby DC
Cawston, Broadland DC
Cawthorne, Barnsley MBC
Cawton, Ryedale DC
Caxton, S Cambs DC
Caynham, S Shropshire DC
Caythorpe, Newark/Sherwood DC
Caythorpe, S Kesteven DC
Cayton, Harrogate BC
Cayton, Scarborough BC
Cefn, Wrexham CBC
Cefn Berain, Conwy CBC
Cefn Brith, Conwy CBC
Cefn Cribwr, Bridgend CBC
Cefn Einion, S Shropshire DC
Cefn Mawr, Wrexham CBC
Cefn Meiriadog, Denbighshire CC
Cefn Sidan, Carmarthenshire CC
Cei Newydd, Ceredigion CC
Ceiriog Ucha, Wrexham CBC
Cellardyke, Fife CI
Cellarhead, Staffs Moorlands DC
Cenarth, Carmarthenshire CC
Central Milton Keynes, Milton
    Keynes CI

Central Twickenham, Richmond
    upon Thames LBC
Ceres, Fife CI
Cerne Abbas, W Dorset DC
Cerrigydrudion, Conwy CBC
Ceulanamaesmawr, Ceredigion
    CC
Chaceley, Tewkesbury BC
Chacewater, Carrick DC
Chackmore, Aylesbury Vale DC
Chacombe, S Northants CI
Chadderton, Oldham MBC
Chaddesden, Derby City
Chaddesley Corbett, Wyre Forest
    DC
Chaddleworth, W Berks DC
Chadlington, W Oxon DC
Chadshunt, Stratford/Avon DC
Chadsmoor, Cannock Chase DC
Chadstone, S Northants CI
Chadwell, Melton BC
Chadwell Heath,
    Barking/Dagenham LBC
Chadwell St Mary, Thurrock BC
Chaffcombe, S Somerset DC
Chagford, W Devon BC
Chaigley, Ribble Valley BC
Chailey, Lewes DC
Chainhurst, Maidstone BC
Chalbury, E Dorset DC
Chaldon, Tandridge DC
Chaldon Herring, Purbeck DC
Chale, Isle of Wight CI
Chale Green, Isle of Wight CI
Chalfont Common, Chiltern DC
Chalfont St Giles, Chiltern DC
Chalfont St Peter, Chiltern DC
Chalford, Stroud DC
Chalgrave, S Beds DC
Chalgrove, S Oxon DC
Chalk, Gravesham BC
Chalk Farm, Camden LBC
Chalksole, Dover DC
Challacombe, N Devon DC
Challock, Ashford BC
Chalton, E Hants DC
Chalton, S Beds DC
Chalvington, Wealden DC
Chamberlayne, Brent LBC
Chance Inn, Fife CI
Chandler's Ford, Eastleigh BC
Chandlers Cross, Three Rivers
    DC
Channelkirk, Scottish Borders CI
Chantry, Mendip DC
Chapel Allerton, Leeds City
Chapel Allerton, Sedgemoor DC
Chapel Amble, N Cornwall DC
Chapel Ascote, Stratford/Avon
    DC

Chapel Brampton, Daventry DC
Chapel Chorlton, Newcastle-u-
    Lyme BC
Chapel en le Frith, High Peak BC
Chapel End, Nuneaton/Bedworth
    BC
Chapel Green, Stratford/Avon DC
Chapel Haddlesey, Selby DC
Chapel Hill, N Kesteven DC
Chapel Lawn, S Shropshire DC
Chapel le Dale, Craven DC
Chapel of Garioch,
    Aberdeenshire CI
Chapel Row, W Berks DC
Chapel St Leonards, E Lindsey
    DC
Chapelhall, N Lanarkshire CI
Chapelton, S Lanarkshire CI
Chapeltown, Blackburn with
    Darwen BC
Chapeltown, Sheffield City
Chapman Sands, Castle Point BC
Chapmanslade, W Wilts DC
Chapmore End, E Herts DC
Chappel, Colchester BC
Chard, S Somerset DC
Chardstock, E Devon DC
Charfield, S Glos CI
Charing, Ashford BC
Charlbury, W Oxon DC
Charlcombe, Bath/N E Somerset
    CI
Charlecote, Stratford/Avon DC
Charlestown, Fife CI
Charlestown, Restormel BC
Charlestown, Highland CI
Charlesworth, High Peak BC
Charleton, S Hams DC
Charley, N W Leics DC
Charlton, Chichester DC
Charlton, Kennet DC
Charlton, N Wilts DC
Charlton, S Northants CI
Charlton, Test Valley BC
Charlton, Wychavon DC
Charlton Adam, S Somerset DC
Charlton Horethorne, S Somerset
    DC
Charlton Kings, Cheltenham BC
Charlton Mackrell, S Somerset
    DC
Charlton Marshall, N Dorset DC
Charlton Musgrove, S Somerset
    DC
Charlton on Otmoor, Cherwell DC
Charltons, Stockton-on-Tees BC
Charlwood, Mole Valley DC
Charminster, W Dorset DC
Charmouth, W Dorset DC
Charndon, Aylesbury Vale DC

Charney Bassett, Vale of White Horse DC
Charnock, Sheffield City
Charnock Richard, Chorley BC
Charsfield, Suffolk C'l DC
Chart Sutton, Maidstone BC
Charter Alley, Basingstoke/Deane BC
Chartham, Canterbury City
Chartridge, Chiltern DC
Charvil, Wokingham DC
Charwelton, Daventry DC
Chase Terrace, Lichfield DC
Chasetown, Lichfield DC
Chastleton, W Oxon DC
Chatburn, Ribble Valley BC
Chatcull, Stafford BC
Chatham Green, Chelmsford BC
Chathill, Berwick-u-Tweed BC
Chattenden, Medway Cl
Chatteris, Fenland DC
Chattisham, Babergh DC
Chatton, Berwick-u-Tweed BC
Chawleigh, Mid Devon DC
Chawston, Bedford BC
Chawton, E Hants DC
Cheadle, Staffs Moorlands DC
Cheadle, Stockport MBC
Cheadle Hulme, Stockport MBC
Cheam, Sutton LBC
Chearsley, Aylesbury Vale DC
Chebsey, Stafford BC
Checkendon, S Oxon DC
Checkley, Staffs Moorlands DC
Checkley cum Wrinehill, Crewe/Nantwich BC
Chedburgh, St Edmundsbury BC
Cheddar, Sedgemoor DC
Cheddington, Aylesbury Vale DC
Cheddleton, Staffs Moorlands DC
Cheddon Fitzpaine, Taunton Deane BC
Chedgrave, S Norfolk DC
Chediston, Suffolk C'l DC
Chedworth, Cotswold DC
Chedzoy, Sedgemoor DC
Cheeseman's Green, Ashford BC
Cheetham Hill, Manchester City
Chelford, Macclesfield BC
Chellaston, Derby City
Chellington, Bedford BC
Chelmarsh, Bridgnorth DC
Chelmondiston, Babergh DC
Chelmorton, Derbys Dales DC
Chelmscote, Stratford/Avon DC
Chelmsford, Chelmsford BC
Chelmsley Wood, Solihull MBC
Chelsea, Kensington/Chelsea Royal Borough
Chelsfield, Bromley LBC

Chelsham, Tandridge DC
Chelsworth, Babergh DC
Cheltenham, Cheltenham BC
Chelveston, E Northants Cl
Chelvey, N Somerset DC
Chelwood, Bath/N E Somerset Cl
Chelwood Gate, Wealden DC
Cheney Longville, S Shropshire DC
Chenies, Chiltern DC
Chepping Wycombe, Wycombe DC
Chepstow, Monmouthshire CC
Cherhill, N Wilts DC
Cherington, Cotswold DC
Cherington, Stratford/Avon DC
Cheriotside, Berwick-u-Tweed BC
Cheriton, Winchester City
Cheriton Bishop, Mid Devon DC
Cheriton Fitzpaine, Mid Devon DC
Cherrington, Telford/Wrekin BC
Cherry Burton, E Riding of Yks
Cherry Green, E Herts DC
Cherry Tree, Blackburn with Darwen BC
Cherry Willingham, W Lindsey DC
Chertsey, Runnymede BC
Cheselbourne, W Dorset DC
Chesham, Chiltern DC
Chesham Bois, Chiltern DC
Cheshunt, Broxbourne BC
Cheslyn Hay, S Staffs Cl
Chessington, Kingston upon Thames Royal Borough
Chester, Chester City
Chester-le-Street, Chester-le-Street DC
Chesterblade, Mendip DC
Chesterfield, Chesterfield BC
Chesterfield, Lichfield DC
Chesterton, Cambridge City
Chesterton, Cherwell DC
Chesterton, Huntingdonshire DC
Chesterton, Stratford/Avon DC
Chesterton Green, Stratford/Avon DC
Chestfield, Canterbury City
Cheswardine, N Shropshire DC
Cheswick, Berwick-u-Tweed BC
Cheswick Green, Solihull MBC
Chetnole, W Dorset DC
Chettiscombe, Mid Devon DC
Chettisham, E Cambs DC
Chettle, N Dorset DC
Chetton, Bridgnorth DC
Chetwode, Aylesbury Vale DC
Chetwynd, Telford/Wrekin BC

Chetwynd Aston, Telford/Wrekin BC
Cheveley, E Cambs DC
Chevening, Sevenoaks DC
Cheverell Magna, Kennet DC
Cheverell Parva, Kennet DC
Chevet, Wakefield MDC
Chevilhorne, Mid Devon DC
Chevington, St Edmundsbury BC
Chew Magna, Bath/N E Somerset Cl
Chew Stoke, Bath/N E Somerset Cl
Chewton Mendip, Mendip DC
Cheylesmore, Coventry City MDC
Chicheley, Milton Keynes Cl
Chichester, Chichester DC
Chickerell, W Dorset DC
Chicklade, Salisbury DC
Chickney, Uttlesford DC
Chicksands, Mid Beds DC
Chiddingfold, Waverley BC
Chiddingly, Wealden DC
Chiddingstone, Sevenoaks DC
Chideock, W Dorset DC
Chidham, Chichester DC
Chieveley, W Berks DC
Chignal, Chelmsford BC
Chignal St James, Chelmsford BC
Chignal Smealey, Chelmsford BC
Chigwell, Epping Forest DC
Chilbolton, Test Valley BC
Chilcomb, Winchester City
Chilcombe, W Dorset DC
Chilcompton, Mendip DC
Chilcote, N W Leics DC
Child Okeford, N Dorset DC
Child's Hill (part), Barnet LBC
Childer Thornton, Ellesmere Port/Neston BC
Childerley, S Cambs DC
Childrey, Vale of White Horse DC
Childs Ercall, N Shropshire DC
Childswickham, Wychavon DC
Childwall, Liverpool City
Chilfrome, W Dorset DC
Chilgrove, Chichester DC
Chilham, Ashford BC
Chillaton, W Devon BC
Chillenden, Dover DC
Chillerton, Isle of Wight Cl
Chillesford, Suffolk C'l DC
Chillingham, Berwick-u-Tweed BC
Chillington, S Hams DC
Chillington, S Somerset DC
Chilmark, Salisbury DC
Chilson, W Oxon DC

Chilsworthy (Nr Holsworthy), Torridge DC
Chilthorne Domer, S Somerset DC
Chilton, Aylesbury Vale DC
Chilton, Babergh DC
Chilton, Sedgefield BC
Chilton, Vale of White Horse DC
Chilton Cantelo, S Somerset DC
Chilton Foliat, Kennet DC
Chilton Polden, Sedgemoor DC
Chilton Trinity, Sedgemoor DC
Chilworth, Test Valley BC
Chimney, W Oxon DC
Chineham, Basingstoke/Deane BC
Chingford, Waltham Forest LBC
Chinley, High Peak BC
Chinnor, S Oxon DC
Chippenham, E Cambs DC
Chippenham, N Wilts DC
Chippenham Without, N Wilts DC
Chipperfield, Dacorum BC
Chipping, E Herts DC
Chipping, Ribble Valley BC
Chipping Barnet, Barnet LBC
Chipping Campden, Cotswold DC
Chipping Hill, Braintree DC
Chipping Norton, W Oxon DC
Chipping Ongar, Epping Forest DC
Chipping Sodbury, S Glos CI
Chipping Warden, S Northants CI
Chipstable, Taunton Deane BC
Chipstead, Reigate/Banstead BC
Chirbury, S Shropshire DC
Chirk, Wrexham CBC
Chirnside, Scottish Borders CI
Chirton, Kennet DC
Chisbury, Kennet DC
Chiselborough, S Somerset DC
Chiseldon, Swindon BC
Chislehampton, S Oxon DC
Chislehurst, Bromley LBC
Chislet, Canterbury City
Chiswell Green, St Albans City/DC
Chiswick, Hounslow LBC
Chisworth, High Peak BC
Chithurst, Chichester DC
Chittering, S Cambs DC
Chitterne, W Wilts DC
Chittlehamholt, N Devon DC
Chittlehampton, N Devon DC
Chivelstone, S Hams DC
Chobham, Surrey Heath BC
Cholderton, Salisbury DC
Cholesbury, Chiltern DC
Chollerford, Tynedale DC
Chollerton, Tynedale DC

Cholmondeley, Crewe/Nantwich BC
Cholmondeston, Crewe/Nantwich BC
Cholsey, S Oxon DC
Chop Gate, Hambleton DC
Chopwell, Gateshead CI
Chorley, Bridgnorth DC
Chorley, Chorley BC
Chorley, Crewe/Nantwich BC
Chorley, Lichfield DC
Chorley, Macclesfield BC
Chorleywood, Three Rivers DC
Chorlton, Chester City
Chorlton, Crewe/Nantwich BC
Chorlton by Backford, Chester City
Chorlton cum Hardy, Manchester City
Choseley, King's Lynn/W Norfolk BC
Chowley, Chester City
Chrishall, Uttlesford DC
Christchurch, Christchurch BC
Christchurch, Fenland DC
Christchurch, Forest of Dean DC
Christian Malford, N Wilts DC
Christleton, Chester City
Christmas Common, S Oxon DC
Christon, N Somerset DC
Christon Bank, Alnwick DC
Christow, Teignbridge DC
Chryston, N Lanarkshire CI
Chudleigh, Teignbridge DC
Chulmleigh, N Devon DC
Chunal, High Peak BC
Church, Hyndburn BC
Church Aston, Telford/Wrekin BC
Church Brampton, Daventry DC
Church Broughton, S Derbys DC
Church Cove, Kerrier DC
Church Crookham, Hart DC
Church Eaton, Stafford BC
Church End, Basingstoke/Deane BC
Church End, Brent LBC
Church End, Chelmsford BC
Church End, Fenland DC
Church End, Mid Beds DC
Church End, S Beds DC
Church End, Uttlesford DC
Church Fenton, Selby DC
Church Gresley, S Derbys DC
Church Hanborough, W Oxon DC
Church Knowle, Purbeck DC
Church Langton, Harborough DC
Church Lawford, Rugby BC
Church Lawton, Congleton BC
Church Leigh, E Staffs BC
Church Lench, Wychavon DC

Church Minshull, Crewe/Nantwich BC
Church Norton, Chichester DC
Church Preen, Shrewsbury/Atcham CI
Church Pulverbatch, Shrewsbury/Atcham CI
Church Shocklach, Chester City
Church Stowe, Daventry DC
Church Stretton, S Shropshire DC
Church Whitfield, Dover DC
Churcham, Forest of Dean DC
Churchdown, Tewkesbury BC
Churchend, Rochford DC
Churchill, N Somerset DC
Churchill, W Oxon DC
Churchill, Wychavon DC
Churchill, Wyre Forest DC
Churchover, Rugby BC
Churchstanton, Taunton Deane BC
Churchstoke, Powys CC
Churchstow, S Hams DC
Churchtown, Coleraine BC
Churchtown, Sefton MBC
Churchtown, Wyre BC
Churt, Waverley BC
Churton by Aldford, Chester City
Churton by Farndon, Chester City
Churwell, Leeds City
Chute, Kennet DC
Chute Forest, Kennet DC
Chyandour, Penwith DC
Cilcain, Flintshire CC
Cilgerran, Pembrokeshire CC
Ciliau Aeron, Ceredigion CC
Cilmery, Powys CC
Cilybebyll, Neath Port Talbot CBC
Cilycwm, Carmarthenshire CC
Cilymaenllwyd, Carmarthenshire CC
Cimla, Neath Port Talbot CBC
Cinderford, Forest of Dean DC
Cirencester, Cotswold DC
Clachaig, Highland CI
Clachan, Highland CI
Clachnaharry, Highland CI
Clachtoll, Highland CI
Clackmannan, Clackmannanshire CI
Clacton on Sea, Tendring DC
Claggan, Highland CI
Claife, S Lakeland DC
Claigan, Highland CI
Clanabogan, Omagh DC
Clandown, Bath/N E Somerset CI
Clanfield, E Hants DC
Clanfield, W Oxon DC
Clanville, Test Valley BC
Clapgate, E Herts DC

Clapham, Arun DC
Clapham, Bedford BC
Clapham, Lambeth LBC
Clapham Austwick, Craven DC
Clappersgate, S Lakeland DC
Clapton, Hackney LBC
Clapton in Gordano, N Somerset DC
Clapton on the Hill, Cotswold DC
Clarborough, Bassetlaw DC
Clare, St Edmundsbury BC
Claremont, Salford City
Clarencefield, Dumfries/Galloway Cl
Clarendon Park, Salisbury DC
Clareton, Harrogate BC
Clarkston, E Renfrewshire Cl
Clashandorran, Highland Cl
Clashmore, Highland Cl
Clashnessie, Highland Cl
Clatt, Aberdeenshire Cl
Clatterbridge, Wirral MBC
Clattercott, Cherwell DC
Clatworthy, W Somerset DC
Claughton, Lancaster City
Claughton, Wirral MBC
Claughton-on-Brock, Wyre BC
Claverdon, Stratford/Avon DC
Claverdon Leys, Stratford/Avon DC
Claverham, N Somerset DC
Clavering, Uttlesford DC
Claverley, Bridgnorth DC
Claverton, Bath/N E Somerset Cl
Claverton, Chester City
Clawson, Melton BC
Clawton, Torridge DC
Claxby, E Lindsey DC
Claxby, W Lindsey DC
Claxby Pluckacre, E Lindsey DC
Claxton, Hartlepool BC
Claxton, Ryedale DC
Claxton, S Norfolk DC
Clay Coton, Daventry DC
Clay Cross, N E Derbys DC
Claybrooke Magna, Harborough DC
Claybrooke Parva, Harborough DC
Claydon, Cherwell DC
Claydon, Mid Suffolk DC
Claygate, Elmbridge BC
Claygate, Maidstone BC
Clayhall, Redbridge LBC
Clayhanger, Mid Devon DC
Clayhanger, Walsall MBC
Clayhidon, Mid Devon DC
Claypole, S Kesteven DC
Claythorn, Glasgow City
Claythorpe, E Lindsey DC

Clayton, Doncaster MBC
Clayton, Hyndburn BC
Clayton, Mid Sussex DC
Clayton le Dale, Ribble Valley BC
Clayton le Moors, Hyndburn BC
Clayton le Woods, Chorley BC
Clayton West, Kirklees MC
Clayworth, Bassetlaw DC
Cleadale, Highland Cl
Cleadon, S Tyneside MBC
Clearwell, Forest of Dean DC
Cleasby, Richmondshire DC
Cleatlam, Teesdale DC
Cleaton Moor, Copeland BC
Cleator, Copeland BC
Cleckheaton, Kirklees MC
Clee St Margaret, S Shropshire DC
Cleedownton, S Shropshire DC
Cleehill, S Shropshire DC
Cleethorpes, N E Lincs Cl
Cleeton St Mary, S Shropshire DC
Cleeve, N Somerset DC
Cleeve Hill, Tewkesbury BC
Cleeve Prior, Wychavon DC
Clehonger, Herefordshire Cl
Cleish, Perth/Kinross Cl
Cleland, N Lanarkshire Cl
Clench Common, Kennet DC
Clenchwarton, King's Lynn/W Norfolk BC
Clent, Bromsgrove DC
Cleobury Mortimer, S Shropshire DC
Cleobury North, Bridgnorth DC
Clephanton, Highland Cl
Clerkenwell, Islington LBC
Clevedon, N Somerset DC
Cleveland, Redcar/Cleveland BC
Cleveleys, Wyre BC
Cleverton, N Wilts DC
Cley next the Sea, N Norfolk DC
Cliburn, Eden DC
Cliddesden, Basingstoke/Deane BC
Cliff, Highland Cl
Cliff End, Rother DC
Cliffe, Medway Cl
Cliffe, Richmondshire DC
Cliffe, Selby DC
Clifford, Herefordshire Cl
Clifford, Leeds City
Clifford Chambers, Stratford/Avon DC
Clifford Hill, Stratford/Avon DC
Clifford's Mesne, Forest of Dean DC
Cliffs End, Thanet DC
Clifton, Calderdale MBC

Clifton, Cherwell DC
Clifton, Derbys Dales DC
Clifton, Eden DC
Clifton, Fylde BC
Clifton, Harrogate BC
Clifton, Malvern Hills DC
Clifton, Mid Beds DC
Clifton, Nottingham City
Clifton Campville, Lichfield DC
Clifton Hampden, S Oxon DC
Clifton Maybank, W Dorset DC
Clifton on Yore, Hambleton DC
Clifton Reynes, Milton Keynes Cl
Clifton upon Dunsmore, Rugby BC
Clifton upon Teme, Malvern Hills DC
Clifton Without, City of York Cl
Cliftonville, Thanet DC
Climping, Arun DC
Clint cum Hamlets, Harrogate BC
Clint Green, Breckland Cl
Clippesby, Gt Yarmouth BC
Clipsham, Rutland CC
Clipson on the Wolds, Rushcliffe BC
Clipston, Daventry DC
Clipstone, Newark/Sherwood DC
Clitheroe, Ribble Valley BC
Clive, N Shropshire DC
Cliviger, Burnley BC
Clocaenog, Denbighshire CC
Clogher, Dungannon & S Tyrone BC
Clophill, Mid Beds DC
Clopton, E Northants Cl
Clopton, Stratford/Avon DC
Clopton, Suffolk C'l DC
Clopton Green, St Edmundsbury BC
Closeburn, Dumfries/Galloway Cl
Closworth, S Somerset DC
Clothall, N Herts DC
Clotton Hoofield, Chester City
Cloughmills, Ballymoney BC
Cloughton, Scarborough BC
Cloughton Newlands, Scarborough BC
Clovelly, Torridge DC
Clovenfords, Scottish Borders Cl
Clovullin, Highland Cl
Clowbridge, Burnley BC
Clowne, Bolsover DC
Clubworthy, N Cornwall DC
Clumber, Bassetlaw DC
Clun, S Shropshire DC
Clunbury, S Shropshire DC
Clune, Highland Cl
Clunes, Highland Cl
Clungunford, S Shropshire DC

Clunton, S Shropshire DC
Cluny, Aberdeenshire CI
Clutton, Bath/N E Somerset CI
Clutton, Chester City
Clydach, Swansea C&C
Clydau, Pembrokeshire CC
Clydebank, W Dunbartonshire CI
Clyffe Pypard, N Wilts DC
Clynder, Argyll/Bute CI
Clynderwen, Carmarthenshire CC
Clyne, Neath Port Talbot CBC
Clynnog, Gwynedd CC
Clyro, Powys CC
Clyst Honiton, E Devon DC
Clyst Hydon, E Devon DC
Clyst St George, E Devon DC
Clyst St Lawrence, E Devon DC
Clyst St Mary, E Devon DC
Coads Green, N Cornwall DC
Coagh, Cookstown DC
Coalbrookdale, Telford/Wrekin BC
Coalburn, S Lanarkshire CI
Coalcleugh, Tynedale DC
Coaley, Stroud DC
Coalhall, E Ayrshire CI
Coalisland, Dungannon & S Tyrone BC
Coalport, Telford/Wrekin BC
Coaltown of Balgonie, Fife CI
Coaltown of Burnturk, Fife CI
Coaltown of Wemyss, Fife CI
Coalville, N W Leics DC
Coalway, Forest of Dean DC
Coanwood, Tynedale DC
Coatbridge, N Lanarkshire CI
Coate, Kennet DC
Coates, Chichester DC
Coates, Cotswold DC
Coates, Fenland DC
Coatham, Redcar/Cleveland BC
Coatham Mundeville, Darlington BC
Coberley, Cotswold DC
Cobham, Elmbridge BC
Cobham, Gravesham BC
Cobley, Bromsgrove DC
Cobnor, Chichester DC
Cock Bevington, Stratford/Avon DC
Cockayne, Ryedale DC
Cockayne Hatley, Mid Beds DC
Cockburnspath, Scottish Borders CI
Cockenzie, E Lothian CI
Cockerham, Lancaster City
Cockermouth, Allerdale BC
Cockernhoe, N Herts DC
Cockfield, Babergh DC
Cockfield, Teesdale DC

Cockfosters, Enfield LBC
Cocking, Chichester DC
Cockington, Torbay CI
Cockley Cley, Breckland CI
Cockpole Green (part), Wokingham DC
Cockshutt, N Shropshire DC
Cockthorpe, N Norfolk DC
Codda, N Cornwall DC
Coddenham, Mid Suffolk DC
Coddington, Chester City
Coddington, Herefordshire CI
Coddington, Newark/Sherwood DC
Codford, W Wilts DC
Codicote, N Herts DC
Codnor, Amber Valley BC
Codsall, S Staffs CI
Codsall Wood, Bridgnorth DC
Coed Eva, Torfaen CBC
Coedffranc, Neath Port Talbot CBC
Coedkernew, Newport City CI
Coedpoeth, Wrexham CBC
Coffee Hall, Milton Keynes CI
Coffinswell, Teignbridge DC
Cofton Hackett, Bromsgrove DC
Cogenhoe, S Northants CI
Coggeshall, Braintree DC
Coillore, Highland CI
Coity Higher, Bridgend CBC
Colan, Restormel BC
Colaton Raleigh, E Devon DC
Colbost, Highland CI
Colburn, Richmondshire DC
Colbury, New Forest DC
Colby, Eden DC
Colby, N Norfolk DC
Colchester, Colchester BC
Cold Ash, W Berks DC
Cold Ashby, Daventry DC
Cold Ashton, S Glos CI
Cold Aston, Cotswold DC
Cold Brayfield, Milton Keynes CI
Cold Christmas, E Herts DC
Cold Hanworth, W Lindsey DC
Cold Hesledon, Easington DC
Cold Hiendley, Wakefield MDC
Cold Higham, S Northants CI
Cold Kirby, Ryedale DC
Cold Newton, Harborough DC
Cold Norton, Maldon DC
Cold Overton, Melton BC
Cold Weston, S Shropshire DC
Coldbackie, Highland CI
Coldean, Brighton/Hove CI
Coldeast, Teignbridge DC
Colden Common, Winchester City
Coldfair Green, Suffolk C'I DC
Coldham, Fenland DC

Coldharbour, Aylesbury Vale DC
Coldharbour, Mole Valley DC
Coldharbour, Purbeck DC
Coldingham, Scottish Borders CI
Coldred, Dover DC
Coldridge, Mid Devon DC
Coldstream, Scottish Borders CI
Coldwaltham, Horsham DC
Cole Green, E Herts DC
Colebatch, S Shropshire DC
Colebrooke, Mid Devon DC
Coleby, N Kesteven DC
Coleby, N Lincs CI
Coleford, Forest of Dean DC
Coleford, Mendip DC
Colehill, E Dorset DC
Coleman's Hatch, Wealden DC
Colemere, N Shropshire DC
Colemore, E Hants DC
Coleorton, N W Leics DC
Coleraine, Coleraine BC
Colerne, N Wilts DC
Colesbourne, Cotswold DC
Colesden, Bedford BC
Coleshill, Chiltern DC
Coleshill, N Warks BC
Coleshill, Vale of White Horse DC
Colgate, Horsham DC
Colgrain, Argyll/Bute CI
Colindale, Barnet LBC
Colinsburgh, Fife CI
Colintraive, Argyll/Bute CI
Colkirk, Breckland CI
Coll, Argyll/Bute CI
Coll, Isle of, Argyll/Bute CI
Collaton St Mary, Torbay CI
Collessie, Fife CI
Collier Row, Havering LBC
Collier Street, Maidstone BC
Colliers End, E Herts DC
Collieston, Aberdeenshire CI
Collingbourne Ducis, Kennet DC
Collingbourne Kingston, Kennet DC
Collingham, Leeds City
Collingham, Newark/Sherwood DC
Collington, Herefordshire CI
Collingtree, Northampton BC
Colloden Moor, Highland CI
Collyweston, E Northants CI
Colmonell, S Ayrshire CI
Colmworth, Bedford BC
Coln Rogers, Cotswold DC
Coln St Aldwyns, Cotswold DC
Coln St Dennis, Cotswold DC
Colnbrook, Slough BC
Colnbrook, Windsor/Maidenhead RB
Colne, Huntingdonshire DC

Colne, Pendle BC
Colne Engaine, Braintree DC
Colney, S Norfolk DC
Colney Heath, St Albans City/DC
Colney Street, St Albans City/DC
Colonsay, Argyll/Bute Cl
Colsterdale, Harrogate BC
Colsterworth, S Kesteven DC
Colston Basset, Rushcliffe BC
Coltishall, Broadland DC
Colton, Lichfield DC
Colton, Selby DC
Colton, S Lakeland DC
Colton, S Norfolk DC
Colvend, Dumfries/Galloway Cl
Colwall, Herefordshire Cl
Colwell, Tynedale DC
Colwich, Stafford BC
Colwick, Gedling BC
Colwinston, Vale of Glamorgan Cl
Colworth, Chichester DC
Colwyn Bay, Conwy CBC
Colyford, E Devon DC
Colyton, E Devon DC
Combe, Herefordshire Cl
Combe, W Berks DC
Combe, W Oxon DC
Combe Fields, Rugby BC
Combe Florey, Taunton Deane
  BC
Combe Hay, Bath/N E Somerset
  Cl
Combe Martin, N Devon DC
Combe Raleigh, E Devon DC
Combe St Nicholas, S Somerset
  DC
Combebow, W Devon BC
Combeinteignhead, Teignbridge
  DC
Comber, Ards BC
Comberbach, Vale Royal BC
Comberton, S Cambs DC
Combhill, Tynedale DC
Combpyne, E Devon DC
Combroke, Stratford/Avon DC
Combs, High Peak BC
Combs, Mid Suffolk DC
Combs Ford, Mid Suffolk DC
Comeytrowe, Taunton Deane BC
Common Moor, Caradon DC
Common Side, Sheffield City
Commondale, Scarborough BC
Compton, Chichester DC
Compton, Guildford BC
Compton, Plymouth City
Compton, W Berks DC
Compton, Winchester City
Compton Abbas, N Dorset DC
Compton Abdale, Cotswold DC
Compton Bassett, N Wilts DC

Compton Beauchamp, Vale of
  White Horse DC
Compton Bishop, Sedgemoor DC
Compton Chamberlayne,
  Salisbury DC
Compton Dando, Bath/N E
  Somerset Cl
Compton Dundon, S Somerset
  DC
Compton Martin, Bath/N E
  Somerset Cl
Compton Pauncefoot, S
  Somerset DC
Compton Scorpion,
  Stratford/Avon DC
Compton Valence, W Dorset DC
Compton Verney, Stratford/Avon
  DC
Compton Wynyates,
  Stratford/Avon DC
Comrie, Fife Cl
Comrie, Perth/Kinross Cl
Conderton, Wychavon DC
Condicote, Cotswold DC
Condorrat, N Lanarkshire Cl
Condover, Shrewsbury/Atcham Cl
Coney Weston, St Edmundsbury
  BC
Coneyhurst, Horsham DC
Coneypark, Falkirk Cl
Coneysthorpe, Ryedale DC
Coneythorpe, Harrogate BC
Congerstone, Hinckley/Bosworth
  BC
Congham, King's Lynn/W Norfolk
  BC
Congleton, Congleton BC
Congresbury, N Somerset DC
Coningsby, E Lindsey DC
Conington, Huntingdonshire DC
Conington, S Cambs DC
Conisbrough, Doncaster MBC
Conisholme, E Lindsey DC
Coniston, E Riding of Yks
Coniston, S Lakeland DC
Coniston Cold, Craven DC
Conistone, Craven DC
Connah's Quay, Flintshire CC
Connel, Argyll/Bute Cl
Conniburrow, Milton Keynes Cl
Connista, Highland Cl
Connor Downs, Penwith DC
Conon Bridge, Highland Cl
Cononley, Craven DC
Conordan, Highland Cl
Consall, Staffs Moorlands DC
Consett, Derwentside DC
Constable Burton, Richmondshire
  DC
Constantine, Kerrier DC

Contin, Highland Cl
Conwy, Conwy CBC
Conyer, Swale BC
Cookbury, Torridge DC
Cookham, Windsor/Maidenhead
  RB
Cookham Dean,
  Windsor/Maidenhead RB
Cookham Rise,
  Windsor/Maidenhead RB
Cookhill, Wychavon DC
Cookley, Suffolk C'l DC
Cookley, Wyre Forest DC
Cookley Green, S Oxon DC
Cooksbridge, Lewes DC
Cooksmill Green, Chelmsford BC
Cookstown, Cookstown DC
Coole Pilate, Crewe/Nantwich BC
Coolham, Horsham DC
Cooling, Medway Cl
Coolnagard, Omagh DC
Coombe, Kingston upon Thames
  Royal Borough
Coombe, N Cornwall DC
Coombe Bissett, Salisbury DC
Coombe Hill, Tewkesbury BC
Coombe Keynes, Purbeck DC
Coombes, Adur DC
Copdock, Babergh DC
Copford, Colchester BC
Copgrove, Harrogate BC
Cople, Bedford BC
Copley, Teesdale DC
Copmanthorpe, City of York Cl
Coppathorne, N Cornwall DC
Coppenhall, S Staffs Cl
Copperhouse, Penwith DC
Coppingford, Huntingdonshire DC
Copplestone, Mid Devon DC
Coppull, Chorley BC
Copsale, Horsham DC
Copster Green, Ribble Valley BC
Copston Magna, Rugby BC
Copt Heath, Solihull MBC
Copt Hewick, Harrogate BC
Copthorne, Mid Sussex DC
Copythorne, New Forest DC
Corarnstilbeg, Highland Cl
Corbet, Banbridge DC
Corbets Tey, Havering LBC
Corbridge, Tynedale DC
Corby, Corby BC
Corby Glen, S Kesteven DC
Coreley, S Shropshire DC
Corfe, Taunton Deane BC
Corfe Castle, Purbeck DC
Corfe Mullen, E Dorset DC
Corfton, S Shropshire DC
Corhampton, Winchester City
Corkerhill, Glasgow City

Corley, N Warks BC
Cornbury, W Oxon DC
Cornelly, Bridgend CBC
Corney, Copeland BC
Cornforth, Sedgefield BC
Cornhill, Aberdeenshire CI
Cornhill, Highland CI
Cornhill on Tweed, Berwick-u-Tweed BC
Cornholme, Calderdale MBC
Cornish Hall End, Braintree DC
Cornsay, Derwentside DC
Cornsay Colliery, Derwentside DC
Corntown, Highland CI
Cornwell, W Oxon DC
Cornwood, S Hams DC
Cornworthy, S Hams DC
Corpach, Highland CI
Corpusty, N Norfolk DC
Corran, Highland CI
Corrie, N Ayrshire CI
Corrimony, Highland CI
Corringham, Thurrock BC
Corringham, W Lindsey DC
Corris, Gwynedd CC
Corry, Highland CI
Corsback, Highland CI
Corscombe, W Dorset DC
Corse, Forest of Dean DC
Corsenside, Tynedale DC
Corsham, N Wilts DC
Corsley, W Wilts DC
Corsock, Dumfries/Galloway CI
Corston, Bath/N E Somerset CI
Corton, Waveney DC
Corton Denham, S Somerset DC
Corwen, Denbighshire CC
Coryates, W Dorset DC
Coryton, Thurrock BC
Coryton, W Devon BC
Cosby, Blaby DC
Cosford, Rugby BC
Cosgrove, S Northants CI
Cosham, Portsmouth City
Cosheston, Pembrokeshire CC
Cossall, Broxtowe BC
Cossington, Charnwood DC
Cossington, Sedgemoor DC
Costessey, S Norfolk DC
Costock, Rushcliffe BC
Coston, Melton BC
Coston, S Norfolk DC
Cotcliffe, Hambleton DC
Cote, W Oxon DC
Cotegill, Eden DC
Cotehill, Carlisle City
Cotes, Charnwood DC
Cotes, Stafford BC
Cotesbach, Harborough DC

Cotgrave, Rushcliffe BC
Cotham, Newark/Sherwood DC
Cotham, Rushcliffe BC
Cotherstone, Teesdale DC
Cothill, Vale of White Horse DC
Cotleigh, E Devon DC
Coton, Nuneaton/Bedworth BC
Coton, S Cambs DC
Coton, Stafford BC
Coton in the Elms, S Derbys DC
Cottam, Bassetlaw DC
Cottam, Preston City
Cottenham, S Cambs DC
Cotterdale, Richmondshire DC
Cottered, E Herts DC
Cotterstock, E Northants CI
Cottesbrooke, Daventry DC
Cottesmore, Rutland CC
Cottingham, Corby BC
Cottingham, E Riding of Yks
Cottisford, Cherwell DC
Cotton, Mid Suffolk DC
Cotton, Staffs Moorlands DC
Cotton End, Bedford BC
Cotwalton, Stafford BC
Coughton, Stratford/Avon DC
Coul of Fairburn, Highland CI
Coulags, Highland CI
Coulby Newham, Middlesbrough CI
Coulin Lodge, Highland CI
Coull, Aberdeenshire CI
Coulnacraggan, Highland CI
Coulsdon, Croydon LBC
Coulston, W Wilts DC
Coulter, S Lanarkshire CI
Coultershaw, Chichester DC
Coulton, Ryedale DC
Cound, Shrewsbury/Atcham CI
Coundon, Coventry City MDC
Countersett, Richmondshire DC
Countesthorpe, Blaby DC
Counthorpe, S Kesteven DC
Countisbury, N Devon DC
Coupar Angus, Perth/Kinross CI
Coupland, Berwick-u-Tweed BC
Courteachan, Highland CI
Courteenhall, S Northants CI
Courtsend, Rochford DC
Cove, Aberdeen City
Cove, Argyll/Bute CI
Cove, Mid Devon DC
Cove, Rushmoor BC
Cove, Highland CI
Covehithe, Waveney DC
Coven, S Staffs CI
Coveney, E Cambs DC
Covenham St Bartholomew, E Lindsey DC

Covenham St Mary, E Lindsey DC
Coventry, Coventry City MDC
Coverack, Kerrier DC
Coverham, Richmondshire DC
Covingham, Swindon BC
Covington, Huntingdonshire DC
Cowan Bridge, Lancaster City
Cowark, Ribble Valley BC
Cowbeech, Wealden DC
Cowbit, S Holland DC
Cowbridge, Vale of Glamorgan CI
Cowdale, High Peak BC
Cowden, Sevenoaks DC
Cowdenbeath, Fife CI
Cowers Lane, Amber Valley BC
Cowes, Isle of Wight CI
Cowesby, Hambleton DC
Cowfold, Horsham DC
Cowick, E Riding of Yks
Cowie, Stirling CI
Cowley, Cotswold DC
Cowley, E Devon DC
Cowley, Hillingdon LBC
Cowling, Craven DC
Cowling, Hambleton DC
Cowlinge, St Edmundsbury BC
Cowplain, E Hants DC
Cowshill, Wear Valley DC
Cox Green, Windsor/Maidenhead RB
Coxall, Herefordshire CI
Coxbench, Amber Valley BC
Coxford, Southampton City
Coxheath, Maidstone BC
Coxhoe, Durham City
Coxley, Mendip DC
Coxwold, Hambleton DC
Coychurch, Bridgend CBC
Coylton, S Ayrshire CI
Coylumbridge, Highland CI
Crackenthorpe, Eden DC
Crackington, N Cornwall DC
Crackleybank, Bridgnorth DC
Crackpot, Richmondshire DC
Cracoe, Craven DC
Cradley, Herefordshire CI
Cradley Heath, Sandwell MBC
Crafthole, Caradon DC
Cragg Vale, Calderdale MBC
Craghead, Derwentside DC
Craig, Angus CI
Craig, Highland CI
Craigavon, Craigavon BC
Craigdarroch, Highland CI
Craigendmuir, E Dunbartonshire CI
Craigendorran, Argyll/Bute CI
Craigie, Perth/Kinross CI
Craigie, S Ayrshire CI

Craiglockhart, Edinburgh City
Craignish, Argyll/Bute CI
Craignure, Argyll/Bute CI
Craigrory, Highland CI
Craigrothie, Fife CI
Craigton, Glasgow City
Craigton, Highland CI
Crail, Fife CI
Crailing, Scottish Borders CI
Crakehall, Hambleton DC
Crambe, Ryedale DC
Cramlington, Blyth Valley BC
Cramond, Edinburgh City
Cranage, Congleton BC
Cranberry, Stafford BC
Cranborne, E Dorset DC
Cranbrook, Tunbridge Wells BC
Cranbrook Common, Tunbridge
    Wells BC
Cranfield, Mid Beds DC
Cranfield, Newry/Mourne DC
Cranford, Hounslow LBC
Cranford, Kettering BC
Cranford St Andrew, Kettering BC
Cranford St John, Kettering BC
Cranham, Stroud DC
Cranhill, Stratford/Avon DC
Crank, St Helens MBC
Cranleigh, Waverley BC
Cranmore, Isle of Wight CI
Cranmore, Mendip DC
Cranoe, Harborough DC
Cransford, Suffolk C'l DC
Cranshaws, Scottish Borders CI
Cransley, Kettering BC
Crantock, Restormel BC
Cranwell, N Kesteven DC
Cranwich, Breckland CI
Cranworth, Breckland CI
Crapstone, W Devon BC
Crask, Highland CI
Crask of Aigas, Highland CI
Craster, Alnwick DC
Craswall, Herefordshire CI
Cratfield, Suffolk C'l DC
Crathie, Aberdeenshire CI
Crathie, Highland CI
Crathorne, Hambleton DC
Craven Arms, S Shropshire DC
Crawford, S Lanarkshire CI
Crawfordjohn, S Lanarkshire CI
Crawley, Crawley BC
Crawley, W Oxon DC
Crawley, Winchester City
Crawley Down, Mid Sussex DC
Crawleyside, Wear Valley DC
Crawshawbooth, Rossendale BC
Cray, Craven DC
Cray, Powys CC
Cray's Pond, S Oxon DC

Crayford, Bexley LBC
Crayke, Hambleton DC
Crays Hill, Basildon DC
Creaton, Daventry DC
Creca, Dumfries/Galloway CI
Credenhill, Herefordshire CI
Crediton, Mid Devon DC
Crediton Hamlets, Mid Devon DC
Cree Valley, Dumfries/Galloway
    CI
Creech St Michael, Taunton
    Deane BC
Creed, Restormel BC
Creekmoor, Poole BC
Creeting St Mary, Mid Suffolk DC
Creeting St Peter, Mid Suffolk DC
Creeton, S Kesteven DC
Cregagh, Castlereagh BC
Creich, Fife CI
Creigiau, Cardiff CC
Crepkill, Highland CI
Creslow, Aylesbury Vale DC
Cressage, Shrewsbury/Atcham CI
Cressbrook, Derbys Dales DC
Cressing, Braintree DC
Cressingham, Breckland CI
Cresswell, Castle Morpeth BC
Creswell, Bolsover DC
Creswell, Stafford BC
Cretingham, Suffolk C'l DC
Crewe, Crewe/Nantwich BC
Crewe Green, Crewe/Nantwich
    BC
Crewkerne, S Somerset DC
Crianlarich, Stirling CI
Criccieth, Gwynedd CC
Crich, Amber Valley BC
Crick, Daventry DC
Cricket St Thomas, S Somerset
    DC
Crickheath, Oswestry BC
Crickhowell, Powys CC
Cricklade, N Wilts DC
Cricklewood (part), Brent LBC
Cricklewood (part), Barnet LBC
Cridling Stubbs, Selby DC
Crieff, Perth/Kinross CI
Criggion, Powys CC
Crigglestone, Wakefield MDC
Crimmond, Aberdeenshire CI
Crimplesham, King's Lynn/W
    Norfolk BC
Crimscote, Stratford/Avon DC
Crimscote Downs, Stratford/Avon
    DC
Cringleford, S Norfolk DC
Cripp's Corner, Rother DC
Cripplesease, Penwith DC
Croachy, Highland CI
Crockenhill, Sevenoaks DC

Crockerhill, Chichester DC
Crockerton, W Wilts DC
Crockey Hill, City of York CI
Crockleford Heath, Tendring DC
Croeserw, Neath Port Talbot CBC
Croesyceiliog, Torfaen CBC
Croft, Blaby DC
Croft, E Lindsey DC
Croft, Herefordshire CI
Croft, Warrington BC
Croftfoot, Glasgow City
Croftnacriech, Highland CI
Crofton, Wakefield MDC
Croft-on-Tees, Richmondshire
    DC
Crofts of Kingscauseway,
    Highland CI
Croglin, Eden DC
Croich, Highland CI
Croick, Highland CI
Cromarty, Highland CI
Crombie, Fife CI
Cromdale, Highland CI
Cromer, E Herts DC
Cromer, N Norfolk DC
Cromford, Derbys Dales DC
Cromhall, S Glos CI
Crompton, Oldham MBC
Cromwell, Newark/Sherwood DC
Cronberry, E Ayrshire CI
Crondall, Hart DC
Cronton, Knowsley MBC
Crook, S Lakeland DC
Crook, Wear Valley DC
Crookedholm, E Ayrshire CI
Crookes, Sheffield City
Crookesmoor, Sheffield City
Crookhall, Derwentside DC
Crookham, Berwick-u-Tweed BC
Crookham Village, Hart DC
Crooklands, S Lakeland DC
Croome, Malvern Hills DC
Cropredy, Cherwell DC
Cropston, Charnwood DC
Cropthorne, Wychavon DC
Cropton, Ryedale DC
Cropwell Bishop, Rushcliffe BC
Cropwell Butler, Rushcliffe BC
Crosby, Allerdale BC
Crosby, Hambleton DC
Crosby, N Lincs CI
Crosby, Sefton MBC
Crosby Garrett, Eden DC
Crosby on Eden, Carlisle City
Crosby Ravensworth, Eden DC
Croscombe, Mendip DC
Crosland Moor, Kirklees MC
Cross at Hand, Maidstone BC
Cross Green, Babergh DC
Cross Green, Stratford/Avon DC

Cross Hills, Craven DC
Cross Houses,
    Shrewsbury/Atcham CI
Cross in Hand, Wealden DC
Cross Lanes, Hambleton DC
Crosscanonby, Allerdale BC
Crossdale Street, N Norfolk DC
Crossens, Sefton MBC
Crossford, Fife CI
Crossford, S Lanarkshire CI
Crossgar, Down DC
Crossgates, Fife CI
Crossgates, Scarborough BC
Crosshill, Fife CI
Crosshill, S Ayrshire CI
Crosshouse, E Ayrshire CI
Crossings, Carlisle City
Crosslanes, Oswestry BC
Crosslee, Renfrewshire CI
Crossmaglen, Newry/Mourne DC
Crossmichael, Dumfries/Galloway
    CI
Crossmoor, Wyre BC
Crossnacreevy, Castlereagh BC
Crosspool, Sheffield City
Crossway Green, Wychavon DC
Crossways, W Dorset DC
Crosthwaite, S Lakeland DC
Croston, Chorley BC
Crostwick, Broadland DC
Crostwight, N Norfolk DC
Crouch End, Haringey LBC
Croughton, Chester City
Croughton, S Northants CI
Crowan, Kerrier DC
Crowborough, Wealden DC
Crowcombe, W Somerset DC
Crowdecote, Derbys Dales DC
Crowell, S Oxon DC
Crowfield, Mid Suffolk DC
Crowfield, S Northants CI
Crowhurst, Rother DC
Crowland, S Holland DC
Crowle, N Lincs CI
Crowle, Wychavon DC
Crowmarsh, S Oxon DC
Crowmarsh Gifford, S Oxon DC
Crown, Highland CI
Crownhill, Milton Keynes CI
Crownhill, Plymouth City
Crownthorpe, S Norfolk DC
Crowshurst, Tandridge DC
Crowthorne, Bracknell Forest BC
Crowton, Vale Royal BC
Croxall, Lichfield DC
Croxby, W Lindsey DC
Croxdale, Durham City
Croxden, E Staffs BC
Croxley Green, Three Rivers DC
Croxton, Breckland CI

Croxton, N Lincs CI
Croxton, S Cambs DC
Croxton, Stafford BC
Croxton Kerrial, Melton BC
Croxton Park, Melton BC
Croy, N Lanarkshire CI
Croy, Highland CI
Croydon, Croydon LBC
Croydon, S Cambs DC
Cruckton, Shrewsbury/Atcham CI
Crucorney, Monmouthshire CC
Cruden, Aberdeenshire CI
Cruden Bay, Aberdeenshire CI
Crudington, Telford/Wrekin BC
Crudwell, N Wilts DC
Crugmeer, N Cornwall DC
Crumlin, Antrim BC
Crumlin, Caerphilly CBC
Crundale, Ashford BC
Cruwys Morchard, Mid Devon DC
Crux Easton, Basingstoke/Deane
    BC
Cryers Hill, Wycombe DC
Crymych, Pembrokeshire CC
Crynant, Neath Port Talbot CBC
Crystal Peaks, Sheffield City
Cuaig, Highland CI
Cubbington, Warwick DC
Cubert, Carrick DC
Cubley, Derbys Dales DC
Cublington, Aylesbury Vale DC
Cuckfield, Mid Sussex DC
Cucklington, S Somerset DC
Cuckmere Valley, Wealden DC
Cuckney, Bassetlaw DC
Cuddesdon, S Oxon DC
Cuddington, Aylesbury Vale DC
Cuddington, Chester City
Cuddington, Vale Royal BC
Cudlipptown, W Devon BC
Cudworth, Barnsley MBC
Cudworth, S Somerset DC
Cuerdale, S Ribble BC
Cuerden, Chorley BC
Cuerdley, Warrington BC
Cuffley, Welwyn Hatfield DC
Cuidrach, Highland CI
Cuil, Highland CI
Culbokie, Highland CI
Culburnie, Highland CI
Culcabock, Highland CI
Culcavy, Lisburn City
Culcharry, Highland CI
Culcheth, Warrington BC
Culduie, Highland CI
Culford, St Edmundsbury BC
Culgaith, Eden DC
Culham, S Oxon DC
Culkein, Highland CI
Culkein Drumbeg, Highland CI

Culkerton, Cotswold DC
Cullen, Moray CI
Cullercoats, N Tyneside CI
Cullicudden, Highland CI
Cullingworth, Bradford MDC
Culloden, Highland CI
Cullompton, Mid Devon DC
Cullyhanna, Newry/Mourne DC
Culmington, S Shropshire DC
Culmstock, Mid Devon DC
Culnaknock, Highland CI
Culpho, Suffolk C'I DC
Culrain, Highland CI
Culross, Fife CI
Culsalmond, Aberdeenshire CI
Culter, Aberdeen City
Cults, Aberdeen City
Cults, Fife CI
Culverthorpe, N Kesteven DC
Culworth, S Northants CI
Cumbernauld, N Lanarkshire CI
Cumberworth, E Lindsey DC
Cumbrae, Isle of, N Ayrshire CI
Cuminestown, Aberdeenshire CI
Cummersdale, Carlisle City
Cummertrees, Dumfries/Galloway
    CI
Cummertrees West,
    Dumfries/Galloway CI
Cummingston, Moray CI
Cumnock, E Ayrshire CI
Cumnor, Vale of White Horse DC
Cumrew, Carlisle City
Cumwhinton, Carlisle City
Cumwhitton, Carlisle City
Cundall, Harrogate BC
Cunningsburgh, Shetland Is CI
Cupar, Fife CI
Cuparmuir, Fife CI
Curbar, Derbys Dales DC
Curbridge, W Oxon DC
Curdridge, Winchester City
Curdworth, N Warks BC
Currey Rivel, S Somerset DC
Currie, Edinburgh City
Curry Mallet, S Somerset DC
Cury, Kerrier DC
Cushendall, Moyle DC
Cushendun, Moyle DC
Cusop, Herefordshire CI
Custom House, Newham LBC
Cutcombe, W Somerset DC
Cut Mill, Chichester DC
Cutnall Green, Wychavon DC
Cutsdean, Cotswold DC
Cutthorpe, N E Derbys DC
Cuxham, S Oxon DC
Cuxton, Medway CI
Cwm, Denbighshire CC

Cwm Cadnant, Isle of Anglesey CC
Cwm Gwaun, Pembrokeshire CC
Cwm Penmachno, Conwy CBC
Cwmamman, Carmarthenshire CC
Cwmavon, Neath Port Talbot CBC
Cwmavon, Torfaen CBC
Cwmbran, Monmouthshire CC
Cwmbran, Torfaen CBC
Cwmgors, Neath Port Talbot CBC
Cwmllynfell, Neath Port Talbot CBC
Cwmynyscoy, Torfaen CBC
Cyffylliog, Denbighshire CC
Cylch y Garn, Isle of Anglesey CC
Cymmer, Neath Port Talbot CBC
Cyncoed, Cardiff CC
Cynffig, Bridgend CBC
Cynwyd, Denbighshire CC
Cynwyl Elfed, Carmarthenshire CC
Cynwyl Gaeo, Carmarthenshire CC
Cyprus, Newham LBC

Dacre, Eden DC
Dacre, Harrogate BC
Dacre Banks, Harrogate BC
Daddry Shield, Wear Valley DC
Dadford, Aylesbury Vale DC
Dadlington, Hinckley/Bosworth BC
Daffy Green, Breckland CI
Dagenham, Barking/Dagenham LBC
Daglingworth, Cotswold DC
Dagnall, Aylesbury Vale DC
Dagworth, Mid Suffolk DC
Dailly, S Ayrshire CI
Dalbeattie, Dumfries/Galloway CI
Dalbury, S Derbys DC
Dalby, E Lindsey DC
Dalby, Melton BC
Dalby cum Skewsby, Hambleton DC
Dalchalm, Highland CI
Dalcharn, Highland CI
Dalchreichart, Highland CI
Dalcross, Highland CI
Dale, Pembrokeshire CC
Dale Abbey, Erewash BC
Dale Head, Eden DC
Dalelia, Highland CI
Dalfaber, Highland CI
Dalgety Bay, Fife CI
Dalham, Forest Heath DC
Dalhavaig, Highland CI

Dalkeith, Midlothian CI
Dallicott, Bridgnorth DC
Dallinghoo, Suffolk C'I DC
Dallington, Rother DC
Dallowgill, Harrogate BC
Dalmally, Argyll/Bute CI
Dalmarnock, Glasgow City
Dalmellington, E Ayrshire CI
Dalmeny, Edinburgh City
Dalmore, Highland CI
Dalmuir, W Dunbartonshire CI
Dalnabreck, Highland CI
Dalneigh, Highland CI
Dalness, Highland CI
Dalreavoch, Highland CI
Dalry, Dumfries/Galloway CI
Dalrymple, E Ayrshire CI
Dalscote, S Northants CI
Dalserf, S Lanarkshire CI
Dalston, Carlisle City
Dalston, Hackney LBC
Dalton, Castle Morpeth BC
Dalton, Dumfries/Galloway CI
Dalton, Hambleton DC
Dalton, Kirklees MC
Dalton, Richmondshire DC
Dalton, Rotherham MBC
Dalton, Tynedale DC
Dalton, W Lancs DC
Dalton Holme, E Riding of Yks
Dalton in Furness, Barrow-in-Furness BC
Dalton le Dale, Easington DC
Dalton on Tees, Richmondshire DC
Dalton Piercy, Hartlepool BC
Dalwhinnie, Highland CI
Dalwood, E Devon DC
Damerham, New Forest DC
Damhead, Midlothian CI
Danbury, Chelmsford BC
Danby, Scarborough BC
Danby Wiske, Hambleton DC
Danderhall, Midlothian CI
Dane End, E Herts DC
Danehill, Wealden DC
Danzey Green, Stratford/Avon DC
Darenth, Dartford BC
Daresbury, Halton BC
Darfield, Barnsley MBC
Dargate, Swale BC
Darlaston, Walsall MBC
Darley, Harrogate BC
Darlingscote, Stratford/Avon DC
Darlington, Darlington BC
Darliston, N Shropshire DC
Darlton, Bassetlaw DC
Darnall, Sheffield City
Darncombe, Scarborough BC

Darnhall, Vale Royal BC
Darnholm, Scarborough BC
Darnley Estate, Glasgow City
Darren Valley, Caerphilly CBC
Darrington, Wakefield MDC
Darsham, Suffolk C'I DC
Dartford, Dartford BC
Dartington, S Hams DC
Dartmoor Forest, W Devon BC
Dartmouth, S Hams DC
Darton, Barnsley MBC
Darvel, E Ayrshire CI
Darwen, Blackburn with Darwen BC
Datchet, Windsor/Maidenhead RB
Datchworth, E Herts DC
Dauntsey, N Wilts DC
Dava, Highland CI
Davenham, Vale Royal BC
Daventry, Daventry DC
Davidstow, N Cornwall DC
Daviot, Aberdeenshire CI
Daviot, Highland CI
Davyhulme, Trafford MBC
Dawley, Telford/Wrekin BC
Dawlish, Teignbridge DC
Dawn, Conwy CBC
Daws Heath, Castle Point BC
Dawsmere, S Holland DC
Daybrook, Gedling BC
Deadwater, Tynedale DC
Deal, Dover DC
Dean, Allerdale BC
Dean, Bedford BC
Dean, Mendip DC
Dean, Winchester City
Dean Lane End, Chichester DC
Dean Prior, S Hams DC
Dean Row, Macclesfield BC
Deane, Basingstoke/Deane BC
Deanland, E Dorset DC
Deans Green, Stratford/Avon DC
Deanscales, Allerdale BC
Deanshanger, S Northants CI
Deanston, Stirling CI
Dearham, Allerdale BC
Dearne, Barnsley MBC
Debach, Suffolk C'I DC
Debden, Uttlesford DC
Debenham, Mid Suffolk DC
Dechmont, W Lothian CI
Deddington, Cherwell DC
Dedham, Colchester BC
Deene, E Northants CI
Deenethorpe, E Northants CI
Deepcar, Sheffield City
Deepdale, S Lakeland DC
Deeping Gate, Peterborough City

Deeping St James, S Kesteven DC
Deeping St Nicholas, S Holland DC
Deer Park, Limavady BC
Deerhurst, Tewkesbury BC
Deerness, Orkney Is Cl
Defford, Wychavon DC
Deganwy, Conwy CBC
Deighton, City of York Cl
Deighton, Hambleton DC
Deighton, Kirklees MC
Deishar, Highland Cl
Delabole, N Cornwall DC
Delamere, Vale Royal BC
Dell, Highland Cl
Dell Quay, Chichester DC
Delph, Oldham MBC
Delting, Shetland Is Cl
Delves Lane, Derwentside DC
Dembleby, N Kesteven DC
Den Bank, Sheffield City
Den of Lindores, Fife Cl
Denaby, Doncaster MBC
Denbigh, Denbighshire CC
Denbigh, Milton Keynes Cl
Denbury, Teignbridge DC
Denby, Amber Valley BC
Denby Dale, Kirklees MC
Denchworth, Vale of White Horse DC
Dene, The, Derwentside DC
Dene Valley, Wear Valley DC
Denford, E Northants Cl
Denge Marsh, Shepway DC
Dengie, Maldon DC
Denham, Mid Suffolk DC
Denham, St Edmundsbury BC
Denham, S Bucks DC
Denhead, Fife Cl
Denholm, Scottish Borders Cl
Denholme, Bradford MDC
Denmead, Winchester City
Dennington, Suffolk C'l DC
Dennistoun, Glasgow City
Denny, Falkirk Cl
Denny Lodge, New Forest DC
Dennyloanhead, Falkirk Cl
Denshaw, Oldham MBC
Denston, St Edmundsbury BC
Denstone, E Staffs BC
Dent, S Lakeland DC
Denton, Darlington BC
Denton, Dover DC
Denton, Harrogate BC
Denton, Huntingdonshire DC
Denton, Lewes DC
Denton, Newcastle City
Denton, S Kesteven DC
Denton, S Norfolk DC

Denton, S Northants Cl
Denton, S Oxon DC
Denton, Tameside MBC
Denton Nether, Carlisle City
Denton Upper, Carlisle City
Denver, King's Lynn/W Norfolk BC
Denwick, Alnwick DC
Deopham, S Norfolk DC
Depden, St Edmundsbury BC
Deppers Bridge, Stratford/Avon DC
Deptford, Lewisham LBC
Deptford, Salisbury DC
Derby, Derby City
Dereham, Breckland Cl
Dergmoney, Omagh DC
Derringstone, Canterbury City
Derrington, Stafford BC
Derry, Derry City
Dersingham, King's Lynn/W Norfolk BC
Dervock, Ballymoney BC
Derwen, Denbighshire CC
Derwent, High Peak BC
Desborough, Kettering BC
Desford, Hinckley/Bosworth BC
Detchant, Berwick-u-Tweed BC
Dethick, Amber Valley BC
Detling, Maidstone BC
Deunant isaf, Conwy CBC
Deuxhill, Bridgnorth DC
Devauden, Monmouthshire CC
Deviock, Caradon DC
Devizes, Kennet DC
Devonport, Plymouth City
Devoran, Carrick DC
Dewlish, W Dorset DC
Dewsall, Herefordshire Cl
Dewsbury, Kirklees MC
Dial Post, Horsham DC
Dibden, New Forest DC
Dibden Purlieu, New Forest DC
Dickleburgh, S Norfolk DC
Didbrook, Tewkesbury BC
Didcot, S Oxon DC
Diddington, Huntingdonshire DC
Diddlebury, S Shropshire DC
Didling, Chichester DC
Didlington, Breckland Cl
Didmarton, Cotswold DC
Didsbury, Manchester City
Digby, N Kesteven DC
Digg, Highland Cl
Diggle, Oldham MBC
Digswell, Welwyn Hatfield DC
Dilham, N Norfolk DC
Dilhorne, Staffs Moorlands DC
Dilston, Tynedale DC
Dilton Marsh, W Wilts DC

Dilwyn, Herefordshire Cl
Dinas Cross, Pembrokeshire CC
Dinas Powys, Vale of Glamorgan Cl
Dinckley, Ribble Valley BC
Dinedor, Herefordshire Cl
Dingley, Kettering BC
Dingwall, Highland Cl
Dinmore, Herefordshire Cl
Dinnington, Newcastle City
Dinnington, Rotherham MBC
Dinnington, S Somerset DC
Dinnington St John's, Rotherham MBC
Dinton, Aylesbury Vale DC
Dinton, Salisbury DC
Diptford, S Hams DC
Dipton, Derwentside DC
Dirleton, E Lothian Cl
Diseworth, N W Leics DC
Dishforth, Harrogate BC
Disley, Macclesfield BC
Diss, S Norfolk DC
Disserth, Powys CC
Distington, Copeland BC
Distington (part), Allerdale BC
Ditcham (part), Chichester DC
Ditcheat, Mendip DC
Ditchford (part), Stratford/Avon DC
Ditchingham, S Norfolk DC
Ditchling, Lewes DC
Dittisham, S Hams DC
Ditton, Tonbridge/Malling BC
Ditton Green, E Cambs DC
Ditton Priors, Bridgnorth DC
Dixton, Tewkesbury BC
Doaghs, Limavady BC
Dobwalls, Caradon DC
Doccombe, Teignbridge DC
Dochgarroch, Highland Cl
Dockenfield, Waverley BC
Docker, S Lakeland DC
Docking, King's Lynn/W Norfolk BC
Docklow, Herefordshire Cl
Dockray, Eden DC
Dodcott cum Wilkesley, Crewe/Nantwich BC
Doddenham, Malvern Hills DC
Doddenhoe End, Uttlesford DC
Dodderhill, Wychavon DC
Doddinghurst, Brentwood BC
Doddington, Berwick-u-Tweed BC
Doddington, Crewe/Nantwich BC
Doddington, Fenland DC
Doddington, N Kesteven DC
Doddington, S Shropshire DC
Doddington, Swale BC
Doddington, Wellingborough BC

Doddiscombsleigh, Teignbridge DC
Dodford, Bromsgrove DC
Dodford, Daventry DC
Dodington, S Glos Cl
Dodleston, Chester City
Dodwell, Stratford/Avon DC
Doe Lea, Bolsover DC
Dogdyke, N Kesteven DC
Dogmersfield, Hart DC
Dolbenmaen, Gwynedd CC
Dolgarrog, Conwy CBC
Dolgellau, Gwynedd CC
Doll, Highland Cl
Dollar, Clackmannanshire Cl
Dolphinton, S Lanarkshire Cl
Dolton, Torridge DC
Dolwen, Conwy CBC
Dolwyddelan, Conwy CBC
Domewood, Tandridge DC
Donaghadee, Ards BC
Donaghmore, Dungannon & S Tyrone BC
Doncaster, Doncaster MBC
Donemana, Strabane DC
Donhead St Andrew, Salisbury DC
Donhead St Mary, Salisbury DC
Donington, Bridgnorth DC
Donington, S Holland DC
Donington on Bain, E Lindsey DC
Donisthorpe, N W Leics DC
Donnington, Chichester DC
Donnington, Cotswold DC
Donnington, Herefordshire Cl
Donnington, Shrewsbury/Atcham Cl
Donnington, Telford/Wrekin BC
Donnington, W Berks DC
Donyatt, S Somerset DC
Dorchester, S Oxon DC
Dorchester, W Dorset DC
Dordon, N Warks BC
Dore, Sheffield City
Dores, Highland Cl
Dorking, Mole Valley DC
Dormans Park, Tandridge DC
Dormansland, Tandridge DC
Dormanstown, Redcar/Cleveland BC
Dormington, Herefordshire Cl
Dormston, Wychavon DC
Dorney, S Bucks DC
Dornie, Highland Cl
Dornoch, Highland Cl
Dornock, Dumfries/Galloway Cl
Dorridge, Solihull MBC
Dorrington, N Kesteven DC
Dorrington, Shrewsbury/Atcham Cl

Dorsington, Stratford/Avon DC
Dorstone, Herefordshire Cl
Dorton, Aylesbury Vale DC
Dosthill, Tamworth BC
Doublebois, Caradon DC
Doughton, Cotswold DC
Douglas, S Lanarkshire Cl
Douglas Water, S Lanarkshire Cl
Doulting, Mendip DC
Doune, Stirling Cl
Doune, Highland Cl
Dounie, Highland Cl
Dousland, W Devon BC
Dove Holes, High Peak BC
Dovenby, Allerdale BC
Dover, Dover DC
Dovercourt, Tendring DC
Doverdale, Wychavon DC
Doveridge, Derbys Dales DC
Dowbridge, Fylde BC
Dowdeswell, Cotswold DC
Dowland, Torridge DC
Dowlish Wake, S Somerset DC
Down Ampney, Cotswold DC
Down Hatherley, Tewkesbury BC
Down St Mary, Mid Devon DC
Downderry, Caradon DC
Downe, Bromley LBC
Downend, Isle of Wight Cl
Downend, S Glos Cl
Downend, W Berks DC
Downfield, Dundee City
Downgate, N Cornwall DC
Downham, Berwick-u-Tweed BC
Downham, Chelmsford BC
Downham, Lewisham LBC
Downham, Ribble Valley BC
Downham Market, King's Lynn/W Norfolk BC
Downham West, King's Lynn/W Norfolk BC
Downhead, Mendip DC
Downhead Park, Milton Keynes Cl
Downhill, Coleraine BC
Downholland, W Lancs DC
Downholme, Richmondshire DC
Downies, Aberdeenshire Cl
Downley, Wycombe DC
Downpatrick, Down DC
Downs Barn, Milton Keynes Cl
Downswood, Maidstone BC
Downton, Herefordshire Cl
Downton, New Forest DC
Downton, Salisbury DC
Dowsby, S Kesteven DC
Dowsdale, S Holland DC
Dowthwaitehead, Eden DC
Doxford Park, Sunderland City
Doynton, S Glos Cl

Drake, Plymouth City
Drakelow, S Derbys DC
Drakes Broughton, Wychavon DC
Draperstown, Magherafelt DC
Draughton, Craven DC
Draughton, Daventry DC
Drax, Selby DC
Draycote, Rugby BC
Draycott, Bridgnorth DC
Draycott, Cotswold DC
Draycott, Erewash BC
Draycott, Mendip DC
Draycott, Staffs Moorlands DC
Draycott in the Clay, E Staffs BC
Drayton, Broadland DC
Drayton, Cherwell DC
Drayton, Harborough DC
Drayton, Portsmouth City
Drayton, S Somerset DC
Drayton, Stratford/Avon DC
Drayton, Vale of White Horse DC
Drayton, Wyre Forest DC
Drayton Bassett, Lichfield DC
Drayton Beauchamp, Aylesbury Vale DC
Drayton Parslow, Aylesbury Vale DC
Drayton St Leonard, S Oxon DC
Dreggie, Highland Cl
Dreghorn, N Ayrshire Cl
Drellingore, Dover DC
Drem, E Lothian Cl
Drewsteignton, W Devon BC
Driby, E Lindsey DC
Driffield, Cotswold DC
Driffield, E Riding of Yks
Drift, Penwith DC
Drigg, Copeland BC
Drighlington, Leeds City
Drimnin, Highland Cl
Drinkstone, Mid Suffolk DC
Drinkstone Green, Mid Suffolk DC
Droitwich, Wychavon DC
Droman, Highland Cl
Dromore, Banbridge DC
Dromore, Omagh DC
Dronfield, N E Derbys DC
Drongan, E Ayrshire Cl
Droxford, Winchester City
Droylsden, Manchester City
Droylsden, Tameside MBC
Druimarbin, Highland Cl
Druimindarroch, Highland Cl
Drum, Conwy CBC
Drumbeg, Lisburn City
Drumbeg, Highland Cl
Drumblade, Aberdeenshire Cl
Drumbo, Lisburn City
Drumbuie, Highland Cl
Drumburgh, Allerdale BC

Drumchork, Highland CI
Drumclog, S Lanarkshire CI
Drumfearn, Highland CI
Drumguish, Highland CI
Drumlithie, Aberdeenshire CI
Drumlough, Lisburn City
Drummond, Highland CI
Drummuie, Highland CI
Drummuir, Aberdeenshire CI
Drumnadrochit, Highland CI
Drumnakilly, Omagh DC
Drumoak, Aberdeenshire CI
Drumoyne, Glasgow City
Drumquin, Omagh DC
Drumragh, Omagh DC
Drumsmittal, Highland CI
Drumsurn, Limavady BC
Drumuie, Highland CI
Drumuillie, Highland CI
Dry Doddington, S Kesteven DC
Dry Drayton, S Cambs DC
Drybeck, Eden DC
Drybrook, Forest of Dean DC
Drymen, Stirling CI
Drynie Park, Highland CI
Drynoch, Highland CI
Dubwath, Allerdale BC
Duck's Cross, Bedford BC
Duckington, Chester City
Ducklington, W Oxon DC
Duckmanton, Chesterfield BC
Duddingston, Edinburgh City
Duddington, E Northants CI
Duddleswell, Wealden DC
Duddo, Berwick-u-Tweed BC
Duddon, Chester City
Duddon Bridge, Copeland BC
Dudleston Heath, N Shropshire DC
Dudley, Dudley MBC
Duffield, Amber Valley BC
Duffryn, Newport City CI
Dufton, Eden DC
Duggleby, Ryedale DC
Duhonw, Powys CC
Duirinish, Highland CI
Duisdalemuir, Highland CI
Duisky, Highland CI
Dukinfield, Tameside MBC
Dulas, Herefordshire CI
Dulcote, Mendip DC
Dulford, E Devon DC
Dull, Perth/Kinross CI
Dullatur, N Lanarkshire CI
Dullingham, E Cambs DC
Dulnain Bridge, Highland CI
Duloe, Caradon DC
Dulverton, W Somerset DC
Dumbarton, W Dunbartonshire CI
Dumbleton, Tewkesbury BC

Dumbreck, Glasgow City
Dumfries, Dumfries/Galloway CI
Dummer, Basingstoke/Deane BC
Dun, Angus CI
Dun Boreraig, Highland CI
Dun Colbost, Highland CI
Dun Colhost, Highland CI
Dunadd, Argyll/Bute CI
Dunan, Highland CI
Dunbar, E Lothian CI
Dunbeath, Highland CI
Dunbeg, Argyll/Bute CI
Dunbeg, Limavady BC
Dunblane, Stirling CI
Dunbog, Fife CI
Duncanston, Highland CI
Dunchideock, Teignbridge DC
Dunchurch, Rugby BC
Duncote, S Northants CI
Duncrun, Limavady BC
Duncton, Chichester DC
Dundee, Dundee City
Dundonald, Castlereagh BC
Dundonald, Fife CI
Dundonald, S Ayrshire CI
Dundonnell, Highland CI
Dundraw, Allerdale BC
Dundreggan, Highland CI
Dundrennan, Dumfries/Galloway CI
Dundrod, Lisburn City
Dundrum, Down DC
Dundry, N Somerset DC
Dunecht, Aberdeenshire CI
Dunfermline, Fife CI
Dunford, Barnsley MBC
Dungannon, Dungannon & S Tyrone BC
Dungeness, Shepway DC
Dungiven, Limavady BC
Dungworth, Sheffield City
Dunham, Bassetlaw DC
Dunham, Breckland CI
Dunham Hill, Chester City
Dunham Town, Trafford MBC
Dunhampton, Wychavon DC
Dunholme, W Lindsey DC
Dunino, Fife CI
Dunipace, Falkirk CI
Dunk's Green, Tonbridge/Malling BC
Dunkeld, Perth/Kinross CI
Dunkerton, Bath/N E Somerset CI
Dunkeswell, E Devon DC
Dunkirk, Swale BC
Dunley, Malvern Hills DC
Dunlop, E Ayrshire CI
Dunloy, Ballymoney BC
Dunmore, Falkirk CI
Dunmore, Limavady BC

Dunmore, Highland CI
Dunmurry, Lisburn City
Dunnerdale, S Lakeland DC
Dunnet, Highland CI
Dunning, Perth/Kinross CI
Dunnington, City of York CI
Dunnington, Stratford/Avon DC
Dunnington Heath, Stratford/Avon DC
Dunnockshaw, Burnley BC
Dunnottar, Aberdeenshire CI
Dunoon, Argyll/Bute CI
Dunrossness, Shetland Is CI
Duns, Scottish Borders CI
Duns Tew, Cherwell DC
Dunsby, S Kesteven DC
Dunscore, Dumfries/Galloway CI
Dunscroft, Doncaster MBC
Dunsden, S Oxon DC
Dunsden Green, S Oxon DC
Dunsfold, Waverley BC
Dunsford, Teignbridge DC
Dunsley, Scarborough BC
Dunsmore, Wycombe DC
Dunsop Bridge, Ribble Valley BC
Dunstable, S Beds DC
Dunstall, E Staffs BC
Dunstan, Alnwick DC
Dunster, W Somerset DC
Dunston, N Kesteven DC
Dunston, S Norfolk DC
Dunston, S Staffs CI
Dunsville, Doncaster MBC
Dunswell, E Riding of Yks
Dunterton, W Devon BC
Duntisbourne Abbots, Cotswold DC
Duntisbourne Leer, Cotswold DC
Duntisbourne Rouse, Cotswold DC
Duntocher, W Dunbartonshire CI
Dunton, Aylesbury Vale DC
Dunton, Mid Beds DC
Dunton, N Norfolk DC
Dunton Bassett, Harborough DC
Dunton Green, Sevenoaks DC
Dunton Wayletts, Basildon DC
Duntulm, Highland CI
Dunure, S Ayrshire CI
Dunvant, Swansea C&C
Dunvegan, Highland CI
Dunwich, Suffolk C'l DC
Dura Den, Fife CI
Durdar, Carlisle City
Durfold Wood (part), Chichester DC
Durham, Durham City
Durisdeer, Dumfries/Galloway CI
Durleigh, Sedgemoor DC
Durleigh Marsh, Chichester DC

Durley, Kennet DC
Durley, Winchester City
Durlock, Dover DC
Durnamuck, Highland Cl
Durness, Highland Cl
Durnford, Salisbury DC
Duror, Highland Cl
Durrington, Salisbury DC
Durrington, Worthing BC
Durris, Aberdeenshire Cl
Dursley, Stroud DC
Durston, Taunton Deane BC
Durweston, N Dorset DC
Duston, Northampton BC
Duthil, Highland Cl
Duton Hill, Uttlesford DC
Dutton, Ribble Valley BC
Dutton, Vale Royal BC
Duxford, S Cambs DC
Dwygyfylchi, Conwy CBC
Dwyriw, Powys CC
Dyffrn Cennen, Carmarthenshire CC
Dyffryn Ardudwy, Gwynedd CC
Dyffryn Arth, Ceredigion CC
Dyffryn Clydach, Neath Port Talbot CBC
Dyke Landward, Moray Cl
Dykehead, N Lanarkshire Cl
Dymchurch, Shepway DC
Dymock, Forest of Dean DC
Dyrham, S Glos Cl
Dysart, Fife Cl
Dyserth, Denbighshire CC

Eabost, Highland Cl
Eabost West, Highland Cl
Eagle, N Kesteven DC
Eaglescliffe, Stockton-on-Tees BC
Eaglesfield, Allerdale BC
Eaglesfield, Dumfries/Galloway Cl
Eaglesham, E Renfrewshire Cl
Eaglestone, Milton Keynes Cl
Eakring, Newark/Sherwood DC
Ealand, N Lincs Cl
Ealing, Ealing LBC
Eamont Bridge, Eden DC
Earby, Pendle BC
Earcroft, Blackburn with Darwen BC
Eardington, Bridgnorth DC
Eardisland, Herefordshire Cl
Eardisley, Herefordshire Cl
Eardiston, Oswestry BC
Earith, Huntingdonshire DC
Earl Shilton, Hinckley/Bosworth BC
Earl Soham, Suffolk C'l DC
Earl Stonham, Mid Suffolk DC

Earl's Green, Mid Suffolk DC
Earle, Berwick-u-Tweed BC
Earlestown, St Helens MBC
Earley, Wokingham DC
Earlish, Highland Cl
Earls Barton, Wellingborough BC
Earls Colne, Braintree DC
Earls Croome, Malvern Hills DC
Earlsdon, Coventry City MDC
Earlsferry, Fife Cl
Earlsfield, Wandsworth LBC
Earlston, Scottish Borders Cl
Earlswood, Reigate/Banstead BC
Earlswood, Stratford/Avon DC
Earlswood Lakes, Stratford/Avon DC
Earn, Perth/Kinross Cl
Earnley, Chichester DC
Earsdon, N Tyneside Cl
Earsham, S Norfolk DC
Earswick, City of York Cl
Eartham, Chichester DC
Easby, Hambleton DC
Easby, Richmondshire DC
Easebourne, Chichester DC
Easenhall, Rugby BC
Easington, Aylesbury Vale DC
Easington, Berwick-u-Tweed BC
Easington, Easington DC
Easington, E Riding of Yks
Easington, Redcar/Cleveland BC
Easington, Ribble Valley BC
Easington, S Oxon DC
Easington Colliery, Easington DC
Easington Lane, Sunderland City
Easington Village, Easington DC
Easingwold, Hambleton DC
Eassie, Angus Cl
East Allington, S Hams DC
East Anstey, N Devon DC
East Ardsley, Leeds City
East Ashling, Chichester DC
East Ayton, Scarborough BC
East Barkwith, E Lindsey DC
East Barnet, Barnet LBC
East Beckham, N Norfolk DC
East Bergholt, Babergh DC
East Bilney, Breckland Cl
East Blatchington, Lewes DC
East Boldre, New Forest DC
East Bolton, Richmondshire DC
East Brendon, W Somerset DC
East Brent, Sedgemoor DC
East Bridgford, Rushcliffe BC
East Brora, Highland Cl
East Buckland, N Devon DC
East Budleigh, E Devon DC
East Burton, Purbeck DC
East Butterwick, N Lincs Cl
East Calder, W Lothian Cl

East Carleton, S Norfolk DC
East Carlton, Corby BC
East Challow, Vale of White Horse DC
East Chelborough, W Dorset DC
East Chevington, Castle Morpeth BC
East Chiltington, Lewes DC
East Chinnock, S Somerset DC
East Chisenbury, Kennet DC
East Clandon, Guildford BC
East Claydon, Aylesbury Vale DC
East Clyne, Highland Cl
East Coker, S Somerset DC
East Compton, Mendip DC
East Cottingwith, E Riding of Yks
East Cowes, Isle of Wight Cl
East Cowton, Hambleton DC
East Cramlington, Blyth Valley BC
East Croachy, Highland Cl
East Dean, Chichester DC
East Dean, Eastbourne BC
East Dean, Test Valley BC
East Dean, Wealden DC
East Dereham, Breckland Cl
East Donyland, Colchester BC
East Down, N Devon DC
East Drayton, Bassetlaw DC
East End, Basingstoke/Deane BC
East End, E Herts DC
East End, New Forest DC
East End, N Somerset DC
East End, W Oxon DC
East Farleigh, Maidstone BC
East Farndon, Daventry DC
East Ferry, W Lindsey DC
East Garston, W Berks DC
East Garton, E Riding of Yks
East Ginge, Vale of White Horse DC
East Goscote, Charnwood DC
East Grafton, Kennet DC
East Grinstead, Mid Sussex DC
East Guldeford, Rother DC
East Haddon, Daventry DC
East Hagbourne, S Oxon DC
East Halton, N Lincs Cl
East Ham, Newham LBC
East Hamlet, S Shropshire DC
East Hanney, Vale of White Horse DC
East Hanningfield, Chelmsford BC
East Hardwick, Wakefield MDC
East Harling, Breckland Cl
East Harlsey, Hambleton DC
East Harptree, Bath/N E Somerset Cl
East Hartford, Blyth Valley BC

East Harting, Chichester DC
East Hatley, S Cambs DC
East Hauxwell, Richmondshire DC
East Hedleyhope, Derwentside DC
East Helmsdale, Highland Cl
East Hendred, Vale of White Horse DC
East Hesterton, Ryedale DC
East Hoathly, Wealden DC
East Holme, Purbeck DC
East Horrington, Mendip DC
East Horsley, Guildford BC
East Huntspill, Sedgemoor DC
East Ilsley, W Berks DC
East Keal, E Lindsey DC
East Kennet, Kennet DC
East Keswick, Leeds City
East Kilbride, S Lanarkshire Cl
East Kintyre, Argyll/Bute Cl
East Kirkby, E Lindsey DC
East Knighton, Purbeck DC
East Knoyle, Salisbury DC
East Langdon, Dover DC
East Langton, Harborough DC
East Langwell, Highland Cl
East Lavington, Chichester DC
East Layton, Richmondshire DC
East Leake, Rushcliffe BC
East Leigh, Mid Devon DC
East Lexham, Breckland Cl
East Lilburn, Berwick-u-Tweed BC
East Linton, E Lothian Cl
East Liss, E Hants DC
East Lothian, E Lothian Cl
East Lulworth, Purbeck DC
East Malling, Tonbridge/Malling BC
East Marden, Chichester DC
East Markham, Bassetlaw DC
East Marton, Craven DC
East Meon, E Hants DC
East Mersea, Colchester BC
East Mey, Highland Cl
East Molesey, Elmbridge BC
East Morton, Bradford MDC
East Newbiggin, Darlington BC
East Norton, Harborough DC
East Ogwell, Teignbridge DC
East Orchard, N Dorset DC
East Ord, Berwick-u-Tweed BC
East Peckham, Tonbridge/Malling BC
East Pennard, Mendip DC
East Portholland (part), Carrick DC
East Portholland (part), Restormel BC

East Portlemouth, S Hams DC
East Prawle, S Hams DC
East Preston, Arun DC
East Putford, Torridge DC
East Quantoxhead, W Somerset DC
East Ravendale, N E Lincs Cl
East Rounton, Hambleton DC
East Rudham, King's Lynn/W Norfolk BC
East Runton, N Norfolk DC
East Ruston, N Norfolk DC
East Saltoun, E Lothian Cl
East Scrafton, Richmondshire DC
East Sheen, Richmond upon Thames LBC
East Stanley, Derwentside DC
East Stockwith, W Lindsey DC
East Stoke, Newark/Sherwood DC
East Stoke, Purbeck DC
East Stour, N Dorset DC
East Stourmouth, Dover DC
East Strathearn, Perth/Kinross Cl
East Studdal, Dover DC
East Suisnish, Highland Cl
East Sutton, Maidstone BC
East Tanfield, Hambleton DC
East Taphouse, Caradon DC
East Thirston, Castle Morpeth BC
East Tisted, E Hants DC
East Tuddenham, Breckland Cl
East Twickenham, Richmond upon Thames LBC
East Tytherley, Test Valley BC
East Village, Mid Devon DC
East Wall, S Shropshire DC
East Walton, King's Lynn/W Norfolk BC
East Wellow, Test Valley BC
East Wemyss, Fife Cl
East Whitburn, W Lothian Cl
East Wickham, Bexley LBC
East Williamston, Pembrokeshire CC
East Winch, King's Lynn/W Norfolk BC
East Wittering, Chichester DC
East Witton, Richmondshire DC
East Woodburn, Tynedale DC
East Woodhay, Basingstoke/Deane BC
East Worlington, N Devon DC
East Worthing, Worthing BC
East Wykeham, E Lindsey DC
Eastbourne, Eastbourne BC
Eastbridge, Suffolk C'l DC
Eastburn, Bradford MDC
Eastbury, W Berks DC
Eastby, Craven DC

Eastchurch, Swale BC
Eastcombe, Stroud DC
Eastcote, Hillingdon LBC
Eastcote, S Northants Cl
Eastcott, Kennet DC
Eastcott, N Cornwall DC
Eastcotts, Bedford BC
Easter Aberchalder, Highland Cl
Easter Ardross, Highland Cl
Easter Boleskine, Highland Cl
Easter Kinkell, Highland Cl
Eastergate, Arun DC
Easterhouse, Glasgow City
Eastern Green, Coventry City MDC
Easterton, Kennet DC
Eastfield, N Lanarkshire Cl
Eastfield, Scarborough BC
Eastgate, Wear Valley DC
Eastham, Wirral MBC
Easthampnett, Chichester DC
Easthope, Bridgnorth DC
Easthorpe, Colchester BC
Easthorpe, Ryedale DC
Easthouses, Midlothian Cl
Eastington, Cotswold DC
Eastington, Mid Devon DC
Eastington, Stroud DC
Eastleach, Cotswold DC
Eastleach Martin, Cotswold DC
Eastleach Turville, Cotswold DC
Eastleaze, Swindon BC
Eastleigh, Eastleigh BC
Eastling, Swale BC
Eastney, Portsmouth City
Eastnor, Herefordshire Cl
Eastoft, N Lincs Cl
Easton, Carlisle City
Easton, Huntingdonshire DC
Easton, Kennet DC
Easton, Mendip DC
Easton, S Kesteven DC
Easton, S Norfolk DC
Easton, Suffolk C'l DC
Easton, Weymouth/Portland BC
Easton Bavents, Waveney DC
Easton Grey, N Wilts DC
Easton in Gordano, N Somerset DC
Easton Maudit, Wellingborough BC
Easton Neston, S Northants Cl
Easton on the Hill, E Northants Cl
Easton Royal, Kennet DC
Eastrea, Fenland DC
Eastriggs, Dumfries/Galloway Cl
Eastrington, E Riding of Yks
Eastry, Dover DC
Eastville, E Lindsey DC
Eastwell, Ashford BC

Eastwell, Melton BC
Eastwick, E Herts DC
Eastwood, Broxtowe BC
Eastwood, Calderdale MBC
Eastwood, Glasgow City
Eastwood, Southend-on-Sea BC
Eathorpe, Warwick DC
Eaton, Bassetlaw DC
Eaton, Chester City
Eaton, Macclesfield BC
Eaton, Melton BC
Eaton, Norwich City
Eaton, S Shropshire DC
Eaton, Vale of White Horse DC
Eaton, Vale Royal BC
Eaton Bishop, Herefordshire Cl
Eaton Bray, S Beds DC
Eaton Constantine,
    Shrewsbury/Atcham Cl
Eaton Hastings, Vale of White
    Horse DC
Eaton under Heywood, S
    Shropshire DC
Eaton upon Tern, N Shropshire
    DC
Eavestone, Harrogate BC
Ebberston, Ryedale DC
Ebbesbourne Wake, Salisbury
    DC
Ebbw Vale, Blaenau Gwent CBC
Ebchester, Derwentside DC
Ebernoe, Chichester DC
Ebford, E Devon DC
Ebrington, Cotswold DC
Ecchinswell, Basingstoke/Deane
    BC
Ecclefechan, Dumfries/Galloway
    Cl
Eccles, Salford City
Eccles, Scottish Borders Cl
Eccles, Tonbridge/Malling BC
Eccles on Sea, N Norfolk DC
Eccles Road, Breckland Cl
Ecclesall, Sheffield City
Ecclesfield, Sheffield City
Eccleshall, Stafford BC
Eccleshill, Blackburn with Darwen
    BC
Ecclesmachan, W Lothian Cl
Eccleston, Chester City
Eccleston, Chorley BC
Eccleston, St Helens MBC
Echt, Aberdeenshire Cl
Eckford, Scottish Borders Cl
Eckington, N E Derbys DC
Eckington, Wychavon DC
Ecton, Wellingborough BC
Edale, High Peak BC
Eday, Orkney Is Cl
Edburton, Horsham DC

Edderton, Highland Cl
Eddleston, Scottish Borders Cl
Edenbridge, Sevenoaks DC
Edenderry, Lisburn City
Edenhall, Eden DC
Edenham, S Kesteven DC
Edensor, Derbys Dales DC
Edenthorpe, Doncaster MBC
Edgbaston, Birmingham City
Edgcote, S Northants Cl
Edgcott, Aylesbury Vale DC
Edge, Chester City
Edge, Stroud DC
Edge End, Forest of Dean DC
Edge Hill, Stratford/Avon DC
Edgebolton, N Shropshire DC
Edgefield, N Norfolk DC
Edgehill, E Staffs BC
Edgeworth, Cotswold DC
Edgmond, Telford/Wrekin BC
Edgton, S Shropshire DC
Edgware, Barnet LBC
Edgworth, Blackburn with Darwen
    BC
Edinbane, Highland Cl
Edinburgh, Edinburgh City
Edingale, Lichfield DC
Edingley, Newark/Sherwood DC
Edingthorpe, N Norfolk DC
Edington, Sedgemoor DC
Edington, W Wilts DC
Edith Weston, Rutland CC
Edlesborough, Aylesbury Vale
    DC
Edleston, Crewe/Nantwich BC
Edlington, Doncaster MBC
Edlington, E Lindsey DC
Edmondsham, E Dorset DC
Edmondsley, Chester-le-Street
    DC
Edmonton, Enfield LBC
Edmundbyers, Wear Valley DC
Ednam, Scottish Borders Cl
Ednaston, Derbys Dales DC
Edrom, Scottish Borders Cl
Edstaston, N Shropshire DC
Edstone, Ryedale DC
Edstone, Stratford/Avon DC
Edvin Loach, Herefordshire Cl
Edwalton, Rushcliffe BC
Edwardstone, Babergh DC
Edwardsville, Merthyr Tydfil CBC
Edwinstowe, Newark/Sherwood
    DC
Edworth, Mid Beds DC
Edwyn Ralph, Herefordshire Cl
Edzell Air Base, Aberdeenshire Cl
Efenechtyd, Denbighshire CC
Effingham, Guildford BC
Efford, Mid Devon DC

Efford, Plymouth City
Egdean, Chichester DC
Egerton, Ashford BC
Egerton, Bolton MBC
Egerton, Crewe/Nantwich BC
Eggborough, Selby DC
Eggbuckland, Plymouth City
Eggington, S Beds DC
Egginton, S Derbys DC
Egglescliffe, Stockton-on-Tees
    BC
Eggleston, Teesdale DC
Eggleston Abbey, Teesdale DC
Eggleton, Herefordshire Cl
Egham, Runnymede BC
Egilsay, Orkney Is Cl
Egleton, Rutland CC
Eglingham, Alnwick DC
Egloshayle, N Cornwall DC
Egloskerry, N Cornwall DC
Eglwysbach, Conwy CBC
Eglwyswrw, Pembrokeshire CC
Eglwys Gymyn, Carmarthenshire
    CC
Egmanton, Newark/Sherwood DC
Egmere, N Norfolk DC
Egremont, Copeland BC
Egton, Scarborough BC
Egton Bridge, Scarborough BC
Egton with Newland, S Lakeland
    DC
Eight Ash Green, Colchester BC
Eilanreach, Highland Cl
Eilean Iarmain, Highland Cl
Elcombe, Swindon BC
Eldene, Swindon BC
Eldernell, Fenland DC
Eldersfield, Malvern Hills DC
Elderslie, Renfrewshire Cl
Eldmire, Hambleton DC
Eldon, Sedgefield BC
Eldroth, Craven DC
Eldwick, Bradford MDC
Elford, Berwick-u-Tweed BC
Elford, Lichfield DC
Elgin, Moray Cl
Elgol, Highland Cl
Elham, Shepway DC
Elie, Fife Cl
Eling, New Forest DC
Elishader, Highland Cl
Elishaw, Tynedale DC
Elkesley, Bassetlaw DC
Elkington, Daventry DC
Elkstone, Cotswold DC
Elkstones, Staffs Moorlands DC
Ellan, Highland Cl
Elland, Calderdale MBC
Ellastone, E Staffs BC
Ellel, Lancaster City

Ellen's Green, Waverley BC
Ellenhall, Stafford BC
Ellerbeck, Hambleton DC
Ellerby, E Riding of Yks
Ellerby, Scarborough BC
Ellerker, E Riding of Yks
Ellerton, E Riding of Yks
Ellerton Abbey, Richmondshire
    DC
Ellerton on Swale, Richmondshire
    DC
Ellesborough, Wycombe DC
Ellesmere, N Shropshire DC
Ellesmere Port, Ellesmere
    Port/Neston BC
Ellesmere Rural, N Shropshire
    DC
Ellinge, Dover DC
Ellingham, Berwick-u-Tweed BC
Ellingham, Breckland Cl
Ellingham, New Forest DC
Ellingham, S Norfolk DC
Ellington, Castle Morpeth BC
Ellington, Huntingdonshire DC
Ellisfield, Basingstoke/Deane BC
Ellistown, N W Leics DC
Ellon, Aberdeenshire Cl
Ellough, Waveney DC
Elloughton, E Riding of Yks
Ellwood, Forest of Dean DC
Elm, Fenland DC
Elm Park, Havering LBC
Elm Tree, Stockton-on-Tees BC
Elmbridge, Wychavon DC
Elmdon, Solihull MBC
Elmdon, Uttlesford DC
Elmdon Heath, Solihull MBC
Elmesthorpe, Blaby DC
Elmham, Breckland Cl
Elmhurst, Lichfield DC
Elmley Castle, Wychavon DC
Elmley Lovett, Wychavon DC
Elmore, Stroud DC
Elmsett, Babergh DC
Elmstead Market, Tendring DC
Elmsted, Shepway DC
Elmstone, Dover DC
Elmstone Hardwicke, Tewkesbury
    BC
Elmswell, Mid Suffolk DC
Elmton, Bolsover DC
Elphin, Highland Cl
Elphinstone, E Lothian Cl
Elsdon, Alnwick DC
Elsenham, Uttlesford DC
Elsfield, S Oxon DC
Elsham, N Lincs Cl
Elsing, Breckland Cl
Elslack, Craven DC
Elsrickle, S Lanarkshire Cl

Elstead, Waverley BC
Elsted, Chichester DC
Elsthorpe, S Kesteven DC
Elston, Newark/Sherwood DC
Elstow, Bedford BC
Elstree, Hertsmere BC
Elstronwick, E Riding of Yks
Elswick, Fylde BC
Elswick, Newcastle City
Elswick Leys, Fylde BC
Elsworth, S Cambs DC
Eltersgill, Teesdale DC
Elterwater, S Lakeland DC
Eltham, Greenwich LBC
Eltham (part), Bexley LBC
Eltisley, S Cambs DC
Elton, Bury MBC
Elton, Chester City
Elton, Derbys Dales DC
Elton, Forest of Dean DC
Elton, Herefordshire Cl
Elton, Huntingdonshire DC
Elton, Rushcliffe BC
Elvanfoot, S Lanarkshire Cl
Elvaston, S Derbys DC
Elveden, Forest Heath DC
Elvington, City of York Cl
Elvington, Dover DC
Elwick, Berwick-u-Tweed BC
Elwick, Hartlepool BC
Elworth, Congleton BC
Elworthy, W Somerset DC
Ely, Cardiff CC
Ely, E Cambs DC
Emberton, Milton Keynes Cl
Embleton, Allerdale BC
Embleton, Alnwick DC
Embo, Highland Cl
Embo Street, Highland Cl
Emborough, Mendip DC
Embsay, Craven DC
Emerson Valley, Milton Keynes Cl
Emersons Green, S Glos Cl
Emery Down, New Forest DC
Emley, Kirklees MC
Emmington, S Oxon DC
Emneth, King's Lynn/W Norfolk
    BC
Emneth Hungate, King's Lynn/W
    Norfolk BC
Empingham, Rutland CC
Empshott, E Hants DC
Emsworth, Havant BC
Enborne, W Berks DC
Enchmarsh, Shrewsbury/Atcham
    Cl
Endcliffe, Sheffield City
Enderby, Blaby DC
Endmoor, S Lakeland DC
Endon, Staffs Moorlands DC

Enfield, Enfield LBC
Enford, Kennet DC
Englefield, W Berks DC
Englefield Green, Runnymede BC
English Bicknor, Forest of Dean
    DC
English Frankton, N Shropshire
    DC
Englishcombe, Bath/N E
    Somerset Cl
Enham Alamein, Test Valley BC
Enmore, Sedgemoor DC
Ennerdale Bridge, Copeland BC
Enniskillen, Fermanagh DC
Ensdon, Shrewsbury/Atcham Cl
Enson, Stafford BC
Enstone, W Oxon DC
Enville, S Staffs Cl
Epperstone, Newark/Sherwood
    DC
Epping, Epping Forest DC
Epping Upland, Epping Forest DC
Eppleby, Richmondshire DC
Epsom, Epsom/Ewell BC
Epwell, Cherwell DC
Epworth, N Lincs Cl
Erbistock, Wrexham CBC
Erbusaig, Highland Cl
Ercall Magna, Telford/Wrekin BC
Erchless Castle, Highland Cl
Erdington, Birmingham City
Eridge Green, Wealden DC
Eriskay, Comhairle Nan Eilean
    Siar
Eriswell, Forest Heath DC
Erith, Bexley LBC
Erlestoke, Kennet DC
Ermington, S Hams DC
Ernesettle, Plymouth City
Erpingham, N Norfolk DC
Erringden, Calderdale MBC
Errogie, Highland Cl
Errol, Perth/Kinross Cl
Erskine, Renfrewshire Cl
Erwarton, Babergh DC
Erwood, Powys CC
Eryholme, Richmondshire DC
Esclusham, Wrexham CBC
Escomb, Wear Valley DC
Escrick, Selby DC
Esh, Derwentside DC
Esh Winning, Durham City
Esh Winning (part), Derwentside
    DC
Esher, Elmbridge BC
Eshott, Castle Morpeth BC
Eshton, Craven DC
Eskadale, Highland Cl
Eskbank, Midlothian Cl
Eskdale, Copeland BC

Eskdalemuir, Dumfries/Galloway Cl
Eskdaleside, Scarborough BC
Esprick, Fylde BC
Essendine, Rutland CC
Essendon, Welwyn Hatfield DC
Essington, S Staffs Cl
Eston, Redcar/Cleveland BC
Estover, Plymouth City
Etal, Berwick-u-Tweed BC
Etchilhampton, Kennet DC
Etchingham, Rother DC
Etchinghill, Cannock Chase DC
Etchinghill, Shepway DC
Etherley, Teesdale DC
Eton, E Staffs BC
Eton, Windsor/Maidenhead RB
Etteridge, Highland Cl
Ettington, Stratford/Avon DC
Etton, E Riding of Yks
Etton, Peterborough City
Ettrick, Scottish Borders Cl
Etwall, S Derbys DC
Euston, St Edmundsbury BC
Euxton, Chorley BC
Evanstown, Bridgend CBC
Evanton, Highland Cl
Evedon, N Kesteven DC
Evelix, Highland Cl
Evenley, S Northants Cl
Evenlode, Cotswold DC
Evenwood, Teesdale DC
Evercreech, Mendip DC
Everdon, Daventry DC
Everingham, E Riding of Yks
Everleigh, Kennet DC
Everley, Scarborough BC
Eversholt, Mid Beds DC
Evershot, W Dorset DC
Eversley, Hart DC
Eversley Cross, Hart DC
Everton, Bassetlaw DC
Everton, Mid Beds DC
Everton, New Forest DC
Evesbatch, Herefordshire Cl
Evesham, Wychavon DC
Evie, Orkney Is Cl
Ewden Village, Sheffield City
Ewell, Epsom/Ewell BC
Ewell Minnis, Dover DC
Ewelme, S Oxon DC
Ewen, Cotswold DC
Ewenny, Vale of Glamorgan Cl
Ewerby, N Kesteven DC
Ewhurst, Rother DC
Ewhurst, Waverley BC
Eworthy, W Devon BC
Ewshot, Hart DC
Ewyas Harold, Herefordshire Cl
Exbourne, W Devon BC

Exbury, New Forest DC
Exelby, Hambleton DC
Exeter, Exeter City
Exford, W Somerset DC
Exhall, Nuneaton/Bedworth BC
Exhall, Stratford/Avon DC
Exminster, Teignbridge DC
Exmoor, W Somerset DC
Exmouth, E Devon DC
Exning, Forest Heath DC
Exton, E Devon DC
Exton, Rutland CC
Exton, W Somerset DC
Exton, Winchester City
Eyam, Derbys Dales DC
Eydon, S Northants Cl
Eye, Herefordshire Cl
Eye, Mid Suffolk DC
Eye, Peterborough City
Eye, S Oxon DC
Eyemouth, Scottish Borders Cl
Eyeworth, Mid Beds DC
Eyhorne Street, Maidstone BC
Eyke, Suffolk C'l DC
Eynesbury Hardwicke, Huntingdonshire DC
Eynort, Highland Cl
Eynsford, Sevenoaks DC
Eynsham, W Oxon DC
Eyre, Highland Cl
Eythorne, Dover DC
Eyton, Herefordshire Cl
Eyton, S Shropshire DC
Eyton upon the Weald Moors, Telford/Wrekin BC

Faccombe, Test Valley BC
Faceby, Hambleton DC
Faddiley, Crewe/Nantwich BC
Fadmoor, Ryedale DC
Faenor, Ceredigion CC
Faichem, Highland Cl
Faifley, W Dunbartonshire Cl
Failsworth, Oldham MBC
Fair Oak, Eastleigh BC
Fairburn, Selby DC
Fairfield, Bromsgrove DC
Fairfield, Bury MBC
Fairfield, Stockton-on-Tees BC
Fairfield, Wyre Forest DC
Fairford, Cotswold DC
Fairford Leys, Aylesbury Vale DC
Fairhaven, Fylde BC
Fairlands, Guildford BC
Fairlie, N Ayrshire Cl
Fairlight, Rother DC
Fairmilehead, Edinburgh City
Fairmuir, Dundee City
Fairoak, Stafford BC
Fairseat, Tonbridge/Malling BC

Fairstead, Braintree DC
Fairwarp, Wealden DC
Fairwater, Cardiff CC
Fairwater, Torfaen CBC
Fairy Cross, Torridge DC
Fairy Glen, Conwy CBC
Fairy Water, Omagh DC
Fakenham, N Norfolk DC
Fakenham Magna, St Edmundsbury BC
Falcutt, S Northants Cl
Faldingworth, W Lindsey DC
Falellan, Highland Cl
Falfield, S Glos Cl
Falkenham, Suffolk C'l DC
Falkirk, Falkirk Cl
Falkland, Fife Cl
Fallin, Stirling Cl
Fallside, N Lanarkshire Cl
Falmer, Lewes DC
Falmouth, Carrick DC
Falstone, Tynedale DC
Fanagmore, Highland Cl
Fangfoss, E Riding of Yks
Fankerton, Falkirk Cl
Far Cotton, Northampton BC
Far Forest, Wyre Forest DC
Far Longdon, Stratford/Avon DC
Farcet, Huntingdonshire DC
Farden, S Shropshire DC
Fareham, Fareham BC
Farewell, Lichfield DC
Faringdon, Vale of White Horse DC
Farington, S Ribble BC
Farlam, Carlisle City
Farleigh, Tandridge DC
Farleigh Hungerford, Mendip DC
Farleigh Wallop, Basingstoke/Deane BC
Farlesthorpe, E Lindsey DC
Farleton, Lancaster City
Farley, Luton BC
Farley, Salisbury DC
Farley, Shrewsbury/Atcham Cl
Farley, Staffs Moorlands DC
Farley Green, Guildford BC
Farley Hill, Wokingham DC
Farleys End, Stroud DC
Farlington, Hambleton DC
Farlington, Portsmouth City
Farlow, Bridgnorth DC
Farmborough, Bath/N E Somerset Cl
Farmcote, Bridgnorth DC
Farmcote, Cotswold DC
Farmington, Cotswold DC
Farmoor, Vale of White Horse DC
Farnborough, Bromley LBC
Farnborough, Rushmoor BC

Farnborough, Stratford/Avon DC
Farnborough, W Berks DC
Farndale East, Ryedale DC
Farndale West, Ryedale DC
Farndish, Bedford BC
Farndon, Chester City
Farndon, Newark/Sherwood DC
Farnham, E Dorset DC
Farnham, Harrogate BC
Farnham, N Dorset DC
Farnham, Suffolk C'l DC
Farnham, Uttlesford DC
Farnham, Waverley BC
Farnham Common, S Bucks DC
Farnham Royal, S Bucks DC
Farnhill, Craven DC
Farningham, Sevenoaks DC
Farnley, Harrogate BC
Farnsfield, Newark/Sherwood DC
Farnworth, Bolton MBC
Farr, Highland Cl
Farraline, Highland Cl
Farringdon, E Devon DC
Farringdon, E Hants DC
Farrington Gurney, Bath/N E
   Somerset Cl
Farsley, Leeds City
Farthinghoe, S Northants Cl
Farthingstone, Daventry DC
Farway, E Devon DC
Fasach, Highland Cl
Fasag, Highland Cl
Fassfern, Highland Cl
Faugh, Carlisle City
Faughanvale, Limavady BC
Fauldhouse, W Lothian Cl
Faulkbourne, Braintree DC
Faulkland, Mendip DC
Fauls, N Shropshire DC
Faversham, Swale BC
Fawcett Forest, S Lakeland DC
Fawdington, Hambleton DC
Fawdon, Newcastle City
Fawfieldhead, Staffs Moorlands
   DC
Fawkham, Sevenoaks DC
Fawler, W Oxon DC
Fawley, New Forest DC
Fawley, W Berks DC
Fawley, Wycombe DC
Fawsley, Daventry DC
Faxfleet, E Riding of Yks
Faygate, Horsham DC
Fazakerley, Liverpool City
Fazeley, Lichfield DC
Feagour, Highland Cl
Fearby, Harrogate BC
Fearn, Highland Cl
Fearnbeg, Highland Cl
Fearnhead, Warrington BC

Fearnmore, Highland Cl
Featherstone, S Staffs Cl
Featherstone, Tynedale DC
Featherstone, Wakefield MDC
Feckenham, Redditch BC
Feeny, Limavady BC
Feering, Braintree DC
Feetham, Richmondshire DC
Feizor, Craven DC
Felbridge, Tandridge DC
Felbrigg, N Norfolk DC
Felcourt, Tandridge DC
Felinfach, Powys CC
Felixkirk, Hambleton DC
Felixstowe, Suffolk C'l DC
Felkington, Berwick-u-Tweed BC
Fell End, Eden DC
Felling, Gateshead Cl
Fellisclife, Harrogate BC
Felmersham, Bedford BC
Felmingham, N Norfolk DC
Felpham, Arun DC
Felsham, Mid Suffolk DC
Felsted, Uttlesford DC
Feltham, Hounslow LBC
Felthorpe, Broadland DC
Felton, Alnwick DC
Felton, Herefordshire Cl
Felton Butler,
   Shrewsbury/Atcham Cl
Feltwell, King's Lynn/W Norfolk
   BC
Fen Ditton, S Cambs DC
Fen Drayton, S Cambs DC
Fen End, Solihull MBC
Fenay Bridge, Kirklees MC
Fencote, Hambleton DC
Fencott, Cherwell DC
Fenham, Newcastle City
Feniscowles, Blackburn with
   Darwen BC
Feniton, E Devon DC
Fenny Bentley, Derbys Dales DC
Fenny Compton, Stratford/Avon
   DC
Fenny Drayton,
   Hinckley/Bosworth BC
Fenny Stratford, Milton Keynes Cl
Fenrother, Castle Morpeth BC
Fenstanton, Huntingdonshire DC
Fenton, Berwick-u-Tweed BC
Fenton, S Kesteven DC
Fenton, Stoke-on-Trent City
Fenton, W Lindsey DC
Fenwick, Berwick-u-Tweed BC
Fenwick, Castle Morpeth BC
Fenwick, Doncaster MBC
Fenwick, E Ayrshire Cl
Feock, Carrick DC
Feorlig, Highland Cl

Ferinquarrie, Highland Cl
Ferndale, Rhondda Cynon Taff
   CBC
Ferintosh, Highland Cl
Ferness, Highland Cl
Fernham, Vale of White Horse
   DC
Fernhill Heath, Wychavon DC
Fernhurst, Chichester DC
Fernilee, High Peak BC
Ferrensby, Harrogate BC
Ferrindonald, Highland Cl
Ferring, Arun DC
Ferrybridge, Wakefield MDC
Ferryden, Angus Cl
Ferryhill, Aberdeen City
Ferryhill, Sedgefield BC
Fersfield, S Norfolk DC
Fersit, Highland Cl
Feshiebridge, Highland Cl
Fetcham, Mole Valley DC
Fetlar, Shetland Is Cl
Fetterangus, Aberdeenshire Cl
Fettercairn, Aberdeenshire Cl
Fetteresso, Aberdeenshire Cl
Fewcott, Cherwell DC
Fewston, Harrogate BC
Ffestiniog, Gwynedd CC
Fiddington, Sedgemoor DC
Fiddington, Tewkesbury BC
Fiddlers Hamlet, Epping Forest
   DC
Field Assarts, W Oxon DC
Field Broughton, S Lakeland DC
Field Dalling, N Norfolk DC
Field Head, Hinckley/Bosworth
   BC
Fifehead Magdalen, N Dorset DC
Fifehead Neville, N Dorset DC
Fifield, W Oxon DC
Fifield, Windsor/Maidenhead RB
Figheldean, Salisbury DC
Filby, Gt Yarmouth DC
Filey, Scarborough BC
Filgrave, Milton Keynes Cl
Filkins, W Oxon DC
Filleigh, N Devon DC
Fillingham, W Lindsey DC
Fillongley, N Warks BC
Filton, S Glos Cl
Fimber, E Riding of Yks
Fincastle, Perth/Kinross Cl
Fincham, King's Lynn/W Norfolk
   BC
Finchampstead, Wokingham DC
Finchdean, E Hants DC
Finchingfield, Braintree DC
Finchley, Barnet LBC
Findern, S Derbys DC
Findhorn, Moray Cl

Findochty, Moray CI
Findon, Aberdeenshire CI
Findon, Arun DC
Finedon, Wellingborough BC
Fingest, Wycombe DC
Finghall, Richmondshire DC
Finglesham, Dover DC
Fingringhoe, Colchester BC
Finham, Coventry City MDC
Finmere, Cherwell DC
Finningham, Mid Suffolk DC
Finningley, Doncaster MBC
Finnis, Banbridge DC
Finsbury Park, Hackney LBC
Finshade, E Northants CI
Finstall, Bromsgrove DC
Finsthwaite, S Lakeland DC
Finstock, W Oxon DC
Fintona, Omagh DC
Fintray, Aberdeenshire CI
Fintry, Dundee City
Fintry, Stirling CI
Fir Vale, Sheffield City
Firbank, S Lakeland DC
Firbeck, Rotherham MBC
Firby, Hambleton DC
Firhill, Highland CI
Firle, Lewes DC
Firsby, E Lindsey DC
Firsdown, Salisbury DC
First Coast, Highland CI
Firth, Orkney Is CI
Fishbourne, Chichester DC
Fishbourne, Isle of Wight CI
Fishburn, Sedgefield BC
Fishermead, Milton Keynes CI
Fishersgate, Adur DC
Fisherstreet, Chichester DC
Fisherton, Highland CI
Fisherwick, Lichfield DC
Fishguard, Pembrokeshire CC
Fishlake, Doncaster MBC
Fishley, Broadland DC
Fishpool, Bury MBC
Fishtoft, Boston BC
Fiskavaig, Highland CI
Fiskerton, Newark/Sherwood DC
Fiskerton, W Lindsey DC
Fittleton, Kennet DC
Fittleworth, Chichester DC
Fitton End, Fenland DC
Fitz, Shrewsbury/Atcham CI
Fitzhead, Taunton Deane BC
Fitzwilliam, Wakefield MDC
Fiunary, Highland CI
Five Ashes, Wealden DC
Five Oak Green, Tunbridge Wells BC
Five Oaks, Horsham DC
Fivehead, S Somerset DC

Fivemiletown, Dungannon & S Tyrone BC
Flackwell Heath, Wycombe DC
Fladbury, Wychavon DC
Flagg, Derbys Dales DC
Flamborough, E Riding of Yks
Flamstead, Dacorum BC
Flansham, Arun DC
Flasby, Craven DC
Flash, Staffs Moorlands DC
Flashader, Highland CI
Flaunden, Dacorum BC
Flawborough, Rushcliffe BC
Flawith, Hambleton DC
Flax Bourton, N Somerset DC
Flaxby, Harrogate BC
Flaxley, Forest of Dean DC
Flaxton, Ryedale DC
Fleckney, Harborough DC
Fledborough, Bassetlaw DC
Fleet, Hart DC
Fleet, W Dorset DC
Fleet Hargate, S Holland DC
Fleet Marston, Aylesbury Vale DC
Fleetwood, Wyre BC
Fleggburgh, Gt Yarmouth BC
Flempton, St Edmundsbury BC
Fletching, Wealden DC
Fleuchary, Highland CI
Flexbury, N Cornwall DC
Flexford, Guildford BC
Flimby, Allerdale BC
Flint, Flintshire CC
Flint Hill, Derwentside DC
Flintham, Rushcliffe BC
Flinton, E Riding of Yks
Flitcham, King's Lynn/W Norfolk BC
Flitton, Mid Beds DC
Flitwick, Mid Beds DC
Flixborough, N Lincs CI
Flixton, Scarborough BC
Flixton, Trafford MBC
Flixton (East), Waveney DC
Flixton (West), Waveney DC
Flockton, Kirklees MC
Flodden, Berwick-u-Tweed BC
Flodigarry, Highland CI
Flookburgh, S Lakeland DC
Floors, Scottish Borders CI
Flordon, S Norfolk DC
Flore, Daventry DC
Flotta, Orkney Is CI
Flotterton, Alnwick DC
Flowton, Mid Suffolk DC
Flushing, Carrick DC
Flyford Flavell, Wychavon DC
Fobbing, Thurrock BC
Fockerby, N Lincs CI
Fodderty, Highland CI

Foggathorpe, E Riding of Yks
Fogo, Scottish Borders CI
Foindle, Highland CI
Foleshill, Coventry City MDC
Folke, W Dorset DC
Folkestone, Shepway DC
Folkingham, S Kesteven DC
Folkington, Wealden DC
Folksworth, Huntingdonshire DC
Folkton, Scarborough BC
Follifoot, Harrogate BC
Folly Gate, W Devon BC
Fonthill Bishop, Salisbury DC
Fonthill Gifford, Salisbury DC
Fontmell Magna, N Dorset DC
Fontwell, Arun DC
Foolow, Derbys Dales DC
Foots Cray, Bexley LBC
Forbes, Aberdeenshire CI
Forcett, Richmondshire DC
Ford, Arun DC
Ford, Aylesbury Vale DC
Ford, Berwick-u-Tweed BC
Ford, Herefordshire CI
Ford, Salisbury DC
Ford, Sefton MBC
Ford, Shrewsbury/Atcham CI
Ford End, Chelmsford BC
Fordbridge, Solihull MBC
Forde Hall, Stratford/Avon DC
Fordell, Fife CI
Forden, Powys CC
Fordham, Colchester BC
Fordham, E Cambs DC
Fordham, King's Lynn/W Norfolk BC
Fordingbridge, New Forest DC
Fordington, E Lindsey DC
Fordoun, Aberdeenshire CI
Fordwells, W Oxon DC
Fordwich, Canterbury City
Fordyce, Aberdeenshire CI
Foregin, Highland CI
Foreglen, Limavady BC
Forehill, S Ayrshire CI
Foremark, S Derbys DC
Forest, Teesdale DC
Forest Gate, Newham LBC
Forest Green, Mole Valley DC
Forest Head, Carlisle City
Forest Hill, Lewisham LBC
Forest Hill, S Oxon DC
Forest in Teesdale, Teesdale DC
Forest Row, Wealden DC
Forest Town, Mansfield DC
Forestburn Gate, Alnwick DC
Forestside, Chichester DC
Forfar, Angus CI
Forge Hammer, Torfaen CBC
Forge Side, Torfaen CBC

Forglen, Aberdeenshire Cl
Forgue, Aberdeenshire Cl
Forkhill, Newry/Mourne DC
Formby, Sefton MBC
Forncett End, S Norfolk DC
Forncett St Mary, S Norfolk DC
Forncett St Peter, S Norfolk DC
Fornham All Saints, St
    Edmundsbury BC
Fornham St Genevieve, St
    Edmundsbury BC
Fornham St Martin, St
    Edmundsbury BC
Forrabury, N Cornwall DC
Forres, Moray Cl
Forsbrook, Staffs Moorlands DC
Forshaw Heath, Stratford/Avon
    DC
Forsinard, Highland Cl
Fort, S Ayrshire Cl
Fort Augustus, Highland Cl
Fort George, Highland Cl
Fort Wiliam, Highland Cl
Forth, S Lanarkshire Cl
Forthampton, Tewkesbury BC
Forton, S Somerset DC
Forton, Stafford BC
Forton, Wyre BC
Fortrose, Highland Cl
Fortuneswell, Weymouth/Portland
    BC
Forward Green, Mid Suffolk DC
Fosbury, Kennet DC
Foscote, Aylesbury Vale DC
Foscote, S Northants Cl
Fosdyke, Boston BC
Fossoway, Perth/Kinross Cl
Fosters Booth, S Northants Cl
Foston, Ryedale DC
Foston, S Derbys DC
Foston, S Kesteven DC
Foston on the Wolds, E Riding of
    Yks
Fotherby, E Lindsey DC
Fotheringhay, E Northants Cl
Foulden, Breckland Cl
Foulden, Scottish Borders Cl
Foulk Stapleford, Chester City
Foulness Island, Rochford DC
Foulridge, Pendle BC
Foulsham, Broadland DC
Fountains Abbey, Harrogate BC
Four Ashes, Mid Suffolk DC
Four Ashes, S Staffs Cl
Four Crosses, S Staffs Cl
Four Elms, Sevenoaks DC
Four Gotes, Fenland DC
Four Lanes, Kerrier DC
Four Marks, E Hants DC
Four Oaks, Rother DC

Four Oaks, Solihull MBC
Four Throws, Tunbridge Wells BC
Fourlanes End, Congleton BC
Fourstones, Tynedale DC
Fovant, Salisbury DC
Foveran, Aberdeenshire Cl
Fowberry Tower, Berwick-u-
    Tweed BC
Fowey, Restormel BC
Fowlis, Angus Cl
Fowlmere, S Cambs DC
Fownhope, Herefordshire Cl
Fox Hollies, Birmingham City
Foxcote, Stratford/Avon DC
Foxearth, Braintree DC
Foxfield, S Lakeland DC
Foxhall, Suffolk C'l DC
Foxhole, Restormel BC
Foxholes, Ryedale DC
Foxley, Breckland Cl
Foxley, N Wilts DC
Foxley, S Northants Cl
Foxton, Harborough DC
Foxton, S Cambs DC
Foxup, Craven DC
Foxwist Green, Vale Royal BC
Foy, Herefordshire Cl
Foyers, Highland Cl
Fraddon, Restormel BC
Fradswell, Stafford BC
Fraisthorpe, E Riding of Yks
Framfield, Wealden DC
Framingham Earl, S Norfolk DC
Framingham Pigot, S Norfolk DC
Framlingham, Suffolk C'l DC
Frampton, Boston BC
Frampton, W Dorset DC
Frampton Cotterell, S Glos Cl
Frampton Mansell, Cotswold DC
Frampton on Severn, Stroud DC
Framsden, Mid Suffolk DC
Framwellgate Moor, Durham City
Franche, Wyre Forest DC
Frankley, Bromsgrove DC
Frankton, Rugby BC
Fransham, Breckland Cl
Frant, Wealden DC
Fraserburgh, Aberdeenshire Cl
Frating Green, Tendring DC
Fratton, Portsmouth City
Frechville, Sheffield City
Freckenham, Forest Heath DC
Freckleton, Fylde BC
Freeby, Melton BC
Freeland, W Oxon DC
Freemantle, Southampton City
Freethorpe, Broadland DC
Freiston, Boston BC
Fremington, N Devon DC
Fremington, Richmondshire DC

Frenchay, S Glos Cl
Frenchbeer, W Devon BC
Frenchmoor, Test Valley BC
Frensham, Waverley BC
Freshbrook, Swindon BC
Freshfield, Sefton MBC
Freshford, Bath/N E Somerset Cl
Freshwater, Isle of Wight Cl
Fressingfield, Mid Suffolk DC
Freston, Babergh DC
Freswick, Highland Cl
Fretherne, Stroud DC
Frettenham, Broadland DC
Freuchie, Fife Cl
Freystrop, Pembrokeshire CC
Friar's Gate, Wealden DC
Friarton, Perth/Kinross Cl
Frickley, Doncaster MBC
Friday Bridge, Fenland DC
Friday Street, Mole Valley DC
Fridays Hill, Chichester DC
Fridaythorpe, E Riding of Yks
Friern Barnet, Barnet LBC
Friesthorpe, W Lindsey DC
Frieth, Wycombe DC
Frilford, Vale of White Horse DC
Frilsham, W Berks DC
Frimley, Surrey Heath BC
Frindsbury Extra, Medway Cl
Fring, King's Lynn/W Norfolk BC
Fringford, Cherwell DC
Frinsted, Maidstone BC
Frinton on Sea, Tendring DC
Friockhelm, Angus Cl
Frisby, Harborough DC
Frisby on the Wreake, Melton BC
Friskney, E Lindsey DC
Friston, Suffolk C'l DC
Friston, Wealden DC
Fritchley, Amber Valley BC
Frith, Teesdale DC
Fritham, New Forest DC
Frithelstock, Torridge DC
Frithelstock Stone, Torridge DC
Frithville, E Lindsey DC
Frittenden, Tunbridge Wells BC
Fritton, Gt Yarmouth BC
Fritton, S Norfolk DC
Fritwell, Cherwell DC
Friz Hill, Stratford/Avon DC
Frizington, Copeland BC
Frocester, Stroud DC
Frodesley, Shrewsbury/Atcham
    Cl
Frodsham, Vale Royal BC
Froggatt, Derbys Dales DC
Froghall, Staffs Moorlands DC
Frogham, Dover DC
Frogmore, S Hams DC
Frolesworth, Harborough DC

Frome, Mendip DC
Frome St Quinton, W Dorset DC
Frome Vauchurch, W Dorset DC
Froncysyllte, Wrexham CBC
Frostenden, Waveney DC
Froxfield, E Hants DC
Froxfield, Kennet DC
Froyle, E Hants DC
Fruithill, Limavady BC
Fryent, Brent LBC
Fryerning, Brentwood BC
Fryston, Wakefield MDC
Fryton, Ryedale DC
Fulbeck, S Kesteven DC
Fulbourn, S Cambs DC
Fulbrook, Stratford/Avon DC
Fulbrook, W Oxon DC
Fulford, City of York Cl
Fulford, Stafford BC
Fulham, Hammersmith/Fulham
    LBC
Fulking, Mid Sussex DC
Full Sutton, E Riding of Yks
Fullarton, Glasgow City
Fullers Slade, Milton Keynes Cl
Fullerton, Test Valley BC
Fulletby, E Lindsey DC
Fulmer, S Bucks DC
Fulmodestone, N Norfolk DC
Fulnetby, W Lindsey DC
Fulready, Stratford/Avon DC
Fulstow, E Lindsey DC
Fulwood, Preston City
Fulwood, Sheffield City
Fundenhall, S Norfolk DC
Funtington, Chichester DC
Funtley, Fareham BC
Furnace, Argyll/Bute Cl
Furnace Wood, Mid Sussex DC
Furneux Pelham, E Herts DC
Furtho, S Northants Cl
Furzton, Milton Keynes Cl
Fyfield, Cotswold DC
Fyfield, Epping Forest DC
Fyfield, Kennet DC
Fyfield, Test Valley BC
Fyfield, Vale of White Horse DC
Fylingdales, Scarborough BC
Fylingthorpe, Scarborough BC
Fyvie, Aberdeenshire Cl

Gabalfa, Cardiff CC
Gaddesby, Melton BC
Gagingwell, W Oxon DC
Gaich, Highland Cl
Gailey, S Staffs Cl
Gainford, Teesdale DC
Gainsborough, W Lindsey DC
Gainsford End, Braintree DC
Gairloch, Highland Cl

Gairlochy, Highland Cl
Gaisgill, Eden DC
Gaitsgill, Carlisle City
Galashiels, Scottish Borders Cl
Galby, Harborough DC
Galgate, Lancaster City
Galley Common,
    Nuneaton/Bedworth BC
Galley Hill, Milton Keynes Cl
Galleywood, Chelmsford BC
Gallowhill, Renfrewshire Cl
Galmisdale, Highland Cl
Galmpton, S Hams DC
Galphay, Harrogate BC
Galston, E Ayrshire Cl
Galtrigill, Highland Cl
Gamblesby, Eden DC
Gamesley, High Peak BC
Gamlingay, S Cambs DC
Gammersgill, Richmondshire DC
Gamrie, Aberdeenshire Cl
Gamston, Bassetlaw DC
Gamston, Rushcliffe BC
Ganarew, Herefordshire Cl
Ganllwyd, Gwynedd CC
Gannaway, Stratford/Avon DC
Gannochy, Perth/Kinross Cl
Gansclet, Highland Cl
Ganstead, E Riding of Yks
Ganthorpe, Ryedale DC
Ganton, Ryedale DC
Gants Hill, Redbridge LBC
Garboldisham, Breckland Cl
Gardenstown, Aberdeenshire Cl
Gardiffaith, Torfaen CBC
Garelochhead, Argyll/Bute Cl
Garford, Vale of White Horse DC
Garforth, Leeds City
Gargrave, Craven DC
Gargunnock, Stirling Cl
Garn Prys, Conwy CBC
Garn yr arw, Torfaen CBC
Garndiffaith, Torfaen CBC
Garnethill, Glasgow City
Garnett Bridge, S Lakeland DC
Garrachan, Highland Cl
Garrafad, Highland Cl
Garras, Kerrier DC
Garrigill, Eden DC
Garriston, Richmondshire DC
Garros, Highland Cl
Garrowhill, Glasgow City
Garrygualach, Highland Cl
Garsdale, S Lakeland DC
Garshall Green, Stafford BC
Garsington, S Oxon DC
Garstang, Wyre BC
Garston, Liverpool City
Garswood, St Helens MBC
Gartcosh, E Dunbartonshire Cl

Gartcraig, Glasgow City
Garth, Wrexham CBC
Garthamlock, Glasgow City
Garthdee, Aberdeen City
Garthorpe, Melton BC
Garthorpe, N Lincs Cl
Gartly, Aberdeenshire Cl
Gartmore, Stirling Cl
Gartness, N Lanarkshire Cl
Gartocharn, W Dunbartonshire Cl
Garton, E Riding of Yks
Garton on the Wolds, E Riding of
    Yks
Gartymore, Highland Cl
Garuald, E Lothian Cl
Garvagh, Coleraine BC
Garve, Highland Cl
Garvestone, Breckland Cl
Garvock, Aberdeenshire Cl
Garw Valley, Bridgend CBC
Garway, Herefordshire Cl
Gasper, Salisbury DC
Gatcombe, Isle of Wight Cl
Gate Burton, W Lindsey DC
Gate Helmsley, Ryedale DC
Gateacre, Liverpool City
Gatebeck, S Lakeland DC
Gateforth, Selby DC
Gatehead, E Ayrshire Cl
Gatehouse of Fleet,
    Dumfries/Galloway Cl
Gateley, Breckland Cl
Gatenby, Hambleton DC
Gateshead, Gateshead Cl
Gatesheath, Chester City
Gateside, Fife Cl
Gateside, N Lanarkshire Cl
Gathurst, Wigan MBC
Gatwick Airport, Crawley BC
Gauldry, Fife Cl
Gaunt's Common, E Dorset DC
Gautby, E Lindsey DC
Gavinton, Scottish Borders Cl
Gawber, Barnsley MBC
Gawcott, Aylesbury Vale DC
Gawsworth, Macclesfield BC
Gawthrop, S Lakeland DC
Gawthwaite, S Lakeland DC
Gaydon, Stratford/Avon DC
Gayhurst, Milton Keynes Cl
Gayle, Richmondshire DC
Gayles, Richmondshire DC
Gayton, King's Lynn/W Norfolk
    BC
Gayton, S Northants Cl
Gayton, Stafford BC
Gayton, Wirral MBC
Gayton le Marsh, E Lindsey DC
Gayton le Wold, E Lindsey DC

Gayton Thorpe, King's Lynn/W Norfolk BC
Gaywood, King's Lynn/W Norfolk BC
Gazeley, Forest Heath DC
Geary, Highland Cl
Gearymore, Highland Cl
Gedding, Mid Suffolk DC
Geddington, Kettering BC
Gedgrave, Suffolk C'l DC
Gedintailor, Highland Cl
Gedling, Gedling BC
Gedney, S Holland DC
Gedney Drove End, S Holland DC
Gedney Dyke, S Holland DC
Gedney Hill, S Holland DC
Geldeston, S Norfolk DC
Gell, Conwy CBC
Gelligaer, Caerphilly CBC
Gellioedd, Conwy CBC
Geltsdale, Carlisle City
Genau'r Glyn, Ceredigion CC
Gentleshaw, Lichfield DC
George Street, Aberdeen City
Georgeham, N Devon DC
Georgenympton, N Devon DC
Georgetown, Dumfries/Galloway Cl
Georgia, Penwith DC
Gergask, Highland Cl
Germansweek, W Devon BC
Germiston, Glasgow City
Germoe, Kerrier DC
Gerrans, Carrick DC
Gerrards Cross, S Bucks DC
Gestingthorpe, Braintree DC
Giants Causeway, Moyle DC
Gibsmere, Newark/Sherwood DC
Gidea Park, Havering LBC
Gidleigh, W Devon BC
Giffard Park, Milton Keynes Cl
Giffnock, E Renfrewshire Cl
Gifford, E Lothian Cl
Giggleswick, Craven DC
Gigha, Argyll/Bute Cl
Gilberdyke, E Riding of Yks
Gilberts Green, Stratford/Avon DC
Gilcrux, Allerdale BC
Gildersome, Leeds City
Gildingwells, Rotherham MBC
Gilesgate, Durham City
Gilesgate Moor, Durham City
Gilfach Goch, Rhondda Cynon Taff CBC
Gilford, Banbridge DC
Gilgarran, Copeland BC
Gillamoor, Ryedale DC
Gillen, Highland Cl

Gilling East, Ryedale DC
Gilling West, Richmondshire DC
Gillingham, Medway Cl
Gillingham, N Dorset DC
Gillingham, S Norfolk DC
Gillway, Tamworth BC
Gilmerton, Edinburgh City
Gilmonby, Teesdale DC
Gilmorton, Harborough DC
Gilnahirk, Castlereagh BC
Gilsland, Tynedale DC
Gilston, E Herts DC
Gimingham, N Norfolk DC
Gipping, Mid Suffolk DC
Girsby, Hambleton DC
Girton, Newark/Sherwood DC
Girton, S Cambs DC
Girvan, S Ayrshire Cl
Gisburn, Ribble Valley BC
Gisburn Forest, Ribble Valley BC
Gisleham, Waveney DC
Gislingham, Mid Suffolk DC
Gissing, S Norfolk DC
Gittisham, E Devon DC
Glackmore, Highland Cl
Gladestry, Powys CC
Gladsmuir, E Lothian Cl
Gladstone, Brent LBC
Glaichbea, Highland Cl
Glaisdale, Scarborough BC
Glamis, Angus Cl
Glan Conwy, Conwy CBC
Glandford, N Norfolk DC
Glanton, Alnwick DC
Glantwymyn, Powys CC
Glanvilles Wootton, N Dorset DC
Glapthorn, E Northants Cl
Glapwell, Bolsover DC
Glasbury, Powys CC
Glascote, Tamworth BC
Glascwm, Powys CC
Glasfryn, Conwy CBC
Glasgow, Glasgow City
Glashvin, Highland Cl
Glasnacardoch, Highland Cl
Glasnakille, Highland Cl
Glasphein, Highland Cl
Glass, Aberdeenshire Cl
Glassford, S Lanarkshire Cl
Glasshouse Hill, Forest of Dean DC
Glasshouses, Harrogate BC
Glasson, Allerdale BC
Glasson, Lancaster City
Glassonby, Eden DC
Glaston, Rutland CC
Glastonbury, Mendip DC
Glatton, Huntingdonshire DC
Glazebrook, Warrington BC
Glazebury, Warrington BC

Glazeley, Bridgnorth DC
Gleadless, Sheffield City
Gleadless Valley, Sheffield City
Gleadsmoss, Macclesfield BC
Gleaston, S Lakeland DC
Glebe, Stockton-on-Tees BC
Glemsford, Babergh DC
Glen, Scottish Borders Cl
Glen Bernisdale, Highland Cl
Glen Heysdal, Highland Cl
Glen Parva, Blaby DC
Glen Tanar, Aberdeenshire Cl
Glen Village, Falkirk Cl
Glenancross, Highland Cl
Glenarm, Larne BC
Glenavy, Lisburn City
Glenbervie, Aberdeenshire Cl
Glenboig, N Lanarkshire Cl
Glenborrodale, Highland Cl
Glenbuchat, Aberdeenshire Cl
Glenbuck, E Ayrshire Cl
Glenburn, Renfrewshire Cl
Glencairn, Dumfries/Galloway Cl
Glencoe, Highland Cl
Glencraig, Fife Cl
Glendale, Highland Cl
Glendaruel, Argyll/Bute Cl
Glenelg, Highland Cl
Glenfarg, Perth/Kinross Cl
Glenfield, Blaby DC
Glenfinnan, Highland Cl
Glengairn, Aberdeenshire Cl
Glengarnock, N Ayrshire Cl
Glengormley, Newtownabbey BC
Glengrasco, Highland Cl
Glenhurich, Highland Cl
Glenlyon, Perth/Kinross Cl
Glenmavis, N Lanarkshire Cl
Glenmore, Highland Cl
Glenmuick Tullich, Aberdeenshire Cl
Glenochil, Clackmannanshire Cl
Glenorchy, Argyll/Bute Cl
Glenridding, Eden DC
Glenrothes, Fife Cl
Glensanda, Highland Cl
Glentham, W Lindsey DC
Glentworth, W Lindsey DC
Glenuig, Highland Cl
Glespin, S Lanarkshire Cl
Glinton, Peterborough City
Glooston, Harborough DC
Glossop, High Peak BC
Gloster Hill, Alnwick DC
Gloucester, Gloucester City
Glusburn, Craven DC
Glympton, W Oxon DC
Glyn Ceiriog, Wrexham CBC
Glyn Tarrell, Powys CC

Glyncorrwg, Neath Port Talbot CBC
Glyncorrwg, West Glamorgan CC
Glynde, Lewes DC
Glyndebourne, Lewes DC
Glynneath, Neath Port Talbot CBC
Glyntraian, Wrexham CBC
Gnosall, Stafford BC
Goadby, Harborough DC
Goadby Marwood, Melton BC
Goathill, W Dorset DC
Goathland, Scarborough BC
Goathurst, Sedgemoor DC
Gobowen, Oswestry BC
Godalming, Waverley BC
Godington, Cherwell DC
Godmanchester, Huntingdonshire DC
Godmanstone, W Dorset DC
Godmersham, Ashford BC
Godney, Mendip DC
Godolphin Cross, Kerrier DC
Godre r Graig, Neath Port Talbot CBC
Godshill, New Forest DC
Godshilll, Isle of Wight Cl
Godstone, Tandridge DC
Goetre Fawr, Monmouthshire CC
Golant, Restormel BC
Golberdon, Caradon DC
Golborne, Wigan MBC
Golborne Bellow, Chester City
Golborne David, Chester City
Golcar, Kirklees MC
Goldcliff, Newport City Cl
Golden Cross, Wealden DC
Golden Green, Tonbridge/Malling BC
Golden Grove, Scarborough BC
Goldenhill, Stoke-on-Trent City
Golders Green, Barnet LBC
Goldhanger, Maldon DC
Goldicote, Stratford/Avon DC
Golding, Shrewsbury/Atcham Cl
Goldsborough, Harrogate BC
Goldsborough, Scarborough BC
Goldshaw Booth, Pendle BC
Goldsithney, Penwith DC
Goldsworth Park, Woking BC
Golgotha, Dover DC
Golspie, Highland Cl
Goltho, W Lindsey DC
Gomeldon, Salisbury DC
Gomersal, Kirklees MC
Gomshall, Guildford BC
Gonalston, Newark/Sherwood DC
Good Easter, Chelmsford BC
Gooderstone, Breckland Cl
Goodleigh, N Devon DC

Goodmanham, E Riding of Yks
Goodnestone, Dover DC
Goodnestone, Swale BC
Goodrich, Herefordshire Cl
Goodrington, Torbay Cl
Goodwick, Pembrokeshire CC
Goodwood, Chichester DC
Goodworth Clatford, Test Valley BC
Goole, E Riding of Yks
Goole Fields, E Riding of Yks
Goonbell, Carrick DC
Goonhavern, Carrick DC
Goose Green, Horsham DC
Gooseham, N Cornwall DC
Goosey, Vale of White Horse DC
Goosnargh, Preston City
Goostrey, Congleton BC
Gorcott Hill, Stratford/Avon DC
Gordon, Scottish Borders Cl
Gordonbush, Highland Cl
Gorebridge, Midlothian Cl
Gorefield, Fenland DC
Gorge, The, Telford/Wrekin BC
Goring, S Oxon DC
Goring by Sea, Worthing BC
Goring Heath, S Oxon DC
Gorleston, Gt Yarmouth BC
Gorse Hill, Swindon BC
Gorseinon, Swansea C&C
Gorslas, Carmarthenshire CC
Gorsley, Forest of Dean DC
Gorstan, Highland Cl
Gorteneorn, Highland Cl
Gortenfern, Highland Cl
Gortin, Omagh DC
Gorton, Manchester City
Gortrush, Omagh DC
Gosbeck, Mid Suffolk DC
Gosberton, S Holland DC
Gosfield, Braintree DC
Gosford, Cherwell DC
Gosforth, Copeland BC
Gosforth, Newcastle City
Gosmore, N Herts DC
Gospel Green, Chichester DC
Gospel Oak, Stratford/Avon DC
Gosport, Gosport BC
Goswick, Berwick-u-Tweed BC
Gotham, Rushcliffe BC
Gotherington, Tewkesbury BC
Goudhurst, Tunbridge Wells BC
Goulceby, E Lindsey DC
Gourdon, Aberdeenshire Cl
Gourock, Inverclyde Cl
Govan, Glasgow City
Goverton, Newark/Sherwood DC
Gowdall, E Riding of Yks
Gowerton, Swansea C&C
Gowkhall, Fife Cl

Goxhill, N Lincs Cl
Grade Ruan, Kerrier DC
Graemsay, Orkney Is Cl
Graffham, Chichester DC
Grafham, Huntingdonshire DC
Grafton, Bromsgrove DC
Grafton, Harrogate BC
Grafton, Herefordshire Cl
Grafton, Kennet DC
Grafton, W Oxon DC
Grafton Flyford, Wychavon DC
Grafton Regis, S Northants Cl
Grafton Underwood, Kettering BC
Grafty Green, Maidstone BC
Graig, Conwy CBC
Graig, Newport City Cl
Grains o' th' Beck, Teesdale DC
Grainsby, E Lindsey DC
Grainthorpe, E Lindsey DC
Grampound, Restormel BC
Granborough, Aylesbury Vale DC
Granby, Milton Keynes Cl
Granby, Rushcliffe BC
Grandborough, Rugby BC
Grandtully, Perth/Kinross Cl
Grange, Allerdale BC
Grange, S Lakeland DC
Grange, Stockton-on-Tees BC
Grange, Wirral MBC
Grange de Lings, W Lindsey DC
Grange Moor, Kirklees MC
Grange of Lindores, Fife Cl
Grange over Sands, S Lakeland DC
Grange Park, S Northants Cl
Grange Park, Swindon BC
Grange Villa, Chester-le-Street DC
Grangemouth, Falkirk Cl
Grangetown, Cardiff CC
Grangetown, Redcar/Cleveland BC
Gransmoor, E Riding of Yks
Grantchester, S Cambs DC
Grantham, S Kesteven DC
Grantley, Harrogate BC
Grantown, Highland Cl
Grantown on Spey, Highland Cl
Grantshouse, Scottish Borders Cl
Grappenhall, Warrington BC
Grasby, W Lindsey DC
Grasmere, S Lakeland DC
Grasscroft, Oldham MBC
Grassendale, Liverpool City
Grassholme, Teesdale DC
Grassington, Craven DC
Grassmoor, N E Derbys DC
Grassthorpe, Newark/Sherwood DC
Grateley, Test Valley BC

Graveley, N Herts DC
Graveley, S Cambs DC
Graveney, Swale BC
Gravenhurst, Mid Beds DC
Gravesend, Gravesham BC
Grayingham, W Lindsey DC
Grayrigg, S Lakeland DC
Grays, Thurrock BC
Grayshott, E Hants DC
Grayswood, Waverley BC
Grazeley, W Berks DC
Grealin, Highland CI
Greasbrough, Rotherham MBC
Greasby, Wirral MBC
Greasley, Broxtowe BC
Great Abington, S Cambs DC
Great Addington, E Northants CI
Great Alne, Stratford/Avon DC
Great Altcar, W Lancs DC
Great Amwell, E Herts DC
Great Asby, Eden DC
Great Ashfield, Mid Suffolk DC
Great Aycliffe, Sedgefield BC
Great Ayton, Hambleton DC
Great Baddow, Chelmsford BC
Great Bardfield, Braintree DC
Great Barford, Bedford BC
Great Barr, Walsall MBC
Great Barrington, Cotswold DC
Great Barton, St Edmundsbury
   BC
Great Bavington, Tynedale DC
Great Bealings, Suffolk C'l DC
Great Bedwyn, Kennet DC
Great Bentley, Tendring DC
Great Billington, S Beds DC
Great Bircham, King's Lynn/W
   Norfolk BC
Great Blakenham, Mid Suffolk DC
Great Bolas, Telford/Wrekin BC
Great Bookham, Mole Valley DC
Great Boughton, Chester City
Great Bourton, Cherwell DC
Great Bowden, Harborough DC
Great Bradley, St Edmundsbury
   BC
Great Braxted, Maldon DC
Great Bricett, Mid Suffolk DC
Great Brickhill, Aylesbury Vale
   DC
Great Brington, Daventry DC
Great Bromley, Tendring DC
Great Broughton, Allerdale BC
Great Broughton, Hambleton DC
Great Budworth, Vale Royal BC
Great Burdon, Darlington BC
Great Burstead, Basildon DC
Great Busby, Hambleton DC
Great Canfield, Uttlesford DC
Great Carlton, E Lindsey DC

Great Casterton, Rutland CC
Great Chart, Ashford BC
Great Chatwell, S Staffs CI
Great Chesterford, Uttlesford DC
Great Cheverell, Kennet DC
Great Chishill, S Cambs DC
Great Clacton, Tendring DC
Great Clifton, Allerdale BC
Great Coates, N E Lincs CI
Great Comberton, Wychavon DC
Great Corby, Carlisle City
Great Cornard, Babergh DC
Great Cowden, E Riding of Yks
Great Coxwell, Vale of White
   Horse DC
Great Cransley, Kettering BC
Great Cressingham, Breckland CI
Great Crosby, Sefton MBC
Great Dalby, Melton BC
Great Dawley, Telford/Wrekin BC
Great Doddington,
   Wellingborough BC
Great Driffield, E Riding of Yks
Great Dunham, Breckland CI
Great Dunmow, Uttlesford DC
Great Durnford, Salisbury DC
Great Easton, Harborough DC
Great Easton, Uttlesford DC
Great Eccleston, Wyre BC
Great Edstone, Ryedale DC
Great Ellingham, Breckland CI
Great Elm, Mendip DC
Great Eversden, S Cambs DC
Great Faringdon, Vale of White
   Horse DC
Great Finborough, Mid Suffolk DC
Great Fransham, Breckland CI
Great Gaddesden, Dacorum BC
Great Gidding, Huntingdonshire
   DC
Great Givendale, E Riding of Yks
Great Glemham, Suffolk C'l DC
Great Glen, Harborough DC
Great Gonerby, S Kesteven DC
Great Gransden, Huntingdonshire
   DC
Great Grimsby, N E Lincs CI
Great Habton, Ryedale DC
Great Hale, N Kesteven DC
Great Hallingbury, Uttlesford DC
Great Hampden, Wycombe DC
Great Hanwood,
   Shrewsbury/Atcham CI
Great Harrowden,
   Wellingborough BC
Great Harwood, Hyndburn BC
Great Haseley, S Oxon DC
Great Hatfield, E Riding of Yks
Great Heck, Selby DC
Great Henny, Braintree DC

Great Hinton, W Wilts DC
Great Hockham, Breckland CI
Great Holland, Tendring DC
Great Holm, Milton Keynes CI
Great Horkesley, Colchester BC
Great Hormead, E Herts DC
Great Horwood, Aylesbury Vale
   DC
Great Houghton, Barnsley MBC
Great Houghton, Northampton
   BC
Great Hucklow, Derbys Dales DC
Great Kelk, E Riding of Yks
Great Kimble, Wycombe DC
Great Kingshill, Wycombe DC
Great Langton, Hambleton DC
Great Leighs, Chelmsford BC
Great Limber, W Lindsey DC
Great Linford, Milton Keynes CI
Great Livermere, St
   Edmundsbury BC
Great Longstone, Derbys Dales
   DC
Great Lumley, Chester-le-Street
   DC
Great Lyth, Shrewsbury/Atcham
   CI
Great Malvern, Malvern Hills DC
Great Maplestead, Braintree DC
Great Marlow, Wycombe DC
Great Massingham, King's
   Lynn/W Norfolk BC
Great Melton, S Norfolk DC
Great Milton, S Oxon DC
Great Missenden, Chiltern DC
Great Mitton, Ribble Valley BC
Great Mongeham, Dover DC
Great Moulton, S Norfolk DC
Great Munden, E Herts DC
Great Musgrave, Eden DC
Great Ness, Shrewsbury/Atcham
   CI
Great Oakley, Corby BC
Great Oakley, Tendring DC
Great Offley, N Herts DC
Great Ormside, Eden DC
Great Orton, Carlisle City
Great Ouseburn, Harrogate BC
Great Oxendon, Daventry DC
Great Packington, N Warks BC
Great Palgrave, Breckland CI
Great Paxton, Huntingdonshire
   DC
Great Plumpton, Fylde BC
Great Plumstead, Broadland DC
Great Ponton, S Kesteven DC
Great Preston, Leeds City
Great Purston, S Northants CI
Great Ribston, Harrogate BC
Great Rissington, Cotswold DC

Great Rollright, W Oxon DC
Great Ryburgh, N Norfolk DC
Great Saling, Braintree DC
Great Salkeld, Eden DC
Great Sampford, Uttlesford DC
Great Sankey, Warrington BC
Great Saredon, S Staffs Cl
Great Shefford, W Berks DC
Great Shelford, S Cambs DC
Great Smeaton, Hambleton DC
Great Snoring, N Norfolk DC
Great Somerford, N Wilts DC
Great Stainton, Darlington BC
Great Stambridge, Rochford DC
Great Staughton,
  Huntingdonshire DC
Great Steeping, E Lindsey DC
Great Stonar, Dover DC
Great Stretton, Harborough DC
Great Strickland, Eden DC
Great Sturton, E Lindsey DC
Great Sutton, Ellesmere
  Port/Neston BC
Great Sutton, S Shropshire DC
Great Swinburne, Tynedale DC
Great Tew, W Oxon DC
Great Tey, Colchester BC
Great Thurlow, St Edmundsbury
  BC
Great Torrington, Torridge DC
Great Tosson, Alnwick DC
Great Totham, Maldon DC
Great Wakering, Rochford DC
Great Waldingfield, Babergh DC
Great Walsingham, N Norfolk DC
Great Waltham, Chelmsford BC
Great Warford, Macclesfield BC
Great Warley, Brentwood BC
Great Washbourne, Tewkesbury
  BC
Great Wenham, Babergh DC
Great Whelnetham, St
  Edmundsbury BC
Great Whittington, Tynedale DC
Great Wigborough, Colchester
  BC
Great Wilbraham, S Cambs DC
Great Wilne, S Derbys DC
Great Wishford, Salisbury DC
Great Witchingham, Broadland
  DC
Great Witcombe, Tewkesbury BC
Great Witley, Malvern Hills DC
Great Wolford, Stratford/Avon DC
Great Wratting, St Edmundsbury
  BC
Great Wymondley, N Herts DC
Great Wyrley, S Staffs Cl
Great Yarmouth, Gt Yarmouth BC
Great Yeldham, Braintree DC

Greatford, S Kesteven DC
Greatham, E Hants DC
Greatham, Hartlepool BC
Greatham, Horsham DC
Greatstone on Sea, Shepway DC
Greatworth, S Northants Cl
Green Fairfield, High Peak BC
Green Hammerton, Harrogate BC
Green Ore, Mendip DC
Green Street Green, Dartford BC
Green Tye, E Herts DC
Greencroft, Derwentside DC
Greendykes, Berwick-u-Tweed
  BC
Greenfield, E Lindsey DC
Greenfield, Mid Beds DC
Greenfield, Oldham MBC
Greenfield, S Oxon DC
Greenford, Ealing LBC
Greengairs, N Lanarkshire Cl
Greenhalgh, Fylde BC
Greenham, W Berks DC
Greenhaugh, Tynedale DC
Greenhead, Tynedale DC
Greenhill, Falkirk Cl
Greenhill, Sheffield City
Greenhithe, Dartford BC
Greenholm, E Ayrshire Cl
Greenholme, Eden DC
Greenhow Hill, Harrogate BC
Greenisland, Carrickfergus BC
Greenland Mains, Highland Cl
Greenlaw, Scottish Borders Cl
Greenleys, Milton Keynes Cl
Greenloaning, Perth/Kinross Cl
Greenmeadow, Torfaen CBC
Greenmount, Bury MBC
Greenock, Inverclyde Cl
Greenodd, S Lakeland DC
Greenrigg, W Lothian Cl
Greens Norton, S Northants Cl
Greenside, Gateshead Cl
Greenstead Green, Braintree DC
Greensted, Epping Forest DC
Greenwich, Greenwich LBC
Greep, Highland Cl
Greet, Tewkesbury BC
Greete, S Shropshire DC
Greetham, E Lindsey DC
Greetham, Rutland CC
Greetland, Calderdale MBC
Greetwell, W Lindsey DC
Greinton, Sedgemoor DC
Grendon, N Warks BC
Grendon, Wellingborough BC
Grendon Bishop, Herefordshire Cl
Grendon Underwood, Aylesbury
  Vale DC
Grendon Warren, Herefordshire
  Cl

Grenoside, Sheffield City
Gresford, Wrexham CBC
Gresham, N Norfolk DC
Gressenhall, Breckland Cl
Gressingham, Lancaster City
Greta Bridge, Teesdale DC
Gretna, Dumfries/Galloway Cl
Gretna Green, Dumfries/Galloway
  Cl
Gretton, Corby BC
Gretton, Tewkesbury BC
Grewelthorpe, Harrogate BC
Greysouthen, Allerdale BC
Greystead, Tynedale DC
Greysteel, Limavady BC
Greystoke, Eden DC
Greystones, Sheffield City
Greywell, Hart DC
Griffithstown, Torfaen CBC
Grigghall, S Lakeland DC
Grimeford, Chorley BC
Grimethorpe, Barnsley MBC
Grimley, Malvern Hills DC
Grimoldby, E Lindsey DC
Grimsargh, Preston City
Grimscote, S Northants Cl
Grimstead, Salisbury DC
Grimsthorpe, S Kesteven DC
Grimston, King's Lynn/W Norfolk
  BC
Grimston, Melton BC
Grimston, Selby DC
Grimstone, Ryedale DC
Grindale, E Riding of Yks
Grindleford, Derbys Dales DC
Grindleton, Ribble Valley BC
Grindlow, Derbys Dales DC
Grindon, Berwick-u-Tweed BC
Grindon, Staffs Moorlands DC
Gringley on the Hill, Bassetlaw
  DC
Grinsdale, Carlisle City
Grinshill, N Shropshire DC
Grinton, Richmondshire DC
Grisedale, S Lakeland DC
Gristhorpe, Scarborough BC
Griston, Breckland Cl
Grittleton, N Wilts DC
Grizebeck, S Lakeland DC
Grizedale, S Lakeland DC
Groby, Hinckley/Bosworth BC
Groes, Conwy CBC
Groombridge, Wealden DC
Grosmont, Monmouthshire CC
Grosmont, Scarborough BC
Groton, Babergh DC
Grove, Bassetlaw DC
Grove, Canterbury City
Grove, Vale of White Horse DC
Grove, Weymouth/Portland BC

Grove End, Stratford/Avon DC
Grove, The, Derwentside DC
Grovesend, Swansea C&C
Grudie, Highland CI
Gruids, Highland CI
Grumbla, Penwith DC
Grundisburgh, Suffolk C'l DC
Guardbridge, Fife CI
Guarlford, Malvern Hills DC
Guestling, Rother DC
Guestwick, Broadland DC
Gugh, Isles of Scilly CI
Guilden Morden, S Cambs DC
Guilden Sutton, Chester City
Guildford, Guildford BC
Guilsborough, Daventry DC
Guilsfield, Powys CC
Guilton, Dover DC
Guisborough, Redcar/Cleveland BC
Guiseley, Leeds City
Guist, Breckland CI
Guiting Power, Cotswold DC
Gulberwick, Shetland Is CI
Gullane, E Lothian CI
Gulval, Penwith DC
Gulworthy, W Devon BC
Gumley, Harborough DC
Gunby, E Lindsey DC
Gunby, S Kesteven DC
Gunnerside, Richmondshire DC
Gunnerton, Tynedale DC
Gunness, N Lincs CI
Gunthorpe, Newark/Sherwood DC
Gunthorpe, N Norfolk DC
Gunthorpe, Rutland CC
Gunthwaite, Barnsley MBC
Gunton, N Norfolk DC
Gunwalloe, Kerrier DC
Gurnard, Isle of Wight CI
Gurney Slade, Mendip DC
Gussage All Saints, E Dorset DC
Gussage St Michael, E Dorset DC
Guston, Dover DC
Guy's Cliffe, Warwick DC
Guy's Head, S Holland DC
Guyhirn, Fenland DC
Guyzance, Alnwick DC
Gwaenysgor, Flintshire CC
Gwaun cae Gurwen, Neath Port Talbot CBC
Gweek, Kerrier DC
Gwehelog Fawr, Monmouthshire CC
Gwennap, Carrick DC
Gwenter, Kerrier DC
Gwernaffield, Flintshire CC
Gwernyfed, Powys CC

Gwernymynydd, Flintshire CC
Gwersyllt, Wrexham CBC
Gwinear, Penwith DC
Gwyddelwern, Denbighshire CC
Gwytherin, Conwy CBC
Gyffin, Conwy CBC

Habberley, Shrewsbury/Atcham CI
Habberley, Wyre Forest DC
Habblesthorpe, Bassetlaw DC
Habergham Eaves, Burnley BC
Habrough, N E Lincs CI
Habton, Ryedale DC
Haccombe with Combe, Teignbridge DC
Haceby, N Kesteven DC
Hacheston, Suffolk C'l DC
Hackenthorpe, Sheffield City
Hackford, Broadland DC
Hackford, S Norfolk DC
Hackforth, Hambleton DC
Hackington, Canterbury City
Hackleton, S Northants CI
Hacklinge, Dover DC
Hackness, Scarborough BC
Hackney, Hackney LBC
Hackthorn, W Lindsey DC
Haconby, S Kesteven DC
Haddenham, Aylesbury Vale DC
Haddenham, E Cambs DC
Haddington, E Lothian CI
Haddington, N Kesteven DC
Haddiscoe, S Norfolk DC
Haddon, Huntingdonshire DC
Haddon, W Somerset DC
Hademore, Lichfield DC
Hadfield, High Peak BC
Hadham Cross, E Herts DC
Hadleigh (Essex), Castle Point BC
Hadleigh (Suffolk), Babergh DC
Hadley, Telford/Wrekin BC
Hadley Wood, Barnet LBC
Hadlow, Tonbridge/Malling BC
Hadlow Down, Wealden DC
Hadnall, N Shropshire DC
Hadstock, Uttlesford DC
Hadzor, Wychavon DC
Hafod Dinbych, Conwy CBC
Haggbeck, Carlisle City
Haggerston, Hackney LBC
Haggs, Falkirk CI
Hagley, Bromsgrove DC
Hagnaby, E Lindsey DC
Hagworthingham, E Lindsey DC
Haigh, Wigan MBC
Haighton, Preston City
Hail Weston, Huntingdonshire DC
Haile, Copeland BC

Hailes, Tewkesbury BC
Hailey, W Oxon DC
Hailsham, Wealden DC
Hainault, Redbridge LBC
Hainford, Broadland DC
Hainton, E Lindsey DC
Haisthorpe, E Riding of Yks
Halam, Newark/Sherwood DC
Halbeath, Fife CI
Halberton, Mid Devon DC
Haldenby, N Lincs CI
Hale, Halton BC
Hale, New Forest DC
Hale, Trafford MBC
Hale, Waverley BC
Halebarns, Trafford MBC
Hales, Newcastle-u-Lyme BC
Hales, S Norfolk DC
Halesowen, Dudley MBC
Halesworth, Waveney DC
Halewood, Knowsley MBC
Halford, Stratford/Avon DC
Halfpenny Green, Bridgnorth DC
Halfpenny Green, S Staffs CI
Halfway, Sheffield City
Halfway, W Berks DC
Halfway Bridge, Chichester DC
Halfway Houses, Swale BC
Halifax, Calderdale MBC
Halkirk, Highland CI
Halkyn, Flintshire CC
Hall Green, Birmingham City
Hallam Head, Sheffield City
Halland, Wealden DC
Hallaton, Harborough DC
Hallatrow, Bath/N E Somerset CI
Hallbankgate, Carlisle City
Hallend, Stratford/Avon DC
Hallglen, Falkirk CI
Hallikeld, Hambleton DC
Hallin, Highland CI
Halling, Medway CI
Hallington, E Lindsey DC
Hallington, Tynedale DC
Halloughton, Newark/Sherwood DC
Hallow, Malvern Hills DC
Hallthwaites, Copeland BC
Hallworthy, N Cornwall DC
Halmer End, Newcastle-u-Lyme BC
Halmore, Stroud DC
Halnaker, Chichester DC
Halsall, W Lancs DC
Halse, S Northants CI
Halse, Taunton Deane BC
Halsetown, Penwith DC
Halsham, E Riding of Yks
Halstead, Braintree DC
Halstead, Harborough DC

Halstead, Sevenoaks DC
Halstock, W Dorset DC
Halstow Marshes, Medway Cl
Haltham, E Lindsey DC
Haltoft End, Boston BC
Halton, Aylesbury Vale DC
Halton, Halton BC
Halton, Lancaster City
Halton East, Craven DC
Halton Gill, Craven DC
Halton Holegate, E Lindsey DC
Halton West, Craven DC
Haltwhistle, Tynedale DC
Halvergate, Broadland DC
Halwell, S Hams DC
Halwill, Torridge DC
Halwill Junction, Torridge DC
Ham, Dover DC
Ham, Kennet DC
Ham, Plymouth City
Ham, Richmond upon Thames
    LBC
Ham, Stroud DC
Ham, Highland Cl
Ham Green, N Somerset DC
Ham Street, Mendip DC
Hamaramore, Highland Cl
Hamaraverin, Highland Cl
Hamble le Rice, Eastleigh BC
Hambleden, Wycombe DC
Hambledon, Waverley BC
Hambledon, Winchester City
Hambleton, Rutland CC
Hambleton, Selby DC
Hambleton, Wyre BC
Hambridge, S Somerset DC
Hambrook, Chichester DC
Hameringham, E Lindsey DC
Hamerton, Huntingdonshire DC
Hamfallow, Stroud DC
Hamilton, S Lanarkshire Cl
Hammer, Chichester DC
Hammersmith,
    Hammersmith/Fulham LBC
Hammerwich, Lichfield DC
Hammoon, N Dorset DC
Hampen, Cotswold DC
Hampnett, Cotswold DC
Hampole, Doncaster MBC
Hampstead, Camden LBC
Hampstead Garden Suburb,
    Barnet LBC
Hampstead Norreys, W Berks DC
Hampsthwaite, Harrogate BC
Hampton, Chester City
Hampton, Richmond upon
    Thames LBC
Hampton, Wychavon DC
Hampton Bishop, Herefordshire
    Cl

Hampton Charles, Herefordshire
    Cl
Hampton Gay, Cherwell DC
Hampton Hill, Richmond upon
    Thames LBC
Hampton in Arden, Solihull MBC
Hampton Lovett, Wychavon DC
Hampton Lucy, Stratford/Avon
    DC
Hampton Nursery, Richmond
    upon Thames LBC
Hampton on the Hill, Warwick DC
Hampton Poyle, Cherwell DC
Hampton Wafer, Herefordshire Cl
Hampton Wick, Richmond upon
    Thames LBC
Hamsey, Lewes DC
Hamstall Ridware, Lichfield DC
Hamstead, Isle of Wight Cl
Hamstead Marshall, W Berks DC
Hamsterley, Teesdale DC
Hamsterley Colliery, Derwentside
    DC
Hamsterley Mill, Derwentside DC
Hamstreet, Ashford BC
Hamworthy, Poole BC
Hanbury, E Staffs BC
Hanbury, Wychavon DC
Hanchurch, Stafford BC
Handbridge, Chester City
Handcross, Mid Sussex DC
Handley, Chester City
Handsacre, Lichfield DC
Handsworth, Birmingham City
Handsworth, Sheffield City
Hanford, N Dorset DC
Hanford, Stoke-on-Trent City
Hanham, S Glos Cl
Hanham Abbots, S Glos Cl
Hankelow, Crewe/Nantwich BC
Hankerton, N Wilts DC
Hankham, Wealden DC
Hanley, Stoke-on-Trent City
Hanley Castle, Malvern Hills DC
Hanley Swan, Malvern Hills DC
Hanlith, Craven DC
Hanmer, Wrexham CBC
Hannah cum Hagnaby, E Lindsey
    DC
Hannington, Basingstoke/Deane
    BC
Hannington, Daventry DC
Hannington, Swindon BC
Hannington Wick, Swindon BC
Hanslope, Milton Keynes Cl
Hanthorpe, S Kesteven DC
Hanwell, Cherwell DC
Hanwell, Ealing LBC
Hanworth, Hounslow LBC
Hanworth, N Norfolk DC

Happisburgh, N Norfolk DC
Hapsford, Chester City
Hapton, Burnley BC
Hapton, S Norfolk DC
Harberton, S Hams DC
Harbertonford, S Hams DC
Harbledown, Canterbury City
Harborne, Birmingham City
Harborough Magna, Rugby BC
Harbottle, Alnwick DC
Harbridge, New Forest DC
Harburn, W Lothian Cl
Harbury, Stratford/Avon DC
Harby, Melton BC
Harby, Newark/Sherwood DC
Harden, Bradford MDC
Hardendale, Eden DC
Hardgate, W Dunbartonshire Cl
Hardham, Horsham DC
Hardingham, Breckland Cl
Hardingstone, Northampton BC
Hardington, Mendip DC
Hardington Mandeville, S
    Somerset DC
Hardley, S Norfolk DC
Hardmead, Milton Keynes Cl
Hardraw, Richmondshire DC
Hardstoft, Bolsover DC
Hardwick, Aylesbury Vale DC
Hardwick, Bassetlaw DC
Hardwick, Cherwell DC
Hardwick, S Cambs DC
Hardwick, S Norfolk DC
Hardwick, Stockton-on-Tees BC
Hardwick, Wellingborough BC
Hardwick, W Lindsey DC
Hardwick, W Oxon DC
Hardwicke, Stroud DC
Hare Street, E Herts DC
Hareby, E Lindsey DC
Hareden, Ribble Valley BC
Harefield, Hillingdon LBC
Harefield, Southampton City
Harelaw, Derwentside DC
Harescombe, Stroud DC
Haresfield, Stroud DC
Harestock, Winchester City
Harewood, Herefordshire Cl
Harewood, Leeds City
Harford, S Hams DC
Hargrave, E Northants Cl
Hargrave, St Edmundsbury BC
Haringey, Haringey LBC
Harker, Carlisle City
Harkstead, Babergh DC
Harlaston, Lichfield DC
Harlaw, Aberdeen City
Harlaxton, S Kesteven DC
Harle Syke, Burnley BC
Harlech, Gwynedd CC

Harlesden, Brent LBC
Harleston, Mid Suffolk DC
Harleston, S Norfolk DC
Harlestone, Daventry DC
Harley, Shrewsbury/Atcham Cl
Harling, Breckland Cl
Harlington, Doncaster MBC
Harlington, Hillingdon LBC
Harlington, Mid Beds DC
Harlosh, Highland Cl
Harlow, Harlow DC
Harlow Hill, Castle Morpeth BC
Harlthorpe, E Riding of Yks
Harlton, S Cambs DC
Harmans Cross, Purbeck DC
Harmby, Richmondshire DC
Harmer Green, Welwyn Hatfield DC
Harmston, N Kesteven DC
Harnhill, Cotswold DC
Harold Hill, Havering LBC
Harold Wood, Havering LBC
Harome, Ryedale DC
Harpenden, St Albans City/DC
Harpford, E Devon DC
Harpham, E Riding of Yks
Harpley, King's Lynn/W Norfolk BC
Harpley, Malvern Hills DC
Harpole, S Northants Cl
Harpsden, S Oxon DC
Harpswell, W Lindsey DC
Harpur Hill, High Peak BC
Harpurhey, Manchester City
Harrapool, Highland Cl
Harray, Orkney Is Cl
Harrietsham, Maidstone BC
Harrington, Allerdale BC
Harrington, E Lindsey DC
Harrington, Kettering BC
Harringworth, E Northants Cl
Harrogate, Harrogate BC
Harrold, Bedford BC
Harrow, Harrow LBC
Harrow on the Hill, Harrow LBC
Harrow Weald, Harrow LBC
Harrowbarrow, Caradon DC
Harrowby Without, S Kesteven DC
Harrowden, Bedford BC
Harston, S Cambs DC
Hart, Hartlepool BC
Hartburn, Castle Morpeth BC
Hartburn, Stockton-on-Tees BC
Hartest, Babergh DC
Hartfield, Wealden DC
Hartford, Vale Royal BC
Hartfordbridge, Hart DC
Hartforth, Richmondshire DC
Harthill, Chester City

Harthill, N Lanarkshire Cl
Harthill, Rotherham MBC
Harting, Chichester DC
Hartington, Derbys Dales DC
Hartington Upper Quarter, High Peak BC
Hartland, Torridge DC
Hartlebury, Wychavon DC
Hartlepool, Hartlepool BC
Hartley, Eden DC
Hartley, Sevenoaks DC
Hartley, Tunbridge Wells BC
Hartley Wespall, Basingstoke/Deane BC
Hartley Wintney, Hart DC
Hartleyburn, Tynedale DC
Hartlington, Craven DC
Hartlip, Swale BC
Hartmount, Highland Cl
Hartoft, Ryedale DC
Harton, Ryedale DC
Harton, S Shropshire DC
Harton, S Tyneside MBC
Hartpury, Forest of Dean DC
Hartshill, N Warks BC
Hartshorne, S Derbys DC
Hartsop, Eden DC
Hartwell, Aylesbury Vale DC
Hartwell, S Northants Cl
Hartwith cum Winsley, Harrogate BC
Hartwood, N Lanarkshire Cl
Harvington, Wychavon DC
Harwell, Vale of White Horse DC
Harwich, Tendring DC
Harwood, Teesdale DC
Harwood Dale, Scarborough BC
Harworth, Bassetlaw DC
Hascombe, Waverley BC
Haselbech, Daventry DC
Haselbury Plucknett, S Somerset DC
Haseley, Warwick DC
Haselor, Stratford/Avon DC
Hasfield, Tewkesbury BC
Haskayne, W Lancs DC
Hasketon, Suffolk C'l DC
Hasland, Chesterfield BC
Hasland, N E Derbys DC
Haslemere, Waverley DC
Haslingbourne, Chichester DC
Haslingden, Hyndburn BC
Haslingfield, S Cambs DC
Haslington, Crewe/Nantwich BC
Hassall, Congleton BC
Hassocks, Mid Sussex DC
Hassop, Derbys Dales DC
Hastingleigh, Ashford BC
Hastings, Hastings BC
Hastingwood, Epping Forest DC

Hastoe, Dacorum BC
Haswell, Easington DC
Hatch, Basingstoke/Deane BC
Hatch Beauchamp, Taunton Deane BC
Hatch End, Harrow LBC
Hatching Green, St Albans City/DC
Hatcliffe, N E Lincs Cl
Hatfield, Doncaster MBC
Hatfield, E Riding of Yks
Hatfield, Herefordshire Cl
Hatfield, Welwyn Hatfield DC
Hatfield Broad Oak, Uttlesford DC
Hatfield Heath, Uttlesford DC
Hatfield Peverel, Braintree DC
Hatfield Woodhouse, Doncaster MBC
Hatford, Vale of White Horse DC
Hatherleigh, W Devon BC
Hathern, Charnwood DC
Hatherop, Cotswold DC
Hathersage, Derbys Dales DC
Hatherton, Crewe/Nantwich BC
Hatherton, S Staffs Cl
Hatley St George, S Cambs DC
Hatton, Amber Valley BC
Hatton, E Lindsey DC
Hatton, S Derbys DC
Hatton, S Shropshire DC
Hatton, Warrington BC
Hatton, Warwick DC
Hatton Bank, Stratford/Avon DC
Hatton Heath, Chester City
Hatton of Cruden, Aberdeenshire Cl
Hatton Rock, Stratford/Avon DC
Haugh, E Lindsey DC
Haugh Head, Berwick-u-Tweed BC
Haugham, E Lindsey DC
Haughley, Mid Suffolk DC
Haughley Green, Mid Suffolk DC
Haughton, Bassetlaw DC
Haughton, Bridgnorth DC
Haughton, Crewe/Nantwich BC
Haughton, Oswestry BC
Haughton, Stafford BC
Haughton Common, Tynedale DC
Haultwick, E Herts DC
Hauxley, Alnwick DC
Hauxton, S Cambs DC
Havant, Havant BC
Havengore Island, Rochford DC
Havens, The, Pembrokeshire CC
Havenstreet, Isle of Wight Cl
Haverah, Harrogate BC
Havercroft, Wakefield MDC
Haverfordwest, Pembrokeshire CC

Havergate Island, Suffolk C'l DC
Haverhill, St Edmundsbury BC
Haverholme, N Kesteven DC
Haverigg, Copeland BC
Haveringland, Broadland DC
Haversham, Milton Keynes C'l
Haverthwaite, S Lakeland DC
Hawarden, Flintshire CC
Hawerby cum Beesby, N E Lincs C'l
Hawes, Richmondshire DC
Hawford, Wychavon DC
Hawick, Scottish Borders C'l
Hawkchurch, E Devon DC
Hawkedon, St Edmundsbury BC
Hawkenbury, Maidstone BC
Hawkesbury, S Glos C'l
Hawkhead, Renfrewshire C'l
Hawkhill, Alnwick DC
Hawkhurst, Tunbridge Wells BC
Hawkinge, Shepway DC
Hawkley, E Hants DC
Hawkridge, W Somerset DC
Hawkshaw, Bury MBC
Hawkshead, S Lakeland DC
Hawkshill Down, Dover DC
Hawkswick, Craven DC
Hawksworth, Rushcliffe BC
Hawkwell, Rochford DC
Hawley, Dartford BC
Hawley, Hart DC
Hawling, Tewkesbury BC
Hawnby, Ryedale DC
Haworth, Bradford MDC
Hawridge, Chiltern DC
Hawsker, Scarborough BC
Hawstead, St Edmundsbury BC
Hawthorn, Easington DC
Hawton, Newark/Sherwood DC
Haxby, City of York C'l
Haxey, N Lincs C'l
Hay on Wye, Powys CC
Hay Street, E Herts DC
Haydock, St Helens MBC
Haydon, Tynedale DC
Haydon, W Dorset DC
Haydon Bridge, Tynedale DC
Haydon Wick, Swindon BC
Haye, Caradon DC
Hayes, Bromley LBC
Hayes, Hillingdon LBC
Hayfield, High Peak BC
Hayhill, E Ayrshire C'l
Hayle, Penwith DC
Hayling Island, Havant BC
Haynes, Mid Beds DC
Hayscastle, Pembrokeshire CC
Hayton, Allerdale BC
Hayton, Bassetlaw DC
Hayton, Carlisle City

Hayton, E Riding of Yks
Hayton's Bent, S Shropshire DC
Haywards Heath, Mid Sussex DC
Haywood, Herefordshire C'l
Haywood, S Norfolk DC
Haywood Oaks, Newark/Sherwood DC
Hazel Grove, Stockport MBC
Hazel Slade, Cannock Chase DC
Hazelbury Bryan, N Dorset DC
Hazeleigh, Maldon DC
Hazeley, Hart DC
Hazelrigg, Berwick-u-Tweed BC
Hazelwood, Amber Valley BC
Hazlemere, Wycombe DC
Hazlerigg, Newcastle City
Hazleton, Cotswold DC
Hazlewood, Craven DC
Hazlewood, Selby DC
Heacham, King's Lynn/W Norfolk BC
Head of Muir, Falkirk C'l
Headbourne Worthy, Winchester City
Headcorn, Maidstone BC
Headingley, Leeds City
Headlam, Teesdale DC
Headley, Basingstoke/Deane BC
Headley, E Hants DC
Headley, Mole Valley DC
Headon cum Upton, Bassetlaw DC
Heads Nook, Carlisle City
Heage, Amber Valley BC
Healaugh, Richmondshire DC
Healey, Harrogate BC
Healey, Tynedale DC
Healeyfield, Derwentside DC
Healing, N E Lincs C'l
Heamoor, Penwith DC
Heanor, Amber Valley BC
Heanton Punchardon, N Devon DC
Heap Bridge, Bury MBC
Heapey, Chorley BC
Heapham, W Lindsey DC
Heast, Highland C'l
Heath, Cardiff CC
Heath, N E Derbys DC
Heath, S Beds DC
Heath, S Shropshire DC
Heath Charnock, Chorley BC
Heath End, Basingstoke/Deane BC
Heath End, Rushmoor BC
Heath End, Stratford/Avon DC
Heath Hayes, Cannock Chase DC
Heath Hill, Bridgnorth DC
Heathall, Dumfries/Galloway C'l

Heathcote, Derbys Dales DC
Heathencote, S Northants C'l
Heather, N W Leics DC
Heatherfield, Highland C'l
Heatherlea, Highland C'l
Heathfield, Richmond upon Thames LBC
Heathfield, S Ayrshire C'l
Heathfield, Teignbridge DC
Heathfield, Wealden DC
Heathrow Airport, Hillingdon LBC
Heathton, Bridgnorth DC
Heathylee, Staffs Moorlands DC
Heaton, Lancaster City
Heaton, Newcastle City
Heaton, Staffs Moorlands DC
Hebburn, S Tyneside MBC
Hebden, Craven DC
Hebden Bridge, Calderdale MBC
Hebden Green, Vale Royal BC
Hebron, Castle Morpeth BC
Heck, Selby DC
Heckfield, Hart DC
Heckingham, S Norfolk DC
Heckington, N Kesteven DC
Heckmondwike, Kirklees MC
Heddington, N Wilts DC
Heddon on the Wall, Castle Morpeth BC
Hedenham, S Norfolk DC
Hedge End, Eastleigh BC
Hedgeley, Alnwick DC
Hedgerley, S Bucks DC
Hedley on the Hill, Tynedale DC
Hednesford, Cannock Chase DC
Hedon, E Riding of Yks
Hedsor, Wycombe DC
Heelands, Milton Keynes C'l
Heeley, Sheffield City
Heggerscales, Eden DC
Heighington, Darlington BC
Heighington, N Kesteven DC
Heights of Kinlochewe, Highland C'l
Heiton, Scottish Borders C'l
Helbeck, Eden DC
Heldon, Moray C'l
Helensburgh, Argyll/Bute C'l
Helford, Kerrier DC
Helhoughton, N Norfolk DC
Helions Bumpstead, Braintree DC
Helland, N Cornwall DC
Hellesdon, Broadland DC
Hellidon, Daventry DC
Hellifield, Craven DC
Hellingly, Wealden DC
Hellington, S Norfolk DC
Helmdon, S Northants C'l
Helmingham, Mid Suffolk DC
Helmsdale, Highland C'l

Helmsley, Ryedale DC
Helmshore, Rossendale BC
Helperby, Hambleton DC
Helperthorpe, Ryedale DC
Helpringham, N Kesteven DC
Helpston, Peterborough City
Helsby, Vale Royal BC
Helsington, S Lakeland DC
Helston, Kerrier DC
Helstone, N Cornwall DC
Helwith Bridge, Craven DC
Hemblington, Broadland DC
Hemel Hempstead, Dacorum BC
Hemingbrough, Selby DC
Hemingby, E Lindsey DC
Hemingford Abbots,
    Huntingdonshire DC
Hemingford Grey,
    Huntingdonshire DC
Hemingstone, Mid Suffolk DC
Hemington, E Northants Cl
Hemington, Mendip DC
Hemington, N W Leics DC
Hemley, Suffolk C'l DC
Hempholme, E Riding of Yks
Hempnall, S Norfolk DC
Hempstead, N Norfolk DC
Hempstead, Uttlesford DC
Hempton, Cherwell DC
Hempton, N Norfolk DC
Hemsby, Gt Yarmouth BC
Hemswell, W Lindsey DC
Hemswell Cliff, W Lindsey DC
Hemsworth, Sheffield City
Hemsworth, Wakefield MDC
Hemyock, Mid Devon DC
Henbury, Bristol City
Henbury, Macclesfield BC
Henderskelfe, Ryedale DC
Hendon, Barnet LBC
Hendon, Sunderland City
Henfield, Horsham DC
Henfynyw, Ceredigion CC
Hengoed, Oswestry BC
Hengrave, St Edmundsbury BC
Henham, Uttlesford DC
Henham, Waveney DC
Henhull, Crewe/Nantwich BC
Henley, Chichester DC
Henley, Mid Suffolk DC
Henley, S Shropshire DC
Henley in Arden, Stratford/Avon
    DC
Henley on Thames, S Oxon DC
Henley Park, Guildford BC
Henllan, Denbighshire CC
Henllan (part), Conwy CBC
Henllanfallteg, Carmarthenshire
    CC
Henllys, Torfaen CBC

Henlow, Mid Beds DC
Hennock, Teignbridge DC
Henny Street, Braintree DC
Henryd, Conwy CBC
Hensall, Selby DC
Henshaw, Tynedale DC
Henstead, Waveney DC
Henstridge, S Somerset DC
Hentland, Herefordshire Cl
Henton, Mendip DC
Henton, S Oxon DC
Henwood, Caradon DC
Hepburn, Berwick-u-Tweed BC
Hepple, Alnwick DC
Hepscott, Castle Morpeth BC
Heptonstall, Calderdale MBC
Hepworth, Kirklees MC
Hepworth, St Edmundsbury BC
Herbrandston, Pembrokeshire CC
Herdings, Sheffield City
Hereford City, Herefordshire Cl
Heribost, Highland Cl
Heribusta, Highland Cl
Heriot, Scottish Borders Cl
Hermiston, Edinburgh City
Hermitage, Chichester DC
Hermitage, W Berks DC
Hermitage, W Dorset DC
Herne, Canterbury City
Herne Bay, Canterbury City
Hernhill, Swale BC
Herodsfoot, Caradon DC
Heronden, Dover DC
Herongate, Brentwood BC
Herons Ghyll, Wealden DC
Heronsgate, Three Rivers DC
Herriard, Basingstoke/Deane BC
Herringby, Gt Yarmouth BC
Herringfleet, Waveney DC
Herringswell, Forest Heath DC
Herrington, Sunderland City
Hersden, Canterbury City
Hersham, Elmbridge BC
Herstmonceux, Wealden DC
Hertford, E Herts DC
Hertford Heath, E Herts DC
Hertingfordbury, E Herts DC
Hesket, Eden DC
Hesket Newmarket, Allerdale BC
Hesketh with Becconsall, W
    Lancs DC
Heskin, Chorley BC
Hesleden, Easington DC
Heslerton, Ryedale DC
Hesleyhurst, Alnwick DC
Heslington, City of York Cl
Hessay, City of York Cl
Hessenford, Caradon DC
Hessett, Mid Suffolk DC
Hessle, E Riding of Yks

Heston, Hounslow LBC
Heswall, Wirral MBC
Hethe, Cherwell DC
Hethel, S Norfolk DC
Hethersett, S Norfolk DC
Hethersgill, Carlisle City
Hethpool, Berwick-u-Tweed BC
Hett, Durham City
Hetton, Craven DC
Hetton, Harrogate BC
Hetton le Hole, Sunderland City
Heugh, Castle Morpeth BC
Heveningham, Suffolk C'l DC
Hever, Sevenoaks DC
Heversham, S Lakeland DC
Hevingham, Broadland DC
Hewelsfield, Forest of Dean DC
Hewick, Harrogate BC
Heworth Without, City of York Cl
Hexham, Tynedale DC
Hexton, N Herts DC
Hexworthy, W Devon BC
Heybridge, Brentwood BC
Heybridge, Maldon DC
Heybridge Basin, Maldon DC
Heydon, Broadland DC
Heydon, S Cambs DC
Heydour, S Kesteven DC
Heysham, Lancaster City
Heyshott, Chichester DC
Heytesbury, W Wilts DC
Heythrop, W Oxon DC
Heywood, Rochdale MBC
Heywood, W Wilts DC
Hibaldstow, N Lincs Cl
Hickleton, Doncaster MBC
Hickling, N Norfolk DC
Hickling, Rushcliffe BC
Hickstead, Mid Sussex DC
High Abbotside, Richmondshire
    DC
High Ackworth, Wakefield MDC
High Bankhill, Eden DC
High Beach, Epping Forest DC
High Bentham, Craven DC
High Bickington, Torridge DC
High Birkwith, Craven DC
High Bishopside, Harrogate BC
High Blantyre, S Lanarkshire Cl
High Bonnybridge, Falkirk Cl
High Bradfield, Sheffield City
High Buston, Alnwick DC
High Catton, E Riding of Yks
High Cogges, W Oxon DC
High Coniscliffe, Darlington BC
High Cross, E Hants DC
High Cross, E Herts DC
High Easter, Uttlesford DC
High Ellington, Harrogate BC
High Ercall, Telford/Wrekin BC

High Garrett, Braintree DC
High Grange, Wear Valley DC
High Green, Sheffield City
High Halden, Ashford BC
High Halstow, Medway Cl
High Ham, S Somerset DC
High Hatton, N Shropshire DC
High Hesket, Eden DC
High Hesledon, Easington DC
High Houses, Richmondshire DC
High Hoyland, Barnsley MBC
High Hunsley, E Riding of Yks
High Hurstwood, Wealden DC
High Kelling, N Norfolk DC
High Laver, Epping Forest DC
High Legh, Macclesfield BC
High Littleton, Bath/N E Somerset
   Cl
High Melton, Doncaster MBC
High Newton, S Lakeland DC
High Newton by the Sea, Alnwick
   DC
High Offley, Stafford BC
High Ongar, Epping Forest DC
High Onn, Stafford BC
High Roothing, Uttlesford DC
High Salvington, Worthing BC
High Shaw, Richmondshire DC
High Spen, Gateshead Cl
High Street, Restormel BC
High Street Green, Mid Suffolk
   DC
High Town, Luton BC
High Toynton, E Lindsey DC
High Trewhitt, Alnwick DC
High Valleyfield, Fife Cl
High Worsall, Hambleton DC
High Wray, S Lakeland DC
High Wych, E Herts DC
High Wycombe, Wycombe DC
Higham, Babergh DC
Higham, Forest Heath DC
Higham, Gravesham BC
Higham, N E Derbys DC
Higham, Pendle BC
Higham Ferrers, E Northants Cl
Higham Hill, Waltham Forest LBC
Higham on the Hill,
   Hinckley/Bosworth BC
Higham Wood, Tonbridge/Malling
   BC
Highampton, W Devon BC
Highams Park, Waltham Forest
   LBC
Highbridge, Sedgemoor DC
Highbridge, Highland Cl
Highbrook, Mid Sussex DC
Highburton, Kirklees MC
Highbury, Islington LBC

Highclere, Basingstoke/Deane
   BC
Highcliffe, Christchurch BC
Higher Ballam, Fylde BC
Higher Hurdsfield, Macclesfield
   BC
Higher Kinnerton, Flintshire CC
Higher Poynton, Macclesfield BC
Higher Town, Isles of Scilly Cl
Higher Walreddon, W Devon BC
Higher Walton, S Ribble BC
Higher Wych, Chester City
Highfield, Gateshead Cl
Highfield, Sheffield City
Highfield, Tendring DC
Highfields, S Cambs DC
Highgate, Haringey LBC
Highland Boath, Highland Cl
Highleadon, Forest of Dean DC
Highleigh, Chichester DC
Highley, Bridgnorth DC
Highmoor, S Oxon DC
Highmoor Cross, S Oxon DC
Highnam, Tewkesbury BC
Highsted, Swale BC
Hightown, Congleton BC
Hightown, Sefton MBC
Hightown Green, Mid Suffolk DC
Highwood, Chelmsford BC
Highworth, Swindon BC
Hilborough, Breckland Cl
Hilden, Lisburn City
Hildenborough, Tonbridge/Malling
   BC
Hildersham, S Cambs DC
Hilderstone, Stafford BC
Hilderthorpe, E Riding of Yks
Hilfield, W Dorset DC
Hilgay, King's Lynn/W Norfolk BC
Hill, S Glos Cl
Hill and Moor, Wychavon DC
Hill Brow (part), Chichester DC
Hill Chorlton, Newcastle-u-Lyme
   BC
Hill Croome, Malvern Hills DC
Hill End, Bridgnorth DC
Hill End, Wear Valley DC
Hill Head, Fareham BC
Hill of Beath, Fife Cl
Hill of Fearn, Highland Cl
Hill Top, New Forest DC
Hillam, Selby DC
Hillborough, Canterbury City
Hillborough, Stratford/Avon DC
Hillbrook, Southampton City
Hilldale, W Lancashire DC
Hilldyke, Boston BC
Hillend, Fife Cl
Hillesden, Aylesbury Vale DC
Hillesley, Stroud DC

Hillhall, Lisburn City
Hillhampton, Malvern Hills DC
Hillhead, Glasgow City
Hilliard's Cross (part), Lichfield
   DC
Hillington, King's Lynn/W Norfolk
   BC
Hillmorton, Rugby BC
Hillpark, Glasgow City
Hillsborough, Lisburn City
Hillsborough, Sheffield City
Hillside, Angus Cl
Hilltown, Dundee City
Hilltown, Newry/Mourne DC
Hilmarton, N Wilts DC
Hilperton, W Wilts DC
Hilsea, Portsmouth City
Hilton, Bridgnorth DC
Hilton, Eden DC
Hilton, Huntingdonshire DC
Hilton, N Dorset DC
Hilton, S Derbys DC
Hilton, Stockton-on-Tees BC
Hilton, Teesdale DC
Hilton, Highland Cl
Hilton of Cadboll, Highland Cl
Himbleton, Wychavon DC
Himley, S Staffs Cl
Hincaster, S Lakeland DC
Hinchley Wood, Elmbridge BC
Hinckley, Hinckley/Bosworth BC
Hinderclay, Mid Suffolk DC
Hinderwell, Scarborough BC
Hindford, Oswestry BC
Hindley, Wigan MBC
Hindley Green, Wigan MBC
Hindlip, Wychavon DC
Hindolveston, N Norfolk DC
Hindon, Salisbury DC
Hindringham, N Norfolk DC
Hingham, S Norfolk DC
Hinstock, N Shropshire DC
Hintlesham, Babergh DC
Hinton, Daventry DC
Hinton, New Forest DC
Hinton, Shrewsbury/Atcham Cl
Hinton, S Glos Cl
Hinton, Stroud DC
Hinton Ampner, Winchester City
Hinton Blewett, Bath/N E
   Somerset Cl
Hinton Charterhouse, Bath/N E
   Somerset Cl
Hinton in the Hedges, S
   Northants Cl
Hinton Martell, E Dorset DC
Hinton on the Green, Wychavon
   DC
Hinton Parva, Swindon BC

Hinton St George, S Somerset DC
Hinton St Mary, N Dorset DC
Hinton Waldrist, Vale of White Horse DC
Hints, Lichfield DC
Hints, S Shropshire DC
Hinwick, Bedford BC
Hinxhill, Ashford BC
Hinxton, S Cambs DC
Hinxworth, N Herts DC
Hipperholme, Calderdale MBC
Hipswell, Richmondshire DC
Hirst, Wansbeck DC
Hirst Courtney, Selby DC
Hirwaun, Rhondda Cynon Taff CBC
Histon, S Cambs DC
Hitcham, Babergh DC
Hitchin, N Herts DC
Hittisleigh, Mid Devon DC
Hixon, Stafford BC
Hoaden, Dover DC
Hoar Cross, E Staffs BC
Hoath, Canterbury City
Hobarris, S Shropshire DC
Hobkirk, Scottish Borders CI
Hobson, Derwentside DC
Hoby, Melton BC
Hockering, Breckland CI
Hockerton, Newark/Sherwood DC
Hockham, Breckland CI
Hockley, Rochford DC
Hockley, Tamworth BC
Hockley Heath, Solihull MBC
Hockliffe, S Beds DC
Hockwold cum Wilton, King's Lynn/W Norfolk BC
Hockworthy, Mid Devon DC
Hoddesdon, Broxbourne BC
Hoddlesden, Blackburn with Darwen BC
Hoddom, Dumfries/Galloway CI
Hodge Hill, Birmingham City
Hodge Lea, Milton Keynes CI
Hodnell, Stratford/Avon DC
Hodnet, N Shropshire DC
Hodsock, Bassetlaw DC
Hoe, Breckland CI
Hoe Gate, Winchester City
Hoff, Eden DC
Hoggeston, Aylesbury Vale DC
Hoghton, Chorley BC
Hoghton (part), S Ribble BC
Hognaston, Derbys Dales DC
Hogshaw, Aylesbury Vale DC
Hogsthorpe, E Lindsey DC
Holbeach, S Holland DC
Holbeach Bank, S Holland DC
Holbeach Drove, S Holland DC

Holbeach St Johns, S Holland DC
Holbeach St Marks, S Holland DC
Holbeach St Matthew, S Holland DC
Holbeck, Bassetlaw DC
Holberrow Green, Wychavon DC
Holbeton, S Hams DC
Holbrook, Amber Valley BC
Holbrook, Babergh DC
Holbrooks, Coventry City MDC
Holburn, Berwick-u-Tweed BC
Holbury Blackfield, New Forest DC
Holcombe, Bury MBC
Holcombe, Mendip DC
Holcombe Brook, Bury MBC
Holcombe Burnell, Teignbridge DC
Holcombe Rogus, Mid Devon DC
Holcot, Daventry DC
Holden, Ribble Valley BC
Holdenby, Daventry DC
Holdfast, Malvern Hills DC
Holdgate, S Shropshire DC
Holdingham, N Kesteven DC
Holford, W Somerset DC
Holker, S Lakeland DC
Holkham, N Norfolk DC
Hollacombe, Torridge DC
Holland Fen, Boston BC
Holland on Sea, Tendring DC
Hollesley, Suffolk CI DC
Hollingbourne, Maidstone BC
Hollinghill, Alnwick DC
Hollington, Derbys Dales DC
Hollingwood, Chesterfield BC
Hollins, Bury MBC
Hollinsclough, Staffs Moorlands DC
Hollinsend, Sheffield City
Hollinswood, Telford/Wrekin BC
Hollinwood, N Shropshire DC
Holloway, Amber Valley BC
Holloway, Islington LBC
Hollowell, Daventry DC
Holly Green, Wycombe DC
Hollybush, E Ayrshire CI
Hollybush, Malvern Hills DC
Hollybush, Torfaen CBC
Hollycombe, Chichester DC
Hollym, E Riding of Yks
Hollyood, Bromsgrove DC
Holm, Orkney Is CI
Holmbury St Mary, Mole Valley DC
Holme, Hambleton DC
Holme, Huntingdonshire DC
Holme, Newark/Sherwood DC
Holme, N Lincs CI
Holme, S Lakeland DC

Holme Abbey, Allerdale BC
Holme Chapel, Burnley BC
Holme East Waver, Allerdale BC
Holme Hale, Breckland CI
Holme Lacy, Herefordshire CI
Holme Low, Allerdale BC
Holme Next the Sea, King's Lynn/W Norfolk BC
Holme on Spalding Moor, E Riding of Yks
Holme on the Wolds, E Riding of Yks
Holme Pierrepont, Rushcliffe BC
Holme St Cuthbert, Allerdale BC
Holme Valley, Kirklees MC
Holmer, Herefordshire CI
Holmes Chapel, Congleton BC
Holmescales, S Lakeland DC
Holmesfield, N E Derbys DC
Holmeswood, W Lancs DC
Holmewood, N E Derbys DC
Holmfirth, Kirklees MC
Holmisdale, Highland CI
Holmpton, E Riding of Yks
Holmrook, Copeland BC
Holmside, Derwentside DC
Holmston, S Ayrshire CI
Holmwood, Mole Valley DC
Holne, S Hams DC
Holnest, W Dorset DC
Holnicote, W Somerset DC
Holsworthy, Torridge DC
Holsworthy Beacon, Torridge DC
Holsworthy Hamlets, Torridge DC
Holt, E Dorset DC
Holt, Malvern Hills DC
Holt, N Norfolk DC
Holt, W Wilts DC
Holt, Wrexham CBC
Holt End, Bromsgrove DC
Holt's Green, N Herts DC
Holtby, City of York CI
Holtby, Hambleton DC
Holton, S Oxon DC
Holton, S Somerset DC
Holton, Waveney DC
Holton cum Beckering, W Lindsey DC
Holton Heath, Purbeck DC
Holton le Clay, E Lindsey DC
Holton le Moor, W Lindsey DC
Holton St Mary, Babergh DC
Holtye, Wealden DC
Holverston, S Norfolk DC
Holwell, Melton BC
Holwell, N Herts DC
Holwell, W Dorset DC
Holwell, W Oxon DC
Holwick, Teesdale DC
Holy Cross, Bromsgrove DC

Holy Island, Berwick-u-Tweed BC
Holybourne, E Hants DC
Holyfield, Epping Forest DC
Holyhead, Isle of Anglesey CC
Holymoorside, N E Derbys DC
Holyport, Windsor/Maidenhead RB
Holystone, Alnwick DC
Holytown, N Lanarkshire Cl
Holywell, Blyth Valley BC
Holywell, Flintshire CC
Holywell, S Kesteven DC
Holywell, W Dorset DC
Holywell Bay (part), Carrick DC
Holywell Bay (part), Restormel BC
Holywell cum Needingworth, Huntingdonshire DC
Holywell Row, Forest Heath DC
Holywood, Dumfries/Galloway Cl
Homersfield, Waveney DC
Honddu Isaf, Powys CC
Honey Hill, Canterbury City
Honeybourne, Wychavon DC
Honeychurch, W Devon BC
Honicknowle, Plymouth City
Honiley, Warwick DC
Honing, N Norfolk DC
Honingham, Broadland DC
Honington, St Edmundsbury BC
Honington, S Kesteven DC
Honington, Stratford/Avon DC
Honiton, E Devon DC
Honley, Kirklees MC
Hoo, Medway Cl
Hoo, Suffolk C'l DC
Hood Grange, Hambleton DC
Hooe, Plymouth City
Hooe, Wealden DC
Hook, E Riding of Yks
Hook, Hart DC
Hook, Kingston upon Thames Royal Borough
Hook, Pembrokeshire CC
Hook End, Brentwood BC
Hook Green, Dartford BC
Hook Norton, Cherwell DC
Hooke, W Dorset DC
Hookwood, Mole Valley DC
Hoole, Chester City
Hoon, S Derbys DC
Hooton, Ellesmere Port/Neston BC
Hooton Levitt, Rotherham MBC
Hooton Pagnell, Doncaster MBC
Hooton Roberts, Rotherham MBC
Hope, Flintshire CC
Hope, High Peak BC
Hope, S Shropshire DC
Hope, Teesdale DC

Hope Bagot, S Shropshire DC
Hope Bowdler, S Shropshire DC
Hope Mansell, Herefordshire Cl
Hope under Dinmore, Herefordshire Cl
Hope Woodlands, High Peak BC
Hopeman, Moray Cl
Hopesay, S Shropshire DC
Hopperton, Harrogate BC
Hopstone, Bridgnorth DC
Hopton, Derbys Dales DC
Hopton, St Edmundsbury BC
Hopton, Stafford BC
Hopton Cangeford, S Shropshire DC
Hopton Castle, S Shropshire DC
Hopton cum Knettishall, St Edmundsbury BC
Hopton on Sea, Gt Yarmouth BC
Hopton Wafers, S Shropshire DC
Hopwas, Lichfield DC
Hopwood, Bromsgrove DC
Horam, Wealden DC
Horbling, S Kesteven DC
Horbury, Wakefield MDC
Horden, Easington DC
Horderley, S Shropshire DC
Hordle, New Forest DC
Hordley, N Shropshire DC
Horham, Mid Suffolk DC
Horkstow, N Lincs Cl
Horley, Cherwell DC
Horley, Reigate/Banstead BC
Hormead, E Herts DC
Horn, Rutland CC
Hornblotton Green, Mendip DC
Hornby, Hambleton DC
Hornby, Lancaster City
Hornby, Richmondshire DC
Horncastle, E Lindsey DC
Hornchurch, Havering LBC
Horncliffe, Berwick-u-Tweed BC
Horndean, E Hants DC
Horndon, Thurrock BC
Horne, Tandridge DC
Horneval, Highland Cl
Horning, N Norfolk DC
Horninghold, Harborough DC
Horninglow, E Staffs BC
Horningsea, S Cambs DC
Horningsham, W Wilts DC
Horningtoft, Breckland Cl
Horns Cross, Torridge DC
Hornsby, Carlisle City
Hornsea, E Riding of Yks
Hornsey, Haringey LBC
Hornton, Cherwell DC
Horrabridge, W Devon BC
Horringer, St Edmundsbury BC
Horsebridge, Test Valley BC

Horsebridge, Wealden DC
Horsebrook, S Staffs Cl
Horsehay, Telford/Wrekin BC
Horseheath, S Cambs DC
Horsehouse, Richmondshire DC
Horsell, Woking BC
Horsenden, Wycombe DC
Horseway, Fenland DC
Horsey, N Norfolk DC
Horsey Island, Tendring DC
Horsford, Broadland DC
Horsforth, Leeds City
Horsham, Horsham DC
Horsham, Malvern Hills DC
Horsham St Faith, Broadland DC
Horsington, E Lindsey DC
Horsington, S Somerset DC
Horsley, Amber Valley BC
Horsley, Stroud DC
Horsley, Tynedale DC
Horsley Cross, Tendring DC
Horsley Woodhouse, Amber Valley BC
Horsleycross Street, Tendring DC
Horsmonden, Tunbridge Wells BC
Horspath, S Oxon DC
Horstead, Broadland DC
Horsted Keynes, Mid Sussex DC
Horton, Aylesbury Vale DC
Horton, Berwick-u-Tweed BC
Horton, E Dorset DC
Horton, Kennet DC
Horton, Ribble Valley BC
Horton, S Glos Cl
Horton, S Northants Cl
Horton, S Somerset DC
Horton, Staffs Moorlands DC
Horton, Windsor/Maidenhead RB
Horton by Malpas, Chester City
Horton cum Studley, Cherwell DC
Horton Heath, Eastleigh BC
Horton in Ribblesdale, Craven DC
Horton Kirby, Sevenoaks DC
Horwich, Bolton MBC
Horwich End, High Peak BC
Horwood, N Devon DC
Hose, Melton BC
Hotham, E Riding of Yks
Hothersall, Ribble Valley BC
Hothfield, Ashford BC
Hoton, Charnwood DC
Hough, Crewe/Nantwich BC
Hough on the Hill, S Kesteven DC
Hougham, S Kesteven DC
Hougham Without, Dover DC
Houghton, Arun DC
Houghton, Carlisle City
Houghton, Huntingdonshire DC

Houghton, King's Lynn/W Norfolk BC
Houghton, Test Valley BC
Houghton Conquest, Mid Beds DC
Houghton le Side, Darlington BC
Houghton le Spring, Sunderland City
Houghton on the Hill, Harborough DC
Houghton Regis, S Beds DC
Houghton St Giles, N Norfolk DC
Houlskye, Scarborough BC
Hound, Eastleigh BC
Hound Green, Hart DC
Houndshill, Stratford/Avon DC
Hounslow, Hounslow LBC
Houston, Renfrewshire CI
Houstry, Highland CI
Hove, Brighton/Hove CI
Hoveringham, Newark/Sherwood DC
Hoveton, N Norfolk DC
Hovingham, Ryedale DC
How, Carlisle City
How Caple, Herefordshire CI
How Green, E Herts DC
Howden, E Riding of Yks
Howden le Wear, Wear Valley DC
Howe, Hambleton DC
Howe, S Norfolk DC
Howe Green, Chelmsford BC
Howe Street, Braintree DC
Howe Street, Chelmsford BC
Howell, N Kesteven DC
Howgate, Midlothian CI
Howgrave, Hambleton DC
Howick, Alnwick DC
Howlett End, Uttlesford DC
Howlown, Eden DC
Howsham, N Lincs CI
Howsham, Ryedale DC
Howwood, Renfrewshire CI
Hoxne, Mid Suffolk DC
Hoxton, Hackney LBC
Hoy, Orkney Is CI
Hoylake, Wirral MBC
Hoyland, Barnsley MBC
Hoylandswaine, Barnsley MBC
Hubberholme, Craven DC
Hubbert's Bridge, Boston BC
Huby, Hambleton DC
Huby, Harrogate BC
Hucclecote, Tewkesbury BC
Hucking, Maidstone BC
Hucknall, Ashfield DC
Huddersfield, Kirklees MC
Huddington, Wychavon DC
Huddleston, Selby DC
Hudswell, Richmondshire DC

Huggate, E Riding of Yks
Hugh Town, Isles of Scilly CI
Hughenden, Wycombe DC
Hughley, Shrewsbury/Atcham CI
Hughton, Highland CI
Hugill, S Lakeland DC
Huish, Kennet DC
Huish, Torridge DC
Huish Champflower, W Somerset DC
Huish Episcopi, S Somerset DC
Hulcote, Mid Beds DC
Hulcote, S Northants CI
Hulcott, Aylesbury Vale DC
Hulland, Derbys Dales DC
Hulland Ward, Derbys Dales DC
Hullavington, N Wilts DC
Hullbridge, Rochford DC
Hulme End, Staffs Moorlands DC
Hulme Walfield, Congleton BC
Hulver Street, Waveney DC
Humber, Herefordshire CI
Humberston, N E Lincs CI
Humbie, E Lothian CI
Humbleton, Berwick-u-Tweed BC
Humbleton, E Riding of Yks
Humby, S Kesteven DC
Hume, Scottish Borders CI
Humshaugh, Tynedale DC
Huncoat, Hyndburn BC
Huncote, Blaby DC
Hunderthwaite, Teesdale DC
Hundleby, E Lindsey DC
Hundleton, Pembrokeshire CC
Hundon, St Edmundsbury BC
Hundred Acres, Winchester City
Hundred End, W Lancs DC
Hungarton, Harborough DC
Hungerford, W Berks DC
Hungerford Newtown, W Berks DC
Hungladder, Highland CI
Hungry Bentley, Derbys Dales DC
Hunmanby, Scarborough BC
Hunnington, Bromsgrove DC
Hunscote, Stratford/Avon DC
Hunsdon, E Herts DC
Hunshelf, Barnsley MBC
Hunsingore, Harrogate BC
Hunsonby, Eden DC
Hunstanton, King's Lynn/W Norfolk BC
Hunstanworth, Wear Valley DC
Hunsterson, Crewe/Nantwich BC
Hunston, Chichester DC
Hunston, Mid Suffolk DC
Hunstrete, Bath/N E Somerset CI
Hunt's Cross, Liverpool City
Hunter's Quay, Argyll/Bute CI

Hunterhill, Renfrewshire CI
Huntingdon, Huntingdonshire DC
Huntingfield, Suffolk C'l DC
Huntington, Chester City
Huntington, City of York CI
Huntington, Herefordshire CI
Huntington, S Staffs CI
Huntley, Forest of Dean DC
Huntly, Aberdeenshire CI
Hunton, Maidstone BC
Hunton, Richmondshire DC
Huntsham, Mid Devon DC
Huntshaw, Torridge DC
Huntspill, Sedgemoor DC
Hunwick, Wear Valley DC
Hunworth, N Norfolk DC
Hurdsfield, Macclesfield BC
Hurleston, Crewe/Nantwich BC
Hurlet, Glasgow City
Hurley, N Warks BC
Hurley, Windsor/Maidenhead RB
Hurlford, E Ayrshire CI
Hurn, Christchurch BC
Hursley, Winchester City
Hurst, Richmondshire DC
Hurst, Wokingham DC
Hurst Green, Ribble Valley BC
Hurst Green, Rother DC
Hurst Green, Tandridge DC
Hurstbourne Priors, Basingstoke/Deane BC
Hurstbourne Tarrant, Test Valley BC
Hurstpierpoint, Mid Sussex DC
Hurstwood, Burnley BC
Hurworth on Tees, Darlington BC
Hury, Teesdale DC
Husbands Bosworth, Harborough DC
Husborne Crawley, Mid Beds DC
Husthwaite, Hambleton DC
Hutchesontown, Glasgow City
Hutleys, Tendring DC
Huttoft, E Lindsey DC
Hutton, Brentwood BC
Hutton, Eden DC
Hutton, N Somerset DC
Hutton, Scottish Borders CI
Hutton, S Ribble BC
Hutton Bonville, Hambleton DC
Hutton Buscel, Scarborough BC
Hutton Conyers, Harrogate BC
Hutton Cranswick, E Riding of Yks
Hutton End, Eden DC
Hutton Hang, Richmondshire DC
Hutton Henry, Easington DC
Hutton le Hole, Ryedale DC
Hutton Magna, Teesdale DC

GAZETTEER

Hutton Mulgrave, Scarborough
BC
Hutton Roof, S Lakeland DC
Hutton Rudby, Hambleton DC
Hutton Sessay, Hambleton DC
Huttons Ambo, Ryedale DC
Huxham, E Devon DC
Huxley, Chester City
Huyton, Knowsley MBC
Hycemoor, Copeland BC
Hyde, New Forest DC
Hyde, Purbeck DC
Hyde, S Beds DC
Hyde, Stroud DC
Hyde, Tameside MBC
Hyde Heath, Chiltern DC
Hyde Park, Sheffield City
Hyde Park, Westminster City
Hydestile, Waverley BC
Hysbackie, Highland Cl
Hythe, New Forest DC
Hythe, Runnymede BC
Hythe, Shepway DC

Ibberton, N Dorset DC
Ible, Derbys Dales DC
Ibrox Cessnock, Glasgow City
Ibsley, New Forest DC
Ibstock, N W Leics DC
Ibstone, Wycombe DC
Ibthorpe, Test Valley BC
Iburndale, Scarborough BC
Ickburgh, Breckland Cl
Ickenham, Hillingdon LBC
Ickford, Aylesbury Vale DC
Ickham, Canterbury City
Ickleford, N Herts DC
Icklesham, Rother DC
Ickleton, S Cambs DC
Icklingham, Forest Heath DC
Ickwell Green, Mid Beds DC
Icomb, Cotswold DC
Idbury, W Oxon DC
Iddesleigh, W Devon BC
Ide, Teignbridge DC
Ideford, Teignbridge DC
Iden, Rother DC
Iden Green, Tunbridge Wells BC
Idlicote, Stratford/Avon DC
Idmiston, Salisbury DC
Idridgehay, Amber Valley BC
Idrigill, Highland Cl
Ifield (part), Horsham DC
Ifold, Chichester DC
Iford, Lewes DC
Ightenhill, Burnley BC
Ightfield, N Shropshire DC
Ightham, Tonbridge/Malling BC
Iken, Suffolk C'l DC
Ilam, Staffs Moorlands DC

Ilchester, S Somerset DC
Ilderton, Berwick-u-Tweed BC
Ilford, Redbridge LBC
Ilfracombe, N Devon DC
Ilkeston, Erewash BC
Ilketshall St Andrew, Waveney
DC
Ilketshall St John, Waveney DC
Ilketshall St Lawrence, Waveney
DC
Ilketshall St Margaret, Waveney
DC
Ilkley, Bradford MDC
Ilkley Moor, Bradford MDC
Illingworth, Calderdale MBC
Illogan, Kerrier DC
Illston on the Hill, Harborough DC
Ilmer, Wycombe DC
Ilmington, Stratford/Avon DC
Ilminster, S Somerset DC
Ilsington, Teignbridge DC
Ilston, Swansea C&C
Ilton, Harrogate BC
Ilton, S Somerset DC
Imber, W Wilts DC
Immingham, N E Lincs Cl
Impington, S Cambs DC
Ince, Ellesmere Port/Neston BC
Ince Blundell, Sefton MBC
Ince in Makerfield, Wigan MBC
Inchinnan, Renfrewshire Cl
Inchmore, Highland Cl
Inchnadamph, Highland Cl
Inchree, Highland Cl
Inchture, Perth/Kinross Cl
Indian Queens, Restormel BC
Ingatestone, Brentwood BC
Ingbirchworth, Barnsley MBC
Ingestre, Stafford BC
Ingham, N Norfolk DC
Ingham, St Edmundsbury BC
Ingham, W Lindsey DC
Ingleby, S Derbys DC
Ingleby Arncliffe, Hambleton DC
Ingleby Barwick, Stockton-on-
Tees BC
Ingleby Greenhow, Hambleton
DC
Ingleton, Craven DC
Ingleton, Teesdale DC
Inglewhite, Preston City
Ingoe, Castle Morpeth BC
Ingoldisthorpe, King's Lynn/W
Norfolk BC
Ingoldmells, E Lindsey DC
Ingoldsby, S Kesteven DC
Ingon, Stratford/Avon DC
Ingram, Berwick-u-Tweed BC
Ingrams Green, Chichester DC
Ingrave, Brentwood BC

Ings, S Lakeland DC
Ingworth, N Norfolk DC
Inkberrow, Wychavon DC
Inkersall, Chesterfield BC
Inkpen, W Berks DC
Innellan, Argyll/Bute Cl
Innerleithen, Scottish Borders Cl
Innerwick, E Lothian Cl
Innes, Moray Cl
Innishael, Argyll/Bute Cl
Innsworth, Tewkesbury BC
Insch, Aberdeenshire Cl
Insh, Highland Cl
Inshegra, Highland Cl
Inskip, Wyre BC
Instow, N Devon DC
Intake, Sheffield City
Intwood, S Norfolk DC
Inver, Highland Cl
Inveralivaig, Highland Cl
Inveralligin, Highland Cl
Inverallochy, Aberdeenshire Cl
Inveraray, Argyll/Bute Cl
Inverarish, Highland Cl
Inverarity, Angus Cl
Inverasdale, Highland Cl
Inverbervie, Aberdeenshire Cl
Invercassley, Highland Cl
Inverchoran, Highland Cl
Inverdruie, Highland Cl
Inveresk, Angus Cl
Inveresk, E Lothian Cl
Inverfarigaig, Highland Cl
Invergarry, Highland Cl
Invergordon, Highland Cl
Invergowrie, Dundee City
Invergowrie, Perth/Kinross Cl
Inverie, Highland Cl
Inverinate, Highland Cl
Inverkeillor, Angus Cl
Inverkeithing, Fife Cl
Inverkeithny, Aberdeenshire Cl
Inverkip, Inverclyde Cl
Inverkirkaig, Highland Cl
Inverlair, Highland Cl
Inverlochy, Highland Cl
Invermoidart, Highland Cl
Invermoriston, Highland Cl
Invernaver, Highland Cl
Inverness, Highland Cl
Inverroy, Highland Cl
Inversanda, Highland Cl
Invershiel, Highland Cl
Invershin, Highland Cl
Invershore, Highland Cl
Inveruglass, Highland Cl
Inverurie, Aberdeenshire Cl
Inwardleigh, W Devon BC
Inworth, Colchester BC

Iochdar, Comhairle Nan Eilean Siar
Iona, Argyll/Bute CI
Iona, Isle of, Argyll/Bute CI
Iping, Chichester DC
Ipplepen, Teignbridge DC
Ipsden, S Oxon DC
Ipstones, Staffs Moorlands DC
Ipswich, Ipswich BC
Irby, Wirral MBC
Irby in the Marsh, E Lindsey DC
Irby upon Humber, N E Lincs CI
Irchester, Wellingborough BC
Ireby, Allerdale BC
Ireby, Lancaster City
Ireleth, Barrow-in-Furness BC
Ireshopeburn, Wear Valley DC
Irlam, Salford City
Irnham, S Kesteven DC
Iron Acton, S Glos CI
Iron Cross, Stratford/Avon DC
Irongray, Dumfries/Galloway CI
Ironville, Amber Valley BC
Irstead, N Norfolk DC
Irthington, Carlisle City
Irthlingborough, E Northants CI
Irthlingborough, Wellingborough BC
Irton, Copeland BC
Irton, Scarborough BC
Irvine, N Ayrshire CI
Isauld, Highland CI
Isfield, Wealden DC
Isham, Wellingborough BC
Islay, Argyll/Bute CI
Isle Abbotts, S Somerset DC
Isle Brewers, S Somerset DC
Isle of Dogs, Tower Hamlets LBC
Isle of Grain, Medway CI
Isle of Sheppey, Swale BC
Isle of Whithorn, Dumfries/Galloway CI
Isleham, E Cambs DC
Isleornsay, Highland CI
Isleworth, Hounslow LBC
Isley Walton, N W Leics DC
Islington, Islington LBC
Islip, Cherwell DC
Islip, E Northants CI
Isycoed, Wrexham CBC
Itchen Abbas, Winchester City
Itchen Stoke, Winchester City
Itchen Valley, Winchester City
Itchenor, Chichester DC
Itchingfield, Horsham DC
Itteringham, N Norfolk DC
Ivegill, Eden DC
Ivelet, Richmondshire DC
Iver, S Bucks DC
Iver Heath, S Bucks DC

Iveston, Derwentside DC
Ivinghoe, Aylesbury Vale DC
Ivinghoe Aston, Aylesbury Vale DC
Ivonbrook Grange, Derbys Dales DC
Ivybridge, S Hams DC
Ivychurch, Shepway DC
Iwade, Swale BC
Iwerne Courtney, N Dorset DC
Iwerne Minster, N Dorset DC
Iwerne Stepleton, N Dorset DC
Ixworth, St Edmundsbury BC
Ixworth Thorpe, St Edmundsbury BC

Jackton, S Lanarkshire CI
Jacobstow, N Cornwall DC
Jacobstowe, W Devon BC
Jamestown, Highland CI
Jamestown, W Dunbartonshire CI
Jamphlars, Fife CI
Janetstown, Highland CI
Jarrow, S Tyneside MBC
Jaywick, Tendring DC
Jed Valley, Scottish Borders CI
Jedburgh, Scottish Borders CI
Jeffreyston, Pembrokeshire CC
Jemimaville, Highland CI
Jericho, Bury MBC
Jerrettspass, Newry/Mourne DC
Jersey Marine, Neath Port Talbot CBC
Jesmond, Newcastle City
Jevington, Wealden DC
John O'Groats, Highland CI
Johnby, Eden DC
Johnshaven, Aberdeenshire CI
Johnston, Pembrokeshire CC
Johnstone, Renfrewshire CI
Johnstonebridge, Dumfries/Galloway CI
Jordanhill, Glasgow City
Jordans, Chiltern DC
Jordanstown, Newtownabbey BC
Jordanthorpe, Sheffield City
Juniper Green, Edinburgh City
Juniper Hill, Cherwell DC
Jura, Argyll/Bute CI

Kaber, Eden DC
Kalewater, Scottish Borders CI
Kalnakill, Highland CI
Kames, Argyll/Bute CI
Katesbridge, Banbridge DC
Kea, Carrick DC
Keadby, N Lincs CI
Keady, Limavady BC
Kearby, Harrogate BC
Kearn, Aberdeenshire CI

Kearsley, Bolton MBC
Kearstwick, S Lakeland DC
Kearton, Richmondshire DC
Keasdon, Craven DC
Keddington, E Lindsey DC
Kedington, St Edmundsbury BC
Kedleston, Amber Valley BC
Kedlock Feus, Fife CI
Keelby, W Lindsey DC
Keele, Newcastle-u-Lyme BC
Keeley Green, Bedford BC
Keevil, W Wilts DC
Kegworth, N W Leics DC
Kehelland, Kerrier DC
Keig, Aberdeenshire CI
Keighley, Bradford MDC
Keinton Mandeville, S Somerset DC
Keir, Dumfries/Galloway CI
Keisby, S Kesteven DC
Keiss, Highland CI
Keistle, Highland CI
Keith, Moray CI
Keithhall, Aberdeenshire CI
Kelbrook, Pendle BC
Kelby, N Kesteven DC
Keld, Eden DC
Keld, Richmondshire DC
Keldholme, Ryedale DC
Kelfield, Selby DC
Kelham, Newark/Sherwood DC
Kelk, E Riding of Yks
Kelleth, Eden DC
Kelleythorpe, E Riding of Yks
Kelling, N Norfolk DC
Kellington, Selby DC
Kelloe, Durham City
Kelloholm, Dumfries/Galloway CI
Kells, Dumfries/Galloway CI
Kelly, W Devon BC
Kelmarsh, Daventry DC
Kelmscott, W Oxon DC
Kelsale, Suffolk C'I DC
Kelsall, Chester City
Kelshall, N Herts DC
Kelso, Scottish Borders CI
Kelstern, E Lindsey DC
Kelston, Bath/N E Somerset CI
Kelton, Dumfries/Galloway CI
Kelty, Fife CI
Kelvedon, Braintree DC
Kelvedon Hatch, Brentwood BC
Kelvin, Glasgow City
Kelvindale, Glasgow City
Kelvingrove, Glasgow City
Kelvinside, Glasgow City
Kelynack, Penwith DC
Kemback, Fife CI
Kemback Bridge, Fife CI
Kemberton, Bridgnorth DC

Kemble, Cotswold DC
Kemerton, Wychavon DC
Kemnay, Aberdeenshire CI
Kempley, Forest of Dean DC
Kemps Green, Stratford/Avon DC
Kempsey, Malvern Hills DC
Kempsford, Cotswold DC
Kempson Hardwick, Bedford BC
Kempston, Bedford BC
Kempstone, Breckland CI
Kempton, S Shropshire DC
Kemsing, Sevenoaks DC
Kemsley, Swale BC
Kenardington, Ashford BC
Kenchester, Herefordshire CI
Kencott, W Oxon DC
Kendal, S Lakeland DC
Kenderchurch, Herefordshire CI
Kendram, Highland CI
Kenfig Hill, Bridgend CBC
Kenilworth, Warwick DC
Kenley, Shrewsbury/Atcham CI
Kenmore, Perth/Kinross CI
Kenmore, Highland CI
Kenn, N Somerset DC
Kenn, Teignbridge DC
Kennerleigh, Mid Devon DC
Kennet, Kennet DC
Kennethmont, Aberdeenshire CI
Kennett, E Cambs DC
Kennford, Teignbridge DC
Kenninghall, Breckland CI
Kennington, Ashford BC
Kennington, Lambeth LBC
Kennington, Vale of White Horse
   DC
Kennishead, Glasgow City
Kennoway, Fife CI
Kenny Hill, Forest Heath DC
Kennythorpe, Ryedale DC
Kensal Rise, Brent LBC
Kensaleyre, Highland CI
Kensington, Kensington/Chelsea
   Royal Borough
Kenswick, Malvern Hills DC
Kensworth, S Beds DC
Kent's Green, Forest of Dean DC
Kent's Oak, Test Valley BC
Kentallen, Highland CI
Kentchurch, Herefordshire CI
Kentford, Forest Heath DC
Kentisbeare, Mid Devon DC
Kentisbury, N Devon DC
Kentish Town, Camden LBC
Kentmere, S Lakeland DC
Kenton, Brent LBC
Kenton, Mid Suffolk DC
Kenton, Newcastle City
Kenton, Teignbridge DC
Kenton (part), Harrow LBC

Kentra, Highland CI
Kents Bank, S Lakeland DC
Kents Hill, Milton Keynes CI
Kenwick, N Shropshire DC
Kenwyn, Carrick DC
Kenyon, Warrington BC
Kepwick, Hambleton DC
Keresley, Coventry City MDC
Keresley, Nuneaton/Bedworth BC
Kerrera, Argyll/Bute CI
Kerridge, Macclesfield BC
Kerris, Penwith DC
Kerrow, Highland CI
Kerry, Powys CC
Kersal, Salford City
Kersall, Newark/Sherwood DC
Kersbrook, E Devon DC
Kersey, Babergh DC
Kersoe, Wychavon DC
Kerswell, E Devon DC
Kerswell Green, Malvern Hills DC
Kesgrave, Suffolk C'l DC
Kessingland, Waveney DC
Keston, Bromley LBC
Keswick, Allerdale BC
Keswick, N Norfolk DC
Keswick, S Norfolk DC
Ketley, Telford/Wrekin BC
Kettering, Kettering BC
Ketteringham, S Norfolk DC
Kettish, Perth/Kinross CI
Kettle Green, E Herts DC
Kettlebaston, Babergh DC
Kettlebridge, Fife CI
Kettlebrook, Tamworth BC
Kettleburgh, Suffolk C'l DC
Kettlehill, Fife CI
Kettleness, Scarborough BC
Kettleshulme, Macclesfield BC
Kettlestone, N Norfolk DC
Kettlethorpe, W Lindsey DC
Kettlewell, Craven DC
Ketton, Rutland CC
Keverstone, Teesdale DC
Kew, Richmond upon Thames
   LBC
Kewstoke, N Somerset DC
Kexbrough, Barnsley MBC
Kexby, City of York CI
Kexby, Selby DC
Kexby, W Lindsey DC
Key Green, Congleton BC
Keyham, Harborough DC
Keyham, Plymouth City
Keyhaven, New Forest DC
Keyingham, E Riding of Yks
Keymer, Mid Sussex DC
Keynsham, Bath/N E Somerset CI
Keysoe, Bedford BC
Keysoe Row, Bedford BC

Keyston, Huntingdonshire DC
Keyworth, Rushcliffe BC
Kibblesworth, Gateshead CI
Kibworth Beauchamp,
   Harborough DC
Kibworth Harcourt, Harborough
   DC
Kidbrooke, Greenwich LBC
Kiddemore Green, S Staffs CI
Kidderminster, Wyre Forest DC
Kiddington, W Oxon DC
Kidlington, Cherwell DC
Kidmore End, S Oxon DC
Kidsgrove, Newcastle-u-Lyme BC
Kidstones, Richmondshire DC
Kidwelly, Carmarthenshire CC
Kielder, Tynedale DC
Kilarrow, Argyll/Bute CI
Kilbarchan, Renfrewshire CI
Kilbirnie, N Ayrshire CI
Kilburn, Amber Valley BC
Kilburn, Brent LBC
Kilburn, Camden LBC
Kilburn, Hambleton DC
Kilby, Blaby DC
Kilchoan, Highland CI
Kilchoman, Argyll/Bute CI
Kilchrenan, Argyll/Bute CI
Kilconquhar, Fife CI
Kilcot, Forest of Dean DC
Kilcoy, Highland CI
Kilcreggan, Argyll/Bute CI
Kildale, Hambleton DC
Kildalton, Argyll/Bute CI
Kildary, Highland CI
Kildonan, N Ayrshire CI
Kildonan, Highland CI
Kildonnan, Highland CI
Kildwick, Craven DC
Kilfinan, Argyll/Bute CI
Kilham, Berwick-u-Tweed BC
Kilham, E Riding of Yks
Kilhoyle, Limavady BC
Kilkhampton, N Cornwall DC
Killamarsh, N E Derbys DC
Killay, Swansea C&C
Killearn, Stirling CI
Killen, Strabane DC
Killen, Highland CI
Killerby, Darlington BC
Killerby, Hambleton DC
Killeter, Strabane DC
Killiecrankie, Perth/Kinross CI
Killilan, Highland CI
Killimster, Highland CI
Killin, Stirling CI
Killinghall, Harrogate BC
Killington, S Lakeland DC
Killowen, Newry/Mourne DC
Killyclogher, Omagh DC

Killyleagh, Down DC
Killyman, Dungannon & S Tyrone BC
Kilmacolm, Inverclyde CI
Kilmaluag, Highland CI
Kilmany, Fife CI
Kilmarie, Highland CI
Kilmarnock, E Ayrshire CI
Kilmaurs, E Ayrshire CI
Kilmelford, Argyll/Bute CI
Kilmeny, Argyll/Bute CI
Kilmersdon, Mendip DC
Kilmeston, Winchester City
Kilmington, E Devon DC
Kilmington, Salisbury DC
Kilmorack, Highland CI
Kilmore, Argyll/Bute CI
Kilmore, Highland CI
Kilmory, Highland CI
Kilmuir, Highland CI
Kilmun, Argyll/Bute CI
Kilndown, Tunbridge Wells BC
Kilnhurst, Rotherham MBC
Kilninver, Argyll/Bute CI
Kilnsea, E Riding of Yks
Kilnsey, Craven DC
Kilnwick, E Riding of Yks
Kilpeck, Herefordshire CI
Kilphedir, Highland CI
Kilpin Pike, E Riding of Yks
Kilrea, Coleraine BC
Kilrenny, Fife CI
Kilsby, Daventry DC
Kilsyth, N Lanarkshire CI
Kiltarlity, Highland CI
Kilton, W Somerset DC
Kilvaxter, Highland CI
Kilve, W Somerset DC
Kilverstone, Breckland CI
Kilvington, Newark/Sherwood DC
Kilwinning, N Ayrshire CI
Kimberley, Broxtowe BC
Kimberley, S Norfolk DC
Kimble, Wycombe DC
Kimble Wick, Wycombe DC
Kimblesworth, Chester-le-Street DC
Kimbolton, Herefordshire CI
Kimbolton, Huntingdonshire DC
Kimcote, Harborough DC
Kimmeridge, Purbeck DC
Kimmerston, Berwick-u-Tweed BC
Kimpton, N Herts DC
Kimpton, Test Valley BC
Kinbeachie, Highland CI
Kinbrace, Highland CI
Kincaple, Fife CI
Kincardine, Fife CI
Kincardine, Highland CI

Kincardine O'Neil, Aberdeenshire CI
Kincraig, Highland CI
Kinellar, Aberdeenshire CI
Kineton, Cotswold DC
Kineton, Stratford/Avon DC
King Edward, Aberdeenshire CI
King Sterndale, High Peak BC
Kings Bromley, Lichfield DC
King's Caple, Herefordshire CI
King's Coughton, Stratford/Avon DC
King's Lynn, King's Lynn/W Norfolk BC
King's Meaburn, Eden DC
King's Moss, St Helens MBC
King's Newnham, Rugby BC
King's Pyon, Herefordshire CI
Kingairloch, Highland CI
Kingfield, Woking BC
Kingham, W Oxon DC
Kinghorn, Fife CI
Kinglassie, Fife CI
Kingmoor, Carlisle City
Kingoodie, Perth/Kinross CI
Kings Cliffe, E Northants CI
Kings Hill, Tonbridge/Malling BC
Kings Langley, Dacorum BC
Kings Norton, Birmingham City
Kings Norton, Harborough DC
Kings Nympton, N Devon DC
Kings Park, Glasgow City
Kings Ripton, Huntingdonshire DC
Kings Somborne, Test Valley BC
Kings Stanley, Stroud DC
Kings Sutton, S Northants CI
Kings Walden, N Herts DC
Kingsbarns, Fife CI
Kingsbridge, S Hams DC
Kingsburgh, Highland CI
Kingsbury, Birmingham City
Kingsbury, Brent LBC
Kingsbury, N Warks BC
Kingsbury Episcopi, S Somerset DC
Kingsclere, Basingstoke/Deane BC
Kingscote, Cotswold DC
Kingscott, Torridge DC
Kingsdon, S Somerset DC
Kingsdown, Dover DC
Kingsdown, Swale BC
Kingseat, Fife CI
Kingsey, Aylesbury Vale DC
Kingsfold, Horsham DC
Kingsford, Wyre Forest DC
Kingsgate, Thanet DC
Kingshurst, Solihull MBC
Kingskerswell, Teignbridge DC

Kingskettle, Fife CI
Kingsland, Herefordshire CI
Kingsley, E Hants DC
Kingsley, Staffs Moorlands DC
Kingsley, Stratford/Avon DC
Kingsley, Vale Royal BC
Kingsley Green, Chichester DC
Kingsnordley, Bridgnorth DC
Kingsnorth, Ashford BC
Kingsnorth, Medway CI
Kingstanding, Birmingham City
Kingsteignton, Teignbridge DC
Kingsteps, Highland CI
Kingsthorpe, Northampton BC
Kingston, Arun DC
Kingston, Canterbury City
Kingston, E Lothian CI
Kingston, Isle of Wight CI
Kingston, Kingston upon Thames Royal Borough
Kingston, Lewes DC
Kingston, New Forest DC
Kingston, Purbeck DC
Kingston, S Cambs DC
Kingston, S Hams DC
Kingston, Stratford/Avon DC
Kingston Bagpuize, Vale of White Horse DC
Kingston Blount, S Oxon DC
Kingston Lisle, Vale of White Horse DC
Kingston on Soar, Rushcliffe BC
Kingston Russell, W Dorset DC
Kingston St Mary, Taunton Deane BC
Kingston Seymour, N Somerset DC
Kingston upon Hull, Kingston upon Hull City
Kingstone, E Staffs BC
Kingstone, Herefordshire CI
Kingstone, S Somerset DC
Kingstown, Carlisle City
Kingswear, S Hams DC
Kingswells, Aberdeen City
Kingswinford, Dudley MBC
Kingswood, Aylesbury Vale DC
Kingswood, Maidstone BC
Kingswood, Reigate/Banstead BC
Kingswood, S Glos CI
Kingswood, Stroud DC
Kingswood, Warwick DC
Kingsworthy, Winchester City
Kington, Wychavon DC
Kington Langley, N Wilts DC
Kington Magna, N Dorset DC
Kington Rural, Herefordshire CI
Kington St Michael, N Wilts DC
Kington Urban, Herefordshire CI
Kingussie, Highland CI

Kingwater, Carlisle City
Kingweston, S Somerset DC
Kinkell, Aberdeenshire Cl
Kinkell, Highland Cl
Kinlet, Bridgnorth DC
Kinloch, Comhairle Nan Eilean Siar
Kinloch, Highland Cl
Kinloch Loggan, Highland Cl
Kinlochbervie, Highland Cl
Kinlocheil, Highland Cl
Kinlocheven, Highland Cl
Kinlochewe, Highland Cl
Kinlochlaggan, Highland Cl
Kinlochleven, Highland Cl
Kinlochmoidart, Highland Cl
Kinlochmore, Highland Cl
Kinloid, Highland Cl
Kinloss, Moray Cl
Kinmel Bay, Conwy CBC
Kinmylies, Highland Cl
Kinnauld, Highland Cl
Kinneff, Aberdeenshire Cl
Kinnerley, Oswestry BC
Kinnersley, Herefordshire Cl
Kinnersley, Malvern Hills DC
Kinning Park, Glasgow City
Kinniside, Copeland BC
Kinnoull, Perth/Kinross Cl
Kinoulton, Rushcliffe BC
Kinross, Perth/Kinross Cl
Kinsbourne Green, St Albans City/DC
Kinsham, Herefordshire Cl
Kinsley, Wakefield MDC
Kintbury, W Berks DC
Kintore, Aberdeenshire Cl
Kinveachy, Highland Cl
Kinver, S Staffs Cl
Kinwarton, Stratford/Avon DC
Kiplin, Hambleton DC
Kippax, Leeds City
Kippen, Stirling Cl
Kirby, Ryedale DC
Kirby Bedon, S Norfolk DC
Kirby Bellars, Melton BC
Kirby Cane, S Norfolk DC
Kirby Cross, Tendring DC
Kirby Grindalythe, Ryedale DC
Kirby Hill, Harrogate BC
Kirby Hill, Richmondshire DC
Kirby Knowle, Hambleton DC
Kirby le Soken, Tendring DC
Kirby Misperton, Ryedale DC
Kirby Muxloe, Blaby DC
Kirby Sigston, Hambleton DC
Kirby Underdale, E Riding of Yks
Kirby Wiske, Hambleton DC
Kirdford, Chichester DC
Kirk Deighton, Harrogate BC

Kirk Ella, E Riding of Yks
Kirk Hammerton, Harrogate BC
Kirk Ireton, Derbys Dales DC
Kirk Langley, Amber Valley BC
Kirk Merrington, Sedgefield BC
Kirk O'Shotts, N Lanarkshire Cl
Kirk Sandall, Doncaster MBC
Kirk Smeaton, Selby DC
Kirkandrews on Eden, Carlisle City
Kirkbampton, Allerdale BC
Kirkbean, Dumfries/Galloway Cl
Kirkbride, Allerdale BC
Kirkburn, E Riding of Yks
Kirkburton, Kirklees MC
Kirkby, Hambleton DC
Kirkby, Knowsley MBC
Kirkby, W Lindsey DC
Kirkby Fleetham, Hambleton DC
Kirkby Green, N Kesteven DC
Kirkby in Ashfield, Ashfield DC
Kirkby in Furness, S Lakeland DC
Kirkby Ireleth, S Lakeland DC
Kirkby la Thorpe, N Kesteven DC
Kirkby Lonsdale, S Lakeland DC
Kirkby Malham, Craven DC
Kirkby Malhamdale, Craven DC
Kirkby Mallory, Hinckley/Bosworth BC
Kirkby Malzeard, Harrogate BC
Kirkby Mills, Ryedale DC
Kirkby on Bain, E Lindsey DC
Kirkby Overblow, Harrogate BC
Kirkby Stephen, Eden DC
Kirkby Thore, Eden DC
Kirkby Underwood, S Kesteven DC
Kirkby Wharfe, Selby DC
Kirkbymoorside, Ryedale DC
Kirkcaldy, Fife Cl
Kirkcambeck, Carlisle City
Kirkcolm, Dumfries/Galloway Cl
Kirkconnel, Dumfries/Galloway Cl
Kirkcowan, Dumfries/Galloway Cl
Kirkcudbright, Dumfries/Galloway Cl
Kirkella, E Riding of Yks
Kirkfieldbank, S Lanarkshire Cl
Kirkgunzeon, Dumfries/Galloway Cl
Kirkham, Fylde BC
Kirkham, Ryedale DC
Kirkharle, Tynedale DC
Kirkhaugh, Tynedale DC
Kirkheaton, Castle Morpeth BC
Kirkheaton, Kirklees MC
Kirkhill, Highland Cl
Kirkintilloch, E Dunbartonshire Cl
Kirkland, Copeland BC
Kirkland, Eden DC

Kirkland, Wyre BC
Kirkleatham, Redcar/Cleveland BC
Kirkley, Waveney DC
Kirklington, Hambleton DC
Kirklington, Newark/Sherwood DC
Kirklinton, Carlisle City
Kirkliston, Edinburgh City
Kirkmabreck, Dumfries/Galloway Cl
Kirkmahoe, Dumfries/Galloway Cl
Kirkmaiden, Dumfries/Galloway Cl
Kirkmichael, S Ayrshire Cl
Kirkmuirhill, S Lanarkshire Cl
Kirknewton, Berwick-u-Tweed BC
Kirknewton, W Lothian Cl
Kirkoswald, Eden DC
Kirkoswald, S Ayrshire Cl
Kirkpatrick Durham, Dumfries/Galloway Cl
Kirkpatrick Fleming, Dumfries/Galloway Cl
Kirkpatrick Juxta, Dumfries/Galloway Cl
Kirkribost, Highland Cl
Kirksanton, Copeland BC
Kirkstead, E Lindsey DC
Kirkstead Bridge, N Kesteven DC
Kirkstyle, Highland Cl
Kirkton, Dundee City
Kirkton of Balmerino, Fife Cl
Kirkton of Skene, Aberdeenshire Cl
Kirkurd, Scottish Borders Cl
Kirkwall, Orkney Is Cl
Kirkwhelpington, Tynedale DC
Kirmington, N Lincs Cl
Kirmond le Mire, W Lindsey DC
Kirn, Argyll/Bute Cl
Kirriemuir, Angus Cl
Kirstead, S Norfolk DC
Kirtling, E Cambs DC
Kirtle, Dumfries & Galloway Cl
Kirtlington, Cherwell DC
Kirtomy, Highland Cl
Kirton, Boston BC
Kirton, Newark/Sherwood DC
Kirton, Suffolk C'l DC
Kirton End, Boston BC
Kirton in Lindsey, N Lincs Cl
Kislingbury, S Northants Cl
Kite Green, Stratford/Avon DC
Kitebrook, Stratford/Avon DC
Kites Hardwick, Rugby BC
Kiveton Park, Rotherham MBC
Knaith, W Lindsey DC
Knaphill, Woking BC

Knapthorpe, Newark/Sherwood DC
Knaptoft, Harborough DC
Knapton, City of York CI
Knapton, N Norfolk DC
Knapton, Ryedale DC
Knapwell, S Cambs DC
Knaresborough, Harrogate BC
Knarsdale, Tynedale DC
Knayton, Hambleton DC
Knebworth, N Herts DC
Kneesall, Newark/Sherwood DC
Kneesworth, S Cambs DC
Kneeton, Rushcliffe BC
Knightcote, Stratford/Avon DC
Knighton, Leicester City
Knighton, Powys CC
Knighton, Stafford BC
Knightsridge, W Lothian CI
Knightswood, Glasgow City
Knightwick, Malvern Hills DC
Knill, Herefordshire CI
Knipton, Melton BC
Knitsley, Derwentside DC
Kniveton, Derbys Dales DC
Knock, Eden DC
Knockan, Highland CI
Knockando, Moray CI
Knockarthur, Highland CI
Knockbreck, Highland CI
Knockentiber, E Ayrshire CI
Knockfarrel, Highland CI
Knockglass, Highland CI
Knockholt, Bromley LBC
Knockholt, Sevenoaks DC
Knockin, Oswestry BC
Knodishall, Suffolk C'I DC
Knolls Green, Macclesfield BC
Knook, W Wilts DC
Knossington, Melton BC
Knott, Highland CI
Knott End on Sea, Wyre BC
Knotting, Bedford BC
Knottingley, Wakefield MDC
Knotty Ash, Liverpool City
Knotty Green, Chiltern DC
Knowbury, S Shropshire DC
Knowesgate, Tynedale DC
Knowle, Bristol City
Knowle, E Devon DC
Knowle, Solihull MBC
Knowle, S Shropshire DC
Knowle Green, Ribble Valley BC
Knowle St Giles, S Somerset DC
Knowlton, Dover DC
Knowlton, E Dorset DC
Knowsley, Knowsley MBC
Knowstone, N Devon DC
Knoydart, Highland CI
Knutsford, Macclesfield BC

Knuzden, Hyndburn BC
Knypersley, Staffs Moorlands DC
Kuggar, Kerrier DC
Kyle, Highland CI
Kyle of Lochalsh, Highland CI
Kyleakin, Highland CI
Kylerhea, Highland CI
Kylesku, Highland CI
Kylestrome, Highland CI
Kyloe, Berwick-u-Tweed BC
Kynnersley, Telford/Wrekin BC

Laceby, N E Lincs CI
Lacey Green, Wycombe DC
Lach Dennis, Vale Royal BC
Lache, Chester City
Lackford, St Edmundsbury BC
Lacock, N Wilts DC
Ladbroke, Stratford/Avon DC
Laddingford, Maidstone BC
Lade Bank, Boston BC
Ladmanlow, High Peak BC
Ladock, Carrick DC
Ladybank, Fife CI
Ladykirk, Scottish Borders CI
Ladywood, Birmingham City
Laga, Highland CI
Laggan, Argyll/Bute CI
Laggan, Highland CI
Lagganlia, Highland CI
Laide, Highland CI
Laindon, Basildon DC
Lair, Highland CI
Lairg, Highland CI
Lairg Muir, Highland CI
Lake, Isle of Wight CI
Lake, Salisbury DC
Lakenheath, Forest Heath DC
Lakes, S Lakeland DC
Lakesend, King's Lynn/W Norfolk BC
Laleham, Spelthorne BC
Laleston, Bridgend CBC
Lamancha, Scottish Borders CI
Lamarsh, Braintree DC
Lamas, Broadland DC
Lambeg, Lisburn City
Lamberhurst, Tunbridge Wells BC
Lamberton, Scottish Borders CI
Lambeth, Lambeth LBC
Lambhill, Glasgow City
Lambley, Gedling BC
Lambley, Tynedale DC
Lambourn, W Berks DC
Lambourne, Epping Forest DC
Lambrigg, S Lakeland DC
Lambs Green, Horsham DC
Lamerton, W Devon BC
Lamesley, Gateshead CI
Lamington, S Lanarkshire CI

Lamington, Highland CI
Lamlash, N Ayrshire CI
Lamonby, Eden DC
Lamorna, Penwith DC
Lamorran (part), Carrick DC
Lamorran (part), Restormel BC
Lampeter, Ceredigion CC
Lampeter Velfrey, Pembrokeshire CC
Lamphey, Pembrokeshire CC
Lamplugh, Copeland BC
Lamport, Daventry DC
Lamyatt, Mendip DC
Lanark, S Lanarkshire CI
Lancaster, Lancaster City
Lanchester, Derwentside DC
Lancing, Adur DC
Landbeach, S Cambs DC
Landcross, Torridge DC
Landewednack, Kerrier DC
Landford, Salisbury DC
Landkey, N Devon DC
Landmoth cum Catto, Hambleton DC
Landrake, Caradon DC
Landulph, Caradon DC
Landward, Fife CI
Landward East, Angus CI
Landward West, Angus CI
Landywood, S Staffs CI
Lane End, Wycombe DC
Lane Top, Sheffield City
Laneast, N Cornwall DC
Laneham, Bassetlaw DC
Lanehead, Tynedale DC
Laneshaw Bridge, Pendle BC
Langal, Highland CI
Langar, Rushcliffe BC
Langbank, Renfrewshire CI
Langcliffe, Craven DC
Langdale End, Scarborough BC
Langdon, Dover DC
Langdon Beck, Teesdale DC
Langenhoe, Colchester BC
Langford, Maldon DC
Langford, Mid Beds DC
Langford, Newark/Sherwood DC
Langford, W Oxon DC
Langford Budville, Taunton Deane BC
Langham, Colchester BC
Langham, Mid Suffolk DC
Langham, N Norfolk DC
Langham, Rutland CC
Langho, Ribble Valley BC
Langholm, Dumfries/Galloway CI
Langlee, Scottish Borders CI
Langleeford, Berwick-u-Tweed BC
Langlees, Falkirk CI

Langley, Chichester DC
Langley, Macclesfield BC
Langley, Maidstone BC
Langley, New Forest DC
Langley, N Herts DC
Langley, Shrewsbury/Atcham Cl
Langley, Slough BC
Langley, S Norfolk DC
Langley, Stratford/Avon DC
Langley, Uttlesford DC
Langley Burrell, N Wilts DC
Langley Green, Stratford/Avon DC
Langley Mill, Amber Valley BC
Langley Moor, Durham City
Langley Park, Derwentside DC
Langleydale, Teesdale DC
Langney Point, Eastbourne BC
Langore, N Cornwall DC
Langport, S Somerset DC
Langridge, Bath/N E Somerset Cl
Langrigg, Allerdale BC
Langrish, E Hants DC
Langriville, E Lindsey DC
Langsett, Barnsley MBC
Langside, Glasgow City
Langstone, Havant BC
Langstone, Newport City Cl
Langthorne, Hambleton DC
Langthorpe, Harrogate BC
Langthwaite, Richmondshire DC
Langtoft, E Riding of Yks
Langtoft, S Kesteven DC
Langton, E Lindsey DC
Langton, Ryedale DC
Langton, Teesdale DC
Langton by Spilsby, E Lindsey DC
Langton by Wragby, E Lindsey DC
Langton Green, Tunbridge Wells BC
Langton Herring, W Dorset DC
Langton Long, N Dorset DC
Langton Matravers, Purbeck DC
Langtree, Torridge DC
Langwathby, Eden DC
Langwith Junction, Bolsover DC
Langworth, W Lindsey DC
Langworthy, Salford City
Lanhydrock, N Cornwall DC
Lanivet, N Cornwall DC
Lanlivery, Restormel BC
Lanner, Kerrier DC
Lanreath, Caradon DC
Lansallos, Caradon DC
Lanteglos, Caradon DC
Lanton, Berwick-u-Tweed BC
Lanton, Scottish Borders Cl
Lapford, Mid Devon DC

Lapley, S Staffs Cl
Lapworth, Warwick DC
Larbert, Falkirk Cl
Larbreck, Fylde BC
Largantea, Limavady BC
Largoward, Fife Cl
Largs, N Ayrshire Cl
Lark Stoke, Stratford/Avon DC
Larkfield, Tonbridge/Malling BC
Larkhall, S Lanarkshire Cl
Larkhill, Salisbury DC
Larkton, Chester City
Larling, Breckland Cl
Larne, Larne BC
Lartington, Teesdale DC
Lasborough, Cotswold DC
Lasham, E Hants DC
Lasswade, Midlothian Cl
Lastingham, Ryedale DC
Latchford, E Herts DC
Latchingdon, Maldon DC
Lathbury, Milton Keynes Cl
Latheron, Highland Cl
Latheronwheel, Highland Cl
Lathom, W Lancs DC
Latimer, Chiltern DC
Latton, N Wilts DC
Lauder, Scottish Borders Cl
Lauderdale, Scottish Borders Cl
Laugharne, Carmarthenshire CC
Laughterton, W Lindsey DC
Laughton, Harborough DC
Laughton, S Kesteven DC
Laughton, Wealden DC
Laughton, W Lindsey DC
Laughton en le Morthen, Rotherham MBC
Launcells, N Cornwall DC
Launceston, N Cornwall DC
Launde, Harborough DC
Launton, Cherwell DC
Laurencekirk, Aberdeenshire Cl
Laurieston, Falkirk Cl
Laurieston, Glasgow City
Lavant, Chichester DC
Lavendon, Milton Keynes Cl
Lavenham, Babergh DC
Lavers, The, Epping Forest DC
Laverstock, Salisbury DC
Laverstoke & Freefolk, Basingstoke/Deane BC
Laverton, Harrogate BC
Laverton, Mendip DC
Laverton, Tewkesbury BC
Law, S Lanarkshire Cl
Lawford, Tendring DC
Lawhitton, N Cornwall DC
Lawkland, Craven DC
Lawley, Telford/Wrekin BC
Lawnhead, Stafford BC

Lawrencetown, Banbridge DC
Lawshall, Babergh DC
Laxdale, Comhairle Nan Eilean Siar
Laxfield, Mid Suffolk DC
Laxton, E Northants Cl
Laxton, E Riding of Yks
Laxton, Newark/Sherwood DC
Laycock, Bradford MDC
Layer Breton, Colchester BC
Layer de la Haye, Colchester BC
Layer Marney, Colchester BC
Layham, Babergh DC
Laysters, Herefordshire Cl
Laytham, E Riding of Yks
Lazenby, Hambleton DC
Lazenby, Redcar/Cleveland BC
Lazonby, Eden DC
Lea, Amber Valley BC
Lea, Crewe/Nantwich BC
Lea, Herefordshire Cl
Lea, N Wilts DC
Lea, Preston City
Lea, S Shropshire DC
Lea, W Lindsey DC
Lea by Backford, Chester City
Lea Marston, N Warks BC
Leabrooks, Amber Valley BC
Leacanashie, Highland Cl
Leachkin, Highland Cl
Lead, Selby DC
Leaden Roding, Uttlesford DC
Leadenhall, Milton Keynes Cl
Leadenham, N Kesteven DC
Leadgate, Derwentside DC
Leadgate, Eden DC
Leadhills, S Lanarkshire Cl
Leafield, W Oxon DC
Leagram, Ribble Valley BC
Leake, Hambleton DC
Leake Commonside, Boston BC
Leake Hurn's End, Boston BC
Lealholm, Scarborough BC
Lealt, Highland Cl
Leamington Hastings, Rugby BC
Leamington Spa, Warwick DC
Leanach, Highland Cl
Learmouth, Berwick-u-Tweed BC
Leasgill, S Lakeland DC
Leasingham, N Kesteven DC
Leasowe, Wirral MBC
Leatherhead, Mole Valley DC
Leathley, Harrogate BC
Leaton, Shrewsbury/Atcham Cl
Leaveland, Swale BC
Leavenheath, Babergh DC
Leavening, Ryedale DC
Lebberston, Scarborough BC
Lechlade, Cotswold DC
Leck, Lancaster City

Leck, Limavady BC
Leckford, Test Valley BC
Leckfurin, Highland CI
Leckhampstead, Aylesbury Vale DC
Leckhampstead, W Berks DC
Leckhampton, Cheltenham BC
Leckmelm, Highland CI
Leconfield, E Riding of Yks
Ledburn, Aylesbury Vale DC
Ledbury, Herefordshire CI
Lednabirichen, Highland CI
Lednagullin, Highland CI
Ledsham, Chester City
Ledsham, Leeds City
Ledston, Leeds City
Ledstone, S Hams DC
Ledwell, W Oxon DC
Lee, N Shropshire DC
Lee, Test Valley BC
Lee Brockhurst, N Shropshire DC
Lee Clump, Chiltern DC
Lee Green, Lewisham LBC
Lee Mill, S Hams DC
Lee Moor, S Hams DC
Lee, The, Chiltern DC
Leebotwood, Shrewsbury/Atcham CI
Leece, S Lakeland DC
Leeds, Leeds City
Leeds, Maidstone BC
Leek, Staffs Moorlands DC
Leek Wootton, Warwick DC
Leekfrith, Staffs Moorlands DC
Leeming, Hambleton DC
Lees, S Derbys DC
Leeswood, Flintshire CC
Legbourne, E Lindsey DC
Legburthwaite, Allerdale BC
Legsby, W Lindsey DC
Leicester, Leicester City
Leicester Forest East, Blaby DC
Leicester Forest West, Blaby DC
Leigh, E Staffs BC
Leigh, Mole Valley DC
Leigh, N Wilts DC
Leigh, Sevenoaks DC
Leigh, S Shropshire DC
Leigh, Tewkesbury BC
Leigh, W Dorset DC
Leigh, Wigan MBC
Leigh Beck, Castle Point BC
Leigh Green, Ashford BC
Leigh on Mendip, Mendip DC
Leigh on Sea, Southend-on-Sea BC
Leigh Park, Havant BC
Leigh Sinton, Malvern Hills DC
Leighfield, Rutland CC
Leighterton, Cotswold DC

Leighton, Crewe/Nantwich BC
Leighton, Mendip DC
Leighton, Shrewsbury/Atcham CI
Leighton, S Beds DC
Leighton Bromswold, Huntingdonshire DC
Leinthall Starkes, Herefordshire CI
Leintwardine, Herefordshire CI
Leire, Harborough DC
Leirinmore, Highland CI
Leiston, Suffolk C'l DC
Leith, Edinburgh City
Leith Hill, Mole Valley DC
Leitholm, Scottish Borders CI
Leitrim, Banbridge DC
Lelant, Penwith DC
Lelley, E Riding of Yks
Lemington, Newcastle City
Lemsford, Welwyn Hatfield DC
Lenborough, Aylesbury Vale DC
Lenchwick, Wychavon DC
Lendalfoot, S Ayrshire CI
Lenham, Maidstone BC
Lennox, Moray CI
Lennoxtown, E Dunbartonshire CI
Lenton, S Kesteven DC
Lentran, Highland CI
Lenzie, E Dunbartonshire CI
Leochel Cushnie, Aberdeenshire CI
Leominster, Herefordshire CI
Leominster East, Herefordshire CI
Leominster South, Herefordshire CI
Leonard Stanley, Stroud DC
Lepe, New Forest DC
Lephin, Highland CI
Leppington, Ryedale DC
Lepton, Kirklees MC
Lerryn, Caradon DC
Lerwick, Shetland Is CI
Lesbury, Alnwick DC
Leslie, Aberdeenshire CI
Leslie, Fife CI
Lesmahagow, S Lanarkshire CI
Lesnewth, N Cornwall DC
Lessingham, N Norfolk DC
Lessonhall, Allerdale BC
Leswalt, Dumfries/Galloway CI
Letchmore Heath, Hertsmere BC
Letchworth, N Herts DC
Letcombe Bassett, Vale of White Horse DC
Letcombe Regis, Vale of White Horse DC
Letham, Angus CI
Letham, Falkirk CI
Letham, Fife CI
Letheringham, Suffolk C'l DC

Letheringsett, N Norfolk DC
Letterewe, Highland CI
Lettermorar, Highland CI
Letters, Highland CI
Letterston, Pembrokeshire CC
Letton, Herefordshire CI
Letty Green, E Herts DC
Letwell, Rotherham MBC
Leuchars, Fife CI
Levedale, S Staffs CI
Leven, E Riding of Yks
Leven, Fife CI
Levens, S Lakeland DC
Levens Green, E Herts DC
Levenshulme, Manchester City
Leverington, Fenland DC
Levern District, Glasgow City
Leverton, Boston BC
Levington, Suffolk C'l DC
Levisham, Ryedale DC
Lew, W Oxon DC
Lewannick, N Cornwall DC
Lewdown, W Devon BC
Lewes, Lewes DC
Leweston, W Dorset DC
Lewis, Comhairle Nan Eilean Siar
Lewisham, Lewisham LBC
Lewiston, Highland CI
Lewknor, S Oxon DC
Lewsey, Luton BC
Lewtrenchard, W Devon BC
Lexham, Breckland CI
Ley, Caradon DC
Ley Hill, Chiltern DC
Leybourne, Tonbridge/Malling BC
Leyburn, Richmondshire DC
Leycett, Newcastle-u-Lyme BC
Leyfields, Tamworth BC
Leyland, S Ribble BC
Leysdown, Swale BC
Leyton, Waltham Forest LBC
Lezant, N Cornwall DC
Leziate, King's Lynn/W Norfolk BC
Lhanbryde, Moray CI
Liberton, Edinburgh City
Lichfield, Lichfield DC
Lickey, Bromsgrove DC
Lickfold, Chichester DC
Liddington, Swindon BC
Liden, Swindon BC
Lidgate, St Edmundsbury BC
Lidlington, Mid Beds DC
Lieurary, Highland CI
Liff, Angus CI
Lifton, W Devon BC
Lighthorne, Stratford/Avon DC
Lighthorne Heath, Stratford/Avon DC

Lighthorne Rough, Stratford/Avon DC

Lightwater, Surrey Heath BC

Lilbourne, Daventry DC

Lilburn Tower, Berwick-u-Tweed BC

Lilford cum Wigsthorpe, E Northants CI

Lilleshall, Telford/Wrekin BC

Lilley, N Herts DC

Lilliesleaf, Scottish Borders CI

Lillings Ambo, Ryedale DC

Lillingstone Dayrell, Aylesbury Vale DC

Lillingstone Lovell, Aylesbury Vale DC

Lillington, W Dorset DC

Lilstock, W Somerset DC

Limavady, Limavady BC

Limbrick, Chorley BC

Limefield, Bury MBC

Limehouse, Tower Hamlets LBC

Limekilns, Fife CI

Limerigg, Falkirk CI

Limington, S Somerset DC

Limpley Stoke, W Wilts DC

Limpsfield, Tandridge DC

Limpsfield Chart, Tandridge DC

Linby, Gedling BC

Linch, Chichester DC

Linchmere, Chichester DC

Lincluden, Dumfries/Galloway CI

Lincoln, Lincoln City

Lindal in Furness (part), Barrow-in-Furness BC

Lindal in Furness (part), S Lakeland DC

Lindale, S Lakeland DC

Lindfield, Mid Sussex DC

Lindford, E Hants DC

Lindley, Kirklees MC

Lindores, Fife CI

Lindsell, Uttlesford DC

Lindsey, Babergh DC

Linford, New Forest DC

Linford, Thurrock BC

Lingdale, Redcar/Cleveland BC

Lingen, Herefordshire CI

Lingfield, Tandridge DC

Lingwood, Broadland DC

Linicro, Highland CI

Linkenholt, Test Valley BC

Linkinhorne, Caradon DC

Linksfield, Aberdeen City

Linlathen, Dundee City

Linley, S Shropshire DC

Linlithgow, W Lothian CI

Linlithgow Bridge, W Lothian CI

Linnie, Highland CI

Linshields, Alnwick DC

Linsidemore, Highland CI

Linslade, Aylesbury Vale DC

Linslade, S Beds DC

Linstead Magna, Suffolk C'I DC

Linstead Parva, Suffolk C'I DC

Linstock, Carlisle City

Linthwaite, Kirklees MC

Linton, Craven DC

Linton, Leeds City

Linton, Maidstone BC

Linton, S Cambs DC

Linton, S Derbys DC

Linton (nr Bromyard), Herefordshire CI

Linton (nr Upton Bishop), Herefordshire CI

Linton on Ouse, Hambleton DC

Linwood, New Forest DC

Linwood, Renfrewshire CI

Linwood, W Lindsey DC

Lionthorn, Falkirk CI

Liphook, E Hants DC

Lisanelly, Omagh DC

Lisburn, Lisburn City

Liscard, Wirral MBC

Liscolman, Moyle DC

Liskeard, Caradon DC

Lismore, Argyll/Bute CI

Liss, E Hants DC

Lissett, E Riding of Yks

Lissington, W Lindsey DC

Liston, Braintree DC

Lisvane/St Mellons, Cardiff CC

Litcham, Breckland DC

Litchborough, S Northants CI

Litchfield, Basingstoke/Deane BC

Litherland, Sefton MBC

Litlington, S Cambs DC

Litlington, Wealden DC

Little Abington, S Cambs DC

Little Addington, E Northants CI

Little Alne, Stratford/Avon DC

Little Amwell, E Herts DC

Little Asby, Eden DC

Little Aston, Lichfield DC

Little Atherfield, Isle of Wight CI

Little Ayton, Hambleton DC

Little Baddow, Chelmsford BC

Little Bardfield, Uttlesford DC

Little Barford, Bedford BC

Little Barningham, N Norfolk DC

Little Barrington, Cotswold DC

Little Barugh, Ryedale DC

Little Bealings, Suffolk C'I DC

Little Bedwyn, Kennet DC

Little Bentley, Tendring DC

Little Berkhamsted, E Herts DC

Little Birch, Herefordshire CI

Little Blakenham, Mid Suffolk DC

Little Bognor, Chichester DC

Little Bollington, Macclesfield BC

Little Bookham, Mole Valley DC

Little Bowden, Harborough DC

Little Bradley, St Edmundsbury BC

Little Brampton, Herefordshire CI

Little Brampton, S Shropshire DC

Little Braxted, Maldon DC

Little Brickhill, Milton Keynes CI

Little Brington, Daventry DC

Little Britain, Stratford/Avon DC

Little Bromley, Tendring DC

Little Broughton, Hambleton DC

Little Budworth, Vale Royal BC

Little Burstead, Basildon DC

Little Busby, Hambleton DC

Little Bytham, S Kesteven DC

Little Canfield, Uttlesford DC

Little Carlton, E Lindsey DC

Little Carlton, Newark/Sherwood DC

Little Casterton, Rutland CC

Little Cawthorpe, E Lindsey DC

Little Chalfont, Chiltern DC

Little Chart, Ashford BC

Little Chesterford, Uttlesford DC

Little Cheverell, Kennet DC

Little Chishill, S Cambs DC

Little Clacton, Tendring DC

Little Clifton, Allerdale BC

Little Comberton, Wychavon DC

Little Common, Rother DC

Little Compton, Stratford/Avon DC

Little Cornard, Babergh DC

Little Cowarne, Herefordshire CI

Little Coxwell, Vale of White Horse DC

Little Cressingham, Breckland CI

Little Cronsley, Kettering BC

Little Crosby, Sefton MBC

Little Dalby, Melton DC

Little Dassett, Stratford/Avon DC

Little Dewchurch, Herefordshire CI

Little Downham, E Cambs DC

Little Driffield, E Riding of Yks

Little Dunham, Breckland CI

Little Dunmow, Uttlesford DC

Little Easton, Uttlesford DC

Little Eaton, Erewash BC

Little Eccleston, Fylde BC

Little Ellingham, Breckland CI

Little Eversden, S Cambs DC

Little Fakenham, St Edmundsbury BC

Little Faringdon, W Oxon DC

Little Fenton, Selby DC

Little Finborough, Mid Suffolk DC

Little Fransham, Breckland CI

Little Gaddesden, Dacorum BC
Little Gidding, Huntingdonshire DC
Little Glemham, Suffolk C'l DC
Little Gransden, S Cambs DC
Little Grimsby, E Lindsey DC
Little Habton, Ryedale DC
Little Hadham, E Herts DC
Little Hale, N Kesteven DC
Little Hallingbury, Uttlesford DC
Little Hampden, Wycombe DC
Little Harrowden, Wellingborough BC
Little Haseley, S Oxon DC
Little Hay, Lichfield DC
Little Hayfield, High Peak BC
Little Haywood, Stafford BC
Little Heath, Welwyn Hatfield DC
Little Henny, Braintree DC
Little Hereford, Herefordshire Cl
Little Hill, Stratford/Avon DC
Little Honington, Stratford/Avon DC
Little Hoole, S Ribble BC
Little Horkesley, Colchester BC
Little Hormead, E Herts DC
Little Horsted, Wealden DC
Little Horwood, Aylesbury Vale DC
Little Houghton, Barnsley MBC
Little Houghton, S Northants Cl
Little Hucklow, Derbys Dales DC
Little Hulton, Salford City
Little Ilford, Newham LBC
Little Kimble, Wycombe DC
Little Kineton, Stratford/Avon DC
Little Kingshill, Chiltern DC
Little Langdale, S Lakeland DC
Little Langton, Hambleton DC
Little Laver, Epping Forest DC
Little Lawford, Rugby BC
Little Leigh, Vale Royal BC
Little Leighs, Chelmsford BC
Little Lever, Bolton MBC
Little Livermere, St Edmundsbury BC
Little London, Basingstoke/Deane BC
Little London, S Holland DC
Little London, Wealden DC
Little Longstone, Derbys Dales DC
Little Luddington, Stratford/Avon DC
Little Lumley, Chester-le-Street DC
Little Malvern, Malvern Hills DC
Little Maplestead, Braintree DC
Little Marcle, Herefordshire Cl
Little Marlow, Wycombe DC

Little Massingham, King's Lynn/W Norfolk BC
Little Melton, S Norfolk DC
Little Milton, S Oxon DC
Little Missenden, Chiltern DC
Little Mitton, Ribble Valley BC
Little Mongeham, Dover DC
Little Morrell, Stratford/Avon DC
Little Munden, E Herts DC
Little Ness, Shrewsbury/Atcham Cl
Little Newsham, Teesdale DC
Little Oakley, Kettering BC
Little Oakley, Tendring DC
Little Orton, Carlisle City
Little Ouse, E Cambs DC
Little Ouseburn, Harrogate BC
Little Packington, N Warks BC
Little Paxton, Huntingdonshire DC
Little Petherick, N Cornwall DC
Little Plumpton, Fylde BC
Little Plumstead, Broadland DC
Little Ponton, S Kesteven DC
Little Preston, Leeds City
Little Purston, S Northants Cl
Little Ribston, Harrogate BC
Little Rissington, Cotswold DC
Little Rogart, Highland Cl
Little Ryburgh, N Norfolk DC
Little Ryle, Alnwick DC
Little Salkeld, Eden DC
Little Sampford, Uttlesford DC
Little Saredon, S Staffs Cl
Little Shelford, S Cambs DC
Little Singleton, Fylde BC
Little Smeaton, Hambleton DC
Little Smeaton, Selby DC
Little Snoring, N Norfolk DC
Little Sodbury, S Glos Cl
Little Somborne, Test Valley BC
Little Somerford, N Wilts DC
Little Stainton, Darlington BC
Little Stanney, Chester City
Little Staughton, Bedford BC
Little Steeping, E Lindsey DC
Little Stonham, Mid Suffolk DC
Little Stretton, Harborough DC
Little Stretton, S Shropshire DC
Little Strickland, Eden DC
Little Sutton, Ellesmere Port/Neston BC
Little Sutton, S Holland DC
Little Tew, W Oxon DC
Little Thetford, E Cambs DC
Little Thorpe, Easington DC
Little Thurlow, St Edmundsbury BC
Little Thurrock, Thurrock BC
Little Torboll, Highland Cl
Little Torrington, Torridge DC

Little Totham, Maldon DC
Little Town, Highland Cl
Little Wakering, Rochford DC
Little Walden, Uttlesford DC
Little Waldingfield, Babergh DC
Little Walsingham, N Norfolk DC
Little Waltham, Chelmsford BC
Little Warford, Macclesfield BC
Little Warley, Brentwood BC
Little Weighton, E Riding of Yks
Little Wenlock, Telford/Wrekin BC
Little Whelnetham, St Edmundsbury BC
Little Wigborough, Colchester BC
Little Wilbraham, S Cambs DC
Little Willicote, Stratford/Avon DC
Little Witchingham, Broadland DC
Little Witley, Malvern Hills DC
Little Wittenham, S Oxon DC
Little Wolford, Stratford/Avon DC
Little Wratting, St Edmundsbury BC
Little Wymondley, N Herts DC
Little Yeldham, Braintree DC
Littleborough, Rochdale MBC
Littlebourne, Canterbury City
Littlebredy, W Dorset DC
Littlebury, Uttlesford DC
Littledale, Lancaster City
Littledean, Forest of Dean DC
Littleferry, Highland Cl
Littleham, Torridge DC
Littlehampton, Arun DC
Littlehempston, S Hams DC
Littlehoughton, Alnwick DC
Littlemill, Highland Cl
Littlemore, Oxford City
Littleover, Derby City
Littleport, E Cambs DC
Littlestone on Sea, Shepway DC
Littlethorpe, Blaby DC
Littlethorpe, Harrogate BC
Littleton, Chester City
Littleton, Winchester City
Littleton Panell, Kennet DC
Littletown, Allerdale BC
Littletown, Durham City
Littlewick Green, Windsor/Maidenhead RB
Littlewood Green, Stratford/Avon DC
Littleworth, Cannock Chase DC
Littleworth, Vale of White Horse DC
Littleworth, Wychavon DC
Litton, Craven DC
Litton, Derbys Dales DC
Litton, Mendip DC
Litton Cheney, W Dorset DC
Liveridge Hill, Stratford/Avon DC

Liverpool, Liverpool City
Liversedge, Kirklees MC
Liverton, Redcar/Cleveland BC
Livesey, Blackburn with Darwen BC
Livingston, W Lothian Cl
Lizard, Kerrier DC
Llanaelhaearn, Gwynedd CC
Llanafanawr, Powys CC
Llanarmon Yn Ial, Denbighshire CC
Llanarth, Ceredigion CC
Llanarth, Monmouthshire CC
Llanarthney, Carmarthenshire CC
Llanasa, Flintshire CC
Llanbadarn Fawr, Powys CC
Llanbadarn Fynydd, Powys CC
Llanbadoc, Monmouthshire CC
Llanbadrig, Isle of Anglesey CC
Llanbedr, Denbighshire CC
Llanbedr, Gwynedd CC
Llanbedr DC, Denbighshire CC
Llanbedr Pont Steffan, Ceredigion CC
Llanbedrog, Gwynedd CC
Llanberis, Gwynedd CC
Llanbister, Powys CC
Llanblethian, Vale of Glamorgan Cl
Llanboidy, Carmarthenshire CC
Llanbradach, Caerphilly CBC
Llanbrynmair, Powys CC
Llancarfan, Vale of Glamorgan Cl
Llancillo, Herefordshire Cl
Llancynfelin, Ceredigion CC
Llandaff, Cardiff CC
Llandaff North, Cardiff CC
Llanddaniel Fab, Isle of Anglesey CC
Llanddarog, Carmarthenshire CC
Llanddeiniolen, Gwynedd CC
Llandderfel, Gwynedd CC
Llanddeusant, Carmarthenshire CC
Llanddew, Powys CC
Llanddewi Brefi, Ceredigion CC
Llanddewi Velfrey, Pembrokeshire CC
Llanddewi Ystradenny, Powys CC
Llanddoged, Conwy CBC
Llanddoged a Maenan, Conwy CBC
Llanddona, Isle of Anglesey CC
Llanddowror, Carmarthenshire CC
Llanddulas, Conwy CBC
Llanddyfnan, Isle of Anglesey CC
Llandegla, Denbighshire CC
Llandegley, Powys CC
Llandeilo, Carmarthenshire CC

Llandinabo, Herefordshire Cl
Llandinam, Powys CC
Llandissilio West, Pembrokeshire CC
Llandough, Vale of Glamorgan Cl
Llandovery, Carmarthenshire CC
Llandow, Vale of Glamorgan Cl
Llandrillo, Denbighshire CC
Llandrillo yn Rhos, Conwy CBC
Llandrindod Wells, Powys CC
Llandrinio, Powys CC
Llandudno, Conwy CBC
Llandudno Junction, Conwy CBC
Llandwrog, Gwynedd CC
Llandybie, Carmarthenshire CC
Llandyfaelog, Carmarthenshire CC
Llandyfriog, Ceredigion CC
Llandygai, Gwynedd CC
Llandyrnog, Denbighshire CC
Llandysilio, Powys CC
Llandysiliogogo, Ceredigion CC
Llandyssil, Powys CC
Llandysul, Ceredigion CC
Llanedi, Carmarthenshire CC
Llanefydd, Conwy CBC
Llanegryn, Gwynedd CC
Llanegwad, Carmarthenshire CC
Llaneilian, Isle of Anglesey CC
Llanelian yn Rhos, Conwy CBC
Llanelidan, Denbighshire CC
Llanelli, Carmarthenshire CC
Llanelli Rural, Carmarthenshire CC
Llanelltyd, Gwynedd CC
Llanelly, Monmouthshire CC
Llanelwedd, Powys CC
Llanengan, Gwynedd CC
Llannerch-y-Medd, Isle of Anglesey CC
Llanerfyl, Powys CC
Llaneugrad, Isle of Anglesey CC
Llanfachraeth, Isle of Anglesey CC
Llanfachreth, Gwynedd CC
Llanfaelog, Isle of Anglesey CC
Llanfaethlu, Isle of Anglesey CC
Llanfair, Gwynedd CC
Llanfair, Vale of Glamorgan Cl
Llanfair ar y bryn, Carmarthenshire CC
Llanfair Caereinion, Powys CC
Llanfair Clydogau, Ceredigion CC
Llanfair DC, Denbighshire CC
Llanfair Mathafarn Eithaf, Isle of Anglesey CC
Llanfair yn Neubwll, Isle of Anglesey CC
Llanfairfechan, Conwy CBC
Llanfairpwll, Isle of Anglesey CC

Llanfairtalhaiarn, Conwy CBC
Llanfairwaterdine, S Shropshire DC
Llanfarian, Ceredigion CC
Llanfechain, Powys CC
Llanferres, Denbighshire CC
Llanfihangel, Powys CC
Llanfihangel Aberbythych, Carmarthenshire CC
Llanfihangel ar Arth, Carmarthenshire CC
Llanfihangel Cwmdu, Powys CC
Llanfihangel Glyn Myfyr, Conwy CBC
Llanfihangel Rhos y Corn, Carmarthenshire CC
Llanfihangel Rhydithon, Powys CC
Llanfihangel y Pennant, Gwynedd CC
Llanfihangel Ystrad, Ceredigion CC
Llanfihangelelesceifiog, Isle of Anglesey CC
Llanfoist Fawr, Monmouthshire CC
Llanfrechfa, Torfaen CBC
Llanfrothen, Gwynedd CC
Llanfrynach, Powys CC
Llanfyllin, Powys CC
Llanfynydd, Carmarthenshire CC
Llanfynydd, Flintshire CC
Llangadog, Carmarthenshire CC
Llangain, Carmarthenshire CC
Llangammarch, Powys CC
Llangan, Vale of Glamorgan Cl
Llangarron, Herefordshire Cl
Llangathen, Carmarthenshire CC
Llangattock, Powys CC
Llangattock Vibon Avel, Monmouthshire CC
Llangedwyn, Powys CC
Llangefni, Isle of Anglesey CC
Llangeinor, Bridgend CBC
Llangeitho, Ceredigion CC
Llangeler, Carmarthenshire CC
Llangelynin, Gwynedd CC
Llangennech, Carmarthenshire CC
Llangennith, Swansea C&C
Llangernyw, Conwy CBC
Llangoed, Isle of Anglesey CC
Llangoedmor, Ceredigion CC
Llangollen, Denbighshire CC
Llangollen Rural, Wrexham CBC
Llangorse, Powys CC
Llangrannog, Ceredigion CC
Llangristiolus, Isle of Anglesey CC
Llangunllo, Powys CC

Llangurig, Powys CC
Llangwm, Conwy CBC
Llangwm, Monmouthshire CC
Llangwm, Pembrokeshire CC
Llangwyryfon, Ceredigion CC
Llangybi, Ceredigion CC
Llangybi, Monmouthshire CC
Llangyfelach, Swansea C&C
Llangyndeyrn, Carmarthenshire CC
Llangynhafal, Denbighshire CC
Llangynidr, Powys CC
Llangyniew, Powys CC
Llangynin, Carmarthenshire CC
Llangynnwr, Carmarthenshire CC
Llangynog, Carmarthenshire CC
Llangynog, Powys CC
Llangynwyd, Bridgend CBC
Llangynwyd Lower, Bridgend CBC
Llangywer, Gwynedd CC
Llanharan, Rhondda Cynon Taff CBC
Llanharry, Rhondda Cynon Taff CBC
Llanhennock, Monmouthshire CC
Llanhilleth, Blaenau Gwent CBC
Llanidan, Isle of Anglesey CC
Llanidloes, Powys CC
Llanidloes Without, Powys CC
Llanigon, Powys CC
Llanilar, Ceredigion CC
Llanishen, Cardiff CC
Llanllawddog, Carmarthenshire CC
Llanllechid, Gwynedd CC
Llanllwchaiarn, Ceredigion CC
Llanllwchaiarn, Powys CC
Llanllwni, Carmarthenshire CC
Llanllyfni, Gwynedd CC
Llanmaes, Vale of Glamorgan CI
Llannefydd, Conwy CBC
Llannor, Gwynedd CC
Llan-non, Carmarthenshire CC
Llanover, Monmouthshire CC
Llanpumsaint, Carmarthenshire CC
Llanrhaeadr, Powys CC
Llanrhaeadr Y C, Denbighshire CC
Llanrhaeadr ym Mochnant, Powys CC
Llanrhian, Pembrokeshire CC
Llanrhidian Higher, Swansea C&C
Llanrhidian Lower, Swansea C&C
Llanrhos, Conwy CBC
Llanrhystud, Ceredigion CC
Llanrothal, Herefordshire CI
Llanrug, Gwynedd CC

Llanrumney, Cardiff CC
Llanrwst, Conwy CBC
Llansadwrn, Carmarthenshire CC
Llansanffraid Glan Conwy, Conwy CBC
Llansannan, Conwy CBC
Llansantffraed, Ceredigion CC
Llansantffraid, Powys CC
Llansawel, Carmarthenshire CC
Llansilin, Powys CC
Llanstadwell, Pembrokeshire CC
Llansteffan, Carmarthenshire CC
Llantarnam, Torfaen CBC
Llantilio Crossenny, Monmouthshire CC
Llantilio Pertholey, Monmouthshire CC
Llantrisant, Rhondda Cynon Taff CBC
Llantrisant Fawr, Monmouthshire CC
Llantwit Fardre, Rhondda Cynon Taff CBC
Llantwit Major, Vale of Glamorgan CI
Llantysilio, Denbighshire CC
Llanuwchllyn, Gwynedd CC
Llanvaches, Newport City CI
Llanveynoe, Herefordshire CI
Llanwarne, Herefordshire CI
Llanwddyn, Powys CC
Llanwenog, Ceredigion CC
Llanwern, Newport City CI
Llanwinio, Carmarthenshire CC
Llanwnda, Gwynedd CC
Llanwnen, Ceredigion CC
Llanwrda, Carmarthenshire CC
Llanwrthwl, Powys CC
Llanwrtyd Wells, Powys CC
Llanyblodwel, Oswestry BC
Llanybydder, Carmarthenshire CC
Llanycil, Gwynedd CC
Llanycrwys, Carmarthenshire CC
Llanymynech, Oswestry BC
Llanynys, Denbighshire CC
Llanyrafon, Torfaen CBC
Llanyre, Powys CC
Llanystumdwy, Gwynedd CC
Llawhaden, Pembrokeshire CC
Llawnt, Oswestry BC
Llay, Wrexham CBC
Lledrod, Ceredigion CC
Llwchwr, Swansea C&C
Llwyn, S Shropshire DC
Llysfaen, Conwy CBC
Llywel, Powys CC
Loandhu, Highland CI
Loanend, Berwick-u-Tweed BC
Loanhead, Midlothian CI

Loans, S Ayrshire CI
Loch Tay, Perth/Kinross CI
Lochailort, Highland CI
Lochaline, Highland CI
Lochanhully, Highland CI
Lochans, Dumfries/Galloway CI
Locharbriggs, Dumfries/Galloway CI
Lochardil, Highland CI
Lochassynt, Highland CI
Lochboisdale, Comhairle Nan Eilean Siar
Lochcarron, Highland CI
Lochearnhead, Stirling CI
Lochee, Dundee City
Lochend, Highland CI
Lochfield, Renfrewshire CI
Lochgelly, Fife CI
Lochgilphead, Argyll/Bute CI
Lochgoil, Argyll/Bute CI
Lochgoilhead, Argyll/Bute CI
Lochinver, Highland CI
Lochmaben, Dumfries/Galloway CI
Lochore, Fife CI
Lochranza, N Ayrshire CI
Lochrutton, Dumfries/Galloway CI
Lochside, Dumfries/Galloway CI
Lochside, Highland CI
Lochslin, Highland CI
Lochwinnoch, Renfrewshire CI
Lochyside, Highland CI
Lockengate, Restormel BC
Lockerbie, Dumfries/Galloway CI
Lockeridge, Kennet DC
Lockerley, Test Valley BC
Locking, N Somerset DC
Lockinge, Vale of White Horse DC
Lockington, E Riding of Yks
Lockington, N W Leics DC
Lockleywood, N Shropshire DC
Locks Heath, Fareham BC
Lockton, Ryedale DC
Lockwood, Redcar/Cleveland BC
Loddington, Harborough DC
Loddington, Kettering BC
Loddiswell, S Hams DC
Loddon, S Norfolk DC
Lode, E Cambs DC
Loders, W Dorset DC
Lodge Moor, Sheffield City
Lodsworth, Chichester DC
Lofthouse, Harrogate BC
Lofthouse Gate, Wakefield MDC
Loftus, Redcar/Cleveland BC
Logan, E Ayrshire CI
Loganlea, W Lothian CI
Loggerheads, Newcastle-u-Lyme BC

Logie Buchan, Aberdeenshire Cl
Logie Coldstone, Aberdeenshire Cl
Logie Hill, Highland Cl
Logie Port, Angus Cl
Lolworth, S Cambs DC
Lonbain, Highland Cl
Londesborough, E Riding of Yks
London Colney, St Albans City/DC
London End, Stratford/Avon DC
Londonthorpe, S Kesteven DC
Londubh, Highland Cl
Lonemore, Highland Cl
Long Ashton, N Somerset DC
Long Bennington, S Kesteven DC
Long Bredy, W Dorset DC
Long Buckby, Daventry DC
Long Clawson, Melton BC
Long Common, Bridgnorth DC
Long Compton, Stafford BC
Long Compton, Stratford/Avon DC
Long Crendon, Aylesbury Vale DC
Long Crichel, E Dorset DC
Long Ditton, Elmbridge BC
Long Drax, Selby DC
Long Eaton, Erewash BC
Long Hanborough, W Oxon DC
Long Hill, High Peak BC
Long Itchington, Stratford/Avon DC
Long Lawford, Rugby BC
Long Load, S Somerset DC
Long Man, Wealden DC
Long Marston, Dacorum BC
Long Marston, Harrogate BC
Long Marston, Stratford/Avon DC
Long Marton, Eden DC
Long Melford, Babergh DC
Long Newnton, Cotswold DC
Long Preston, Craven DC
Long Riston, E Riding of Yks
Long Stratton, S Norfolk DC
Long Sutton, Hart DC
Long Sutton, S Holland DC
Long Sutton, S Somerset DC
Long Thurlow, Mid Suffolk DC
Long Whatton, N W Leics DC
Long Wittenham, S Oxon DC
Longborough, Cotswold DC
Longbridge, Birmingham City
Longbridge Deverill, W Wilts DC
Longburton, W Dorset DC
Longcot, Vale of White Horse DC
Longcroft, Falkirk Cl
Longden, Shrewsbury/Atcham Cl
Longdendale, Tameside MBC
Longdon, Lichfield DC

Longdon, Malvern Hills DC
Longdon on Tern, Telford/Wrekin BC
Longdowns, Kerrier DC
Longfield, Dartford BC
Longford, Coventry City MDC
Longford, Derbys Dales DC
Longford, Neath Port Talbot CBC
Longford, N Shropshire DC
Longford, Telford/Wrekin BC
Longford, Tewkesbury BC
Longforgan, Perth/Kinross Cl
Longformacus, Scottish Borders Cl
Longframlington, Alnwick DC
Longham, Breckland Cl
Longham, E Dorset DC
Longhirst, Castle Morpeth BC
Longhope, Forest of Dean DC
Longhorsley, Castle Morpeth BC
Longhoughton, Alnwick DC
Longley, Sheffield City
Longley Green, Malvern Hills DC
Longnewton, Stockton-on-Tees BC
Longney, Stroud DC
Longniddry, E Lothian Cl
Longnor, Shrewsbury/Atcham Cl
Longnor, Staffs Moorlands DC
Longparish, Test Valley BC
Longridge, Ribble Valley BC
Longridge, W Lothian Cl
Longridge Towers, Berwick-u-Tweed DC
Longriggend, N Lanarkshire Cl
Longsdon, Staffs Moorlands DC
Longside, Aberdeenshire Cl
Longsleddale, S Lakeland DC
Longslow, N Shropshire DC
Longstanton, S Cambs DC
Longstock, Test Valley BC
Longstowe, S Cambs DC
Longthorpe, Peterborough City
Longton, S Ribble BC
Longton, Stoke-on-Trent City
Longtown, Carlisle City
Longtown, Herefordshire Cl
Longville in the Dale, S Shropshire DC
Longwell Green, S Glos Cl
Longwick, Wycombe DC
Longwitton, Castle Morpeth BC
Longworth, Vale of White Horse DC
Lonmay, Aberdeenshire Cl
Lonmore, Highland Cl
Looe, Caradon DC
Loose, Maidstone BC
Loosley Row, Wycombe DC
Lopen, S Somerset DC

Lopham, Breckland Cl
Loppington, N Shropshire DC
Lorbottle, Alnwick DC
Lordington, Chichester DC
Loreburn, Dumfries/Galloway Cl
Lorton, Allerdale BC
Loscoe, Amber Valley BC
Lossiemouth, Moray Cl
Lostock, Bolton MBC
Lostock Gralam, Vale Royal BC
Lostock Hall, S Ribble BC
Lostwithiel, Restormel BC
Lothbeg, Highland Cl
Lothersdale, Craven DC
Lothmore, Highland Cl
Loudwater, Wycombe DC
Loughborough, Charnwood DC
Loughbrickland, Banbridge DC
Loughton, Epping Forest DC
Loughton, Milton Keynes Cl
Lound, Bassetlaw DC
Lound, S Kesteven DC
Lound, Waveney DC
Loundsley Green, Chesterfield BC
Lount, N W Leics DC
Louth, E Lindsey DC
Lovacott, N Devon DC
Love Clough, Rossendale BC
Loversall, Doncaster MBC
Loves Green, Chelmsford BC
Lovington, S Somerset DC
Low Abbotside, Richmondshire DC
Low Bentham, Craven DC
Low Bishopside, Harrogate BC
Low Bradfield, Sheffield City
Low Bradley, Craven DC
Low Braithwaite, Eden DC
Low Brunton, Tynedale DC
Low Burnham, N Lincs Cl
Low Coniscliffe, Darlington BC
Low Dinsdale, Darlington BC
Low Dovengill, Eden DC
Low Gate, Tynedale DC
Low Heskett, Eden DC
Low Hesleyhurst, Alnwick DC
Low Leighton, High Peak BC
Low Mill, Ryedale DC
Low Row, Carlisle City
Low Row, Richmondshire DC
Low Toynton, E Lindsey DC
Low Valleyfield, Fife Cl
Low Westwood, Derwentside DC
Low Worsall, Hambleton DC
Lowca, Copeland BC
Lowdham, Newark/Sherwood DC
Lowedges, Sheffield City
Lower Allithwaite, S Lakeland DC
Lower Arboll, Highland Cl

Lower Assendon, S Oxon DC
Lower Badcall, Highland CI
Lower Beeding, Horsham DC
Lower Benefield, E Northants CI
Lower Binton, Stratford/Avon DC
Lower Boddington, S Northants CI
Lower Braes, Falkirk CI
Lower Brailes, Stratford/Avon DC
Lower Breakish, Highland CI
Lower Broadheath, Malvern Hills DC
Lower Brynamman, Neath Port Talbot CBC
Lower Bullingham, Herefordshire CI
Lower Cam, Stroud DC
Lower Chelmscote, Stratford/Avon DC
Lower Clopton, Stratford/Avon DC
Lower Darwen, Blackburn with Darwen BC
Lower Diabaig, Highland CI
Lower Dounreay, Highland CI
Lower Down, S Shropshire DC
Lower Drummond, Highland CI
Lower Dunsforth, Harrogate BC
Lower Eythorne, Dover DC
Lower Farringdon, E Hants DC
Lower Forge, Bridgnorth DC
Lower Frankton, N Shropshire DC
Lower Froyle, E Hants DC
Lower Gledfield, Highland CI
Lower Goldstone, Dover DC
Lower Green, N Norfolk DC
Lower Green, W Berks DC
Lower Halistra, Highland CI
Lower Halstow, Swale BC
Lower Hardres, Canterbury City
Lower Harpton, Herefordshire CI
Lower Hartsay, Amber Valley BC
Lower Heyford, Cherwell DC
Lower Higham, Gravesham BC
Lower Holker, S Lakeland DC
Lower Ingon, Stratford/Avon DC
Lower Kinnerton, Chester City
Lower Langford, N Somerset DC
Lower Largo, Fife CI
Lower Lemington, Cotswold DC
Lower Meon, Stratford/Avon DC
Lower Milovaig, Highland CI
Lower Moor, Wychavon DC
Lower Nazeing, Epping Forest DC
Lower Netchwood, Bridgnorth DC
Lower New Inn, Torfaen CBC
Lower Ollach, Highland CI
Lower Penn, S Staffs CI

Lower Pennington, New Forest DC
Lower Peover, Vale Royal BC
Lower Pitkerrie, Highland CI
Lower Quinton, Stratford/Avon DC
Lower Raydon, Babergh DC
Lower Sapey, Malvern Hills DC
Lower Shiplake, S Oxon DC
Lower Shuckburgh, Stratford/Avon DC
Lower Slaughter, Cotswold DC
Lower Stoke, Medway CI
Lower Stondon, Mid Beds DC
Lower Sundon, S Beds DC
Lower Swell, Cotswold DC
Lower Thurlton, S Norfolk DC
Lower Tysoe, Stratford/Avon DC
Lower Upham, Winchester City
Lower Vexford, W Somerset DC
Lower Washburn, Harrogate BC
Lower Waterston, W Dorset DC
Lower Wawensmere, Stratford/Avon DC
Lower Wield, E Hants DC
Lower Withington, Macclesfield BC
Lower Woodend, Wycombe DC
Lowesby, Harborough DC
Lowestoft, Waveney DC
Loweswater, Allerdale BC
Lowfield, Sheffield City
Lowgates, Chesterfield BC
Lowgill, Lancaster City
Lowgill, S Lakeland DC
Lowick, Berwick-u-Tweed BC
Lowick, E Northants CI
Lowick, S Lakeland DC
Lowlands, Torfaen CBC
Lowside Quarter, Copeland BC
Lowsonford, Warwick DC
Lowther, Eden DC
Lowthorpe, E Riding of Yks
Lowton, Wigan MBC
Loxbeare, Mid Devon DC
Loxhill, Waverley BC
Loxhore, N Devon DC
Loxley, Sheffield City
Loxley, Stratford/Avon DC
Loxton, N Somerset DC
Loxwood, Chichester DC
Lubbesthorpe, Blaby DC
Lubenham, Harborough DC
Lubinvullin, Highland CI
Luccombe, W Somerset DC
Luccombe Village, Isle of Wight CI
Lucker, Berwick-u-Tweed BC
Luckington, N Wilts DC
Lucklawhill, Fife CI

Lucton, Herefordshire CI
Ludborough, E Lindsey DC
Luddenden, Calderdale MBC
Luddenham, Swale BC
Luddesdown, Gravesham BC
Luddington, E Northants CI
Luddington, N Lincs CI
Luddington, Stratford/Avon DC
Ludford, E Lindsey DC
Ludford, S Shropshire DC
Ludgershall, Aylesbury Vale DC
Ludgershall, Kennet DC
Ludgvan, Penwith DC
Ludham, N Norfolk DC
Ludlow, S Shropshire DC
Ludstone, Bridgnorth DC
Ludworth, Durham City
Luffield Abbey, Aylesbury Vale DC
Luffincott, Torridge DC
Lugar, E Ayrshire CI
Lugton, E Ayrshire CI
Lugwardine, Herefordshire CI
Luib, Highland CI
Luing, Argyll/Bute CI
Lullington, Mendip DC
Lullington, S Derbys DC
Lulsley, Malvern Hills DC
Lumby, Selby DC
Lumley, Chichester DC
Lumphanan, Aberdeenshire CI
Lumphinnans, Fife CI
Lumsden, Aberdeenshire CI
Lunanhead, Angus CI
Luncarty, Perth/Kinross CI
Lund, E Riding of Yks
Lund, Selby DC
Lundie, Angus CI
Lundin Links, Fife CI
Lundy Island, Torridge DC
Lunedale, Teesdale DC
Lunnasting, Shetland Is CI
Lunsford's Cross, Rother DC
Luppitt, E Devon DC
Lupton, S Lakeland DC
Lurgashall, Chichester DC
Lusby, E Lindsey DC
Luss, Argyll/Bute CI
Lusta, Highland CI
Lustleigh, Teignbridge DC
Luston, Herefordshire CI
Luthrie, Fife CI
Luton, Luton BC
Luton, Medway CI
Lutterworth, Harborough DC
Lutton, E Northants CI
Lutton, S Holland DC
Luttons, Ryedale DC
Luxborough, W Somerset DC
Luxulyan, Restormel BC

Lybster, Highland CI
Lydbrook, Forest of Dean DC
Lydbury North, S Shropshire DC
Lydd, Shepway DC
Lydden, Dover DC
Lyddington, Rutland CC
Lydeard St Lawrence, Taunton
   Deane BC
Lydford, Mendip DC
Lydford, W Devon BC
Lydgate, Calderdale MBC
Lydgate, Sheffield City
Lydham, S Shropshire DC
Lydiard Millicent, N Wilts DC
Lydiard Tregoz, N Wilts DC
Lydiate, Sefton MBC
Lydlinch, N Dorset DC
Lydney, Forest of Dean DC
Lye, Dudley MBC
Lye Green, Chiltern DC
Lye Green, Stratford/Avon DC
Lyford, Vale of White Horse DC
Lymbridge Green, Shepway DC
Lyme Handley, Macclesfield BC
Lyme Regis, W Dorset DC
Lyminge, Shepway DC
Lymington, New Forest DC
Lyminster, Arun DC
Lymm, Warrington BC
Lymore, New Forest DC
Lympne, Shepway DC
Lympsham, Sedgemoor DC
Lympstone, E Devon DC
Lynchat, Highland CI
Lynclys, Oswestry BC
Lyndhurst, New Forest DC
Lyndhurst, Newark/Sherwood DC
Lyndon, Rutland CC
Lyne, Runnymede BC
Lyne, Scottish Borders CI
Lyne of Gorthleck, Highland CI
Lyneal, N Shropshire DC
Lyneham, N Wilts DC
Lyneham, W Oxon DC
Lynemouth, Castle Morpeth BC
Lynesack, Teesdale DC
Lynford, Breckland CI
Lyng, Breckland CI
Lyng, Sedgemoor DC
Lynmouth, N Devon DC
Lynsted, Swale BC
Lynton, N Devon DC
Lynwilg, Highland CI
Lyonshall, Herefordshire CI
Lypiatt, Stroud DC
Lytchett Matravers, Purbeck DC
Lytchett Minster, Purbeck DC
Lyth, S Lakeland DC
Lytham St Anne's, Fylde BC
Lythe, Scarborough BC

Mabe, Kerrier DC
Mablethorpe, E Lindsey DC
Macclesfield, Macclesfield BC
Macduff, Aberdeenshire CI
Macefen, Chester City
Machen, Caerphilly CBC
Machrie, N Ayrshire CI
Machrihanish, Argyll/Bute CI
Machynlleth, Powys CC
Mackworth, Amber Valley BC
Mackworth, Derby City
Macmerry, E Lothian CI
Macosquin, Coleraine BC
Maddiston, Falkirk CI
Madehurst, Arun DC
Madeley, Newcastle-u-Lyme BC
Madeley, Telford/Wrekin BC
Madingley, S Cambs DC
Madley, Herefordshire CI
Madresfield, Malvern Hills DC
Madron, Penwith DC
Maelor South, Wrexham CBC
Maenclochog, Pembrokeshire CC
Maentwrog, Gwynedd CC
Maer, Newcastle-u-Lyme BC
Maesbrook, Oswestry BC
Maesbury Marsh, Oswestry BC
Maescar, Powys CC
Maesteg, Bridgend CBC
Maesycwmmer, Caerphilly CBC
Magdalen Laver, Epping Forest
   DC
Maghaberry, Lisburn City
Magham Down, Wealden DC
Maghera, Magherafelt DC
Magherafelt, Magherafelt DC
Magheramore, Limavady BC
Maghull, Sefton MBC
Magor, Monmouthshire CC
Maida Vale, Westminster City
Maiden Bradley, Salisbury DC
Maiden Law, Derwentside DC
Maiden Newton, W Dorset DC
Maidenhead,
   Windsor/Maidenhead RB
Maidens, S Ayrshire CI
Maidenwell, E Lindsey DC
Maidford, S Northants CI
Maids Moreton, Aylesbury Vale
   DC
Maidstone, Maidstone BC
Maidwell, Daventry DC
Mainstone, S Shropshire DC
Maisemore, Tewkesbury BC
Maker, Caradon DC
Makerstoun, Scottish Borders CI
Malborough, S Hams DC
Malden Rushett, Kingston upon
   Thames Royal Borough

Maldon, Maldon DC
Malham, Craven DC
Malham Moor, Craven DC
Maligar, Highland CI
Malin Bridge, Sheffield City
Mallaig, Highland CI
Mallaigmore, Highland CI
Mallaigvaig, Highland CI
Mallerstang, Eden DC
Mallusk, Newtownabbey BC
Mallwyd, Gwynedd CC
Malmesbury, N Wilts DC
Malpas, Carrick DC
Malpas, Chester City
Maltby, Rotherham MBC
Maltby, Stockton-on-Tees BC
Maltby le Marsh, E Lindsey DC
Maltman's Hill, Ashford BC
Malton, Derwentside DC
Malton, Ryedale DC
Malvern, Malvern Hills DC
Malvern Link, Malvern Hills DC
Malvern Wells, Malvern Hills DC
Mamhead, Teignbridge DC
Manaccan, Kerrier DC
Manafon, Powys CC
Manaton, Teignbridge DC
Manby, E Lindsey DC
Mancetter, N Warks BC
Manchester, Manchester City
Mandale, Stockton-on-Tees BC
Manea, Fenland DC
Manfield, Richmondshire DC
Mangotsfield, S Glos CI
Mangrove Green, N Herts DC
Mankinholes, Calderdale MBC
Manley, Vale Royal BC
Manningford, Kennet DC
Manningford Bohune, Kennet DC
Manningford Bruce, Kennet DC
Mannings Heath, Horsham DC
Mannington, N Norfolk DC
Manningtree, Tendring DC
Mannofield, Aberdeen City
Manor, Brent LBC
Manor, Scottish Borders CI
Manor, Sheffield City
Manor Park, Newham LBC
Manorbier, Pembrokeshire CC
Manordeifi, Pembrokeshire CC
Manordeilo/Salem,
   Carmarthenshire CC
Mansell Gamage, Herefordshire
   CI
Mansell Lacy, Herefordshire CI
Mansergh, S Lakeland DC
Mansewood, Glasgow City
Mansfield, Mansfield DC
Mansfield Woodhouse, Mansfield
   DC

Mansriggs, S Lakeland DC
Manston, N Dorset DC
Manston, Thanet DC
Manthorpe, S Kesteven DC
Manton, Kennet DC
Manton, N Lincs CI
Manton, Rutland CC
Manuden, Tendring DC
Manuden, Uttlesford DC
Maperton, S Somerset DC
Mapesbury, Brent LBC
Maple Cross, Three Rivers DC
Maplebeck, Newark/Sherwood
 DC
Mapledurham, S Oxon DC
Mapledurwell,
 Basingstoke/Deane BC
Maplehurst, Horsham DC
Mapperley, Amber Valley BC
Mapperton, W Dorset DC
Mappleborough Green,
 Stratford/Avon DC
Mappleton, Derbys Dales DC
Mappleton, E Riding of Yks
Mappowder, N Dorset DC
Marazion, Penwith DC
Marbury, Crewe/Nantwich BC
Marbury, Vale Royal BC
March, Fenland DC
Marcham, Vale of White Horse
 DC
Marchamley, N Shropshire DC
Marchington, E Staffs BC
Marchwiel, Wrexham CBC
Marchwood, New Forest DC
Marden, Chichester DC
Marden, Herefordshire CI
Marden, Kennet DC
Marden, Maidstone BC
Marden Ash, Epping Forest DC
Mardu, S Shropshire DC
Marefield, Harborough DC
Mareham le Fen, E Lindsey DC
Mareham on the Hill, E Lindsey
 DC
Maresfield, Wealden DC
Margam, Neath Port Talbot CBC
Margam Moors, Neath Port
 Talbot CBC
Margaret Marsh, N Dorset DC
Margaret Roding, Uttlesford DC
Margaretting, Chelmsford BC
Margate, Thanet DC
Marham, King's Lynn/W Norfolk
 BC
Marhamchurch, N Cornwall DC
Marholm, Peterborough City
Mariansleigh, N Devon DC
Marishader, Highland CI
Marishes, Ryedale DC

Mark, Sedgemoor DC
Mark Cross, Wealden DC
Markbeech, Sevenoaks DC
Markby, E Lindsey DC
Markenfield Hall, Harrogate BC
Market Bosworth,
 Hinckley/Bosworth BC
Market Deeping, S Kesteven DC
Market Drayton, N Shropshire DC
Market Harborough, Harborough
 DC
Market Lavington, Kennet DC
Market Overton, Rutland CC
Market Rasen, W Lindsey DC
Market Stainton, E Lindsey DC
Market Weighton, E Riding of Yks
Market Weston, St Edmundsbury
 BC
Markfield, Hinckley/Bosworth BC
Markham Clinton, Bassetlaw DC
Markinch, Fife CI
Markington, Harrogate BC
Marks Tey, Colchester BC
Marksbury, Bath/N E Somerset CI
Markwell, Caradon DC
Markyate, Dacorum BC
Marlborough, Kennet DC
Marlcliff, Stratford/Avon DC
Marldon, S Hams DC
Marlesford, Suffolk C'l DC
Marley, Chichester DC
Marley, Dover DC
Marley Green, Crewe/Nantwich
 BC
Marlingford, S Norfolk DC
Marloes, Pembrokeshire CC
Marlow, Wycombe DC
Marlow Bottom, Wycombe DC
Marlston cum Lache, Chester City
Marnham, Bassetlaw DC
Marnhull, N Dorset DC
Marnoch, Aberdeenshire CI
Marple, Stockport MBC
Marr, Doncaster MBC
Marraway, Stratford/Avon DC
Marrel, Highland CI
Marrick, Richmondshire DC
Marsden, Kirklees MC
Marsett, Richmondshire DC
Marsh, E Devon DC
Marsh Baldon, S Oxon DC
Marsh Chapel, E Lindsey DC
Marsh Farm, Luton BC
Marsh Gibbon, Aylesbury Vale
 DC
Marsh Green, E Devon DC
Marsh Green, Telford/Wrekin BC
Marsh House, Stockton-on-Tees
 BC
Marshalswick, St Albans City/DC

Marsham, Broadland DC
Marshborough, Dover DC
Marshbrook, S Shropshire DC
Marshfield, Newport City CI
Marshfield, S Glos CI
Marshgate, N Cornwall DC
Marshland St James, King's
 Lynn/W Norfolk BC
Marshside, Canterbury City
Marshside, Sefton MBC
Marshwood, W Dorset DC
Marske, Richmondshire DC
Marske by the Sea,
 Redcar/Cleveland BC
Marston, Kennet DC
Marston, S Kesteven DC
Marston, S Oxon DC
Marston, Stafford BC
Marston, Vale Royal BC
Marston Doles, Stratford/Avon
 DC
Marston Green, Solihull MBC
Marston Jabbett,
 Nuneaton/Bedworth BC
Marston Magna, S Somerset DC
Marston Meysey, N Wilts DC
Marston Montgomery, Derbys
 Dales DC
Marston Moretaine, Mid Beds DC
Marston on Dove, S Derbys DC
Marston St Lawrence, S
 Northants CI
Marston Trussel, Daventry DC
Marstow, Herefordshire CI
Marsworth, Aylesbury Vale DC
Martello, Tendring DC
Marten, Kennet DC
Marthall, Macclesfield BC
Martham, Gt Yarmouth BC
Martin, Dover DC
Martin, New Forest DC
Martin, N Kesteven DC
Martin Drove End, New Forest
 DC
Martin Hussingtree, Wychavon
 DC
Martin Mill, Dover DC
Martindale, Eden DC
Martinhoe, N Devon DC
Martinsthorpe, Rutland CC
Martlesham, Suffolk C'l DC
Martletwy, Pembrokeshire CC
Martley, Malvern Hills DC
Martock, S Somerset DC
Marton, Barrow-in-Furness BC
Marton, Harrogate BC
Marton, Macclesfield BC
Marton, Rugby BC
Marton, Ryedale DC
Marton, S Shropshire DC

Marton, Vale Royal BC
Marton, W Lindsey DC
Marton cum Grafton, Harrogate BC
Marton cum Moxby, Hambleton DC
Marton le Moor, Harrogate BC
Martons Both, Craven DC
Marwood, N Devon DC
Marwood, Teesdale DC
Mary Tavy, W Devon BC
Marybank, Highland CI
Maryburgh, Highland CI
Maryculter, Aberdeenshire CI
Marykirk, Aberdeenshire CI
Maryport, Allerdale BC
Marystow, W Devon BC
Masham, Harrogate BC
Mashbury, Chelmsford BC
Masongill, Craven DC
Mastin Moor, Chesterfield BC
Mastrick, Aberdeen City
Matching, Epping Forest DC
Matching Green, Epping Forest DC
Matching Tye, Epping Forest DC
Matfen, Castle Morpeth BC
Matfield, Tunbridge Wells BC
Mathern, Monmouthshire CC
Mathon Rural, Herefordshire CI
Mathry, Pembrokeshire CC
Matlaske, N Norfolk DC
Matlock, Derbys Dales DC
Matterdale End, Eden DC
Mattersey, Bassetlaw DC
Mattingley, Hart DC
Mattishall, Breckland CI
Mauchline, E Ayrshire CI
Maud, Aberdeenshire CI
Maugersbury, Cotswold DC
Maugherhay, Sheffield City
Maulden, Mid Beds DC
Maulds Meaburn, Eden DC
Maunby, Hambleton DC
Mautby, Gt Yarmouth BC
Mavesyn Ridware, Lichfield DC
Mavis Enderby, E Lindsey DC
Mawbray, Allerdale BC
Mawddwy, Gwynedd CC
Mawdesley, Chorley BC
Mawgan, Kerrier DC
Mawgan in Pydar, Restormel BC
Mawla, Carrick DC
Mawnan, Kerrier DC
Mawr, Swansea C&C
Maxey, Peterborough City
Maxstoke, N Warks BC
Maxton, Scottish Borders CI
Maxworthy, N Cornwall DC
Maybole, S Ayrshire CI

Mayfield, E Staffs BC
Mayfield, Midlothian CI
Mayfield, Highland CI
Mayfield, Wealden DC
Mayford, Woking BC
Maylands, Maldon DC
Mayobridge, Newry/Mourne DC
Mays Wood, Stratford/Avon DC
Maze, Lisburn City
Meadle, Wycombe DC
Meadowfield, Durham City
Meadowhall, Sheffield City
Meadowtown, S Shropshire DC
Meal Bank, S Lakeland DC
Mealo, Allerdale BC
Mealsgate, Allerdale BC
Mearbeck, Craven DC
Meare, Mendip DC
Mearley, Ribble Valley BC
Mears Ashby, Wellingborough BC
Measham, N W Leics DC
Meathop, S Lakeland DC
Meaux, E Riding of Yks
Meavy, W Devon BC
Mechell, Isle of Anglesey CC
Medbourne, Harborough DC
Medburn, Castle Morpeth BC
Meddon (nr Hartland), Torridge DC
Medlar, Fylde BC
Medmenham, Wycombe DC
Medomsley, Derwentside DC
Medstead, E Hants DC
Meerbrook, Staffs Moorlands DC
Meering, Newark/Sherwood DC
Meersbrook, Sheffield City
Meesden, E Herts DC
Meeth, W Devon BC
Meidrim, Carmarthenshire CC
Meifod, Powys CC
Meigh, Newry/Mourne DC
Meigle, Perth/Kinross CI
Meir, Stoke-on-Trent City
Meir Heath, Stafford BC
Melbecks, Richmondshire DC
Melbourn, S Cambs DC
Melbourne, E Riding of Yks
Melbourne, S Derbys DC
Melbury Abbas, N Dorset DC
Melbury Bubb, W Dorset DC
Melbury Osmond, W Dorset DC
Melbury Sampford, W Dorset DC
Melchbourne, Bedford BC
Melchet Park, Test Valley BC
Melcombe Horsey, W Dorset DC
Melcombe Regis,
 Weymouth/Portland BC
Meldon, Castle Morpeth BC
Meldon, W Devon BC
Meldreth, S Cambs DC

Meldrum, Aberdeenshire CI
Melin y coed, Conwy CBC
Melincrythan, Neath Port Talbot CBC
Melindwr, Ceredigion CC
Melkinthorpe, Eden DC
Melkridge, Tynedale DC
Melksham, W Wilts DC
Melling, Lancaster City
Melling, Sefton MBC
Mellis, Mid Suffolk DC
Mellon Charles, Highland CI
Mellon Udrigle, Highland CI
Mellor, Ribble Valley BC
Mells, Mendip DC
Mells, Suffolk C'I DC
Melmerby, Eden DC
Melmerby, Harrogate BC
Melmerby, Richmondshire DC
Melplash, W Dorset DC
Melrose, Scottish Borders CI
Melsonby, Richmondshire DC
Meltham, Kirklees MC
Melton, Suffolk C'I DC
Melton Constable, N Norfolk DC
Melton Mowbray, Melton BC
Melton Ross, N Lincs CI
Meltonby, E Riding of Yks
Melvaig, Highland CI
Melverley, Oswestry BC
Melvich, Highland CI
Membury, E Devon DC
Menabilly, Restormel BC
Menai Bridge, Isle of Anglesey CC
Mendham, Mid Suffolk DC
Mendlesham, Mid Suffolk DC
Menheniot, Caradon DC
Menstrie, Clackmannanshire CI
Mentmore, Aylesbury Vale DC
Menwith, Harrogate BC
Menzieshill, Dundee City
Meoble, Highland CI
Meole Brace,
 Shrewsbury/Atcham CI
Meonstoke, Winchester City
Meopham, Gravesham BC
Mepal, E Cambs DC
Meppershall, Mid Beds DC
Mere, Macclesfield BC
Mere, N Kesteven DC
Mere, Salisbury DC
Mereclough, Burnley BC
Mereworth, Tonbridge/Malling BC
Meriden, Solihull MBC
Merkadale, Highland CI
Merkinch, Highland CI
Merley, Poole BC
Merlins Bridge, Pembrokeshire CC

Merrington, Shrewsbury/Atcham CI
Merriott, S Somerset DC
Merrivale, W Devon BC
Merrybent, Darlington BC
Merrymeet, Caradon DC
Mersea Island, Colchester BC
Mersham, Ashford BC
Merstham, Reigate/Banstead BC
Merston, Chichester DC
Merstone, Isle of Wight CI
Merthyr Cynog, Powys CC
Merthyr Mawr, Bridgend CBC
Merthyr Tydfil, Merthyr Tydfil CBC
Merthyr Vale, Merthyr Tydfil CBC
Merton, Breckland CI
Merton, Cherwell DC
Merton, Torridge DC
Mertoun, Scottish Borders CI
Meshaw, N Devon DC
Messing, Colchester BC
Messing cum Inworth, Colchester BC
Messingham, N Lincs CI
Metfield, Mid Suffolk DC
Metheringham, N Kesteven DC
Methil, Fife CI
Methilhill, Fife CI
Methley, Leeds City
Methlick, Aberdeenshire CI
Methven, Perth/Kinross CI
Methwold, King's Lynn/W Norfolk BC
Methwold Hythe, King's Lynn/W Norfolk BC
Mettingham, Waveney DC
Mevagissey, Restormel BC
Meysey Hampton, Cotswold DC
Mial, Highland CI
Michaelchurch, Herefordshire CI
Michaelchurch Escley, Herefordshire CI
Michaelston, Vale of Glamorgan CI
Michaelstone y Fedw, Newport City CI
Michaelstow, N Cornwall DC
Micheldever, Winchester City
Michelmersh, Test Valley BC
Mickfield, Mid Suffolk DC
Mickle Trafford, Chester City
Mickleby, Scarborough BC
Micklefield, Leeds City
Micklefield, Wycombe DC
Mickleham, Mole Valley DC
Mickleover, Derby City
Mickleton, Cotswold DC
Mickleton, Teesdale DC
Mickletown, Leeds City
Mid Atholl, Perth/Kinross CI

Mid Calder, W Lothian CI
Mid Clyth, Highland CI
Mid Craigie, Dundee City
Mid Holmwood, Mole Valley DC
Mid Strome, Highland CI
Mid Wharfedale, Harrogate BC
Middle Assendon, S Oxon DC
Middle Aston, Cherwell DC
Middle Barton, W Oxon DC
Middle Claydon, Aylesbury Vale DC
Middle Littleton, Wychavon DC
Middle Rasen, W Lindsey DC
Middle Tysoe, Stratford/Avon DC
Middlebie, Dumfries/Galloway CI
Middlebrook, Bolton MBC
Middlecroft, Chesterfield BC
Middlefield, Stratford/Avon DC
Middleham, Richmondshire DC
Middlehope, S Shropshire DC
Middlemarsh, W Dorset DC
Middlesbrough, Middlesbrough CI
Middlesmoor, Harrogate BC
Middlestone, Sedgefield BC
Middlestown, Kirklees MC
Middleton, Berwick-u-Tweed BC
Middleton, Braintree DC
Middleton, Castle Morpeth BC
Middleton, Corby BC
Middleton, Harrogate BC
Middleton, King's Lynn/W Norfolk BC
Middleton, Lancaster City
Middleton, Leeds City
Middleton, N Warks BC
Middleton, Oswestry BC
Middleton, Rochdale MBC
Middleton, Ryedale DC
Middleton, S Lakeland DC
Middleton, S Shropshire DC
Middleton, Suffolk C'l DC
Middleton, Test Valley BC
Middleton Baggot, Bridgnorth DC
Middleton by Wirksworth, Derbys Dales DC
Middleton by Youlgrave, Derbys Dales DC
Middleton Cheney, S Northants CI
Middleton Green, E Staffs BC
Middleton in Teesdale, Teesdale DC
Middleton on Leven, Hambleton DC
Middleton on Sea, Arun DC
Middleton on the Hill, Herefordshire CI
Middleton on the Wolds, E Riding of Yks
Middleton Priors, Bridgnorth DC

Middleton St George, Darlington BC
Middleton Scriven, Bridgnorth DC
Middleton Stoney, Cherwell DC
Middleton Tyas, Richmondshire DC
Middlewich, Congleton BC
Middlewood, Sheffield City
Middlezoy, Sedgemoor DC
Middop, Ribble Valley BC
Middridge, Sedgefield BC
Midfield, Highland CI
Midgeholme, Carlisle City
Midgham, W Berks DC
Midgley, Calderdale MBC
Midhopestones, Sheffield City
Midhurst, Chichester DC
Midlem, Scottish Borders CI
Midloe, Huntingdonshire DC
Midmar, Aberdeenshire CI
Midsomer Norton, Bath/N E Somerset CI
Midtown, Highland CI
Midville, E Lindsey DC
Migdale, Highland CI
Migneint, Conwy CBC
Milborne Port, S Somerset DC
Milborne St Andrew, N Dorset DC
Milbourne, Castle Morpeth BC
Milburn, Eden DC
Milcombe, Cherwell DC
Milcote, Stratford/Avon DC
Milden, Babergh DC
Mildenhall, Forest Heath DC
Mildenhall, Kennet DC
Mile End, Aberdeen City
Mile End, Forest of Dean DC
Mile House, Stockton-on-Tees BC
Milebush, Maidstone BC
Mileham, Breckland CI
Milfield, Berwick-u-Tweed BC
Milford, Amber Valley BC
Milford, Stafford BC
Milford, Torridge DC
Milford, Waverley BC
Milford Haven, Pembrokeshire CC
Milford on Sea, New Forest DC
Milkwall, Forest of Dean DC
Mill Bank, Calderdale MBC
Mill Corner, Rother DC
Mill End, N Herts DC
Mill End, Wycombe DC
Mill Green, Brentwood BC
Mill Green, N Shropshire DC
Mill Hill, Barnet LBC
Mill Side, S Lakeland DC
Milland, Chichester DC
Millbank, Highland CI

Millbridge, Waverley BC
Millbrook, Caradon DC
Millbrook, Mid Beds DC
Millcraig, Highland CI
Millerston, E Dunbartonshire CI
Millholme, S Lakeland DC
Millhouses, Sheffield City
Millington, E Riding of Yks
Millington, Macclesfield BC
Millmeece, Stafford BC
Millnain, Highland CI
Millom, Copeland BC
Millom Without, Copeland BC
Millport, N Ayrshire CI
Millthrop, S Lakeland DC
Milltimber, Aberdeen City
Millwall, Tower Hamlets LBC
Milmonivaig, Highland CI
Milnafua, Highland CI
Milnathort, Perth/Kinross CI
Milngavie, E Dunbartonshire CI
Milnrow, Rochdale MBC
Milnthorpe, S Lakeland DC
Milson, S Shropshire DC
Milstead, Swale BC
Milston, Salisbury DC
Milton, Carlisle City
Milton, Cherwell DC
Milton, Fife CI
Milton, Glasgow City
Milton, Portsmouth City
Milton, S Cambs DC
Milton, Stoke-on-Trent City
Milton, Highland CI
Milton, Vale of White Horse DC
Milton, W Dunbartonshire CI
Milton Abbas, N Dorset DC
Milton Abbot, W Devon BC
Milton Bryan, Mid Beds DC
Milton Clevedon, Mendip DC
Milton Combe, W Devon BC
Milton Damerel, Torridge DC
Milton Ernest, Bedford BC
Milton Green, Chester City
Milton Keynes, Milton Keynes CI
Milton Lilbourne, Kennet DC
Milton Malsor, S Northants CI
Milton of Balgonie, Fife CI
Milton of Campsie, E
    Dunbartonshire CI
Milton Regis, Swale BC
Milton under Wychwood, W Oxon
    DC
Milverton, Taunton Deane BC
Milwich, Stafford BC
Minchinhampton, Stroud DC
Mindrum, Berwick-u-Tweed BC
Minehead, W Somerset DC
Minera, Wrexham CBC
Minety, N Wilts DC

Mingarrypark, Highland CI
Miningsby, E Lindsey DC
Minions, Caradon DC
Minishant, S Ayrshire CI
Minley Manor, Hart DC
Minshull Vernon, Crewe/Nantwich
    BC
Minskip, Harrogate BC
Minstead, New Forest DC
Minsted, Chichester DC
Minster, N Cornwall DC
Minster, Swale BC
Minster, Thanet DC
Minster Lovell, W Oxon DC
Minsteracres, Tynedale DC
Minsterley, Shrewsbury/Atcham
    CI
Minsterworth, Tewkesbury BC
Minterne Magna, W Dorset DC
Minting, E Lindsey DC
Mintlaw, Aberdeenshire CI
Minton, S Shropshire DC
Mirfield, Kirklees MC
Miserden, Stroud DC
Misson, Bassetlaw DC
Misterton, Bassetlaw DC
Misterton, Harborough DC
Misterton, S Somerset DC
Mistley, Tendring DC
Mitchel Troy, Monmouthshire CC
Mitcheldean, Forest of Dean DC
Mitford, Castle Morpeth BC
Mitford Bridge, Stratford/Avon DC
Mithian, Carrick DC
Mitton, S Staffs CI
Mixbury, Cherwell DC
Mixon, Staffs Moorlands DC
Mobberley, Macclesfield BC
Moccas, Herefordshire CI
Mochdre, Conwy CBC
Mochdre, Powys CC
Mockerkin, Allerdale BC
Modbury, S Hams DC
Moddershall, Stafford BC
Model Village, Stratford/Avon DC
Modsarie, Highland CI
Moel Llyn, Conwy CBC
Moel Seisiog, Conwy CBC
Moelfre, Isle of Anglesey CC
Moelfre Isaf, Conwy CBC
Moelfre Uchaf, Conwy CBC
Moffat, Dumfries/Galloway CI
Mogerhanger, Mid Beds DC
Moira, Lisburn City
Mol chlach, Highland CI
Molash, Ashford BC
Mold, Flintshire CC
Molecomb, Chichester DC
Molehill Green, Uttlesford DC
Molendinar, Glasgow City

Molescroft, E Riding of Yks
Molesworth, Huntingdonshire DC
Molland, N Devon DC
Mollington, Cherwell DC
Mollington, Chester City
Mollinsburn, E Dunbartonshire CI
Monewden, Suffolk C'l DC
Moneydie, Perth/Kinross CI
Moneymore, Cookstown DC
Moneyreagh, Castlereagh BC
Moniack, Highland CI
Monifieth, Angus CI
Monikie, Angus CI
Monimail, Fife CI
Monk Fryston, Selby DC
Monk Sherborne,
    Basingstoke/Deane BC
Monk Soham, Mid Suffolk DC
Monk's Heath, Macclesfield BC
Monkhopton, Bridgnorth DC
Monkland, Herefordshire CI
Monkleigh, Torridge DC
Monkokehampton, W Devon BC
Monks Eleigh, Babergh DC
Monks Horton, Shepway DC
Monks Kirby, Rugby BC
Monks Risborough, Wycombe DC
Monksilver, W Somerset DC
Monkston, Milton Keynes CI
Monkstown, Newtownabbey BC
Monkton, E Devon DC
Monkton, S Ayrshire CI
Monkton, Thanet DC
Monkton Up Wimborne, E Dorset
    DC
Monkton Combe, Bath/N E
    Somerset CI
Monkton Farleigh, W Wilts DC
Monkwood, E Hants DC
Monmouth, Monmouthshire CC
Monnington on Wye,
    Herefordshire CI
Monquhittor, Aberdeenshire CI
Montacute, S Somerset DC
Montford, Shrewsbury/Atcham CI
Montgomery, Powys CC
Montrose, Angus CI
Montsale, Maldon DC
Monxton, Test Valley BC
Monyash, Derbys Dales DC
Monymusk, Aberdeenshire CI
Moodiesburn, N Lanarkshire CI
Moor End, Wycombe DC
Moor Green, E Herts DC
Moor Monkton, Harrogate BC
Moor Park, Three Rivers DC
Moorby, E Lindsey DC
Moore, Halton BC
Moorends, Doncaster MBC
Moorfoot, Midlothian CI

Moorhouse, Carlisle City
Moorhouse, Newark/Sherwood DC
Moorlinch, Sedgemoor DC
Moorsholm, Redcar/Cleveland BC
Moorside, Derwentside DC
Moorside, Oldham MBC
Moorthorpe, Wakefield MDC
Moortown, Isle of Wight CI
Moortown, W Lindsey DC
Mop End, Chiltern DC
Morangie, Highland CI
Morar, Highland CI
Morborne, Huntingdonshire DC
Morchard Bishop, Mid Devon DC
Morcombelake, W Dorset DC
Morcott, Rutland CC
Morda, Oswestry BC
Morden, Merton LBC
Morden, Purbeck DC
Mordiford, Herefordshire CI
Mordington, Scottish Borders CI
Mordon, Sedgefield BC
More, S Shropshire DC
More Crichel, E Dorset DC
Morebath, Mid Devon DC
Morecambe, Lancaster City
Moredon, Swindon BC
Morefield, Highland CI
Moreleigh, S Hams DC
Moresby, Copeland BC
Morestead, Winchester City
Moreton, Epping Forest DC
Moreton, Herefordshire CI
Moreton, Purbeck DC
Moreton, S Oxon DC
Moreton, Wirral MBC
Moreton Corbet, N Shropshire DC
Moreton in Marsh, Cotswold DC
Moreton Jefferies, Herefordshire CI
Moreton Morrell, Stratford/Avon DC
Moreton on Lugg, Herefordshire CI
Moreton Paddox, Stratford/Avon DC
Moreton Pinkney, S Northants CI
Moreton Saye, N Shropshire DC
Moreton Valence, Stroud DC
Moretonhampstead, Teignbridge DC
Morland, Eden DC
Morley, Erewash BC
Morley, Leeds City
Morley, Teesdale DC
Morley Green, Macclesfield BC
Morley St Botolph, S Norfolk DC
Morningside, Edinburgh City

Morningthorpe, S Norfolk DC
Morpeth, Castle Morpeth BC
Morston, N Norfolk DC
Mortehoe, N Devon DC
Mortimer, W Berks DC
Mortimer West End, Basingstoke/Deane BC
Mortlake, Richmond upon Thames LBC
Morton, Newark/Sherwood DC
Morton, N E Derbys DC
Morton, N Kesteven DC
Morton, Oswestry BC
Morton, S Kesteven DC
Morton, W Lindsey DC
Morton Bagot, Stratford/Avon DC
Morton on Swale, Hambleton DC
Morton on the Hill, Broadland DC
Morton Palms, Darlington BC
Morton Tinmouth, Teesdale DC
Morvah, Penwith DC
Morval, Caradon DC
Morville, Bridgnorth DC
Morwenstow, N Cornwall DC
Mosborough, Sheffield City
Moscow, E Ayrshire CI
Mose, Bridgnorth DC
Mosedale, Eden DC
Moseley, Birmingham City
Moseley, Malvern Hills DC
Moss, Doncaster MBC
Moss, Highland CI
Moss Bank, St Helens MBC
Moss Side, Fylde BC
Moss Side, Highland CI
Mossblown, S Ayrshire CI
Mossend, N Lanarkshire CI
Mosside, Moyle DC
Mossley, Newtownabbey BC
Mossley, Tameside MBC
Mossley Hill, Liverpool City
Mosspark, Glasgow City
Mosstodloch, Moray CI
Mosterton, W Dorset DC
Moston, Chester City
Moston, Congleton BC
Mostyn, Flintshire CC
Motcombe, N Dorset DC
Motherby, Eden DC
Motherwell, N Lanarkshire CI
Mottingham, Bromley LBC
Mottisfont, Test Valley BC
Mottistone, Isle of Wight CI
Mottram St Andrew, Macclesfield BC
Mouldsworth, Chester City
Moulin, Perth/Kinross CI
Moulsford, S Oxon DC
Moulsoe, Milton Keynes CI
Moulton, Daventry DC

Moulton, Forest Heath DC
Moulton, Richmondshire DC
Moulton, S Holland DC
Moulton, Vale Royal BC
Moulton St Mary, Broadland DC
Moulton Seas End, S Holland DC
Mount, Carrick DC
Mount Blair, Perth/Kinross CI
Mount Bures, Colchester BC
Mount Ellen, E Dunbartonshire CI
Mount Florida, Glasgow City
Mount Gould, Plymouth City
Mount Hawke, Carrick DC
Mount High, Highland CI
Mount Melville, Fife CI
Mount Pleasant, Merthyr Tydfil CBC
Mount Pleasant, Torfaen CBC
Mount Vernon, Glasgow City
Mountain Ash, Rhondda Cynon Taff CBC
Mountfield, Rother DC
Mountgerald, Highland CI
Mountjoy, Restormel BC
Mountnessing, Brentwood BC
Mountsorrel, Charnwood DC
Mourne, Newry/Mourne DC
Mousehole, Penwith DC
Mouswald, Dumfries/Galloway CI
Mowsley, Harborough DC
Moy, Dungannon & S Tyrone BC
Moy, Highland CI
Moy Hall, Highland CI
Moyles Court, New Forest DC
Much Birch, Herefordshire CI
Much Cowarne, Herefordshire CI
Much Dewchurch, Herefordshire CI
Much Hadham, E Herts DC
Much Hoole, S Ribble BC
Much Marcle, Herefordshire CI
Much Wenlock, Bridgnorth DC
Muchalls, Aberdeenshire CI
Muchelney, S Somerset DC
Muchlarnick, Caradon DC
Muckhart, Clackmannanshire CI
Mucklestone, Newcastle-u-Lyme BC
Muckleton, N Shropshire DC
Muckton, E Lindsey DC
Mudeford, Christchurch BC
Mudford, S Somerset DC
Mugeary, Highland CI
Mugginton, Amber Valley BC
Muggleswick, Derwentside DC
Muie, Highland CI
Muir of Ord, Highland CI
Muir of Tarradale, Highland CI
Muirhead, Angus CI
Muirhead, N Lanarkshire CI

Muirhouses, Falkirk CI
Muirkirk, E Ayrshire CI
Muirshearlich, Highland CI
Muker, Richmondshire DC
Mulbarton, S Norfolk DC
Mull, Isle of, Argyll/Bute CI
Mullagh, Limavady BC
Mullaghbane, Newry/Mourne DC
Mullion, Kerrier DC
Mumbles, Swansea C&C
Mumby, E Lindsey DC
Muncaster, Copeland BC
Mundesley, N Norfolk DC
Mundford, Breckland CI
Mundham, S Norfolk DC
Mundon, Maldon DC
Mungrisdale, Eden DC
Munlochy, Highland CI
Munsley, Herefordshire CI
Munslow, S Shropshire DC
Murcott, Cherwell DC
Murieston, W Lothian CI
Murroes, Angus CI
Murrow, Fenland DC
Mursley, Aylesbury Vale DC
Murton, Berwick-u-Tweed BC
Murton, City of York CI
Murton, Easington DC
Murton, Eden DC
Musbury, E Devon DC
Muscoates, Ryedale DC
Musgrave, Eden DC
Musselburgh, E Lothian CI
Muston, Melton BC
Muston, Scarborough BC
Mustow Green, Wyre Forest DC
Muswell Hill, Haringey LBC
Mutford, Waveney BC
Muthill, Perth/Kinross CI
Mwdwl Eithin, Conwy CBC
Myddfai, Carmarthenshire CC
Myddle, N Shropshire DC
Myerscough, Wyre BC
Mylor, Carrick DC
Mynachlogddu, Pembrokeshire
   CC
Myndtown, S Shropshire DC
Mynydd Bodrochwyn, Conwy
   CBC
Mynydd Cribau, Conwy CBC
Mynydd Marian, Conwy CBC
Myrelandhorn, Highland CI
Mytchett, Surrey Heath BC
Mytholm, Calderdale MBC
Mytholmroyd, Calderdale MBC
Mythop, Fylde BC
Myton on Swale, Hambleton DC

Naburn, City of York CI
Nackington, Canterbury City

Nacton, Suffolk C'l DC
Nafferton, E Riding of Yks
Nailsea, N Somerset DC
Nailstone, Hinckley/Bosworth BC
Nailsworth, Stroud DC
Nairn, Highland CI
Nancegollan, Kerrier DC
Nancledra, Penwith DC
Nangreaves, Bury MBC
Nannerch, Flintshire CC
Nanpean, Restormel BC
Nanstallon, N Cornwall DC
Nantcwnlle, Ceredigion CC
Nantglyn, Denbighshire CC
Nantmawr, Oswestry BC
Nantmel, Powys CC
Nantwich, Crewe/Nantwich BC
Nantyglo, Blaenau Gwent CBC
Nantymoel, Bridgend CBC
Napchester, Dover DC
Naphill, Wycombe DC
Nappa, Craven DC
Napton Fields, Stratford/Avon DC
Napton Holt, Stratford/Avon DC
Napton on the Hill, Stratford/Avon
   DC
Narberth, Pembrokeshire CC
Narborough, Blaby DC
Narborough, Breckland CI
Narford, Breckland CI
Naseby, Daventry DC
Nash, Aylesbury Vale DC
Nash, Dover DC
Nash, Herefordshire CI
Nash, Newport City CI
Nash, S Shropshire DC
Nash Lee, Wycombe DC
Nash Mills, Dacorum BC
Nassington, E Northants CI
Nasty, E Herts DC
Nateby, Eden DC
Nateby, Wyre BC
Natland, S Lakeland DC
Naughton, Babergh DC
Naunton, Cotswold DC
Naunton Beauchamp, Wychavon
   DC
Navenby, N Kesteven DC
Navestock, Brentwood BC
Navidale, Highland CI
Nawton, Ryedale DC
Nayland, Babergh DC
Nazeing, Epping Forest DC
Nazeing Gate, Epping Forest DC
Neasham, Darlington BC
Neath, Neath Port Talbot CBC
Neath Hill, Milton Keynes CI
Neatishead, N Norfolk DC
Nebo, Conwy CBC
Nebsworth, Stratford/Avon DC

Nechells, Birmingham City
Necton, Breckland CI
Nedd, Highland CI
Nedging Tye, Babergh DC
Needham, S Norfolk DC
Needham Market, Mid Suffolk DC
Neen Savage, Bridgnorth DC
Neen Sollars, S Shropshire DC
Neenton, Bridgnorth DC
Nefyn, Gwynedd CC
Neilston, E Renfrewshire CI
Nelson, Caerphilly CBC
Nelson, Pendle BC
Nempnett Thrubwell, Bath/N E
   Somerset CI
Nenthead, Eden DC
Nenthorn, Scottish Borders CI
Nercwys, Flintshire CC
Neroche, Taunton Deane BC
Nesbit, Berwick-u-Tweed BC
Ness, Comhairle Nan Eilean Siar
Ness, Ellesmere Port/Neston BC
Ness, Ryedale DC
Nesscliffe, Shrewsbury/Atcham CI
Nesting, Shetland Is CI
Neston, Ellesmere Port/Neston
   BC
Netchwood, Bridgnorth DC
Nether Alderley, Macclesfield BC
Nether Broughton, Melton BC
Nether Burrow, Lancaster City
Nether Cerne, W Dorset DC
Nether Compton, W Dorset DC
Nether Edge, Sheffield City
Nether Green, Sheffield City
Nether Haugh, Rotherham MBC
Nether Heyford, S Northants CI
Nether Kellet, Lancaster City
Nether Langwith, Bassetlaw DC
Nether Padley, Derbys Dales DC
Nether Poppleton, City of York CI
Nether Row, Allerdale BC
Nether Silton, Hambleton DC
Nether Staveley, S Lakeland DC
Nether Stowey, Sedgemoor DC
Nether Wallop, Test Valley BC
Nether Whitacre, N Warks BC
Nether Winchendon, Aylesbury
   Vale DC
Nether Worton, W Oxon DC
Nether Wyresdale, Wyre BC
Netheravon, Kennet DC
Netherburn, S Lanarkshire CI
Netherbury, W Dorset DC
Netherby, Carlisle City
Netherby, Harrogate BC
Netherend, Forest of Dean DC
Netherexe, E Devon DC
Netherfield, Milton Keynes CI
Netherfield, Rother DC

Netherhampton, Salisbury DC
Netherseal, S Derbys DC
Netherthong, Kirklees MC
Netherthorpe, Sheffield City
Netherton, Alnwick DC
Netherton, Sefton MBC
Netherton, Teignbridge DC
Netherton, Wakefield MDC
Netherton, Wychavon DC
Nethertown, Copeland BC
Nethertown, Highland Cl
Netherwitton, Castle Morpeth BC
Nethy Bridge, Highland Cl
Nethybridge, Highland Cl
Netley Marsh, New Forest DC
Netterfield, Gedling BC
Nettlebed, S Oxon DC
Nettlebridge, Mendip DC
Nettlecombe, W Somerset DC
Nettleden, Dacorum BC
Nettleham, W Lindsey DC
Nettlestead, Maidstone BC
Nettlestead, Mid Suffolk DC
Nettlestone, Isle of Wight Cl
Nettleton, N Wilts DC
Nettleton, W Lindsey DC
Nevern, Pembrokeshire CC
Nevill Holt, Harborough DC
New Abbey, Dumfries/Galloway
    Cl
New Aberdour, Aberdeenshire Cl
New Alresford, Winchester City
New Ash Green, Sevenoaks DC
New Barn, Dartford BC
New Barnet, Barnet LBC
New Bradwell, Milton Keynes Cl
New Brancepeth, Durham City
New Brighton, Wirral MBC
New Buckenham, Breckland Cl
New Byth, Aberdeenshire Cl
New Cheriton, Winchester City
New Cross, Lewisham LBC
New Cumnock, E Ayrshire Cl
New Deer, Aberdeenshire Cl
New Earswick, City of York Cl
New Edlington, Doncaster MBC
New Ellerby, E Riding of Yks
New End, Stratford/Avon DC
New Farnley, Leeds City
New Ferry, Wirral MBC
New Forest, Richmondshire DC
New Frankley, Birmingham City
    Cl
New Galloway,
    Dumfries/Galloway Cl
New Gilston, Fife Cl
New Grimsby, Isles of Scilly Cl
New Hampton, Herefordshire Cl
New Hartley, Blyth Valley BC
New Haw, Runnymede BC

New Holland, N Lincs Cl
New Houghton, Bolsover DC
New Houses, Craven DC
New Hutton, S Lakeland DC
New Hythe, Tonbridge/Malling BC
New Inn, Torfaen CBC
New Invention, S Shropshire DC
New Kyo, Derwentside DC
New Lanark, S Lanarkshire Cl
New Leake, E Lindsey DC
New Luce, Dumfries/Galloway Cl
New Machar, Aberdeenshire Cl
New Malden, Kingston upon
    Thames Royal Borough
New Marske, Redcar/Cleveland
    BC
New Mill, Dacorum BC
New Mills, Carrick DC
New Mills, High Peak BC
New Mills, Macclesfield BC
New Mills, Highland Cl
New Milton, New Forest DC
New Moat, Pembrokeshire CC
New Pitsligo, Aberdeenshire Cl
New Polzeath, N Cornwall DC
New Radnor, Powys CC
New Romney, Shepway DC
New Rossington, Doncaster MBC
New Sauchie, Clackmannanshire
    Cl
New Silksworth, Sunderland City
New Southgate, Enfield LBC
New Stevenston, N Lanarkshire
    Cl
New Tredegar, Caerphilly CBC
New Waltham, N E Lincs Cl
New Whittington, Chesterfield BC
New Wimpole, S Cambs DC
New Winton, E Lothian Cl
New Yatt, W Oxon DC
New York, N Tyneside Cl
Newall, Harrogate BC
Newark, Peterborough City
Newark on Trent,
    Newark/Sherwood DC
Newarthill, N Lanarkshire Cl
Newbald, E Riding of Yks
Newbattle, Midlothian Cl
Newbiggin, Eden DC
Newbiggin, Richmondshire DC
Newbiggin, S Lakeland DC
Newbiggin, Teesdale DC
Newbiggin by the Sea, Wansbeck
    DC
Newbiggin on Lune, Eden DC
Newbigging, Angus Cl
Newbold, Chesterfield BC
Newbold, N W Leics DC
Newbold Astbury cum Moreton,
    Congleton BC

Newbold on Avon, Rugby BC
Newbold on Stour, Stratford/Avon
    DC
Newbold Pacey, Stratford/Avon
    DC
Newbold Verdon,
    Hinckley/Bosworth BC
Newborough, E Staffs BC
Newborough, Peterborough City
Newbottle, S Northants Cl
Newbourne, Suffolk C'l DC
Newbridge, Caerphilly CBC
Newbridge, Dumfries/Galloway Cl
Newbridge, Edinburgh City
Newbridge, Isle of Wight Cl
Newbridge, New Forest DC
Newbridge, Penwith DC
Newbrough, Tynedale DC
Newbuildings, Mid Devon DC
Newburgh, Aberdeenshire Cl
Newburgh, Fife Cl
Newburgh, Hambleton DC
Newburgh, W Lancs DC
Newburn, Newcastle City
Newbury, W Berks DC
Newby, Craven DC
Newby, Eden DC
Newby, Hambleton DC
Newby, Harrogate BC
Newby, Scarborough BC
Newby Bridge, S Lakeland DC
Newby East, Carlisle City
Newby Wiske, Hambleton DC
Newcarron, Falkirk Cl
Newcastle, Down DC
Newcastle Emlyn,
    Carmarthenshire CC
Newcastle Higher, Bridgend CBC
Newcastle on Clun, S Shropshire
    DC
Newcastle under Lyme,
    Newcastle-u-Lyme BC
Newcastle upon Tyne, Newcastle
    City
Newcastleton, Scottish Borders
    Cl
Newchapel, Tandridge DC
Newchurch, Isle of Wight Cl
Newchurch, Shepway DC
Newchurch/Merthyr,
    Carmarthenshire CC
Newchurch in Pendle, Pendle BC
Newdigate, Mole Valley DC
Newell Green, Bracknell Forest
    BC
Newenden, Ashford BC
Newent, Forest of Dean DC
Newfield, Highland Cl
Newgate, N Norfolk DC
Newhall, Crewe/Nantwich BC

Newhall, S Derbys DC
Newham, Berwick-u-Tweed BC
Newhaven, Lewes DC
Newhills, Aberdeen City
Newholm, Scarborough BC
Newick, Lewes DC
Newington, Shepway DC
Newington, S Oxon DC
Newington, Southwark LBC
Newington, Swale BC
Newland, Forest of Dean DC
Newland, Malvern Hills DC
Newland, Selby DC
Newland, S Lakeland DC
Newland, Wakefield MDC
Newland, Wokingham DC
Newlands, Glasgow City
Newlands, Scottish Borders Cl
Newlands, Highland Cl
Newlands, Tynedale DC
Newlands of Geise, Highland Cl
Newlyn, Penwith DC
Newmachar, Aberdeenshire Cl
Newmains, N Lanarkshire Cl
Newmarket, Forest Heath DC
Newmills, Fife Cl
Newmilns, E Ayrshire Cl
Newmore, Highland Cl
Newnham, Basingstoke/Deane BC
Newnham, Daventry DC
Newnham, Forest of Dean DC
Newnham, N Herts DC
Newnham, Stratford/Avon DC
Newnham, Swale BC
Newnham Regis, Rugby BC
Newport, E Riding of Yks
Newport, Gt Yarmouth BC
Newport, Isle of Wight Cl
Newport, Newport City Cl
Newport, Pembrokeshire CC
Newport, Stroud DC
Newport, Telford/Wrekin BC
Newport, Highland Cl
Newport, Uttlesford DC
Newport on Tay, Fife Cl
Newport Pagnell, Milton Keynes Cl
Newquay, Ceredigion CC
Newquay, Restormel BC
Newry, Newry/Mourne DC
Newsham, Hambleton DC
Newsham, Richmondshire DC
Newsholme, E Riding of Yks
Newsholme, Ribble Valley BC
Newsome, Kirklees MC
Newstead, Berwick-u-Tweed BC
Newstead, Gedling BC
Newthorpe, Selby DC
Newtimber, Mid Sussex DC

Newtoft, W Lindsey DC
Newton, Babergh DC
Newton, Barrow-in-Furness BC
Newton, Breckland Cl
Newton, E Staffs BC
Newton, Fenland DC
Newton, Hambleton DC
Newton, Herefordshire Cl
Newton, Kettering BC
Newton, Lancaster City
Newton, N Kesteven DC
Newton, Ribble Valley BC
Newton, Rugby BC
Newton, Rushcliffe BC
Newton, Ryedale DC
Newton, S Ayrshire Cl
Newton, S Cambs DC
Newton, S Lakeland DC
Newton, S Norfolk DC
Newton, Highland Cl
Newton, Tynedale DC
Newton, Vale Royal BC
Newton, W Lothian Cl
Newton, Fylde BC
Newton (nr Leominster), Herefordshire Cl
Newton (nr Longtown), Herefordshire Cl
Newton Abbot, Teignbridge DC
Newton Arlosh, Allerdale BC
Newton Aycliffe, Sedgefield BC
Newton Bewley, Hartlepool BC
Newton Blossomville, Milton Keynes Cl
Newton Bromswold, E Northants Cl
Newton by Tattenhall, Chester City
Newton by Toft, W Lindsey DC
Newton Ferrers, S Hams DC
Newton Flotman, S Norfolk DC
Newton Grange, Derbys Dales DC
Newton Hall, Durham City
Newton Harcourt, Harborough DC
Newton Kyme cum Toulston, Selby DC
Newton le Willows, Richmondshire DC
Newton le Willows, St Helens MBC
Newton Longville, Aylesbury Vale DC
Newton Mearns, E Renfrewshire Cl
Newton Morrell, Richmondshire DC
Newton Mulgrave, Scarborough BC
Newton of Ardtoe, Highland Cl

Newton on Derwent, E Riding of Yks
Newton on Ouse, Hambleton DC
Newton on the Moor, Alnwick DC
Newton on Trent, W Lindsey DC
Newton Poppleford, E Devon DC
Newton Purcell, Cherwell DC
Newton Regis, N Warks BC
Newton Reigny, Eden DC
Newton St Cyres, Mid Devon DC
Newton St Faith, Broadland DC
Newton St Loe, Bath/N E Somerset Cl
Newton St Petrock, Torridge DC
Newton Solney, S Derbys DC
Newton Stacey, Test Valley BC
Newton Stewart, Dumfries/Galloway Cl
Newton Tony, Salisbury DC
Newton Tracey, N Devon DC
Newton under Roseberry, Redcar/Cleveland BC
Newton Valence, E Hants DC
Newtongrange, Midlothian Cl
Newtonhill, Aberdeenshire Cl
Newtonhill, Highland Cl
Newtonmore, Highland Cl
Newtown, Alnwick DC
Newtown, Basingstoke/Deane BC
Newtown, Berwick-u-Tweed BC
Newtown, Isle of Wight Cl
Newtown, New Forest DC
Newtown, Poole BC
Newtown, Powys CC
Newtown, Staffs Moorlands DC
Newtown, Stockton-on-Tees BC
Newtown, Test Valley BC
Newtown, Winchester City
Newtown in St Martin, Kerrier DC
Newtown Linford, Charnwood DC
Newtown St Boswells, Scottish Borders Cl
Newtownabbey, Newtownabbey BC
Newtownards, Ards BC
Newtownbreda, Castlereagh BC
Newtownhamilton, Newry/Mourne DC
Newtownsaville, Omagh DC
Newtownstewart, Strabane DC
Newtyle, Angus Cl
Neyland, Pembrokeshire CC
Nicholashayne, Mid Devon DC
Nicholforest, Carlisle City
Nidd, Harrogate BC
Nigg, Aberdeen City
Nigg, Highland Cl
Nigg Ferry, Highland Cl
Nine Ashes, Epping Forest DC
Ninebanks, Tynedale DC

Ninfield, Wealden DC
Ningwood, Isle of Wight CI
Niton, Isle of Wight CI
No Man's Heath, Chester City
No Place, Derwentside DC
Nobottle, Daventry DC
Nocton, N Kesteven DC
Noke, Cherwell DC
Nolton, Pembrokeshire CC
Nomansland, Mid Devon DC
Noneley, N Shropshire DC
Nonikiln, Highland CI
Nonington, Dover DC
Nook, Carlisle City
Norbiton, Kingston upon Thames
  Royal Borough
Norbury, Crewe/Nantwich BC
Norbury, Croydon LBC
Norbury, Derbys Dales DC
Norbury, S Shropshire DC
Norbury, Stafford BC
Norchard, Wychavon DC
Nordelph, King's Lynn/W Norfolk
  BC
Norden, Rochdale MBC
Nordley, Bridgnorth DC
Norfolk Park, Sheffield City
Norham, Berwick-u-Tweed BC
Norley, Vale Royal BC
Norleywood, New Forest DC
Normanby, N Lincs CI
Normanby, Ryedale DC
Normanby by Spital, W Lindsey
  DC
Normanby le Wold, W Lindsey
  DC
Normandy, Guildford BC
Normanton, Derby City
Normanton, Newark/Sherwood
  DC
Normanton, Rutland CC
Normanton, S Kesteven DC
Normanton, Wakefield MDC
Normanton le Heath, N W Leics
  DC
Normanton on Soar, Rushcliffe
  BC
Normanton on the Wolds,
  Rushcliffe BC
Normanton on Trent, Bassetlaw
  DC
Normanton Springs, Sheffield City
Normoss, Fylde BC
Norris Hill, N W Leics DC
North, Weymouth/Portland BC
North Ashton (part), St Helens
  MBC
North Aston, Cherwell DC
North Baddesley, Test Valley BC
North Ballachulish, Highland CI

North Barrow, S Somerset DC
North Berwick, E Lothian CI
North Boarhunt, Winchester City
North Bovey, Teignbridge DC
North Bradley, W Wilts DC
North Cadbury, S Somerset DC
North Carlton, W Lindsey DC
North Cave, E Riding of Yks
North Central,
  Weymouth/Portland BC
North Cerney, Cotswold DC
North Charlton, Alnwick DC
North Cheriton, S Somerset DC
North Claines, Wychavon DC
North Cliffe, E Riding of Yks
North Clifton, Newark/Sherwood
  DC
North Coates, E Lindsey DC
North Cockerington, E Lindsey
  DC
North Cove, Waveney DC
North Cowton, Richmondshire DC
North Crawley, Milton Keynes CI
North Cray, Bexley LBC
North Creake, King's Lynn/W
  Norfolk BC
North Curry, Taunton Deane BC
North Dalton, E Riding of Yks
North Deighton, Harrogate BC
North Duffield, Selby DC
North Elkington, E Lindsey DC
North Elmham, Breckland CI
North Elmsall, Wakefield MDC
North End, Portsmouth City
North Erradale, Highland CI
North Fambridge, Maldon DC
North Fenham, Newcastle City
North Ferriby, E Riding of Yks
North Foreland, Thanet DC
North Frodingham, E Riding of
  Yks
North Gorley, New Forest DC
North Gosforth, Newcastle City
North Greetwell, W Lindsey DC
North Grimston, Ryedale DC
North Harris, Comhairle Nan
  Eilean Siar
North Harrow, Harrow LBC
North Hayling, Havant BC
North Heath, Horsham DC
North Hill, N Cornwall DC
North Hinksey, Vale of White
  Horse DC
North Holmwood, Mole Valley DC
North Huish, S Hams DC
North Hykeham, N Kesteven DC
North Kelsey, W Lindsey DC
North Kessock, Highland CI
North Killingholme, N Lincs CI
North Kilvington, Hambleton DC

North Kilworth, Harborough DC
North Knapdale, Argyll/Bute CI
North Kyme, N Kesteven DC
North Lee, Wycombe DC
North Leigh, W Oxon DC
North Leverton, Bassetlaw DC
North Littleton, Wychavon DC
North Lodge, Chester-le-Street
  DC
North Lopham, Breckland CI
North Luffenham, Rutland CC
North Marden, Chichester DC
North Marlbrook, Bromsgrove DC
North Marston, Aylesbury Vale
  DC
North Meols, W Lancs DC
North Molton, N Devon DC
North Moreton, S Oxon DC
North Mundham, Chichester DC
North Muskham,
  Newark/Sherwood DC
North Mymms, Welwyn Hatfield
  DC
North Newbald, E Riding of Yks
North Newington, Cherwell DC
North Newnton, Kennet DC
North Nibley, Stroud DC
North Ormsby, E Lindsey DC
North Otterington, Hambleton DC
North Owersby, W Lindsey DC
North Perrott, S Somerset DC
North Petherton, Sedgemoor DC
North Petherwin, N Cornwall DC
North Pickenham, Breckland CI
North Piddle, Wychavon DC
North Poorton, W Dorset DC
North Prospect, Plymouth City
North Queensferry, Fife CI
North Rauceby, N Kesteven DC
North Reston, E Lindsey DC
North Rigton, Harrogate BC
North Rode, Macclesfield BC
North Ronaldsay, Orkney Is CI
North Runcton, King's Lynn/W
  Norfolk BC
North Scale, Barrow-in-Furness
  BC
North Scarle, N Kesteven DC
North Seaton, Wansbeck DC
North Shields, N Tyneside CI
North Shoebury, Southend-on-
  Sea BC
North Somercotes, E Lindsey DC
North Stainley, Harrogate BC
North Stainmore, Eden DC
North Stoke, Bath/N E Somerset
  CI
North Stoke, S Oxon DC
North Street, Swale BC

North Sunderland, Berwick-u-Tweed BC
North Tamerton, N Cornwall DC
North Tawton, W Devon BC
North Templar, Glasgow City
North Thoresby, E Lindsey DC
North Tidworth, Kennet DC
North Tolsta, Comhairle Nan Eilean Siar
North Tuddenham, Breckland CI
North Uist, Comhairle Nan Eilean Siar
North Walsham, N Norfolk DC
North Waltham, Basingstoke/Deane BC
North Warnborough, Hart DC
North Weald Bassett, Epping Forest DC
North Weston, N Somerset DC
North Wheatley, Bassetlaw DC
North Wick, Bath/N E Somerset CI
North Widcombe, Bath/N E Somerset CI
North Willingham, W Lindsey DC
North Wingfield, N E Derbys DC
North Witham, S Kesteven DC
North Woolwich, Newham LBC
North Wootton, King's Lynn/W Norfolk BC
North Wootton, Mendip DC
North Wootton, W Dorset DC
North Wraxall, N Wilts DC
Northall, Aylesbury Vale DC
Northallerton, Hambleton DC
Northam, Torridge DC
Northampton, Northampton BC
Northaw, Welwyn Hatfield DC
Northbay, Comhairle Nan Eilean Siar
Northborough, Peterborough City
Northbourne, Dover DC
Northchapel, Chichester DC
Northchurch, Dacorum BC
Northcott, Torridge DC
Northend, Bath/N E Somerset CI
Northend, Stratford/Avon DC
Northfield, Birmingham City
Northfield, Stockton-on-Tees BC
Northfleet, Gravesham BC
Northgate, S Holland DC
Northiam, Rother DC
Northill, Mid Beds DC
Northington, Winchester City
Northleach, Cotswold DC
Northleigh, E Devon DC
Northlew, W Devon BC
Northmavine, Shetland Is CI
Northmoor, W Oxon DC
Northolt, Ealing LBC

Northop, Flintshire CC
Northop Hall, Flintshire CC
Northorpe, S Kesteven DC
Northorpe, W Lindsey DC
Northowram, Calderdale MBC
Northrepps, N Norfolk DC
Northville, Torfaen CBC
Northway, Tewkesbury BC
Northwich, Vale Royal BC
Northwold, King's Lynn/W Norfolk BC
Northwood, Derbys Dales DC
Northwood, Hillingdon LBC
Northwood, Isle of Wight CI
Northwood, N Shropshire DC
Northwood Green, Forest of Dean DC
Norton, Bassetlaw DC
Norton, Bridgnorth DC
Norton, Daventry DC
Norton, Doncaster MBC
Norton, Herefordshire CI
Norton, Isle of Wight CI
Norton, Mid Suffolk DC
Norton, N Wilts DC
Norton, Powys CC
Norton, Sheffield City
Norton, Shrewsbury/Atcham CI
Norton, S Shropshire DC
Norton, Stockton-on-Tees BC
Norton, Swale BC
Norton, Tewkesbury BC
Norton, Wychavon DC
Norton Bavant, W Wilts DC
Norton Canes, Cannock Chase DC
Norton Canon, Herefordshire CI
Norton Conyers, Harrogate BC
Norton Disney, N Kesteven DC
Norton Fitzwarren, Taunton Deane BC
Norton Grange, Stockton-on-Tees BC
Norton Green, Isle of Wight CI
Norton Hawkfield, Bath/N E Somerset CI
Norton Heath, Epping Forest DC
Norton in Hales, N Shropshire DC
Norton Juxta Kempsey, Wychavon DC
Norton juxta Twycross, Hinckley/Bosworth BC
Norton le Clay, Harrogate BC
Norton Lees, Sheffield City
Norton Lindsey, Warwick DC
Norton Malreward, Bath/N E Somerset CI
Norton Mandeville, Epping Forest DC
Norton on Derwent, Ryedale DC

Norton Radstock, Bath/N E Somerset CI
Norton St Philip, Mendip DC
Norton sub Hamdon, S Somerset DC
Norton Subcourse, S Norfolk DC
Norwell, Newark/Sherwood DC
Norwich, Norwich City
Norwood, Sheffield City
Norwood Hill, Mole Valley DC
Noseley, Harborough DC
Noss, Highland CI
Noss Mayo, S Hams DC
Nostell, Wakefield MDC
Nosterfield, Hambleton DC
Nostie, Highland CI
Notgrove, Cotswold DC
Notting Hill, Kensington/Chelsea Royal Borough
Nottingham, Nottingham City
Notton, Wakefield MDC
Nounsley, Braintree DC
Nowton, St Edmundsbury BC
Nox, Shrewsbury/Atcham CI
Nuffield, S Oxon DC
Nun Monkton, Harrogate BC
Nunburnholme, E Riding of Yks
Nuneaton, Nuneaton/Bedworth BC
Nuneham Courtenay, S Oxon DC
Nunney, Mendip DC
Nunnington, Ryedale DC
Nunnykirk, Alnwick DC
Nunthorpe, Middlesbrough CI
Nunwick, Tynedale DC
Nursling, Test Valley BC
Nutbourne, Chichester DC
Nutbourne, Horsham DC
Nutfield, Tandridge DC
Nuthall, Broxtowe BC
Nuthampstead, N Herts DC
Nuthurst, Horsham DC
Nuthurst, Stratford/Avon DC
Nutley, Basingstoke/Deane BC
Nutley, Wealden DC
Nutwell, Doncaster MBC
Nybster, Highland CI
Nyewood, Chichester DC
Nymet Rowland, Mid Devon DC
Nympsfield, Stroud DC
Nynehead, Taunton Deane BC
Nythe, Swindon BC
Nyton, Arun DC

Oad Street, Swale BC
Oadby, Oadby/Wigston BC
Oakamoor, Staffs Moorlands DC
Oakdale, Poole BC
Oake, Taunton Deane BC
Oakenclough, Wyre BC

Oakengates, Telford/Wrekin BC
Oakenshaw, Wear Valley DC
Oakerthorpe, Amber Valley BC
Oakfield, Torfaen CBC
Oakford, Mid Devon DC
Oakgrove, Macclesfield BC
Oakham, Rutland CC
Oakhanger, E Hants DC
Oakhill, Mendip DC
Oakington, S Cambs DC
Oaklands, E Herts DC
Oakley, Aylesbury Vale DC
Oakley, Basingstoke/Deane BC
Oakley, Bedford BC
Oakley, Mid Suffolk DC
Oakley, Fife CI
Oakley Green,
    Windsor/Maidenhead RB
Oakmere, Vale Royal BC
Oakridge, Stroud DC
Oaksey, N Wilts DC
Oaksford, Torfaen CBC
Oakshaw Ford, Carlisle City
Oakthorpe, N W Leics DC
Oakwood, Neath Port Talbot CBC
Oakworth, Bradford MDC
Oape, Highland CI
Oare, Swale BC
Oare, W Somerset DC
Oasby, S Kesteven DC
Oatlands, Elmbridge BC
Oban, Argyll/Bute CI
Oborne, W Dorset DC
Obsdale Park, Highland CI
Oby, Gt Yarmouth BC
Occaney, Harrogate BC
Occold, Mid Suffolk DC
Ochiltree, E Ayrshire CI
Ochtrelure, Dumfries/Galloway CI
Ockbrook, Erewash BC
Ockham, Guildford BC
Ockle, Highland CI
Ockley, Mole Valley DC
Ocle Pychard, Herefordshire CI
Octon, E Riding of Yks
Odcombe, S Somerset DC
Odd Down, Bath/N E Somerset CI
Odd Rode, Congleton BC
Oddendale, Eden DC
Oddingley, Wychavon DC
Oddington, Cherwell DC
Oddington, Cotswold DC
Odell, Bedford BC
Odiham, Hart DC
Odstock, Salisbury DC
Odstone, Hinckley/Bosworth BC
Offa, Wrexham CBC
Offchurch, Warwick DC
Offcote, Derbys Dales DC
Offenham, Wychavon DC

Offerton Estate, Stockport MBC
Offham, Tonbridge/Malling BC
Offley, N Herts DC
Offord Cluny, Huntingdonshire
    DC
Offord d'Arcy, Huntingdonshire
    DC
Offton, Mid Suffolk DC
Offwell, E Devon DC
Ogbourne Maizey, Kennet DC
Ogbourne St Andrew, Kennet DC
Ogbourne St George, Kennet DC
Ogle, Castle Morpeth BC
Ogmore Vale, Bridgend CBC
Ogmore Valley, Bridgend CBC
Ogwell, Teignbridge DC
Okeford Fitzpaine, N Dorset DC
Okehampton, W Devon BC
Okehampton Hamlets, W Devon
    BC
Okeover, E Staffs BC
Okewoodhill, Mole Valley DC
Olantigh, Ashford BC
Old, Daventry DC
Old Aberdeen, Aberdeen City
Old Alresford, Winchester City
Old Basing, Basingstoke/Deane
    BC
Old Bewick, Berwick-u-Tweed BC
Old Bolsover, Bolsover DC
Old Brampton, N E Derbys DC
Old Buckenham, Breckland CI
Old Burghclere,
    Basingstoke/Deane BC
Old Byland, Ryedale DC
Old Catton, Broadland DC
Old Cleeve, W Somerset DC
Old Clipstone, Newark/Sherwood
    DC
Old Colwyn, Conwy CBC
Old Dalby, Melton BC
Old Darnley, Glasgow City
Old Deer, Aberdeenshire CI
Old Drumchapel, Glasgow City
Old Ellerby, E Riding of Yks
Old Farm Park, Milton Keynes CI
Old Ford, Tower Hamlets LBC
Old Glossop, High Peak BC
Old Hall Green, E Herts DC
Old Hunstanton, King's Lynn/W
    Norfolk BC
Old Hutton, S Lakeland DC
Old Kea, Carrick DC
Old Kilpatrick, W Dunbartonshire
    CI
Old Knebworth, N Herts DC
Old Laund Booth, Pendle BC
Old Leake, Boston BC
Old Luce, Dumfries/Galloway CI
Old Malton, Ryedale DC

Old Marston, Oxford City
Old Milverton, Warwick DC
Old Newton, Mid Suffolk DC
Old Park, Telford/Wrekin BC
Old Radnor, Powys CC
Old Rayne, Aberdeenshire CI
Old Romney, Shepway DC
Old Somerby, S Kesteven DC
Old Stratford, S Northants CI
Old Stratford, Stratford/Avon DC
Old Swarland, Alnwick DC
Old Town, S Lakeland DC
Old Town, Swindon BC
Old Trafford, Trafford MBC
Old Warden, Mid Beds DC
Old Weston, Huntingdonshire DC
Old Whittington, Chesterfield BC
Old Windsor,
    Windsor/Maidenhead RB
Old Woking, Woking BC
Oldberrow, Stratford/Avon DC
Oldborough, Mid Devon DC
Oldbrook, Milton Keynes CI
Oldbury, Bridgnorth DC
Oldbury, Sandwell MBC
Oldbury on Severn, S Glos CI
Oldbury on the Hill, Cotswold DC
Oldcotes, Bassetlaw DC
Oldfield, Wychavon DC
Oldford, Mendip DC
Oldham, Oldham MBC
Oldhamstocks, E Lothian CI
Oldhurst, Huntingdonshire DC
Oldland, S Glos CI
Oldmeldrum, Aberdeenshire CI
Oldshore Beg, Highland CI
Oldshoremore, Highland CI
Oldstead, Ryedale DC
Oldtown, Highland CI
Olivers Battery, Winchester City
Ollersett, High Peak BC
Ollerton, Macclesfield BC
Ollerton, Newark/Sherwood DC
Ollerton, N Shropshire DC
Olney, Milton Keynes CI
Olton, Solihull MBC
Olveston, S Glos CI
Omagh, Omagh DC
Ombersley, Wychavon DC
Ompton, Newark/Sherwood DC
Onecote, Staffs Moorlands DC
Onehouse, Mid Suffolk DC
Ongar, Epping Forest DC
Onibury, S Shropshire DC
Onich, Highland CI
Onllwyn, Neath Port Talbot CBC
Onneley, Newcastle-u-Lyme BC
Opinan, Highland CI
Orby, E Lindsey DC
Orchard Leigh, Chiltern DC

Orcheston, Salisbury DC
Orcop, Herefordshire CI
Ord, Berwick-u-Tweed BC
Ord, Highland CI
Ordiquhill, Aberdeenshire CI
Ordsall, Salford City
Ore, Hastings BC
Orelton, Herefordshire CI
Oreton, Bridgnorth DC
Orford, Suffolk C'l DC
Orford, Warrington BC
Organford, Purbeck DC
Orgreave, Rotherham MBC
Orkney, Orkney Is CI
Orlestone, Ashford BC
Orlingbury, Wellingborough BC
Ormesby, Redcar/Cleveland BC
Ormesby St Margaret, Gt
    Yarmouth BC
Ormesby St Michael, Gt
    Yarmouth BC
Ormiscaig, Highland CI
Ormiston, E Lothian CI
Ormsaigbeg, Highland CI
Ormsaigmore, Highland CI
Ormskirk, W Lancs DC
Orphir, Orkney Is CI
Orpington, Bromley LBC
Orrell, Sefton MBC
Orrell, Wigan MBC
Orsett, Thurrock BC
Orslow, S Staffs CI
Orston, Rushcliffe BC
Orton, Carlisle City
Orton, Eden DC
Orton, Kettering BC
Orton Longueville, Peterborough
    City
Orton on the Hill,
    Hinckley/Bosworth BC
Orton Waterville, Peterborough
    City
Orwell, S Cambs DC
Osbaldeston, Ribble Valley BC
Osbaldwick, City of York CI
Osbaston, Hinckley/Bosworth BC
Osbournby, N Kesteven DC
Oscott, Birmingham City
Oscroft, Chester City
Ose, Highland CI
Osgathorpe, N W Leics DC
Osgodby, Hambleton DC
Osgodby, Scarborough BC
Osgodby, Selby DC
Osgodby, S Kesteven DC
Osgodby, W Lindsey DC
Oskaig, Highland CI
Osleston, S Derbys DC
Osmaston, Derbys Dales DC
Osmington, W Dorset DC

Osmotherley, Hambleton DC
Osmotherley, S Lakeland DC
Ospisdale, Highland CI
Ospringe, Swale BC
Ossett, Wakefield MDC
Ossington, Newark/Sherwood DC
Ostend, Maldon DC
Osterley, Hounslow LBC
Oswaldkirk, Ryedale DC
Oswaldtwistle, Hyndburn BC
Oswestry, Oswestry BC
Otford, Sevenoaks DC
Otham, Maidstone BC
Othery, Sedgemoor DC
Otley, Leeds City
Otley, Suffolk C'l DC
Otterbourne, Winchester City
Otterburn, Craven DC
Otterburn, Tynedale DC
Otterden, Maidstone BC
Otterford, Taunton Deane BC
Otterham, N Cornwall DC
Otterhampton, Sedgemoor DC
Ottershaw, Runnymede BC
Otterton, E Devon DC
Ottery St Mary, E Devon DC
Ottringham, E Riding of Yks
Oughtershaw, Craven DC
Oughterside, Allerdale BC
Oughtibridge, Sheffield City
Oulston, Hambleton DC
Oulton, Allerdale BC
Oulton, Broadland DC
Oulton, Stafford BC
Oulton, Waveney DC
Oulton Broad, Waveney DC
Oundle, E Northants CI
Ousby, Eden DC
Ousden, St Edmundsbury BC
Ouseburn, Harrogate BC
Ousefleet, E Riding of Yks
Ouston, Chester-le-Street DC
Out Newton, E Riding of Yks
Out Rawcliffe, Wyre BC
Outgate, S Lakeland DC
Outhgill, Eden DC
Outhill, Stratford/Avon DC
Outlane, Kirklees MC
Outseats, Derbys Dales DC
Outwell, King's Lynn/W Norfolk
    BC
Outwood, Bury MBC
Outwood, Tandridge DC
Outwood, Wakefield MDC
Outwoods, E Staffs BC
Ovenden, Calderdale MBC
Over, S Cambs DC
Over Alderley, Macclesfield BC
Over Burrow, Lancaster City
Over Compton, W Dorset DC

Over Dinsdale, Hambleton DC
Over Haddon, Derbys Dales DC
Over Kellet, Lancaster City
Over Kiddington, W Oxon DC
Over Norton, W Oxon DC
Over Peover, Macclesfield BC
Over Silton, Hambleton DC
Over Staveley, S Lakeland DC
Over Stowey, Sedgemoor DC
Over Wallop, Test Valley BC
Over Whitacre, N Warks BC
Over Wyresdale, Lancaster City
Overbury, Wychavon DC
Overdale, Telford/Wrekin BC
Overseal, S Derbys DC
Overstone, Daventry DC
Overstrand, N Norfolk DC
Overthorpe, S Northants CI
Overton, Basingstoke/Deane BC
Overton, Chester City
Overton, Hambleton DC
Overton, Kennet DC
Overton, Lancaster City
Overton, Winchester City
Overton, Wrexham CBC
Overtown, N Lanarkshire CI
Oving, Aylesbury Vale DC
Oving, Chichester DC
Ovingdean, Brighton/Hove CI
Ovingham, Tynedale DC
Ovington, Braintree DC
Ovington, Breckland CI
Ovington, Teesdale DC
Ovington, Tynedale DC
Owenkillew, Omagh DC
Ower, New Forest DC
Owermoigne, W Dorset DC
Owlerton, Sheffield City
Owlpen, Stroud DC
Owmby by Spital, W Lindsey DC
Owslebury, Winchester City
Owston, Doncaster MBC
Owston, Harborough DC
Owston Ferry, N Lincs CI
Owstwick, E Riding of Yks
Owthorpe, Rushcliffe BC
Owton Manor, Hartlepool BC
Oxborough, Breckland CI
Oxcliffe, Lancaster City
Oxen Park, S Lakeland DC
Oxenhall, Forest of Dean DC
Oxenholme, S Lakeland DC
Oxenhope, Bradford MDC
Oxenton, Tewkesbury BC
Oxenwood, Kennet DC
Oxford, Oxford City
Oxhill, Derwentside DC
Oxhill, Stratford/Avon DC
Oxley, Wolverhampton MBC
Oxley's Green, Rother DC

Oxnam, Scottish Borders Cl
Oxney, Isle of, Ashford BC
Oxshott, Elmbridge BC
Oxspring, Barnsley MBC
Oxted, Tandridge DC
Oxton, Newark/Sherwood DC
Oxton, Scottish Borders Cl
Oxton, Selby DC
Oxton, Wirral MBC
Oxwick, Breckland Cl
Oyne, Aberdeenshire Cl
Ozleworth, Cotswold DC

Packington, Lichfield DC
Packington, N W Leics DC
Padbury, Aylesbury Vale DC
Paddington, Westminster City
Paddlesworth, Shepway DC
Paddock, Kirklees MC
Paddock Wood, Tunbridge Wells
    BC
Paddolgreen, N Shropshire DC
Padiham, Burnley BC
Padside, Harrogate BC
Padstow, N Cornwall DC
Padworth, W Berks DC
Pagham, Arun DC
Paglesham, Rochford DC
Paignton, Torbay Cl
Pailton, Rugby BC
Painscastle, Powys CC
Painshawfield, Tynedale DC
Painswick, Stroud DC
Painter's Forstal, Swale BC
Pairc, Comhairle Nan Eilean Siar
Paisley, Renfrewshire Cl
Pakefield, Waveney DC
Pakenham, Mid Suffolk DC
Pakenham, St Edmundsbury BC
Palestine, Test Valley BC
Palewell, Richmond upon
    Thames LBC
Palgrave, Breckland Cl
Palgrave, Mid Suffolk DC
Palmer's Green, Enfield LBC
Palterton, Bolsover DC
Pamber End, Basingstoke/Deane
    BC
Pamber Green,
    Basingstoke/Deane BC
Pamphill, E Dorset DC
Pampisford, S Cambs DC
Pancrasweek, Torridge DC
Pandy Tudur, Conwy CBC
Panfield, Braintree DC
Pangbourne, W Berks DC
Pannal, Harrogate BC
Panshanger, Welwyn Hatfield DC
Pant, Oswestry BC
Panton, E Lindsey DC

Papa Westray, Orkney Is Cl
Papcastle, Allerdale BC
Papigoe, Highland Cl
Papplewick, Gedling BC
Papworth Everard, S Cambs DC
Papworth St Agnes, S Cambs DC
Par, Restormel BC
Parbold, W Lancs DC
Parbrook, Mendip DC
Pardshaw, Allerdale BC
Parham, Horsham DC
Parham, Suffolk C'l DC
Park, Glasgow City
Park, Sheffield City
Park, Swindon BC
Park Bernisdale, Highland Cl
Park Corner, S Oxon DC
Park Gate, Fareham BC
Park Hill, Sheffield City
Park Street, St Albans City/DC
Parkend, Forest of Dean DC
Parkeston, Tendring DC
Parkfield, Stockton-on-Tees BC
Parkgate, Antrim BC
Parkgate, Ellesmere Port/Neston
    BC
Parkgate, Mole Valley DC
Parkham, Torridge DC
Parkhead, Glasgow City
Parkhead, Sheffield City
Parkhouse, Glasgow City
Parkhurst, Isle of Wight Cl
Parkstone, Poole BC
Parkwoon Springs, Sheffield City
Parlington, Leeds City
Parracombe, N Devon DC
Parson Cross, Sheffield City
Parson Drove, Fenland DC
Parsons Green,
    Hammersmith/Fulham LBC
Partick, Glasgow City
Partington, Trafford MBC
Partney, E Lindsey DC
Parton, Copeland BC
Parton, Dumfries/Galloway Cl
Parwich, Derbys Dales DC
Passenham, S Northants Cl
Paston, N Norfolk DC
Patcham, Brighton/Hove Cl
Patching, Arun DC
Patchway, S Glos Cl
Pateley Bridge, Harrogate BC
Pathhead, Midlothian Cl
Pathlow, Stratford/Avon DC
Patmore Heath, E Herts DC
Patna, E Ayrshire Cl
Patney, Kennet DC
Patrick Brompton, Richmondshire
    DC
Patrington, E Riding of Yks

Patrington Haven, E Riding of
    Yks
Patrixbourne, Canterbury City
Patshull, S Staffs Cl
Patterdale, Eden DC
Pattingham, S Staffs Cl
Pattishall, S Northants Cl
Patton Bridge, S Lakeland DC
Paul, Penwith DC
Paulerspury, S Northants Cl
Paull, E Riding of Yks
Paulsgrove, Portsmouth City
Paulton, Bath/N E Somerset Cl
Pauntley, Forest of Dean DC
Pauperhaugh, Alnwick DC
Pavenham, Bedford BC
Pawlett, Sedgemoor DC
Pawston, Berwick-u-Tweed BC
Paxford, Cotswold DC
Paxton, Scottish Borders Cl
Payhembury, E Devon DC
Paythorne, Ribble Valley BC
Peacehaven, Lewes DC
Peak Dale, High Peak BC
Peak Forest, High Peak BC
Peakirk, Peterborough City
Peartree, Southampton City
Peartree Bridge, Milton Keynes Cl
Pease Pottage, Mid Sussex DC
Peasedown St John, Bath/N E
    Somerset Cl
Peasemore, W Berks DC
Peasenhall, Suffolk C'l DC
Peaslake, Guildford BC
Peasmarsh, Rother DC
Peat Inn, Fife Cl
Peatling Magna, Harborough DC
Peatling Parva, Harborough DC
Peaton, S Shropshire DC
Pebmarsh, Braintree DC
Pebworth, Wychavon DC
Pecket Well, Calderdale MBC
Peckforton, Crewe/Nantwich BC
Peckham, Southwark LBC
Peckleton, Hinckley/Bosworth BC
Pednor, Chiltern DC
Peebles, Scottish Borders Cl
Peel Hill, Fylde BC
Pegswood, Castle Morpeth BC
Pegwell Bay, Thanet DC
Peinaha, Highland Cl
Peinchorran, Highland Cl
Peiness, Highland Cl
Peinlich, Highland Cl
Peinmore, Highland Cl
Peldon, Colchester BC
Pelenna, Neath Port Talbot CBC
Pelsall, Walsall MBC
Pelton, Chester-le-Street DC
Pelutho, Allerdale BC

Pelynt, Caradon DC
Pemberton, Wigan MBC
Pembridge, Herefordshire CI
Pembroke, Pembrokeshire CC
Pembroke Dock, Pembrokeshire CC
Pembury, Tunbridge Wells BC
Pen lwyn, Torfaen CBC
Pen Selwood, S Somerset DC
Pen y Bedw, Conwy CBC
Pen y Bont Fawr, Powys CC
Penally, Pembrokeshire CC
Penare, Restormel BC
Penarth, Vale of Glamorgan CI
Penbryn, Ceredigion CC
Pencaer, Pembrokeshire CC
Pencaitland, E Lothian CI
Pencarreg, Carmarthenshire CC
Pencoed, Bridgend CBC
Pencombe, Herefordshire CI
Pencoyd, Herefordshire CI
Pendeen, Penwith DC
Pendine, Carmarthenshire CC
Pendlebury, Salford City
Pendleton, Ribble Valley BC
Pendleton, Salford City
Pendock, Malvern Hills DC
Pendoggett, N Cornwall DC
Pendoylan, Vale of Glamorgan CI
Penge, Bromley LBC
Penhill, Swindon BC
Penhow, Newport City CI
Penhurst, Rother DC
Penicuik, Midlothian CI
Penistone, Barnsley MBC
Penketh, Warrington BC
Penkridge, S Staffs CI
Penllergaer, Swansea C&C
Penllyn, Vale of Glamorgan CI
Penmachno, Conwy CBC
Penmaenmawr, Conwy CBC
Penmynydd, Isle of Anglesey CC
Penn, Chiltern DC
Penn Hill, Poole BC
Penn Street, Chiltern DC
Pennal, Gwynedd CC
Pennant, Conwy CBC
Pennard, Swansea C&C
Pennerley, S Shropshire DC
Pennington, New Forest DC
Pennington, S Lakeland DC
Penny Bridge, S Lakeland DC
Pennyland, Milton Keynes CI
Pennymoor, Mid Devon DC
Penpillick, Restormel BC
Penpol, Carrick DC
Penpont, Dumfries/Galloway CI
Penrhyn Bay, Conwy CBC
Penrhyndeudraeth, Gwynedd CC
Penrhynside, Conwy CBC

Penrice, Swansea C&C
Penrith, Eden DC
Penrose, N Cornwall DC
Penruddock, Eden DC
Penryn (part), Carrick DC
Penryn (part), Kerrier DC
Pensarn, Conwy CBC
Pensby, Wirral MBC
Pensford, Bath/N E Somerset CI
Penshaw, Sunderland City
Penshurst, Sevenoaks DC
Pensifiler, Highland CI
Pensilva, Caradon DC
Pentewan, Restormel BC
Pentir, Gwynedd CC
Pentire, Restormel BC
Pentlow, Braintree DC
Pentney, King's Lynn/W Norfolk BC
Penton Grafton, Test Valley BC
Penton Mewsey, Test Valley BC
Pentraeth, Isle of Anglesey CC
Pentre, Oswestry BC
Pentre Bont, Conwy CBC
Pentre Llyn Cymmer, Conwy CBC
Pentrebach, Merthyr Tydfil CBC
Pentrefelin, Conwy CBC
Pentrefoelas, Conwy CBC
Pentrepiod, Torfaen CBC
Pentrich, Amber Valley BC
Pentridge, E Dorset DC
Pentwyn, Cardiff CC
Pentyrch, Cardiff CC
Penwithick, Restormel BC
Penwortham, S Ribble BC
Penybont, Powys CC
Penycae, Wrexham CBC
Penyffordd, Flintshire CC
Penygarn, Torfaen CBC
Penygroes, Gwynedd CC
Penyrheol, Caerphilly CBC
Penzance, Penwith DC
Peopleton, Wychavon DC
Peover Heath, Macclesfield BC
Peover Inferior, Macclesfield BC
Peper Harow, Waverley BC
Peplow, N Shropshire DC
Perivale, Ealing LBC
Perlethorpe cum Budby, Newark/Sherwood DC
Perranarworthal, Carrick DC
Perranporth, Carrick DC
Perranuthnoe, Penwith DC
Perranzabuloe, Carrick DC
Perry, Huntingdonshire DC
Perry Barr, Birmingham City
Perry Green, E Herts DC
Pershore, Wychavon DC
Pertenhall, Bedford BC

Perth, Perth/Kinross CI
Perthy, N Shropshire DC
Perton, S Staffs CI
Peter Tavy, W Devon BC
Peterborough, Peterborough City
Peterchurch, Herefordshire CI
Peterhead, Aberdeenshire CI
Peterlee, Easington DC
Peters Green, N Herts DC
Peters Marland, Torridge DC
Petersfield, E Hants DC
Petersham, Richmond upon Thames LBC
Peterston Super Ely, Vale of Glamorgan CI
Peterstow, Herefordshire CI
Petham, Canterbury City
Petrockstowe, Torridge DC
Pett, Rother DC
Pettaugh, Mid Suffolk DC
Pettinain, S Lanarkshire CI
Pettistree, Suffolk C'l DC
Petton, Mid Devon DC
Petton, N Shropshire DC
Petts Wood, Bromley LBC
Petworth, Chichester DC
Pevensey, Wealden DC
Peverell, Plymouth City
Pewsey, Kennet DC
Phillack, Penwith DC
Philleigh, Carrick DC
Philpstoun, W Lothian CI
Phoenix Green, Hart DC
Pica, Copeland BC
Pickenham, Breckland CI
Pickering, Ryedale DC
Pickering Nook, Derwentside DC
Picket Piece, Test Valley BC
Picket Post, New Forest DC
Pickhill, Hambleton DC
Picklescott, Shrewsbury/Atcham CI
Pickmere, Macclesfield BC
Pickup Bank, Blackburn with Darwen BC
Pickwell, Melton BC
Pickworth, Rutland CC
Pickworth, S Kesteven DC
Picton, Chester City
Picton, Hambleton DC
Piddinghoe, Lewes DC
Piddington, Cherwell DC
Piddington, S Northants CI
Piddington, Wycombe DC
Piddlehinton, W Dorset DC
Piddletrenthide, W Dorset DC
Pidley cum Fenton, Huntingdonshire DC
Piercebridge, Darlington BC
Pigdon, Castle Morpeth BC

Pikehall, Derbys Dales DC
Pilgrims Hatch, Brentwood BC
Pilham, W Lindsey DC
Pillaton, Caradon DC
Pillerton Hersey, Stratford/Avon DC
Pillerton Priors, Stratford/Avon DC
Pilley, Barnsley MBC
Pilling, Wyre BC
Pillowell, Forest of Dean DC
Pilning, S Glos CI
Pilsbury, Derbys Dales DC
Pilsdon, W Dorset DC
Pilsley, Derbys Dales DC
Pilsley, N E Derbys DC
Pilton, E Northants CI
Pilton, Mendip DC
Pilton, Rutland CC
Pilton West, N Devon DC
Pimhill, Shrewsbury/Atcham CI
Pimlico, Westminster City
Pimperne, N Dorset DC
Pinchbeck, S Holland DC
Pinchbeck West, S Holland DC
Pineham, Dover DC
Pinehurst, Swindon BC
Pinewood, Babergh DC
Pinner, Harrow LBC
Pinvin, Wychavon DC
Pinwherry, S Ayrshire CI
Pinxton, Bolsover DC
Pipe and Lyde, Herefordshire CI
Pipe Aston, Herefordshire CI
Piperhill, Highland CI
Pipewell, Kettering BC
Pirbright, Guildford BC
Pirton, N Herts DC
Pirton, Wychavon DC
Pishill, S Oxon DC
Pistyll, Gwynedd CC
Pitcalnie, Highland CI
Pitcaple, Aberdeenshire CI
Pitch Green, Wycombe DC
Pitch Place, Guildford BC
Pitchcombe, Stroud DC
Pitchcott, Aylesbury Vale DC
Pitchford, Shrewsbury/Atcham CI
Pitchill, Stratford/Avon DC
Pitcombe, S Somerset DC
Pitgrudy, Highland CI
Pitlochry, Perth/Kinross CI
Pitmaduthy, Highland CI
Pitmedden, Aberdeenshire CI
Pitminster, Taunton Deane BC
Pitney, S Somerset DC
Pitscottie, Fife CI
Pitsea, Basildon DC
Pitsford, Daventry DC
Pitsligo, Aberdeenshire CI

Pitsmoor, Sheffield City
Pitstone, Aylesbury Vale DC
Pittenweem, Fife CI
Pitteuchar, Fife CI
Pittington, Durham City
Pittnetrail, Highland CI
Pittodrie, Aberdeen City
Pitton, Salisbury DC
Pitullie, Aberdeenshire CI
Pity Me, Durham City
Pixey Green, Mid Suffolk DC
Pixley, Herefordshire CI
Place Newton, Ryedale DC
Plains, N Lanarkshire CI
Plaish, Shrewsbury/Atcham CI
Plaistow, Chichester DC
Plaistow, Newham LBC
Plaitford, Test Valley BC
Plantation, Lisburn City
Plasnewydd, Cardiff CC
Plastow Green,
    Basingstoke/Deane BC
Platt, Tonbridge/Malling BC
Plawsworth, Chester-le-Street DC
Plaxtol, Tonbridge/Malling BC
Play Hatch, S Oxon DC
Playden, Rother DC
Playford, Suffolk C'l DC
Plealey, Shrewsbury/Atcham CI
Plean, Stirling CI
Pleasington, Blackburn with
    Darwen BC
Pleasley, Bolsover DC
Plenmeller, Tynedale DC
Pleshey, Chelmsford BC
Plockton, Highland CI
Plompton, Harrogate BC
Plowden, S Shropshire DC
Ploxgreen, Shrewsbury/Atcham CI
Pluckley, Ashford BC
Plumbland, Allerdale BC
Plumbley, Sheffield City
Plumbridge, Strabane DC
Plumley, Macclesfield BC
Plumpton, Eden DC
Plumpton, Lewes DC
Plumpton, S Northants CI
Plumpton Head, Eden DC
Plumptons, Fylde DC
Plumstead, Greenwich LBC
Plumstead, N Norfolk DC
Plumtree, Rushcliffe BC
Plungar, Melton BC
Plush, W Dorset DC
Plymouth, Plymouth City
Plympton, Plymouth City
Plympton Erne, Plymouth City
Plympton St Mary, Plymouth City
Plymstock, Plymouth City

Plymstock Dunstone, Plymouth City
Plymstock Radford, Plymouth City
Plymtree, E Devon DC
Pockley, Ryedale DC
Pocklington, E Riding of Yks
Pode Hole, S Holland DC
Podington, Bedford BC
Podmore, Stafford BC
Point, Comhairle Nan Eilean Siar
Point Clear, Tendring DC
Pointon, S Kesteven DC
Polbain, Highland CI
Polbeth, W Lothian CI
Polebrook, E Northants CI
Polegate, Wealden DC
Poles, Highland CI
Polesworth, N Warks BC
Polglass, Highland CI
Polgooth, Restormel BC
Poling, Arun DC
Polkerris, Restormel BC
Pollington, E Riding of Yks
Polloch, Highland CI
Pollockshaws, Glasgow City
Pollok, Glasgow City
Pollokshields, Glasgow City
Pollosgan, Highland CI
Polmaily, Highland CI
Polmassick, Restormel BC
Polmont, Falkirk CI
Polnessan, E Ayrshire CI
Polnish, Highland CI
Polperro, Caradon DC
Polsham, Mendip DC
Polstead, Babergh DC
Polstead Heath, Babergh DC
Poltimore, E Devon DC
Polwarth, Scottish Borders CI
Polyphant, N Cornwall DC
Polzeath, N Cornwall DC
Ponders End, Enfield LBC
Pondersbridge, Fenland DC
Ponsanooth, Kerrier DC
Ponsonby, Copeland BC
Pont Cyfyng, Conwy CBC
Pont y pant, Conwy CBC
Pontardawe, Neath Port Talbot CBC
Pontarddulais, Swansea C&C
Pontarfynach, Ceredigion CC
Pontefract, Wakefield MDC
Ponteland, Castle Morpeth BC
Pontesbury, Shrewsbury/Atcham CI
Ponthir, Torfaen CBC
Pontlliw, Swansea C&C
Pontneathvaughan, Neath Port Talbot CBC

Pontnewydd, Torfaen CBC
Pontrhydyfen, Neath Port Talbot CBC
Pontrhydyrun, Torfaen CBC
Ponts Green, Rother DC
Pontsticill, Merthyr Tydfil CBC
Pontyberem, Carmarthenshire CC
Pontyclun, Rhondda Cynon Taff CBC
Pontycymmer, Bridgend CBC
Pontymoel, Torfaen CBC
Pontypool, Torfaen CBC
Pontypridd, Rhondda Cynon Taff CBC
Pooksgreen, New Forest DC
Pool, Kerrier DC
Pool in Wharfedale, Leeds City
Pool Crofts, Highland CI
Poole, Crewe/Nantwich BC
Poole, Poole BC
Poole Keynes, Cotswold DC
Poolewe, Highland CI
Pooley Bridge, Eden DC
Poolhill, Forest of Dean DC
Poolsbrook, Chesterfield BC
Popham, Basingstoke/Deane BC
Poplar, Tower Hamlets LBC
Porchfield, Isle of Wight CI
Poringland, S Norfolk DC
Porkellis, Kerrier DC
Porlock, W Somerset DC
Port an eorna, Highland CI
Port Askaig, Argyll/Bute CI
Port Bannatyne, Argyll/Bute CI
Port Charlotte, Argyll/Bute CI
Port Ellen, Argyll/Bute CI
Port Eynon, Swansea C&C
Port Glasgow, Inverclyde CI
Port Henderson, Highland CI
Port Isaac, N Cornwall DC
Port Mor, Highland CI
Port Mulgrave, Scarborough BC
Port Seton, E Lothian CI
Port Sunlight, Wirral MBC
Port Talbot, Neath Port Talbot CBC
Port William, Dumfries/Galloway CI
Portaferry, Ards BC
Portballintrae, Coleraine BC
Portbury, N Somerset DC
Portchester, Fareham BC
Portesham, W Dorset DC
Portgate, W Devon BC
Portgaverne, N Cornwall DC
Portgordon, Moray CI
Portgower, Highland CI
Porth, Rhondda Cynon Taff CBC
Porth Navas, Kerrier DC

Porthallow, Kerrier DC
Porthcawl, Bridgend CBC
Porthcothan, N Cornwall DC
Porthcurno, Penwith DC
Porthleven, Kerrier DC
Porthmadog, Gwynedd CC
Porthmeor, Penwith DC
Porthoustock, Kerrier DC
Porthpean, Restormel BC
Porthtowan (part), Carrick DC
Porthtowan (part), Kerrier DC
Portington, E Riding of Yks
Portinscale, Allerdale BC
Portishead, N Somerset DC
Portknockie, Moray CI
Portland, Weymouth/Portland BC
Portlethen, Aberdeenshire CI
Portloe, Carrick DC
Portmahomack, Highland CI
Portmoak, Perth/Kinross CI
Portmore, New Forest DC
Portnahaven, Argyll/Bute CI
Portnalong, Highland CI
Portnaluchaig, Highland CI
Portobello, Stratford/Avon DC
Porton, Salisbury DC
Portormin, Highland CI
Portpatrick, Dumfries/Galloway CI
Portquin, N Cornwall DC
Portrack, Stockton-on-Tees BC
Portreath, Kerrier DC
Portree, Highland CI
Portrush, Coleraine BC
Portscatho, Carrick DC
Portsea, Portsmouth City
Portskerra, Highland CI
Portskewett, Monmouthshire CC
Portslade, Brighton/Hove CI
Portsmouth, Portsmouth City
Portsoy, Aberdeenshire CI
Portstewart, Coleraine BC
Portuairk, Highland CI
Portvasgo, Highland CI
Portway, Bromsgrove DC
Portway, Stratford/Avon DC
Portwrinkle, Caradon DC
Poslingford, St Edmundsbury BC
Possilpark, Glasgow City
Postcombe, S Oxon DC
Postern, Amber Valley BC
Postling, Shepway DC
Postwick, Broadland DC
Potsgrove, Mid Beds DC
Pott Row, King's Lynn/W Norfolk BC
Pott Shrigley, Macclesfield BC
Potten End, Dacorum BC
Potter Heigham, N Norfolk DC
Potterhanworth, N Kesteven DC
Potterne, Kennet DC

Potterne Wick, Kennet DC
Potters Marston, Blaby DC
Potterspury, S Northants CI
Potterton, Aberdeenshire CI
Potto, Hambleton DC
Potton, Mid Beds DC
Potton Island, Rochford DC
Poughill, Mid Devon DC
Poughill, N Cornwall DC
Poulshot, Kennet DC
Poulton, Chester City
Poulton, Cotswold DC
Poulton, Warrington BC
Poulton le Fylde, Wyre BC
Pound Bank, Wyre Forest DC
Poundon, Aylesbury Vale DC
Poundstock, N Cornwall DC
Powburn, Alnwick DC
Powderham, Teignbridge DC
Powerstock, W Dorset DC
Powick, Malvern Hills DC
Poxwell, W Dorset DC
Poy Street Green, Mid Suffolk DC
Poyle, Cherwell DC
Poyle, Slough BC
Poynings, Mid Sussex DC
Poyntington, W Dorset DC
Poynton, Macclesfield BC
Praa Sands, Kerrier DC
Prabost, Highland CI
Pratt's Bottom, Bromley LBC
Praze an Beeble, Kerrier DC
Predannack Wollas, Kerrier DC
Preees Higher Heath, N Shropshire DC
Prees, N Shropshire DC
Preesall, Wyre BC
Preese, Fylde BC
Preesgweene, Oswestry BC
Premnay, Aberdeenshire CI
Prendwick, Alnwick DC
Prenton, Wirral MBC
Prescot, Knowsley MBC
Prescote, Cherwell DC
Prescott, Tewkesbury BC
Preshute, Kennet DC
Pressen, Berwick-u-Tweed BC
Prestatyn, Denbighshire CC
Prestbury, Cheltenham BC
Prestbury, Macclesfield BC
Presteigne, Powys CC
Presthope, Bridgnorth DC
Prestleigh, Mendip DC
Preston, Berwick-u-Tweed BC
Preston, Brent LBC
Preston, Cotswold DC
Preston, Dover DC
Preston, E Riding of Yks
Preston, N Herts DC
Preston, Preston City

Preston, Rutland CC
Preston, Scottish Borders Cl
Preston, Stockton-on-Tees BC
Preston, Teignbridge DC
Preston, Weymouth/Portland BC
Preston Bagot, Stratford/Avon DC
Preston Bissett, Aylesbury Vale
DC
Preston Brockhurst, N Shropshire
DC
Preston Brook, Halton BC
Preston Candover,
Basingstoke/Deane BC
Preston Capes, Daventry DC
Preston Deanery, S Northants Cl
Preston Green, Stratford/Avon
DC
Preston on Stour, Stratford/Avon
DC
Preston on Wye, Herefordshire Cl
Preston Patrick, S Lakeland DC
Preston Richard, S Lakeland DC
Preston St Mary, Babergh DC
Preston under Scar,
Richmondshire DC
Preston upon the Weald Moors,
Telford/Wrekin BC
Preston Wynne, Herefordshire Cl
Prestonpans, E Lothian Cl
Prestwich, Bury MBC
Prestwick, S Ayrshire Cl
Prestwold, Charnwood DC
Prestwood, Chiltern DC
Prestwood, S Staffs Cl
Prickwillow, E Cambs DC
Priddy, Mendip DC
Priest Hutton, Lancaster City
Priestland, E Ayrshire Cl
Primrose Green, Breckland Cl
Primrose Valley, Scarborough BC
Princes Risborough, Wycombe
DC
Princethorpe, Rugby BC
Princetown, W Devon BC
Prinsted, Chichester DC
Priors Dean, E Hants DC
Priors Hardwick, Stratford/Avon
DC
Priors Marston, Stratford/Avon
DC
Priorslee, Telford/Wrekin BC
Priston, Bath/N E Somerset Cl
Prittlewell, Southend-on-Sea BC
Privett, E Hants DC
Probus, Carrick DC
Prospect, Allerdale BC
Prudhoe, Tynedale DC
Publow, Bath/N E Somerset Cl
Puckeridge, E Herts DC
Puckington, S Somerset DC

Pucklechurch, S Glos Cl
Pudding Norton, N Norfolk DC
Puddington, Chester City
Puddington, Mid Devon DC
Puddledock, Breckland Cl
Puddletown, W Dorset DC
Pudlestone, Herefordshire Cl
Pudsey, Leeds City
Pulborough, Horsham DC
Pulford, Chester City
Pulham, N Dorset DC
Pulham Market, S Norfolk DC
Pulham St Mary, S Norfolk DC
Pulloxhill, Mid Beds DC
Pulverbatch, Shrewsbury/Atcham
Cl
Pumpherston, W Lothian Cl
Puncheston, Pembrokeshire CC
Puncknowle, W Dorset DC
Punnetts Town, Wealden DC
Purbrook, Winchester City
Purdis Farm, Suffolk C'l DC
Purfleet, Thurrock BC
Puriton, Sedgemoor DC
Purleigh, Maldon DC
Purley, Croydon LBC
Purley on Thames, W Berks DC
Purlogue, S Shropshire DC
Purse Caundle, W Dorset DC
Purslow, S Shropshire DC
Purston Jaglin, Wakefield MDC
Purton, Forest of Dean DC
Purton, N Wilts DC
Pury End, S Northants Cl
Pusey, Vale of White Horse DC
Putley, Herefordshire Cl
Putney, Wandsworth LBC
Puttenham, Guildford BC
Puxley, S Northants Cl
Puxton, N Somerset DC
Pwllheli, Gwynedd CC
Pye Green, Cannock Chase DC
Pyecombe, Mid Sussex DC
Pyle, Bridgend CBC
Pyle, Isle of Wight Cl
Pylle, Mendip DC
Pymoor, E Cambs DC
Pyrford, Woking BC
Pyrton, S Oxon DC
Pytchley, Kettering BC
Pyworthy, Torridge DC

Quabbs, S Shropshire DC
Quadring, S Holland DC
Quainton, Aylesbury Vale DC
Quakers Yard, Merthyr Tydfil
CBC
Quaking Houses, Derwentside
DC
Quantock Vale, W Somerset DC

Quarff, Shetland Is Cl
Quarles, N Norfolk DC
Quarley, Test Valley BC
Quarme, W Somerset DC
Quarndon, Amber Valley BC
Quarnford, Staffs Moorlands DC
Quarrendon, Aylesbury Vale DC
Quarrington, N Kesteven DC
Quarrington Hill, Durham City
Quarter, S Lanarkshire Cl
Quarter Bach, Carmarthenshire
CC
Quatford, Bridgnorth DC
Quatt, Bridgnorth DC
Quatt Malvern, Bridgnorth DC
Quebec, Derwentside DC
Quedgeley, Gloucester City
Queen Adelaide, E Cambs DC
Queen Camel, S Somerset DC
Queen Charlton, Bath/N E
Somerset Cl
Queen's Cross, Aberdeen City
Queen's Park, Brent LBC
Queenborough, Swale BC
Queenhill, Malvern Hills DC
Queensbury, Brent LBC
Queensferry, Flintshire CC
Queenslie, Glasgow City
Queensnympton, N Devon DC
Queenzieburn, N Lanarkshire Cl
Quendon, Uttlesford DC
Queniborough, Charnwood DC
Quenington, Cotswold DC
Quernmore, Lancaster City
Quethiock, Caradon DC
Quidenham, Breckland Cl
Quidhampton,
Basingstoke/Deane BC
Quidhampton, Salisbury DC
Quinton, Birmingham City
Quinton, S Northants Cl
Quinton, Stratford/Avon DC
Quintrell Downs, Restormel BC
Quorn, Charnwood DC

Raasay, Highland Cl
Raby, Teesdale DC
Raby, Wirral MBC
Rackenford, N Devon DC
Rackham, Horsham DC
Rackheath, Broadland DC
Racton, Chichester DC
Radbourne, S Derbys DC
Radbourne, Stratford/Avon DC
Radbrook, Stratford/Avon DC
Radcliffe, Alnwick DC
Radcliffe, Bury MBC
Radcliffe on Trent, Rushcliffe BC
Radclive, Aylesbury Vale DC
Radcot, W Oxon DC

Raddery, Highland Cl
Radernie, Fife Cl
Radford, Coventry City MDC
Radford Semele, Warwick DC
Radipole, Weymouth/Portland BC
Radlett, Hertsmere BC
Radley, Vale of White Horse DC
Radnage, Wycombe DC
Radstock, Bath/N E Somerset Cl
Radstone, S Northants Cl
Radway, Stratford/Avon DC
Radwell, Bedford BC
Radwell, N Herts DC
Radwinter, Uttlesford DC
Radyr/St Fagans, Cardiff CC
Ragdale, Melton BC
Raglan, Monmouthshire CC
Ragnall, Bassetlaw DC
Rainford, St Helens MBC
Rainham, Havering LBC
Rainham, Medway Cl
Rainhill, St Helens MBC
Rainow, Macclesfield BC
Rainton, Harrogate BC
Rainworth, Newark/Sherwood DC
Raisbeck, Eden DC
Raithby, E Lindsey DC
Raithby cum Maltby, E Lindsey
  DC
Rake, Chichester DC
Ralston, Renfrewshire Cl
Ramasaig, Highland Cl
Rame, Caradon DC
Rampisham, W Dorset DC
Rampside, Barrow-in-Furness BC
Rampton, Bassetlaw DC
Rampton, S Cambs DC
Ramsbottom, Bury MBC
Ramsbury, Kennet DC
Ramscraigs, Highland Cl
Ramsdean, E Hants DC
Ramsdell, Basingstoke/Deane BC
Ramsden, W Oxon DC
Ramsden Bellhouse, Basildon DC
Ramsden Crays, Basildon DC
Ramsden Heath, Chelmsford BC
Ramsey, Huntingdonshire DC
Ramsey, Tendring DC
Ramsgate, Thanet DC
Ramsgreave, Ribble Valley BC
Ramsholt, Suffolk C'l DC
Ramshorn, E Staffs BC
Ranby, Bassetlaw DC
Ranby, E Lindsey DC
Rand, W Lindsey DC
Rand Grange, Hambleton DC
Randalstown, Antrim BC
Randlay, Telford/Wrekin BC
Randwick, Stroud DC
Rangemore, E Staffs BC

Rangeworthy, S Glos Cl
Rankinston, E Ayrshire Cl
Ranmoor, Sheffield City
Ranmore, Mole Valley DC
Rannoch, Perth/Kinross Cl
Ranochan, Highland Cl
Ranskill, Bassetlaw DC
Ranton, Stafford BC
Ranworth, Broadland DC
Rasharkin, Ballymoney BC
Raskelf, Hambleton DC
Rastrick, Calderdale MBC
Ratagan, Highland Cl
Ratby, Hinckley/Bosworth BC
Ratcliffe on Soar, Rushcliffe BC
Ratcliffe on the Wreake,
  Charnwood DC
Rathen, Aberdeenshire Cl
Rathfriland, Banbridge DC
Rathillet, Fife Cl
Rathlin Island, Moyle DC
Rathmell, Craven DC
Ratho, Edinburgh City
Rathven, Moray Cl
Ratley, Stratford/Avon DC
Ratling, Dover DC
Ratlinghope, S Shropshire DC
Rattery, S Hams DC
Rattlesden, Mid Suffolk DC
Rattray, Perth/Kinross Cl
Raughton Head, Carlisle City
Raunds, E Northants Cl
Ravarnet, Lisburn City
Raveleys, The, Huntingdonshire
  DC
Ravenfield, Rotherham MBC
Ravenglass, Copeland BC
Ravenhill, Cannock Chase DC
Raveningham, S Norfolk DC
Ravenscar, Scarborough BC
Ravensden, Bedford BC
Ravenseat, Richmondshire DC
Ravenshead, Gedling BC
Ravensmoor, Crewe/Nantwich
  BC
Ravensthorpe, Daventry DC
Ravenstone, Milton Keynes Cl
Ravenstone, N W Leics DC
Ravenstonedale, Eden DC
Ravenstown, S Lakeland DC
Ravensworth, Richmondshire DC
Raw, Scarborough BC
Rawcliffe, City of York Cl
Rawcliffe Bridge, E Riding of Yks
Rawdon, Leeds City
Rawmarsh, Rotherham MBC
Rawnsley, Cannock Chase DC
Rawreth, Rochford DC
Rawridge, E Devon DC
Rawtenstall, Rossendale BC

Raydon, Babergh DC
Raylees, Alnwick DC
Rayleigh, Rochford DC
Rayne, Aberdeenshire Cl
Rayne, Braintree DC
Rayners Lane, Harrow LBC
Raynham, N Norfolk DC
Reach, E Cambs DC
Reach, S Beds DC
Read, Ribble Valley BC
Reading, Reading BC
Reading Street, Ashford BC
Reagill, Eden DC
Rearquhar, Highland Cl
Rearsby, Charnwood DC
Reay, Highland Cl
Rechullin, Highland Cl
Red Dial, Allerdale BC
Red Hill, Stratford/Avon DC
Red Lodge, Forest Heath DC
Redbourn, St Albans City/DC
Redbourne, N Lincs Cl
Redbourne Cheney, Swindon BC
Redbridge, Southampton City
Redbrook, Forest of Dean DC
Redcar, Redcar/Cleveland BC
Redding, Falkirk Cl
Reddingmuirhead, Falkirk Cl
Reddish, Stockport MBC
Redditch, Redditch BC
Rede, St Edmundsbury BC
Redenhall, S Norfolk DC
Redesmouth, Tynedale DC
Redford, Chichester DC
Redford, Teesdale DC
Redgorton, Perth/Kinross Cl
Redgrave, Mid Suffolk DC
Redhill, Gedling BC
Redhill, Reigate/Banstead BC
Redisham, Waveney DC
Redlingfield, Mid Suffolk DC
Redlynch, Salisbury DC
Redmarley, Forest of Dean DC
Redmarshall, Stockton-on-Tees
  BC
Redmile, Melton BC
Redmire, Richmondshire DC
Redmoor, Restormel BC
Rednal, Oswestry BC
Redpoint, Highland Cl
Redruth, Kerrier DC
Redwick, Newport City Cl
Redworth, Darlington BC
Reed, N Herts DC
Reedham, Broadland DC
Reedley Hallows, Pendle BC
Reedness, E Riding of Yks
Reepham, Broadland DC
Reepham, W Lindsey DC
Reeth, Richmondshire DC

Reiff, Highland CI
Reigate, Reigate/Banstead BC
Reighton, Scarborough BC
Reiss, Highland CI
Rejerrah, Carrick DC
Remenham, Wokingham DC
Rempstone, Rushcliffe BC
Remusaig, Highland CI
Rendall, Orkney Is CI
Rendcomb, Cotswold DC
Rendham, Suffolk C'I DC
Rendlesham, Suffolk C'I DC
Renfrew, Renfrewshire CI
Renhold, Bedford BC
Rennington, Alnwick DC
Renton, W Dunbartonshire CI
Renwick, Eden DC
Repps, Gt Yarmouth BC
Repton, S Derbys DC
Resaurie, Highland CI
Resolis, Highland CI
Resolven, Neath Port Talbot CBC
Retew, Restormel BC
Retford, Bassetlaw DC
Rettendon, Chelmsford BC
Revesby, E Lindsey DC
Rewe, E Devon DC
Reydon, Waveney DC
Reymerston, Breckland CI
Reynoldston, Swansea C&C
Rhayader, Powys CC
Rhenetra, Highland CI
Rhiconich, Highland CI
Rhicullen, Highland CI
Rhigos, Rhondda Cynon Taff
    CBC
Rhilochan, Highland CI
Rhiroy, Highland CI
Rhitongue, Highland CI
Rhives, Highland CI
Rhiwbina, Cardiff CC
Rhodes Mannis, Shepway DC
Rhodesia, Bassetlaw DC
Rhos, Neath Port Talbot CBC
Rhos on Sea, Conwy CBC
Rhos y mawn, Conwy CBC
Rhoscolyn, Isle of Anglesey CC
Rhosddu, Wrexham CBC
Rhosllanerchrugog, Wrexham
    CBC
Rhossili, Swansea C&C
Rhosybol, Isle of Anglesey CC
Rhosyr, Isle of Anglesey CC
Rhu, Argyll/Bute CI
Rhuddlan, Denbighshire CC
Rhue, Highland CI
Rhuvoult, Highland CI
Rhyd y Foel, Conwy CBC
Rhydd, Malvern Hills DC
Rhydlydan, Conwy CBC

Rhydycroesau, Oswestry BC
Rhydyfro, Neath Port Talbot CBC
Rhyl, Denbighshire CC
Rhymney, Caerphilly CBC
Rhynie, Aberdeenshire CI
Ribbesford, Wyre Forest DC
Ribble Banks, Craven DC
Ribble Head, Craven DC
Ribbleton, Preston City
Ribby, Fylde BC
Ribchester, Ribble Valley BC
Riber, Derbys Dales DC
Riby, W Lindsey DC
Riccall, Selby DC
Richard's Castle (Herefordshire),
    Herefordshire CI
Richards Castle, S Shropshire
    DC
Richborough Port, Dover DC
Richmond, Richmondshire DC
Richmond, Sheffield City
Richmond Hill, Richmond upon
    Thames LBC
Richmond Town, Richmond upon
    Thames LBC
Rickinghall Inferior, Mid Suffolk
    DC
Rickinghall Superior, Mid Suffolk
    DC
Rickling, Uttlesford DC
Rickmansworth, Three Rivers DC
Riddings, Amber Valley BC
Riddlecombe, Torridge DC
Riddlesden, Bradford MDC
Riddlesworth, Breckland CI
Ridge, Hertsmere BC
Ridge, Purbeck DC
Ridgewell, Braintree DC
Ridgewood, Wealden DC
Ridgmont, Mid Beds DC
Ridgway, S Shropshire DC
Riding, Tynedale DC
Ridley, Crewe/Nantwich BC
Ridlington, N Norfolk DC
Ridlington, Rutland CC
Ridsdale, Tynedale DC
Rienachait, Highland CI
Rievaulx, Ryedale DC
Rigg, Dumfries/Galloway CI
Riggend, N Lanarkshire CI
Rigmaden Park, S Lakeland DC
Rigsby, E Lindsey DC
Rigside, S Lanarkshire CI
Rileyhill (part), Lichfield DC
Rillington, Ryedale DC
Rimington, Ribble Valley BC
Rimpton, S Somerset DC
Rimswell, E Riding of Yks
Ring's End, Fenland DC
Ringinglow, Sheffield City

Ringland, Broadland DC
Ringmer, Lewes DC
Ringmore, S Hams DC
Ringsend, Coleraine BC
Ringsfield, Waveney DC
Ringshall Stocks, Mid Suffolk DC
Ringstead, E Northants CI
Ringstead, King's Lynn/W Norfolk
    BC
Ringstead, W Dorset DC
Ringway, Manchester City
Ringwood, New Forest DC
Ringwould, Dover DC
Rinsey, Kerrier DC
Ripe, Wealden DC
Ripley, Amber Valley BC
Ripley, Guildford BC
Ripley, Harrogate BC
Ripley, New Forest DC
Riplingham, E Riding of Yks
Ripon, Harrogate BC
Rippingale, S Kesteven DC
Ripple, Dover DC
Ripple, Malvern Hills DC
Ripponden, Calderdale MBC
Rireavach, Highland CI
Risby, N Lincs CI
Risby, St Edmundsbury BC
Risca, Caerphilly CBC
Rise, E Riding of Yks
Risegate, S Holland DC
Riseholme, W Lindsey DC
Riseley, Bedford BC
Rishangles, Mid Suffolk DC
Rishton, Hyndburn BC
Rishworth, Calderdale MBC
Risinghurst, Oxford City
Risley, Erewash BC
Risley, Warrington BC
Risplith, Harrogate BC
Riston, E Riding of Yks
Rivar, Kennet DC
Rivenhall, Braintree DC
River, Chichester DC
River, Dover DC
Riverhead, Sevenoaks DC
Riverside, Cardiff CC
Rivington, Chorley BC
Rixton, Warrington BC
Roade, S Northants CI
Roadside, Highland CI
Roag, Highland CI
Roath, Cardiff CC
Roberton, S Lanarkshire CI
Robertsbridge, Rother DC
Roberttown, Kirklees MC
Robin Hood's Bay, Scarborough
    BC
Roborough (nr Winkleigh),
    Torridge DC

Roby, Knowsley MBC
Rocester, E Staffs BC
Roch, Pembrokeshire CC
Rochdale, Rochdale MBC
Roche, Restormel BC
Rochester, Medway Cl
Rochester, Tynedale DC
Rochven, Highland Cl
Rock, Alnwick DC
Rock, N Cornwall DC
Rock, Wyre Forest DC
Rockbeare, E Devon DC
Rockbourne, New Forest DC
Rockcliffe, Carlisle City
Rockfield, Highland Cl
Rockhampton, S Glos Cl
Rockhill, S Shropshire DC
Rockingham, Corby BC
Rockland St Mary, S Norfolk DC
Rockland St Peter, Breckland Cl
Rocklands, Breckland Cl
Rockley, Kennet DC
Rockwell, Dundee City
Rockwell End, Wycombe DC
Rodborough, Stroud DC
Rodd, Herefordshire Cl
Roddam, Berwick-u-Tweed BC
Rode, Mendip DC
Rode Heath, Congleton BC
Rodeheath, Macclesfield BC
Roden, Telford/Wrekin BC
Rodhuishd, W Somerset DC
Rodington, Telford/Wrekin BC
Rodmarton, Cotswold DC
Rodmell, Lewes DC
Rodmersham, Swale BC
Rodney Stoke, Mendip DC
Rodsley, Derbys Dales DC
Roe Green, Brent LBC
Roeburndale, Lancaster City
Roecliffe, Harrogate BC
Roehampton, Wandsworth LBC
Roffey, Horsham DC
Rogart, Highland Cl
Rogate, Chichester DC
Rogerstone, Newport City Cl
Rogiet, Monmouthshire CC
Rokeby, Teesdale DC
Roker, Sunderland City
Rollesby, Gt Yarmouth BC
Rolleston, Harborough DC
Rolleston, Newark/Sherwood DC
Rolleston, Sheffield City
Rolleston on Dove, E Staffs BC
Rollright, W Oxon DC
Rolston, E Riding of Yks
Rolvenden, Ashford BC
Romaldkirk, Teesdale DC
Romanby, Hambleton DC
Romansleigh, N Devon DC

Romesdal, Highland Cl
Romford, Havering LBC
Romiley, Stockport MBC
Romney Marsh, Shepway DC
Romsey, Test Valley BC
Romsey Extra, Test Valley BC
Romsley, Bridgnorth DC
Romsley, Bromsgrove DC
Rookhope, Wear Valley DC
Rookley, Isle of Wight Cl
Rookwith, Hambleton DC
Roos, E Riding of Yks
Roosebeck, S Lakeland DC
Rootfield, Highland Cl
Rope, Crewe/Nantwich BC
Ropley, E Hants DC
Ropsley, S Kesteven DC
Rorrington, S Shropshire DC
Rose, Carrick DC
Rose Ash, N Devon DC
Roseacre, Fylde BC
Rosebank, S Lanarkshire Cl
Rosedale, Ryedale DC
Roseden, Berwick-u-Tweed BC
Rosehall, Highland Cl
Rosehearty, Aberdeenshire Cl
Rosehill, N Shropshire DC
Roseisle, Moray Cl
Rosemarket, Pembrokeshire CC
Rosemarkie, Highland Cl
Rosemount, Aberdeen City
Rosenannon, Restormel BC
Rosewell, Midlothian Cl
Roseworth, Stockton-on-Tees BC
Rosgill, Eden DC
Roskhill, Highland Cl
Rosley, Allerdale BC
Roslin, Midlothian Cl
Rosliston, S Derbys DC
Rosneath, Argyll/Bute Cl
Ross, Berwick-u-Tweed BC
Ross on Wye, Herefordshire Cl
Ross Rural, Herefordshire Cl
Rossendale, Rossendale BC
Rossett, Wrexham CBC
Rossie, Fife Cl
Rossington, Doncaster MBC
Rostherne, Macclesfield BC
Rosthwaite, Allerdale BC
Roston, Derbys Dales DC
Rostrevor, Newry/Mourne DC
Rosyth, Fife Cl
Rothbury, Alnwick DC
Rotherby, Melton BC
Rotherfield, Wealden DC
Rotherfield Greys, S Oxon DC
Rotherfield Peppard, S Oxon DC
Rotherham, Rotherham MBC
Rothersthorpe, S Northants Cl
Rotherwick, Hart DC

Rothes, Moray Cl
Rothesay, Argyll/Bute Cl
Rothienorman, Aberdeenshire Cl
Rothley, Alnwick DC
Rothley, Charnwood DC
Rothwell, Kettering BC
Rothwell, Leeds City
Rothwell, W Lindsey DC
Rotsea, E Riding of Yks
Rottingdean, Brighton/Hove Cl
Rottington, Copeland BC
Roudham, Breckland Cl
Rough Haugh, Highland Cl
Rougham, Breckland Cl
Rougham, St Edmundsbury BC
Roughlee Booth, Pendle BC
Roughsike, Carlisle City
Roughton, E Lindsey DC
Roughton, N Norfolk DC
Round Island, Isles of Scilly Cl
Roundhay, Leeds City
Roundhurst, Chichester DC
Roundway, Kennet DC
Roundwood, Brent LBC
Rounton, Hambleton DC
Rous Lench, Wychavon DC
Rousay, Orkney Is Cl
Rousdon, E Devon DC
Rousham, W Oxon DC
Routh, E Riding of Yks
Row, N Cornwall DC
Row, Crosthwaite, S Lakeland DC
Rowarth, High Peak BC
Rowborough, Stratford/Avon DC
Rowde, Kennet DC
Rowen, Conwy CBC
Rowfant, Mid Sussex DC
Rowfoot, Tynedale DC
Rowhedge, Colchester BC
Rowhook, Horsham DC
Rowington, Warwick DC
Rowland, Derbys Dales DC
Rowlands Castle, E Hants DC
Rowlands Gill, Gateshead Cl
Rowley, E Riding of Yks
Rowley, S Shropshire DC
Rowley Regis, Sandwell MBC
Rowlstone, Herefordshire Cl
Rowly, Waverley BC
Rowney Green, Bromsgrove DC
Rownhams, Test Valley BC
Rowsham, Aylesbury Vale DC
Rowsley, Derbys Dales DC
Rowston, N Kesteven DC
Rowton, Chester City
Rowton, Telford/Wrekin BC
Rowtown, Runnymede BC
Roxbourne, Harrow LBC
Roxburgh, Scottish Borders Cl

Roxby, Hambleton DC
Roxby, N Lincs Cl
Roxby, Scarborough BC
Roxby cum Risby, N Lincs Cl
Roxeth, Harrow LBC
Roxholm, N Kesteven DC
Roxton, Bedford BC
Roxwell, Chelmsford BC
Royal Four Towns,
    Dumfries/Galloway Cl
Royal Oak, Scarborough BC
Royal Tunbridge Wells,
    Tunbridge Wells BC
Roybridge, Highland Cl
Royden, Wirral MBC
Roydon, Epping Forest DC
Roydon, King's Lynn/W Norfolk
    BC
Roydon, S Norfolk DC
Royston, Barnsley MBC
Royston, N Herts DC
Royton, Oldham MBC
Ruabon, Wrexham CBC
Ruan Minor, Kerrier DC
Ruanlanihorne, Carrick DC
Ruardean, Forest of Dean DC
Ruchazie, Glasgow City
Ruchill, Glasgow City
Ruckcroft, Eden DC
Ruckinge, Ashford BC
Ruckley, Shrewsbury/Atcham Cl
Rudbaxton, Pembrokeshire CC
Rudby, Hambleton DC
Ruddington, Rushcliffe BC
Rudford, Forest of Dean DC
Rudge, Bridgnorth DC
Rudgwick, Horsham DC
Rudheath, Vale Royal BC
Rudry, Caerphilly CBC
Rudston, E Riding of Yks
Rudyard, Staffs Moorlands DC
Rufford, Newark/Sherwood DC
Rufford, W Lancs DC
Rufforth, City of York Cl
Rugby, Rugby BC
Rugeley, Cannock Chase DC
Ruilick, Highland Cl
Ruisaurie, Highland Cl
Ruishton, Taunton Deane BC
Ruislip, Hillingdon LBC
Rumburgh, Waveney DC
Rumer Hill, Stratford/Avon DC
Rumford, Falkirk Cl
Rumford, N Cornwall DC
Rumney, Cardiff CC
Runcton, Chichester DC
Runcton Holme, King's Lynn/W
    Norfolk BC
Runham, Gt Yarmouth BC
Runswick Bay, Scarborough BC

Runwell, Chelmsford BC
Ruscombe, Stroud DC
Ruscombe, Wokingham DC
Rush Green, E Herts DC
Rushall, Kennet DC
Rushall, S Norfolk DC
Rushbrook, Stratford/Avon DC
Rushbrooke, St Edmundsbury BC
Rushbury, S Shropshire DC
Rushden, E Northants Cl
Rushden, N Herts DC
Rushford, Stratford/Avon DC
Rushlake Green, Wealden DC
Rushmere, Waveney DC
Rushmere St Andrew, Suffolk C'l
    DC
Rushmoor, Waverley BC
Rushock, Wyre Forest DC
Rushton, Kettering BC
Rushton, Shrewsbury/Atcham Cl
Rushton, Staffs Moorlands DC
Rushton, Vale Royal BC
Rushton Spencer, Staffs
    Moorlands DC
Rushwick, Malvern Hills DC
Rushyford, Sedgefield BC
Ruskington, N Kesteven DC
Rusland, S Lakeland DC
Rusper, Horsham DC
Ruspidge, Forest of Dean DC
Russell's Water, S Oxon DC
Rusthall, Tunbridge Wells BC
Rustington, Arun DC
Ruston, Scarborough BC
Ruston Parva, E Riding of Yks
Ruswarp, Scarborough BC
Ruthall, Bridgnorth DC
Rutherglen, S Lanarkshire Cl
Ruthin, Denbighshire CC
Ruthven, Highland Cl
Ruthvoes, Restormel BC
Ruthwell, Dumfries/Galloway Cl
Ruyton xi Towns, Oswestry BC
Ryal, Castle Morpeth BC
Ryarsh, Tonbridge/Malling BC
Ryburgh, N Norfolk DC
Rychraggan, Highland Cl
Rydal, S Lakeland DC
Rydale, Dumfries/Galloway Cl
Ryde, Isle of Wight Cl
Rye, Rother DC
Rye Foreign, Rother DC
Ryhall, Rutland CC
Ryhill, Wakefield MDC
Ryhope, Sunderland City
Rylstone, Craven DC
Ryme Intrinseca, W Dorset DC
Ryston, King's Lynn/W Norfolk
    BC

Ryther cum Ossendyke, Selby
    DC
Ryton, Bridgnorth DC
Ryton, Forest of Dean DC
Ryton, Ryedale DC
Ryton on Dunsmore, Rugby BC

Saasaig, Highland Cl
Sabden, Ribble Valley BC
Sacombe, E Herts DC
Sacombe Green, E Herts DC
Sacriston, Chester-le-Street DC
Sadberge, Darlington BC
Saddington, Harborough DC
Saddlebow, King's Lynn/W
    Norfolk BC
Saddleworth, Oldham MBC
Sadgill, S Lakeland DC
Saffron Walden, Uttlesford DC
Saham Toney, Breckland Cl
Saighton, Chester City
St Abbs, Scottish Borders Cl
St Agnes, Carrick DC
St Agnes, Isles of Scilly Cl
St Aidans, Stockton-on-Tees BC
St Albans, St Albans City/DC
St Allen, Carrick DC
St Andrews, Brent LBC
St Andrews, Fife Cl
St Andrews, Orkney Is Cl
St Ann Without, Lewes DC
St Annes, Fylde BC
St Anthony in Meneage, Kerrier
    DC
St Arvans, Monmouthshire CC
St Asaph, Denbighshire CC
St Athan, Vale of Glamorgan Cl
St Austell, Restormel BC
St Bees, Copeland BC
St Blaise, Restormel BC
St Boswells, Scottish Borders Cl
St Breock, N Cornwall DC
St Breward, N Cornwall DC
St Briavels, Forest of Dean DC
St Brides, Pembrokeshire CC
St Brides Major, Vale of
    Glamorgan Cl
St Brides Minor, Bridgend CBC
St Brides Super Ely, Vale of
    Glamorgan Cl
St Bridget's Beckermet, Copeland
    BC
St Budeaux, Plymouth City
St Buryan, Penwith DC
St Cadocs, Torfaen CBC
St Catherine, Bath/N E Somerset
    Cl
St Clears, Carmarthenshire CC
St Cleer, Caradon DC
St Clement, Carrick DC

St Clether, N Cornwall DC
St Columb Major, Restormel BC
St Columb Minor, Restormel BC
St Combs, Aberdeenshire CI
St Cuthbert Out, Mendip DC
St Cuthbert Without, Carlisle City
St Cuthberts, Stockton-on-Tees BC
St Cyrus, Aberdeenshire CI
St Davids, Pembrokeshire CC
St Day, Carrick DC
St Day, Kerrier DC
St Dennis, Restormel BC
St Devereux, Herefordshire CI
St Dials, Torfaen CBC
St Dogmaels, Pembrokeshire CC
St Dominic, Caradon DC
St Donats, Vale of Glamorgan CI
St Endellion, N Cornwall DC
St Enoder, Restormel BC
St Erme, Carrick DC
St Erth, Penwith DC
St Erth Praze, Penwith DC
St Ervan, N Cornwall DC
St Eval, N Cornwall DC
St Ewe, Restormel BC
St Fergus, Aberdeenshire CI
St Fillans, Perth/Kinross CI
St Florence, Pembrokeshire CC
St Gennys, N Cornwall DC
St George, Conwy CBC
St Georges, Telford/Wrekin BC
St Georges, Vale of Glamorgan CI
St Germans, Caradon DC
St Giles, Richmondshire DC
St Giles in the Wood, Torridge DC
St Giles on the Heath, Torridge DC
St Gluvias, Kerrier DC
St Goran, Restormel BC
St Harmon, Powys CC
St Helen, Isles of Scilly CI
St Helen Auckland, Wear Valley DC
St Helen Without, Vale of White Horse DC
St Helens, Isle of Wight CI
St Helens, St Helens MBC
St Hilary, Penwith DC
St Hill, Mid Sussex DC
St Ippolyts, N Herts DC
St Ishmael, Carmarthenshire CC
St Ishmaels, Pembrokeshire CC
St Issey, N Cornwall DC
St Ive, Caradon DC
St Ives, E Dorset DC
St Ives, Huntingdonshire DC
St Ives, Penwith DC

St James, Medway CI
St John, Caradon DC
St John Without, Lewes DC
St John's Beckermet, Copeland BC
St John's Castlerigg, Allerdale BC
St John's Highway, King's Lynn/W Norfolk BC
St John's Town of Dalry, Dumfries/Galloway CI
St John's Wood, Westminster City
St Johns, Woking BC
St Johns, Worcester City
St Juliot, N Cornwall DC
St Just, Penwith DC
St Just in Roseland, Carrick DC
St Keverne, Kerrier DC
St Kew, N Cornwall DC
St Keyne, Caradon DC
St Lawrence, Isle of Wight CI
St Lawrence, Maldon DC
St Leonards, E Dorset DC
St Leonards, Fylde BC
St Leonards, Hastings BC
St Levan, Penwith DC
St Lukes, Southampton City
St Mabyn, N Cornwall DC
St Margaret's at Cliffe, Dover DC
St Margaret's Hope, Orkney Is CI
St Margarets, Herefordshire CI
St Martha, Guildford BC
St Martin, Caradon DC
St Martin, Kerrier DC
St Martin's, Isles of Scilly CI
St Martin's, Richmondshire DC
St Martins, Oswestry BC
St Martins Without, Peterborough City
St Mary Bourne, Basingstoke/Deane BC
St Mary Cray, Bromley LBC
St Mary Hoo, Medway CI
St Mary in the Marsh, Shepway DC
St Mary Out Liberty, Pembrokeshire CC
St Mary's, Isles of Scilly CI
St Mary's Bay, Shepway DC
St Mary's Marsh, Medway CI
St Mawes, Carrick DC
St Mawgan, Restormel BC
St Mellion, Caradon DC
St Merryn, N Cornwall DC
St Mewan, Restormel BC
St Michael, St Albans City/DC
St Michael Caerhays, Restormel BC
St Michael Penkivel, Carrick DC
St Michael's Mount, Penwith DC

St Michaels, Ashford BC
St Michaels' on Wyre, Wyre BC
St Minver, N Cornwall DC
St Minver Lowlands, N Cornwall DC
St Monans, Fife CI
St Neot, Caradon DC
St Neots, Huntingdonshire DC
St Neots Rural, Huntingdonshire DC
St Newlyn East, Carrick DC
St Nicholas, Vale of Glamorgan CI
St Nicholas at Wade, Thanet DC
St Olaves, Gt Yarmouth BC
St Osyth, Tendring DC
St Paul Malmesbury Without, N Wilts DC
St Paul's Cray, Bromley LBC
St Paul's Walden, N Herts DC
St Peter, Plymouth City
St Peter the Great, Worcester City
St Peters, Thanet DC
St Pinnock, Caradon DC
St Raphael's, Brent LBC
St Sampson, Restormel BC
St Stephen, St Albans City/DC
St Stephen in Brannel, Restormel BC
St Stephens, N Cornwall DC
St Teath, N Cornwall DC
St Thomas Rural, N Cornwall DC
St Tudy, N Cornwall DC
St Veep, Caradon DC
St Wenn, Restormel BC
St Weonards, Herefordshire CI
St Werburgh, Medway CI
St Winnow, Caradon DC
Saintbury, Cotswold DC
Saintfield, Down DC
Salcombe, S Hams DC
Salcombe Regis, E Devon DC
Salcott, Colchester BC
Sale, Trafford MBC
Sale Green, Wychavon DC
Saleby, E Lindsey DC
Salehurst, Rother DC
Salen, Highland CI
Salesbury, Ribble Valley BC
Salford, Mid Beds DC
Salford, Salford City
Salford, W Oxon DC
Salford Priors, Stratford/Avon DC
Salfords, Reigate/Banstead BC
Salhouse, Broadland DC
Saline, Fife CI
Salisbury, Salisbury DC
Sallachy, Highland CI
Salle, Broadland DC

Salmonby, E Lindsey DC
Salperton, Cotswold DC
Salph End, Bedford BC
Salsburgh, N Lanarkshire Cl
Salt, Stafford BC
Saltash, Caradon DC
Saltburn, Highland Cl
Saltburn by the Sea,
    Redcar/Cleveland BC
Saltby, Melton BC
Saltcoats, N Ayrshire Cl
Saltdean, Lewes DC
Salterforth, Pendle BC
Saltfleet Haven, E Lindsey DC
Saltfleetby All Saints, E Lindsey
    DC
Saltfleetby St Clements, E
    Lindsey DC
Saltfleetby St Peter, E Lindsey
    DC
Saltford, Bath/N E Somerset Cl
Salthouse, N Norfolk DC
Saltmarshe, E Riding of Yks
Saltmarshe, Herefordshire Cl
Saltney, Flintshire CC
Salton, Ryedale DC
Saltrens (nr Monkleigh), Torridge
    DC
Saltwick, Castle Morpeth BC
Saltwood, Shepway DC
Salwarpe, Wychavon DC
Sambourne, Stratford/Avon DC
Sambrook, Telford/Wrekin BC
Samesfield, Herefordshire Cl
Samlesbury, S Ribble BC
Sampford Arundel, Taunton
    Deane BC
Sampford Brett, W Somerset DC
Sampford Courtenay, W Devon
    BC
Sampford Peverell, Mid Devon
    DC
Sampford Spiney, W Devon BC
Samson, Isles of Scilly Cl
Sanachan, Highland Cl
Sancreed, Penwith DC
Sancton, E Riding of Yks
Sand, Highland Cl
Sand Hutton, Ryedale DC
Sandavore, Highland Cl
Sanday, Orkney Is Cl
Sandbach, Congleton BC
Sandbank, Argyll/Bute Cl
Sandend, Aberdeenshire Cl
Sanderstead, Croydon LBC
Sandfields, Neath Port Talbot
    CBC
Sandford, Eden DC
Sandford, Mid Devon DC
Sandford, N Somerset DC

Sandford, Purbeck DC
Sandford on Thames, S Oxon DC
Sandford Orcas, W Dorset DC
Sandford St Martin, W Oxon DC
Sandgate, Shepway DC
Sandhaven, Aberdeenshire Cl
Sandhills, Oxford City
Sandhoe, Tynedale DC
Sandholme, Boston BC
Sandholme, E Riding of Yks
Sandhurst, Bracknell Forest BC
Sandhurst, Tewkesbury BC
Sandhurst, Tunbridge Wells BC
Sandhutton, Hambleton DC
Sandiacre, Erewash BC
Sandiway, Vale Royal BC
Sandleheath, New Forest DC
Sandleigh, Vale of White Horse
    DC
Sandling, Maidstone BC
Sandness, Shetland Is Cl
Sandon, Chelmsford BC
Sandon, N Herts DC
Sandon, Stafford BC
Sandown, Isle of Wight Cl
Sandplace, Caradon DC
Sandridge, St Albans City/DC
Sandringham, King's Lynn/W
    Norfolk BC
Sands, Guildford BC
Sandsend, Scarborough BC
Sandsting, Shetland Is Cl
Sandtoft, N Lincs Cl
Sandwell, Birmingham City
Sandwich, Dover DC
Sandwick, Comhairle Nan Eilean
    Siar
Sandwick, Eden DC
Sandwick, Orkney Is Cl
Sandwick, Shetland Is Cl
Sandwith, Copeland BC
Sandy, Mid Beds DC
Sandyford, Newcastle City
Sandygate, Sheffield City
Sangobeg, Highland Cl
Sangomore, Highland Cl
Sanna, Highland Cl
Sanquhar, Dumfries/Galloway Cl
Santon, Copeland BC
Santon Downham, Forest Heath
    DC
Sapcote, Blaby DC
Sapiston, St Edmundsbury BC
Sapperton, Cotswold DC
Sapperton, S Kesteven DC
Sarclet, Highland Cl
Saredon, S Staffs Cl
Sarisbury, Fareham BC
Sarratt, Three Rivers DC
Sarsden, W Oxon DC

Satley, Derwentside DC
Satterleigh, N Devon DC
Satterthwaite, S Lakeland DC
Saughall, Chester City
Saul, Stroud DC
Saundby, Bassetlaw DC
Saundersfoot, Pembrokeshire CC
Saunderton, Wycombe DC
Saunderton Lee, Wycombe DC
Sausthorpe, E Lindsey DC
Saval, Highland Cl
Savernake, Kennet DC
Sawbridgeworth, E Herts DC
Sawdon, Scarborough BC
Sawley, Erewash BC
Sawley, Harrogate BC
Sawley, Ribble Valley BC
Sawrey, S Lakeland DC
Sawston, S Cambs DC
Sawtry, Huntingdonshire DC
Saxby, Melton BC
Saxby, W Lindsey DC
Saxby All Saints, N Lincs Cl
Saxelbye, Melton BC
Saxhams, The, St Edmundsbury
    BC
Saxilby, W Lindsey DC
Saxlingham, N Norfolk DC
Saxlingham Nethergate, S
    Norfolk DC
Saxmundham, Suffolk C'l DC
Saxon Street, E Cambs DC
Saxondale, Rushcliffe BC
Saxtead, Suffolk C'l DC
Saxthorpe, N Norfolk DC
Saxton cum Scarthingwell, Selby
    DC
Sayers Common, Mid Sussex DC
Scackleton, Ryedale DC
Scaftworth, Bassetlaw DC
Scagglethorpe, Ryedale DC
Scalby, Scarborough BC
Scaldwell, Daventry DC
Scaleby, Carlisle City
Scales, Eden DC
Scales, Fylde BC
Scales, S Lakeland DC
Scalford, Melton BC
Scaling (part), Scarborough BC
Scalloway, Shetland Is Cl
Scalpay, Comhairle Nan Eilean
    Siar
Scalthwaiterigg, S Lakeland DC
Scamblesby, E Lindsey DC
Scamodale, Highland Cl
Scampston, Ryedale DC
Scampton, W Lindsey DC
Scapa, Orkney Is Cl
Scarborough, Scarborough BC
Scarcliffe, Bolsover DC

Scarcroft, Leeds City
Scarfskerry, Highland Cl
Scargill, Teesdale DC
Scarisbrick, W Lancs DC
Scarning, Breckland Cl
Scarrington, Rushcliffe BC
Scarth Hill, W Lancs DC
Scarva, Banbridge DC
Scawby, N Lincs Cl
Scawton, Ryedale DC
Scaynes Hill, Mid Sussex DC
Scholar Green, Congleton BC
Scholes, Kirklees MC
Scholes, Leeds City
Scleddau, Pembrokeshire CC
Scole, S Norfolk DC
Scone, Perth/Kinross Cl
Sconser, Highland Cl
Scopwick, N Kesteven DC
Scoraig, Highland Cl
Scorborough, E Riding of Yks
Scoriton, S Hams DC
Scorrier (part), Carrick DC
Scorrier (part), Kerrier DC
Scorton, Richmondshire DC
Scorton, Wyre BC
Scosthrop, Craven DC
Scotby, Carlisle City
Scotch Corner, Richmondshire DC
Scotforth, Lancaster City
Scothern, W Lindsey DC
Scots' Gap, Castle Morpeth BC
Scotsburn, Highland Cl
Scotstoun, Glasgow City
Scotstown, Highland Cl
Scotswood, Newcastle City
Scott Willoughby, N Kesteven DC
Scotter, W Lindsey DC
Scotterthorpe, W Lindsey DC
Scottlethorpe, S Kesteven DC
Scotton, Harrogate BC
Scotton, Richmondshire DC
Scotton, W Lindsey DC
Scottow, N Norfolk DC
Scoulton, Breckland Cl
Scourie, Highland Cl
Scrabster, Highland Cl
Scrainwood, Alnwick DC
Scrane End, Boston BC
Scraptoft, Harborough DC
Scratby, Gt Yarmouth BC
Scrayingham, Ryedale DC
Scredington, N Kesteven DC
Scremerston, Berwick-u-Tweed BC
Screveton, Rushcliffe BC
Scrivelsby, E Lindsey DC
Scriven, Harrogate BC
Scrooby, Bassetlaw DC

Scropton, S Derbys DC
Scruton, Hambleton DC
Sculthorpe, N Norfolk DC
Scunthorpe, N Lincs Cl
Sea Palling, N Norfolk DC
Seaboard, Highland Cl
Seaborough, W Dorset DC
Seacombe, Wirral MBC
Seafield, S Ayrshire Cl
Seafield, W Lothian Cl
Seaford, Lewes DC
Seaforth, Sefton MBC
Seagrave, Charnwood DC
Seagry, N Wilts DC
Seaham, Easington DC
Seahouses, Berwick-u-Tweed BC
Seal, Sevenoaks DC
Sealand, Flintshire CC
Seale, Guildford BC
Seamer, Hambleton DC
Seamer, Scarborough BC
Seamill, N Ayrshire Cl
Seapatrick, Banbridge DC
Searby, W Lindsey DC
Seasalter, Canterbury City
Seascale, Copeland BC
Seathwaite, S Lakeland DC
Seaton, Aberdeen City
Seaton, Allerdale BC
Seaton, Caradon DC
Seaton, Easington DC
Seaton, E Devon DC
Seaton, E Riding of Yks
Seaton, Rutland CC
Seaton Carew, Hartlepool BC
Seaton Delaval, Blyth Valley BC
Seaton Ross, E Riding of Yks
Seaton Sluice, Blyth Valley BC
Seave Green, Hambleton DC
Seaview, Isle of Wight Cl
Seavington St Mary, S Somerset DC
Seavington St Michael, S Somerset DC
Seawick, Tendring DC
Sebastopol, Torfaen CBC
Sebergham, Allerdale BC
Seckington, N Warks BC
Second Coast, Highland Cl
Sedbergh, S Lakeland DC
Sedbury, Richmondshire DC
Sedbusk, Richmondshire DC
Sedge Fen, Forest Heath DC
Sedgeberrow, Wychavon DC
Sedgebrook, S Kesteven DC
Sedgefield, Sedgefield BC
Sedgeford, King's Lynn/W Norfolk BC
Sedgehill, Salisbury DC
Sedgley Park, Bury MBC

Sedgwick, S Lakeland DC
Sedlescombe, Rother DC
Seedfield, Bury MBC
Seedley, Salford City
Seend, Kennet DC
Seer Green, Chiltern DC
Seething, S Norfolk DC
Sefton, Sefton MBC
Sefton Park, Liverpool City
Seghill, Blyth Valley BC
Seighford, Stafford BC
Seil, Argyll/Bute Cl
Seisdon, S Staffs Cl
Selattyn, Oswestry BC
Selborne, E Hants DC
Selby, Selby DC
Selham, Chichester DC
Selhurst, Croydon LBC
Selkirk, Scottish Borders Cl
Sellack, Herefordshire Cl
Sellafield, Copeland BC
Sellindge, Shepway DC
Selling, Swale BC
Selly Oak, Birmingham City
Selmeston, Wealden DC
Selsdon, Croydon LBC
Selsey, Chichester DC
Selsfield Common, Mid Sussex DC
Selside, Craven DC
Selside, S Lakeland DC
Selston, Ashfield DC
Selwood, Mendip DC
Selworthy, W Somerset DC
Semer, Babergh DC
Semington, W Wilts DC
Semley, Salisbury DC
Sempringham, S Kesteven DC
Send, Guildford BC
Seneley Green, St Helens MBC
Sennen, Penwith DC
Sessay, Hambleton DC
Sesswick, Wrexham CBC
Setchey, King's Lynn/W Norfolk BC
Setley, New Forest DC
Setmurthy, Allerdale BC
Settle, Craven DC
Settrington, Ryedale DC
Seven Sisters, Neath Port Talbot CBC
Sevenhampton, Cotswold DC
Sevenoaks, Sevenoaks DC
Sevenoaks Weald, Sevenoaks DC
Severn Beach, S Glos Cl
Severn Stoke, Malvern Hills DC
Sevington, Ashford BC
Sewards End, Uttlesford DC

Sewardstonebury, Epping Forest DC
Sewerby, E Riding of Yks
Sexhow, Hambleton DC
Sezincote, Cotswold DC
Sgeir Iosal, Highland Cl
Sgoir Beag, Highland Cl
Shabbington, Aylesbury Vale DC
Shackerstone, Hinckley/Bosworth BC
Shackleford, Guildford BC
Shadforth, Durham City
Shadingfield, Waveney DC
Shadoxhurst, Ashford DC
Shadwell, Leeds City
Shadwell, Tower Hamlets LBC
Shaftesbury, N Dorset DC
Shafton, Barnsley MBC
Shalbourne, Kennet DC
Shalcombe, Isle of Wight Cl
Shalden, E Hants DC
Shaldon, Teignbridge DC
Shalfleet, Isle of Wight Cl
Shalford, Braintree DC
Shalford, Guildford BC
Shalford Green, Braintree DC
Shalmsford Street, Canterbury City
Shalstone, Aylesbury Vale DC
Shandon, Argyll/Bute Cl
Shandwick, Highland Cl
Shangton, Harborough DC
Shanklin, Isle of Wight Cl
Shap, Eden DC
Shapinsay, Orkney Is Cl
Shapwick, E Dorset DC
Shapwick, Sedgemoor DC
Shard End, Birmingham City
Shardlow, S Derbys DC
Shareshill, S Staffs Cl
Sharlston, Wakefield MDC
Sharnbrook, Bedford BC
Sharnford, Blaby DC
Sharoe Green, Preston City
Sharow, Harrogate BC
Sharpenhoe, S Beds DC
Sharperton, Alnwick DC
Sharpham, Mendip DC
Sharpness, Stroud DC
Sharpthorne, Mid Sussex DC
Sharrington, N Norfolk DC
Sharrow, Sheffield City
Shatterford, Wyre Forest DC
Shatterling, Dover DC
Shaugh Prior, S Hams DC
Shavington, Crewe/Nantwich BC
Shavington Park, N Shropshire DC
Shaw, Oldham MBC
Shaw, Swindon BC

Shaw, W Berks DC
Shaw cum Donnington, W Berks DC
Shawbost, Comhairle Nan Eilean Siar
Shawbury, N Shropshire DC
Shawell, Harborough DC
Shawford, Winchester City
Shawforth, Rossendale BC
Shawlands, Glasgow City
Shearsby, Harborough DC
Shebbear, Torridge DC
Shebdon, Stafford BC
Sheddocksley, Aberdeen City
Shedfield, Winchester City
Sheen, Staffs Moorlands DC
Sheepscombe, Stroud DC
Sheepstor, W Devon BC
Sheepwash, Torridge DC
Sheepy Magna, Hinckley/Bosworth BC
Sheepy Parva, Hinckley/Bosworth BC
Sheering, Epping Forest DC
Sheerness, Swale BC
Sheerwater, Woking BC
Sheet, E Hants DC
Sheffield, Sheffield City
Sheffield Park, Wealden DC
Shefford, Mid Beds DC
Sheigra, Highland Cl
Sheinton, Shrewsbury/Atcham Cl
Shelderton, S Shropshire DC
Sheldon, Birmingham City
Sheldon, Derbys Dales DC
Sheldon, E Devon DC
Sheldwich, Swale BC
Shelfanger, S Norfolk DC
Shelfield, Stratford/Avon DC
Shelfield Green, Stratford/Avon DC
Shelford, Rushcliffe BC
Shelland, Mid Suffolk DC
Shelley, Babergh DC
Shelley, Kirklees MC
Shellingford, Vale of White Horse DC
Shellow Bowells, Epping Forest DC
Shelsley Beauchamp, Malvern Hills DC
Shelsley Kings, Malvern Hills DC
Shelsley Walsh, Malvern Hills DC
Shelswell, Cherwell DC
Shelton, Bedford BC
Shelton, Rushcliffe BC
Shelton, S Norfolk DC
Shelve, S Shropshire DC
Shenfield, Brentwood BC
Shenington, Cherwell DC

Shenley, Hertsmere BC
Shenley Brook End, Milton Keynes Cl
Shenley Church End, Milton Keynes Cl
Shenley Lodge, Milton Keynes Cl
Shenleybury, Hertsmere BC
Shenington, Cherwell DC
Shennington, Stratford/Avon DC
Shenstone, Lichfield DC
Shenstone, Wyre Forest DC
Shenton, Hinckley/Bosworth BC
Shepherd's Bush, Hammersmith/Fulham LBC
Shepherd's Green, S Oxon DC
Shepherdswell, Dover DC
Shepley, Kirklees MC
Shepperton, Spelthorne BC
Sheppey, Isle of, Swale BC
Shepreth, S Cambs DC
Shepshed, Charnwood DC
Shepton Beauchamp, S Somerset DC
Shepton Mallet, Mendip DC
Shepton Montague, S Somerset DC
Shepway, Maidstone BC
Sheraton, Easington DC
Sherborne, Cotswold DC
Sherborne, W Dorset DC
Sherborne St John, Basingstoke/Deane BC
Sherbourne, Warwick DC
Sherbourne Hill, Stratford/Avon DC
Sherburn, Durham City
Sherburn, Ryedale DC
Sherburn in Elmet, Selby DC
Shere, Guildford BC
Shereford, N Norfolk DC
Sherfield English, Test Valley BC
Sherfield on Loddon, Basingstoke/Deane BC
Sherford, S Hams DC
Sheriff Hutton, Ryedale DC
Sheriffhales, Bridgnorth DC
Sheringham, N Norfolk DC
Sherington, Milton Keynes Cl
Shermanbury, Horsham DC
Shernborne, King's Lynn/W Norfolk BC
Sherrington, W Wilts DC
Sherston, N Wilts DC
Shettleston, Glasgow City
Shevington, Wigan MBC
Sheviock, Caradon DC
Shiel Bridge, Highland Cl
Shield Row, Derwentside DC
Shieldaig, Highland Cl
Shieldhill, Falkirk Cl

GAZETTEER

Shielfoot, Highland Cl
Shifford, W Oxon DC
Shifnal, Bridgnorth DC
Shilbottle, Alnwick DC
Shildon, Sedgefield BC
Shillingford, Mid Devon DC
Shillingford, S Oxon DC
Shillingford St George,
    Teignbridge DC
Shillinglee, Chichester DC
Shillingstone, N Dorset DC
Shillington, Mid Beds DC
Shillmoor, Alnwick DC
Shilton, Rugby BC
Shilton, W Oxon DC
Shimpling, Babergh DC
Shimpling, S Norfolk DC
Shimpling Street, Babergh DC
Shincliffe, Durham City
Shiney Row, Sunderland City
Shinfield, Wokingham DC
Shingay cum Wendy, S Cambs
    DC
Shipbourne, Tonbridge/Malling
    BC
Shipdham, Breckland Cl
Shipham, Sedgemoor DC
Shiphay, Torbay Cl
Shiplake, S Oxon DC
Shipley, Amber Valley BC
Shipley, Bradford MDC
Shipley, Bridgnorth DC
Shipley, Horsham DC
Shipmeadow, Waveney DC
Shippon, Vale of White Horse DC
Shipston on Stour, Stratford/Avon
    DC
Shipton, Bridgnorth DC
Shipton, Hambleton DC
Shipton Bellinger, Test Valley BC
Shipton Gorge, W Dorset DC
Shipton Green, Chichester DC
Shipton Moyne, Cotswold DC
Shipton on Cherwell, Cherwell
    DC
Shipton under Wychwood, W
    Oxon DC
Shiptonthorpe, E Riding of Yks
Shirburn, S Oxon DC
Shirdley Hill, W Lancs DC
Shirebrook, Bolsover DC
Shiregreen, Sheffield City
Shirehampton, Bristol City
Shirenewton, Monmouthshire CC
Shireoaks, Bassetlaw DC
Shirland, N E Derbys DC
Shirlett, Bridgnorth DC
Shirley, Derbys Dales DC
Shirley, Solihull MBC
Shirley, Southampton City

Shirrell Heath, Winchester City
Shirwell, N Devon DC
Shobdon, Herefordshire Cl
Shobnall, E Staffs BC
Shobrooke, Mid Devon DC
Shocklach Oviatt, Chester City
Shoeburyness, Southend-on-Sea
    BC
Sholden, Dover DC
Sholing, Southampton City
Sholver, Oldham MBC
Shoreditch, Hackney LBC
Shoreham, Sevenoaks DC
Shoreham by Sea, Adur DC
Shoresdean, Berwick-u-Tweed
    BC
Shoreswood, Berwick-u-Tweed
    BC
Shorne, Gravesham BC
Shortlanesend, Carrick DC
Shorwell, Isle of Wight Cl
Shoscombe, Bath/N E Somerset
    Cl
Shotesham, S Norfolk DC
Shotley, Babergh DC
Shotley Low Quarter, Tynedale
    DC
Shotover, S Oxon DC
Shottermill (part), Chichester DC
Shottery, Stratford/Avon DC
Shottesbrooke,
    Windsor/Maidenhead RB
Shotteswell, Stratford/Avon DC
Shottisham, Suffolk C'l DC
Shottle, Amber Valley BC
Shotton, Berwick-u-Tweed BC
Shotton, Easington DC
Shotton, Flintshire CC
Shotton, Teesdale DC
Shotts, N Lanarkshire Cl
Shotwick, Chester City
Shotwick Park, Chester City
Shouldham, King's Lynn/W
    Norfolk BC
Shouldham Thorpe, King's
    Lynn/W Norfolk BC
Shoulton, Malvern Hills DC
Shrawardine,
    Shrewsbury/Atcham Cl
Shrawley, Malvern Hills DC
Shrewley, Warwick DC
Shrewsbury, Shrewsbury/Atcham
    Cl
Shrewton, Salisbury DC
Shripney, Arun DC
Shrivenham, Vale of White Horse
    DC
Shropham, Breckland Cl
Shudy Camps, S Cambs DC
Shulishadermor, Highland Cl

Shulista, Highland Cl
Shurdington, Tewkesbury BC
Shurlock Row,
    Windsor/Maidenhead RB
Shurton, W Somerset DC
Shustoke, N Warks BC
Shute, E Devon DC
Shutford, Cherwell DC
Shutlanger, S Northants Cl
Shuttington, N Warks BC
Shuttlewood, Bolsover DC
Sibbertoft, Daventry DC
Sibdon Carwood, S Shropshire
    DC
Sibford Ferris, Cherwell DC
Sibford Gower, Cherwell DC
Sible Hedingham, Braintree DC
Sibsey, E Lindsey DC
Sibson, Hinckley/Bosworth BC
Sibson cum Stibbington,
    Huntingdonshire DC
Sibthorpe, Rushcliffe BC
Sibton, Suffolk C'l DC
Sicklinghall, Harrogate BC
Sidbury, Bridgnorth DC
Sidbury, E Devon DC
Sidcup, Bexley LBC
Siddington, Cotswold DC
Siddington, Macclesfield BC
Sidestrand, N Norfolk DC
Sidford, E Devon DC
Sidlesham, Chichester DC
Sidley, Rother DC
Sidlow, Reigate/Banstead BC
Sidmouth, E Devon DC
Sigglesthorne, E Riding of Yks
Sighthill, Glasgow City
Signet, W Oxon DC
Silchester, Basingstoke/Deane
    BC
Sileby, Charnwood DC
Silecroft, Copeland BC
Silk Willoughby, N Kesteven DC
Silkstone, Barnsley MBC
Silloth, Allerdale BC
Silpho, Scarborough BC
Silsden, Bradford MDC
Silsoe, Mid Beds DC
Silton, N Dorset DC
Silver End, Braintree DC
Silverdale, Lancaster City
Silverdale, Newcastle-u-Lyme BC
Silverstone, S Northants Cl
Silverton, Mid Devon DC
Silvertown, Newham LBC
Simister, Bury MBC
Simmondley, High Peak BC
Simonburn, Tynedale DC
Simonstone, Ribble Valley BC
Simonswood, W Lancs DC

Simpson, Milton Keynes Cl
Simshill, Glasgow City
Sinderby, Hambleton DC
Sinderhope, Tynedale DC
Singleton, Ashford BC
Singleton, Chichester DC
Singleton, Fylde BC
Singlewell, Gravesham BC
Sinnington, Ryedale DC
Sinton Green, Malvern Hills DC
Sion Mills, Strabane DC
Sisland, S Norfolk DC
Sissinghurst, Tunbridge Wells BC
Siston, S Glos Cl
Sithney, Kerrier DC
Sitlington, Wakefield MDC
Sittingbourne, Swale BC
Six Ashes, Bridgnorth DC
Six Ashes, S Staffs Cl
Six Mile Bottom (part), S Cambs DC
Sixhills, W Lindsey DC
Sixmilecross, Omagh DC
Sixpenny Handley, E Dorset DC
Sizewell, Suffolk C'l DC
Skeabost Bridge, Highland Cl
Skeeby, Richmondshire DC
Skeffington, Harborough DC
Skeffling, E Riding of Yks
Skegby, Ashfield DC
Skegness, E Lindsey DC
Skelbo, Highland Cl
Skelbroke, Doncaster MBC
Skelding, Harrogate BC
Skeldyke, Boston BC
Skellingthorpe, N Kesteven DC
Skellow, Doncaster MBC
Skelmanthorpe, Kirklees MC
Skelmersdale, W Lancs DC
Skelmorlie, N Ayrshire Cl
Skelpick, Highland Cl
Skelsmergh, S Lakeland DC
Skelton, City of York Cl
Skelton, Eden DC
Skelton, Harrogate BC
Skelton, Redcar/Cleveland BC
Skelton, Richmondshire DC
Skelwith Bridge, S Lakeland DC
Skendleby, E Lindsey DC
Skene, Aberdeenshire Cl
Skerne, E Riding of Yks
Skerray, Highland Cl
Skerries, Shetland Is Cl
Skewen, Neath Port Talbot CBC
Skewsby, Hambleton DC
Skeyton, N Norfolk DC
Skidbrooke, E Lindsey DC
Skidby, E Riding of Yks
Skilgate, W Somerset DC
Skillington, S Kesteven DC

Skinburness, Allerdale BC
Skinflats, Falkirk Cl
Skinidin, Highland Cl
Skinnand, N Kesteven DC
Skinnerton, Highland Cl
Skinnet, Highland Cl
Skinningrove, Redcar/Cleveland BC
Skipness, Argyll/Bute Cl
Skipsea, E Riding of Yks
Skipton, Craven DC
Skipton on Swale, Hambleton DC
Skipwith, Selby DC
Skirlaugh, E Riding of Yks
Skirling, Scottish Borders Cl
Skirmett, Wycombe DC
Skirpenbeck, E Riding of Yks
Skirwith, Eden DC
Skirza, Highland Cl
Sklebo Muir, Highland Cl
Skulamus, Highland Cl
Skullomie, Highland Cl
Skutterskelfe, Hambleton DC
Skye of Curr, Highland Cl
Slackhall, High Peak BC
Slad, Stroud DC
Slade Green, Bexley LBC
Slaggyford, Tynedale DC
Slaidburn, Ribble Valley BC
Slains, Aberdeenshire Cl
Slaithwaite, Kirklees MC
Slaley, Tynedale DC
Slammanan, Falkirk Cl
Slapton, Aylesbury Vale DC
Slapton, S Hams DC
Slapton, S Northants Cl
Slaugham, Mid Sussex DC
Slawston, Harborough DC
Sleaford, E Hants DC
Sleaford, N Kesteven DC
Sleagill, Eden DC
Sleapford, Telford/Wrekin BC
Sleat, Highland Cl
Slebech, Pembrokeshire CC
Sledge Green, Malvern Hills DC
Sledmere, E Riding of Yks
Sleightholme, Teesdale DC
Sleights, Scarborough BC
Sleningford, Harrogate BC
Slepe, Purbeck DC
Slickly, Highland Cl
Slimbridge, Stroud DC
Slindon, Arun DC
Slindon, Stafford BC
Slinfold, Horsham DC
Slingsby, Ryedale DC
Slip End, S Beds DC
Slipton, E Northants Cl
Slitting Mill, Cannock Chase DC
Sloley, N Norfolk DC

Sloothby, E Lindsey DC
Slough, Slough BC
Sluggan, Highland Cl
Slyne, Lancaster City
Smailholm, Scottish Borders Cl
Small Dale, High Peak BC
Small Dole, Horsham DC
Small Heath, Birmingham City
Small Hythe, Ashford BC
Small Isles, Highland Cl
Smallbridge, Rochdale MBC
Smallburgh, N Norfolk DC
Smalley, Amber Valley BC
Smallfield, Tandridge DC
Smallridge, E Devon DC
Smallwood, Congleton BC
Smannell, Test Valley BC
Smardale, Eden DC
Smarden, Ashford BC
Smeeth, Ashford BC
Smeeton Westerby, Harborough DC
Smestow, S Staffs Cl
Smethcott, Shrewsbury/Atcham Cl
Smethwick, Sandwell MBC
Smirisary, Highland Cl
Smisby, S Derbys DC
Smith's Wood, Solihull MBC
Smithfield, Carlisle City
Smithills, Bolton MBC
Smithincott, Mid Devon DC
Smithstown, Highland Cl
Smithton, Highland Cl
Snailbeach, S Shropshire DC
Snailwell, E Cambs DC
Snainton, Scarborough BC
Snaith, E Riding of Yks
Snape, Hambleton DC
Snape, Suffolk C'l DC
Snarestone, N W Leics DC
Snarford, W Lindsey DC
Snargate, Shepway DC
Snatchwood, Torfaen CBC
Snave, Shepway DC
Sneaton, Scarborough BC
Sneatonthorpe, Scarborough BC
Snelland, W Lindsey DC
Snelson, Macclesfield BC
Snelston, Derbys Dales DC
Snetterton, Breckland Cl
Snettisham, King's Lynn/W Norfolk BC
Snibston, N W Leics DC
Snitter, Alnwick DC
Snitterby, W Lindsey DC
Snitterfield, Stratford/Avon DC
Snittlegarth, Allerdale BC
Snitton, S Shropshire DC
Snodland, Tonbridge/Malling BC

Snowdonia, Conwy CBC
Snowford, Stratford/Avon DC
Snowshill, Tewkesbury BC
Soberton, Winchester City
Sockbridge, Eden DC
Sockburn, Darlington BC
Sodbury, S Glos Cl
Softley, Teesdale DC
Soham, E Cambs DC
Soho, Birmingham City
Soho, Westminster City
Solihull, Solihull MBC
Solitote, Highland Cl
Sollers Hope, Herefordshire Cl
Solport, Carlisle City
Solva, Pembrokeshire CC
Somerby, Melton BC
Somerby, W Lindsey DC
Somercotes, Amber Valley BC
Somerford, Christchurch BC
Somerford, Congleton BC
Somerford, S Staffs Cl
Somerford Booths, Congleton BC
Somerford Keynes, Cotswold DC
Somerley, Chichester DC
Somerleyton, Waveney DC
Somers Town, Camden LBC
Somersal Herbert, Derbys Dales
  DC
Somersby, E Lindsey DC
Somersham, Huntingdonshire DC
Somersham, Mid Suffolk DC
Somerton, Babergh DC
Somerton, Cherwell DC
Somerton, Gt Yarmouth BC
Somerton, S Somerset DC
Sompting, Adur DC
Sonning, Wokingham DC
Sonning Common, S Oxon DC
Sopley, New Forest DC
Sopworth, N Wilts DC
Sorn, E Ayrshire Cl
Sotby, E Lindsey DC
Sothall, Sheffield City
Sotherton, Waveney DC
Sotterley, Waveney DC
Soudley, Forest of Dean DC
Sough, Pendle BC
Soulbury, Aylesbury Vale DC
Soulby, Eden DC
Souldern, Cherwell DC
Souldrop, Bedford BC
Sound, Crewe/Nantwich BC
Sourton, W Devon BC
Soutergate, S Lakeland DC
South Acre, Breckland Cl
South Alkham, Dover DC
South Alloa, Falkirk Cl
South Ballachulish, Highland Cl

South Bank, Redcar/Cleveland
  BC
South Barrow, S Somerset DC
South Bedburn, Teesdale DC
South Benfleet, Castle Point BC
South Brent, S Hams DC
South Cadbury, S Somerset DC
South Carlton, W Lindsey DC
South Cave, E Riding of Yks
South Cerney, Cotswold DC
South Charlton, Alnwick DC
South Cliffe, E Riding of Yks
South Clifton, Newark/Sherwood
  DC
South Clunes, Highland Cl
South Cockerington, E Lindsey
  DC
South Cove, Waveney DC
South Cowal, Argyll/Bute Cl
South Cowton, Hambleton DC
South Creake, King's Lynn/W
  Norfolk BC
South Croxton, Charnwood DC
South Cuil, Highland Cl
South Dalton, E Riding of Yks
South Darenth, Sevenoaks DC
South Darley, Derbys Dales DC
South Duffield, Selby DC
South Elkington, E Lindsey DC
South Elmham All Saints,
  Waveney DC
South Elmham St Cross,
  Waveney DC
South Elmham St James,
  Waveney DC
South Elmham St Margaret,
  Waveney DC
South Elmham St Mary, Waveney
  DC
South Elmham St Michael,
  Waveney DC
South Elmham St Nicholas,
  Waveney DC
South Elmham St Peter,
  Waveney DC
South Elmsall, Wakefield MDC
South End, Barrow-in-Furness
  BC
South Erradale, Highland Cl
South Fambridge, Rochford DC
South Fawley, W Berks DC
South Ferriby, N Lincs Cl
South Garvan, Highland Cl
South Godstone, Tandridge DC
South Gorley, New Forest DC
South Gosforth, Newcastle City
South Green, Basildon DC
South Hanningfield, Chelmsford
  BC

South Harris, Comhairle Nan
  Eilean Siar
South Harrow, Harrow LBC
South Harting, Chichester DC
South Hayling, Havant BC
South Heath, Chiltern DC
South Heighton, Lewes DC
South Hetton, Easington DC
South Hiendley, Wakefield MDC
South Hill, Caradon DC
South Hinksey, Vale of White
  Horse DC
South Holme, Ryedale DC
South Holmwood, Mole Valley DC
South Huish, S Hams DC
South Hykeham, N Kesteven DC
South Hylton, Sunderland City
South Kelsey, W Lindsey DC
South Kessock, Highland Cl
South Killingholme, N Lincs Cl
South Kilvington, Hambleton DC
South Kilworth, Harborough DC
South Kirkby, Wakefield MDC
South Knapdale, Argyll/Bute Cl
South Kyme, N Kesteven DC
South Leigh, W Oxon DC
South Leverton, Bassetlaw DC
South Littleton, Wychavon DC
South Lopham, Breckland Cl
South Luffenham, Rutland CC
South Marston, Swindon BC
South Milford, Selby DC
South Milton, S Hams DC
South Mimms, Hertsmere BC
South Molton, N Devon DC
South Moor, Derwentside DC
South Moreton, S Oxon DC
South Mundham, Chichester DC
South Muskham,
  Newark/Sherwood DC
South Newbald, E Riding of Yks
South Newington, Cherwell DC
South Newton, Salisbury DC
South Normanton, Bolsover DC
South Norwood, Croydon LBC
South Nutfield, Tandridge DC
South Ockendon, Thurrock BC
South Ormsby cum Kesby, E
  Lindsey DC
South Otterington, Hambleton DC
South Oxhey, Three Rivers DC
South Perrott, W Dorset DC
South Petherton, S Somerset DC
South Petherwin, N Cornwall DC
South Pickenham, Breckland Cl
South Pool, S Hams DC
South Rauceby, N Kesteven DC
South Reston, E Lindsey DC
South Ronaldsay, Orkney Is Cl

South Runcton, King's Lynn/W Norfolk BC
South Scarle, Newark/Sherwood DC
South Shields, S Tyneside MBC
South Somercotes, E Lindsey DC
South Stainley, Harrogate BC
South Stainmore, Eden DC
South Stanley, Derwentside DC
South Stoke, Arun DC
South Stoke, S Oxon DC
South Tawton, W Devon BC
South Thoresby, E Lindsey DC
South Tidworth, Kennet DC
South Twickenham, Richmond upon Thames LBC
South Walsham, Broadland DC
South Warnborough, Hart DC
South Weald, Brentwood BC
South Weston, S Oxon DC
South Wheatley, Bassetlaw DC
South Wheatley, N Cornwall DC
South Widcombe, Bath/N E Somerset CI
South Wigston, Oadby/Wigston BC
South Willingham, E Lindsey DC
South Wingfield, Amber Valley BC
South Witham, S Kesteven DC
South Wonston, Winchester City
South Woodford, Redbridge LBC
South Woodham Ferrers, Chelmsford BC
South Wootton, King's Lynn/W Norfolk BC
South Wraxall, W Wilts DC
South Zeal, W Devon BC
Southall, Ealing LBC
Southam, Stratford/Avon DC
Southam, Tewkesbury BC
Southam Fields, Stratford/Avon DC
Southam Holt, Stratford/Avon DC
Southampton, Southampton City
Southborough, Tunbridge Wells BC
Southbourne, Bournemouth BC
Southbourne, Chichester DC
Southburgh, Breckland CI
Southburn, E Riding of Yks
Southchurch, Southend-on-Sea BC
Southdean, Scottish Borders CI
Southease, Lewes DC
Southend, Argyll/Bute CI
Southend on Sea, Southend-on-Sea BC
Southern Green, N Herts DC

Southerness, Dumfries/Galloway CI
Southery, King's Lynn/W Norfolk BC
Southey Green, Sheffield City
Southfleet, Dartford BC
Southgate, Enfield LBC
Southgate (part), Barnet LBC
Southill, Mid Beds DC
Southleigh, E Devon DC
Southminster, Maldon DC
Southmoor, Vale of White Horse DC
Southoe, Huntingdonshire DC
Southolt, Mid Suffolk DC
Southorpe, Peterborough City •
Southowram, Calderdale MBC
Southport, Sefton MBC
Southrepps, N Norfolk DC
Southrop, Cotswold DC
Southrope Green, Basingstoke/Deane BC
Southsea, Portsmouth City
Southstoke, Bath/N E Somerset CI
Southville, Torfaen CBC
Southwaite, Eden DC
Southwark, Southwark LBC
Southwater, Horsham DC
Southway, Mendip DC
Southway, Plymouth City
Southwell, Newark/Sherwood DC
Southwell, Weymouth/Portland BC
Southwick, Adur DC
Southwick, Dumfries/Galloway CI
Southwick, E Northants CI
Southwick, Sunderland City
Southwick, W Wilts DC
Southwick, Winchester City
Southwold, Waveney DC
Southwood, Mendip DC
Sowerby, Calderdale MBC
Sowerby, Hambleton DC
Sowerby, Wyre BC
Sowerby Bridge, Calderdale MBC
Sowerby under Cotcliffe, Hambleton DC
Sowton, E Devon DC
Soyal, Highland CI
Spa Common, N Norfolk DC
Spalding, S Holland DC
Spaldington, E Riding of Yks
Spaldwick, Huntingdonshire DC
Spalford, Newark/Sherwood DC
Spanby, N Kesteven DC
Sparcells, Swindon BC
Sparham, Breckland CI
Spark Bridge, S Lakeland DC
Sparkbrook, Birmingham City

Sparkford, S Somerset DC
Sparkhill, Birmingham City
Sparkwell, S Hams DC
Sparrowpit, High Peak BC
Sparsholt, Vale of White Horse DC
Sparsholt, Winchester City
Spaunton, Ryedale DC
Spaxton, Sedgemoor DC
Spean Bridge, Highland CI
Speen, W Berks DC
Speen, Wycombe DC
Speeton, Scarborough BC
Speke, Liverpool City
Speldhurst, Tunbridge Wells BC
Spellbrook, E Herts DC
Spelsbury, W Oxon DC
Spencers Wood, Wokingham DC
Spennithorne, Richmondshire DC
Spennymoor, Sedgefield BC
Spernal, Stratford/Avon DC
Spetchley, Wychavon DC
Spetisbury, N Dorset DC
Spexhall, Waveney DC
Speybank, Highland CI
Speybridge, Highland CI
Spilsby, E Lindsey DC
Spindlestone, Berwick-u-Tweed BC
Spinningdale, Highland CI
Spitalfields, Tower Hamlets LBC
Spithurst, Lewes DC
Spittal, Berwick-u-Tweed BC
Spittal, Pembrokeshire CC
Spittal, Highland CI
Spittalfield, Perth/Kinross CI
Spixworth, Broadland DC
Splott, Cardiff CC
Spofforth, Harrogate BC
Spondon, Derby City
Spooner Row, S Norfolk DC
Spoonley Gate, Bridgnorth DC
Sporle, Breckland CI
Spott, E Lothian CI
Spratton, Daventry DC
Spreyton, W Devon BC
Spridlington, W Lindsey DC
Springboig, Glasgow City
Springburn, Glasgow City
Springfield, Chelmsford BC
Springfield, Dumfries/Galloway CI
Springfield, Fife CI
Springfield, Milton Keynes CI
Springfield, Highland CI
Springside, N Ayrshire CI
Springthorpe, W Lindsey DC
Sproatley, E Riding of Yks
Sproston, Vale Royal BC
Sprotborough, Doncaster MBC
Sproughton, Babergh DC

Sprouston, Scottish Borders Cl
Sproxton, Melton BC
Sproxton, Ryedale DC
Sproxton, S Kesteven DC
Spurstow, Crewe/Nantwich BC
Sringston, W Somerset DC
Stacey Bushes, Milton Keynes Cl
Stackpole, Pembrokeshire CC
Staddlethorpe, E Riding of Yks
Stadhampton, S Oxon DC
Staffield, Eden DC
Staffin, Highland Cl
Stafford, Stafford BC
Stagsden, Bedford BC
Stain, E Lindsey DC
Stainborough, Barnsley MBC
Stainburn, Harrogate BC
Stainby, S Kesteven DC
Staincross, Barnsley MBC
Staindrop, Teesdale DC
Staines, Spelthorne BC
Staines Green, E Herts DC
Stainfield, S Kesteven DC
Stainfield, W Lindsey DC
Stainforth, Craven DC
Stainforth, Doncaster MBC
Staining, Fylde BC
Stainland, Calderdale MBC
Stainmore, Eden DC
Stainsacre, Scarborough BC
Stainsby, Stockton-on-Tees BC
Stainton, Doncaster MBC
Stainton, Eden DC
Stainton, Middlesbrough Cl
Stainton, Richmondshire DC
Stainton, S Lakeland DC
Stainton, Teesdale DC
Stainton by Langworth, W
   Lindsey DC
Stainton le Vale, W Lindsey DC
Staintondale, Scarborough BC
Stair, E Ayrshire Cl
Staithes, Scarborough BC
Stalbridge, N Dorset DC
Stalham, N Norfolk DC
Staling Bank, Richmondshire DC
Stalisfield, Swale BC
Stallingborough, N E Lincs Cl
Stalmine, Wyre BC
Stalybridge, Tameside MBC
Stambourne, Braintree DC
Stambourne Green, Braintree DC
Stambridge, Rochford DC
Stamford, S Kesteven DC
Stamford Bridge, E Riding of Yks
Stamfordham, Castle Morpeth BC
Stanborough, Welwyn Hatfield
   DC
Stanbridge, E Dorset DC
Stanbridge, S Beds DC

Standburn, Falkirk Cl
Standeford, S Staffs Cl
Standen, Ashford BC
Standford, E Hants DC
Standish, Stroud DC
Standish, Wigan MBC
Standlake, W Oxon DC
Standon, E Herts DC
Standon, Stafford BC
Standon, Winchester City
Stane, N Lanarkshire Cl
Stanfield, Breckland Cl
Stanford, Breckland Cl
Stanford, Mid Beds DC
Stanford, Shepway DC
Stanford Bishop, Herefordshire Cl
Stanford Dingley, W Berks DC
Stanford in the Vale, Vale of
   White Horse DC
Stanford le Hope, Thurrock BC
Stanford on Avon, Daventry DC
Stanford on Soar, Rushcliffe BC
Stanford Rivers, Epping Forest
   DC
Stanghow, Redcar/Cleveland BC
Stanhoe, King's Lynn/W Norfolk
   BC
Stanhope, Ashford BC
Stanhope, Wear Valley DC
Stanion, Corby BC
Stank, Hambleton DC
Stanley, Derwentside DC
Stanley, Erewash BC
Stanley, Perth/Kinross Cl
Stanley, Staffs Moorlands DC
Stanley, Wakefield MDC
Stanmore, Harrow LBC
Stanmore, W Berks DC
Stannah, Wyre BC
Stanningfield, St Edmundsbury
   BC
Stanninghall, Broadland DC
Stannington, Castle Morpeth BC
Stannington, Sheffield City
Stansfield, St Edmundsbury BC
Stanstead, Babergh DC
Stanstead Abbotts, E Herts DC
Stanstead St Margarets, E Herts
   DC
Stansted, Tonbridge/Malling BC
Stansted Mountfitchet, Uttlesford
   DC
Stanthorne, Vale Royal BC
Stanton, Castle Morpeth BC
Stanton, E Staffs BC
Stanton, St Edmundsbury BC
Stanton, Tewkesbury BC
Stanton by Bridge, S Derbys DC
Stanton by Dale, Erewash BC

Stanton Drew, Bath/N E
   Somerset Cl
Stanton Fitzwarren, Swindon BC
Stanton Harcourt, W Oxon DC
Stanton Hill, Ashfield DC
Stanton in Peak, Derbys Dales
   DC
Stanton Lacy, S Shropshire DC
Stanton Long, Bridgnorth DC
Stanton on the Wolds, Rushcliffe
   BC
Stanton Prior, Bath/N E Somerset
   Cl
Stanton St Bernard, Kennet DC
Stanton St Gabriel, W Dorset DC
Stanton St John, S Oxon DC
Stanton St Quintin, N Wilts DC
Stanton under Bardon,
   Hinckley/Bosworth BC
Stanton upon Hine Heath, N
   Shropshire DC
Stanton Wick, Bath/N E Somerset
   Cl
Stantonbury, Milton Keynes Cl
Stanwardine in the Fields, N
   Shropshire DC
Stanway, Colchester BC
Stanway, Tewkesbury BC
Stanwell, Spelthorne BC
Stanwick, E Northants Cl
Stanwick St John, Richmondshire
   DC
Stanwix Rural, Carlisle City
Stapehill, E Dorset DC
Stapeley, Crewe/Nantwich BC
Stapenhill, E Staffs BC
Staple, Dover DC
Staple Hill, S Glos Cl
Staplecross, Rother DC
Staplefield, Mid Sussex DC
Stapleford, Broxtowe BC
Stapleford, E Herts DC
Stapleford, Melton BC
Stapleford, N Kesteven DC
Stapleford, Salisbury DC
Stapleford, S Cambs DC
Stapleford Abbotts, Epping Forest
   DC
Stapleford Tawney, Epping
   Forest DC
Staplegrove, Taunton Deane BC
Staplehurst, Maidstone BC
Staplers, Isle of Wight Cl
Stapleton, Bristol City
Stapleton, Carlisle City
Stapleton, Herefordshire Cl
Stapleton, Hinckley/Bosworth BC
Stapleton, Richmondshire DC
Stapleton, Selby DC
Stapleton, Shrewsbury/Atcham Cl

Staploe, Bedford BC
Star, Fife Cl
Starbotton, Craven DC
Starcross, Teignbridge DC
Starmore, Harborough DC
Starston, S Norfolk DC
Startforth, Teesdale DC
Statenborough, Dover DC
Stathern, Melton BC
Station Town, Easington DC
Staunton, Newark/Sherwood DC
Staunton (Coleford), Forest of Dean DC
Staunton (Glos), Forest of Dean DC
Staunton Harold, N W Leics DC
Staunton on Arrow, Herefordshire Cl
Staunton on Wye, Herefordshire Cl
Staveley, Chesterfield BC
Staveley, Harrogate BC
Staveley, S Lakeland DC
Staveley in Cartmel, S Lakeland DC
Staverton, Daventry DC
Staverton, S Hams DC
Staverton, Tewkesbury BC
Staverton, W Wilts DC
Stawell, Sedgemoor DC
Stawley, Taunton Deane BC
Staxigoe, Highland Cl
Staynall, Wyre BC
Staythorpe, Newark/Sherwood DC
Steane, S Northants Cl
Stearsby, Hambleton DC
Stebbing, Uttlesford DC
Stedham, Chichester DC
Steelend, Fife Cl
Steep, E Hants DC
Steeple, Maldon DC
Steeple, Purbeck DC
Steeple Ashton, W Wilts DC
Steeple Aston, Cherwell DC
Steeple Barton, W Oxon DC
Steeple Bumpstead, Braintree DC
Steeple Claydon, Aylesbury Vale DC
Steeple Gidding, Huntingdonshire DC
Steeple Langford, Salisbury DC
Steeple Morden, S Cambs DC
Steeton, Bradford MDC
Steeton, Selby DC
Stelling Minnis, Shepway DC
Stenhousemuir, Falkirk Cl
Stenigot, E Lindsey DC
Stenness, Orkney Is Cl
Stenscholl, Highland Cl

Stenson, S Derbys DC
Stenson Fields, S Derbys DC
Stenton, E Lothian Cl
Stenton, Fife Cl
Steppingley, Mid Beds DC
Stepps, N Lanarkshire Cl
Sterndale Moor, High Peak BC
Sternfield, Suffolk C'l DC
Stert, Kennet DC
Stetchworth, E Cambs DC
Stevenage, Stevenage BC
Stevenston, N Ayrshire Cl
Steventon, Basingstoke/Deane BC
Steventon, Vale of White Horse DC
Stevington, Bedford BC
Stewartby, Bedford BC
Stewarton, E Ayrshire Cl
Stewartstown, Cookstown DC
Stewkley, Aylesbury Vale DC
Stewton, E Lindsey DC
Steyning, Horsham DC
Stibb, N Cornwall DC
Stibb Cross, Torridge DC
Stibb Green, Kennet DC
Stibbard, N Norfolk DC
Stichill, Scottish Borders Cl
Sticker, Restormel BC
Stickford, E Lindsey DC
Sticklepath, W Devon BC
Stickney, E Lindsey DC
Stiffkey, N Norfolk DC
Stifford, Thurrock BC
Stillingfleet, Selby DC
Stillington, Hambleton DC
Stilton, Huntingdonshire DC
Stinchcombe, Stroud DC
Stinsford, W Dorset DC
Stirchley, Telford/Wrekin BC
Stirling, Stirling Cl
Stirton, Craven DC
Stisted, Braintree DC
Stithians, Kerrier DC
Stivichall, Coventry City MDC
Stixwould, E Lindsey DC
Stoak, Chester City
Stobo, Scottish Borders Cl
Stoborough, Purbeck DC
Stobswell, Dundee City
Stobswood, Castle Morpeth BC
Stock, Chelmsford BC
Stock, Wychavon DC
Stockbridge, Test Valley BC
Stockbridge Village, Knowsley MBC
Stockbury, Maidstone BC
Stockcross, W Berks DC
Stockdalewath, Carlisle City
Stockeld, Harrogate BC

Stockerston, Harborough DC
Stocket, Aberdeen City
Stocking Pelham, E Herts DC
Stockingford, Nuneaton/Bedworth BC
Stockland, E Devon DC
Stockland Bristol, Sedgemoor DC
Stockland Green, Birmingham City
Stockleigh English, Mid Devon DC
Stockleigh Pomeroy, Mid Devon DC
Stocklinch, S Somerset DC
Stockport, Stockport MBC
Stocksbridge, Sheffield City
Stocksfield, Tynedale DC
Stockton, Bridgnorth DC
Stockton, S Norfolk DC
Stockton, Stratford/Avon DC
Stockton, W Wilts DC
Stockton Heath, Warrington BC
Stockton on Tees, Stockton-on-Tees BC
Stockton on the Forest, City of York Cl
Stockwell, Lambeth LBC
Stockwood, W Dorset DC
Stodmarsh, Canterbury City
Stody, N Norfolk DC
Stoer, Highland Cl
Stogumber, W Somerset DC
Stogursey, W Somerset DC
Stoke, Basingstoke/Deane BC
Stoke, Chester City
Stoke, Crewe/Nantwich BC
Stoke, Havant BC
Stoke, Medway Cl
Stoke, Plymouth City
Stoke, Coventry City MDC
Stoke (nr Hartland), Torridge DC
Stoke Abbott, W Dorset DC
Stoke Albany, Kettering BC
Stoke Ash, Mid Suffolk DC
Stoke Bardolph, Gedling BC
Stoke Bruerne, S Northants Cl
Stoke by Clare, St Edmundsbury BC
Stoke by Nayland, Babergh DC
Stoke Canon, E Devon DC
Stoke Charity, Winchester City
Stoke Climsland, N Cornwall DC
Stoke d'Abernon, Elmbridge BC
Stoke Doyle, E Northants Cl
Stoke Dry, Rutland CC
Stoke Edith, Herefordshire Cl
Stoke Ferry, King's Lynn/W Norfolk BC
Stoke Fleming, S Hams DC
Stoke Gabriel, S Hams DC

Stoke Gifford, S Glos CI

Stoke Golding, Hinckley/Bosworth BC

Stoke Goldington, Milton Keynes CI

Stoke Hammond, Aylesbury Vale DC

Stoke Heath, Bromsgrove DC

Stoke Holy Cross, S Norfolk DC

Stoke Lacy, Herefordshire CI

Stoke Lyne, Cherwell DC

Stoke Mandeville, Aylesbury Vale DC

Stoke Newington, Hackney LBC

Stoke Orchard, Tewkesbury BC

Stoke Poges, S Bucks DC

Stoke Prior, Bromsgrove DC

Stoke Prior, Herefordshire CI

Stoke Rivers, N Devon DC

Stoke Rochford, S Kesteven DC

Stoke Row, S Oxon DC

Stoke St Gregory, Taunton Deane BC

Stoke St Mary, Taunton Deane BC

Stoke St Michael, Mendip DC

Stoke St Milborough, S Shropshire DC

Stoke sub Hamdon, S Somerset DC

Stoke Talmage, S Oxon DC

Stoke Trister, S Somerset DC

Stoke upon Tern, N Shropshire DC

Stoke upon Trent, Stoke-on-Trent City

Stoke Wake, N Dorset DC

Stokeham, Bassetlaw DC

Stokeinteignhead, Teignbridge DC

Stokenchurch, Wycombe DC

Stokenham, S Hams DC

Stokesay, S Shropshire DC

Stokesby, Gt Yarmouth BC

Stokesley, Hambleton DC

Stolford, W Somerset DC

Ston Easton, Mendip DC

Stondon, Mid Beds DC

Stondon Massey, Brentwood BC

Stone, Aylesbury Vale DC

Stone, Dartford BC

Stone, Stafford BC

Stone, Stroud DC

Stone, Wyre Forest DC

Stone Rural, Stafford BC

Stonebridge, Brent LBC

Stone-cum-Ebony, Ashford BC

Stonegate, Rother DC

Stonegrave, Ryedale DC

Stonehall, Dover DC

Stonehaugh, Tynedale DC

Stonehaven, Aberdeenshire CI

Stonehenge, Salisbury DC

Stonehouse, S Lanarkshire CI

Stonehouse, Stroud DC

Stonehouse, Tynedale DC

Stoneleigh, Epsom/Ewell BC

Stoneleigh, Warwick DC

Stonely, Huntingdonshire DC

Stones Green, Tendring DC

Stonesby, Melton BC

Stonesfield, W Oxon DC

Stoneton, Stratford/Avon DC

Stoney Cross, New Forest DC

Stoney Middleton, Derbys Dales DC

Stoney Stanton, Blaby DC

Stoney Stratton, Mendip DC

Stoney Thorpe, Stratford/Avon DC

Stoneyburn, W Lothian CI

Stoneygate, Leicester City

Stoneyhills, Maldon DC

Stoneykirk, Dumfries/Galloway CI

Stoneywood, Falkirk CI

Stonham Aspal, Mid Suffolk DC

Stonham Parva, Mid Suffolk DC

Stonor, S Oxon DC

Stonton Wyville, Harborough DC

Stony Stratford, Milton Keynes CI

Stonydelph, Tamworth BC

Stoodleigh, Mid Devon DC

Stopham, Chichester DC

Stopsley, Luton BC

Storeton, Wirral MBC

Storiths, Craven DC

Stornoway, Comhairle Nan Eilean Siar

Storrington, Horsham DC

Storrs, S Lakeland DC

Storth, S Lakeland DC

Stotfold, Mid Beds DC

Stottesdon, Bridgnorth DC

Stoughton, Chichester DC

Stoughton, Guildford BC

Stoughton, Harborough DC

Stoulton, Wychavon DC

Stour Provost, N Dorset DC

Stourbridge, S Staffs CI

Stourmouth, Dover DC

Stourpaine, N Dorset DC

Stourport on Severn, Wyre Forest DC

Stourton, Salisbury DC

Stourton, S Staffs CI

Stourton, Stratford/Avon DC

Stourton Caundle, N Dorset DC

Stoven, Waveney DC

Stow, Scottish Borders CI

Stow, W Lindsey DC

Stow Bardolph, King's Lynn/W Norfolk BC

Stow Bedon, Breckland CI

Stow cum Quy, S Cambs DC

Stow Longa, Huntingdonshire DC

Stow Maries, Maldon DC

Stow on the Wold, Cotswold DC

Stowbridge, King's Lynn/W Norfolk BC

Stowe, Aylesbury Vale DC

Stowe, S Kesteven DC

Stowe, S Shropshire DC

Stowe by Chartley, Stafford BC

Stowe ix Churches, Daventry DC

Stowey Sutton, Bath/N E Somerset CI

Stowford, W Devon BC

Stowlangtoft, Mid Suffolk DC

Stowmarket, Mid Suffolk DC

Stowood, S Oxon DC

Stowting, Shepway DC

Stowupland, Mid Suffolk DC

Strabane, Strabane DC

Strachan, Aberdeenshire CI

Strachur, Argyll/Bute CI

Stradbroke, Mid Suffolk DC

Stradbroke, Sheffield City

Stradishall, St Edmundsbury BC

Stradreagh, Limavady BC

Stradsett, King's Lynn/W Norfolk BC

Stragglethorpe, N Kesteven DC

Straid, Newtownabbey BC

Straiton, S Ayrshire CI

Stramshall, E Staffs BC

Stranocum, Ballymoney BC

Stranraer, Dumfries/Galloway CI

Stratfield Mortimer, W Berks DC

Stratfield Saye, Basingstoke/Deane BC

Stratfield Turgis, Basingstoke/Deane BC

Stratford, Newham LBC

Stratford St Andrew, Suffolk C'l DC

Stratford St Mary, Babergh DC

Stratford Tony, Salisbury DC

Stratford upon Avon, Stratford/Avon DC

Strath, Highland CI

Strathan, Highland CI

Strathan Skerray, Highland CI

Strathaven, S Lanarkshire CI

Strathblane, Stirling CI

Strathbungo, Glasgow City

Strathcarron, Highland CI

Strathconon, Highland CI

Strathcoul, Highland CI

Strathdon, Aberdeenshire CI

Stratheden, Fife CI

Stratherrick, Highland CI
Strathisla, Moray CI
Strathkinness, Fife CI
Strathmartine, Angus CI
Strathmiglo, Fife CI
Strathpeffer, Highland CI
Strathtay, Perth/Kinross CI
Strathy, Highland CI
Strathyre, Stirling CI
Stratton, Cotswold DC
Stratton, N Cornwall DC
Stratton, W Dorset DC
Stratton Audley, Cherwell DC
Stratton Hall, Suffolk C'l DC
Stratton on the Fosse, Mendip DC
Stratton St Margaret, Swindon BC
Stratton St Michael, S Norfolk DC
Stratton Strawless, Broadland DC
Streat, Lewes DC
Streatham, Lambeth LBC
Streatley, S Beds DC
Streatley, S Oxon DC
Streatley, W Berks DC
Street, Mendip DC
Street End, Chichester DC
Streethay, Lichfield DC
Streetly, Walsall MBC
Strefford, S Shropshire DC
Strelley, Broxtowe BC
Strensall, City of York CI
Strensham, Wychavon DC
Strete, S Hams DC
Stretford, Herefordshire CI
Stretford, Trafford MBC
Strethall, Uttlesford DC
Stretham, E Cambs DC
Strettington, Chichester DC
Stretton, Chester City
Stretton, E Staffs BC
Stretton, N E Derbys DC
Stretton, Rutland CC
Stretton, S Shropshire DC
Stretton, Warrington BC
Stretton Baskerville, Rugby BC
Stretton en le Field, N W Leics DC
Stretton Grandison, Herefordshire CI
Stretton Heath, Shrewsbury/Atcham CI
Stretton on Dunsmore, Rugby BC
Stretton on Fosse, Stratford/Avon DC
Stretton Sugwas, Herefordshire CI
Stretton under Fosse, Rugby BC
Stretton Westwood, Bridgnorth DC

Stretton Westwood, Shrewsbury/Atcham CI
Strichen, Aberdeenshire CI
Strickland Ketel, S Lakeland DC
Strickland Roger, S Lakeland DC
Stringston, W Somerset DC
Strixton, Wellingborough BC
Stroat, Forest of Dean DC
Stromeferry, Highland CI
Stromemore, Highland CI
Stromness, Orkney Is CI
Stronaba, Highland CI
Stronchreggan, Highland CI
Strone, Argyll/Bute CI
Strone, Highland CI
Stronsay, Orkney Is CI
Strontian, Highland CI
Strood Green, Chichester DC
Strood Green, Mole Valley DC
Stroud, E Hants DC
Stroud, Stroud DC
Struan, Perth/Kinross CI
Struan, Highland CI
Struanmore, Highland CI
Strubby, E Lindsey DC
Strule, Omagh DC
Strumpshaw, Broadland DC
Struy, Highland CI
Stuartfield, Aberdeenshire CI
Stubbington, Fareham BC
Stubton, S Kesteven DC
Stuchbury, S Northants CI
Stuckton, New Forest DC
Studdal, Dover DC
Studham, S Beds DC
Studland, Purbeck DC
Studley, Stratford/Avon DC
Studley Green, Wycombe DC
Studley Roger, Harrogate BC
Stukeleys, Huntingdonshire DC
Stuntney, E Cambs DC
Sturbridge, Stafford BC
Sturmer, Braintree DC
Sturminster Marshall, E Dorset DC
Sturminster Newton, N Dorset DC
Sturry, Canterbury City
Sturston, Breckland CI
Sturton by Stow, W Lindsey DC
Sturton Grange, Leeds City
Sturton le Steeple, Bassetlaw DC
Stuston, Mid Suffolk DC
Stutton, Babergh DC
Stutton, Selby DC
Styal, Macclesfield BC
Styrrup, Bassetlaw DC
Subberthwaite, S Lakeland DC
Suckley, Malvern Hills DC
Sudborough, E Northants CI
Sudbourne, Suffolk C'l DC

Sudbrooke, W Lindsey DC
Sudbury, Babergh DC
Sudbury, Brent LBC
Sudbury, Derbys Dales DC
Sudbury Court, Brent LBC
Sudeley, Tewkesbury BC
Suffield, N Norfolk DC
Suffield, Scarborough BC
Sugnall, Stafford BC
Suisnish, Highland CI
Suladale, Highland CI
Sulby, Daventry DC
Sulgrave, S Northants CI
Sulham, W Berks DC
Sulhamstead, W Berks DC
Sullington, Horsham DC
Sully, Vale of Glamorgan CI
Summerbridge, Harrogate BC
Summercourt, Restormel BC
Summerfield, Dover DC
Summerhouse, Darlington BC
Summerseat, Bury MBC
Sun Rising, Stratford/Avon DC
Sunbiggin, Eden DC
Sunbury, Spelthorne BC
Sunderland, Sunderland City
Sunderland Bridge, Durham City
Sundon, S Beds DC
Sundon Park, Luton BC
Sundridge, Sevenoaks DC
Sunk Island, E Riding of Yks
Sunningdale, Windsor/Maidenhead RB
Sunninghill, Windsor/Maidenhead RB
Sunningwell, Vale of White Horse DC
Sunniside, Gateshead CI
Sunniside, Wear Valley DC
Sunnybrae, Orkney Is CI
Sunnyside, Mid Sussex DC
Surbiton, Kingston upon Thames Royal Borough
Surfleet, S Holland DC
Surlingham, S Norfolk DC
Sustead, N Norfolk DC
Susworth, W Lindsey DC
Suton, S Norfolk DC
Sutterton, Boston BC
Sutton, Bassetlaw DC
Sutton, Bridgnorth DC
Sutton, Chichester DC
Sutton, E Cambs DC
Sutton, E Lindsey DC
Sutton, Hambleton DC
Sutton, Herefordshire CI
Sutton, Macclesfield BC
Sutton, Mid Beds DC
Sutton, N Norfolk DC
Sutton, N Shropshire DC

Sutton, Peterborough City
Sutton, Plymouth City
Sutton, Rochford DC
Sutton, Rushcliffe BC
Sutton, Stafford BC
Sutton, Suffolk C'l DC
Sutton, Sutton LBC
Sutton, Vale Royal BC
Sutton, W Oxon DC
Sutton at Hone, Dartford BC
Sutton Bassett, Kettering BC
Sutton Benger, N Wilts DC
Sutton Bonington, Rushcliffe BC
Sutton Bridge, S Holland DC
Sutton by Dover, Dover DC
Sutton Cheney,
  Hinckley/Bosworth BC
Sutton Courtenay, Vale of White
  Horse DC
Sutton Crosses, S Holland DC
Sutton cum Duckmanton, N E
  Derbys DC
Sutton Four Oaks, Birmingham
  City
Sutton Howgrave, Hambleton DC
Sutton in Ashfield, Ashfield DC
Sutton in Craven, Craven DC
Sutton Lane Ends, Macclesfield
  BC
Sutton Leach, St Helens MBC
Sutton Maddock, Bridgnorth DC
Sutton Mandeville, Salisbury DC
Sutton New Hall, Birmingham City
Sutton on Derwent, E Riding of
  Yks
Sutton on Hull, Kingston upon
  Hull City
Sutton on the Forest, Hambleton
  DC
Sutton on the Hill, S Derbys DC
Sutton on Trent,
  Newark/Sherwood DC
Sutton St Edmund, S Holland DC
Sutton St James, S Holland DC
Sutton Scotney, Winchester City
Sutton under Brailes,
  Stratford/Avon DC
Sutton under Whitestonecliffe,
  Hambleton DC
Sutton upon Tern, N Shropshire
  DC
Sutton Valence, Maidstone BC
Sutton Veny, W Wilts DC
Sutton Vesey, Birmingham City
Sutton Waldron, N Dorset DC
Swaby, E Lindsey DC
Swadlincote, S Derbys DC
Swaffham, Breckland Cl
Swaffham Bulbeck, E Cambs DC
Swaffham Prior, E Cambs DC

Swafield, N Norfolk DC
Swainby, Hambleton DC
Swainsthorpe, S Norfolk DC
Swainswick, Bath/N E Somerset
  Cl
Swalcliffe, Cherwell DC
Swalecliffe, Canterbury City
Swallow, W Lindsey DC
Swallowcliffe, Salisbury DC
Swallowfield, Wokingham DC
Swanage, Purbeck DC
Swanbourne, Aylesbury Vale DC
Swanland, E Riding of Yks
Swanley, Sevenoaks DC
Swanmore, Winchester City
Swannington, Broadland DC
Swannington, N W Leics DC
Swanscombe, Dartford BC
Swansea, Swansea C&C
Swanton Abbott, N Norfolk DC
Swanton Morley, Breckland Cl
Swanton Novers, N Norfolk DC
Swanwick, Amber Valley BC
Swarby, W Somerset DC
Swardeston, S Norfolk DC
Swarkestone, S Derbys DC
Swarland, Alnwick DC
Swarthmoor, S Lakeland DC
Swaton, N Kesteven DC
Swavesey, S Cambs DC
Sway, New Forest DC
Swayfield, S Kesteven DC
Swaything, Southampton City
Sweffling, Suffolk C'l DC
Swell, Cotswold DC
Swepstone, N W Leics DC
Swerford, W Oxon DC
Swettenham, Congleton BC
Swilland, Suffolk C'l DC
Swillington, Leeds City
Swimbridge, N Devon DC
Swinbrook, W Oxon DC
Swinden, Craven DC
Swinderby, N Kesteven DC
Swindon, Cheltenham BC
Swindon, S Staffs Cl
Swindon, Swindon BC
Swine, E Riding of Yks
Swinefleet, E Riding of Yks
Swineshead, Bedford BC
Swineshead, Boston BC
Swineshead Bridge, Boston BC
Swinethorpe, N Kesteven DC
Swiney, Highland Cl
Swinfen, Lichfield DC
Swinford, Harborough DC
Swingfield, Shepway DC
Swinhoe, Berwick-u-Tweed BC
Swinhope, W Lindsey DC
Swinithwaite, Richmondshire DC

Swinscoe, Staffs Moorlands DC
Swinstead, S Kesteven DC
Swinton, Glasgow City
Swinton, Harrogate BC
Swinton, Rotherham MBC
Swinton, Ryedale DC
Swinton, Salford City
Swinton, Scottish Borders Cl
Swithland, Charnwood DC
Swordale, Highland Cl
Swordly, Highland Cl
Sworton Heath, Macclesfield BC
Swyncombe, S Oxon DC
Swynnerton, Stafford BC
Swyre, W Dorset DC
Syde, Cotswold DC
Sydenham, Lewisham LBC
Sydenham, S Oxon DC
Sydenham Damerel, W Devon
  BC
Syderstone, King's Lynn/W
  Norfolk BC
Sydling St Nicholas, W Dorset DC
Sydmonton, Basingstoke/Deane
  BC
Syerston, Newark/Sherwood DC
Sykehouse, Doncaster MBC
Sykes, Ribble Valley BC
Syleham, Mid Suffolk DC
Symington, S Ayrshire Cl
Symington, S Lanarkshire Cl
Symondsbury, W Dorset DC
Syre, Highland Cl
Syreford, Cotswold DC
Syresham, S Northants Cl
Syston, Charnwood DC
Syston, S Kesteven DC
Sytch House Green, Bridgnorth
  DC
Sytchampton, Wychavon DC
Sywell, Wellingborough BC

Tabley, Macclesfield BC
Tackley, W Oxon DC
Tacolneston, S Norfolk DC
Tadcaster, Selby DC
Taddington, Derbys Dales DC
Tadley, Basingstoke/Deane BC
Tadlow, S Cambs DC
Tadmarton, Cherwell DC
Tadworth, Reigate/Banstead BC
Taffs Well, Rhondda Cynon Taff
  CBC
Taibach, Neath Port Talbot CBC
Tain, Highland Cl
Takeley, Uttlesford DC
Talaton, E Devon DC
Talgarth, Powys CC
Talisker, Highland Cl
Talke, Newcastle-u-Lyme BC

Talkin, Carlisle City
Talladale, Highland Cl
Tallentire, Allerdale BC
Talley, Carmarthenshire CC
Tallington, S Kesteven DC
Talmine, Highland Cl
Talsarnau, Gwynedd CC
Talskiddy, Restormel BC
Talton, Stratford/Avon DC
Talybont on Usk, Powys CC
Talywain, Torfaen CBC
Tamfourhill, Falkirk Cl
Tamlaght, Limavady BC
Tamniaran, Limavady BC
Tamworth, Tamworth BC
Tan y fron, Conwy CBC
Tandridge, Tandridge DC
Tanfield, Derwentside DC
Tanfield Lea, Derwentside DC
Tangley, Test Valley BC
Tangmere, Chichester DC
Tankersley, Barnsley MBC
Tannington, Mid Suffolk DC
Tannochside, N Lanarkshire Cl
Tansley, Derbys Dales DC
Tansor, E Northants Cl
Tantobie, Derwentside DC
Tanton, Hambleton DC
Tanworth in Arden,
    Stratford/Avon DC
Tap o' Noth, Aberdeenshire Cl
Taplow, S Bucks DC
Tapton, Sheffield City
Tarbert, Argyll/Bute Cl
Tarbet, Highland Cl
Tarbock Green, Knowsley MBC
Tarbolton, S Ayrshire Cl
Tarbrax, S Lanarkshire Cl
Tarland, Aberdeenshire Cl
Tarleton, W Lancs DC
Tarlscough, W Lancs DC
Tarlton, Cotswold DC
Tarnacre, Wyre BC
Tarporley, Vale Royal BC
Tarrant Crawford, N Dorset DC
Tarrant Gunville, N Dorset DC
Tarrant Hinton, N Dorset DC
Tarrant Keyneston, N Dorset DC
Tarrant Launceston, N Dorset DC
Tarrant Monkton, N Dorset DC
Tarrant Rawston, N Dorset DC
Tarrant Rushton, N Dorset DC
Tarring Neville, Lewes DC
Tarrington, Herefordshire Cl
Tarset, Tynedale DC
Tarskavaig, Highland Cl
Tattershall, E Lindsey DC
Tarves, Aberdeenshire Cl
Tarvin, Chester City
Tasburgh, S Norfolk DC

Tasley, Bridgnorth DC
Taston, W Oxon DC
Tatenhill, E Staffs BC
Tatershall, E Lindsey DC
Tatershall Thorpe, E Lindsey DC
Tatham, Lancaster City
Tathwell, E Lindsey DC
Tatsfield, Tandridge DC
Tattenhall, Chester City
Tattenhoe, Milton Keynes Cl
Tatterford, N Norfolk DC
Tattersett, N Norfolk DC
Tattershall Bridge, N Kesteven
    DC
Tattingstone, Babergh DC
Tattle Bank, Stratford/Avon DC
Tatton, Macclesfield BC
Tatworth, S Somerset DC
Taunton, Taunton Deane BC
Taverham, Broadland DC
Tavistock, W Devon BC
Tawe Uchaf, Powys CC
Tawstock, N Devon DC
Taxal, High Peak BC
Tayinloan, Argyll/Bute Cl
Taynton, W Oxon DC
Taynton, Forest of Dean DC
Taynuilt, Argyll/Bute Cl
Tayport, Fife Cl
Tealby, W Lindsey DC
Tealing, Angus Cl
Teangue, Highland Cl
Tebay, Eden DC
Tebworth, S Beds DC
Tedburn St Mary, Teignbridge DC
Teddington, Richmond upon
    Thames LBC
Teddington, Tewkesbury BC
Tedstone Delamere,
    Herefordshire Cl
Tedstone Wafer, Herefordshire Cl
Teeton, Daventry DC
Teffont, Salisbury DC
Teigh, Rutland CC
Teigngrace, Teignbridge DC
Teignmouth, Teignbridge DC
Telford, Telford/Wrekin BC
Tellisford, Mendip DC
Telscombe, Lewes DC
Templand, Dumfries/Galloway Cl
Temple Bruer, N Kesteven DC
Temple Cloud, Bath/N E
    Somerset Cl
Temple Ewell, Dover DC
Temple Grafton, Stratford/Avon
    DC
Temple Guiting, Cotswold DC
Temple Hardewyke,
    Stratford/Avon DC

Temple High Grange, N Kesteven
    DC
Temple Hirst, Selby DC
Temple Normanton, N E Derbys
    DC
Temple Sowerby, Eden DC
Temple, The, Lisburn City
Templecombe, S Somerset DC
Templemoyle, Limavady BC
Templepatrick, Antrim BC
Templeton, Mid Devon DC
Templeton, Pembrokeshire CC
Templetown, Derwentside DC
Tempsford, Mid Beds DC
Ten Mile Bank, King's Lynn/W
    Norfolk BC
Tenby, Pembrokeshire CC
Tendring, Tendring DC
Tenterden, Ashford BC
Terling, Braintree DC
Termon, Omagh DC
Ternhill, N Shropshire DC
Terregles, Dumfries/Galloway Cl
Terrick, Wycombe DC
Terrington, Ryedale DC
Terrington St Clement, King's
    Lynn/W Norfolk BC
Terrington St John, King's
    Lynn/W Norfolk BC
Terry's Green, Stratford/Avon DC
Testerton, N Norfolk DC
Teston, Maidstone BC
Tetbury, Cotswold DC
Tetbury Upton, Cotswold DC
Tetchill, N Shropshire DC
Tetcott, Torridge DC
Tetford, E Lindsey DC
Tetney, E Lindsey DC
Tetsworth, S Oxon DC
Tettenhall, S Staffs Cl
Tetworth, Huntingdonshire DC
Teversal, Ashfield DC
Teversham, S Cambs DC
Tewin, E Herts DC
Tewkesbury, Tewkesbury BC
Teynham, Swale BC
Thakeham, Horsham DC
Thame, S Oxon DC
Thames Ditton, Elmbridge BC
Thamesmead (part), Bexley LBC
Thanington, Canterbury City
Thankerton, S Lanarkshire Cl
Tharston, S Norfolk DC
Thatcham, W Berks DC
Thatto Heath, St Helens MBC
Thaxted, Uttlesford DC
Theakston, Hambleton DC
Thealby, N Lincs Cl
Theale, W Berks DC
Thearne, E Riding of Yks

Theberton, Suffolk C'l DC
Thedden Grange, E Hants DC
Theddingworth, Harborough DC
Theddlethorpe, E Lindsey DC
Theddlethorpe All Saints, E
  Lindsey DC
Thelbridge, Mid Devon DC
Thelnetham, St Edmundsbury BC
Thelveton, S Norfolk DC
Thelwall, Warrington BC
Themelthorpe, Broadland DC
Thenford, S Northants Cl
Therfield, N Herts DC
Thetford, Breckland Cl
Theydon Bois, Epping Forest DC
Theydon Garnon, Epping Forest
  DC
Theydon Mount, Epping Forest
  DC
Thimbleby, E Lindsey DC
Thimbleby, Hambleton DC
Thirkleby, Hambleton DC
Thirlby, Hambleton DC
Thirlwall, Tynedale DC
Thirn, Hambleton DC
Thirsk, Hambleton DC
Thirston, Castle Morpeth BC
Thistleton, Fylde BC
Thistleton, Rutland CC
Thixendale, Ryedale DC
Thockrington, Tynedale DC
Tholomas Drove, Fenland DC
Tholthorpe, Hambleton DC
Thomley, S Oxon DC
Thompson, Breckland Cl
Thonock, W Lindsey DC
Thoralby, Richmondshire DC
Thoresthorpe, E Lindsey DC
Thoresway, W Lindsey DC
Thorganby, Selby DC
Thorganby, W Lindsey DC
Thorgill, Ryedale DC
Thorington, Suffolk C'l DC
Thorlby, Craven DC
Thorley, E Herts DC
Thorley Street, E Herts DC
Thormanby, Hambleton DC
Thornaby, Stockton-on-Tees BC
Thornaby on Tees, Stockton-on-
  Tees BC
Thornaby Village, Stockton-on-
  Tees BC
Thornage, N Norfolk DC
Thornborough, Aylesbury Vale
  DC
Thornborough, Hambleton DC
Thornbury, Herefordshire Cl
Thornbury, S Glos Cl
Thornbury (nr Holsworthy),
  Torridge DC

Thornby, Daventry DC
Thorncliffe, Staffs Moorlands DC
Thorncombe, W Dorset DC
Thorncombe Street, Waverley BC
Thorndon, Mid Suffolk DC
Thorndon Cross, W Devon BC
Thorne, Doncaster MBC
Thorner, Leeds City
Thorney, Newark/Sherwood DC
Thorney, Peterborough City
Thorney Hill, New Forest DC
Thorney Island, Chichester DC
Thornford, W Dorset DC
Thorngumbald, E Riding of Yks
Thornham, King's Lynn/W Norfolk
  BC
Thornham Magna, Mid Suffolk
  DC
Thornham Parva, Mid Suffolk DC
Thornhaugh, Peterborough City
Thornhill, Copeland BC
Thornhill, Dumfries/Galloway Cl
Thornhill, High Peak BC
Thornhill, Kirklees MC
Thornhill, Southampton City
Thornhill, Stirling Cl
Thornhill, Torfaen CBC
Thornhill Edge, Kirklees MC
Thornholme, E Riding of Yks
Thornley, Easington DC
Thornley, Wear Valley DC
Thornley with Wheatley, Ribble
  Valley BC
Thornliebank, E Renfrewshire Cl
Thorns, St Edmundsbury BC
Thornsett, High Peak BC
Thornthwaite, Allerdale BC
Thornthwaite, Harrogate BC
Thornton, Aylesbury Vale DC
Thornton, Berwick-u-Tweed BC
Thornton, Bradford MDC
Thornton, E Lindsey DC
Thornton, E Riding of Yks
Thornton, Fife Cl
Thornton, Hinckley/Bosworth BC
Thornton, Middlesbrough Cl
Thornton, Sefton MBC
Thornton, Stratford/Avon DC
Thornton, Wyre BC
Thornton Curtis, N Lincs Cl
Thornton Heath, Croydon LBC
Thornton Hough, Wirral MBC
Thornton in Craven, Craven DC
Thornton in Lonsdale, Craven DC
Thornton le Beans, Hambleton
  DC
Thornton le Clay, Ryedale DC
Thornton le Dale, Ryedale DC
Thornton le Fen, E Lindsey DC
Thornton le Moor, Hambleton DC

Thornton le Moor, W Lindsey DC
Thornton le Moors, Chester City
Thornton le Street, Hambleton
  DC
Thornton on the Hill, Hambleton
  DC
Thornton Rust, Richmondshire
  DC
Thornton Steward,
  Richmondshire DC
Thornton Watlass, Hambleton DC
Thorntonhall, S Lanarkshire Cl
Thornville, Harrogate BC
Thornwood, Glasgow City
Thornwood Common, Epping
  Forest DC
Thoroton, Rushcliffe BC
Thorp, Hambleton DC
Thorp Arch, Leeds City
Thorpe, Craven DC
Thorpe, Derbys Dales DC
Thorpe, E Lindsey DC
Thorpe, Eden DC
Thorpe, Newark/Sherwood DC
Thorpe, Runnymede BC
Thorpe Abbotts, S Norfolk DC
Thorpe Achurch, E Northants Cl
Thorpe Arnold, Melton BC
Thorpe Audlin, Wakefield MDC
Thorpe Bassett, Ryedale DC
Thorpe Bay, Southend-on-Sea
  BC
Thorpe by Water, Rutland CC
Thorpe Constantine, Lichfield DC
Thorpe End, Broadland DC
Thorpe Green, Babergh DC
Thorpe Hesley, Rotherham MBC
Thorpe in Balne, Doncaster MBC
Thorpe in the Glebe, Rushcliffe
  BC
Thorpe Langton, Harborough DC
Thorpe le Fallows, W Lindsey DC
Thorpe le Soken, Tendring DC
Thorpe Malsor, Kettering BC
Thorpe Mandeville, S Northants
  Cl
Thorpe Market, N Norfolk DC
Thorpe Marriott, Broadland DC
Thorpe Morieux, Babergh DC
Thorpe next Haddowe, S Norfolk
  DC
Thorpe on the Hill, N Kesteven
  DC
Thorpe St Andrew, Broadland DC
Thorpe St Peter, E Lindsey DC
Thorpe Salvin, Rotherham MBC
Thorpe Satchville, Melton BC
Thorpe Thewles, Stockton-on-
  Tees BC
Thorpe Tilney, N Kesteven DC

Thorpe Underwood, Harrogate BC
Thorpe Waterville, E Northants Cl
Thorpe Willoughby, Selby DC
Thorpeness, Suffolk C'l DC
Thorrington, Tendring DC
Thorverton, Mid Devon DC
Thrandeston, Mid Suffolk DC
Thrapston, E Northants Cl
Threapland, Allerdale BC
Threapwood, Chester City
Three Gates, Stratford/Avon DC
Three Hammers, N Cornwall DC
Three Holes, King's Lynn/W Norfolk BC
Three Legged Cross, E Dorset DC
Three Mile Cross, Wokingham DC
Threekingham, N Kesteven DC
Threemilestone, Carrick DC
Threemiletown, W Lothian Cl
Threlkeld, Eden DC
Threshfield, Craven DC
Thrimby, Eden DC
Thringarth, Teesdale DC
Thringstone, N W Leics DC
Thrintoft, Hambleton DC
Thriplow, S Cambs DC
Throcking, E Herts DC
Throckley, Newcastle City
Throckmorton, Wychavon DC
Throphill, Castle Morpeth BC
Thropton, Alnwick DC
Througham, Stroud DC
Throwleigh, W Devon BC
Throwley, Swale BC
Thrumpton, Rushcliffe BC
Thrumster, Highland Cl
Thrunton, Alnwick DC
Thrupp, Cherwell DC
Thrupp, Stroud DC
Thruscross, Harrogate BC
Thrushelton, W Devon BC
Thrussington, Charnwood DC
Thruxton, Herefordshire Cl
Thruxton, Test Valley BC
Thrybergh, Rotherham MBC
Thundersley, Castle Point BC
Thundridge, E Herts DC
Thurcaston, Charnwood DC
Thurcroft, Rotherham MBC
Thurdon, N Cornwall DC
Thurgarton, Newark/Sherwood DC
Thurgarton, N Norfolk DC
Thurgoland, Barnsley MBC
Thurlaston, Blaby DC
Thurlaston, Rugby BC
Thurlby, N Kesteven DC

Thurlby, S Kesteven DC
Thurleigh, Bedford BC
Thurlestone, S Hams DC
Thurloxton, Sedgemoor DC
Thurlstone, Barnsley MBC
Thurlton, S Norfolk DC
Thurmaston, Charnwood DC
Thurnby, Harborough DC
Thurne, Gt Yarmouth BC
Thurnham, Lancaster City
Thurnham, Maidstone BC
Thurning, E Northants Cl
Thurning, N Norfolk DC
Thurnscoe, Barnsley MBC
Thursby, Allerdale BC
Thursford, N Norfolk DC
Thursley, Waverley BC
Thurso, Highland Cl
Thurso East, Highland Cl
Thurstaston, Wirral MBC
Thurston, Mid Suffolk DC
Thurstonfield, Carlisle City
Thurstonland, Kirklees MC
Thurton, S Norfolk DC
Thurvaston, S Derbys DC
Thwaite, Mid Suffolk DC
Thwaite, N Norfolk DC
Thwaite, Richmondshire DC
Thwaite St Mary, S Norfolk DC
Thwing, E Riding of Yks
Tibberton, Forest of Dean DC
Tibberton, Telford/Wrekin BC
Tibberton, Wychavon DC
Tibenham, S Norfolk DC
Tibshelf, Bolsover DC
Tibthorpe, E Riding of Yks
Ticehurst, Rother DC
Tichborne, Winchester City
Tickencote, Rutland CC
Tickenham, N Somerset DC
Tickhill, Doncaster MBC
Ticklerton, S Shropshire DC
Ticknall, S Derbys DC
Tickton, E Riding of Yks
Tidcombe, Kennet DC
Tiddington, S Oxon DC
Tiddington, Stratford/Avon DC
Tidebrook, Wealden DC
Tideford, Caradon DC
Tidenham, Forest of Dean DC
Tideswell, Derbys Dales DC
Tidmarsh, W Berks DC
Tidmington, Stratford/Avon DC
Tidpit, New Forest DC
Tidworth, Kennet DC
Tiers Cross, Pembrokeshire CC
Tiffield, S Northants Cl
Tighnabruaich, Argyll/Bute Cl
Tilbrook, Huntingdonshire DC
Tilbury, Thurrock BC

Tilbury Juxta Clare, Braintree DC
Tile Cross, Solihull MBC
Tilehurst, W Berks DC
Tilery, Stockton-on-Tees BC
Tilford, Waverley BC
Tillicoultry, Clackmannanshire Cl
Tillingham, Maldon DC
Tillington, Chichester DC
Tillside, Berwick-u-Tweed BC
Tillydrone, Aberdeen City
Tilmanstone, Dover DC
Tilney All Saints, King's Lynn/W Norfolk BC
Tilney High End, King's Lynn/W Norfolk BC
Tilney St Lawrence, King's Lynn/W Norfolk BC
Tilshead, Salisbury DC
Tilstock, N Shropshire DC
Tilston, Chester City
Tilsworth, S Beds DC
Tilton on the Hill, Harborough DC
Tilty, Uttlesford DC
Timberland, N Kesteven DC
Timbersbrook, Congleton BC
Timberscombe, W Somerset DC
Timble, Harrogate BC
Timperley, Trafford MBC
Timsbury, Bath/N E Somerset Cl
Timsbury, Test Valley BC
Timworth, St Edmundsbury BC
Tincleton, W Dorset DC
Tindale, Carlisle City
Tingewick, Aylesbury Vale DC
Tingley, Leeds City
Tingrith, Mid Beds DC
Tingwall, Shetland Is Cl
Tinhay, W Devon BC
Tinkers Bridge, Milton Keynes Cl
Tinkersley, Derbys Dales DC
Tinshill, Leeds City
Tinsley, Sheffield City
Tintagel, N Cornwall DC
Tintern, Monmouthshire CC
Tintinhull, S Somerset DC
Tintwistle, High Peak BC
Tinwald, Dumfries/Galloway Cl
Tinwell, Rutland CC
Tipperty, Aberdeenshire Cl
Tipps End, Fenland DC
Tipton, Dudley MBC
Tipton, Sandwell MBC
Tipton St John, E Devon DC
Tiptree, Colchester BC
Tiree, Isle of, Argyll/Bute Cl
Tirley, Tewkesbury BC
Tirril, Eden DC
Tirryside, Highland Cl
Tirymynach, Ceredigion CC
Tisbury, Salisbury DC

Tissington, Derbys Dales DC
Titchfield, Fareham BC
Titchmarsh, E Northants CI
Titchwell, King's Lynn/W Norfolk BC
Titley, Herefordshire CI
Titlington, Alnwick DC
Titsey, Tandridge DC
Tittesworth, Staffs Moorlands DC
Tittleshall, Breckland CI
Tiverton, Chester City
Tiverton, Mid Devon DC
Tivetshall St Margaret, S Norfolk DC
Tivetshall St Mary, S Norfolk DC
Tixall, Stafford BC
Tixover, Rutland CC
Tobermory, Argyll/Bute CI
Tockenham, N Wilts DC
Tockholes, Blackburn with Darwen BC
Tockwith, Harrogate BC
Todber, N Dorset DC
Toddington, S Beds DC
Toddington, Tewkesbury BC
Todenham, Cotswold DC
Todhills, Carlisle City
Todmorden, Calderdale MBC
Todwick, Rotherham MBC
Toft, Macclesfield BC
Toft, S Cambs DC
Toft, S Kesteven DC
Toft Monks, S Norfolk DC
Toft Newton, W Lindsey DC
Toftrees, N Norfolk DC
Toftwood, Breckland CI
Togston, Alnwick DC
Tokers Green, S Oxon DC
Tokyngton, Brent LBC
Tollard Royal, Salisbury DC
Tollcross, Glasgow City
Toller Fratrum, W Dorset DC
Toller Porcorum, W Dorset DC
Tollerton, Hambleton DC
Tollerton, Rushcliffe BC
Tollesbury, Maldon DC
Tolleshunt D'Arcy, Maldon DC
Tolleshunt Knights, Maldon DC
Tolleshunt Major, Maldon DC
Tolpuddle, W Dorset DC
Tolvah, Highland CI
Tolworth, Kingston upon Thames Royal Borough
Tomatin, Highland CI
Tomich, Highland CI
Tomintoul, Moray CI
Tomlow, Stratford/Avon DC
Tonbridge, Tonbridge/Malling BC
Tong, Bridgnorth DC
Tonge, N W Leics DC

Tonge, Swale BC
Tongham, Guildford BC
Tongland, Dumfries/Galloway CI
Tongue, Highland CI
Tongwell, Milton Keynes CI
Tonmawr, Neath Port Talbot CBC
Tonna, Neath Port Talbot CBC
Tonwell, E Herts DC
Tonypandy, Rhondda Cynon Taff CBC
Tonyrefail, Rhondda Cynon Taff CBC
Toomebridge, Antrim BC
Toot Baldon, S Oxon DC
Toot Hill, Epping Forest DC
Toothill, Swindon BC
Toothill, Test Valley BC
Tooting, Wandsworth LBC
Topcliffe, Hambleton DC
Topcroft, S Norfolk DC
Tophill East, Weymouth/Portland BC
Tophill West, Weymouth/Portland BC
Toppesfield, Braintree DC
Torbryan, Teignbridge DC
Tore, Highland CI
Torgulbin, Highland CI
Torksey, W Lindsey DC
Torlundy, Highland CI
Tormarton, S Glos CI
Tormore, Highland CI
Tornagrain, Highland CI
Torness, Highland CI
Torpenhow, Allerdale BC
Torphins, Aberdeenshire CI
Torpichen, W Lothian CI
Torpoint, Caradon DC
Torquay, Torbay CI
Torran, Highland CI
Torrance, E Dunbartonshire CI
Torridon, Highland CI
Torrin, Highland CI
Torrington, Torridge DC
Torrisdale, Highland CI
Torroble, Highland CI
Torroy, Highland CI
Torry, Aberdeen City
Torryburn, Fife CI
Torthorwald, Dumfries/Galloway CI
Tortworth, S Glos CI
Torvaig, Highland CI
Torver, S Lakeland DC
Torwood, Falkirk CI
Torworth, Bassetlaw DC
Toryglen, Glasgow City
Toscaig, Highland CI
Toseland, Huntingdonshire DC
Tosside, Ribble Valley BC

Tostock, Mid Suffolk DC
Totaig, Highland CI
Totardor, Highland CI
Tote, Highland CI
Totegan, Highland CI
Tothill, E Lindsey DC
Totland, Isle of Wight CI
Totley, Sheffield City
Totnes, S Hams DC
Toton, Broxtowe BC
Totscore, Highland CI
Tottenham, Haringey LBC
Tottenhill, King's Lynn/W Norfolk BC
Totteridge, Barnet LBC
Totteridge, Wycombe DC
Totternhoe, S Beds DC
Totterton, S Shropshire DC
Tottington, Breckland CI
Tottington, Bury MBC
Totton, New Forest DC
Tough, Aberdeenshire CI
Toulvaddie, Highland CI
Tournaig, Highland CI
Tovil, Maidstone BC
Tow Law, Wear Valley DC
Towcester, S Northants CI
Towednack, Penwith DC
Tower Hamlets, Tower Hamlets LBC
Towersey, S Oxon DC
Townhead, Eden DC
Townhead, Glasgow City
Townhill, Fife CI
Townshend, Kerrier DC
Towrie, Aberdeenshire CI
Towthorpe, City of York CI
Towton, Selby DC
Towyn, Abergele, Conwy CBC
Toxteth, Liverpool City
Toy's Hill, Sevenoaks DC
Toynton All Saints, E Lindsey DC
Toynton St Peter, E Lindsey DC
Traboe, Kerrier DC
Tradespark, Highland CI
Trafford Park, Trafford MBC
Trallong, Powys CC
Tranent, E Lothian CI
Tranmere, Wirral MBC
Trantlebeg, Highland CI
Trantlemore, Highland CI
Tranwell, Castle Morpeth BC
Traps Green, Stratford/Avon DC
Traquair, Scottish Borders CI
Trawden, Pendle BC
Trawsfynydd, Gwynedd CC
Trawsgoed, Ceredigion CC
Treales, Fylde BC
Trearddur, Isle of Anglesey CC
Trebanos, Neath Port Talbot CBC

Trebartha, N Cornwall DC
Trebetherick, N Cornwall DC
Treborough, W Somerset DC
Trebudannon, Restormel BC
Treburly, N Cornwall DC
Trecoed, Powys CC
Trecwn, Pembrokeshire CC
Tredavoe, Penwith DC
Tredegar, Blaenau Gwent CBC
Tredington, Stratford/Avon DC
Tredinnick, N Cornwall DC
Tredrizzick, N Cornwall DC
Treen, Penwith DC
Treeton, Rotherham MBC
Tref Alaw, Isle of Anglesey CC
Trefechan, Merthyr Tydfil CBC
Trefeglwys, Powys CC
Trefeurig, Ceredigion CC
Treflach, Oswestry BC
Treflys, Powys CC
Trefnant, Denbighshire CC
Trefriw, Conwy CBC
Tregadillett, N Cornwall DC
Tregaron, Ceredigion CC
Tregeare, N Cornwall DC
Tregidden, Kerrier DC
Tregole, N Cornwall DC
Tregonetha, Restormel BC
Tregony, Carrick DC
Tregurrian, Restormel BC
Tregynon, Powys CC
Treharris, Merthyr Tydfil CBC
Treknow, N Cornwall DC
Trelan, Kerrier DC
Trelash, N Cornwall DC
Trelawny, Plymouth City
Trelawnyd, Flintshire CC
Trelech, Carmarthenshire CC
Trelewis, Merthyr Tydfil CBC
Treligga, N Cornwall DC
Trelights, N Cornwall DC
Trelill, N Cornwall DC
Trelissick, Carrick DC
Trellech United, Monmouthshire
  CC
Tremail, N Cornwall DC
Tremaine, N Cornwall DC
Tremar, Caradon DC
Tremeirchion, Denbighshire CC
Trenance, Restormel BC
Trenarren, Restormel BC
Trench, Telford/Wrekin BC
Treneglos, N Cornwall DC
Trent, W Dorset DC
Trentishoe, N Devon DC
Treorchy, Rhondda Cynon Taff
  CBC
Tresco, Isles of Scilly CI
Trescott, S Staffs CI
Trescowe, Kerrier DC

Tresham, Stroud DC
Tresillian, Carrick DC
Treskinnick Cross, N Cornwall DC
Tresmeer, N Cornwall DC
Tressady, Highland CI
Treswell, Bassetlaw DC
Trethewey, Penwith DC
Trethurgy, Restormel BC
Tretire, Herefordshire CI
Treuddyn, Flintshire CC
Trevalga, N Cornwall DC
Trevanson, N Cornwall DC
Trevarren, Restormel BC
Trevarrick, Restormel BC
Trevellas, Carrick DC
Treverbyn, Restormel BC
Treverva, Kerrier DC
Trevethin, Torfaen CBC
Treville, Herefordshire CI
Treviscoe, Restormel BC
Trevone, N Cornwall DC
Trevor, Wrexham CBC
Trewalchmai, Isle of Anglesey CC
Trewarmett, N Cornwall DC
Trewarthenick, Carrick DC
Trewassa, N Cornwall DC
Trewellard, Penwith DC
Trewen, N Cornwall DC
Trewern, Powys CC
Trewidland, Caradon DC
Trewint, N Cornwall DC
Trewithian, Carrick DC
Trewoon, Restormel BC
Treyarnon, N Cornwall DC
Treyford, Chichester DC
Tricketts Cross, E Dorset DC
Trigon, Purbeck DC
Trillick, Omagh DC
Trimdon, Easington DC
Trimdon, Sedgefield BC
Trimingham, N Norfolk DC
Trimley St Martin, Suffolk C'l DC
Trimley St Mary, Suffolk C'l DC
Trimpley, Wyre Forest DC
Trimsaran, Carmarthenshire CC
Tring, Dacorum BC
Trislaig, Highland CI
Trispen, Carrick DC
Tritlington, Castle Morpeth BC
Troedyraur, Ceredigion CC
Troedyrhiw, Merthyr Tydfil CBC
Trofarth, Conwy CBC
Trondra, Shetland Is CI
Troon, Kerrier DC
Troon, S Ayrshire CI
Trongate, Glasgow City
Troqueer Landward,
  Dumfries/Galloway CI
Troston, St Edmundsbury BC
Trottiscliffe, Tonbridge/Malling BC

Trotton, Chichester DC
Troutbeck, Eden DC
Troutbeck, S Lakeland DC
Troutbeck Bridge, S Lakeland DC
Trow Green, Forest of Dean DC
Trowbridge, Cardiff CC
Trowbridge, W Wilts DC
Trowell, Broxtowe BC
Trowse Newton, S Norfolk DC
Trudoxhill, Mendip DC
Trull, Taunton Deane BC
Trumpington, Cambridge City
Trunch, N Norfolk DC
Truro, Carrick DC
Trusham, Teignbridge DC
Trusley, S Derbys DC
Trysull, S Staffs CI
Tubney, Vale of White Horse DC
Tuckhill, Bridgnorth DC
Tuddenham, Breckland CI
Tuddenham, Forest Heath DC
Tuddenham, Suffolk C'l DC
Tuddenham St Martin, Suffolk C'l
  DC
Tudeley, Tunbridge Wells BC
Tudhoe, Sedgefield BC
Tudweiliog, Gwynedd CC
Tugby, Harborough DC
Tugford, S Shropshire DC
Tullibardine, Perth/Kinross CI
Tullibody, Clackmannanshire CI
Tullich Muir, Highland CI
Tulloch, Perth/Kinross CI
Tulloch, Highland CI
Tullybrisland, Limavady BC
Tullynessle, Aberdeenshire CI
Tulse Hill, Lambeth LBC
Tumby, E Lindsey DC
Tummel, Perth/Kinross CI
Tunbridge Wells, Tunbridge Wells
  BC
Tunstall, E Riding of Yks
Tunstall, Lancaster City
Tunstall, Richmondshire DC
Tunstall, Stoke-on-Trent City
Tunstall, Suffolk C'l DC
Tunstall, Swale BC
Tunstead, N Norfolk DC
Tunworth, Basingstoke/Deane BC
Tupholme, E Lindsey DC
Tupton, N E Derbys DC
Tur Langton, Harborough DC
Turgis Green, Basingstoke/Deane
  BC
Turkdean, Cotswold DC
Turnastone, Herefordshire CI
Turnberry, S Ayrshire CI
Turnditch, Amber Valley BC
Turners Hill, Mid Sussex DC
Turnerspuddle, Purbeck DC

Turnworth, N Dorset DC
Turriff, Aberdeenshire Cl
Tursdale, Durham City
Turton Bottom, Blackburn with Darwen BC
Turvey, Bedford BC
Turville, Wycombe DC
Turweston, Aylesbury Vale DC
Tushingham, Chester City
Tusmore, Cherwell DC
Tutbury, E Staffs BC
Tutnall, Bromsgrove DC
Tuttington, Broadland DC
Tuxford, Bassetlaw DC
Twechar, E Dunbartonshire Cl
Tweedbank, Scottish Borders Cl
Tweedmouth, Berwick-u-Tweed BC
Twelveheads, Carrick DC
Twemlow, Congleton BC
Twenty, S Kesteven DC
Twerton, Bath/N E Somerset Cl
Twickenham, Richmond upon Thames LBC
Twigworth, Tewkesbury BC
Twin Rivers, E Riding of Yks
Twineham, Mid Sussex DC
Twinhoe, Bath/N E Somerset Cl
Twinstead, Braintree DC
Twiston, Ribble Valley BC
Twitchen, N Devon DC
Twitchen, S Shropshire DC
Twitham, Dover DC
Two Dales, Derbys Dales DC
Two Gates, Tamworth BC
Two Locks, Torfaen CBC
Two Mile Ash, Milton Keynes Cl
Twycross, Hinckley/Bosworth BC
Twyford, Aylesbury Vale DC
Twyford, Breckland Cl
Twyford, Melton BC
Twyford, S Derbys DC
Twyford, Winchester City
Twyford, Wokingham DC
Twynholm, Dumfries/Galloway Cl
Twyning, Tewkesbury BC
Twywell, E Northants Cl
Ty nant, Conwy CBC
Tyberton, Herefordshire Cl
Tydd Gote, S Holland DC
Tydd St Giles, Fenland DC
Tydd St Mary, S Holland DC
Tyldesley, Wigan MBC
Tyler Hill, Canterbury City
Tylers Green, Chiltern DC
Tylers Green, Epping Forest DC
Tyndrum, Stirling Cl
Tyneham, Purbeck DC
Tynemouth, N Tyneside Cl
Tynewater, Midlothian Cl

Tyninghame, E Lothian Cl
Tynron, Dumfries/Galloway Cl
Tyrie, Aberdeenshire Cl
Tyringham, Milton Keynes Cl
Tysoe, Stratford/Avon DC
Tythby, Rushcliffe BC
Tytherington, Mendip DC
Tytherington, S Glos Cl
Tytherleigh, E Devon DC
Tywardreath and Par, Restormel BC
Tywyn, Gwynedd CC
Tywyn, Deganwy, Conwy CBC

Ubbeston, Suffolk C'l DC
Ubley, Bath/N E Somerset Cl
Uckarby, Richmondshire DC
Uckfield, Wealden DC
Uckington, Tewkesbury BC
Uddingston, S Lanarkshire Cl
Udimore, Rother DC
Udny, Aberdeenshire Cl
Udny Green, Aberdeenshire Cl
Udny Station, Aberdeenshire Cl
Uffculme, Mid Devon DC
Uffington, Shrewsbury/Atcham Cl
Uffington, S Kesteven DC
Uffington, Vale of White Horse DC
Ufford, Peterborough City
Ufford, Suffolk C'l DC
Ufton, Stratford/Avon DC
Ufton Nervet, W Berks DC
Ugborough, S Hams DC
Uggeshall, Waveney DC
Ugglebarnby, Scarborough BC
Ugley, Uttlesford DC
Ugthorpe, Scarborough BC
Uig, Comhairle Nan Eilean Siar
Uig, Highland Cl
Uigshader, Highland Cl
Ulbster, Highland Cl
Ulceby, E Lindsey DC
Ulceby, N Lincs Cl
Ulcombe, Maidstone BC
Uldale, Allerdale BC
Uley, Stroud DC
Ulgham, Castle Morpeth BC
Ullapool, Highland Cl
Ullenhall, Stratford/Avon DC
Ullenwood, Cotswold DC
Ulleskelf, Selby DC
Ullesthorpe, Harborough DC
Ulley, Rotherham MBC
Ullingswick, Herefordshire Cl
Ullinish, Highland Cl
Ullock, Allerdale BC
Ulnes Walton, Chorley BC
Ulpha, Copeland BC
Ulpha, S Lakeland DC

Ulrome, E Riding of Yks
Ulting, Maldon DC
Ulverscroft, Charnwood DC
Ulverston, S Lakeland DC
Umberslade, Stratford/Avon DC
Unapool, Highland Cl
Uncheril, Highland Cl
Underbarrow, S Lakeland DC
Underhill, Weymouth/Portland BC
Underskiddaw, Allerdale BC
Undley, Forest Heath DC
Undy, Monmouthshire CC
Unst, Shetland Is Cl
Unstone, N E Derbys DC
Unsworth, Bury MBC
Unthank, Eden DC
Unverinate, Highland Cl
Up Cerne, W Dorset DC
Up Hatherly, Cheltenham BC
Up Holland, W Lancs DC
Up Marden, Chichester DC
Up Nately, Basingstoke/Deane BC
Up Somborne, Test Valley BC
Up Sydling, W Dorset DC
Upavon, Kennet DC
Upchurch, Swale DC
Uphall, W Lothian Cl
Uphall Station, W Lothian Cl
Upham, Winchester City
Uphill, N Somerset DC
Uplaw Moor, E Renfrewshire Cl
Upleadon, Forest of Dean DC
Upleatham, Redcar/Cleveland BC
Uplees, Swale BC
Uploders, W Dorset DC
Uplowman, Mid Devon DC
Uplyme, E Devon DC
Upminster, Havering LBC
Upottery, E Devon DC
Uppat, Highland Cl
Upper Affcot, S Shropshire DC
Upper Ardchronie, Highland Cl
Upper Arley, Wyre Forest DC
Upper Aston, Bridgnorth DC
Upper Astrop, S Northants Cl
Upper Badcall, Highland Cl
Upper Basildon, W Berks DC
Upper Beeding, Horsham DC
Upper Benefield, E Northants Cl
Upper Bentley, Bromsgrove DC
Upper Bighouse, Highland Cl
Upper Boddington, S Northants Cl
Upper Brailes, Stratford/Avon DC
Upper Breakish, Highland Cl
Upper Broughton, Rushcliffe BC
Upper Bucklebury, W Berks DC
Upper Caldecote, Mid Beds DC

Upper Chelmscote, Stratford/Avon DC
Upper Chute, Kennet DC
Upper Clatford, Test Valley BC
Upper Clopton, Stratford/Avon DC
Upper Cwmbran, Torfaen CBC
Upper Dean, Bedford BC
Upper Denby, Barnsley MBC
Upper Deverills, W Wilts DC
Upper Diabaig, Highland CI
Upper Dicker, Wealden DC
Upper Drummond, Highland CI
Upper Dunsforth, Harrogate BC
Upper Elkstone, Staffs Moorlands DC
Upper End, High Peak BC
Upper Farmcote, Bridgnorth DC
Upper Farringdon, E Hants DC
Upper Framilode, Stroud DC
Upper Froyle, E Hants DC
Upper Gills, Highland CI
Upper Gravenhurst, Mid Beds DC
Upper Green, W Berks DC
Upper Hackney, Derbys Dales DC
Upper Halistra, Highland CI
Upper Hambleton, Rutland CC
Upper Hardres, Canterbury City
Upper Hartfield, Wealden DC
Upper Heath, S Shropshire DC
Upper Helmsley, Ryedale DC
Upper Heyford, Cherwell DC
Upper Heyford, S Northants CI
Upper Hill, Herefordshire CI
Upper Hopton, Kirklees MC
Upper Hulme, Staffs Moorlands DC
Upper Killay, Swansea C&C
Upper Lambourn, W Berks DC
Upper Largo, Fife CI
Upper Ludstone, Bridgnorth DC
Upper Lybster, Highland CI
Upper Milcote, Stratford/Avon DC
Upper Milovaig, Highland CI
Upper Nidderdale, Harrogate BC
Upper North Dean, Wycombe DC
Upper Ollach, Highland CI
Upper Poppleton, City of York CI
Upper Quinton, Stratford/Avon DC
Upper Rawcliffe, Wyre BC
Upper Sapey, Herefordshire CI
Upper Sheringham, N Norfolk DC
Upper Shuckburgh, Stratford/Avon DC
Upper Slaughter, Cotswold DC
Upper Stondon, Mid Beds DC
Upper Stowe, Daventry DC
Upper Street, New Forest DC

Upper Sundon, S Beds DC
Upper Swainswick, Bath/N E Somerset CI
Upper Swell, Cotswold DC
Upper Tean, Staffs Moorlands DC
Upper Teviotdale, Scottish Borders CI
Upper Tullich, Highland CI
Upper Tweed, Scottish Borders CI
Upper Tysoe, Stratford/Avon DC
Upper Upham, Kennet DC
Upper Wawensmoor, Stratford/Avon DC
Upper Weald, Milton Keynes CI
Upper Wield, E Hants DC
Upper Winchendon, Aylesbury Vale DC
Upper Woodford, Salisbury DC
Upperthong, Kirklees MC
Upperthorpe, Sheffield City
Upperton, Chichester DC
Uppertown, Highland CI
Uppingham, Rutland CC
Uppington, Shrewsbury/Atcham CI
Upsall, Hambleton DC
Upshire, Epping Forest DC
Upstreet, Canterbury City
Upthorpe, St Edmundsbury BC
Upton, Aylesbury Vale DC
Upton, Broadland DC
Upton, Hinckley/Bosworth BC
Upton, Huntingdonshire DC
Upton, Newark/Sherwood DC
Upton, Northampton BC
Upton, Peterborough City
Upton, Purbeck DC
Upton, Slough BC
Upton, Stratford/Avon DC
Upton, Test Valley BC
Upton, Vale of White Horse DC
Upton, Wakefield MDC
Upton, W Dorset DC
Upton, W Lindsey DC
Upton, W Oxon DC
Upton, W Somerset DC
Upton, Wirral MBC
Upton Bishop, Herefordshire CI
Upton by Chester, Chester City
Upton Cressett, Bridgnorth DC
Upton Grey, Basingstoke/Deane BC
Upton Lovell, W Wilts DC
Upton Magna, Shrewsbury/Atcham CI
Upton Noble, Mendip DC
Upton Pyne, E Devon DC
Upton St Leonards, Stroud DC
Upton Scudamore, W Wilts DC

Upton Snodsbury, Wychavon DC
Upton upon Severn, Malvern Hills DC
Upton Warren, Wychavon DC
Upton Wood, Dover DC
Upwaltham, Chichester DC
Upware, E Cambs DC
Upwell, King's Lynn/W Norfolk BC
Upwick Green, E Herts DC
Upwood, Huntingdonshire DC
Urchfont, Kennet DC
Urlay Nook, Stockton-on-Tees BC
Urmston, Trafford MBC
Urpeth, Chester-le-Street DC
Urr, Dumfries/Galloway CI
Urra, Hambleton DC
Urswick, S Lakeland DC
Ushaw Moor, Durham City
Usk, Monmouthshire CC
Usselby, W Lindsey DC
Utkinton, Vale Royal BC
Utley, Bradford MDC
Utterby, E Lindsey DC
Uttoxeter, E Staffs BC
Uxbridge, E Staffs BC
Uxbridge, Hillingdon LBC
Uzmaston, Pembrokeshire CC

Vale of Allen, E Dorset DC
Vale of Grwyney, Powys CC
Vale of Leven, W Dunbartonshire CI
Valley, Isle of Anglesey CC
Valtos, Highland CI
Van, Caerphilly CBC
Vange, Basildon DC
Varteg, Torfaen CBC
Vatten, Highland CI
Venn Ottery, E Devon DC
Vennington, Shrewsbury/Atcham CI
Ventnor, Isle of Wight CI
Vernham Street, Test Valley BC
Vernolds Common, S Shropshire DC
Verwood, E Dorset DC
Veryan, Carrick DC
Vickerstown, Barrow-in-Furness BC
Victoria, E Staffs BC
Victoria, Stockton-on-Tees BC
Viewpark, N Lanarkshire CI
Vinehall Street, Rother DC
Virginia Water, Runnymede BC
Virginstowe, Torridge DC
Virley, Colchester BC
Vobster, Mendip DC
Vowchurch, Herefordshire CI

Waberthwaite, Copeland BC

Wackerfield, Teesdale DC
Wacton, Herefordshire CI
Wacton, S Norfolk DC
Wadborough, Wychavon DC
Waddesdon, Aylesbury Vale DC
Waddingham, W Lindsey DC
Waddington, N Kesteven DC
Waddington, Ribble Valley BC
Waddingworth, E Lindsey DC
Waddon Hill, Stratford/Avon DC
Wadebridge, N Cornwall DC
Wadenhoe, E Northants CI
Wadesmill, E Herts DC
Wadhurst, Wealden DC
Wadsley, Sheffield City
Wadsley Bridge, Sheffield City
Wadsworth, Calderdale MBC
Wadworth, Doncaster MBC
Waen, Denbighshire CC
Wainfelin, Torfaen CBC
Wainfleet All Saints, E Lindsey DC
Wainfleet St Mary, E Lindsey DC
Wainhouse Corner, N Cornwall DC
Wainstalls, Calderdale MBC
Waitby, Eden DC
Waithe, E Lindsey DC
Wakefield, Wakefield MDC
Wakerley, E Northants CI
Wakes Colne, Colchester BC
Walberswick, Suffolk C'l DC
Walberton, Arun DC
Walburn, Richmondshire DC
Walcot, N Kesteven DC
Walcot, S Shropshire DC
Walcot, Swindon BC
Walcote, Harborough DC
Walcote, Stratford/Avon DC
Walcott, N Kesteven DC
Walcott, N Norfolk DC
Walden, Richmondshire DC
Walden Stubbs, Selby DC
Walderton, Chichester DC
Walditch, W Dorset DC
Waldridge, Chester-le-Street DC
Waldringfield, Suffolk C'l DC
Waldron, Wealden DC
Wales, Rotherham MBC
Walesby, Newark/Sherwood DC
Walesby, W Lindsey DC
Walford, Herefordshire CI
Walford, N Shropshire DC
Walgherton, Crewe/Nantwich BC
Walgrave, Daventry DC
Walkden, Salford City
Walker, Newcastle City
Walkerburn, Scottish Borders CI
Walkergate, Newcastle City
Walkeringham, Bassetlaw DC

Walkerith, W Lindsey DC
Walkern, E Herts DC
Walkhampton, W Devon BC
Walkingham Hill, Harrogate BC
Walkington, E Riding of Yks
Walkley, Sheffield City
Walkley Bank, Sheffield City
Wall, Lichfield DC
Wall, Tynedale DC
Wall under Heywood, S Shropshire DC
Wallacestone, Falkirk CI
Wallacewell, Glasgow City
Wallasey, Wirral MBC
Wallerthwaite, Harrogate BC
Wallingford, S Oxon DC
Wallington, Castle Morpeth BC
Wallington, N Herts DC
Wallington, Sutton LBC
Wallingwells, Bassetlaw DC
Wallis Wood, Mole Valley DC
Walls, Orkney Is CI
Walls, Shetland Is CI
Wallsend, N Tyneside CI
Wallyford, E Lothian CI
Walmer, Dover DC
Walmer Bridge, S Ribble BC
Walmersley, Bury MBC
Walmsgate, E Lindsey DC
Walnut Tree, Milton Keynes CI
Walpole, King's Lynn/W Norfolk BC
Walpole, Suffolk C'l DC
Walpole Cross Keys, King's Lynn/W Norfolk BC
Walpole Highway, King's Lynn/W Norfolk BC
Walpole St Andrew, King's Lynn/W Norfolk BC
Walpole St Peter, King's Lynn/W Norfolk BC
Walsall, Walsall MBC
Walsall Wood, Walsall MBC
Walsden, Calderdale MBC
Walsgrave, Coventry City MDC
Walsham le Willows, Mid Suffolk DC
Walshaw, Bury MBC
Walshford, Harrogate BC
Walsingham, N Norfolk DC
Walsoken, King's Lynn/W Norfolk BC
Walters Ash, Wycombe DC
Walterstone, Herefordshire CI
Waltham, Canterbury City
Waltham, N E Lincs CI
Waltham Abbey, Epping Forest DC
Waltham Chase, Winchester City
Waltham Cross, Broxbourne BC

Waltham Forest, Waltham Forest LBC
Waltham on the Wolds, Melton BC
Waltham St Lawrence, Windsor/Maidenhead RB
Walthamstow, Waltham Forest LBC
Walton, Carlisle City
Walton, Chesterfield BC
Walton, Harborough DC
Walton, Leeds City
Walton, Mendip DC
Walton, Milton Keynes CI
Walton, N E Derbys DC
Walton, Stratford/Avon DC
Walton, Stratford/Avon DC
Walton, Suffolk C'l DC
Walton, Telford/Wrekin BC
Walton, Tendring DC
Walton, Wakefield MDC
Walton, Warrington BC
Walton Cardiff, Tewkesbury BC
Walton in Gordano, N Somerset DC
Walton le Dale, S Ribble BC
Walton on Thames, Elmbridge BC
Walton on the Hill, Stafford BC
Walton on the Naze, Tendring DC
Walton on the Wolds, Charnwood DC
Walton on Trent, S Derbys DC
Walworth, Darlington BC
Walworth, Southwark LBC
Walwyns Castle, Pembrokeshire CC
Wambrook, S Somerset DC
Wamphray, Dumfries/Galloway CI
Wanborough, Guildford BC
Wanborough, Swindon BC
Wandsworth, Wandsworth LBC
Wangford, Forest Heath DC
Wangford, Waveney DC
Wanings Green, Stratford/Avon DC
Wanlip, Charnwood DC
Wanlockhead Village, Dumfries/Galloway CI
Wansford, E Riding of Yks
Wansford, Peterborough City
Wanstrow, Mendip DC
Wantage, Vale of White Horse DC
Wantisden, Suffolk C'l DC
Wappenbury, Warwick DC
Wappenham, S Northants CI
Wapping, Tower Hamlets LBC
Warbleton, Wealden DC
Warborough, S Oxon DC

Warboys, Huntingdonshire DC
Warbstow, N Cornwall DC
Warburton, Trafford MBC
Warcop, Eden DC
Ward Green, Mid Suffolk DC
Warden, Swale BC
Warden, Tynedale DC
Wardington, Cherwell DC
Wardle, Crewe/Nantwich BC
Wardle, Rochdale MBC
Wardley, Chichester DC
Wardley, Rutland CC
Wardley Green, Chichester DC
Wardlow, Derbys Dales DC
Wardy Hill, E Cambs DC
Ware, E Herts DC
Wareham, Purbeck DC
Wareham St Martin, Purbeck DC
Warehorne, Ashford BC
Waren Mill, Berwick-u-Tweed BC
Warenford, Berwick-u-Tweed BC
Wareside, E Herts DC
Waresley, Huntingdonshire DC
Warfield, Bracknell Forest BC
Wargrave, Wokingham DC
Warham, N Norfolk DC
Waringsford, Banbridge DC
Wark, Berwick-u-Tweed BC
Wark, Tynedale DC
Warkleigh, N Devon DC
Warkton, Kettering BC
Warkworth, Alnwick DC
Warkworth, S Northants Cl
Warlaby, Hambleton DC
Warleggan, Caradon DC
Warley, Brentwood BC
Warley, Sandwell MBC
Warlingham, Tandridge DC
Warmfield, Wakefield MDC
Warmingham, Crewe/Nantwich
    BC
Warmington, E Northants Cl
Warmington, Stratford/Avon DC
Warminster, W Wilts DC
Warmley, S Glos Cl
Warmsworth, Doncaster MBC
Warmwell, W Dorset DC
Warndon, Worcester City
Warnford, Winchester City
Warnham, Horsham DC
Warningcamp, Arun DC
Warninglid, Mid Sussex DC
Warren, Macclesfield BC
Warren Row,
    Windsor/Maidenhead RB
Warren Street, Maidstone BC
Warrenpoint, Newry/Mourne DC
Warrenton, Berwick-u-Tweed BC
Warrington, Milton Keynes Cl
Warrington, Warrington BC

Warsash, Fareham BC
Warsill, Harrogate BC
Warslow, Staffs Moorlands DC
Warsop, Mansfield DC
Warter, E Riding of Yks
Warthill, Ryedale DC
Wartling, Wealden DC
Wartnaby, Melton BC
Warton, Alnwick DC
Warton, Fylde BC
Warton, Lancaster City
Warwick, Warwick DC
Warwick Bridge, Carlisle City
Warwick on Eden, Carlisle City
Wasdale, Copeland BC
Washaway, N Cornwall DC
Washbrook, Babergh DC
Washburn, Harrogate BC
Washfield, Mid Devon DC
Washford, W Somerset DC
Washford Pyne, Mid Devon DC
Washing Bay, Dungannon & S
    Tyrone BC
Washingborough, N Kesteven DC
Washingley, Huntingdonshire DC
Washington, Horsham DC
Washington, Sunderland City
Washwood Heath, Birmingham
    City
Wasing, W Berks DC
Wasperton, Warwick DC
Wass, Ryedale DC
Watchet, W Somerset DC
Watchfield, Vale of White Horse
    DC
Watchgate, S Lakeland DC
Watendlath, Allerdale BC
Water Eaton, Cherwell DC
Water End, Dacorum BC
Water End, Welwyn Hatfield DC
Water Newton, Huntingdonshire
    DC
Water Orton, N Warks BC
Water Stratford, Aylesbury Vale
    DC
Water Yeat, S Lakeland DC
Waterbeach, S Cambs DC
Waterbeck, Dumfries/Galloway Cl
Waterfoot, E Renfrewshire Cl
Waterfoot, Moyle DC
Waterfoot, Rossendale BC
Waterford, E Herts DC
Watergall, Stratford/Avon DC
Waterhead, Carlisle City
Waterhead, S Lakeland DC
Waterhouses, Durham City
Waterhouses, Staffs Moorlands
    DC
Wateringbury, Tonbridge/Malling
    BC

Waterlip, Mendip DC
Waterloo, Poole BC
Waterloo, Sefton MBC
Waterloo, Highland Cl
Waterlooville, Havant BC
Watermead, Aylesbury Vale DC
Waterperry, S Oxon DC
Waters Upton, Telford/Wrekin BC
Watersfield, Horsham DC
Waterside, E Ayrshire Cl
Waterside, E Dunbartonshire Cl
Waterside, E Staffs BC
Waterstein, Highland Cl
Waterstock, S Oxon DC
Waterthorpe, Sheffield City
Watford, Daventry DC
Watford, Watford BC
Wath, Harrogate BC
Wath upon Dearne, Rotherham
    MBC
Watlington, King's Lynn/W Norfolk
    BC
Watlington, S Oxon DC
Watten, Highland Cl
Wattisfield, Mid Suffolk DC
Wattisham, Babergh DC
Watton, Breckland Cl
Watton, E Riding of Yks
Watton at Stone, E Herts DC
Waun Afon, Torfaen CBC
Waunfawr, Gwynedd CC
Wavendon, Milton Keynes Cl
Wavendon Gate, Milton Keynes
    Cl
Waverley, Glasgow City
Waverton, Allerdale BC
Waverton, Chester City
Wavertree, Liverpool City
Wawne, E Riding of Yks
Waxham, N Norfolk DC
Waxholme, E Riding of Yks
Wayford, S Somerset DC
Wealdstone, Harrow LBC
Weare, Sedgemoor DC
Weare Giffard, Torridge DC
Wearhead, Wear Valley DC
Weasdale, Eden DC
Weasenham All Saints, Breckland
    Cl
Weasenham St Peter, Breckland
    Cl
Weaste, Salford City
Weaverham, Vale Royal BC
Weaverthorpe, Ryedale DC
Webheath, Bromsgrove DC
Weddicar, Copeland BC
Weddington, Nuneaton/Bedworth
    BC
Wedmore, Sedgemoor DC
Wednesbury, Sandwell MBC

Wednesfield, Walsall MBC
Weecar, Newark/Sherwood DC
Weedon, Aylesbury Vale DC
Weedon Bec, Daventry DC
Weedon Lois, S Northants Cl
Weeford, Lichfield DC
Week St Mary, N Cornwall DC
Weekley, Kettering BC
Weeley, Tendring DC
Weeley Heath, Tendring DC
Weem, Perth/Kinross Cl
Weeping Cross, Stafford BC
Weethley, Stratford/Avon DC
Weethley Bank, Stratford/Avon
 DC
Weethley Gate, Stratford/Avon
 DC
Weeting, Breckland Cl
Weeton, E Riding of Yks
Weeton, Fylde BC
Weeton, Harrogate BC
Weisdale, Shetland Is Cl
Welbeck, Bassetlaw DC
Welborne, S Norfolk DC
Welbourn, N Kesteven DC
Welburn (Kirkbymoorside),
 Ryedale DC
Welburn (Malton), Ryedale DC
Welbury, Hambleton DC
Welby, S Kesteven DC
Welcombe, Torridge DC
Weldon, Corby BC
Welford, Daventry DC
Welford, W Berks DC
Welford on Avon, Stratford/Avon
 DC
Welford Pastures, Stratford/Avon
 DC
Welham, Harborough DC
Welham Green, Welwyn Hatfield
 DC
Well, E Lindsey DC
Well, Hambleton DC
Well, Hart DC
Welland, Malvern Hills DC
Wellbank, Angus Cl
Wellesbourne, Stratford/Avon DC
Wellesbourne Hastings,
 Stratford/Avon DC
Wellesbourne Mountford,
 Stratford/Avon DC
Wellhouse, Glasgow City
Welling, Bexley LBC
Wellingborough, Wellingborough
 BC
Wellingham, Breckland Cl
Wellingore, N Kesteven DC
Wellington, Herefordshire Cl
Wellington, Taunton Deane BC
Wellington, Telford/Wrekin BC

Wellington Heath, Herefordshire
 Cl
Wellington Without, Taunton
 Deane BC
Wellow, Bath/N E Somerset Cl
Wellow, Isle of Wight Cl
Wellow, Newark/Sherwood DC
Wellow, Test Valley BC
Wellpond Green, E Herts DC
Wells, Mendip DC
Wells next the Sea, N Norfolk DC
Welney, King's Lynn/W Norfolk
 BC
Welsh Bicknor, Herefordshire Cl
Welsh End, N Shropshire DC
Welsh Newton, Herefordshire Cl
Welsh St Donats, Vale of
 Glamorgan Cl
Welshampton, N Shropshire DC
Welshpool, Powys CC
Welton, Allerdale BC
Welton, Daventry DC
Welton, E Riding of Yks
Welton, W Lindsey DC
Welton le Marsh, E Lindsey DC
Welton le Wold, E Lindsey DC
Welwick, E Riding of Yks
Welwyn, Welwyn Hatfield DC
Welwyn Garden City, Welwyn
 Hatfield DC
Wem, N Shropshire DC
Wem Rural, N Shropshire DC
Wembdon, Sedgemoor DC
Wembley, Brent LBC
Wembley Central, Brent LBC
Wembury, S Hams DC
Wembworthy, Mid Devon DC
Wemyss Bay, Inverclyde Cl
Wenden Lofts, Uttlesford DC
Wendens Ambo, Uttlesford DC
Wendlebury, Cherwell DC
Wendling, Breckland Cl
Wendover, Aylesbury Vale DC
Wendron, Kerrier DC
Wendy, S Cambs DC
Wenham Magna, Babergh DC
Wenham Parva, Babergh DC
Wenhaston, Suffolk C'l DC
Wenlli, Conwy CBC
Wennington, Lancaster City
Wensley, Derbys Dales DC
Wensley, Richmondshire DC
Wentbridge, Wakefield MDC
Wentloog, Newport City Cl
Wentnor, S Shropshire DC
Wentworth, E Cambs DC
Wentworth, Rotherham MBC
Wenvoe, Vale of Glamorgan Cl
Weobley, Herefordshire Cl
Weoley, Birmingham City

Wereham, King's Lynn/W Norfolk
 BC
Wergs, S Staffs Cl
Werrington, N Cornwall DC
Werrington, Staffs Moorlands DC
Wervin, Chester City
Wesham, Fylde BC
Wessington, N E Derbys DC
West Acre, King's Lynn/W Norfolk
 BC
West Allen, Tynedale DC
West Allerdean, Berwick-u-Tweed
 BC
West Alvington, S Hams DC
West Anstey, N Devon DC
West Ashby, E Lindsey DC
West Ashling, Chichester DC
West Ashton, W Wilts DC
West Auckland, Wear Valley DC
West Ayton, Scarborough BC
West Bagborough, Taunton
 Deane BC
West Barkwith, E Lindsey DC
West Beckham, N Norfolk DC
West Bergholt, Colchester BC
West Bilney, King's Lynn/W
 Norfolk BC
West Bolton, Richmondshire DC
West Bradford, Ribble Valley BC
West Bradley, Mendip DC
West Bretton, Wakefield MDC
West Bridgford, Rushcliffe BC
West Bromwich, Sandwell MBC
West Buckland, N Devon DC
West Buckland, Taunton Deane
 BC
West Burton, Bassetlaw DC
West Burton, Richmondshire DC
West Butterwick, N E Lincs Cl
West Byfleet, Woking BC
West Caister, Gt Yarmouth BC
West Calder, W Lothian Cl
West Camel, S Somerset DC
West Carse, Perth/Kinross Cl
West Challow, Vale of White
 Horse DC
West Chelborough, W Dorset DC
West Chevington, Castle Morpeth
 BC
West Chiltington, Horsham DC
West Chinnock, S Somerset DC
West Clandon, Guildford BC
West Close Booth, Pendle BC
West Clyne, Highland Cl
West Coker, S Somerset DC
West Compton, Mendip DC
West Compton, W Dorset DC
West Cornforth, Sedgefield BC
West Crewkerne, S Somerset DC
West Curry, N Cornwall DC

West Curthwaite, Allerdale BC
West Dean, Chichester DC
West Dean, Salisbury DC
West Dean, Test Valley BC
West Deeping, S Kesteven DC
West Derby, Liverpool City
West Dereham, King's Lynn/W Norfolk BC
West Ditchburn, Alnwick DC
West Don, Aberdeen City
West Down, N Devon DC
West Drayton, Bassetlaw DC
West Drayton, Hillingdon LBC
West Dunnet, Highland CI
West End, Bedford BC
West End, Dundee City
West End, Eastleigh BC
West End, Harrogate BC
West End, N Somerset DC
West End, Surrey Heath BC
West End Green, Basingstoke/Deane BC
West Farleigh, Maidstone BC
West Felton, Oswestry BC
West Fen, E Lindsey DC
West Firle, Lewes DC
West Firsby, W Lindsey DC
West Fleetham, Berwick-u-Tweed BC
West Ginge, Vale of White Horse DC
West Grafton, Kennet DC
West Green, Hart DC
West Grinstead, Horsham DC
West Haddlesey, Selby DC
West Haddon, Daventry DC
West Hagbourne, S Oxon DC
West Hallam, Erewash BC
West Halton, N Lincs CI
West Halton, N Lincs CI
West Ham, Newham LBC
West Hanney, Vale of White Horse DC
West Hanningfield, Chelmsford BC
West Hardwick, Wakefield MDC
West Harlsey, Hambleton DC
West Harptree, Bath/N E Somerset CI
West Harrow, Harrow LBC
West Hatch, Taunton Deane BC
West Hauxwell, Richmondshire DC
West Heath, Rushmoor BC
West Helmsdale, Highland CI
West Hendred, Vale of White Horse DC
West Hesterton, Ryedale DC
West Hill, E Devon DC
West Hoathly, Mid Sussex DC

West Holme, Purbeck DC
West Horndon, Brentwood BC
West Horrington, Mendip DC
West Horsley, Guildford BC
West Hougham, Dover DC
West Huntspill, Sedgemoor DC
West Hyde, Three Rivers DC
West Ilsley, W Berks DC
West Itchenor, Chichester DC
West Keal, E Lindsey DC
West Kilbride, N Ayrshire CI
West Kingsdown, Sevenoaks DC
West Kintyre, Argyll/Bute CI
West Kirby, Wirral MBC
West Knighton, W Dorset DC
West Knoyle, Salisbury DC
West Kyo, Derwentside DC
West Langdon, Dover DC
West Langton, Harborough DC
West Langwell, Highland CI
West Lavington, Chichester DC
West Lavington, Kennet DC
West Layton, Richmondshire DC
West Leake, Rushcliffe BC
West Lexham, Breckland CI
West Lilling, Ryedale DC
West Linton, Scottish Borders CI
West Loch Fyne, Argyll/Bute CI
West Lulworth, Purbeck DC
West Lutton, Ryedale DC
West Lynn, King's Lynn/W Norfolk BC
West Malling, Tonbridge/Malling BC
West Malvern, Malvern Hills DC
West Marden, Chichester DC
West Markham, Bassetlaw DC
West Marton, Craven DC
West Meon, Winchester City
West Mersea, Colchester BC
West Molesey, Elmbridge BC
West Monkton, Taunton Deane BC
West Moors, E Dorset DC
West Newbiggin, Darlington BC
West Newton, E Riding of Yks
West Newton, King's Lynn/W Norfolk BC
West Ogwell, Teignbridge DC
West Orchard, N Dorset DC
West Overton, Kennet DC
West Parley, E Dorset DC
West Peckham, Tonbridge/Malling BC
West Pelton, Chester-le-Street DC
West Pennard, Mendip DC
West Pontnewydd, Torfaen CBC
West Portholland (part), Carrick DC

West Portholland (part), Restormel BC
West Putford, Torridge DC
West Quantock, W Somerset DC
West Quantoxhead, W Somerset DC
West Rainton, Durham City
West Rasen, W Lindsey DC
West Ravendale, N E Lincs CI
West Raynham, N Norfolk DC
West Rounton, Hambleton DC
West Row, Forest Heath DC
West Rudham, King's Lynn/W Norfolk BC
West Runton, N Norfolk DC
West Scrafton, Richmondshire DC
West Stafford, W Dorset DC
West Stockwith, Bassetlaw DC
West Stoke, Chichester DC
West Stonesdale, Richmondshire DC
West Stour, N Dorset DC
West Stourmouth, Dover DC
West Stow, St Edmundsbury BC
West Stowell, Kennet DC
West Strathan, Highland CI
West Street, Dover DC
West Street, Maidstone BC
West Tanfield, Hambleton DC
West Thorney, Chichester DC
West Thurrock, Thurrock BC
West Tisbury, Salisbury DC
West Tisted, E Hants DC
West Torrington, E Lindsey DC
West Town, N Somerset DC
West Twickenham, Richmond upon Thames LBC
West Tytherley, Test Valley BC
West Walton, King's Lynn/W Norfolk BC
West Wellow, Test Valley BC
West Wemyss, Fife CI
West Wick, N Somerset DC
West Wickham, Bromley LBC
West Wickham, S Cambs DC
West Winch, King's Lynn/W Norfolk BC
West Wittering, Chichester DC
West Witton, Richmondshire DC
West Woodburn, Tynedale DC
West Woodhay, W Berks DC
West Woodlands, Mendip DC
West Worldham, E Hants DC
West Wratting, S Cambs DC
West Wycombe, Wycombe DC
Westbarns, E Lothian CI
Westbere, Canterbury City
Westborough, S Kesteven DC
Westbourne, Bournemouth BC

Westbourne, Chichester DC
Westbourne, Havant BC
Westbury, Aylesbury Vale DC
Westbury, Shrewsbury/Atcham Cl
Westbury, W Wilts DC
Westbury on Severn, Forest of Dean DC
Westbury sub Mendip, Mendip DC
Westby, Fylde BC
Westcliff on Sea, Southend-on-Sea BC
Westcombe, Mendip DC
Westcot Barton, W Oxon DC
Westcote, Cotswold DC
Westcott, Aylesbury Vale DC
Westcott, Mole Valley DC
Westdean, Wealden DC
Wester Aberchalder, Highland Cl
Wester Arboll, Highland Cl
Wester Gruinards, Highland Cl
Westerdale, Scarborough BC
Westerdale, Highland Cl
Westerfield, Suffolk C'l DC
Westerham, Sevenoaks DC
Westerhope, Newcastle City
Westerkirk, Dumfries/Galloway Cl
Westerleigh, S Glos Cl
Westerton, Chichester DC
Westfield, Breckland Cl
Westfield, Rother DC
Westfield, Sheffield City
Westfield, Highland Cl
Westfield, W Lothian Cl
Westfield, Woking BC
Westford, Highland Cl
Westgate, N Norfolk DC
Westgate, Wear Valley DC
Westgate on Sea, Thanet DC
Westhall, Waveney DC
Westham, Wealden DC
Westham East, Weymouth/Portland BC
Westham North, Weymouth/Portland BC
Westham West, Weymouth/Portland BC
Westhampnett, Chichester DC
Westhay, Mendip DC
Westhead, W Lancs DC
Westhide, Herefordshire Cl
Westhill, Aberdeenshire Cl
Westhill, Highland Cl
Westhope, S Shropshire DC
Westhorpe, Mid Suffolk DC
Westhorpe, S Holland DC
Westhoughton, Bolton MBC
Westhouse, Craven DC
Westhumble, Mole Valley DC
Westlea, Swindon BC

Westleigh, Mid Devon DC
Westleigh, N Devon DC
Westleton, Suffolk C'l DC
Westley, St Edmundsbury BC
Westley Waterless, E Cambs DC
Westlinton, Carlisle City
Westmarsh, Dover DC
Westmeston, Lewes DC
Westmill, E Herts DC
Westminster, Westminster City
Westnewton, Allerdale BC
Weston, Bath/N E Somerset Cl
Weston, Bridgnorth DC
Weston, Crewe/Nantwich BC
Weston, E Hants DC
Weston, Harrogate BC
Weston, Newark/Sherwood DC
Weston, N Herts DC
Weston, N Shropshire DC
Weston, S Holland DC
Weston, S Northants Cl
Weston, Stafford BC
Weston, Waveney DC
Weston, W Berks DC
Weston, Weymouth/Portland BC
Weston Beggard, Herefordshire Cl
Weston by Welland, Kettering BC
Weston Colville, S Cambs DC
Weston Corbett, Basingstoke/Deane BC
Weston Green, Elmbridge BC
Weston Green, S Cambs DC
Weston Hills, S Holland DC
Weston Jones, Stafford BC
Weston Longville, Broadland DC
Weston Lullingfields, N Shropshire DC
Weston Nr Honiton, E Devon DC
Weston Nr Sidmouth, E Devon DC
Weston on Avon, Stratford/Avon DC
Weston on the Green, Cherwell DC
Weston on Trent, S Derbys DC
Weston Patrick, Basingstoke/Deane BC
Weston Rhyn, Oswestry BC
Weston Sub Edge, Cotswold DC
Weston super Mare, N Somerset DC
Weston Turville, Aylesbury Vale DC
Weston under Lizard, S Staffs Cl
Weston under Penyard, Herefordshire Cl
Weston under Redcastle, N Shropshire DC

Weston under Wetherley, Warwick DC
Weston Underwood, Amber Valley BC
Weston Underwood, Milton Keynes Cl
Westonbirt, Cotswold DC
Westoning, Mid Beds DC
Westonzoyland, Sedgemoor DC
Westow, Ryedale DC
Westport, S Somerset DC
Westquarter, Falkirk Cl
Westray, Orkney Is Cl
Westrill, Harborough DC
Westruther, Scottish Borders Cl
Westry, Fenland DC
Westville, E Lindsey DC
Westward, Allerdale BC
Westward Ho!, Torridge DC
Westwell, Ashford BC
Westwell, W Oxon DC
Westwick, Harrogate BC
Westwick, N Norfolk DC
Westwick, S Cambs DC
Westwick, Teesdale DC
Westwood, W Wilts DC
Westwood, Wychavon DC
Westwood Heath, Coventry City MDC
Westwoodside, N Lincs Cl
Wetheral, Carlisle City
Wetherby, Leeds City
Wetherden, Mid Suffolk DC
Wetheringsett, Mid Suffolk DC
Wethersfield, Braintree DC
Wettenhall, Crewe/Nantwich BC
Wetton, Staffs Moorlands DC
Wetwang, E Riding of Yks
Wexcombe, Kennet DC
Wexham, S Bucks DC
Wexham Court, Slough BC
Weybourne, N Norfolk DC
Weybread, Mid Suffolk DC
Weybridge, Elmbridge BC
Weyhill, Test Valley BC
Weymouth, Weymouth/Portland BC
Weymouth East, Weymouth/Portland BC
Weymouth West, Weymouth/Portland BC
Whaddon, Aylesbury Vale DC
Whaddon, Salisbury DC
Whaddon, S Cambs DC
Whaddon, Stroud DC
Whale, Eden DC
Whaley, Bolsover DC
Whaley Bridge, High Peak BC
Whalley, Ribble Valley BC
Whalsay, Shetland Is Cl

Whalton, Castle Morpeth BC
Wham, Craven DC
Whaplode, S Holland DC
Whaplode Drove, S Holland DC
Wharfe, Craven DC
Wharles, Fylde BC
Wharncliffe Side, Sheffield City
Wharram le Street, Ryedale DC
Wharton, Eden DC
Whashton, Richmondshire DC
Whatcote, Stratford/Avon DC
Whatfield, Babergh DC
Whatley, Mendip DC
Whatlington, Rother DC
Whatstandwell, Amber Valley BC
Whatton, Rushcliffe BC
Whaw, Richmondshire DC
Wheatacre, S Norfolk DC
Wheatcroft, Amber Valley BC
Wheatfield, S Oxon DC
Wheathampstead, St Albans
  City/DC
Wheathill, S Shropshire DC
Wheatley, E Hants DC
Wheatley, S Oxon DC
Wheatley Booth, Pendle BC
Wheatley Hill, Easington DC
Wheaton Aston, S Staffs CI
Wheatsheaf Enclosure,
  Chichester DC
Wheeler End, Wycombe DC
Wheelerstreet, Waverley BC
Wheelock, Congleton BC
Wheelton, Chorley BC
Wheldrake, City of York CI
Whelford, Cotswold DC
Whempstead, E Herts DC
Whenby, Hambleton DC
Whepstead, St Edmundsbury BC
Wherstead, Babergh DC
Wherwell, Test Valley BC
Whessoe, Darlington BC
Whetsted, Tunbridge Wells BC
Whetstone, Barnet LBC
Whetstone, Blaby DC
Whicham, Copeland BC
Whichford, Stratford/Avon DC
Whiddon Down, W Devon BC
Whilton, Daventry DC
Whimple, E Devon DC
Whimpwell Green, N Norfolk DC
Whinburgh, Breckland CI
Whinfell, S Lakeland DC
Whippingham, Isle of Wight CI
Whipsnade, S Beds DC
Whirlow, Sheffield City
Whisby, N Kesteven DC
Whissendine, Rutland CC
Whissonsett, Breckland CI
Whistley Green, Wokingham DC

Whiston, Knowsley MBC
Whiston, Rotherham MBC
Whiston, S Northants CI
Whiston, S Staffs CI
Whiston, Staffs Moorlands DC
Whitbeck, Copeland BC
Whitbourne, Herefordshire CI
Whitburn, S Tyneside MBC
Whitburn, W Lothian CI
Whitby, Ellesmere Port/Neston
  BC
Whitby, Scarborough BC
Whitchurch, Aylesbury Vale DC
Whitchurch, Basingstoke/Deane
  BC
Whitchurch, Bath/N E Somerset
  CI
Whitchurch, Herefordshire CI
Whitchurch, N Shropshire DC
Whitchurch, Stratford/Avon DC
Whitchurch, W Devon BC
Whitchurch/Tongwynlais, Cardiff
  CC
Whitchurch Canonicorum, W
  Dorset DC
Whitchurch Hill, S Oxon DC
Whitchurch on Thames, S Oxon
  DC
Whitchurch Rural, N Shropshire
  DC
Whitcombe, W Dorset DC
Whitcott Keysett, S Shropshire
  DC
White Colne, Braintree DC
White Coppice, Chorley BC
White Island, Isles of Scilly CI
White Kirkley, Wear Valley DC
White Lackington, W Dorset DC
White Ladies Aston, Wychavon
  DC
White le Head, Derwentside DC
White Notley, Braintree DC
White Roothing, Uttlesford DC
White Waltham,
  Windsor/Maidenhead RB
Whiteabbey, Newtownabbey BC
Whitebridge, Highland CI
Whitechapel, Preston City
Whitechapel, Tower Hamlets LBC
Whitecraig, E Lothian CI
Whitecroft, Forest of Dean DC
Whitecross, Newry/Mourne DC
Whitefield, Bury MBC
Whiteford, Aberdeenshire CI
Whitegate, Vale Royal BC
Whitehaugh, Renfrewshire CI
Whitehaven, Copeland BC
Whitehead, Carrickfergus BC
Whitehill, E Hants DC
Whitehills, Aberdeenshire CI

Whitehouse, Newtownabbey BC
Whiteinch, Glasgow City
Whitekirk, E Lothian CI
Whitelackington, S Somerset DC
Whiteleaf, Wycombe DC
Whiteley, Fareham BC
Whiteley, Winchester City
Whiteness, Shetland Is CI
Whiteparish, Salisbury DC
Whiterow, Highland CI
Whiteshill, Stroud DC
Whiteside, Tynedale DC
Whitesmith, Wealden DC
Whitestaunton, S Somerset DC
Whitestone, Nuneaton/Bedworth
  BC
Whitestone, Teignbridge DC
Whiteway, Stroud DC
Whitewell, Ribble Valley BC
Whitfield, Dover DC
Whitfield, Dundee City
Whitfield, High Peak BC
Whitfield, S Northants CI
Whitfield, Tynedale DC
Whitford, E Devon DC
Whitford, Flintshire CC
Whitgift, E Riding of Yks
Whitgreave, Stafford BC
Whithorn, Dumfries/Galloway CI
Whiting Bay, N Ayrshire CI
Whitland, Carmarthenshire CC
Whitle, High Peak BC
Whitleigh, Plymouth City
Whitletts, S Ayrshire CI
Whitley, Selby DC
Whitley, Vale Royal BC
Whitley Bay, N Tyneside CI
Whitley Row, Sevenoaks DC
Whitlingham, S Norfolk DC
Whitlock's End, Solihull MBC
Whitminster, Stroud DC
Whitmore, Newcastle-u-Lyme BC
Whitnage, Mid Devon DC
Whitnash, Warwick DC
Whitney on Wye, Herefordshire
  CI
Whitrigg, Allerdale BC
Whitsbury, New Forest DC
Whitsome, Scottish Borders CI
Whitstable, Canterbury City
Whitstone, N Cornwall DC
Whittingham, Alnwick DC
Whittingham, Preston City
Whittingslow, S Shropshire DC
Whittington, Cotswold DC
Whittington, Lancaster City
Whittington, Lichfield DC
Whittington, Oswestry BC
Whittington, S Staffs CI
Whittington, Tynedale DC

Whittington, Wychavon DC
Whittington Moor, Chesterfield BC
Whittle le Woods, Chorley BC
Whittlebury, S Northants CI
Whittlesey, Fenland DC
Whittlesford, S Cambs DC
Whitton, Alnwick DC
Whitton, Mid Suffolk DC
Whitton, N Lincs CI
Whitton, Powys CC
Whitton, Richmond upon Thames LBC
Whitton, S Shropshire DC
Whitton, Stockton-on-Tees BC
Whittonditch, Kennet DC
Whittonstall, Tynedale DC
Whitwell, Bolsover DC
Whitwell, Broadland DC
Whitwell, Hambleton DC
Whitwell, Isle of Wight CI
Whitwell, N Herts DC
Whitwell, Rutland CC
Whitwell on the Hill, Ryedale DC
Whitwood, Wakefield MDC
Whitworth, Rossendale BC
Whixall, N Shropshire DC
Whixley, Harrogate BC
Whorlton, Hambleton DC
Whorlton, Teesdale DC
Whygate, Tynedale DC
Whyteleafe, Tandridge DC
Wibdon, Forest of Dean DC
Wibtoft, Rugby BC
Wichenford, Malvern Hills DC
Wichling, Maidstone BC
Wick, Arun DC
Wick, Bournemouth BC
Wick, S Glos CI
Wick, Highland CI
Wick, Vale of Glamorgan CI
Wick, Wychavon DC
Wick St Lawrence, N Somerset DC
Wicken, E Cambs DC
Wicken, S Northants CI
Wicken Bonhunt, Uttlesford DC
Wickenby, W Lindsey DC
Wickersley, Rotherham MBC
Wickford, Basildon DC
Wickham, W Berks DC
Wickham, Winchester City
Wickham Bishops, Maldon DC
Wickham Bushes, Dover DC
Wickham Market, Suffolk C'l DC
Wickham St Paul, Braintree DC
Wickham Skeith, Mid Suffolk DC
Wickhambreaux, Canterbury City
Wickhambrook, St Edmundsbury BC

Wickhamford, Wychavon DC
Wicklewood, S Norfolk DC
Wickmere, N Norfolk DC
Wickwar, S Glos CI
Widdington, Uttlesford DC
Widdrington, Castle Morpeth BC
Wide Open, N Tyneside CI
Widecombe in the Moor, Teignbridge DC
Wideford, Orkney Is CI
Widegates, Caradon DC
Widemouth Bay, N Cornwall DC
Widewell, Plymouth City
Widford, E Herts DC
Widford, W Oxon DC
Widley, Winchester City
Widmerpool, Rushcliffe BC
Widnes, Halton BC
Widworthy, E Devon DC
Wield, E Hants DC
Wigan, Wigan MBC
Wiggaton, E Devon DC
Wiggenhall St Germans, King's Lynn/W Norfolk BC
Wiggenhall St Mary Magdalen, King's Lynn/W Norfolk BC
Wiggenhall St Mary the Virgin, King's Lynn/W Norfolk BC
Wigginton, Cherwell DC
Wigginton, City of York CI
Wigginton, Dacorum BC
Wigginton, Lichfield DC
Wigglesworth, Craven DC
Wiggonby, Allerdale BC
Wiggonholt, Horsham DC
Wighill, Harrogate BC
Wighton, N Norfolk DC
Wigmore, Herefordshire CI
Wigmore, Medway CI
Wigsley, Newark/Sherwood DC
Wigsthorpe, E Northants CI
Wigston, Oadby/Wigston BC
Wigston Parva, Blaby DC
Wigtoft, Boston BC
Wigton, Allerdale BC
Wigtown, Dumfries/Galloway CI
Wilbarston, Kettering BC
Wilberfoss, E Riding of Yks
Wilburton, E Cambs DC
Wilby, Breckland CI
Wilby, Mid Suffolk DC
Wilby, Wellingborough BC
Wilcot, Kennet DC
Wildboarclough, Macclesfield BC
Wilde Street, Forest Heath DC
Wilden, Bedford BC
Wildhern, Test Valley BC
Wildmore, E Lindsey DC
Wildon Grange, Hambleton DC
Wildsworth, W Lindsey DC

Wilford, Nottingham City
Wilkesley, Crewe/Nantwich BC
Wilkieston, W Lothian CI
Willand, Mid Devon DC
Willaston, Crewe/Nantwich BC
Willen, Milton Keynes CI
Willen Park, Milton Keynes CI
Willenhall, Coventry City MDC
Willenhall, Walsall MBC
Willerby, E Riding of Yks
Willerby, Ryedale DC
Willersey, Cotswold DC
Willersley, Herefordshire CI
Willesborough Lees, Ashford BC
Willesden Green, Brent LBC
Willey, Bridgnorth DC
Willey, Herefordshire CI
Willey, Rugby BC
Williamsburgh, Renfrewshire CI
Williamscot, Cherwell DC
Willian, N Herts DC
Willicote, Stratford/Avon DC
Willimoteswick, Tynedale DC
Willingale, Epping Forest DC
Willingdon, Eastbourne BC
Willingdon, Wealden DC
Willingham, S Cambs DC
Willingham, Waveney DC
Willingham by Stow, W Lindsey DC
Willington, Bedford BC
Willington, N Tyneside CI
Willington, S Derbys DC
Willington, Stratford/Avon DC
Willington, Wear Valley DC
Willington, Wrexham CBC
Willisham, Mid Suffolk DC
Willitoft, E Riding of Yks
Williton, W Somerset DC
Willoughby, E Lindsey DC
Willoughby, Rugby BC
Willoughby on the Wolds, Rushcliffe BC
Willoughby Waterleys, Harborough DC
Willoughton, W Lindsey DC
Wills Pastures, Stratford/Avon DC
Wilmcote, Stratford/Avon DC
Wilmington, Dartford BC
Wilmington, E Devon DC
Wilmington, Wealden DC
Wilmslow, Macclesfield BC
Wilnecote, Tamworth BC
Wilpshire, Ribble Valley BC
Wilsden, Bradford MDC
Wilsford, Kennet DC
Wilsford, N Kesteven DC
Wilsford, Salisbury DC
Wilshamstead, Bedford BC
Wilstead, Bedford BC

Wilsthorpe, S Kesteven DC
Wilstrop, Harrogate BC
Wilton, Copeland BC
Wilton, Kennet DC
Wilton, Redcar/Cleveland BC
Wilton, Ryedale DC
Wilton, Salisbury DC
Wimbish, Uttlesford DC
Wimblebury, Cannock Chase DC
Wimbledon, Merton LBC
Wimblington, Fenland DC
Wimbolds Trafford, Chester City
Wimboldsley, Vale Royal BC
Wimborne, E Dorset DC
Wimborne Minster, E Dorset DC
Wimborne St Giles, E Dorset DC
Wimbotsham, King's Lynn/W Norfolk BC
Wimpole, S Cambs DC
Wimpstone, Stratford/Avon DC
Wincanton, S Somerset DC
Winceby, E Lindsey DC
Wincham, Vale Royal BC
Winchburgh, W Lothian CI
Winchcombe, Tewkesbury BC
Winchelsea, Rother DC
Winchester, Winchester City
Winchfield, Hart DC
Winchmore Hill, Chiltern DC
Winchmore Hill, Enfield LBC
Wincle, Macclesfield BC
Wincobank, Sheffield City
Wincot Lands, Stratford/Avon DC
Windermere, S Lakeland DC
Winderton, Stratford/Avon DC
Windhill, Highland CI
Windle, St Helens MBC
Windlesham, Surrey Heath BC
Windlestone, Sedgefield BC
Windley, Amber Valley BC
Windmill Hill, Wealden DC
Windmill Naps, Stratford/Avon DC
Windrush, Cotswold DC
Windsor, Windsor/Maidenhead RB
Windygates, Fife CI
Windyridge, Rushcliffe BC
Wineham, Horsham DC
Winestead, E Riding of Yks
Winfarthing, S Norfolk DC
Winford, Isle of Wight CI
Winford, N Somerset DC
Winfortin, Herefordshire CI
Winfrith Newburgh, Purbeck DC
Wing, Aylesbury Vale DC
Wing, Rutland CC
Wingate, Easington DC
Wingates, Alnwick DC
Wingates, Bolton MBC
Wingerworth, N E Derbys DC

Wingfield, Mid Suffolk DC
Wingfield, S Beds DC
Wingfield, W Wilts DC
Wingham, Dover DC
Wingham Well, Dover DC
Wingrave, Aylesbury Vale DC
Winkburn, Newark/Sherwood DC
Winkfield, Bracknell Forest BC
Winkhill, Staffs Moorlands DC
Winkleigh, Torridge DC
Winksley, Harrogate BC
Winmarleigh, Wyre BC
Winnersh, Wokingham DC
Winscales, Allerdale BC
Winscombe, N Somerset DC
Winsford, W Somerset DC
Winsford, Vale Royal BC
Winsham, S Somerset DC
Winshill, E Staffs BC
Winsick, N E Derbys DC
Winskill, Eden DC
Winslade, Basingstoke/Deane BC
Winsley, W Wilts DC
Winslow, Aylesbury Vale DC
Winslow, Herefordshire CI
Winson, Cotswold DC
Winster, Derbys Dales DC
Winster, S Lakeland DC
Winston, Mid Suffolk DC
Winston, Teesdale DC
Winstone, Cotswold DC
Winstree Hundred, Colchester BC
Winterborne Came, W Dorset DC
Winterborne Clenston, N Dorset DC
Winterborne Herringstone, W Dorset DC
Winterborne Houghton, N Dorset DC
Winterborne Kingston, N Dorset DC
Winterborne Monkton, W Dorset DC
Winterborne St Martin, W Dorset DC
Winterborne Stickland, N Dorset DC
Winterborne Whitechurch, N Dorset DC
Winterborne Zelston, N Dorset DC
Winterbourne, Salisbury DC
Winterbourne, S Glos CI
Winterbourne, W Berks DC
Winterbourne Abbas, W Dorset DC
Winterbourne Bassett, Kennet DC
Winterbourne Monkton, Kennet DC

Winterbourne Steepleton, W Dorset DC
Winterbourne Stoke, Salisbury DC
Winterburn, Craven DC
Winteringham, N Lincs CI
Winterley, Crewe/Nantwich BC
Wintersett, Wakefield MDC
Wintershil, Winchester City
Winterslow, Salisbury DC
Winterton, N Lincs CI
Winterton on Sea, Gt Yarmouth BC
Winthorpe, Newark/Sherwood DC
Winton, Eden DC
Winton, Hambleton DC
Winton, Salford City
Wintringham, Ryedale DC
Winwick, Daventry DC
Winwick, Huntingdonshire DC
Winwick, Warrington BC
Wirksworth, Derbys Dales DC
Wirral, The, Wirral MBC
Wirswall, Crewe/Nantwich BC
Wisbech, Fenland DC
Wisbech St Mary, Fenland DC
Wisborough Green, Chichester DC
Wiseton, Bassetlaw DC
Wisewood, Sheffield City
Wishaw, N Lanarkshire CI
Wishaw, N Warks BC
Wisley, Guildford BC
Wispington, E Lindsey DC
Wissett, Waveney DC
Wissington, Babergh DC
Wistanstow, S Shropshire DC
Wistanswick, N Shropshire DC
Wistaston, Crewe/Nantwich BC
Wiston, Horsham DC
Wiston, Pembrokeshire CC
Wistow, Harborough DC
Wistow, Huntingdonshire DC
Wistow, Selby DC
Wiswell, Ribble Valley BC
Witcham, E Cambs DC
Witchampton, E Dorset DC
Witchford, E Cambs DC
Witham, Braintree DC
Witham Friary, Mendip DC
Witham on the Hill, S Kesteven DC
Witham St Hughs, N Kesteven DC
Withcall, E Lindsey DC
Witheridge, N Devon DC
Witherley, Hinckley/Bosworth BC
Withern, E Lindsey DC
Withernsea, E Riding of Yks
Withernwick, E Riding of Yks

Withersfield, St Edmundsbury BC
Witherslack, S Lakeland DC
Withiel, N Cornwall DC
Withiel Florey, W Somerset DC
Withington, Cotswold DC
Withington, Herefordshire Cl
Withington, Shrewsbury/Atcham Cl
Withleigh, Mid Devon DC
Withnell, Chorley BC
Withybrook, Rugby BC
Withycombe, W Somerset DC
Withyham, Wealden DC
Withypool, W Somerset DC
Witley, Waverley BC
Witnesham, Suffolk C'l DC
Witney, W Oxon DC
Wittenham, S Oxon DC
Wittering, Peterborough City
Wittersham, Ashford BC
Witton, N Norfolk DC
Witton Gilbert, Durham City
Witton le Wear, Wear Valley DC
Wiveliscombe, Taunton Deane BC
Wivelsfield, Lewes DC
Wivenhoe, Colchester BC
Wiverton, Rushcliffe BC
Wiveton, N Norfolk DC
Wix, Tendring DC
Wixford, Stratford/Avon DC
Wixoe, St Edmundsbury BC
Woburn, Mid Beds DC
Woburn Sands, Milton Keynes Cl
Wokefield, W Berks DC
Woking, Woking BC
Wokingham, Wokingham DC
Wokingham Without, Wokingham DC
Wold Newton, E Riding of Yks
Wold Newton, N E Lincs Cl
Woldingham, Tandridge DC
Wolferlow, Herefordshire Cl
Wolferton, King's Lynn/W Norfolk BC
Wolfhampcote, Rugby BC
Wolfscastle, Pembrokeshire CC
Wollaston, Shrewsbury/Atcham Cl
Wollaston, Wellingborough BC
Wolsingham, Wear Valley DC
Wolston, Rugby BC
Wolverhampton, Wolverhampton MBC
Wolverley, N Shropshire DC
Wolverley, Wyre Forest DC
Wolverton, Basingstoke/Deane BC
Wolverton, Dover DC
Wolverton, Milton Keynes Cl

Wolverton, Stratford/Avon DC
Wolvey, Rugby BC
Wolviston, Stockton-on-Tees BC
Wombleton, Ryedale DC
Wombourne, S Staffs Cl
Wombwell, Barnsley MBC
Womenswold, Canterbury City
Womersley, Selby DC
Wonersh, Waverley BC
Wonson, W Devon BC
Wonston, Winchester City
Wooburn, Wycombe DC
Wooburn Green, Wycombe DC
Wooburn Moor, Wycombe DC
Wood Burcote, S Northants Cl
Wood Dalling, Broadland DC
Wood End, E Herts DC
Wood End, N Warks BC
Wood End, Stratford/Avon DC
Wood Enderby, E Lindsey DC
Wood Green, Haringey LBC
Wood Norton, N Norfolk DC
Woodacott Cross, Torridge DC
Woodale, Richmondshire DC
Woodbank, Chester City
Woodbastwick, Broadland DC
Woodbeck, Bassetlaw DC
Woodborough, Gedling BC
Woodborough, Kennet DC
Woodbridge, Suffolk C'l DC
Woodbury, E Devon DC
Woodbury Salterton, E Devon DC
Woodchester, Stroud DC
Woodchurch, Ashford BC
Woodcote, S Oxon DC
Woodcote, Telford/Wrekin BC
Woodcott, Basingstoke/Deane BC
Woodditton, E Cambs DC
Woodeaton, Cherwell DC
Woodeaton, S Oxon DC
Woodend, Copeland BC
Woodend, S Northants Cl
Woodford, E Northants Cl
Woodford, N Cornwall DC
Woodford, Salisbury DC
Woodford Green, Redbridge LBC
Woodford Halse, Daventry DC
Woodgate, Arun DC
Woodgate, Breckland Cl
Woodgate, Bromsgrove DC
Woodgreen, New Forest DC
Woodhall, E Lindsey DC
Woodhall, Richmondshire DC
Woodhall Spa, E Lindsey DC
Woodham, Aylesbury Vale DC
Woodham, Runnymede BC
Woodham, Woking BC
Woodham Ferrers, Chelmsford BC

Woodham Mortimer, Maldon DC
Woodham Walter, Maldon DC
Woodhill, Bridgnorth DC
Woodhorn, Wansbeck DC
Woodhouse, Sheffield City
Woodhouse, Wakefield MDC
Woodhouse Eaves, Charnwood DC
Woodhurst, Huntingdonshire DC
Woodland, Teesdale DC
Woodland, Teignbridge DC
Woodlands, Dumfries/Galloway Cl
Woodlands, E Dorset DC
Woodlands Park, Windsor/Maidenhead RB
Woodlands St Mary, W Berks DC
Woodleigh, S Hams DC
Woodlesford, Leeds City
Woodley, Wokingham DC
Woodmancote, Chichester DC
Woodmancote, Cotswold DC
Woodmancote, Horsham DC
Woodmancote, Tewkesbury BC
Woodmans Green, Chichester DC
Woodmansey, E Riding of Yks
Woodmansterne, Reigate/Banstead BC
Woodnesborough, Dover DC
Woodnewton, E Northants Cl
Woodplumpton, Preston City
Woodrising, Breckland Cl
Woodseats, Sheffield City
Woodseaves, N Shropshire DC
Woodseaves, Stafford BC
Woodsend, Kennet DC
Woodsetts, Rotherham MBC
Woodsford, W Dorset DC
Woodside, Allerdale BC
Woodside, Fife Cl
Woodside, Glasgow City
Woodstock, W Oxon DC
Woodthorpe, Charnwood DC
Woodthorpe, Chesterfield BC
Woodthorpe, E Lindsey DC
Woodthorpe, Gedling BC
Woodthorpe, Sheffield City
Woodton, S Norfolk DC
Woodville, S Derbys DC
Woodwalton, Huntingdonshire DC
Woodyates, E Dorset DC
Wookey, Mendip DC
Wool, Purbeck DC
Woolaston, Forest of Dean DC
Woolaston, Oswestry BC
Woolavington, Sedgemoor DC
Woolbeding, Chichester DC
Wooler, Berwick-u-Tweed BC
Woolfardisworthy, Torridge DC

Woolhampton, W Berks DC
Woolhope, Herefordshire Cl
Woolland, N Dorset DC
Woolley, Huntingdonshire DC
Woolley, Wakefield MDC
Woolmer Green, Welwyn Hatfield DC
Woolpit, Mid Suffolk DC
Woolscott, Rugby BC
Woolsery, Torridge DC
Woolsington, Newcastle City
Woolstanwood, Crewe/Nantwich BC
Woolstaston, Shrewsbury/Atcham Cl
Woolsthorpe by Belvoir, S Kesteven DC
Woolston, S Shropshire DC
Woolston, Southampton City
Woolston, Warrington BC
Woolstone, Milton Keynes Cl
Woolstone, Vale of White Horse DC
Woolton, Liverpool City
Woolton Hill, Basingstoke/Deane BC
Woolverstone, Babergh DC
Woolverton, Mendip DC
Woolwell, S Hams DC
Woolwich, Greenwich LBC
Wooperton, Berwick-u-Tweed BC
Woore, N Shropshire DC
Wooton, N Lincs Cl
Wootton, Bedford BC
Wootton, Bridgnorth DC
Wootton, Dover DC
Wootton, E Staffs BC
Wootton, New Forest DC
Wootton, Northampton BC
Wootton, Vale of White Horse DC
Wootton, W Oxon DC
Wootton Bassett, N Wilts DC
Wootton Bridge, Isle of Wight Cl
Wootton Common, Isle of Wight Cl
Wootton Courtenay, W Somerset DC
Wootton Fitzpaine, W Dorset DC
Wootton Rivers, Kennet DC
Wootton St Lawrence, Basingstoke/Deane BC
Wootton Wawen, Stratford/Avon DC
Worcester, Worcester City
Worcester Park, Sutton LBC
Worcester Park (part), Epsom/Ewell BC
Wordwell, St Edmundsbury BC
Worfield, Bridgnorth DC
Workington, Allerdale BC

Worksop, Bassetlaw DC
Worlaby, N Lincs Cl
World's End, W Berks DC
Worldham, E Hants DC
Worle, N Somerset DC
Worleston, Crewe/Nantwich BC
Worlingham, Waveney DC
Worlington, Forest Heath DC
Worlingworth, Mid Suffolk DC
Wormbridge, Herefordshire Cl
Wormegay, King's Lynn/W Norfolk BC
Wormhill, High Peak BC
Wormingford, Colchester BC
Worminghall, Aylesbury Vale DC
Wormington, Tewkesbury BC
Worminster, Mendip DC
Wormit, Fife Cl
Wormleighton, Stratford/Avon DC
Wormley West End, E Herts DC
Wormshill, Maidstone BC
Wormsley, Herefordshire Cl
Worplesdon, Guildford BC
Worrall, Sheffield City
Worsbrough, Barnsley MBC
Worsley, Salford City
Worstead, N Norfolk DC
Worsthorne, Burnley BC
Worston, Ribble Valley BC
Worth, Dover DC
Worth, Macclesfield BC
Worth, Mid Sussex DC
Worth Matravers, Purbeck DC
Wortham, Mid Suffolk DC
Worthen, S Shropshire DC
Worthenbury, Wrexham CBC
Worthing, Breckland Cl
Worthing, Worthing BC
Worthington, N W Leics DC
Wortley, Barnsley MBC
Worton, Kennet DC
Worton, W Oxon DC
Wortwell, S Norfolk DC
Wothersome, Leeds City
Wotherton, S Shropshire DC
Wothorpe, Peterborough City
Wotter, S Hams DC
Wotton, Mole Valley DC
Wotton under Edge, Stroud DC
Wotton Underwood, Aylesbury Vale DC
Woughton, Milton Keynes Cl
Wouldham, Tonbridge/Malling BC
Wrabness, Tendring DC
Wragby, E Lindsey DC
Wramplingham, S Norfolk DC
Wrangaton, S Hams DC
Wrangle, Boston BC
Wrawby, N Lincs Cl
Wraxall, Mendip DC

Wraxall, N Somerset DC
Wraxall, W Dorset DC
Wray, Lancaster City
Wraysbury, Windsor/Maidenhead RB
Wrayton, Lancaster City
Wrea Green, Fylde BC
Wreay, Eden DC
Wrekenton, Gateshead Cl
Wrelton, Ryedale DC
Wrenbury, Crewe/Nantwich BC
Wreningham, S Norfolk DC
Wrentham, Waveney DC
Wrenthorpe, Wakefield MDC
Wressle, E Riding of Yks
Wrestlingworh, Mid Beds DC
Wretham, Breckland Cl
Wretton, King's Lynn/W Norfolk BC
Wrexham, Wrexham CBC
Wrightington, W Lancs DC
Wrinehill, Newcastle-u-Lyme BC
Wrington, N Somerset DC
Writtle, Chelmsford BC
Wrockwardine, Telford/Wrekin BC
Wrockwardine Wood, Telford/Wrekin BC
Wroot, N Lincs Cl
Wrotham, Tonbridge/Malling BC
Wrotham Heath, Tonbridge/Malling BC
Wroughton, Swindon BC
Wroxall, Isle of Wight Cl
Wroxall, Warwick DC
Wroxeter, Shrewsbury/Atcham Cl
Wroxham, Broadland DC
Wroxton, Cherwell DC
Wyaston, Derbys Dales DC
Wyatts Green, Brentwood BC
Wyberton, Boston BC
Wyboston, Bedford DC
Wybourn, Sheffield City
Wybunbury, Crewe/Nantwich BC
Wych Cross, Wealden DC
Wychbold, Wychavon DC
Wyche, Malvern Hills DC
Wychnor, E Staffs BC
Wychwood, W Oxon DC
Wyck Rissington, Cotswold DC
Wycliffe, Teesdale DC
Wycombe Marsh, Wycombe DC
Wyddial, E Herts DC
Wye, Ashford BC
Wyham cum Cadeby, E Lindsey DC
Wyke, Bridgnorth DC
Wyke Regis, Weymouth/Portland BC
Wyke, The, Bridgnorth DC
Wykeham, Scarborough BC

Wyken, Coventry City MDC
Wykey, Oswestry BC
Wylam, Tynedale DC
Wylye, Salisbury DC
Wymering, Portsmouth City
Wymeswold, Charnwood DC
Wymington, Bedford BC
Wymondham, Melton BC
Wymondham, S Norfolk DC
Wymondley, N Herts DC
Wyndford, Glasgow City
Wynford Eagle, W Dorset DC
Wyre, Orkney Is Cl
Wyre Piddle, Wychavon DC
Wysall, Rushcliffe BC
Wythall, Bromsgrove DC
Wytham, Vale of White Horse DC
Wythburn, Allerdale BC
Wythop, Allerdale BC
Wyton, Huntingdonshire DC
Wyverstone, Mid Suffolk DC
Wyville cum Hungerton, S
    Kesteven DC

Y Felinheli, Gwynedd CC
Y Ferwig, Ceredigion CC
Yaddlethorpe, N Lincs Cl
Yafford, Isle of Wight Cl
Yafforth, Hambleton DC
Yalding, Maidstone BC
Yanwath, Eden DC
Yanworth, Cotswold DC
Yapham, E Riding of Yks
Yapton, Arun DC
Yarburgh, E Lindsey DC
Yarcombe, E Devon DC
Yardley, Birmingham City
Yardley Gobion, S Northants Cl
Yardley Hastings, S Northants Cl
Yarkhill, Herefordshire Cl
Yarlet, Stafford BC
Yarlington, S Somerset DC
Yarm, Stockton-on-Tees BC
Yarmouth, Isle of Wight Cl
Yarnfield, Stafford BC
Yarningale, Stratford/Avon DC
Yarnscombe, Torridge DC
Yarnscombe, Torridge DC
Yarnton, Cherwell DC
Yarpole, Herefordshire Cl
Yarrow, Scottish Borders Cl
Yarwell, E Northants Cl
Yate, S Glos Cl
Yateley, Hart DC
Yattendon, W Berks DC
Yatton, Herefordshire Cl
Yatton, N Somerset DC
Yatton Keynell, N Wilts DC
Yaverland, Isle of Wight Cl
Yawl, E Devon DC

Yaxham, Breckland Cl
Yaxley, Huntingdonshire DC
Yaxley, Mid Suffolk DC
Yazor, Herefordshire Cl
Yeading, Hillingdon LBC
Yeadon, Leeds City
Yealand Conyers, Lancaster City
Yealand Redmayne, Lancaster
    City
Yealmpton, S Hams DC
Yearsley, Hambleton DC
Yeaton, Shrewsbury/Atcham Cl
Yeaveley, Derbys Dales DC
Yedingham, Ryedale DC
Yeldersley, Derbys Dales DC
Yelford, W Oxon DC
Yell, Shetland Is Cl
Yelling, Huntingdonshire DC
Yellington, Alnwick DC
Yelvertoft, Daventry DC
Yelverton, S Norfolk DC
Yelverton, W Devon BC
Yeolmbridge, N Cornwall DC
Yeovil, S Somerset DC
Yeovil Without, S Somerset DC
Yeovilton, S Somerset DC
Yetholm, Scottish Borders Cl
Yetminster, W Dorset DC
Yettington, E Devon DC
Yielden, Bedford BC
Yiewsley, Hillingdon LBC
Ynsawdre, Bridgend CBC
Ynysbwl, Rhondda Cynon Taff
    CBC
Ynysowen, Merthyr Tydfil CBC
Yockleton, Shrewsbury/Atcham
    Cl
Yokefleet, E Riding of Yks
Yoker South, Glasgow City
York, City of York Cl
Yorkhill, Glasgow City
Yorkletts, Canterbury City
Yorkley, Forest of Dean DC
Yorton, N Shropshire DC
Youlgreave, Derbys Dales DC
Youlthorpe, E Riding of Yks
Youlton, Hambleton DC
Yoxall, E Staffs BC
Yoxford, Suffolk C'l DC
Ysbyty Ifan, Conwy CBC
Ysbyty Ystwyth, Ceredigion CC
Ysceifiog, Flintshire CC
Yscir, Powys CC
Ysgubor Y Coed, Ceredigion CC
Ystalyfera, Neath Port Talbot
    CBC
Ystrad Fflur, Ceredigion CC
Ystrad Meurig, Ceredigion CC
Ystrad Mynach, Caerphilly CBC
Ystradfellte, Powys CC

Ystradgynlais, Powys CC

Zeals, Salisbury DC
Zelah, Carrick DC
Zennor, Penwith D

INDEX

INDEX

INDEX

INDEX

INDEX